THE *unofficial* GUIDE®

TO Walt Disney World®

2025

BECKY GANDILLON
with BOB SEHLINGER *and* LEN TESTA

(Walt Disney World is officially known as Walt Disney World Resort.)

Please note that prices fluctuate in the course of time and that travel information changes under the impact of many factors that influence the travel industry. We therefore suggest that you email or call ahead for confirmation when making your travel plans. Every effort has been made to ensure the accuracy of information throughout this book, and the contents of this publication are believed to be correct at the time of printing. Nevertheless, the publishers cannot accept responsibility for errors or omissions, for changes in details given in this guide, or for the consequences of any reliance on the information provided by the same. Assessments of attractions and so forth are based upon the authors' own experiences; therefore, descriptions given in this guide necessarily contain an element of subjective opinion, which may not reflect the publisher's opinion or dictate a reader's own experience on another occasion. Readers are invited to write the publisher with ideas, comments, and suggestions for future editions. There is a risk of contracting COVID-19 in any public space. The Unofficial Guides are not liable for any illness or injury. Consult a physician regarding your risk factors before booking travel.

The Unofficial Guides
An imprint of AdventureKEEN
2204 First Ave. S., Ste. 102
Birmingham, AL 35233

To contact us from within the United States, please call 800-678-7006 or fax 877-374-9016. You may also email us at info@theunofficialguides.com. Reach us on social media at TheUnofficialGuides on Facebook, Instagram, Pinterest, and Threads; TheUGSeries on X; and TheUnofficialGuideSeries on YouTube.

AdventureKEEN also publishes its books in a variety of electronic formats. Some content that appears in print may not be available in electronic formats.

Cover design by Scott McGrew
Text design by Vertigo Design

ISBN: 978-1-62809-153-3 (pbk.); eISBN: 978-1-62809-154-0 (ebook)

Distributed by Publishers Group West

Manufactured in China

5 4 3 2

COME CHECK US OUT!

Supplement your valuable guidebook with tips, news, and deals by visiting our websites:

theunofficialguides.com
touringplans.com

Sign up for the Unofficial Guide newsletter for even more travel tips and special offers.

Join the conversation on social media:

 TheUGSeries

 TheUnofficialGuides

 TheUnofficialGuides

 TheUnofficialGuides

 TheUnofficialGuideSeries

 TheUnofficialGuides

Other Unofficial Guides

The Disneyland Story: The Unofficial Guide to the Evolution of Walt Disney's Dream

Universal vs. Disney: The Unofficial Guide to American Theme Parks' Greatest Rivalry

The Unofficial Guide to Disney Cruise Line

The Unofficial Guide to Disneyland

The Unofficial Guide to Las Vegas

The Unofficial Guide to Universal Orlando

The Unofficial Guide to Washington, D.C.

LIST *of* MAPS *and* DIAGRAMS

CONTENTS

INTRODUCTION

FOR *the* LOVE *of* DISNEY

DEAR READER, we've been writing *The Unofficial Guide to Walt Disney World* since 1986—before one of our authors was even born! You've really got to love a place to study it for that long—and we do. Millions of you do too. Comments like these arrive in our messages every day:

"It took a lot of planning, but this was easily the best family vacation we ever had."

"I thought the commercials about the "most magical place on earth" were cheesy and overblown. And then I visited with my own kids and I can't believe I doubted."

"We just got back home and we're already planning another trip."

Disney's theme parks are among the most iconic vacation destinations. They skillfully combine unmatched imagination and storytelling with new technologies, all presented with a touch of pixie dust. Walt Disney World is also a purpose-built city: a place engineered from the ground up to entertain, amaze, and inspire.

WHY DISNEY WORLD NEEDS *a* 572-PAGE GUIDEBOOK

WE KNOW WHAT YOU'RE THINKING. What have I gotten myself into? Why on earth do I need a textbook-size tome of information, suggestions, recommendations, and—gulp—data for one family vacation? Is all of this even necessary?

If it's your first visit, we think so.

The thing that surprises most Walt Disney World visitors is that a vacation here requires much more planning and effort than probably any other vacation they've taken.

Why? A lot of it has to do with scale and capacity. Some of the best experiences at Disney World simply don't have the capacity to serve the 60,000 people who visit the Magic Kingdom on an average day.

The best restaurants can't handle that many people, and the best rides have queues that would spill out all over everywhere if everyone tried to experience them. This results in vastly different experiences for the visitors who do their homework and make their plans and reservations . . . and for those who don't. A reader from Louisiana, understands:

I don't know how people do Disney without this information. I felt sorry seeing people so excited to get into the parks and only then realize that a little homework beforehand would've saved their trip.

We see your panic level starting to rise. Take a deep breath. If you love theme parks, Disney World is as good as it gets. If you arrive without knowing anything and make every possible mistake, there's a really good chance that you'll still have a wonderful vacation. All of the planning we cover here is just to guard against the small chance of disappointment, and to maximize your fun—while hopefully minimizing the cost and time spent in lines.

The ultimate goal of this book is to help you avoid potential problems, and to point out opportunities for greatness that you might not have known about. We're here to help you turn a great vacation into a particularly amazing one.

A mom from Kentucky who hadn't been to Disney in over a decade came back with this to say:

I was convinced that I already knew everything I needed to know about Disney and that this book was overkill—boy was I wrong. There is so much to learn!

WHAT MAKES THIS BOOK DIFFERENT?

THE ADVICE IN THIS BOOK is different from what you'll find by scrolling TikTok, random Googling, or reading other books, in three important ways.

First, the team behind this book is totally independent of the Walt Disney Company, Walt Disney World, and all other parts of the Disney corporate organization. We don't get any free trips, gifts, special favors, invitations, or other compensation from Disney; we pay for everything we review. Disney doesn't request, influence, edit, or approve anything you'll read here.

That means that we stay totally unbiased. If a restaurant serves bad food, an experience is overpriced, or a ride isn't worth the wait, we say so. No need to guess at what our motivation might be.

Second, we use data, science, and technology to help solve the problems that everyone encounters at Walt Disney World. The Disney theme parks are the ultimate problem-solving opportunity for numbers nerds like us: it's the most meticulously well-run environment anywhere. For example, lines for rides and restaurants that seem chaotic at first actually form in predictable ways at predictable times. That makes it possible for us to study them—and predict them.

You might be surprised that Disney-related questions like "How can I spend less time in line?" or "What rides should my kids try?" are active areas of research in schools around the world, and similar business problems pop up in corporate America every day. The authors and researchers who contribute to this book have years—even decades—of academic and professional experience in these areas and use them to help you. And don't worry—we'll translate all of those numbers and science into easy-to-understand, actionable advice.

The third way this book is different is the amount of time and money that goes into making it. Disney research is a full-time job for a lot of our core team. Over the years, we've spent millions of dollars and many thousands of hours reviewing and analyzing Disney World's hotels, rides, crowds, and restaurants. No other book or website commits the people, skills, or budget to do anything like the research you'll find here. The only other organization that does the same level of analysis on Disney World is Disney itself. And we will tell you what they won't.

HOW *to* USE THIS BOOK

THE BEST WAY TO USE THIS BOOK is to read the introductory chapters, then scan the topics of the remaining chapters to get a feel for the kinds of questions each chapter answers. Read in depth the chapters most important to you. Then, as you plan your trip, you can refer back to sections as they become relevant to you.

We've organized the chapters so that they appear in the same sequence and timeline that you'll use to plan and take your trip. For example, Part 2 contains advice on what you need to know to start planning your trip. The next few chapters guide you through choosing a hotel, finding good places to eat, and picking the best rides and entertainment in the parks.

Each chapter starts with **Key Questions,** a list of some FAQs that visitors have about Walt Disney World. For each question, we've listed where in the chapter you can find the answers.

KEY QUESTIONS ANSWERED IN THIS CHAPTER
- Where can I find a planning checklist and timeline? *(page 21)*
- What are the six most important tips for avoiding lines at Disney World? *(page 40)*
- What is the Genie+ ride reservation system, and how do I use it? *(page 49)*

Of course, each chapter answers more questions than the ones we highlight. You can skim each chapter's section headings to see if a particular topic is relevant to you.

Some subjects, such as how Disney accommodates guests in wheelchairs, are relevant across multiple parts of your vacation. These subjects are usually covered in depth in one chapter (in this case, Part 8, "Tips for Varied Circumstances"), with cross-references in other chapters when they're needed.

Most topics are covered in great detail. For example, Disney World has hundreds of attractions, from simple spinners you might find at your local town carnival to massive super-headliners, the likes of which you've never seen. Understanding these rides and how they're run will help you decide what's worth your time.

THE *UNOFFICIAL GUIDE* TEAM

ALLOW US TO INTRODUCE THE PEOPLE who work on this book, except for our dining critic, who shall remain anonymous:

- **BECKY GANDILLON** Author
- **BOB SEHLINGER** Coauthor and publisher
- **LEN TESTA** Coauthor
- **FRED HAZELTON** Statistician
- **JIM HILL** Disney Dish contributor

- **DAVID DAVIES** Webmaster, TouringPlans.com
- **TRAVIS BRYANT** Webmaster, TheUnofficialGuides.com
- **KAREN TURNBOW, PhD** Child psychologist

CONTRIBUTORS
Bella Cannuscio
Christina Harrison
Bob Jacobs
Seth Kubersky
Colin McManus
Brian McNichols
Liliane J. Opsomer
Amy Schinner
Laurel Stewart
Bethany Vinton
Deb Wills

DATA COLLECTORS
Chantale Brazeau
Christine Harrison
Giovanna Harrison
Ivonne Ramos
Darcie Vance
Rich Vosburgh
Kelly Whitman

HOTEL INSPECTOR
Darcie Vance

EDITORIAL AND ART
- **KATE JOHNSON** Managing editor
- **ANNIE LONG** Layout
- **JENNA BARRON, REBECCA HENDERSON, SUSAN McWILLIAMS, ANDREW MOLLENKOF** Proofreaders
- **SCOTT McGREW** Cover design
- **STEVE JONES, CASSANDRA POERTNER** Cartography
- **POTOMAC INDEXING** Indexing (**Joanne Sprott,** team leader)

YOUR UNOFFICIAL WALT DISNEY WORLD TOOLBOX

WHEN IT COMES TO WALT DISNEY WORLD, a family with two toddlers in diapers (bless your heart) needs different advice than a couple going to the EPCOT International Flower & Garden Festival.

To meet the needs of our diverse readers, we've created this guide. We call *The Unofficial Guide to Walt Disney World*, at 572 pages, the "Big Book." It provides the detailed information that anyone traveling to Walt Disney World needs to plan a super vacation. It's the cornerstone of your trip planning.

As thorough as we try to make the main guide, though, there just isn't enough space for all the tips and resources that may be useful to certain readers. Therefore, we've developed two additional guides that provide information tailored to specific visitors:

The Unofficial Guide to Disney Cruise Line, by Tammy Whiting with Erin Foster and Len Testa, presents advice for first-time cruisers; money-saving tips for booking your cruise; and detailed profiles for restaurants, shows, and nightclubs, along with deck plans and thorough coverage of the ports visited by Disney Cruise Line.

The Unofficial Guide to Universal Orlando, by Seth Kubersky, is the most comprehensive guide to Universal Orlando Resort in print. At more than 400 pages, it's the perfect tool for understanding and enjoying Universal's ever-expanding complex of theme parks, a water park, resort hotels, nightclubs, and restaurants. The guide includes field-tested touring plans that will save you hours of standing in line.

CORRECTIONS, UPDATES, AND BREAKING NEWS

WE EXPECT THIS 2025 EDITION to be available through fall 2025. The first set of updates was started in the spring of 2024 and incorporates Disney's current operating procedures at press time. An up-to-date summary of book changes is available at theugseries.com/wdwupdates.

LETTERS AND COMMENTS FROM READERS

MANY READERS WRITE TO US with comments or to share their own tips for visiting Disney World. Their feedback is regularly incorporated into the *Guide* and contributes to its ongoing improvement. If you write to us or complete our reader survey, we won't release your name or address to anyone. If you're willing to have your comments quoted in the *Guide,* be sure to tell us where you're from.

Speaking of comments, from the thousands of letters, emails, and surveys we receive, a little over 10% contain comments. Of that 10%, an even smaller percentage are useful and well written. Quotable comments are like gold to us. If a comment hits the nail on the head, it's unlikely that we'll receive a more well-written and more insightful one. If a better comment hasn't been submitted recently, the older one remains in the next edition because it best serves our readers.

Online Reader Survey

TouringPlans.com hosts a questionnaire you can use to give feedback on your Walt Disney World visit. Access it at touringplans.com/walt -disney-world/survey. This questionnaire lets every member of your party, regardless of age, tell us what they think about attractions, hotels, restaurants, and more. The responses we get are critical to the updating of our book and recommendations.

You can also print out the reader survey and mail it to us at the following address:

Reader Survey
The Unofficial Guide to Walt Disney World
2204 First Ave. S., Ste. 102
Birmingham, AL 35233

Finally, if you'd like to review this book on Amazon, go to theug series.com/2025reviews.

How to Contact the Authors

Becky Gandillon, Bob Sehlinger, and Len Testa
The Unofficial Guide to Walt Disney World
2204 First Ave. S., Ste. 102
Birmingham, AL 35233
info@theunofficialguides.com
Facebook: TheUnofficialGuides | X: @TheUGSeries

When you write, please put your mailing address on both your letter and your envelope—the two sometimes get separated. It's also a good idea to include your phone number. If you email us, please tell us where you're from.

Derek Burgan is our food consigliere. Brad Huber developed the latest version of our Lines app. Todd Perlmutter, Bryan Klinck, and EJJ skillfully debugged the touring plan software. Lines' chat is moderated by the fabulous Weasus, missoverexcited, and PrincipalTinker.

We'd like to say thanks to these folks for their assistance with fact-checking and research: Robert Bloom, Shannon Bohn, Dani Dennison, Anne Densk, Alyssa Drake, Erin Foster, Scott Gustin, Jennifer Heymont, Erin Jenkins, Lauren Macvane, David McDonough, and Carlye Wisel. Thanks also to Jamie Holding and his GitHub repository (github.com/cubehouse/themeparks). Thanks to John Tierney, who knows more about DVC rentals and water treatment than any one human has a right to know.

Finally, to everyone at Walt Disney Parks and Resorts who follows our research from a distance, even if they can't say it: We love you too. You make the magic.

THE IMPORTANCE OF BEING SERIOUS

SOME READERS ARE ASTONISHED that seemingly functional adults would spend so much time on critical analyses of a theme park. But most of us do plenty of reading and research before buying a car or a major appliance, and a Disney World vacation costs more than a dishwasher.

On top of that, the Disney advertising machine is immensely powerful, and we think it's important that when Disney's marketing says its theme parks and restaurants are "world-class" and its artists are "legends," it's important to hold it accountable for those words.

One of the ways we do that is to point out whether the things Disney is doing today meet the standards it has set for itself. When we say that Rise of the Resistance in Disney's Hollywood Studios is the best theme park ride Disney has made in at least 30 years, it's because we believe it meets the highest of Disney's ideals dating back to Walt himself. Likewise, if we complain about an expansive and violent pirate raid of a Caribbean island mysteriously pausing for an auction that sets the price of chickens, it's because those things don't make sense in the stories Disney has already established. And at Disney, storytelling is key.

THE IMPORTANCE OF BEING GOOFY

WHAT MAKES WRITING ABOUT WALT DISNEY WORLD so much fun is that the Disney executives have to take everything so seriously. Day to day, they debate momentous decisions with far-reaching consequences: Will Pluto look silly in a silver cape? What possible color schemes can we come up with for our next batch in the never-ending parade of spirit jerseys? What "big anniversary" can we celebrate next?

Unofficially, we think having a sense of humor is important. This guidebook has one, and it's probably necessary that you do too—not just to use this book but to have the most fun possible at Walt Disney World. Think of *The Unofficial Guide* as your private trainer getting your sense of humor in shape. It will help you understand the importance of being goofy.

PART 1

WALT DISNEY WORLD:
An Overview

KEY QUESTIONS ANSWERED IN THIS CHAPTER

- What is Walt Disney World? *(see below)*
- How big is Walt Disney World? *(see below and next page)*
- What's the difference between the different theme parks? *(page 8)*
- What do these new words and acronyms mean? *(page 17)*

WHAT IS DISNEY WORLD?

WE MAY BE BIASED, but we think Walt Disney World (WDW), in Orlando, Florida, is the best collection of theme parks anywhere. Its size, quality, theming, and ambition go far beyond that of any other amusement park or theme park you may have seen.

You might be familiar with commercials for Disney's theme parks. These are great at showing families bonding over exciting rides and meeting famous characters, but 30-second ads don't convey where to find those rides and characters, how long you'll stand in line, or how much money this magical visit will cost. That's where this book comes in. We give you all of the information you need to know, in a format that you can refer back to as you continue to plan, book, and then take your vacation.

Let's start with the basics! Walt Disney World has four theme parks. If you think of Walt Disney World, the park that probably comes to mind is the **Magic Kingdom**—the first one built and the one most people think of when they hear the words *Disney World*. The other three theme parks are **EPCOT, Disney's Hollywood Studios,** and **Disney's Animal Kingdom.**

Walt Disney World also boasts two water parks, **Blizzard Beach** and **Typhoon Lagoon.** But wait, there's more: over three dozen hotels and a campground; more than 100 restaurants; a massive year-round sports center; an outdoor mall/entertainment/hotel complex called **Disney Springs;** six convention centers; four golf courses; and an array of spas, recreation options, and other activities. Phew!

HOW BIG IS WALT DISNEY WORLD?

WALT DISNEY WORLD IS *MASSIVE*—around 43 square miles, about double the size of Manhattan and slightly smaller than Miami.

We like to use the theme parks as rough guideposts for the locations of other places within Walt Disney World. For example, the **Magic Kingdom Resort Area** is about 7 square miles and contains the Magic Kingdom theme park and nearby hotels, restaurants, golf courses, and entertainment.

The theme parks are miles apart, separated by barely-developed Central Florida swampland—so you'll either need a car to get around or you can use the Walt Disney World transportation system's fleet of buses, boats, vans, monorails, and aerial gondolas (the Skyliner). Disney World's bus system is the third largest in Florida, behind Jacksonville's and Miami's. Its transportation system is so large (and complex) that Part 9 of this book is dedicated to it.

Because of Walt Disney World's size and everything there is to do, it would take at least two weeks to thoroughly explore most of it. Two weeks at Disney is way outside of the budget for most families, so we'll tell you the best things to see in the time you have available.

THE MAJOR THEME PARKS

The Magic Kingdom

Opened in 1971, the Magic Kingdom is the original Walt Disney World theme park. Here you'll find **Cinderella Castle**, along with other entertainment and rides, mostly featuring Disney characters. It's only one piece of Disney World, but it remains the heart.

The Magic Kingdom is divided into six "lands" arranged around a central hub. First you come to **Main Street, U.S.A.,** which connects the park entrance with the hub. Arranged clockwise around the hub are **Adventureland, Frontierland, Liberty Square, Fantasyland,** and **Tomorrowland.** The Magic Kingdom has more rides, shows, and entertainment than any other WDW theme park. A comprehensive tour would take two days, but a tour of the highlights (and more) can be done in one full day.

Three resorts—the **Contemporary** and **Grand Floridian Resorts, Polynesian Village,** and their villa units (**Bay Lake Tower, The Villas at the Grand Floridian,** and **Disney's Polynesian Villas and Bungalows**)— are connected to the Magic Kingdom by monorail and boat. Three other hotels—**Shades of Green** (for the US military and their families), **Wilderness Lodge** (including the **Boulder Ridge Villas** and **Copper Creek Villas & Cabins**), and **Fort Wilderness Resort & Campground**— are located nearby but are served by boat and bus instead of monorail.

EPCOT

Opened in 1982, EPCOT is twice as big as the Magic Kingdom. The "front" (southern) part consists of three areas (**World Discovery, World Celebration,** and **World Nature**) with giant pavilions themed to human creativity, technological advancement, and the natural world; **World Showcase,** the "back" (northern) part, is arranged around a 40-acre lagoon and presents the architectural, social, and cultural heritages of almost a dozen nations, with each country represented by its own pavilion. EPCOT has recently been undergoing a revitalization that aims to increase its appeal among families with young children, which typically means the introduction of more Disney characters.

The EPCOT resorts—the **BoardWalk Inn & Villas, Dolphin, Swan, Swan Reserve, Yacht & Beach Club Resorts,** and **Beach Club Villas**—are within a 5- to 15-minute walk of the International Gateway, a secondary entrance to the theme park located in World Showcase. The hotels are also linked to EPCOT and Disney's Hollywood Studios by boat and walkway. EPCOT is connected to the Magic Kingdom and its hotels by monorail. An elevated gondola system called the **Skyliner** links EPCOT and Disney's Hollywood Studios to Disney's Pop Century, Art of Animation, Caribbean Beach, and Riviera Resorts. In case you can't tell, this is one of the most well-connected areas of the entire resort, and a personal favorite of our authors.

Disney's Hollywood Studios

Opened in 1989 in an area slightly larger than the Magic Kingdom, Disney's Hollywood Studios (DHS) has two main sections. About half of the space is a theme park focused on the motion picture, music, and television industries. Highlights include a re-creation of Hollywood and Sunset Boulevards from Hollywood's Golden Age, several rides and musical shows, and a movie stunt show.

The other half is made up of two immersive movie-themed lands. **Toy Story Land** opened in 2018 with three themed rides for children. **Star Wars: Galaxy's Edge** opened in 2019 and is an incredibly immersive area that has two state-of-the-art, large rides for older children, teens, and adults.

DHS is connected to other Walt Disney World areas by highway, boat, and Skyliner but not by monorail. Guests can park in DHS's parking lot or commute by bus; guests at EPCOT resort hotels can reach DHS by boat, on foot, or by Skyliner.

Disney's Animal Kingdom

About five times the size of the Magic Kingdom, Disney's Animal Kingdom is the largest park. It combines zoological exhibits with rides, shows, and live entertainment. The park is arranged in a hub-and-spoke configuration somewhat like the Magic Kingdom. A tropical rainforest serves as "Main Street," funneling visitors to **Discovery Island,** the park's hub. Dominated by the park's icon, the 14-story-tall, hand-carved **Tree of Life,** Discovery Island offers services, shopping, and dining. From there, guests can access the themed areas: **Africa, Asia, DinoLand U.S.A.,** and **Pandora.** Discovery Island, Africa, and DinoLand U.S.A. opened in 1998, followed by Asia in 1999. Africa is over 100 acres just by itself and is home to free-roaming herds in a re-creation of the Serengeti Plain.

Pandora—The World of Avatar, based on James Cameron's *Avatar* film franchise, is the most significant recent expansion. Its biggest draw may be the scenery—including "floating mountains" and glow-in-the-dark plants—which Disney has replicated from the movie. See Part 13 for full details.

continued on page 14

South Orlando

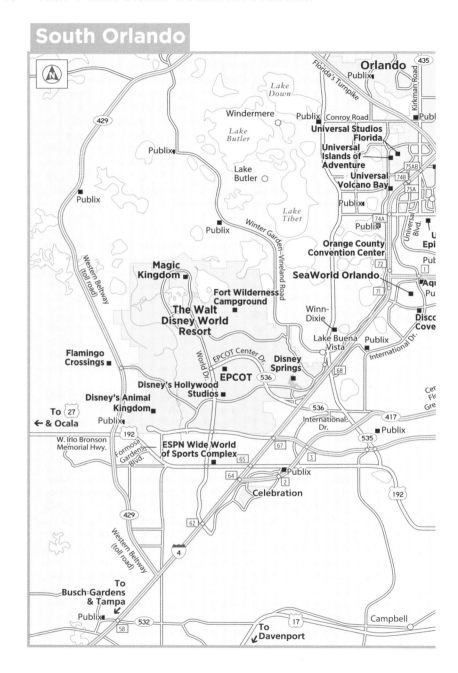

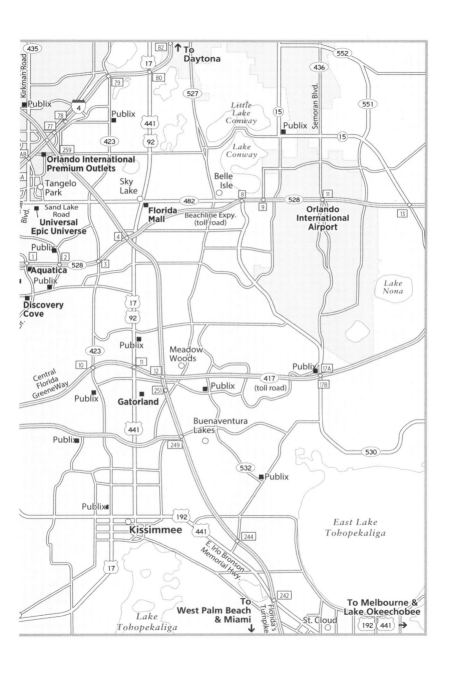

Walt Disney World

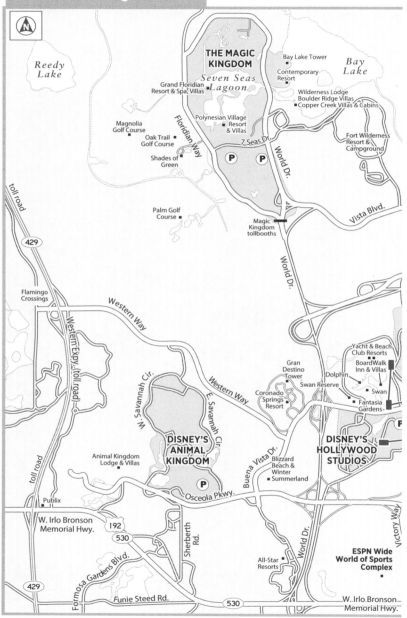

Reedy Lake

THE MAGIC KINGDOM

Seven Seas Lagoon

Bay Lake Tower
Contemporary Resort

Bay Lake

Grand Floridian Resort & Spa, Villas

Wilderness Lodge
Boulder Ridge Villas
Copper Creek Villas & Cabins

Magnolia Golf Course

Polynesian Village Resort & Villas

Fort Wilderness Resort & Campground

Oak Trail Golf Course

7 Seas Dr.

Floridian Way

Shades of Green

World Dr.

Vista Blvd.

toll road

429

Palm Golf Course

Magic Kingdom tollbooths

World Dr.

Flamingo Crossings

Western Way

Western Expy. (toll road)

Yacht & Beach Club Resorts

BoardWalk Inn & Villas

Gran Destino Tower

Dolphin

Swan Reserve

Swan

W. Savannah Cir.

Western Way

Coronado Springs Resort

Fantasia Gardens

E. Savannah Cir.

DISNEY'S ANIMAL KINGDOM

Animal Kingdom Lodge & Villas

DISNEY'S HOLLYWOOD STUDIOS

Buena Vista Dr.

Blizzard Beach & Winter Summerland

toll road

Publix

Osceola Pkwy.

W. Irlo Bronson Memorial Hwy.

192

530

Sherberth Rd.

World Dr.

Victory Way

ESPN Wide World of Sports Complex

All-Star Resorts

429

Formosa Gardens Blvd.

Funie Steed Rd.

530

W. Irlo Bronson Memorial Hwy.

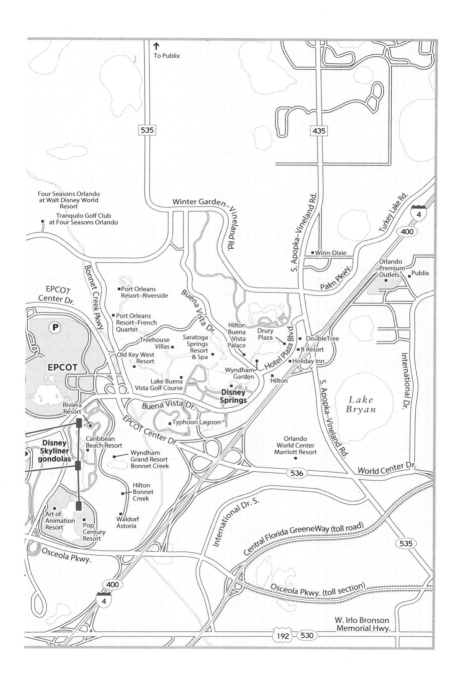

continued from page 9

Disney's Animal Kingdom has its own parking lot and is connected to other Walt Disney World destinations by the Disney bus system. Although no hotels lie within walking distance of Animal Kingdom, the **All-Star Resorts, Animal Kingdom Lodge & Villas,** and **Coronado Springs Resort** are all nearby.

THE WATER PARKS

DISNEY WORLD HAS TWO WATER PARKS: **Typhoon Lagoon** and **Blizzard Beach.** Opened in 1989, Typhoon Lagoon is known for its wave pool capable of making 6-foot waves. Blizzard Beach opened in 1995 and features more slides. Both parks pay careful attention to atmosphere and theme. Typhoon Lagoon and Blizzard Beach have their own parking lots and can be reached by Disney bus.

OTHER WALT DISNEY WORLD VENUES

Disney Springs

Themed as a Florida waterfront town, Disney Springs consists of four areas, each with shopping, dining, and entertainment: the Marketplace, on the east side; the West Side, on (surprise!) the west side; Town Center; and The Landing, on the waterfront.

The Marketplace contains the country's largest Disney merchandise store; upscale and specialty shops, and many restaurants. **The West Side** is a diverse mix of nightlife, shopping, dining, and entertainment, including a **Cirque du Soleil** show exclusive to Disney World. And **Town Center** hosts a wide variety of well-known brands, from Anthropologie and Free People to Levi's and Under Armour.

The Landing offers more shopping and arguably the best dining options in Disney Springs. These include **The Boathouse,** an upscale waterfront seafood eatery that also serves great steaks; **Morimoto Asia**, a high-quality, midpriced restaurant from Iron Chef Masaharu Morimoto; **Chef Art Smith's Homecomin',** a restaurant from Florida native Art Smith that features local farm-to-table ingredients and traditional Southern cooking; and **Wine Bar George,** serving tasty Mediterranean small plates and a well-curated list of affordable wines.

Disney Springs has three multistory parking garages, with short walks to the middle of the action. It is also accessible via Disney transportation from Disney resort hotels and theme parks.

Disney's BoardWalk

Near EPCOT, the BoardWalk is an idealized replica of a 1930s East Coast waterfront resort. It features upscale restaurants, shops and galleries, and a brewpub. In the evening, a nightclub with dueling pianos and a DJ dance club join the lineup (both are for guests age 21 and up only). Anyone can enjoy the BoardWalk for free, but the piano bar has a cover charge at night. This area is anchored by the **BoardWalk Inn & Villas.**

The BoardWalk is within walking distance of the EPCOT resorts, EPCOT's International Gateway entrance, and Disney's Hollywood

WHAT'S NEW AT WALT DISNEY WORLD

LAST YEAR OR SO

- *Luminous,* a new nighttime fireworks show for **EPCOT** opened in late 2023.
- A major expansion of the **Polynesian Village Resort,** for Disney Vacation Club members, should open on the Seven Seas Lagoon in 2024.
- **Tiana's Bayou Adventure,** a retheming of the Splash Mountain log flume ride, opened in the Magic Kingdom's Frontierland in 2024.

LAST 2 YEARS

- **Journey of Water, Inspired by Moana,** an outdoor interactive water play area, opened in EPCOT in October 2023
- **Tron Lightcycle/Run,** an outdoor roller-coaster, opened in the Magic Kingdom's Tomorrowland in April 2023.

LAST 5 YEARS

- **Guardians of the Galaxy: Cosmic Rewind,** the world's longest indoor roller-coaster, opened in EPCOT in 2022.
- Disney's paid **Genie+** and **Individual Lightning Lane** ride reservation systems debuted, replacing FastPass+.
- Disney's **Early Theme Park Entry** and **Extended Evening Theme Park Hours** debuted, replacing the Extra Magic Hours program.
- EPCOT opened a new nighttime show, *Harmonious,* in October 2021 (since closed), along with **Remy's Ratatouille Adventure,** a ride based on the Pixar film *Ratatouille.*
- The **Magic Kingdom** debuted a new nighttime show, *Disney Enchantment,* in October 2021 (since closed).
- The **Star Wars: Galactic Starcruiser** hotel opened in 2022 . . . and closed in September 2023.
- The land **Star Wars: Galaxy's Edge** opened in Disney's Hollywood Studios (DHS), with two new state-of-the-art rides (**Star Wars: Rise of the Resistance** and *Millennium Falcon:* **Smugglers Run**) and *Star Wars*–themed dining options.
- DHS opened **Mickey & Minnie's Runaway Railway,** an immersive 3D ride through the new Mickey Mouse cartoon universe.

LAST 10 YEARS

- **Disney's Riviera Resort,** a Disney Vacation Club property, opened in 2019 adjacent to the Caribbean Beach Resort. Connecting the Riviera to EPCOT and DHS is the new **Disney Skyliner** elevated gondola system, which also links Disney's Pop Century, Art of Animation, and Caribbean Beach Resorts with each other and those theme parks.
- **Disney's Coronado Springs Resort** opened the 15-story **Gran Destino Tower** in 2019, with more-upscale guest rooms and dining options.
- EPCOT unveiled the food-and-arts-themed **International Festival of the Arts,** which takes place in January and February.
- DHS opened **Toy Story Land,** with two new rides: **Alien Swirling Saucers,** a variation on an amusement park spinning ride, and **Slinky Dog Dash,** a mild roller coaster that's more fun than it might seem at first glance.
- Disney's Animal Kingdom added its sixth "land," **Pandora—The World of Avatar.** It features two attractions (**Avatar Flight of Passage,** a thrilling flight simulator, and **Na'vi River Journey,** a gentle boat ride) and glowing "bioluminescent" plants. The adventurous restaurant **Tiffins** opened with the accompanying **Nomad Lounge.**
- **Copper Creek Villas & Cabins** at **Disney's Wilderness Lodge Resort** opened, adding refurbished Disney Vacation Club rooms and two-bedroom cabins along Bay Lake, as well as **Geyser Point Bar & Grill.**
- EPCOT saw the opening of **Frozen Ever After,** a ride based on the popular film *Frozen,* in World Showcase's Norway Pavilion.

Studios. Boat transportation is available to and from EPCOT and Disney's Hollywood Studios, the Skyliner connects the BoardWalk to the Studios and the hotels on its route, and buses serve other Walt Disney World locations.

WHAT'S NEW AT WALT DISNEY WORLD

Disneyland is something that will never be finished. It's something that I can keep developing. It will be a live, breathing thing that will need change.

—Walt Disney

WHAT WALT SAID OF DISNEYLAND is also true of Disney World. The table on page 15 shows all the major changes that have taken place at Walt Disney World in the last 2, 5, and 10 years.

THE PEOPLE OF WALT DISNEY WORLD

DISNEY'S EMPLOYEES are called **cast members.** These are the people who can make or break a vacation with their service. Fortunately, Disney staff often go the extra mile to make your visit special, as the following two readers share.

First, from a family from Illinois who received assistance for a health emergency:

On our first day at the resort, our 6-year-old grandson woke up with a deep cough, fever, and kind of wheezing. Our daughter-in-law contacted the desk and found that WDW provided a shuttle to a local prompt-care facility. As it turned out, the shuttle wasn't available, so they called a cab instead and covered the cost! Our grandson was able to be seen by a physician and received medication that allowed him to get better and salvage the trip. We can't say enough about what the staff and WDW did for us that day! They were terrific!

And a family from Michigan had this to relate:

We had a very unexpected and wonderful surprise waiting in our stroller after the Country Bear Jamboree. Out of nearly 30 strollers, ours had been visited by Santa Mickey while we were in the show. We came out to a stroller decorated with silly bands, Christmas ornaments, and a snowman Mickey plush toy. Our 5-year-old son, not to mention the rest of our party, were delighted. Just another way that WDW goes one more step to make a magical experience.

POCKET TRANSLATOR FOR COMMON DISNEY ABBREVIATIONS

IT MAY COME AS A SURPRISE to many, but Walt Disney World has its own somewhat peculiar language. On the opposite page are some abbreviations and slang you're likely to encounter, both in this guide and in the larger Disney community.

COMMON ABBREVIATIONS

ADR Advance Dining Reservation	**ETPE** Early Theme Park Entry (formerly Morning Extra Magic Hours, or Morning EMH)
BG Boarding group (for newer rides such as Tron Lightcycle/Run)	**EETPH** Extended Evening Theme Park Hours (formerly Evening Extra Magic Hours, or Evening EMH)
CM Cast member	**I-DRIVE** International Drive (a major Orlando thoroughfare)
DCL Disney Cruise Line	**MDE** My Disney Experience mobile app
DHS Disney's Hollywood Studios	**TTC** Ticket and Transportation Center
DTS Disney Transportation System	**WDI** Walt Disney Imagineering
DVC Disney Vacation Club	**WDW** Walt Disney World

THE DISNEY LEXICON IN A NUTSHELL

ATTRACTION Ride or theater show

ATTRACTION HOST Ride operator

BACKSTAGE Behind the scenes, out of view of customers

CAST MEMBER Employee

CHARACTER Disney character impersonated by an employee

COSTUME Work attire or uniform

DARK RIDE Indoor ride

FACE CHARACTER A character who doesn't wear a head-covering costume (Snow White, Cinderella, Jasmine, and the like)

GREETER Employee positioned at an attraction entrance

GUEST Customer/visitor

HIDDEN MICKEYS Frontal silhouette of Mickey's head worked subtly into the design of buildings, railings, golf greens, attractions, and just about anything else

OFF-SITE HOTEL A hotel located outside of Walt Disney World's boundaries

ON-SITE HOTEL A hotel located inside Walt Disney World's boundaries and served by Disney's transportation network

ONSTAGE In full view of customers

PRESHOW Entertainment at an attraction before the feature presentation

SOFT OPENING The opening of a park or attraction before its stated opening date

PART 2

PLANNING *before* YOU LEAVE HOME

KEY QUESTIONS ANSWERED IN THIS CHAPTER

- Where can I find a planning checklist and timeline? *(page 21)*
- What is My Disney Experience, and how do I use it? *(page 24)*
- When is Disney World least crowded and most crowded? *(page 29)*
- What are Early Theme Park Entry and Extended Evening Theme Park Hours, and how do I use them? *(page 30)*
- What special events are scheduled while I'm at Walt Disney World? *(page 32)*
- How can I contact someone at Disney with questions? *(page 34)*

Visiting Walt Disney World is a bit like childbirth—you never really believe what people tell you, but once you have been through it yourself, you know exactly what they were saying!

—Hilary Wolfe, a mother and
Unofficial Guide reader from Wales

GATHERING INFORMATION

IN ADDITION TO THIS GUIDE, we recommend that you visit our sister website, **TouringPlans.com.** The blog posts there can keep you up-to-date with breaking news and even more data for your Walt Disney World vacation.

TouringPlans.com complements and augments the information in this book, and it provides real-time personalized services that are impossible to build into a book. The book is your comprehensive reference guide; TouringPlans.com is your personal concierge. You can sign up for free at touringplans.com/walt-disney-world/join/basic.

With that free access, you'll be able to create custom touring plans, follow them in the parks, and get updates to them if conditions change while you're there. You'll also find current information on attractions, shows, restaurants, crowds, park hours, and more. A few of the site's features require a small subscription fee to access, such as a detailed, day-by-day crowd calendar and a service that sends your hotel-room request directly to Disney. That fee covers the costs of the extra people, technology, and external services it takes to provide them.

Below is a brief rundown of some things you'll find on the site. We only share it because we regularly receive many requests asking us for tools and information that don't fit into the book but are already available on the site for free.

TICKET DISCOUNTS A free, customizable search helps you find the cheapest tickets for your specific trip dates and needs. A typical family of four saves around $130 on average by purchasing admission after using the tool.

CUSTOM TOURING PLANS Some of the best and most well-tested touring plans are found in the *Unofficial Guides*. They've been used by millions of families over the years, usually with excellent results. That said, they often depend on arriving at the park early, and they're built to accommodate the general public. Your family or traveling party might want to visit different attractions or tour only in the afternoon and evening. In those cases, and for others with unique circumstances, we provide custom touring plans online.

The free online plans will also allow you to input any Genie+ return times, if you have them, to minimize your wait in line throughout the day. Online plans also work with Disney's Disability Access Service (see page 314).

A DETAILED 365-DAY CROWD CALENDAR FOR EACH THEME PARK Subscribers can see which parks will be the least crowded every day of their trip, using a 1–10 scale. You can also view historical crowd data and check the accuracy of the predictions.

HOTEL-ROOM VIEWS AND ROOM-REQUEST SERVICE TouringPlans .com has photos of the views from every Disney-owned hotel room in Walt Disney World—more than 35,000 images in all—and it'll give you the exact wording to use to request a specific room. If you're a subscriber, it'll even automatically email your request to Disney 30 days before you arrive. A couple who regularly uses the service writes:

We don't always get a room that matches our request, but when we do, the results are worth attempting it every time. Nothing beats walking to the window in your "standard view" secret-Savanna room at Animal Kingdom Lodge and seeing a giraffe greeting you there, while you're saving several hundred dollars a night compared to the more expensive room.

Disney tries to accommodate your request, and most of the requests sent on behalf of readers are honored in full or partially, but sometimes Disney just can't make it work. Feel fortunate if you get what you asked for.

GENIE+/INDIVIDUAL LIGHTNING LANE INFORMATION The site shows which reservations are the most useful and will automatically suggest the best ones for your touring plans.

ANSWERS TO YOUR TRIP-PLANNING QUESTIONS The TouringPlans online community includes tens of thousands of Disney fans and repeat travelers willing to help with your vacation plans. Ask questions in the forum and offer your own helpful tips.

LINES APP This in-park app is available on the Apple App Store and the Google Play Store. For years, Lines has been one of the highest-rated Disney World apps for Apple and Android devices—higher than even Disney's own apps. Designed to accompany you in the park, Lines has lots of interesting, free features and provides ride and park information that Disney doesn't, including:

- **Posted and actual wait times at attractions.** Lines is the only Disney app that displays both posted wait times and the estimated actual wait times. The wait time you see posted outside of a ride is sometimes much longer than the actual wait time, often because Disney is trying to do crowd control. With Lines, you can make better decisions about whether to get in line.
- **"Ride now or wait" recommendations.** Lines shows you whether ride wait times are likely to get longer or shorter. If you find a long line at a particular attraction, Lines tells you the best time to come back.
- **Real-time updates while you're in a park.** Lines automatically updates your custom touring plan to reflect actual crowd conditions at a given moment. You can also restart your plan and add or change attractions, breaks, meals, and more.

Seeing actual wait times can also help set kids' expectations about how long they'll be in line, as this family from New Jersey found:

The Lines app had the actual wait time nailed almost every single time we consulted it. My kids used Lines on their phones and felt like they were in on a huge adult secret.

The *Unofficial Guide* and TouringPlans.com, along with the Lines app, are designed to work together as a comprehensive planning and touring resource.

This mom from Missouri used all the tools available to her:

The Unofficial Guide *was the perfect place to start planning our vacation (actually our honeymoon). After reading the book, I had a good idea of what hotels I was interested in, and I had must-do and must-eat places somewhat picked out. I then took the knowledge from the book and switched to the website to personalize our touring plans and use as a reference when needed. The book and the website together made our trip INCREDIBLE.*

Our website, **TheUnofficialGuides.com,** is dedicated to news about our guidebooks and features a blog with posts from *Unofficial Guide* authors. You can also sign up for the **"Unofficial Guides Newsletter,"** which contains more travel tips. We also recommend that you check out the following:

1. **Walt Disney World Resort vacation-planning videos.** You can watch online videos advertising Walt Disney World's offerings at plandisney.disney .go.com/plandisney-video-library.

2. *Guide for Guests with Disabilities.* An overview of services and options for guests with disabilities is available at disneyworld.disney.go.com/guest -services/guests-with-disabilities; at Guest Relations when entering the parks, at resort front desks, and at wheelchair-rental areas (for locations, see the "Services" sidebar in each theme park chapter).

YOUR DISNEY TRIP-PLANNING TIMELINE: THE QUICK-START GUIDE TO USING THE *GUIDE*

AS YOU GO THROUGH THIS BOOK, you'll see many references to date-specific planning milestones for your trip. For example, you can make Disney dining reservations 60 days before your arrival. You might be wondering about other important dates for your Disney trip, too, so on the next few pages, we've provided a comprehensive timeline that represents the major research, decisions, and tasks that happen when preparing for a Walt Disney World vacation. Within each milestone, you'll find a reference to the section in this book that has the information you need for that milestone, and/or links to TouringPlans.com for additional information.

Most Disney trips involve about a dozen important dates to remember. If you've started planning more than 11 months before your trip, you'll have plenty of time to do research ahead of those dates. If you're traveling within the next couple of months, you'll want to move a bit quicker.

Do you really need to do this? Absolutely—the demand for things like restaurants can easily outpace their capacity, and you may not get to experience them at all without planning and making reservations. A popular character meal such as Topolino's Terrace can accommodate only a tiny percentage of the people who want to eat there.

Making dining reservations as soon as possible is vital if you want to eat at good (or popular) restaurants. Other reservations, such as those for spas or recreational activities, are important to consider too. Your best bet is always to research early and make reservations as soon as Disney allows.

How to Plan in a Hurry

We get variations on this email a lot:

> *AH! Our first Disney trip is in three weeks, and I just found out about the* Unofficial Guide. *I had no idea about all the research and reservations I needed to do! Am I too late?*

You'll be fine. You'll still want to go through the timeline, because those steps are important—you'll just work through them all on a tighter schedule.

9–12 Months Before Your Trip

You may already have a general idea of when you want to visit Disney World. What the trip will cost you, however, can be a surprise. Take a couple of evenings to plan a budget and an approximate time of year to travel, and to narrow down your hotel choices.

- **Establish a budget**. See pages 58–60 for an idea of how much Disney vacation you can get for $1,500–$4,000, for various family sizes. You can also go to disneyworld.disney.go.com and put in some sample dates to see package prices in your cart without purchasing.

- **Figure out when to go and where to stay.** Begin researching resorts (see Part 5) and the best times of year to visit (see page 27).

- **Brush up on discounts.** Disney releases certain discounts around the same time every year. Check mousesavers.com for a list of these regular discounts, when they're usually announced, and the travel dates they cover at theugseries.com/wdw-discounts. Also see the section on hotel discounts beginning on page 82 in Part 5.

- **Create an account at My Disney Experience** (see page 25). You'll need it to make hotel, dining, and (potentially) ride reservations later.

- **Make a preliminary hotel reservation.** This typically requires a deposit equal to one night's cost and guarantees you a room. Staying on-site gets you early and (at select resorts) late access to the theme parks, offering a substantial advantage in avoiding long lines (see page 30). You can change or cancel without penalty for several months while you continue your research.

- **Disney Vacation Club (DVC)** members can make reservations at their home resorts starting 11 months before their trip. See page 83 for information on how to rent points from a DVC member.

- **Investigate whether trip insurance makes sense for your situation.** If you'll be traveling to Disney World during peak hurricane season (August and September), it is almost certainly worthwhile. Third-party policies, such as those from insuremytrip.com, are usually cheaper than Disney's trip insurance and are often more comprehensive. In the post-pandemic era, almost all trips should be insured for trip cancellation or interruption, and for medical emergencies.

- **If you're not a US citizen, make sure your family's passports and visas are in order.** Passports typically need to be valid for six months beyond your travel dates. An electronic US visa is typically good for two years from the date of issue, if you need one. See esta.cbp.dhs.gov/esta to check whether your country participates in the US's visa waiver program. As of 2024, you must apply for a visa (or waiver) at least 72 hours prior to arrival.

7–9 Months Before Your Trip

Now is the time to start thinking about where you'll be eating and what you want to do in the theme parks.

- **Purchase your park tickets** at least this far in advance (see page 63 for ticket and add-on details). TouringPlans' Least Expensive Ticket Calculator (touringplans.com/walt-disney-world/ticket-calculator) will find you the best discounts on Disney tickets. This helps you lock in prices before any potential increases.

- **Link your tickets to your My Disney Experience account** so that all tickets and reservations are linked together.

- **Disney Vacation Club** members can make resort reservations outside their home resorts starting seven months before their trip.

- **Check the best days to visit each park.** Use the Disney World Crowd Calendar (touringplans.com/walt-disney-world/crowd-calendar) to select the parks you'll visit on each day of your trip.

4–6 Months Before Your Trip

Get familiar with Disney's rides, shows, and attractions, and start planning what you'll see each day.

- **Review the attractions and shows** in the Magic Kingdom (see page 363), EPCOT (see page 403), Disney's Animal Kingdom (see page 433), and Disney's Hollywood Studios (see page 458).

- **Make a list of must-see attractions in each park.** If you're unsure whether your child should experience a particular attraction, see our Small-Child Fright-Potential Table on pages 304–306. See the table on page 307 for a list of height requirements for the attractions.

- **Review our touring plans** (see page 546) and use them to begin putting together a touring strategy for each park. You can also use the touring plan software at touringplans.com/walt-disney-world/touring-plans.

180 Days Before Your Trip

Use this time to research Disney's restaurants and dining options.

- **Get familiar with Disney World restaurants** (see Part 6) so you're ready when Disney's dining reservation system opens at your 60-day mark. See touringplans.com/walt-disney-world/dining for current restaurant ratings, menus, and prices at every Disney restaurant, all searchable.

- **Get familiar with the Disney Dining Plan** (see page 205). If you're planning to stay at a Disney hotel, you'll need to figure out if the plan will save you any money on the meals you're interested in.

120 Days Before Your Trip

As your vacation approaches, it's time to make concrete arrangements for your days in the theme parks.

- **Save money on stroller rentals in the parks** (if you'll need a stroller) by renting from a third-party company; see page 297 for our recommendations. You can also **save on wheelchair and ECV rentals** this way; see page 316 for details and recommendations.

60 Days Before Your Trip

Now you can start making restaurant, tour, spa, and other reservations.

- **Make reservations for sit-down dining** beginning at 5:45 a.m. Eastern time online at disneyworld.disney.go.com/dining, or at 6:45 a.m. by phone (see page 208 for tips): ☎ 407-WDW-DINE (939-3463). If you're staying at a Walt Disney World resort, you can make reservations for up to 10 days of your trip today. You have a better chance of getting what you want if you use the website instead of calling.

- **Make reservations for the following:**
  Theme park tours: ☎ 407-WDW-TOUR (939-8687)
  Recreational activities such as boating: ☎ 407-WDW-PLAY (939-7529)
  Spa treatments: ☎ 407-WDW-SPAS (939-7727)
  Bibbidi Bobbidi Boutique (page 503): ☎ 407-WDW-STYL (939-7895)

- **Start a walking regimen** to prepare for the 7–10 miles per day you may be walking in the parks. See page 290 for more on that.

- **If you decide not to go to Disney World,** you typically have 30 days to cancel most Disney vacation packages without a penalty; room-only reservations can be canceled without a penalty until eight days before your trip. See page 80 for a review of Disney's cancellation policies.

- **Start online check-in** at disneyworld.disney.go.com/trip/online-check-in, if you're staying at a Disney-owned hotel. Doing this in advance means you'll be able to head directly to your hotel room upon arrival, without having to stop at the front desk.

45 Days Before Your Trip

- **Final payment for room-only reservations** is due if you book online within 45 days of arrival (payment of room-only reservations booked farther out isn't due until check-in).

- **Order your MagicBands** (see page 70), if desired.

- **If you're flying,** make arrangements for your transfer between the airport and your hotel (see page 328).

- **If you want to switch resorts** or make more dining reservations, now is a good time to check on both.

30 Days Out

- **Send your room request to Disney.** TouringPlans can do this for you automatically (see page 19).

- Final payment is due for Disney vacation packages.
- Sign up for Disney's Disability Access Service (see page 314), if needed. You'll be able to make two ride reservations in advance. See theugseries .com/get-wdw-das for more details.
- Confirm park hours and finish preliminary touring plans.
- Download the Lines app so you can follow your chosen touring plan and get updates in the parks.
- Arrange to stop delivery of mail and newspapers.
- Arrange for pet or house sitters.

2 Weeks Out

- Arrange grocery delivery to your resort (see page 362).
- If you're flying to the US from another country, complete the Advance Passenger Information and Secure Flight (APIS) process at least 72 hours before your flight. You should be able to do this through your airline's website; otherwise, make sure your travel agent has your information. You'll need to provide the address where you'll be staying in the United States, so have that information handy when you complete this form.
- Check that you have enough prescription medication.
- If staying at a Disney Good Neighbor hotel, ensure your hotel reservation appears in the "Resort Hotel" section of the My Disney Experience app or website. This is how Disney knows you're eligible for Early Theme Park Entry or Extended Evening Theme Park Hours (see page 30).

8 Days Out

- For 2025 arrival dates, this is typically your last chance to **cancel Disney room-only reservations** without penalty. Call ☎ 407-W-DISNEY (407-934-7639).

6 Days Out

- Check the weather forecast.
- Start packing. Good shoes are especially important.

5 Days Out

- For 2024 arrival dates, this is typically your last chance to **cancel Disney room-only reservations** without penalty. Call ☎ W-DISNEY (407-934-7639).

4 Days Out

- Purchase Disney's Memory Maker photo package (see page 359) at least three days in advance to ensure that all photos are linked as soon as you arrive. You'll also get a discount if you buy your package in advance.

The Day Before

- Check in for your flight online.
- Finish your Disney resort online check-in, if you haven't already done so, at disneyworld.disney.go.com/trip/online-check-in.
- Cancel any unneeded dining or baby- or pet-sitting reservations.
- Do one last check of park hours and weather.

DISNEY ONLINE: OFFICIAL AND OTHERWISE

A SUITE OF HIGH-TECH ENHANCEMENTS to Disney's theme parks and hotels, known as **MyMagic+,** includes optional wristbands (**MagicBands**) that function as admission tickets, hotel keys, and credit cards. MyMagic+ also integrates Disney's dining and ride reservation systems. It requires you to make detailed decisions about every day of your trip, sometimes months in advance, if you want to visit popular attractions and avoid long waits. Dining reservations, for instance, require you to know the exact time you want to eat, and where, two months before you arrive.

The Walt Disney World website (disneyworld.disney.go.com) and the **My Disney Experience** (**MDE**) mobile app are the glue that binds this all together. Because you must plan so much before you leave home, we cover the basics of both the website and the app in the next section. MagicBand information starts on page 70. Details on Disney's ride reservation systems—**Genie+** and **Individual Lightning Lane**—and Disney's other new way of waiting in lines, called **boarding groups** or **virtual queues,** start on page 49. Finally, Disney's **"free Genie"** itinerary-planning service, which you absolutely should *not* use, is described on page 53.

My Disney Experience on the Disney World Website

The web version of MDE (disneyworld.disney.go.com/plan) allows you to make hotel, dining, ride, and some recreation reservations; buy admission; and get park hours, attraction information, and much more.

TECHNICAL PROBLEMS Disney World's website is so unreliable that most visitors are familiar with the various "broken" page screens and keep track of how many times they encounter "Stitch ate my page" vs. "The Seven Dwarfs are working on it." If you run into technical issues on Disney's website, the first thing to do is try using your browser's private or incognito mode. Disney's website often places so many cookies on your computer that it appears to break its own systems. If that doesn't work and human intervention is required, call ☎ 407-939-4357 in the US or ☎ 0800 169 0749 in the UK for help.

Set aside several hours to get any issues resolved. Disney's phone systems are regularly understaffed, and stories abound of long waits for support. This is especially true on days when big events are released.

BEFORE YOU BEGIN Set aside at least 30–40 minutes to complete this process. Make sure you have the following items on hand:

- A valid admission ticket or confirmation number for everyone in your group
- Your hotel reservation number, if you're staying on-site (including the Swan, Swan Reserve, Dolphin, and Disney Springs hotels)
- A computer, smartphone, or tablet connected to the internet
- An email account that you can access easily while traveling
- The dates, times, and confirmation numbers of any dining or recreation reservations you've made

If you're coordinating travel plans with friends or family who live elsewhere, you'll also need the following information:

- The names and (optional) email addresses of the people you're traveling with
- The dates and times of any dining or recreation reservations they've made

GETTING STARTED Go to disneyworld.disney.go.com/plan and click "Create Account." You'll be asked for your email address, along with your name, billing address, and birth date. (Disney uses your billing address to send your hotel reservation information, if applicable, and to charge your credit card for anything you purchase.)

Once you've created an account, the website will display a page with links to other steps in the planning process. These steps are described next. If the website shows you different screens and options when you sign in, click the "My Disney Experience" icon in the upper-right corner of the page and look for similar wording.

DISNEY HOTEL INFORMATION If you're staying at a Disney hotel, select "Resort Hotel" and then "Link Reservation." Enter your reservation number. This associates your MDE account with your hotel stay in Disney's computer systems. If you've booked a travel package that includes theme park admission, Disney computers will automatically link the admission to your MDE account, allowing you to skip the "Linking Tickets" step. If you've booked a Disney hotel through a third-party site like Expedia, that site should send you a Disney reservation number to use here. It can take up to a week for third-party sites to send Disney your booking information, so be patient and plan ahead.

REGISTER FRIENDS AND FAMILY Click the "Family & Friends" icon; then enter the names and ages of everyone traveling with you. You can do this later, too, but you'll need this information when you make your park and dining reservations.

LINKING TICKETS You will need to have purchased theme park tickets for each member of your group and linked them to each member's MDE profile before making some reservations.

If you haven't purchased your tickets, do so now. See page 68 for where to find better deals on tickets. Once purchased, you can add these tickets to MDE just like tickets bought directly from Disney.

If you've already purchased tickets but have not linked them, click the "Park Tickets" widget, then click on "Link Tickets," and follow the instructions.

MAKING DINING RESERVATIONS In My Disney Experience, click the "Dining" icon, then the "Make a Reservation" link. (You may have to reenter your travel dates.) First, you'll need to indicate how many people are dining. Then, you'll choose a date and a time range for when you'd like to dine. A list of every Walt Disney World eatery will be displayed. Use the filtering criteria at the top of the page to narrow the list. Once you've settled on a restaurant, click the time of the reservation you'd like to book. To complete your reservation, you'll also need to enter a credit card number to hold your reservation. If you want to make other dining reservations, you'll need to repeat this process for each one.

My Disney Experience Mobile App

In addition to its website, Disney offers an app called My Disney Experience, available on the Apple App Store and the Google Play Store. It includes park hours, attraction operating hours and descriptions, wait times for buses, restaurant hours with descriptions and menus, the ability to make dining and ride reservations, GPS-based directions, counter-service meal ordering, the locations of park

unofficial **TIP**
Some features of MDE, including mobile ordering, may not be available on older devices.

photographers, and more. You'll definitely want to download the app and familiarize yourself with all of its features before your trip.

Our Recommended Websites

Searching online for Disney information is like navigating an immense maze for a tiny piece of cheese: You may find a lot of dead ends before you get what you want. Our picks follow.

BEST Q&A SITE planDisney, formerly Walt Disney World's Mom's Panel, is made up of Disney World veterans chosen from among more than 10,000 applicants each year. The panelists have a website, plandisney.disney.go.com, where they offer tips and discuss how to plan a Disney World vacation. Several panelists have specialized experience in areas such as runDisney or traveling with sports groups. Some speak languages other than English, too.

BEST MONEY-SAVING SITE MouseSavers (mousesavers.com) keeps an updated list of discounts for use at Disney World resorts, separated into categories such as "For the general public" and "For residents of certain states." Anyone who calls or books online can use a current discount. The savings can be considerable—as much as 40%. The site also offers deals on rental cars and non-Disney hotels in the area, along with a calendar showing when Disney sales typically launch.

BEST SITE FOR CAR-RENTAL DEALS AutoSlash (autoslash.com) will use every available discount code for every car company in Orlando to find you the best deal. See page 330 for more on car rentals.

BEST DISNEY DISCUSSION BOARDS There are tons of these; among the most active boards are **disboards.com; forums.wdwmagic.com; forum .touringplans.com;** and, for Brits, **thedibb.co.uk** (*DIBB* stands for "Disney Information Bulletin Board").

WHEN *to* GO *to* WALT DISNEY WORLD

SELECTING THE TIME OF YEAR FOR YOUR VISIT

WALT DISNEY WORLD IS BUSIEST from the weekend before Christmas Day until the first weekend in January. The next-busiest times are spring break (early March–early April, plus the week before Easter when Easter is later); Thanksgiving week; and February during Presidents' Day and Mardi Gras. You'll also see shorter bursts of crowds in early June as public-school summer vacations start, and on three-day weekends, such as Columbus Day and Veterans Day.

The least busy time *historically* is Labor Day through early October. In addition, the last two weeks of October and the first week of November are usually less crowded than average, as are the weeks after Thanksgiving and before Christmas. The weeks between late April and Memorial Day have lower crowds than the weeks on either side.

The biggest rule of thumb is that Walt Disney World is less crowded (and less expensive) when most kids are in school. That said, Disney has become adept at loading off-peak periods with special events, conventions, food festivals, and the like; discounts on rooms and dining during slower periods also figure in.

In short: Disney World can be busy at any time, and you'll need to look beyond the time of year to pinpoint the least crowded dates. For a calendar of scheduled events, visit theugseries.com/wdwevents.

DON'T FORGET AUGUST Kids go back to school pretty early in Florida (and in a lot of other places). This makes mid- to late August a good time for families who can't vacation during the school year . . . and don't mind the oppressive heat.

A New Jersey mother of two school-age children spells it out:

> *The end of August is the PERFECT time to go (just watch out for hurricanes; it's the season). There were virtually no wait times, 20 minutes at the most.*

PLANNING FOR FLORIDA WEATHER

> *Why is the world's best theme park in the world's worst climate?*
>
> —A reader from Oregon

LONG BEFORE WALT DISNEY WORLD EXISTED, tourists visited Florida year-round to enjoy the temperate climate. The best weather months are generally November through March (see the table below). Fall is usually dry, but spring and summer are wet. Rain is possible anytime, usually in the form of scattered thunderstorms, but an entire day lost to steady rain is unusual.

SUMMER TEMPERATURES CAN FEEL LIKE 120°F If your weather app says it's 95°F in Orlando, it's warmer if you're standing in the sun, and hotter still if you're wearing dark-colored clothing.

Florida's humidity makes the heat feel worse because it prevents your sweat from evaporating to cool you off. During summer in the Magic Kingdom, you'll commonly experience Heat Indexes ("feels-like temperatures") above 110°F, and we've measured highs of 122°F. How hot is that? A steak cooked rare is considered done at 130°F.

WALT DISNEY WORLD CLIMATE

	JAN	FEB	MAR	APR	MAY	JUN	JUL	AUG	SEP	OCT	NOV	DEC
AVERAGE DAILY HIGH												
	72°F	75°F	79°F	84°F	88°F	91°F	92°F	91°F	89°F	85°F	78°F	75°F
AVERAGE DAILY MAX HEAT INDEX (COMBINED EFFECT OF HEAT AND HUMIDITY)												
	72°F	75°F	81°F	92°F	106°F	119°F	121°F	120°F	111°F	96°F	79°F	75°F
AVERAGE DAILY TEMPERATURE												
	62°F	64°F	68°F	74°F	79°F	82°F	84°F	83°F	82°F	77°F	69°F	65°F
AVERAGE DAILY HUMIDITY												
	71%	68%	65%	64%	65%	75%	79%	80%	80%	73%	71%	73%
AVERAGE RAINFALL PER MONTH												
	2.1"	1.9"	2.5"	2.2"	2.7"	6.1"	6.0"	6.6"	5.5"	2.4"	1.2"	1.6"
NUMBER OF DAYS OF RAIN PER MONTH												
	4	4	5	4	6	12	13	14	11	5	3	4

Source: climate-data.org

CROWD CALENDAR

DISNEY WORLD'S ATTENDANCE is normally almost 59 million guests per year—an average of around 161,000 guests per day. That makes tips for avoiding crowds invaluable. Besides which month or week to visit, you should also think about the best park to visit on each day of your stay.

Disney regularly adjusts things like resort discounts, park capacity, and park hours in order to entice more people or adjust capacity if things are looking uncrowded. Because of that, it's not possible to include an accurate calendar of crowds in this book. To stay updated, you can find a calendar covering the next year at touringplans.com /walt-disney-world/crowd-calendar. For each date, you'll find a crowd-level index based on a 1–10 scale, with 1 being least crowded and 10 being most crowded. The calendar is based on how long you'll wait in line and takes into account all holidays, special events, and more, as described in the next section.

Keeping the online Crowd Calendar updated requires year-round work. As a result, there is a subscription fee for full access. Much of the rest of the website is free, and owners of the current edition of this guide are eligible for a discount on the subscription. See page 18 for more information about TouringPlans.com.

Even on a "slow" day, you will certainly see posted wait times of 1 hour or more for popular rides such as Seven Dwarfs Mine Train in the Magic Kingdom, Avatar Flight of Passage in Disney's Animal Kingdom, Remy's Ratatouille Adventure and Frozen Ever After in EPCOT, and Star Wars: Rise of the Resistance and Slinky Dog Dash in DHS.

HOW TOURINGPLANS DETERMINES CROWD LEVELS AND BEST DAYS

A number of factors contribute to the models used to predict both crowd levels and the best days to visit each theme park.

Data used to predict crowd levels:

- Recent wait times, which are given high importance
- Historical theme park hours from the same time period in past years

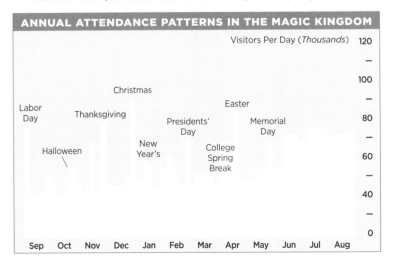

- Future hotel-room bookings in the Orlando area
- Disney's special-events calendar (for example, the Magic Kingdom's Halloween and Christmas parties)
- Legal holidays in the United States
- Public-school schedules, weighted by distance from Florida and tourism rates

TouringPlans also collects thousands of wait times from every ride in every Disney park daily, including posted and actual times. *Popular Science* did a nice article several years ago on the data science behind their predictions; read it at popsci.com/touring-plan-app-disney-lines.

SPRING BREAK AND HOLIDAY CROWDS

MANY FAMILIES HAVE NO CHOICE but to visit Disney World during a busy time. Much of this book, in fact, is dedicated to helping readers who visit during busier times enjoy the experience. Armed with knowledge and some strategy, you can have a great time whenever you go.

Disney World experiences its highest demand during holiday periods. If you visit during spring break or a major holiday, the first thing you need to know is that the theme parks' guest capacity is not infinite. Disney allocates park capacity so that guests staying at its hotels and those who have bought date-specific tickets in advance have priority for park entry.

Christmas and New Year's at the Theme Parks

Don't expect to see all the attractions in a single day at any park during this most crowded period. That said, Disney's Animal Kingdom is usually the least crowded park during the winter holidays, especially on New Year's Eve because it closes hours earlier than any other park. EPCOT is a good choice, too, because it has about twice the acreage and typically lower crowds than the Magic Kingdom. (It also has fewer attractions, but many of them are high-capacity shows and rides.)

New Year's Eve is the busiest day of the year in the Magic Kingdom. The park stages New Year's Eve fireworks on both December 30 and December 31 for those who either wish to see fireworks in multiple parks or don't want to be caught in the crowds. If you stay until midnight, expect it to take 1–3 hours to get back to your hotel by bus or car. We suggest getting a room at a Magic Kingdom monorail resort (the **Contemporary, Grand Floridian,** or **Polynesian Village**), which have walking paths as well. If you're visiting EPCOT or the Studios for New Year's Eve, we suggest the **BoardWalk Inn, BoardWalk Villas, Yacht Club, Beach Club, Swan, Swan Reserve,** or **Dolphin,** all within walking distance of those parks. Even the Skyliner will be swamped beyond its capacity.

EARLY THEME PARK ENTRY

EARLY THEME PARK ENTRY (aka Early Entry or ETPE) is a perk for guests staying at Disney resort hotels, including the Swan, Dolphin, and Swan Reserve; Shades of Green; the Four Seasons; Disney Springs hotels; and Hilton hotels in Bonnet Creek. Those guests can enter any of Disney's theme parks 30 minutes earlier than official park operating hours every day.

WHAT'S REQUIRED? A valid ticket or MagicBand is required to enter the park. Make sure you have your reservation linked to your My Disney Experience account.

DISNEY SPRINGS AND GOOD NEIGHBOR HOTELS The Early Entry benefit is offered to guests staying at Disney Springs hotels and select Disney Good Neighbor hotels (see table on page 77). But Disney's computer systems don't always know this, which can lead to confusion at the park entrance. The computer systems of Disney and the Good Neighbor hotels are supposed to communicate these details through Disney's My Disney Experience (MDE) system. If you're staying at a Good Neighbor hotel eligible for Early Entry, ensure that your reservation number appears in MDE at least a week before you arrive.

If these computer systems don't communicate properly before your trip, your experience at the gates may vary. We've heard stories of families calling hotels to get confirmation. On our family's most recent stay at the Swan, scanning in for Early Entry worked every day of the trip, other than the very last one at EPCOT. On that morning, the cast member just asked us what our hotel was and then to produce a key. After that, we were allowed into the park.

HOW DOES EARLY ENTRY WORK? Eligible resort guests are invited to enter any theme park 30 minutes before the general public. During this time, guests should be able to enjoy select attractions. In the Magic Kingdom, for example, you should find attractions open in Fantasyland and Tomorrowland.

In practice, we think on-site guests should arrive at their chosen park's entrance about an hour before official opening. That gets you at the very front of the crowd, ready to go to your first attraction as soon as the park opens. And Disney often opens the park a bit earlier than 30 minutes in advance, giving you even more of a bonus.

During holidays and other busy times, some parks open to regular guests at 8 a.m. and Early Entry begins at 7:30 a.m., so you'll need to be at the park entrance no later than 7 a.m. You won't be alone in doing this, but because relatively few people are willing to get up that early for a theme park, your first few hours in the parks will be (wait for it) magical.

How Early Entry Affects Attendance at the Theme Parks

Because Early Entry is offered at every park, every day, Disney resort guests are spread out more evenly among the parks, and Disney can dangle this benefit of staying on-site in front of potential hotel guests.

If you're staying at an eligible resort, remember these three things about Early Entry:

1. The Magic Kingdom has more attractions open for Early Entry than any other park. We think the Magic Kingdom's Early Entry, coupled with a good touring plan, is the most worthwhile of any park's.

2. Early Entry is especially useful when Disney opens new rides.

3. Early Entry is a big advantage when using the standby line at popular attractions such as Star Wars: Rise of the Resistance in Disney's Hollywood

Studios; Frozen Ever After and Remy's Ratatouille Adventure in EPCOT; and Avatar Flight of Passage in Animal Kingdom.

WHAT'S THE CATCH? The disadvantage of Early Entry for on-site guests is that they must now wake up and get moving earlier to beat the crowds. Off-site guests are considerably disadvantaged by the Early Entry program—they are guaranteed to have thousands of on-site guests already in front of them at any theme park they visit, every day. When popular attractions, such as Tron Lightcycle/Run, eventually convert to standby queues, it's a safe bet that their lines will be hours long well before the first off-site guest even sets foot inside the park.

To mitigate the effect of Early Entry on off-site guests, we've added off-site versions of the touring plans to this book. Be aware, however, that even with an optimal touring plan, off-site guests may wait several more hours in line per day than on-site guests, due to the head start those on-site guests have.

EXTENDED EVENING THEME PARK HOURS

EXTENDED EVENING THEME PARK HOURS (EETPH) is the much more limited post-park-closing version of Early Entry; it's offered much less frequently and to many fewer guests. Typically held on one night per week and, for now, only at certain parks, EETPH allows only guests staying at Disney's Deluxe and DVC resorts two extra hours in that park after official closing. Thus, if the Magic Kingdom closes at 9 p.m. to regular guests, the park will operate Extended Hours from 9 to 11 p.m. for guests at Disney Deluxe or DVC resorts only.

During EETPH, Disney sets up checkpoints throughout the park, such as the entrance to each attraction, to verify that guests entering are eligible for the program. Disney scans your MagicBand or plastic ticket to verify your resort.

The advantage of EETPH is that so few guests qualify that lines are usually exceptionally short. In late December 2022, we managed to see 10 attractions in the Magic Kingdom during EETPH, waiting a total of 31 minutes in line. In comparison, those same 10 attractions would've taken almost 7 hours to see during that day. In EPCOT, it's a little harder to take advantage of the time since the major attractions are so far apart. At the first-ever EETPH in Animal Kingdom in late 2023, Expedition Everest and Avatar Flight of Passage were both walk-on attractions for the second hour.

THE WALT DISNEY WORLD CALENDAR

DISNEY CELEBRATES SPECIAL EVENTS throughout the year. Some events commemorate major holidays, while others are designed by Disney to boost attendance during otherwise-slow times of year.

JANUARY Usually held the second weekend after New Year's, the **Walt Disney World Marathon** attracts thousands of runners and their families every year. You can find information on all Disney running events at rundisney.com.

Another winter event is the **EPCOT International Festival of the Arts.** Running from the first full week of January until the third full week of February, the festival (which is included as part of your park admission) highlights the visual, performing, and culinary arts, with live performances, creative cuisine, and workshops to build your own creative skills. See pages 221, 223, and 509 for more information.

FEBRUARY Black History Month is celebrated throughout Walt Disney World with displays, artisans, storytellers, and entertainers.

In 2025, **Presidents' Day** is Monday, February 17, which will make the entire Valentine's Day/Presidents' Day weekend very crowded.

MARCH In 2025, **Mardi Gras** is Tuesday, March 4, which will significantly increase crowds starting at the very beginning of the month. The **EPCOT International Flower & Garden Festival,** which runs March–May, showcases exotic floral displays—the 30 million blooms from some 1,200 species will make your eyes pop. The festival also features food and beverage kiosks, making it more like fall's International Food & Wine Festival (see August, below), only with impressive Disney-themed topiaries.

APRIL Easter is April 20, 2025. Because it's so late this year, expect spring break crowds to be a little more spread out than normal from mid-March through the week of Easter.

JUNE Gay Days, an unofficial gathering of LGBTQ people from around the world, has been happening annually since 1991. Organizers say previous Gay Days have attracted close to 200,000 visitors and their friends and families. For additional information, visit gaydays.com.

JULY July Fourth used to be one of the most crowded seasons of the year, but thanks to the incredibly hot weather and the increasing interest in other parts of the year, that is no longer the case.

AUGUST The **EPCOT International Food & Wine Festival** is usually held in the World Showcase from August to late November. The celebration represents the cuisines of six continents and may include demonstrations, wine seminars, tastings, and more. Many activities are included in EPCOT admission, though some are by reservation only and require separate tickets. See page 221 for more information about the festival.

Mickey's Not So Scary Halloween Party, in the Magic Kingdom, is typically held on select nights between mid-August and November 1, 7 p.m.–midnight. Ticket holders can get into the park starting at 4 p.m. The festivities include trick-or-treating in costume, parades, live music, storytelling, and a fireworks show. See page 397 for more information on this popular event.

NOVEMBER The **Wine and Dine Half-Marathon** early in this month revolves around a 13.1-mile race that ends with a nighttime party amid the EPCOT International Food & Wine Festival. The 2024 event will be the October 31–November 3. Veterans Day and Jersey Week (when many East Coast schools have several days or an entire week off) also occur in early November, significantly boosting crowds for a week.

DECEMBER The annual **Disney Parks Christmas Day Parade,** televised on December 25, is usually taped in the Magic Kingdom in November or the first week of December. The parade ties up pedestrian traffic on Main Street, U.S.A., all day. In 2023, this taping happened on November 12.

EPCOT's holiday celebration, **EPCOT International Festival of the Holidays,** typically runs late November–late December and includes food booths similar to those present in World Showcase during the Festival of the Arts, Food & Wine, and Flower & Garden Festivals.

Disney's Very Merry Christmas Party takes place on select evenings in November and December, 7 p.m.–midnight (after regular hours; ticketed guests can get into the park starting at 4 p.m.). The event includes attractions; stage shows featuring Disney characters; unlimited complimentary snacks and drinks; a holiday-themed fireworks show; carolers; "a magical snowfall on Main Street"; white lights on Cinderella Castle; and live entertainment.

WDW ADDRESSES

GENERAL INFORMATION
WDW Guest Communications, PO Box 10040, Lake Buena Vista, FL 32830-0040
☎ 407-560-2544; wdw.guest.communications@disneyworld.com or
guest.services@disneyworld.com
General online help: disneyworld.disney.go.com/help/email

CONVENTION AND BANQUET INFORMATION (aka Group Sales)
Walt Disney World Resort South, PO Box 10000, Lake Buena Vista, FL 32830-1000
☎ 321-939-7129; disneymeetings.com

DISNEY IMAGINATION CAMPUS (youth programs)
☎ 321-939-7560; disneycampus.com

WALT DISNEY WORLD TICKET MAIL ORDER
☎ 407-566-4985; ticket.inquiries@disneyworld.com

WDW PHONE NUMBERS

General Information ☎ 407-824-4321 or 407-824-2222

General Information for Deaf and Hard-of-Hearing Guests (TTY) ☎ 407-827-5141

Accommodations/Central Reservations ☎ 407-934-7639

Advance Dining Reservations ☎ 407-939-3463

Advent Health Centra Care (urgent-care clinic) ☎ 407-390-1888 (Kissimmee);
☎407-934-2273 (Lake Buena Vista); ☎ 407-291-8975 (Universal–Dr. Phillips)

All-Star Movies Resort ☎ 407-939-7000

All-Star Music Resort ☎ 407-939-6000

All-Star Sports Resort ☎ 407-939-5000

AMC Movies at Disney Springs ☎ 407-827-1308

Animal Kingdom Lodge & Villas–Jambo House ☎ 407-938-3000
Kidani Village ☎ 407-938-7400

Art of Animation Resort ☎ 407-938-7000

Beach Club Resort ☎ 407-934-8000

Beach Club Villas ☎ 407-934-8000

Blizzard Beach Information ☎ 407-560-3400

BoardWalk Inn and Villas ☎ 407-939-6200

Caribbean Beach Resort ☎ 407-934-3400

Car Rentals ☎ 407-824-3470, ext. 1

Contemporary Resort and Bay Lake Tower ☎ 407-824-1000

Convention Information ☎ 321-939-7129

WDW PHONE NUMBERS (continued)

Coronado Springs Resort ☎ 407-939-1000

Disney Institute ☎ 321-939-4600

Disney Springs Information ☎ 407-939-5277

ESPN Wide World of Sports Complex ☎ 407-939-1500

Fantasia Gardens and Fairways Miniature Golf ☎ 407-560-4870

Fort Wilderness Resort & Campground ☎ 407-824-2900

Golf Reservations and Information ☎ 407-939-4653

Grand Floridian Resort & Spa/Grand Floridian Villas ☎ 407-824-3000

Group Camping ☎ 407-939-7807

Guided Tour Information ☎ 407-939-8687

Guided VIP Solo Tours ☎ 407-560-4033

House of Blues Tickets and Information ☎ 407-934-2583

Lost and Found (for articles lost yesterday or before; for same day, go to Guest Relations, front desk, or disneyworld.com/lostandfound) ☎ 407-824-4245

Merchandise Guest Services ☎ 877-560-6477

Old Key West Resort ☎ 407-827-7700

Outdoor Recreation Reservations and Information ☎ 407-939-7529

Polynesian Village Resort ☎ 407-824-2000

Polynesian Village Villas ☎ 407-824-3500

Pop Century Resort ☎ 407-938-4000

Port Orleans Resort–French Quarter ☎ 407-934-5000

Port Orleans Resort–Riverside ☎ 407-934-6000

Riviera Resort ☎ 407-828-7030

Resort Dining ☎ 407-939-3463

Saratoga Springs Resort & Spa, Treehouse Villas ☎ 407-827-1100

Security ☎ 407-560-7959 (routine); ☎ 407-560-1990 (urgent)

Shades of Green ☎ 407-824-3400 or 407-824-3600

Special Requests for Guests with Disabilities ☎ 407-560-2547 (voice)

Telecommunication for the Deaf Reservations (TTY) ☎ 407-827-5141

Walt Disney Travel Company ☎ 407-939-6244

Walt Disney World Dolphin ☎ 407-934-4000

Walt Disney World Swan ☎ 407-934-3000

Walt Disney World Swan Reserve ☎ 407-934-3000

Walt Disney World Ticket Inquiries ☎ 407-939-7679

Weather Information ☎ 407-827-4545

Wilderness Lodge/Boulder Ridge & Copper Creek Villas ☎ 407-824-3200

Winter Summerland Miniature Golf ☎ 407-560-3000

Wrecker Service (7 a.m.–11 p.m.; if closed, call Security) ☎ 407-824-0976

Yacht Club Resort ☎ 407-934-7000

PART 3

MAKING *the* MOST *of* YOUR TIME

KEY QUESTIONS ANSWERED IN THIS CHAPTER

- How long does it take to see Walt Disney World? *(see below)*
- What are standby queues, boarding groups, Disney's Genie/Genie+, and Individual Lightning Lane, and how do I use them? *(page 49)*
- What are the six most important tips for avoiding lines at Disney World? *(page 40)*
- What are touring plans, and how do I use them? *(page 42)*

ALLOCATING TIME

THE VACATION THAT FIGHTS BACK

A WHIRLWIND TOUR of Disney's four theme parks and two water parks takes at least **six full days** and a level of stamina typically reserved for running a marathon. A British man, thinking we exaggerated, measured how far he walked and found this:

> *Our visits to the theme parks were spread over five days, during which my wife and I (ages 51 and 55) walked a total of 68 miles for an average of 13 miles per day!*

You'll soon discover that at Walt Disney World, less is more. Take the parks in small doses, with time for swimming and/or rest and relaxation in between. Forcing yourself to go fast will just make everyone cranky and tired. It's exhausting to rise at dawn and run around a theme park for 8–10 hours day after day. Sooner or later (usually sooner), you hit the wall. To avoid that, use one or both of these tips:

1. Take at least a morning off (preferably an entire day) after two consecutive days in the parks.
2. Return to your hotel for at least a 2-hour break each day you're in the parks.

The key to any sleep-in day is to set up a touring plan (see page 42). To get you started, we've created **late-start touring plans** for Animal Kingdom. Check them out at theugseries.com/sleepin-animalkingdom.

This Virginia family recommends taking it slow and easy:

We spent eight days in Disney, and it was totally worth it. A longer trip, believe it or not, eliminates the happy death march—we cut our stress by 90%. Each day, we took some sort of break: a morning swim, an afternoon nap, a sit-down snack in a restaurant. The end result was that the kids got to see/ride everything they wanted without exhausting themselves (or us)—or spending most of their days in line. And we had almost zero tantrums (really!).

The rest of this section will help you decide which park to see first, when to arrive, how to build breaks and naps into your schedule, and what to do on the first and last days of your trip.

WHICH PARK SHOULD YOU SEE FIRST?

THE ANSWER TO THIS QUESTION DEPENDS on the time of year you visit, the length of your stay, and who you're traveling with.

If you start in **Magic Kingdom,** you start your trip off with the wow factor. This is the classic Disney day. But you could be overwhelmed trying to cram this busiest park into your first day when you're still adjusting to Disney vacation mode.

EPCOT is designed to open your eyes to see and appreciate other perspectives. But it's also the park that requires the most walking and could wear you out before your vacation has even really begun.

Disney's Hollywood Studios has some of the best individual attractions of any park, which can make it a hit with the thrill seekers or *Star Wars* fans in your family. But it also has the most attraction downtime of any park, and the longest overall wait times, which add up to a significant risk of starting off your vacation on an unlucky sour note.

Animal Kingdom is the most relaxed of any park—and the hottest. You could start with the relaxing day or save it for later in your vacation when you need a breather.

OPERATING HOURS

THE DISNEY WORLD WEBSITE typically publishes park hours around 60–75 days in advance, but schedule adjustments can happen at any time, including the day of your visit. Check disneyworld.disney .go.com or the My Disney Experience app for exact hours before you arrive. Off-season, parks may be open as few as 10 hours (9 a.m.–7 p.m.), while at busy times (particularly holidays) they may operate for more than 13 hours. The parks used to have much more staggered opening times, but recently it seems that most parks open at 9 a.m. during the offseason, with a little variation during busier times.

Opening Time

When you search Disney's website for park hours, you'll usually find the times at which the park is open to the general public. For example, when Disney says the Magic Kingdom is open from 9 a.m. to 9 p.m., that means the gates open to all ticket holders at 9 a.m. However, Early Theme Park Entry (see page 30) means it opens at 8:30 a.m. for Disney hotel guests. Disney often opens the parks to these guests even earlier, say 8:15 a.m. But because off-site guests aren't eligible for Early Entry, they are likely to be held at the park entrance until the official opening time, regardless of when on-site guests are admitted.

Closing Time

Attraction queues shut down at approximately the official closing time. Some shopping venues, such as Main Street, U.S.A., in the Magic Kingdom, stay open 30–60 minutes after the rest of the park has closed.

THE PRACTICALITY OF RETURNING TO YOUR HOTEL FOR REST

MANY READERS WRITE ABOUT the practicality of departing the theme park for a nap and swim at the hotel.

A dad from Washington made the following request:

I would like to see nearness to the parks emphasized in your accommodation guide. We tried going back to the hotel for midday breaks, but it was too time-consuming. By the time you got to the car, negotiated traffic, rested, and reversed the process to get back to the park, it took 2–3 hours for a short rest and was not worth it!

In Part 5, you'll find a table (pages 194–199) that lists the commuting times to each of the Disney theme parks from many popular hotels within 20 miles of Walt Disney World.

How long will it take you to get from a theme park to your hotel by car? At Animal Kingdom, Hollywood Studios, and EPCOT, you can get to your car in the parking lot in about 15–20 minutes. From the Magic Kingdom, it will take you 40–50 minutes. Obviously, if you're at the farthest point from the park entrance, it will take even longer. Once in your car, you'll be able to commute to most US 192 hotels, all Disney World hotels, all Lake Buena Vista hotels, and most hotels along the I-4 corridor and south International Drive (I-Drive) in 20 minutes or less. It will take about the same time to reach hotels on I-Drive north of Sand Lake Road and in the Universal Orlando area. So, for most people, the one-way commute, including walking, will average 40–45 minutes.

ARRIVAL AND DEPARTURE DAYS: WHAT TO DO WHEN YOU HAVE ONLY HALF A DAY

ON ARRIVAL AND DEPARTURE DAYS, you will probably have only part of a day for touring or other vacation activities. It's a common problem: You roll into the World about 1 p.m., excited and ready to go—but where?

The first question: Do you feel comfortable using a full day's admission when you have less than a full day to tour? The incremental cost to add another day is under $20 if you're visiting for four or more days but $90 for one to three days (see table on pages 64–65 for the breakdown). The crowd level that day, your arrival time, and the parks' closing times are important considerations.

Opting for a Partial Day at the Theme Parks

If you decide to use one day's admission on a half day or less, refer to the **Lines** app or the posted wait times in the My Disney Experience App to see the least crowded park to visit.

One option—if you can reach the park before 1 p.m. and stay until closing (usually 7 p.m.)—is Disney's Animal Kingdom, which requires the least amount of time to tour. You'll find shorter lines for Avatar Flight of Passage, Kilimanjaro Safaris, and Expedition Everest in the late afternoon on all but the busiest days of the year. You just won't have time to do all of the shows during one afternoon.

Another option is to experience Disney's Hollywood Studios' secondary attractions, such as Star Tours—The Adventures Continue, any live shows and entertainment, and shopping on your partial day, leaving your full day for the park's headliner attractions.

Whenever you arrive at a theme park after noon, you should go to higher-capacity attractions where waiting time is relatively shorter, even during the most crowded part of the day. Our clip-out Touring Plan Companions in the back of the book list attractions in each of the Disney parks that require the least waiting during the most crowded part of the day. Although the lines for these attractions may seem long, they move quickly.

Alternatives to the Theme Parks on Arrival Day

Before you head out for fun on arrival day, you must check in and unpack, and you could detour to the grocery or convenience store to buy snacks, drinks, and breakfast food. At all Disney resorts and many non-Disney hotels, you can't occupy your room until after 3 p.m. (4 p.m. for DVC resorts); however, many properties will check you in and store your luggage before that.

The least expensive way to spend your arrival day is to check in, unpack, do your chores, and relax at your hotel swimming pool.

Another daytime option is a trip to a **water park** (see Part 15), and in 2025, this is an even more worthwhile option, because booking a vacation package through Disney will get you into a water park for free on your arrival day. If the park is open late and you get hungry, you'll find ample fast food.

If none of the above options sound appealing, consider minigolf (see page 514) or entertainment at Disney Springs (see page 503).

In the Evening

Dinner provides a great opportunity to plan the next day's activities. If you're hungry for entertainment, too, consider **Disney Springs**. It includes **Cirque du Soleil** (see page 500) and **Raglan Road** (see page 269), an Irish pub with live music and good food, among other diversions.

Departure Days

Departure days don't seem to cause as much indecision as arrival days. If you want to visit a theme park on your departure day, get up early and be at a park when it opens. If you have plenty of time, check out and store your luggage with the bell desk or in your car. Or, if you can arrange a late checkout, you might want to return to your hotel for a shower and change of clothes before your trip home. Departure day is a great time to plan a longer breakfast or brunch at a resort, especially if you want a chance to explore one of the Deluxe or DVC resorts that offer great dining options.

HOW *to* AVOID LONG WAITS *in* LINE

LONG LINES ARE USUALLY THE TOP COMPLAINT among theme park guests—not the quality of the rides, the cost, or the food. It's fair to say that one of the main purposes of the *Unofficial Guide* is to save you time in line. It's what the book is most famous for, and what most of our team's day-to-day work revolves around.

Disney has gone on record saying the average Magic Kingdom guest experiences around 10 of that park's 50-ish attractions in a one-day visit, about one ride per hour. Disney considers everything from headliner rides, like Seven Dwarfs Mine Train, to evening fireworks to the Main Street, U.S.A., piano player as one of those 10. Using the advice and touring plans in this book, we're confident you'll see 20 or more attractions in the same amount of time. How do we do that? By minimizing waiting.

There are six keys to avoiding long lines at Disney World. We elaborate on each these in the remainder of this chapter.

1. Decide in advance what you really want to see (see below).
2. Arrive early (see opposite page).
3. Know what to expect when you arrive (see page 42).
4. Use a touring plan (see page 42).
5. Understand how standby queues, boarding groups, Genie+, and Individual Lightning Lane work (see page 49).
6. Use the single-rider line if one is available (see page 56).

DECIDE IN ADVANCE WHAT YOU REALLY WANT TO SEE

DISNEY'S ATTRACTIONS RANGE from midway-type rides like you'd find at your local carnival to high-tech extravaganzas found nowhere else. To help you decide which to see, we describe each theme park and its attractions in detail. In each description, we include our evaluation of the attraction and give it an overall star rating; the opinions of Disney World guests are also expressed as star ratings, with five stars being the highest rating. We also use the following categories to help you understand the size and scope of the different attractions:

SUPER-HEADLINERS The best attractions the theme park has to offer. They represent the cutting edge of attraction technology and design. When you get back from Walt Disney World and people ask, "Did you go on so-and-so?" this is what they'll be talking about.

HEADLINERS Multimillion-dollar, full-scale, themed adventures and theater presentations that are modern in technology and design and employ a full range of special effects.

MAJOR ATTRACTIONS More modestly themed adventures with state-of-the-art technologies. Or larger-scale attractions of older design.

MINOR ATTRACTIONS Midway-type rides, small "dark" rides (cars on a track, zigzagging through the dark), small theater presentations, transportation rides, and elaborate walk-through attractions.

DIVERSIONS Exhibits, both passive and interactive, including playgrounds, video arcades, and street theater.

Not every attraction fits neatly into these descriptions, but it's a handy way to compare any two.

A Word About Disney Thrill Rides

Readers of all ages should try to be open-minded about Disney "thrill rides." Compared to those at other theme parks, the Disney attractions are generally quite tame, with more emphasis on sights, atmosphere, and special effects than on the motion, speed, or feel of the ride. While we suggest you take Disney's pre-ride warnings seriously, we also recognize that Disney even classifies Frozen Ever After as a thrill ride because it has a drop in the boat ride—even though the drop is very tame and thousands of visitors experience it every day.

Expedition Everest, Rock 'n' Roller Coaster, and Tron Lightcycle/Run, however, are a different story. These are serious coasters that are faster and more intense than Space Mountain or Big Thunder Mountain.

Mission: Space, a high-tech spinning simulation ride in EPCOT, is a toss-up (pun intended)—it absolutely has the potential to make you sick, as do the Star Tours simulator and the spinning Guardians of the Galaxy: Cosmic Rewind.

ARRIVE EARLY! ARRIVE EARLY! ARRIVE EARLY!

THIS IS THE MOST IMPORTANT KEY to efficient touring and avoiding long lines. First thing in the morning, there are fewer people and almost no lines. The same four rides you experience in 1 hour in the early morning in the Magic Kingdom can take as long as 3 hours after 10:30 a.m.

Eat breakfast before you arrive; don't waste prime touring time sitting in a restaurant or waiting in line to order.

You gain a big advantage if you're already past the tapstiles when the park opens. While everyone else is stuck in line waiting for the people ahead to find their admission media and figure out how the tapstiles work, the lucky few (hundreds) already in the park will be in line for their first attraction. You'll probably be done and on your way to your second before many of them are even in the park, and with a good plan you'll be able to stay ahead of them for the rest of the day.

The earlier a park opens, the greater your advantage. This is because most vacationers won't make the effort to rise early and get to a park before it opens. Many fewer people are willing to make an 8 a.m. opening than a 9 a.m. opening. If you visit during the offseason and are staying at a Disney resort, arrive at the tapstiles 60 minutes before official opening (to take advantage of the Early Theme Park Entry benefit for Disney hotel guests). If you're staying off-site, arrive 30 minutes before official opening to get into the park as soon as it officially opens.

During holiday periods, Disney resort guests should arrive 60–70 minutes early, and off-site guests, 40–50 minutes early. By arriving, we mean be through security and at the tapstiles at the recommended time. One time-saving tip: Hold your bag away from your body as you walk through the security screening. This lowers the chance that you'll get pulled for a bag check.

Many readers share their experiences about getting to the parks before opening, such as this mom from Tennessee:

I didn't want to believe the hype about rope drop [park opening]. It's too difficult to get everyone up and to the parks that early on vacation! But on the one day I was able to get us there on time, we experienced double what we were able to do on any other day. Next Disney vacation, everyone has an early bedtime so we can do more rope drops!

It's important to note that Disney's Early Theme Park Entry program (see page 30) greatly reduces the rope-drop advantage for off-site guests, as there will already be thousands of people in line in front of you. The one exception is at Magic Kingdom, where Adventureland, Frontierland, and Liberty Square don't open until regular park opening anyway.

If getting the kids up earlier than usual causes crankiness that will put a damper on your day, don't worry—you'll have a great time no matter when you get to the park. Many families with young children have found that it's better to accept the relative inefficiencies of arriving at the park a bit late than to jar the children out of their routine. A mom of teens from Mississippi agrees:

I would have loved to experience the uncrowded early morning in the parks, but it wasn't worth the surly attitudes of our teenage crew. They were more than happy to stay up late, so we would try to avoid long lines during the day and then go to the big headliners in the last hour the park was open instead.

KNOW WHAT TO EXPECT WHEN YOU ARRIVE

BECAUSE MOST OF THE TOURING PLANS hinge on arriving before the park opens, you need to know about opening procedures. Disney transportation to the parks begins 1–1½ hours before official opening. The parking lots open about an hour before the park does. Each park has an entrance plaza outside the tapstiles, where you'll remain until the park opens.

unofficial **TIP**
The facts and figures in our books come from years of data collection and analysis by expert statisticians, programmers, field researchers, and lifelong Disney enthusiasts.

Disney typically allows Disney hotel guests into the parks roughly 30–50 minutes before official opening time (off-site guests may be directed to a holding area outside the park until official opening). This prevents dense crowds from forming around the admission tapstiles. Once inside, guests are typically held at various points in the park until it opens, a process called rope drop. Once the park is open, you can walk immediately to your first attraction.

USE A TOURING PLAN

WE KNOW FROM RESEARCH that theme park visitors' overall satisfaction is strongly tied to the number of attractions they're able to experience. So to help you have the best theme park day, we developed field-tested touring plans: step-by-step itineraries that allow readers to experience as many attractions as possible with the least amount of waiting.

We're confident that the touring plans in this book can save you 4 hours or more of standing in line in a full park day, and they allow you to see more attractions. How do they do this? The answer is *data*. Numbers and math are powerful!

You may be surprised to learn that the problem of avoiding lines in theme parks is very similar to everyday situations faced by companies around the world. For example, it's almost the exact problem FedEx and UPS have when trying to deliver packages efficiently (you're the driver; the rides you want to ride are the customers that need to be visited; and the time you spend walking and waiting in line is the travel time to the next customer).

Because this kind of situation is common, it gets studied and solved widely in schools and corporations, mainly in the fields of mathematics, operations research, and computer science. Bob used his experience teaching college operations research to come up with the first Disney touring plans in this book. Years later, Bob helped Len while Len was writing his master's thesis on efficient computer techniques for this kind of problem. Becky has been solving related problems for companies around the country for years in her "real job" as a data and analytics consultant.

Let's summarize and say that in the years since we started this journey, we've assembled a full-time team of data scientists, programmers, and researchers (and spent millions of dollars) to figure out how to avoid lines at Disney World.

This research has been recognized by both the travel industry and academe, having been cited by such diverse sources as *Popular Science, The Atlanta Journal-Constitution, The Dallas Morning News,* the Mathematical Association of America, *Money, The New York Times,* Operations Research Forum, *Travel Weekly, USA Today,* and *Wired,* along with the BBC, CBS News, Fox News, and the Travel Channel. The methodology behind the touring plans was also used as a case study in the book *Numbers Rule Your World,* by Kaiser Fung, an expert in business analytics and data visualization.

So that's a touring plan: a step-by-step guide to avoiding lines, just for you, that is supported by a team of well-funded, obsessive, Disney data fans with lots and lots of math.

We get a ton of reader mail commenting on touring plans. First, an Ohio family felt the wind in their sails:

> *The whole time we were in the Magic Kingdom, following the touring plan, it seemed that we were traveling in front of a hurricane— we'd wait 10 minutes or so for an attraction (or less—sometimes we just walked right on), but when we got out and started moving on to the next one, we could see the line building for what we just did.*

A family of four from Kentucky had this to say:

> *If there is one cult in this world I could join, it would be the staff of the* Unofficial Guide. *I tell everyone going to Disney to use this book and the awesome app. Years ago, we tried to convince friends to use the book, but they were scared off by the highly structured nature of the touring plans. We happened to see them at Disney during a late summer afternoon. Our family had enjoyed a full day with lots of rides and no more than a 20-minute wait. They had been on two total rides, standing in line over 1½ hours each time. They were miserable, and already considering escaping back to the hotel.*

A mom from Arkansas gave the touring plans a shot:

This is our fifth family trip to WDW, and this was my first time to use a touring plan. I have read the books and been a member of Lines for years. However, I never bought into the demands of the touring plan. After this last trip, I am officially a fan! I cannot express to you how much better our trip was since we followed a plan. We accomplished more in the first hour of Magic Kingdom than we used to accomplish in 3 hours. My family will use touring plans from now on.

A woman from Tennessee used the touring plans as a litmus test for her fiancé:

Your book has helped me plan two amazing trips to Disney World. My first trip there, I went in blind. My second trip, I discovered your book and used your touring plans. My third trip, I used the [Lines app] and had the best trip of my life! My fiancé just informed me that we can't go "every year." I think I'm going to have to break it off with him.

Variables That Affect the Success of the Touring Plans

How much time you'll save with any of the plans can be affected by how early you arrive at the parks; how quickly you move from attraction to attraction; how many breaks you take; when, where, and how you eat (counter service vs. table service); and whether you have young children in your tour group, among other factors. **Rider Switch** (see page 303), also known as "child swap," among other things, inhibits families with little ones from moving quickly through height-restricted attractions.

UNEXPECTED RIDE CLOSURES Some things are beyond your control. A perfect example of this is rides that don't open on time or suddenly stop running at some point during the day. For example, Test Track, an automobile-based thrill ride in EPCOT, can run about 30 cars at a time. But it's a decades-old outdoor ride with fragile technology that doesn't seem to handle Florida's humidity (or thunderstorms) very well.

Test Track has unscheduled downtime (when the ride isn't working) about 7 out of every 10 days, for ride breakdowns or weather. On average, it's unavailable to guests for around 1 hour per day. To get Test Track running again, the staff might begin the ride with 10 or 20 cars before going to full capacity; on these days, you'll have a long wait even if you're among the first to get back in line.

Breakdowns have more impact at parks with fewer attractions, such as Hollywood Studios and EPCOT. At the Studios, Rock 'n' Roller Coaster averages 90 minutes of downtime per day; Rise of the Resistance over an hour; Slinky Dog Dash and Mickey & Minnie's Runaway Railway, over 45 minutes each; and Tower of Terror, around 20. So, the Studios has nine rides, and five of them are unreliable.

It's not better at EPCOT, where, in addition to the high downtime at Test Track, noted in the table on the opposite page, Frozen Ever After and Remy's Ratatouille Adventure both average 45 minutes of downtime per day; Journey into Imagination with Figment, over 30 minutes; and Spaceship Earth, around 25. Close to half of the park's rides are unreliable. On bad days, multiple headliner attractions break down simultaneously, as this reader from Connecticut experienced:

What took tons of time was down attractions. It seems like almost everything was down: Kilimanjaro Safaris at Animal Kingdom; Soarin', Spaceship Earth, and Remy's Ratatouille Adventure when we visited EPCOT; and Rise of the Resistance and Smugglers Run at the Studios.

At least Smugglers Run handled it well. They gave us a pass to re-ride without waiting. In the welcome video when we re-rode, the guy said, "Oh, I didn't expect you to come back after the incident. Good to see you again." That was amazing.

RIDE BREAKDOWNS AND LIGHTNING LANE All of Disney's least reliable rides use Lightning Lane. The combination of downtime and Lightning Lane makes standby waits everywhere in the park substantially worse. If a ride like Test Track breaks down for 2 hours, thousands of guests who would've ridden it end up going to another attraction—like Soarin' Around the World or Frozen Ever After. Something like half of those Test Track guests were using Lightning Lane, and Disney gives them the opportunity to use that reservation at any other attraction. But those other attractions already have full lines thanks to the displaced crowds. The only way to fit the Lightning Lane guests from Test Track into other Lightning Lanes is to put them ahead of standby guests. This makes the standby guests wait even longer because an entirely different ride broke down.

Of course, some of those standby guests will end up purchasing Genie+ or Individual Lightning Lane to avoid these suddenly longer lines around the park. That makes the problem of subsequent ride breakdowns larger, because more people will be using Lightning Lane. A vicious cycle!

Because of this, if you really want to experience Rise of the Resistance, we recommend purchasing Individual Lightning Lane for it on all but the least-crowded days. Rise breaks down for a little over an hour per day on average. Typically, it has around one major outage per day, with each outage lasting about an hour. When Rise breaks down, Disney usually kicks out everyone in line and tells them to try back "later" when the ride is running again. (This process is called "dumping the queue.") If you're a particularly unlucky standby guest, you can spend an hour in line, get dumped, come back later, and repeat the same frustration.

The touring plans in this book consider ride reliability when choosing which attraction to visit first each morning. And if you're following a touring plan on the Lines app, you can tap "Optimize" at any

ATTRACTIONS THAT FREQUENTLY EXPERIENCE OUTAGES		
ATTRACTION AND THEME PARK	**AVERAGE DOWNTIME PER DAY (IN MINUTES)**	**LIKELIHOOD RIDE IS DOWN AT SOME POINT DURING THE DAY**
Rock 'n' Roller Coaster *(Hollywood Studios)*	90	75%
Test Track *(EPCOT)*	70	75%
Star Wars: Rise of the Resistance *(Hollywood Studios)*	70	80%
Space Mountain *(Magic Kingdom)*	65	60%
Pirates of the Caribbean *(Magic Kingdom)*	65	50%
The Magic Carpets of Aladdin *(Magic Kingdom)*	60	50%

time of day to have the plan adjust automatically to avoid the problem areas or attractions.

If you're following a printed touring plan, it's safe to assume that a ride outage will affect your plan at some point during the day. Our advice is to check the My Disney Experience app or the Lines app for current wait times throughout the rest of the park and then adjust your plan accordingly.

WEATHER One variable we can't predict accurately within a book is the weather. When lightning or heavy rains are nearby, Disney will close many (if not all) outdoor rides for safety. The effect on ride wait times when this happens is similar to having a whole set of unexpected ride breakdowns at once. Indoor attractions become incredibly popular, or people cut their losses and leave the park.

Customize Your Touring Plans

The attractions included in this book's touring plans are the most popular, as determined by more than 1 million reader surveys. If you've never been to Walt Disney World, we suggest using these plans as a starting point. They're designed to help you see the best Disney attractions with as little waiting in line as possible and have been field-tested by millions of families.

If you are a return visitor, your favorite attractions may be different. One way to customize the plans is to go to **TouringPlans.com** to create personalized versions. Tell the software the date, time, and park you've chosen to visit, along with the attractions you want to see. Your custom plan will tell you, for your specific travel date, the exact order in which you should visit attractions to minimize your waits in line. If you decide to use Disney's Genie+ ride reservation system, the plans incorporate whichever reservations you get into the itinerary (likewise for Individual Lightning Lane purchases). The touring plans also support Rider Switch on rides with height restrictions (see page 303). Besides attractions, you can schedule meals, breaks, entertainment, and more. You can even tell the software how fast you plan to walk, and it'll make the necessary adjustments.

These custom touring plans get some reviews from readers and TouringPlans.com subscribers. From an Alberta, Canada reader:

We love the ability to personalize the touring plans! Because we rarely arrive at park opening, we can't use the ones printed in the book. The personalized plans let us reduce wait times and eliminate arguing about what we are going to do next. Everyone can see their "big" attraction coming up on the plan, and we know we'll get to them all.

From a Virginia mom:

The touring plans helped make our vacation perfect! We visited WDW over spring break, the week before Easter. It was CROWDED. We saw signs for 90- to 120-minute waits on some of the rides. Using our touring plans, we only waited for 30 minutes once. Other than that, our longest wait was 20 minutes, and most of our other waits were 0–10 minutes. We would have had a completely different vacation without the touring plans. They were lifesavers!

Alternatively, some changes in the standard touring plans are simple enough to make on your own. If a plan calls for an attraction you're not interested in, simply skip it and move on to the next one. You can also substitute similar attractions in the same area of the park. If a plan calls for, say, riding Dumbo and you'd rather not, but you would enjoy the Mad Tea Party (which is not in the plan), then go ahead and substitute that for Dumbo. As long as the substitution is an attraction that has a similar wait time and duration and is near the attraction called for in the touring plan, you won't compromise the overall effectiveness of the plan.

What the Touring Plans Assume

Millions of families have used touring plans. For an audience that large, we have to make some assumptions around how most guests will behave on their vacation. For example, we know that only around 25% of theme park guests arrive in time for park opening. If we assumed everyone was going to show up that early, we'd be wrong 75% of the time. So when we have to make these decisions, we often look at the benefits of being right as compared to the consequences of being wrong.

For example, a touring plan may not have you go immediately to a super-headliner at rope drop if we predict that the line will back up quickly but have a shorter wait sometime later in the day. However, if you're right at the rope and one of the first 50 or 100 people in the queue, you should head to the super-headliner every time.

But we wouldn't want to assume that everyone reading this book will be among the first 50 people in line for a park's opening—we'd be wrong hundreds of times for every one time we were right. We'll tell you the benefits of being at the front of the pack, but we assume that you'll be somewhere in the middle or toward the back of the initial wave of guests. That's the more realistic scenario for most readers.

The good news is that no matter what you ride first, the touring plan software can handle it. Just tell it which ride you've completed and ask it to reoptimize your plan. The rest of your day will be planned out, no matter where you went first and how long it took.

What to Do If You Lose the Thread

If unforeseen events interrupt a plan:

1. If you're following a touring plan in the Lines app, just mark any attractions you've already done as completed and tap "Optimize" when you're ready to start touring again. The app will figure out the best possible plan for the remainder of your day.

2. If you're following a printed touring plan, skip a step on the plan for every 20 minutes you're delayed. For example, if you lose your phone and spend an hour hunting for it, skip three steps and pick up from there.

3. Forget the plan and organize the remainder of your day using the standby wait times listed in My Disney Experience or the Lines app, or consult the Clip-Out Touring Plan Companions starting on page 565.

"Bouncing Around"

Disney generally tries to place its most popular rides on opposite sides of the park. In the Magic Kingdom, for example, these attractions are positioned almost as far apart as possible—in the north, east, and west corners of the park—so that guests are more evenly distributed throughout the day.

It's often possible to save a lot of time in line by walking across the park to catch one of these rides when crowds are low. Some readers object to this crisscrossing. A woman from Georgia, told us she "got dizzy from all the bouncing around." Believe us, we empathize.

In general, the touring plans recommend crossing the park only if it'll save you more than 1 minute in line for every 1 minute of extra walking. (If you prefer some other trade-off, the software can help.)

We sometimes recommend crossing the park to see a newly opened ride; in these cases, a special trip to visit the attraction early avoids much longer waits later. Also, live shows, especially at the Studios and Animal Kingdom, sometimes have performance schedules so at odds with each other (and the rest of the park's schedule) that geographically organized touring is impossible.

If you want to experience headliner attractions in one day without long waits, you can see those first (requires crisscrossing the park) or squeeze in visits during the last 2 hours the park is open, as long as the rides don't have significant downtime.

Touring Plan Rejection

We suggest sticking to the plans religiously, especially in the mornings, if you're visiting during busy times. The consequence of touring spontaneity in peak season is hours of standing in line. However, some folks don't respond well to the rigidity of a touring plan. If you encounter this problem with someone in your party, communication is key, as this reader from Michigan found out:

The one thing I will suggest is if one member of the family is doing most of the research and planning (like I did), that they communicate what the book/touring plans suggest. I failed to do this and it led to some, shall we say, tense moments between my husband and me on our first day. However, once he realized how much time we were saving, he understood why I was so bent on following the touring plans.

One of our all-time favorite letters came from a Nebraska couple. One of them was a planner, and one clearly wasn't. They were both experienced negotiators, as their letter shows:

We created our own 4.25-by-5.5-inch guidebook for our trip that included a number of pages from the TouringPlans.com website. This was the first page:

THE TYPE-A SPOUSE'S BILL OF RIGHTS
1. We will not see everything in one vacation.
2. Len Testa will not be vacationing with us. His plans don't schedule time for benches. Ours may.
3. We may deviate from the touring plans at some point. Really.
4. Even if it isn't on the Disney Dining Plan, a funnel cake or other snack may be purchased without a grouchy face from the nonpurchasing spouse.
5. Sometimes, sitting by the pool may sound more fun than going to a park, show, or other scheduled event. On this vacation, that will be fine.
6. "But I thought we were going to . . . " is a phrase that must be stricken from the discussion of any plans that had not been previously discussed as a couple.
7. Other items may be added as circumstances dictate at the parks.

It was a much happier vacation with these generally understood principles in writing.

How Early Theme Park Entry, Extended Evening Theme Park Hours, and Special Events Work with the Touring Plans

With Early Theme Park Entry, Disney resort guests are admitted to all four Disney theme parks at least 30 minutes before official park opening. Off-site resort guests who enter the parks at official opening will find thousands of on-site guests already ahead of them in lines.

To mitigate the effect of Early Entry on off-site guests, we've added off-site versions of several touring plans. And the free touring plan software (see touringplans.com/walt-disney-world/touring-plans) will optimize touring plans that begin at any time of day.

During Extended Evening Theme Park Hours (see page 32) and After Hours events, crowds are so low that a touring plan isn't needed—just head to the nearest attraction that interests you. Generally, Halloween and Christmas parties will also have low wait times. Parties tend to attract guests who are interested in the special entertainment.

STANDBY QUEUES, BOARDING GROUPS, GENIE+, INDIVIDUAL LIGHTNING LANE, AND GENIE

NOTE: Significant changes to the Genie+ ride reservation system, announced after the first printing of this edition, will take effect July 24, 2024. Please see theugseries.com/wdwupdates for details.

PRIOR TO 2021, Disney ran a *free* ride reservation system called FastPass+ that allowed you to reserve a spot on an attraction for a specific day and time. You could book a reservation at a specific ride, for a specific 1-hour time window, up to two months before your trip.

In 2021, Disney decided to monetize this process by charging money to wait less. The result is an unprecedented, unpopular, unwieldy system for navigating the theme parks. There are now at least four different Disney processes for waiting in line at rides. Each method has its own set of rules, often put in place for Disney's benefit, not yours.

Here are the ways you can wait in line at Walt Disney World:

STANDBY QUEUES This is the way most people are familiar with: You get in a line for a ride, and you wait until it's your turn to ride. It doesn't cost anything, and the wait-time sign in front of the attraction gives you some idea of how long you're going to be waiting.

As we went to press, it was rare for any Walt Disney World ride not to operate a standby queue. The last two not to operate one were Tron Lightcycle/Run in the Magic Kingdom and Guardians of the Galaxy: Cosmic Rewind in EPCOT, which used boarding groups (see below) exclusively when they opened and for some time afterward.

COST: Standby queues are free with park admission.

BOARDING GROUPS/VIRTUAL QUEUES A boarding group, or virtual queue, is a virtual line without a guaranteed return time. They're typically used at new, popular rides, so it's possible you'll see them at Tiana's Bayou Adventure when it opens in the Magic Kingdom. Here's how it works: At exactly 7 a.m. on the day of your visit, you'll use

RIDE RESERVATION SYSTEM DEFINITIONS	
LIGHTNING LANE	An alternative to the standby line at some rides. Comes in two flavors: Genie+ and Individual.
GENIE+	A way of using the Lightning Lane at most (but not all) of the popular rides in each park, for a single additional upcharge per person per day.
INDIVIDUAL LIGHTNING LANE (ILL)	Another way of using the Lighting Lane, available for a per-attraction fee, for one or two of the most popular rides in each park. It's a way for Disney to charge more than it would for Genie+ while shortening the lines at a park's top attractions.

My Disney Experience (MDE) to request a boarding group. If you're successful, you'll get a boarding group number and a rough estimate of how long you must wait until your group is called.

You need to be fast and lucky: Boarding groups for Tron are often fully allocated for the entire day within 10 seconds of 7 a.m. So many people try to get a boarding group that it is essentially a lottery as to who gets in. And if anything goes wrong, your chance to experience the ride is almost certainly gone. (A second group of reservations is available at 1 p.m., using the same process; however, these reservations are less likely to be called to ride.)

If the ride is running smoothly, boarding groups typically start getting called within 30 minutes of park opening, beginning with boarding group 1. The MDE app will display the current range of boarding groups that are able to ride. When your group is called, the app will alert you so you can return.

Boarding groups are used at rides that Disney thinks are likely to break down often, or where it wants to control the length of the standby queue. Because new rides may not have worked out all their bugs, Disney isn't confident that it can give guests a specific time to return and ride. For example, suppose Disney gave you a specific time of 1–2 p.m. to ride Tron. If Tron breaks down and is unavailable between 1 and 2 p.m., then at 2 p.m., the ride must accommodate everyone who didn't get to ride between 1 and 2, plus everyone who was scheduled to ride between 2 and 3 p.m. There's not enough ride capacity to do that (and Disney doesn't want to run the ride at half capacity in anticipation of breakdowns either). Boarding groups solve this problem by not attaching a specific return time to your virtual wait.

COST: Boarding groups are free with park admission.

GENIE+ AND LIGHTNING LANE *(aka paid FastPass+)* Genie+ is a paid version of Disney's former FastPass+ system. Built as a feature in the My Disney Experience app, using it costs $20–$35 per person, per day. The price varies by day and by park: Genie+ costs more on busier days and at more popular parks.

As we went to press, you could only purchase Genie+ on the day of your park visit. That means you have to make separate, daily purchases for each day you plan to use it. (Disney has said it's working on changing this aspect of the system.)

Disney can limit the number of guests who purchase Genie+. While that doesn't happen often, if you want to be absolutely certain you have it, you can purchase Genie+ at midnight on the day of your park visit to guarantee you can make reservations. You must also be back online at 6:55 a.m. to start making Genie+ reservations at 7 a.m.

Paying for Genie+ lets you make reservations to skip the standby line. At participating attractions, Genie+ will show you the next available return time at each attraction, such as 1–2 p.m. or 1:15–2:15 p.m. You'll pick the attraction where the return time works best for your day and where you think you'll be avoiding a significant wait.

When you return to ride, you'll use the Lightning Lane—a separate line that's faster than the standby line. Guests in this line are given priority to board. Almost all popular attractions offer Genie+ (or Individual Lightning Lane; see below).

With Genie+, Disney appears to normally allocate 50% of a ride's hourly capacity to Genie+ riders. But because Genie+ costs real money, we also believe Disney has set an upper goal on how long people will wait in the Lightning Lane—something like "no more than 10 minutes." And that means that if the Genie+ gets backed up, Disney will take up to 99 guests from the Genie+ line for every 1 guest it takes from the standby line. If you're in the standby line when that happens, it can be endlessly frustrating.

The number of Lightning Lane reservations available is limited, so Lightning Lane doesn't eliminate the need to wake up early. Because Lightning Lane reservations are offered only on the day of your visit, it's possible for a ride to run out of Lightning Lane reservations or desirable return times before you even arrive at the park.

Guests can make reservations starting at 7 a.m. That is also the time at which on-site guests can purchase Individual Lightning Lane access (off-site guests have to wait until park opening) and when everyone can make boarding group reservations. We're not sure why Disney scheduled these critical, mutually exclusive tasks for the exact same time of day—we suspect it's that nobody who made the decision ever had to do this for themselves. We're hoping staggering the times is on the list of potential changes to Genie+.

Speaking of boarding groups, Genie+ isn't available on rides that use boarding groups. For those, you'll need Individual Lightning Lane.

IS GENIE+ WORTH THE COST? It all depends. We recommend using Genie+ in the Magic Kingdom and Hollywood Studios under most crowd conditions. We're not ready to say that a family of four should spend $120 (or even $80) on Genie+ in EPCOT or Animal Kingdom, though: EPCOT has fewer rides and they're spaced far apart, limiting the amount of time you'd save using Genie+ beyond what you'd get just by showing up early and hitting the key attractions first. And Animal Kingdom has few enough attractions with long waits that you can easily follow a plan to avoid waits without paying. For specific advice on how best to use Genie+ at each park, read the Genie+ section in that park's chapter.

Most reader comments we get on Genie+ are negative, focusing on the cost and the constant need to use smartphones:

Genie+ makes everyone miserable. If you don't have it, you resent all the people flying by you, the unpredictable wait times, and the feeling that you're somehow less than everyone else. If you have it, you sacrifice any sense of being "in the moment" because your face is constantly buried in your phone working to plan your next Lightning Lane. And when there's a wait in the LL line, you feel like you just wasted all your money. The whole system has added a level of sadness to the Happiest Place on Earth. You end up feeling like everyone's out for themselves and just gross.

—A reader from Ohio

Disney World is still magical but far less enjoyable with Genie+. We visited during a relatively off-peak time, and had we not bought Lightning Lane reservations, our waits for the popular rides would've been over an hour within 30–60 minutes of park opening on most days.

—A family from Missouri

And regarding phone usage, a visitor from Pennsylvania says:

Vacation was less than magical this time. I'm not entirely sure why, but I think it had something to do with working my phone so much. I am not high-tech, but I was able to do mobile ordering, Genie+, and ILL with few problems. But my phone became the focus too many times during the day instead of the park.

These folks from Ohio agree:

I don't need an app or map to know how to navigate the parks, and I still spent 22 hours MORE TIME on my phone during our VACATION. An entire day, staring at MDE and mobile ordering. Something's gotta give.

The bad news: Disney says that about 50% of park guests are using these reservations, which earns the company tens of millions of dollars per year. Genie isn't going away or getting cheaper anytime soon.

Genie+ Guidelines

- Park tickets are required to obtain Lightning Lane return times.
- You may hold only one Genie+ Lightning Lane reservation at a time (unless 2 hours have passed since you obtained your last Genie+ reservation) and/or up to two reservations for Individual Lightning Lane attractions. The only other exception to this rule is that there is no limit to the number of Replacement Lightning Lane reservations (see opposite page) you can simultaneously hold.
- You shouldn't make a Genie+ reservation unless it can save you 30 minutes or more at an attraction or if a nearby ride is distributing immediate return times.
- Always check the return period before obtaining your reservation. Keep an eye out for attractions whose Lightning Lane return time is immediate, or at least sooner than the standby wait.
- Don't count on Lightning Lane being available for popular attractions after noon during busier times of year. This especially applies to Slinky Dog Dash, Remy's Ratatouille Adventure, Frozen Ever After, and Test Track.
- Make sure everyone in your party has their own Lightning Lane return time. Reservations are tied to each individual ticket and may not be transferred.
- You can obtain a second Genie+ return time (1) as soon as you enter the Lightning Lane of your first, (2) 2 hours after you obtained your last Genie+ reservation, or (3) when your unused Genie+ return-time window

has expired. You can maximize efficiency by getting your next Lightning Lane return time while waiting to board the previous one.

- Be mindful of your Lightning Lane return time, and plan intervening activities accordingly. You may use your Genie+ Lightning Lane entry 5 minutes before its start time and up to 15 minutes after it expires. This unadvertised grace period is typically the only exception to your return window.

- Attractions typically do not dispense Lightning Lane reservations while they are closed for technical difficulties or special events.

- If an attraction is unavailable due to technical difficulties during your return window, your Lightning Lane automatically converts to a Replacement Lightning Lane pass. Replacement passes remain valid for use until closing time at that attraction (if it reopens) or at selected other Lightning Lane attractions in the same park. If the original return window was near closing time, the Replacement pass may be valid the next day.

- You may want to pick one member of your party to handle everyone's tickets and Lightning Lane reservations on their phone. This gives your group the option of splitting up while retaining access to each other's plans; however, each person must still use their own ticket to enter the park or redeem Lightning Lane reservations.

COST: Genie+ is $20–$35 per person per day.

INDIVIDUAL LIGHTNING LANE (ILL) You'll have to pay separately to get on a new or popular ride, even if you've already purchased Genie+. If Tron offers boarding groups but you didn't get one, or if you want to avoid a potential 2-hour wait at Avatar Flight of Passage, Disney will offer you a chance to ride at a price, by using ILL.

Purchasing an ILL in MDE is straightforward. Passes are sold per-person, and guests are limited to two per day. When it's your time to ride, you'll be directed to the Lightning Lane to board.

You don't need to purchase Genie+ to purchase ILL. Likewise, purchasing ILL does not get you access to the other Genie+ attractions.

At press time, these were the Individual Lightning Lane attractions in each park:

- **Magic Kingdom** Seven Dwarfs Mine Train and Tron Lightcycle/Run
- **EPCOT** Guardians of the Galaxy: Cosmic Rewind
- **Hollywood Studios** Star Wars: Rise of the Resistance
- **Animal Kingdom** Avatar Flight of Passage

COST: Varies by attraction, day of year, and time of day. The lowest cost we've seen recently for an ILL is $10, at Seven Dwarfs Mine Train. The highest cost (so far) is $25 at Rise of the Resistance. We expect these prices to increase.

IS ILL WORTH THE COST? For certain rides. The table on the next page shows how much time you're likely to save at each ILL attraction on a busy day, along with the maximum cost we've seen for that ILL.

As a rough estimate, the highest-priced one-day park ticket costs about $15 per hour you're in the park (assuming $170 for the ticket over 11 hours). So, any ILL that costs less than around $15.40 per hour saved is a good deal. No Individual Lightning Lane meets that criterion under average crowd conditions.

DISNEY GENIE (MINUS THE PLUS) Disney announced the "free Genie" itinerary-planning feature of the MDE app in 2019 and said little

INDIVIDUAL LIGHTNING LANE (ILL) SAVINGS ANALYSIS			
ATTRACTION	**AVERAGE MINUTES IN LINE SAVED ON AVERAGE**	**HIGHEST COST**	**COST PER SAVED MINUTE/HOUR**
Avatar Flight of Passage *Animal Kingdom*	42	$17	$0.40/$24
Seven Dwarfs Mine Train *Magic Kingdom*	29	$12	$0.41/$25
Star Wars: Rise of the Resistance* *Hollywood Studios*	37	$25	$0.68/$41
Guardians of the Galaxy *EPCOT*	19	$17	$0.89/$54
Tron Lightcycle/Run *Magic Kingdom*	15	$20	$1.33/$80

Note: ILL prices (at press time) don't include tax.

*We still recommend that readers determined to ride Rise of the Resistance purchase an ILL for it. As noted on page 45, Rise breaks down often enough that using the standby line risks wasting too much time and never riding.

more about it for the next two years. Originally, Genie sounded a lot like our computer-optimized touring plans: You'd tell Genie what rides you want to ride, and Genie would plan your day to minimize your wait in line.

But that's not at all what Genie does. In fact, Genie is one of the worst products Disney has ever produced. Its real purpose isn't to plan your day—because it doesn't. It's to serve Disney's park management needs. To understand why requires a little background.

Back in the days of FastPass+, the widespread use of the free reservations adeptly spread crowds away from headliners (where they had reservations anyway) to typically lower-wait attractions where they spent their time in line until they could use those reservations.

Now consider Genie+ instead. It costs money, so fewer people use it. That means Disney loses the all-important crowd distribution that FastPass+ provided. The risk to Disney's operations is that guests just queue up for Disney's best, most popular rides, resulting in long lines, while other attractions sit underused.

That's where "free Genie" comes in—it suggests lower-rated, less popular attractions to guests who wouldn't have otherwise visited and directs crowds away from the parks' most popular attractions. This has been proven repeatedly in our field-testing. For example, we tested Genie one day in Hollywood Studios. Arriving at 8:30 a.m., in time for Early Entry, Len fired up the Genie app to get Genie's recommendations. Here was the morning itinerary that Genie suggested:

9:30 a.m. Ride Toy Story Mania!

10:20 a.m. Buy a droid in Galaxy's Edge.

11:10 a.m. Eat lunch at Ronto Roasters.

That's right, reader: Genie knew Len was in the park at 8:30 a.m. At that hour, waits at Tower of Terror, Rock 'n' Roller Coaster, and Toy Story Mania! were well below 5 minutes (we had another researcher ride them to check). Despite no lines at these headliners, Genie suggested just one ride in the first 3½ hours Len was in the park.

Genie also tried to upsell Len on the benefits of Genie+ and Individual Lightning Lane purchases, and suggested he buy a $100

Star Wars droid. All told, Genie immediately suggested three ways for Len to spend money before noon, but only one ride.

Somehow, it got worse. When Len declined Genie's suggestion to buy a droid at 10:20 a.m., Genie then suggested the following four attractions instead:

- *Walt Disney Presents*
- *Disney Junior Play and Dance!*
- Lightning McQueen's Racing Academy
- Alien Swirling Saucers

Let us point out that Genie suggested that Len—a middle-aged man touring alone—see two stage shows designed expressly for small children or go on a midway-style spinner also designed for small children. Setting aside the ick factor, these are also four of the lowest-rated attractions in the park.

The afternoon portion of Len's Genie's itinerary looked like this:

12:10 p.m. Ride *Millennium Falcon:* Smugglers Run.

2:00 p.m. Experience Star Tours—The Adventures Continue.

2:35 p.m. Ride Star Wars: Rise of the Resistance (using standby line).

4:30 p.m. Ride Alien Swirling Saucers.

5:35 p.m. See *Muppet*Vision 3D.*

6:00 p.m. Eat dinner at ABC Commissary.

6:40 p.m. See the *Vacation Fun* Mickey Mouse movie.

7:30 p.m. Ride The Twilight Zone Tower of Terror.

8:45 p.m. Watch the *Wonderful World of Animation* projection show.

Rise of the Resistance broke down before Len could ride it, and Genie swapped Rise out for Slinky Dog Dash. Even though Rise resumed operation shortly after, Genie never suggested it to Len again that day.

It's worth noting that Genie's initial 12½-hour plan didn't include Mickey & Minnie's Runaway Railway, Slinky Dog Dash, or Rock 'n' Roller Coaster—some of the park's highest-rated attractions for his age group. And while Len eventually got on Slinky, he missed out on Rise of the Resistance. So in a full day in the park, with plenty of time, Len experienced just three of the top five rides.

What happened to Len in the Studios isn't unusual: In every park where we've tried Genie, it asked us for preferences and produced an itinerary that ignored all or most of those choices.

Other readers have chimed in with similar experiences. Here's one from a family from Wisconsin:

> *We were VERY disappointed with the new Genie app. It was tedious to use, not intuitive, and showed us things we could care less about and could not remove from our screens. How many times in a day must we tell the app that we don't want to go to Swiss Family Treehouse?*

Another odd Genie behavior is that there doesn't seem to be a way to tell it when you want to leave the park. It assumes you'll be in the park until it closes. Obviously, it's harder to make an itinerary with a time constraint. But it's also safe to say that Disney wants you in the park all day, so you'll spend as much money as possible.

We've heard that guest satisfaction survey results for Genie are terrible. One insider described them as "disastrous" and "far below even the lowest expectations." That's not surprising.

As we see it, Genie is two parts crowd control for Disney park operations, two parts upselling engine, and *maybe* one part planning app. Genie is unlikely to get you to all of a park's highest-rated attractions. Needless to say, we don't think it's a substitute for a good touring plan. We don't think it's good, period.

COST: The basic version of Genie is free. It is still not worth using.

USE THE SINGLE-RIDER LINE *(if available)*

THIS TIME-SAVER, a line for individuals riding alone, is available at **Test Track** in EPCOT, **Expedition Everest** in Animal Kingdom, and **Rock 'n' Roller Coaster Starring Aerosmith** and *Millennium Falcon: Smugglers Run* at Hollywood Studios. The objective is to fill odd spaces left by groups that don't quite fill the ride vehicle. Because there aren't many singles and most groups are unwilling to split up, single-rider lines are almost always incredibly short. The one exception is at Rock 'n' Roller Coaster, where the single-rider line will regularly close when it's longer than the standby queue.

MAKING *the* MOST *of* YOUR MONEY

When you're immersed in it and not paying attention to how you're being fleeced, it's still amazing.

—A reader from Maryland

ALLOCATING MONEY

HOW MUCH DOES A DISNEY VACATION COST?

EVERY YEAR, WE HEAR FROM tens of thousands of families who are either planning or just back from a Disney vacation, and we talk with travel agents who hear from thousands more. The thing that surprises these families the most is how much their trip ends up costing.

To help you avoid that surprise, we've created the table on pages 58–60. It shows how much Disney vacation you get for $1,500, $2,000, $3,000, and $4,000, for families of various sizes. Each price category contains a list of hotel options (off-site budget, Disney Value, Disney Moderate, or Disney Deluxe) and meal types (counter-service or sit-down). These options illustrate the trade-offs you should consider when planning your trip—and there *will* be trade-offs. Here's an example for a family of two adults and one child with a $2,000 budget, excluding transportation:

OPTION A One full day at a Disney theme park, two days of table-service meals, and two nights at a Disney Deluxe resort

OPTION B Three full days at Disney's theme parks, three days of counter-service meals, and two nights at a budget off-site motel

continued on page 61

WHAT YOU PAY AND WHAT YOU GET AT WDW

2 ADULTS/$4,000

BUDGET OPTION ($4,004)
• 9 days theme park admission, parking
• 9 nights at a budget off-site motel
• 2 CS meals, 7 TS meals

VALUE OPTION ($4,044)
• 8 days theme park admission
• 8 nights at a Disney Value resort
• 6 CS meals, 2 TS meals

MODERATE OPTION ($3,959)
• 6 days theme park admission
• 6 nights at a Disney Moderate resort
• 3 CS meals, 3 TS meals

DELUXE OPTION ($4,028)
• 4 days theme park admission
• 5 nights at a Disney Deluxe resort
• 4 CS meals

2 ADULTS, 2 KIDS/$4,000

BUDGET OPTION ($4,097)
• 5 days theme park admission, parking
• 5 nights at a budget off-site motel
• 5 CS meals

VALUE OPTION ($3,968)
• 4 days theme park admission
• 4 nights at a Disney Value resort
• 3 CS meals, 1 TS meal

MODERATE OPTION ($3,806)
• 3 days theme park admission
• 4 nights at a Disney Moderate resort
• 3 TS meals

DELUXE OPTION ($4,012)
• 3 days theme park admission
• 3 nights at a Disney Deluxe resort
• 1 CS meal, 2 TS meals

2 ADULTS, 1 KID/$4,000

BUDGET OPTION ($4,024)
• 7 days theme park admission, parking
• 8 nights at a budget off-site motel
• 7 CS meals

VALUE OPTION ($4,021)
• 5 days theme park admission
• 6 nights at a Disney Value resort
• 3 CS meals, 2 TS meals

MODERATE OPTION ($3,955)
• 4 days theme park admission
• 5 nights at a Disney Moderate resort
• 2 CS meals, 2 TS meals

DELUXE OPTION ($3,979)
• 3 days theme park admission
• 4 nights at a Disney Deluxe resort
• 3 TS meals

3 ADULTS/$4,000

BUDGET OPTION ($4,081)
• 7 days theme park admission, parking
• 7 nights at a budget off-site motel
• 7 CS meals

VALUE OPTION ($3,970)
• 5 days theme park admission
• 5 nights at a Disney Value resort
• 3 CS meals, 2 TS meals

MODERATE OPTION ($3,999)
• 4 days theme park admission
• 4 nights at a Disney Moderate resort
• 4 CS meals

DELUXE OPTION ($3,995)
• 3 days theme park admission
• 4 nights at a Disney Deluxe resort
• 1 CS meal, 2 TS meals

3 ADULTS, 1 KID/$4,000

BUDGET OPTION ($4,061)
• 4 days theme park admission, parking
• 5 nights at a budget off-site motel
• 1 CS meal, 3 TS meals

VALUE OPTION ($3,951)
• 4 days theme park admission
• 4 nights at a Disney Value resort
• 4 CS meals

MODERATE OPTION ($3,924)
• 3 days theme park admission
• 4 nights at a Disney Moderate resort
• 3 TS meals

DELUXE OPTION ($3,993)
• 3 days theme park admission
• 3 nights at a Disney Deluxe resort
• 2 CS meals, 1 TS meal

2 ADULTS/$3,000

BUDGET OPTION ($2,971)
• 7 days theme park admission, parking
• 7 nights at a budget off-site motel
• 7 CS meals

VALUE OPTION ($3,132)
• 5 days theme park admission
• 6 nights at a Disney Value resort
• 6 CS meals

MODERATE OPTION ($2,904)
• 4 days theme park admission
• 4 nights at a Disney Moderate resort
• 2 CS meals, 2 TS meals

DELUXE OPTION ($2,891)
• 3 days theme park admission
• 3 nights at a Disney Deluxe resort
• 3 TS meals

2 ADULTS, 2 KIDS/$3,000

BUDGET OPTION ($2,986)
• 3 days theme park admission, parking
• 4 nights at a budget off-site motel
• 4 CS meals

VALUE OPTION ($3,144)
• 3 days theme park admission
• 3 nights at a Disney Value resort
• 1 CS meal, 2 TS meals

MODERATE OPTION ($2,943)
• 2 days theme park admission
• 3 nights at a Disney Moderate resort
• 3 TS meals

DELUXE OPTION ($3,021)
• 2 days theme park admission
• 3 nights at a Disney Deluxe resort
• 2 CS meals

CS = counter service   TS = table service

WHAT YOU PAY AND WHAT YOU GET AT WDW

WHAT YOU PAY AND WHAT YOU GET AT WDW *(continued)*

2 ADULTS, 1 KID/$3,000	3 ADULTS/$3,000
BUDGET OPTION ($3,049) • 4 days theme park admission, parking • 5 nights at a budget off-site motel • 5 CS meals	**BUDGET OPTION ($2,967)** • 4 days theme park admission, parking • 5 nights at a budget off-site motel • 4 CS meals
VALUE OPTION ($3,131) • 4 days theme park admission • 4 nights at a Disney Value resort • 4 CS meals	**VALUE OPTION ($2,915)** • 3 days theme park admission • 4 nights at a Disney Value resort • 3 CS meals, 1 TS meal
MODERATE OPTION ($2,914) • 3 days theme park admission • 3 nights at a Disney Moderate resort • 3 TS meals	**MODERATE OPTION ($2,929)** • 3 days theme park admission • 3 nights at a Disney Moderate resort • 1 CS meal, 2 TS meals
DELUXE OPTION ($2,979) • 2 days theme park admission • 3 nights at a Disney Deluxe resort • 1 CS meal, 2 TS meals	**DELUXE OPTION ($2,971)** • 2 days theme park admission • 3 nights at a Disney Deluxe resort • 2 CS meals, 1 TS meal

3 ADULTS, 1 KID/$3,000	
BUDGET OPTION ($3,120) • 3 days theme park admission, parking • 3 nights at a budget off-site motel • 3 TS meals	**MODERATE OPTION ($2,938)** • 2 days theme park admission • 3 nights at a Disney Moderate resort • 1 CS meal, 2 TS meals
VALUE OPTION ($3,006) • 3 days theme park admission • 3 nights at a Disney Value resort • 3 CS meals	**DELUXE OPTION ($3,063)** • 2 days theme park admission • 3 nights at a Disney Deluxe resort • 2 CS meals

2 ADULTS/$2,000	2 ADULTS, 2 KIDS/$2,000
BUDGET OPTION ($2,070) • 4 days theme park admission, parking • 4 nights at a budget off-site motel • 4 CS meals	**BUDGET OPTION ($2,081)** • 2 days theme park admission, parking • 3 nights at a budget off-site motel • 2 TS meals
VALUE OPTION ($2,006) • 3 days theme park admission • 4 nights at a Disney Value resort • 3 CS meals	**VALUE OPTION ($2,065)** • 2 days theme park admission • 2 nights at a Disney Value resort • 1 CS meal, 1 TS meal
MODERATE OPTION ($2,097) • 3 days theme park admission • 3 nights at a Disney Moderate resort • 3 CS meals	**MODERATE OPTION ($1,806)** • 1 day theme park admission • 2 nights at a Disney Moderate resort • 2 TS meals
DELUXE OPTION ($1,929) • 2 days theme park admission • 2 nights at a Disney Deluxe resort • 2 TS meals	**DELUXE OPTION ($2,065)** • 2 days theme park admission • 1 night at a Disney Deluxe resort • 2 CS meals

2 ADULTS, 1 KID/$2,000	3 ADULTS/$2,000
BUDGET OPTION ($2,060) • 3 days theme park admission, parking • 2 nights at a budget off-site motel • 3 CS meals	**BUDGET OPTION ($2,036)** • 2 days theme park admission, parking • 3 nights at a budget off-site motel • 2 TS meals
VALUE OPTION ($2,027) • 2 days theme park admission • 3 nights at a Disney Value resort • 2 CS meals, 1 TS meal	**VALUE OPTION ($2,026)** • 2 days theme park admission • 3 nights at a Disney Value resort • 2 TS meals
MODERATE OPTION ($2,057) • 2 days theme park admission • 3 nights at a Disney Moderate resort • 2 CS meals	**MODERATE OPTION ($2,024)** • 2 days theme park admission • 2 nights at a Disney Moderate resort • 2 TS meals
DELUXE OPTION ($1,925) • 1 day theme park admission • 2 nights at a Disney Deluxe resort • 2 TS meals	**DELUXE OPTION ($1,938)** • 2 days theme park admission • 1 night at a Disney Deluxe resort • 2 TS meals

CS = counter service   TS = table service

continued on next page

continued from previous page

WHAT YOU PAY AND WHAT YOU GET AT WDW *(continued)*

3 ADULTS, 1 KID/$2,000

BUDGET OPTION ($2,083)
- 2 days theme park admission, parking
- 2 nights at a budget off-site motel
- 2 TS meals

VALUE OPTION ($2,007)
- 2 days theme park admission
- 2 nights at a Disney Value resort
- 2 CS meals

MODERATE OPTION ($1,911)
- 2 days theme park admission
- 1 night at a Disney Moderate resort
- 2 CS meals

DELUXE OPTION ($2,035)
- 1 day theme park admission
- 2 nights at a Disney Deluxe resort
- 2 CS meals

2 ADULTS/$1,500

BUDGET OPTION ($1,574)
- 3 days theme park admission, parking
- 3 nights at a budget off-site motel
- 3 CS meals

VALUE OPTION ($1,522)
- 3 days theme park admission
- 3 nights at a Disney Value resort
- 3 CS meals

MODERATE OPTION ($1,468)
- 2 days theme park admission
- 2 nights at a Disney Moderate resort
- 1 CS meal, 1 TS meal

DELUXE OPTION ($1,451)
- 2 days theme park admission
- 1 night at a Disney Deluxe resort
- 2 TS meals

2 ADULTS, 2 KIDS/$1,500

BUDGET OPTION ($1,428)
- 1 day theme park admission, parking
- 2 nights at a budget off-site motel
- 2 TS meals

VALUE OPTION ($1,519)
- 1 day theme park admission
- 2 nights at a Disney Value resort
- 1 CS meal, 1 TS meal

MODERATE OPTION ($1,497)
- 1 day theme park admission
- 2 nights at a Disney Moderate resort
- 1 TS meal

DELUXE OPTION ($1,411)
- 1 day theme park admission
- 1 night at a Disney Deluxe resort
- 1 TS meal

2 ADULTS, 1 KID/$1,500

BUDGET OPTION ($1,504)
- 2 days theme park admission, parking
- 3 nights at a budget off-site motel
- 2 CS meals

VALUE OPTION ($1,485)
- 2 days theme park admission
- 1 night at a Disney Value resort
- 1 CS meal, 1 TS meal

MODERATE OPTION ($1,494)
- 2 days theme park admission
- 1 night at a Disney Moderate resort
- 2 CS meals

DELUXE OPTION ($1,198)
- 1 day theme park admission
- 1 night at a Disney Deluxe resort
- 1 TS meal

3 ADULTS/$1,500

BUDGET OPTION ($1,546)
- 2 days theme park admission, parking
- 3 nights at a budget off-site motel
- 2 CS meals

VALUE OPTION ($1,545)
- 2 days theme park admission
- 1 night at a Disney Value resort
- 2 CS meals

MODERATE OPTION ($1,536)
- 2 days theme park admission
- 1 night at a Disney Moderate resort
- 2 CS meals

DELUXE OPTION ($1,238)
- 1 day theme park admission
- 1 night at a Disney Deluxe resort
- 1 TS meal

3 ADULTS, 1 KID/$1,500

BUDGET OPTION ($1,502)
- 1 day theme park admission, parking
- 2 nights at a budget off-site motel
- 2 TS meals

VALUE OPTION ($1,575)
- 1 day theme park admission
- 2 nights at a Disney Value resort
- 1 CS meal, 1 TS meal

MODERATE OPTION ($1,537)
- 1 day theme park admission
- 2 nights at a Disney Moderate resort
- 1 TS meal

DELUXE OPTION ($1,451)
- 1 day theme park admission
- 1 night at a Disney Deluxe resort
- 1 TS meal

CS = counter service   TS = table service

continued from page 57

In this case, and in general, your choice is between (1) a nicer hotel or (2) a longer trip (more time in the parks) at a cheaper hotel. You may also get better meals if you cut costs in other categories.

If you'd like to plug in your own numbers, you can download our spreadsheet at theugseries.com/wdwyouget2025. Ticket prices are based on Disney's February 2024 costs and include tax. All hotel prices are quoted for summer nights in 2024 and include tax. What you'll pay may be higher, depending on what time of year you visit.

Here are the assumptions we made to go along with actual prices from Disney's website:

- Children are ages 3–9; adults are age 10 and up.
- One night at a non-Disney budget hotel—the Quality Inn & Suites by the Parks—booked through the hotel, costs $77.
- One night at any of Disney's All-Star Resorts (all had the cheapest Disney Value resort rates at press time) costs $188 on the WDW website.
- One night at Disney's Coronado Springs Resort (the cheapest Disney Moderate resort at the time) costs $282 using Disney's website.
- One night in a studio at Disney's Old Key West (the cheapest Disney Deluxe/Disney Vacation Club resort at press time) costs $478 using Disney's website.
- A day's worth of counter-service meals, plus one snack, costs $60 for adults and $44 for kids.
- A counter-service breakfast and lunch, a snack, and a sit-down dinner costs $95 per adult and $60 per child.

For most trips in these price ranges, theme park admission ranges from 35% to 60% of the cost of a trip, regardless of family size. If you're not staying at a Deluxe resort, it's safe to assume that ticket costs will take half of your budget (again, excluding transportation).

It's a different story for off-site hotels, which lack services like free shuttles and extra time in the theme parks. Excellent third-party resorts, such as the **Sheraton Vistana** and **Marriott's Harbour Lake,** offer *two-bedroom* rooms at rates up to 65% less than those of Disney's cheapest one-bedroom Deluxe hotels. But if you pick one of these off-site locations, make sure to factor in the cost of a car, parking, and gas.

How to Save Over $600 on Your Trip

In this book, you'll find many techniques for saving money on a Walt Disney World vacation, including finding an inexpensive hotel, discounts on park tickets, and budget-friendly restaurants. But sometimes you can do all of that and *still* need to cut your overall costs to stay within your budget.

Let's go over some "bonus" things you can do to potentially save over $600 on your Disney vacation. For each of these tips, assume a family of four traveling to Walt Disney World for a one-week (six-day, seven-night) vacation. Our sample family includes two adults and two children ages 4 and 7.

TIP 1: RESEARCH AND PREPARE FOR THE WEATHER

It can rain at Disney World at any time of year, and it can get unbearably hot and surprisingly cold. Bring your own rain ponchos, sweatshirts, and/or neck fans instead of buying at the parks.

Don't buy 2 adult ponchos x $12 and 2 kids' ponchos x $10 = **$44**
Do buy 4 ponchos at local dollar store = **$5**
SAVINGS $44 – $5 = **$39**

Don't buy 2 adult sweatshirts x $60 and 2 kids' sweatshirts x $40 = **$200** (*ouch*)
Do bring yours from home, or buy 4 Disney sweatshirts outside the parks ($25 x adult and $15 x kid) = **$80**
SAVINGS $200 – $80 = **$120**

Don't buy 2 neck fans for the family to share x $30 = **$60**
Do buy 2 neck fans in advance x $16 = **$32**
SAVINGS $60 – $32 = **$28**

TIP 2: BUY TICKETS IN ADVANCE . . . FAR IN ADVANCE

Disney is pretty predictable about raising ticket prices every year. The good news is this lets you plan ahead and purchase your park tickets in advance.

Don't wait until a couple of months out to buy park tickets
Do buy tickets in advance either from Disney or from one of our recommended ticket wholesalers (see page 67)
AVERAGE SAVINGS $25 x 4 tickets = **$100**

TIP 3: BRING YOUR OWN STROLLER OR RENT FROM A THIRD PARTY (RATHER THAN DISNEY)

Our sample family wants a stroller for their 4-year-old in the parks. Disney strollers are cheap but bulky and uncomfortable. They'll do in a pinch, but you can do better for your money.

Don't rent a stroller for $13 per day (length-of-stay rate) x 6 days = **$78**
Do buy 1 umbrella stroller outside the parks (much more comfortable and convenient) = **$32**
Or rent 1 Baby Jogger City Mini stroller or similar from a third-party company (MUCH more comfortable and convenient; see page 296) = **$75**
SAVINGS $3 to $46, plus whining avoidance

TIP 4: STAY HYDRATED FOR FREE

All Disney restaurants (not food carts) will give you a free cup of ice water. Instead of wasting money on bottled water or sugary drinks, this is an easy way to save some cash. For our sample family, let's assume that everyone wants to drink something other than water at breakfast and that the kids' meals will include a drink at lunch and dinner. Only the adults will drink free water, and we'll assume they each skip one bottled water and one soda at a meal per day.

Don't buy 1 beverage and 1 bottled water at $4.49 each x 2 adults x 6 days = **$108**
Do drink free water instead = **$0**
SAVINGS $108 – $0 = **$108**

TIP 5: BRING YOUR OWN SNACKS AND SODAS

It's amazing how much you can save by bringing your own nonperishable snacks and drinks into the park. You can bring them from home or get groceries delivered to your room. You can choose fun things that are different from what you would normally feed your kids at home so that the snacks are still a treat, just less expensive.

Don't buy 1 snack at $6 each and 1 soda at $4.49 each x 4 people x
6 days = **$252**
Do bring your own snacks and sodas = **$60**
SAVINGS $252 – $60 = **$192**

TIP 6: EAT BREAKFAST IN YOUR ROOM
This saves you time and a small fortune. As with snacks and sodas, you can
bring them from home or order in groceries. It's quick, easy, and cheap.

Don't buy one $13 breakfast platter + one $7 yogurt parfait + two $8 kids'
Mickey waffle meals + four $3.79 milks x 6 days = **$307**
Do bring your own breakfast, including paper bowls, napkins, plastic
spoons, cereal, breakfast pastries, mini doughnuts, cereal bars, fruit, juice,
and milk = **$90**
SAVINGS $307 – $90 = **$217**

TOTAL SAVINGS $647–$782 *($108–$131 per day)*

Three More Tips from Becky

1. Buy your tickets online from one of the sellers listed on page 67. Get
   tickets only for the number of days you plan to visit, skipping any add-ons.
   You can even time your tickets to take advantage of date-based pricing
   (see below).

2. Rent a condo or vacation home close to the parks if you
   want more space for less money. You'll have a longer
   and less convenient commute to the parks, but you'll
   get much more bang for your buck. Just check traffic
   patterns using a mapping app that displays traffic, such
   as Google Maps, before you book.

3. Buy discounted Disney apparel and souvenirs from one
   of Orlando's two **Disney Character Warehouse** outlets
   (theugseries.com/disneyoutlets). Even better, purchase
   for kids beforehand, then surprise them during the vacation. They'll still be
   excited about souvenirs, and you will avoid Disney gift shop sticker shock.

unofficial **TIP**
Look up your potential
vacation rental's address
at park opening and
closing times to see
what traffic you might
encounter when driving
to and from the parks.

WALT DISNEY WORLD ADMISSION TICKETS

DISNEY OFFERS THOUSANDS of theme park ticket options, ranging from the humble (yet somehow still expensive) **1-Day Base Ticket,**
which is good for a single day's entry into one Disney theme park,
to the blinged-out **Incredi-Pass,** good for 365 days of admission into
every Disney theme park and more attractions. See pages 64–65 for
a summary of the most common admission types.

DATE-BASED PRICING AND OTHER SURCHARGES

DISNEY USES DATE-BASED PRICING for theme park tickets, meaning prices fluctuate depending on the date, similar to the way you could
pay more or less for hotels and flights depending on when you want to
travel. Additionally, 1-day tickets for the Magic Kingdom usually cost
more than tickets for the other parks.

Tickets are generally most expensive when kids are out of school:
Christmas and other holidays, spring break, and summer vacation.

WDW THEME PARK TICKET OPTIONS

	1-DAY	2-DAY	3-DAY	4-DAY	5-DAY
USE WITHIN: 1 DAY	4 DAYS	5 DAYS	7 DAYS	8 DAYS
BASE TICKET AGES 3-9					
ALL PARKS: $111-$196	$234-$353	$360-$521	$473-$663	$509-$741
—	($117-$177/day)	($120-$174/day)	($118-$166/day)	($102-$148/day)
BASE TICKET AGE 10+					
ALL PARKS: $116-$201	$245-$362	$375-$535	$491-$681	$530-$763
—	($123-$181/day)	($125-$178/day)	($123-$170/day)	($106-$153/day)

Base Ticket admits guest to one theme park each day of use. Tickets must be used within the number of days shown in the "Use Within" row above.

PARK HOPPER					
AGES 3-9: $193-$265 AGE 10+: $199-$271	$314-$443 $324-$453	$440-$610 $455-$625	$564-$764 $582-$782	$600-$843 $620-$864

Park Hopper option entitles guest to visit more than one theme park on each day of use. See below for details.

WATER PARK AND SPORTS					
AGES 3-9: NOT SOLD AGE 10+: NOT SOLD	$309-$427 $318-$437	$435-$594 $449-$649	$548-$737 $566-$755	$584-$816 $605-$837

Water Park and Sports entitles you to a specified number of visits (between 1 and 10) to a choice of entertainment and recreation venues. It's a flat $75 fee to add to any ticket for any age and any ticket length.

PARK HOPPER PLUS					
AGES 3-9: $215-$286 AGE 10+: $221-$292	$335-$464 $345-$474	$461-$632 $476-$647	$585-$785 $603-$803	$621-$864 $642-$885
1 visit	2 visits	3 visits	4 visits	5 visits

Park Hopper Plus option entitles guest to a specified number of visits (1-10) to a choice of entertainment and recreation venues, plus the Park Hopper option above. PHP tickets expire 1 day later than the "Use Within" days above.

Less-expensive tickets are available during nonholiday periods when kids are in school (January and February, for example) and during peak hurricane season in September.

You must tell Disney the first date you plan to visit a theme park or water park. Your ticket price will be based on that starting date, the number of days you plan to visit theme parks or water parks, and whether you plan to visit more than one theme park per day.

If you reschedule your vacation from days when tickets are more expensive to days when they are less expensive, Disney will not refund the difference in price—but they will charge you the difference if you need to move from less expensive to more expensive days.

TICKET ADD-ONS

THREE TICKET ADD-ON OPTIONS are available with your park admission, each at an additional cost:

PARK HOPPER Lets you visit more than one theme park per day. The cost is usually $90–$100 on top of the base ticket price. The longer your stay, the less it costs per day. For example, as an add-on to a 7-Day Base Ticket, the flat fee works out to around $14 a day for

NOTE: ALL TICKET AND ADD-ON PRICES INCLUDE 6.5% SALES TAX.				
6-DAY	**7-DAY**	**8-DAY**	**9-DAY**	**10-DAY**
9 DAYS	10 DAYS	12 DAYS	13 DAYS	14 DAYS
BASE TICKET AGES 3–9				
$526–$786	$543–$807	$582–$831	$606–$844	$625–$865
($88–$131/day)	($78–$115/day)	($73–$104/day)	($67–$94/day)	($63–$87/day)
BASE TICKET AGE 10+				
$548–$808	$565–$831	$605–$854	$630–$867	$650–$889
($91–$135/day)	($81–$119/day)	($76–$107/day)	($70–$96/day)	($65–$89/day)
Park choices are Magic Kingdom, EPCOT, Disney's Hollywood Studios, or Disney's Animal Kingdom.				
PARK HOPPER				
$617–$887 $638–$910	$634–$909 $655–$932	$672–$932 $696–$956	$697–$945 $720–$970	$716–$966 $740–$991
Park choices are any combination of Magic Kingdom, EPCOT, Disney's Hollywood Studios, or Disney's Animal Kingdom on each day of use.				
WATER PARK AND SPORTS				
$601–$861 $622–$883	$616–$882 $639–$906	$656–$905 $680–$929	$681–$918 $704–$943	$700–$940 $724–$964
Choices are Disney's Blizzard Beach water park, Disney's Typhoon Lagoon water park, Oak Trail Golf Course, ESPN Wide World of Sports Complex, and Fantasia Gardens and Fairways or Winter Summerland minigolf.				
PARK HOPPER PLUS				
$638–$909 $659–$931	$655–$930 $677–$953	$694–$953 $717–$977	$718–$966 $641–$991	$737–$988 $762–$1,012
6 visits	7 visits	8 visits	9 visits	10 visits
Choices are Disney's Blizzard Beach water park, Disney's Typhoon Lagoon water park, Oak Trail Golf Course, ESPN Wide World of Sports Complex, or Fantasia Gardens and Fairways or Winter Summerland minigolf.				

park-hopping privileges; as an add-on to a 2-Day Base Ticket, the fee can be $45 a day. If you want to be able to change parks after lunch or hit up EPCOT every night for dining, this is the add-on you need. Keep in mind that you can't choose to park-hop for just a day or two and not pay for the upgrade on other days. It's all-or-nothing.

WATER PARK AND SPORTS This $75 (including tax) option provides daily entry to Blizzard Beach, Typhoon Lagoon, Oak Trail Golf Course, Fantasia Gardens and Fairways and Winter Summerland minigolf, and the ESPN Wide World of Sports Complex.

PARK HOPPER PLUS The Park Hopper Plus (PHP) option combines the Park Hopper and Water Park and Sports add-ons. This option costs $90–$122 more than a Base Ticket, including tax, which is cheaper than the combined cost of the two options purchased separately.

You can't change how many Park Hopper/Water Park/PHP admissions you can buy with either option; the number is fixed, and unused days aren't refundable. You can, however, skip Park Hopper/Water Park/PHP entirely and buy an individual admission to any of the venues listed above—that's frequently the best deal if you're not park-hopping and want to visit just Typhoon Lagoon and/or Blizzard Beach once.

If you buy a ticket but then decide later that you want to add the Park Hopper/PHP option, you can do so. But keep in mind that Disney doesn't prorate the cost: If you add Park Hopper/PHP on the last day of your trip, you'll pay the same price as if you'd bought it before you left home.

WHEN TICKETS EXPIRE
(for tickets dated August 13, 2021, and later)

ALONG WITH IMPLEMENTING date-based pricing, Disney has shortened the amount of time you have to use your tickets. Whereas previously all tickets expired 14 days from the date of first use, ticket expiration is now based on how many days you're visiting the theme parks and water parks, as shown in the table below.

For example, if you purchase a basic 4-Day Base Ticket and specify that you'll start using it on June 1, 2025, you must complete your four theme park visits by midnight June 7, 2025. *Once you start using your ticket, any unused admissions expire even if you don't use them.*

If you purchase a ticket and don't use any of it before it expires, you can apply the amount paid for that ticket toward the purchase of a new ticket at current prices, provided the new ticket's price is the same cost (or more) of the expired ticket.

WHEN TICKETS EXPIRE										
DAYS ON BASE TICKET	1	2	3	4	5	6	7	8	9	10
DAYS TILL TICKET EXPIRES FROM FIRST USE (WITHOUT PARK HOPPER PLUS)	Expires after first use	4	5	7	8	9	10	12	13	14
DAYS TILL TICKET EXPIRES FROM FIRST USE (WITH PARK HOPPER PLUS)	1	5	6	8	9	10	11	13	14	15

ANNUAL PASSES

ANNUAL PASSES PROVIDE UNLIMITED USE of the major theme parks for one year. Pass holders can add water park access for $105. Four versions are available (prices are for age 3 and up and include tax):

- The **Pixie Dust Pass** ($439; Florida residents only) lets you have up to three simultaneous park reservations. The Pixie Dust Pass has the most blockout dates, or dates when the pass cannot be used (almost all weekends are off-limits, plus a week or two around every major holiday and chunks of time around minor holidays).

- The **Pirate Pass** ($799; Florida residents only) includes four simultaneous park reservations. It has fewer weekend blockout dates than the Pixie Dust Pass but retains blockout dates for every major and minor holiday.

- The **Sorcerer Pass** ($999; Florida residents and Disney Vacation Club members only) includes five simultaneous park reservations. The only blockout dates are the Wednesday–Saturday around Thanksgiving, and the two weeks surrounding Christmas and New Year's.

- The **Incredi-Pass** ($1,449; available to everyone) includes five simultaneous park reservations and has no blockout dates.

Note that while park reservations are no longer required for date-based tickets, they are still required for certain types of admission, including Annual Passes.

Annual Pass holders also get some perks, including free parking; hotel, dining, and merchandise discounts; and seasonal offers such as a dedicated entrance line at the parks. They can also visit the parks after 2 p.m. without needing a reservation (except on Saturdays and Sundays in the Magic Kingdom). Beginning in 2024, Annual Pass holders were also given "good-to-go" days when no park reservations were needed at all. Annual Passes are not valid for special events. See disneyworld.disney.go.com/passes for details.

WHERE TO PURCHASE DISNEY WORLD TICKETS

TICKETS ARE AVAILABLE at Disney resorts and theme parks, Disney Store locations, and disneyworld.disney.go.com for the prices shown on pages 76–77. (If you purchase on arrival, you will incur a $21.30-per-ticket surcharge for tickets of three days or longer.)

unofficial **TIP**
If you order physical tickets in advance, allow enough time for them to be mailed to your home.

If you're trying to keep your vacation costs to an absolute minimum, consider using a third-party wholesaler, such as **Boardwalk Ticketing** (board walkticketing.com) or **Tripster** (☎ 888-590-5910; tripster.com), especially for trips of three or more park days. All tickets are brand-new, and the savings can easily exceed $200 for a family of four. Vendors will provide you with electronic tickets just like Disney does, so you'll be able to make hotel, dining, and ride reservations through the My Disney Experience website, though you may have to wait up to a week to do so when ordering from a third party (see pages 25–26).

You might be wondering why Disney gives third-party wholesalers such large discounts on tickets. The answer is volume. Disney knows most visitors will pay full price for tickets, so there's no incentive to offer them a discount. However, Disney also knows that there are lots of shoppers who will visit only if they can get a deal. Disney uses third-party wholesalers to offer discounted tickets to those shoppers, so it doesn't have to offer discounts to the general public. It's a win–win–win: The discount shoppers get their deal, Disney maximizes its revenue, and third-party companies earn a little bit too.

Tripster offers discounted tickets for almost all Central Florida attractions, including Disney, Universal, and SeaWorld. Boardwalk Ticketing offers them only for Disney. Discounts for the major theme parks range from about 6% to 12%; tickets for other attractions are more deeply discounted.

Finally, tickets are available at some non-Disney hotels and shopping centers and through independent ticket brokers. Because Disney admissions are only marginally discounted in the Orlando area, the chief reason to buy from an independent broker is convenience. Offers of free or heavily discounted tickets abound, but the catch is they generally require you to attend a time-share sales presentation.

Where *Not* to Buy Tickets and Passes

unofficial **TIP**
Also steer clear of passes offered on eBay and Craigslist.

In addition to the many authorized resellers of Disney admissions, there are quite a few unauthorized ones. They buy up unused days on legitimately purchased park passes and resell them as if they were brand-new.

These resellers insist that you specify the exact days you plan to use the ticket. They already know, of course, how many days are left on the pass and when it expires. If you tell them that you plan to use it tomorrow and the next two days, then they'll sell you a ticket that has three days left on it and expires in three days. Because they don't tell you this, you might assume that the usual five-day expiration period applies from the date of first use. If you skip a day instead of using the pass on the next three consecutive days, you'll find out that it expires before you thought it would.

HOW TO SAVE MONEY ON DISNEY WORLD TICKETS

DISNEY'S DATE-BASED PRICING SCHEME is the most complicated system ever used for ticket purchases. It is so complicated, in fact, that the TouringPlans team wrote a computer program to analyze all the options and look for loopholes in the new pricing rules. Try their **Ticket Price Comparison Tool** (theugseries.com/ug-ticketcalculator), which aggregates ticket prices from Disney and a number of online ticket vendors. Answer a few questions about the size of your party and the parks you intend to visit, and the calculator will identify your four cheapest ticket options. It will also show you how much you'll save versus buying at the gate.

The program will also make recommendations for considerations other than price. For example, Annual Passes might cost more, but Disney often offers substantial resort discounts and other deals to Annual Pass holders. These resort discounts, especially during the off-season, can more than offset the price of the pass.

The Ticket Price Comparison Tool will automatically use all of the tips below and more. If you'd rather do the research yourself, here's what you'll need to consider:

1. BUY PARK TICKETS BEFORE YOU GET TO THE PARKS. As mentioned previously, if you buy at the theme parks, Disney adds a surcharge of $21.30 to park tickets with three or more days of admission.

2. BUY FROM A THIRD-PARTY WHOLESALER. As we've noted, Disney contracts with third-party ticket vendors to offer discounts to consumers who'll visit only if they can get a deal. By using other companies, Disney doesn't have to offer those discounts directly to people who'd visit anyway. These vendors sign contracts with Disney and provide the same tickets you'd purchase at Walt Disney World. See previous page for the vendors we recommend.

3. MEMBERS OF THE US MILITARY AND FLORIDA RESIDENTS GET SPECIAL DISCOUNTS. Disney's recent deal for US military personnel included a 4-Day Park Hopper for $350, substantially less than the $719 regular price. Florida resident discounts aren't as steep, but they're better than anything the general public gets.

4. SET YOUR TICKET'S START DATE EARLIER THAN YOUR ARRIVAL DATE. Suppose you're visiting for a long weekend (Thursday–Sunday) and you're buying four-day tickets. You'd naturally pick Thursday as your ticket's start date. But remember that four-day park tickets are valid for seven days. If you're visiting at the start of a busy (i.e., expensive) season, setting your ticket start date to Monday or Tuesday can save you money.

5. IF YOU'RE VISITING ONLY ONE WATER PARK, buy a separate water park ticket instead of purchasing the Water Park and Sports add-on. The break-even point on the Water Park and Sports option is two water park visits.

6. VISIT A WATER PARK ON YOUR FIRST OR LAST DAY. Say your trip starts at the end of a busy period and you're already planning one water park visit. Visiting the water park on your first day allows you to set your theme park start date one day later, saving money on your date-based ticket. Conversely, if your trip ends at the beginning of a busy season, go to the water park on the last day of your trip and set your theme park start date a day earlier.

Ticket Deals for Canada Residents

Disney often discounts theme park admission for Canada residents by setting the Canadian dollar at par with the US dollar. The exchange rate as of this writing is $1 CAD equals $0.76 USD, so this deal effectively boosts the value of the Loonie by around 33%. Visit disneyworld.disney .go.com/en_ca/special-offers to see the latest offers.

Ticket Deals for United Kingdom Residents

In the UK, Disney offers advance-purchase tickets that aren't available in the United States. As we went to press, you can get 14-Day **Ultimate Tickets** starting at £519 for adults and £499 for kids—the same price as a 7-Day Ultimate Ticket. Ultimate Tickets provide unlimited admission to major and minor parks, along with park-hopping privileges to the major parks. Ultimate Tickets expire 14 days after first use. To find out more, call ☎ 0800-169-0730 from the UK or 407-566-4985 within the US (Monday–Friday, 9 a.m.–8 p.m.; Saturday, 9 a.m.–7 p.m.; and Sunday, 10 a.m.–4 p.m.) or see disneyholidays.co.uk/walt-disney-world or the **Disney Information Bulletin Board** (thedibb.co.uk).

Discounts Available to Certain Groups and Individuals

DISNEY VACATION CLUB Members get a discount on Annual Passes.

CONVENTION-GOERS Disney World, Universal Orlando, SeaWorld, and other Orlando-area parks sometimes set up a web link where you can purchase discounted afternoon and evening admissions. This link should be included in your convention materials.

DISNEY CORPORATE SPONSORS If you work for one of these, you may be eligible for discounted admissions or perks at the parks. Check with your workplace's employee-benefits office.

FLORIDA RESIDENTS get substantial savings on virtually all tickets. You'll need to prove Florida residency with a valid driver's license or state identification card.

MILITARY, DEPARTMENT OF DEFENSE, CIVIL SERVICE Active-duty and retired military, Department of Defense (DOD) civilian employees, some civil-service employees, and dependents of these groups can buy Disney multiday admissions at a 9%–10% discount. Military personnel can buy discounted admission for nonmilitary guests if the military member accompanies the nonmilitary guest. If a group seeks the discount, at least half of the group's members must be eligible.

DISNEY IMAGINATION CAMPUS Disney runs educational programs for K–12 students; these programs also offer ticket discounts (with restrictions). Visit disneycampus.com.

DISNEY TICKET PRICE INCREASES

DISNEY USUALLY RAISES TICKET PRICES once or twice a year. Hikes were announced in February and December 2022, February 2020, March 2019, February and September 2018, and February 2014–2017.

unofficial **TIP**
Save money on tickets by planning ahead— buy them before the next price increase.

Prices on all tickets went up an average of almost 9% in 2022, 6% in 2020, 4% in 2019, 9% in 2018, and 7% in 2017. For your budget, assume an increase of around 10% per year to be safe.

FOR ADDITIONAL INFORMATION ON TICKETS

IF YOU HAVE A QUESTION regarding tickets that can be addressed only with a person-to-person conversation, call **Disney Ticket Inquiries** at ☎ 407-566-4985 or email ticket.inquiries@disneyworld.com. If you call, be aware that you may spend considerable time on hold; if you email, it can take up to three days to get a response. Fortunately, the ticket section of the Disney World website, disneyworld.disney.go.com /tickets, is refreshingly straightforward in showing how ticket prices break down.

TICKETS AND MAGICBANDS

WE'VE USED THE WORD *TICKET* to describe that thing you carry around as proof of your admission purchase. In fact, there are three forms of Disney admission media—none of which is a ticket.

One admission medium, the **MagicBand,** is a wristband about the size and shape of a small wristwatch. It contains a tiny radio frequency identification (RFID) chip that stores a link to the record of your admission purchase in Disney's computers. Your MagicBand also functions as your Disney hotel-room key, and it can (optionally) work as a credit card for most food and merchandise purchases.

MagicBands are available for purchase for about $15 if you're staying on-site. Most people now purchase the new generation, called **MagicBand+.** These are available for purchase for around $25–$40 if you are staying on-site, or $35–$50 if you are staying off-site. MagicBand+ does everything the original MagicBand does, but it will also light up and make sounds during certain interactions, like entering the park, waving at a statue, or watching a nighttime spectacular.

Each member of your family gets their own MagicBand with a unique serial number. The wristbands are removable, resizable, and waterproof, and they have ventilation holes for cooling. You can choose your colors and personalize your bands when you order them at the Disney World website. Even more designs are available throughout the parks and at shopdisney.com.

Along with the wristband, each family member will be asked to select a four-digit PIN for purchases. See opposite page for details.

If you don't want a MagicBand, you're staying off-property, or you bought your admission from a third-party vendor, your second "ticket" option is a **Key to the World** (**KTTW**) **Card,** which is a flexible, credit card–size piece of plastic with an embedded RFID chip.

Your third option is to use the **My Disney Experience** (MDE) app on your Bluetooth-enabled smartphone. This option allows you to tap your smartphone or smartwatch for admission at park entrances, the same way you tap your phone for payments at stores and restaurants.

Of the three options, we think the MagicBands and KTTW Cards are the fastest and easiest to use. The main problem with using the MDE app is that it's far slower to take out your phone, open the app, and find the right screen to do what you want. And that's assuming you don't have to connect to Wi-Fi, log into the app, or remember the password you used.

RFID for Payment, Genie+, Hotel-Room Access, and Photos

Disney's hotel-room doors have RFID readers, allowing you to enter your room simply by tapping your wristband or KTTW Card against the reader, or by telling the MDE app to open the door. RFID readers are also installed at virtually every Disney cash register on-property, allowing you to pay for food, drinks, ride reservations, and souvenirs by tapping your MagicBand/KTTW Card against the reader. For in-person purchases, you'll be asked to verify your identity by entering your PIN on a small keypad.

The MDE app requires that you enable Bluetooth transmitting and receiving for tickets, photos, ride reservations, and payments. (Note that doing so will allow your location to be tracked while you're using the app.)

If you're using Disney's **Memory Maker** service (see page 359), your MagicBand or KTTW Card serves as the link between your photos and your family. Each photographer carries an RFID reader on which you tap

> *unofficial* **TIP**
> Disney strongly encourages guests to use contactless methods of payment while in the World. These include MagicBands, ApplePay, Google Pay, credit cards, and debit cards.

your MagicBand, KTTW Card, or phone after having your photo taken. The computers that run the Memory Maker system will link your photos to you, and you'll be able to view them on the Disney World website.

Disney's onboard ride-photo computers incorporate RFID technology too. As you begin down the big drop near the finale of Tiana's Bayou Adventure, for example, sensors read the serial number on your MagicBand (or detect the Bluetooth signal sent from the MDE app on your phone) and pass it to Tiana's cameras. When those cameras snap your family plunging past the photo spot, they attach your MagicBands' serial numbers to the photo, allowing you to see your ride photos together after you've returned home. Because ride sensors may not pick up the signal from an RFID card or a phone sitting in a wallet or purse, we think onboard ride photos require MagicBands.

PRIVACY CONCERNS Many people are understandably wary of multi-national corporations tracking their movements. As noted earlier, guests who prefer not to wear MagicBands or not to download the

MDE app can instead obtain KTTW Cards, which are somewhat harder to track (RFID-blocking wallets are available online).

OPTIONAL EXPENSES

WHICH SPECIAL EVENTS ARE WORTH THE MONEY?

AS A WAY TO "SELL" THE SAME THEME PARK RIDES multiple times per day, Disney constantly experiments with offers of extra time in the parks that require buying separate admission. For example, before the pandemic, the Magic Kingdom hosted a preopening event, regular park hours, and then another event after the park closed to regular guests, all on the same day.

The scope of the events varies: Morning events usually include access to all the rides in just one land, plus breakfast. Evening events typically include most of a park's attractions. Holiday-themed events are held in the evening and include special entertainment, parades, fireworks, and decorations in addition to access to almost all of the park's rides; complimentary snacks are usually offered as well. (Guests with tickets to evening events are typically admitted starting around 4 p.m., allowing them to catch a few extra hours in the parks too.)

Disney restricts the number of tickets sold for these events, from a few hundred at the morning events to less than 30,000 (we've heard) for the Halloween and Christmas events. As a result, wait times for rides at most of these are usually 15 minutes or less. Hyperpopular rides, such as Seven Dwarfs Mine Train or Slinky Dog Dash, will undoubtedly have longer waits, but they'll still be much shorter than waits during the day. What you're paying for, therefore, is shorter lines (and often unique entertainment).

We think all the events have some value to guests with limited time. To help you decide whether they are worth the cost, we've summarized each below, in the (rough) order we recommend them.

1. MICKEY'S NOT SO SCARY HALLOWEEN PARTY (Magic Kingdom; select days mid-August–November 1, 7 p.m.–midnight, with ticketed guests allowed into the park starting at 4 p.m.; ticket prices were $109–$199 per person in 2023). With holiday-themed characters and performers, the Magic Kingdom's Halloween parade is the best in Walt Disney World. The event also includes decorations throughout the park; special (often rare) character sightings; fireworks; and occasional, light retheming of a few attractions, plus a boatload of candy, if you're interested.

2. DISNEY'S VERY MERRY CHRISTMAS PARTY (Magic Kingdom; select days early November–late December, 7 p.m.–midnight, with ticketed guests allowed into the park starting at 4 p.m.; ticket prices were $159–$199 per person in 2023). Like the Halloween party, the Christmas party offers holiday decorations and a special parade and fireworks, plus unique shows and live performances by Disney characters. The Halloween party is ranked higher because it offers more for a lower price, but the Christmas party is admittedly pure magic.

3. JOLLYWOOD NIGHTS (Disney's Hollywood Studios; select days early November–late December, 8:30 p.m.–12:30 a.m., with ticketed guests allowed into the park starting at 7 p.m.; ticket prices were $159–$179 per person in 2023). This is the only holiday party offered at Walt Disney World that doesn't include complimentary snacks. But it has unique characters, unbelievably good stage shows, immersive holiday décor, incredible food options, and walk-ons for most of the popular Hollywood Studios attractions. It had some hiccups in its first year, but we expect great things in the future.

4. MAGIC KINGDOM AFTER HOURS (Magic Kingdom; 3 hours after regular park closing; select Mondays and Thursdays; $155–$175 per person). Yes, it's up to $175 for 3 hours in the park, but the high cost keeps crowds low. Most rides will have wait times of 5 minutes or less, meaning that the number of rides you can visit depends largely on how fast you can walk between them and how long the rides last.

5. DISNEY'S HOLLYWOOD STUDIOS AFTER HOURS (Disney's Hollywood Studios; 3 hours after regular park closing; typically Wednesday but days of week vary; $155–$175 per person). If you can't get up early for Rise of the Resistance and you're visiting during a busy time of year, this is the most direct way to experience the ride (multiple times!) with short waits. Plus, nighttime rides on Tower of Terror and Slinky Dog Dash are vastly different than daytime rides. Prices went up significantly for this event starting in 2024, but it offers the shortest waits you'll find at Hollywood Studios.

6. EPCOT AFTER HOURS (EPCOT; 3 hours after regular park closing; typically Thursday, but days of week vary; $149–$159 per person). Like at Hollywood Studios, this is the way to see the park's headliners without long lines. Waits are usually so short that the limiting factor for how many rides you'll experience is likely to be the walking distance between Remy's and Guardians of the Galaxy. Because rides are so spread out and there are fewer long-wait attractions to absorb crowds, we think EPCOT After Hours is the least worthwhile of the After Hours options.

7. DISNEY H2O GLOW AFTER HOURS (Typhoon Lagoon; 3 hours after regular park closing; typically Saturdays mid-May–early September; days vary; $75–$80 per person). During months with warmer nights, Disney offers after-hours admission to Typhoon Lagoon. Besides the glow-in-the-dark visuals at the wave pool, this event offers some of the shortest lines you'll likely find at a Disney water park.

PART 5

ACCOMMODATIONS

KEY QUESTIONS ANSWERED IN THIS CHAPTER

The BASIC CONSIDERATIONS

LOCATING A SUITABLE HOTEL OR CONDO is critical to planning any Walt Disney World vacation. The basic question is whether to stay at a hotel located inside Disney World (**on-site**) or not (**off-site**).

Around 86% of *Unofficial Guide* readers stay on-site during their trips. On top of the convenience and the amenities, readers say they enjoy "being in the Disney bubble"— that is, the special magic and convenience associated with staying inside the World. "I feel more a part of everything and less like a visitor," one guest writes. We agree.

> *unofficial* **TIP**
> We recommend that most readers' first choice for lodging be an on-site hotel at Walt Disney World. The incremental extra cost is generally more than offset by the room quality, amenities, transportation, and theme park benefits.

The primary reasons to stay off-site are cost and space. Walt Disney World room rates vary from about $150 on a slow weeknight at what Disney calls its Value resorts to over $2,000 per night during the holidays at its Deluxe properties. Off-site but nearby, clean, bare-bones motel rooms can be had for as little as $70 a night (see page 192). Lodging prices can change, but it's possible to get a hotel room comparable to one at a Moderate Disney resort for half the cost during holidays, or a room twice the size for the same money, all within a 15-minute drive of the parks.

There are advantages to staying outside Disney World and driving or taking a hotel shuttle to the theme parks. Meals can be less expensive, and rooming outside the World makes you more likely to visit other Orlando-area attractions and eating spots. **Universal Studios** and **Universal Islands of Adventure, Kennedy Space Center Visitor Complex, SeaWorld,** and **Gatorland** are well worth your attention.

Because Walt Disney World is so large, some off-property hotels are actually closer in both time and distance to some of the theme parks than other Disney resorts are. Check our Hotel Information Table on page 194–199, which lists commuting times from both Disney and non-Disney hotels.

If you're looking for the cheapest room possible on the premise that "it's just a place to sleep," please read our discussion on page 192 first. Our research indicates that most people are happier *not* booking the cheapest room, even when taking the extra cost into account.

THE LATEST IN LODGING

AT THE TIME OF THIS WRITING, Disney was offering significant hotel discounts throughout 2024. With only one new attraction opening in the next few years (**Tiana's Bayou Adventure** in 2024), Disney will probably continue to discount rooms to give people an incentive to visit. This means you may be able to stretch your lodging budget.

Speaking of stretching your budget, if you're planning to stay at a Disney Moderate or Deluxe resort, it's possible to get an equivalent or superior room by renting **Disney Vacation Club** (**DVC**) points instead of paying cash (see page 83). In the table on page 91, for example, note that it can be less expensive to rent a one-bedroom villa in Animal Kingdom Lodge than it is to pay cash for a smaller standard room. Likewise, renting a two-bedroom villa at the Grand Floridian

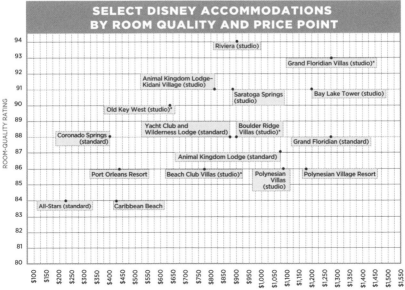

is often less expensive than paying for a standard room at one of the resort's outer buildings. If renting DVC points for an on-site room is still outside your budget, see "The Best Off-Site Hotels for Families," page 181, for the best alternatives.

THE BENEFITS OF STAYING IN THE WORLD

GUESTS WHO STAY ON DISNEY PROPERTY enjoy privileges and amenities unavailable to those staying off-site. Though some of these perks are advertising gimmicks, others are real and valuable. Here are the benefits and what they mean:

1. CONVENIENCE Commuting to the theme parks using the Disney transportation system is easy (though not always fast), especially if you stay in a hotel that offers monorail, boat, or Skyliner access.

2. EARLY ACCESS TO ATTRACTION AND RESTAURANT RESERVATIONS Guests at Disney resorts can make **Individual Lightning Lane** reservations (see page 49) starting at 7 a.m.; off-site guests must wait until the park opens. Guests staying on-property can also make dining reservations 60 days before they arrive and then an additional 10 days into their trip.

3. EARLY THEME PARK ENTRY Disney resort guests—along with guests of the **Swan, Dolphin, Swan Reserve, Shades of Green, Signia by Hilton Orlando Bonnet Creek, Waldorf Astoria Orlando, Four Seasons,** and **Disney Springs Resort Area** hotels—enjoy extra time in the theme parks not available to off-site guests. In many cases, this means shorter waits in line for Disney's most popular rides. See page 30 for details.

4. EXTENDED EVENING THEME PARK HOURS Guests staying at Disney Deluxe resorts and DVC properties, plus the **Dolphin, Swan, Swan Reserve,** and **Shades of Green,** get two extra hours in the theme parks after they close to regular guests. At the time of this writing, Extended Evening Theme Park Hours were offered one or two days per week in various parks. See page 32 for details.

5. FREE PARKING Disney resort guests pay nothing to park in theme park lots—this saves you $30 per day. Likewise, Disney doesn't charge a fee for overnight parking at its resorts, unlike most off-site hotels.

6. GOLFING PRIVILEGES Disney guests can get priority tee times at the on-property golf courses.

7. NO RESORT FEES Unlike many hotels outside of Walt Disney World, the on-site hotels don't charge a nightly resort fee on top of their advertised rates.

THE PROS AND CONS OF STAYING ON-SITE

1. COST You should expect to pay **$150–$175 per night** (including taxes and fees), depending on time of year, for a clean, safe, well-maintained hotel room near Disney World. In this price range, on-site hotels come out ahead. Rooms at the **Pop Century Resort,** for example, cost $195–$365 (before discounts) throughout the year. For even less, you could stay at the **All-Star Resorts,** all of which have been refurbished to look and feel almost exactly like the rooms at Pop Century. Still, for Skyliner access, I prefer Pop Century even with its slightly higher cost.

DISNEY RESORT PRIVILEGES AT A GLANCE

HOTEL	ILL RESERVATIONS	RESTAURANT RESERVATIONS	EARLY THEME PARK ENTRY	EXTENDED EVENING HOURS
Disney resort hotels and Disney Vacation Club (DVC) properties	Starting at 7 a.m.	Up to 70 days out	Yes	Deluxe, DVC only
Disney Springs Resort Area (DSRA) hotels*	Park opening	60 days out	Yes	No
Four Seasons Orlando	Park opening	60 days out	Yes	No
Shades of Green	Starting at 7 a.m.	60 days out	Yes	Yes
Signia by Hilton Orlando Bonnet Creek	Park opening	60 days out	Yes	No
Swan, Dolphin, and Swan Reserve	Starting at 7 a.m.	60 days out	Yes	Yes
Waldorf Astoria Orlando	Park opening	60 days out	Yes	No
Non-Disney hotels	Park opening	60 days out	No	No

* DoubleTree Suites by Hilton, Drury Plaza Hotel Orlando, Hilton Orlando Buena Vista Palace, Hilton Orlando Lake Buena Vista, Holiday Inn Orlando–Disney Springs, Renaissance Orlando Resort and Spa (formerly B Resort & Spa), and Wyndham Garden Lake Buena Vista

Note: All table-service restaurants at Disney Springs and the Swan, Dolphin, and Swan Reserve are independently owned and run, as are a handful of other restaurants around the parks (such as Patina Restaurant Group's Tutto Italia and Via Napoli in EPCOT). These non-Disney-owned restaurants take Advance Dining Reservations, but many also accept reservations directly or through OpenTable.com, meaning 1) they may have tables available even when Disney says they don't and 2) depending on the restaurant, you may not have to prebook with a credit card or pay a no-show fee when you make reservations outside of the Disney system.

Off-site hotels and homes are often better deals for families looking for more space, or high-end lodging and service, for the same money. For instance, Disney's cheapest family suite, at the **Art of Animation Resort,** sleeps six and costs $460–$840 per night. A comparable room at the **Sonesta ES Suites Lake Buena Vista** costs around $200–$325 per night, depending on the time of year. Renting a three-bedroom condo in Kissimmee is even cheaper: around $160–$260 per night. In 2024, my family spent four nights at a two-bedroom condo in Oakwater Resort for less than $100 a night. We had two bedrooms, two bathrooms, two walk-in closets, laundry machines, a full kitchen, and a living room. And we were less than 15 minutes from any of the theme parks! You can afford a longer trip with those savings—a fact that more than offsets the on-site perks.

Similarly, the cheapest room at Disney's flagship **Grand Floridian Resort & Spa** costs about $780–$1,280. The cheapest room at the **Four Seasons Resort Orlando** (near the Magic Kingdom) is at the upper end of that range. But the Four Seasons room is larger and better in every way, with restaurants generally as good as or better than the Grand Floridian's, along with superior customer service. And the pools are like their own water park.

While we think Disney's least expensive hotels are worth the extra cost versus staying off-site, we continue to receive an increasing number of negative reader comments. The vast majority are about the lack of value found at Disney's more expensive hotels. A reader from Illinois is an example:

Before the pandemic, we stayed on-site at Disney resorts every time. I'm planning our first trip back, and I just don't think paying on-site prices makes sense anymore. No Magical Express from the airport, no more Fastpass+ selections. And we're not early risers, so Early Entry won't help us either.

It's the same story at Disney's Deluxe resorts, according to this reader from Texas:

We stayed at the Grand-freaking-Floridian, were on the app at 6:59 every morning, and still had a tough time getting the ride reservations we wanted. As Disney veterans, after two or three days we had figured out what works and what doesn't, but a novice family would walk away from a WDW vacation today with a very bad taste in their mouths.

Dining reservations were impossible to get via normal channels. Service at the hotel was better than last time, but still not worth $770 a night for a lagoon-view room.

Quite frankly, we agree that Disney's Deluxe hotels—the Grand Floridian and Contemporary in particular—are overpriced. At both of these locations, what you're paying for is the ability to walk to the Magic Kingdom.

The Hotel Information Table on pages 194–199 includes the cost range for both on-site and off-site hotels at a glance.

2. EASE OF ACCESS Even if you do stay in Walt Disney World, you're dependent on some mode of transportation. It may be less stressful to use the Disney transportation system, but, with the exception of getting to the Magic Kingdom, the fastest, most efficient, most flexible way to get around is usually by car. If you're in EPCOT, for example, and you want to take your cranky kids back to the Contemporary for a nap, forget the monorail. You'll get back much faster by car.

The Disney transportation system is like most public transportation with its pros and cons, and users must expect inconveniences, including vehicles that arrive and depart on *their* schedule, not yours; the occasional need to transfer; multiple stops; time lost loading and unloading passengers; and other people just as desperate to catch a ride as you are.

If you plan to have a car, traffic on I-4 is the largest potential problem with staying at an off-site hotel, especially if you're coming or going during rush hours. The closer your off-site hotel is to Disney property, the less risk there is in being stuck in I-4 traffic. Secondary roads, such as Turkey Lake Road, Palm Parkway, International Drive, and Universal Boulevard, can help get you around that traffic.

A Kentucky dad was pleasantly surprised by the short commute:

My wife read in another guidebook that it can take 2 hours to commute to the parks if you stay outside Walt Disney World. I guess it could take 2 hours if you stayed in Tampa, but from our hotel on US 192, we could commute to any of the parks except the Magic Kingdom and have at least one ride under our belt in about an hour.

For commuting times from our recommended off-site hotels, see our Hotel Information Table on pages 194–199.

3. FOOD COSTS A few off-site hotels' prices include some sort of free breakfast, ranging from fruit and pastries to pancakes, microwavable waffles, bacon, and eggs. The Disney hotels don't. Depending on how hungry your family is in the morning, eating breakfast at your off-site hotel can save you a minimum of $6–$16 per person per day versus breakfast in the parks. Or you can get groceries delivered to wherever you're staying. My family does grocery delivery to our room whether we're staying off-site or on-site, and it saves us a significant amount of money, especially on breakfast foods.

4. YOUNG CHILDREN Although the hassle of commuting to most non-World hotels is only slightly (if at all) greater than that of commuting to Disney hotels, a definite peace of mind results from staying in the World. Disney resorts are used to catering to kids, much more so than any hotels in the "real world."

5. SPLITTING UP If you're in a party that will probably split up to tour (as frequently happens in families with teens or children of widely varying ages), staying in the World offers more transportation options and, thus, more independence. Mom and Dad can take the car and return to the hotel for a relaxed dinner and early bedtime while the teens remain in the park for extra rides.

6. VISITING OTHER ORLANDO-AREA ATTRACTIONS If you also plan to visit Universal Orlando, SeaWorld, Kennedy Space Center, or other area attractions, it may be more convenient to stay outside of Walt Disney World or to split your stay.

The DISNEY RESORTS

DISNEY RESORTS 101

BEFORE YOU MAKE ANY DECISIONS, understand these basics regarding Disney resorts.

Disney has four main categories of resorts: **Value, Moderate, Deluxe,** and **DVC Villa.** It's a handy system that we'll use in discussing both Disney and off-site hotels. A fifth category, **Campground,** is exclusive to the campsites at **Fort Wilderness Resort.**

Value resorts are the least expensive Disney-owned hotels. They also have the smallest rooms and most limited amenities.

Moderate resorts are a step up from the Values in guest-room quality, amenities, and cost.

Deluxe resorts are Disney's top-of-the-line hotels, boasting extensive theming; luxurious rooms; and superior on-site dining, recreation, and services.

Disney Vacation Club (DVC) resorts (or DVC Villas) offer suites, some with full kitchens. DVC resorts—several of which are attached to Deluxe resorts—equal or surpass Deluxe resorts in quality. They can also be a better value.

MAKING RESERVATIONS Whether you book your hotel room through Disney, a travel agent, the internet, a tour operator, or an organization like AAA,

*un*official **TIP**
Keep in mind that Disney Reservation Center and Walt Disney Travel Company representatives don't have detailed personal knowledge of the resorts.

*un*official **TIP**
If you must book by phone, call before 11 a.m. or after 3 p.m. Eastern.

you can often save by reserving the room by itself, instead of as part of a vacation package. This is known as a **room-only reservation.** Though later on in this chapter we'll scrutinize the advantages and disadvantages of buying a package (see page 174), we'll go ahead and tell you now that Disney World packages at list price rarely save you any money.

We recommend that you book your trip through a travel agent or the Walt Disney World website (disneyworld.disney.go.com) instead of calling the Disney Reservation Center (DRC). Not only is booking online much faster than booking by phone, but DRC reservationists are also focused on selling you a Walt Disney Travel Company package. Even if you insist that all you want is the room, they'll try to persuade you to bundle it with some small extra, like a minigolf pass, so that your purchase can be counted as a package—this lets Disney apply various restrictions and cancellation policies that you wouldn't be saddled with if you bought just the room by itself.

If for some reason you must book your vacation on the phone, a careful shopper from Indiana advises both wariness and toughness:

> *Making reservations through* 407-W-DISNEY *is like buying a car: You need to know the sales tricks, have a firm idea of what you want, and be prepared to walk away if you don't get it at a price you're willing to pay.*

CANCELLATION POLICIES Regarding cancellation, know that there are some trade-offs. If you book a package and then cancel 2–29 days before arrival, you lose your $200 deposit. If you cancel a day or less before arrival, you lose the entire package cost. If you reserve only a room and cancel fewer than eight days before arrival (a new stricter policy in 2025—it used to be five days), you lose your deposit of one night's room charge. Further, Disney imposes a $50 fee, plus a $15 processing fee, for changing your package's details—such as adjusting travel dates, moving to a cheaper resort, or adding a discount code—30 days or fewer before your trip.

YOUR HOTEL-ROOM VIEW Rates at Disney hotels vary by season (see page 63) and from room to room according to view. Furthermore, each Disney resort has its own seasonal calendar that varies depending on the resort. Beyond the choice of a specific resort and the seasonal impact on pricing, the biggest factor in how much you'll pay is the view that you choose.

Standard view, the most ambiguous category, crops up at almost every Disney resort. It's usually interpreted as a view of infrastructure or unremarkable scenery. At Animal Kingdom Lodge, for example, you have savanna views, water views, and standard views. Savanna views overlook the replicated African veldt, water views overlook the swimming pool, and value and standard views usually offer stunning vistas of . . . rooftops and parking lots.

With a standard view, however, you can at least pinpoint what you *won't* be seeing. Each resort has little quirks with its definition of "water view." At the Grand Floridian, for example, rooms with views of Seven Seas Lagoon are sensibly called "lagoon view" rooms, while those with views of the marina or pools are lumped together with other "resort view" rooms (no standard-view rooms here).

The Yacht Club Resort, like the Grand Floridian, is on a lake and has a pool and a marina. Lake and quiet pool views are both water-view rooms, but you have to upgrade to Club Level to get a guaranteed view of Stormalong Bay! And at Wilderness Lodge, a water view could be the pool, a waterfall, Bay Lake, or even Copper Creek.

For many readers, a good view is essential to enjoying their room. Getting the view you want, however, doesn't necessarily mean that you'll have the *experience* you want, as a New York couple points out:

> We stayed in the Conch Key building at the Grand Floridian. The view was lovely, but we could hear the boat's horn blasting every 20 minutes, 7 a.m.–midnight. It was obnoxious and kept us up.

TouringPlans.com's **Hotel Room Views** project uses more than 35,000 photos to show the view from every Disney-owned hotel room in Walt Disney World, plus instructions on how to request each room. It also has interactive maps for every building in every resort, so you can search for rooms by cost, view, walking distance, noise, accessibility, and more. Visit touringplans.com/walt-disney-world/hotels to see photos of the rooms we recommend in this chapter.

HOW TO GET THE ROOM YOU WANT Disney won't guarantee a specific room when you book but will post your request on your reservation record. The easiest way to make a request is to use the Hotel Room Views tool described above. Select the room you want, and your request will be automatically emailed to Disney 30 days before you arrive.

Our experience indicates that making a request with just a single room number doesn't work well. Frequently that one single room isn't available, and you've given no additional information as to why that room was preferable. To increase your odds of getting the room you want, tell the reservationist (or your travel agent) *to the letter* what characteristics and amenities you desire.

unofficial **TIP**
A week or two before you arrive, call your resort's front desk. Call late in the evening when they're not so busy and reconfirm the requests that by now should be appearing in their computer system.

Be politely assertive when speaking to any Disney agent. Specify the type of view you're looking for. Similarly, state clearly such preferences as a particular floor, a room near restaurants, or a room away from elevators and ice machines. If you have a long list of preferences, type it in order of importance and email, fax, or snail-mail it to the hotel. Include your contact information and your reservation-confirmation number. Be brief, though: Disney's reservation system has a limited amount of space to store what you write.

Someone from Disney's Centralized Inventory Management team, or the resort itself, will assign your room. You can call back in a few days to make sure your preferences were posted to your record.

We'll provide the information needed for each resort to frame your requests, including a resort map and our recommendations for specific rooms or buildings. A dash (–) indicates a range of rooms.

Readers say the hotel-request service works about two out of three times. Disney's room assigners tell us that the most common reasons for not getting the exact room requested are as follows:

- **Someone is already in the requested room.** This is common during holidays and other busy times. It helps to list several alternatives.

- **Asking to get into your room early (before 3 or 4 p.m.).** Unless you say otherwise, the front desk will assume that any room currently available overrides your earlier requests.

- **Listing only rooms that are more expensive than the one you paid for.** It doesn't hurt to ask for an upgrade, but make sure you've given the room assigners a fallback option based on what you've bought.

- **Unclear requests.** We've read multipage requests with sentences about room preferences embedded in paragraphs relating the life stories of everyone in the group, and requests with enough picky stuff to rule out every room in the hotel. Make sure your requests are *succinct* and *realistic.*

HOW TO GET DISCOUNTS ON LODGING

THERE ARE SO MANY GUEST ROOMS in and around Disney World that competition is brisk, and everyone, including Disney, cuts deals to fill them. Disney, however, has a unique way of managing its room inventory. To uphold the brand integrity of its hotels, Disney prefers to use enticements rather than discounts. For example, in the past Disney has included a Free Dining benefit if you reserved a certain number of nights at rack rate and has offered special deals only by email to returning guests. Consequently, many of the "normal" strategies for getting discounted rates at most hotels don't work well for Disney hotels.

One of TouringPlans' major ongoing research projects is to identify sellers with the steepest discounts on Disney hotel rooms. Those discounts are almost certainly found through sites that offer last-minute, one- to four-night DVC deals—where *last-minute* typically means "within 90 days." If you're willing to stay at any Disney hotel as long as it's a great deal, see "Rent Disney Vacation Club Points" on page 83 for details.

Note: Discounts may be limited to a certain number of rooms or certain dates. Rooms at deep discounts tend to get snatched up quickly, so don't take too long to decide what you want to do.

1. HUNT FOR SEASONAL SAVINGS Save 15%–35% per night or more on a Disney hotel room by visiting during the slower times of year. However, Disney has so many seasons in its calendar that it's hard to keep up; plus, the dates for each "season" vary among resorts. Disney also changes the price of its hotel rooms with the day of the week, charging more for the same room on Friday and Saturday nights. The rate hikes can range from $13 to over $100 per room, per night. It may require some legwork and being flexible on your travel dates, but there are usually deals to be found.

2. ALWAYS RESEARCH SPECIALS Even after booking, keep an eye out for discounts that could be applied to your reservation. A family from Massachusetts benefitted from their continued research:

I booked our trip online with Disney using a special-offer discount we had received in the mail. Two months before our trip, and after I had already paid in full, Disney ran a special that was even better than the one I had booked. I gave them a call, and they politely, quickly, and efficiently credited the difference.

Specials can include discounts on vacation packages in addition to discounts on rooms. Discounts on park admission or dining packages can be substantial, depending on the number of people in your traveling party or where you're staying.

3. READ THE BANNERS ON DISNEY'S WEBSITE As we went to press, Disney's website listed all the discounts running for the general public. The trick is knowing where to look. In Disney's case, visit disney world.disney.go.com/resorts. The link to the discounts page is found in the banner above all of your search information—where you'll be tempted to just scroll past to get to where you want.

4. INVESTIGATE INTERNET SELLERS Expedia (expedia.com), **Hotwire** (hotwire.com), **Priceline** (priceline.com) and its **Express Deals** section (theugseries.com/priceline-express), and **Travelocity** (travelocity.com) offer discounted rooms at Disney hotels, but usually at a price close to the rate you can get from the Walt Disney Travel Company or Walt Disney World Central Reservations. Most breaks are in the 7%–25% range. *Always check these websites' prices against Disney's.*

5. RENT DISNEY VACATION CLUB POINTS The **Disney Vacation Club** (**DVC**) is Disney's time-share program. There are 13 DVC resorts: **Animal Kingdom Villas, Bay Lake Tower at the Contemporary Resort, Beach Club Villas, BoardWalk Villas, Boulder Ridge Villas, The Cabins at Fort Wilderness, Copper Creek Villas & Cabins, Grand Floridian Villas, Old Key West Resort, Polynesian Villas & Bungalows, Riviera Resort, Saratoga Springs Resort & Spa,** and **Treehouse Villas at Saratoga Springs**. Construction on a 14th DVC resort, a tower for the **Polynesian Village,** should be completed by the end of 2024.

DVC members buy a number of annual "points" that they use to pay for their Disney accommodations. Sometimes members opt to "rent" (sell) their points instead of using them. Though Disney is not involved in the transaction, it allows this practice. The typical rental rate is $15–$19 per point, depending on the resort and time of year, when you deal with members directly; third-party brokers charge $18–$21 per point for hosting the buying-and-selling market and offering credit card payments.

Last-minute deals can bring the price down to the $8–$12 range. For example, in late 2023 my family booked a last-minute offer for a standard-view, two-bedroom Animal Kingdom Villa for around $300 per night, all-in. Disney's rack rate for the room was $1,151, so the DVC points represented almost a 75% discount. At other times, we've stayed in studios at Animal Kingdom Lodge for $90 per night (in September) and at the Polynesian for $170 per night (in January).

Staying in a standard-view studio for six nights during summer 2024 in Animal Kingdom Lodge & Villas currently costs $3,391 if you're paying with cash. The same room costs a DVC member 57 points. If you rented those points at $21 per point, that studio would cost you $1,197—a savings of more than $2,000. Put another way: That $1,197 bill would be cheaper than a room at any on-site resort (other than the All-Stars) for the same night.

Likewise, you can gain a lot more space for the same budget by renting points. If you're a family of six people or more, a two-bedroom villa in Animal Kingdom Lodge sleeps eight. While it costs around $620 per night (at $21 per point), a family suite at Art of Animation costs $630 (without discounts). For $10 *less* per night, you get more than double the space—1,170 square feet in Animal Kingdom versus 565 at Art of Animation—and better amenities.

LAST-MINUTE DVC DEALS The website **DVCReservations.com** emails a newsletter roughly every week with steeply discounted DVC rooms available within the next 90 days. These discounts are, by a wide margin, the best generally available deals you can find on Disney hotel rooms: typically 35%–60% off Disney's rates. We've seen instances where the least expensive room on-property was a 376-square-foot DVC rental villa at Old Key West or Saratoga Springs, not a 260-square-foot Value resort room such as Pop Century or the All-Stars.

RENTING POINTS FROM AN OWNER VS. A THIRD PARTY As mentioned, you have two options when renting points: Go through a third-party broker or deal directly with a DVC member. For a fixed rate of around $18–$21 per point, **David's Vacation Club Rentals** (dvc request.com) will match your request for a specific resort and dates to its available supply. David's per-point rate is higher than if you did the legwork yourself, but they take requests months in advance, and they notify you as soon as something becomes available; plus, they take credit cards.

In addition to David's, some readers, like this one from Missouri, have had good results with the **DVC Rental Store** (dvcrentalstore.com):

> *We rented DVC points for this trip through the DVC Rental Store, and we had a wonderful experience. Unlike David's, they don't make you pay the entire cost upon booking. For our stay at Boulder Ridge Villas, we paid just over half what we were planning to pay for the Wilderness Lodge.*

When you deal directly with the DVC member, you pay the member directly, such as by certified check (few members take credit cards). The member makes a reservation in your name and pays Disney the requisite number of points. Arrangements vary, but again, the going rate is around $15–$19 per point. Trust is required from both parties. Usually, your reservation is documented by a confirmation sent from Disney to the owner and then passed along to you. Though the deal you cut is strictly up to you and the owner, you should always insist on receiving the confirmation number before making more than a one-night deposit.

*un*official **TIP**
To enhance your chances of receiving a PIN-code offer, you need to get your name and street or email address into the Disney system.

We suggest checking one of the online Disney discussion boards (such as Disboards.com) if you're not picky about where you stay and when you go and you're willing to put in the effort to ask around. If you're trying to book a particular resort, especially during a busy time of year, it's usually easier to just use an established third-party site.

6. CRACK THE (PIN) CODE Disney maintains a list of recent visitors as well as those who have inquired about a Disney World vacation. During slow times of the year, Disney will send these folks personalized discounts by direct mail and email. Each offer is uniquely identified by a long string of letters and numbers called a PIN code. This code is required to get the discount—thus, it can't be shared—and Disney will verify that the street or email address that the code was sent to is yours.

To get your name into the Disney system for a PIN code, call ☎ 407-W-DISNEY (934-7639) and request written info. If you've been to Disney World before, your name and address will, of course, already be on record, but you won't be as likely to receive a PIN-code offer as you would by calling and requesting that information be mailed to you.

Or go to disneyworld.disney.go.com and sign up to automatically be sent offers and news at your email address. You might also consider getting a **Disney Rewards Visa card,** which entitles you to exclusive discounts (visit disneyrewards.com for details). One version of the card is free, and the other has a $49 annual fee.

7. DISNEY-SPECIALIST TRAVEL AGENTS Disney vacations are so popular that entire travel agencies specialize in just Disney theme park trips and cruises. Even large, general-travel agencies such as AAA often have dedicated agents with specialized, up-to-date knowledge of what's going on at the parks.

Three obvious situations where it makes sense to engage a travel agent are as follows:

1. This is one of your first trips to Walt Disney World and you'd like to talk to someone objective in person.
2. You're looking to save time in evaluating several different scenarios, such as which of two discounts saves the most money.
3. You want someone else to keep checking for a better deal than what you already have.

We can't emphasize enough how much time (and money) a travel agent will save you in those last two scenarios. If you're trying to compare, say, the cost difference between a Value and a Moderate resort with a particular discount that may not be available at all resorts on all dates, you could easily spend an hour working through different combinations to find the best deal. We think most people give up far before finishing, potentially wasting a lot of money. Good travel agents will do this for you at no charge (because they'll earn a commission from Disney when you book through them).

8. ORGANIZATIONS AND AUTO CLUBS Disney has developed time-limited programs with some auto clubs and organizations. AAA, for example, can often offer discounts on hotels and packages comparable to those Disney offers its Annual Pass holders. Such deals come and go, but the market suggests there will be more. If you're a member of AARP, AAA, or any travel or auto club, ask whether the group has a program before shopping elsewhere.

9. ROOM UPGRADES Sometimes a room upgrade is as good as a discount. If you're visiting Disney World during a slower time, book the least expensive room your discounts will allow. When checking in, ask politely about being upgraded to a room with a more expensive view. A fair percentage of the time, you'll get one at no additional charge or at a deep discount. Understand, however, that a room upgrade should be considered a favor. Hotels are under no obligation to upgrade you, so if your request is not met, accept the decision graciously.

10. MILITARY DISCOUNTS Shades of Green Armed Forces Recreation Center, near the Grand Floridian Resort & Spa, offers luxury accommodations at rates based on a service member's rank, as well as attraction tickets to the theme parks (see profile on page 124). For rates and other information, call ☎ 888-593-2242 or visit shades ofgreen.org.

11. YEAR-ROUND DISCOUNTS AT MARRIOTT RESORTS Members of the military, government workers, teachers, nurses, and AAA members can save on rooms at the Dolphin, Swan, and Swan Reserve (when space is available, of course). Plus, Marriott Bonvoy members can use points to book stays. Call ☎ 888-828-8850 or visit swandolphin .com and click on "Special Offers."

CHOOSING A WALT DISNEY WORLD HOTEL

IF YOU WANT TO STAY IN THE WORLD but don't know which hotel to choose, the most important factors to consider are as follows:

1. **Room quality** (see below)
2. **Transportation** (see page 88)
3. **Cost** (see page 89)
4. **Pools and amenities** (see page 90)
5. **Location/distance from parks** (see page 90)
6. **Theme** (see page 93)
7. **Dining options** (see page 94)
8. **The size of your room vs. the size of your group** (see page 96)

1. ROOM QUALITY Many Disney hotel rooms are among the best designed anywhere. Plus, they're maintained much better than the average hotel room in Orlando. All rooms have minifridges and free, reliable Wi-Fi, along with coffee makers in the DVC units.

As Disney refurbishes its hotel rooms, it also reexamines how modern families use these spaces. As a simple example, new rooms have 5–10 built-in USB charging ports to accommodate everyone's cell phones and tablets, and beds have plenty of space for storing large empty suitcases underneath.

Not surprisingly, many readers rate Disney's Deluxe and DVC rooms highest for quality, but some Value and Moderate rooms rate even higher. The text that follows provides context for these room-quality ratings. In addition, the table on the opposite page shows how the Walt Disney World hotels stack up as far as room quality.

VALUE RESORTS Room quality in this category is highest at the **All-Star Resorts,** where the entire room configuration has changed in the last few years. Carpet has been replaced with vinyl plank flooring. Queen beds are standard, and king beds are available. In rooms with two queen beds, one bed can fold into the wall when not in use, exposing a desk; this frees up around 36 square feet of space in these 260-square-foot rooms—a 14% increase. In addition, bathrooms are brighter and more open, and more storage is available in the living areas.

ROOM-QUALITY RATINGS FOR THE DISNEY RESORTS	
SWAN RESERVE | 94	PORT ORLEANS FRENCH QUARTER | 88
RIVIERA | 94	
BOULDER RIDGE VILLAS (studio) | 92	BOARDWALK VILLAS (studio) | 88
SHADES OF GREEN | 92	ANIMAL KINGDOM LODGE (studio) | 87
ANIMAL KINGDOM VILLAS–KIDANI VILLAGE (studio) | 91	ALL-STAR MUSIC | 86
GRAND FLORIDIAN VILLAS (studio) | 91	POLYNESIAN VILLAGE RESORT | 86
SARATOGA SPRINGS RESORT (studio) | 91	ANIMAL KINGDOM VILLAS–JAMBO HOUSE (studio) | 86
BAY LAKE TOWER (studio) | 91	BEACH CLUB VILLAS (studio) | 86
OLD KEY WEST (studio) | 90	POLYNESIAN VILLAS (studio) | 86
CABINS AT FORT WILDERNESS | 90	SWAN | 86
COPPER CREEK VILLAS (studio) | 89	BEACH CLUB RESORT | 86
CONTEMPORARY | 89	PORT ORLEANS RIVERSIDE | 84
YACHT CLUB | 88	ALL-STAR SPORTS | 84
CORONADO SPRINGS | 88	CARIBBEAN BEACH | 84
BOARDWALK INN | 88	ART OF ANIMATION | 83
TREEHOUSE VILLAS | 88	DOLPHIN | 82
WILDERNESS LODGE | 88	ALL-STAR MOVIES | 82
GRAND FLORIDIAN RESORT | 88	POP CENTURY | 80

Art of Animation's room quality is in the middle of the pack for the Disney Value resorts. Rooms are clean and functional, but because the resort opened in 2012, they're not old enough to need the updates that Pop and the All-Stars have gotten and thus feel dated in comparison. **Pop Century** falls to the bottom of the list this year since its updates happened a while ago, and people consistently rate the family suites at Art of Animation higher than the normal rooms at Pop Century.

MODERATE RESORTS Readers rate the rooms at **Coronado Springs** the highest of any Moderate resort. These rooms have been modernized with vinyl plank flooring, plenty of desk space, excellent lighting, and doors separating the bathroom area from the main living space.

Readers rate the rooms at **Port Orleans French Quarter** the second-highest. Rooms at French Quarter have flooring similar to that at Coronado Springs but don't have the newest storage or bathroom makeovers. We think French Quarter's rooms are rated highly because this resort is the smallest and most intimate of the Moderates, and that atmosphere carries over to the room ratings.

Port Orleans Riverside and **Caribbean Beach** have the lowest-rated Moderate rooms. All rooms in Riverside have vinyl flooring. One section, Alligator Bayou, has an updated bathroom design and a new drop-down twin bed for a fifth child. However, the furniture design in these rooms is rustic (to fit the theming) and lacks the modern conveniences found in the updated Value resorts.

Caribbean Beach recently got a welcome upgrade, including a conversion of its *Pirates of the Caribbean*–themed rooms in the Trinidad section to a *Little Mermaid* theme. These updates use lighter, brighter color schemes and bring foldout and drop-down bed options to rooms that previously had two fixed beds. Like the renovations at the

Value resorts, this update modernized and increased the functionality of the rooms at Caribbean Beach. Our one word of caution is that, because of its size, many Caribbean Beach reno efforts get stopped before all rooms are finished. We believe this happened again with the most recent renovations, so if you're booking here, ask specifically for a refurbished room.

Disney's most recent addition to the Moderate category is **Gran Destino Tower** at Coronado Springs, which offers some of the best-designed bathrooms in this category. Even better, Gran Destino's Club Level rooms—with access to the fabulous private **Chronos Club** lounge—are the cheapest Club Level rooms on-property. If you're looking to try one of these rooms, Gran Destino is a great place to start.

DELUXE RESORTS Rooms at the **Swan Reserve** are rated the highest in this category. These are incredibly new and well appointed. I don't expect they'll stay at the very top long-term, but they will still age well and be a contender in the above-average category for a while.

Other above-average Deluxe rooms are found at **Shades of Green, Contemporary, Yacht Club, Wilderness Lodge, Grand Floridian,** and **BoardWalk Inn.** Those at **Animal Kingdom Lodge–Jambo House** are rated average. The lowest-rated rooms are found at the Dolphin.

Animal Kingdom Lodge & Villas, BoardWalk Inn, and **Wilderness Lodge,** along with the **Contemporary, Grand Floridian, Polynesian Village,** and **Yacht & Beach Club Resorts** and **Gran Destino Tower** at Coronado Springs, boast **Club Level** (concierge) floors. Benefits include personalized trip planning and a lounge stocked with small bites to graze on. This New Jersey reader, however, found the snacks on the skimpy side:

> *We found the Club Level food offerings limited and carefully metered out. Tiny plates were replenished slowly. Given that Club Level is a significant extra expense, we didn't appreciate being told how much we could eat and when.*

DVC RESORTS Disney's highest-rated rooms are found at its time-share resorts. Topping the list are **Riviera Resort** and **Boulder Ridge Villas.** Opened in late 2019, the Riviera is Disney's newest DVC resort. With above-average on-site dining and Skyliner access to EPCOT and Hollywood Studios, it's a positive (and pricey) addition to Disney's resort lineup. The large, stylish rooms are, in our opinion, the best of any Disney-owned hotel. The Boulder Ridge Villas just received a new refurbishment that makes them among some of the most usable and beautiful rooms at the DVC resorts.

Almost all other DVC resorts have rooms rated above average: **Animal Kingdom Lodge–Kidani Village, Grand Floridian Villas, Saratoga Springs, Bay Lake Tower, Old Key West, Copper Creek Villas & Cabins at Wilderness Lodge,** and **BoardWalk Villas.** The BoardWalk Villas were recently refurbished but don't share the same level of functionality or theming as other newly upgraded rooms.

2. TRANSPORTATION If you'll be driving, your Disney hotel's transportation isn't especially important unless you plan to spend most of your time in the Magic Kingdom (because almost any Disney transportation beats parking at the Transportation and Ticket Center). If you haven't decided whether you want a car for your Disney vacation, see "How to Travel Around the World" (see page 336).

The hotels our readers rate highest for Disney transportation are **Polynesian Village, Grand Floridian, Riviera,** and **Pop Century.** The Polynesian and Grand Floridian connect to the Magic Kingdom and EPCOT by monorail. These resorts use buses to get to other destinations on-property. The Riviera and Pop Century connect to Caribbean Beach and Art of Animation Resorts, Disney's Hollywood Studios, and EPCOT via the Skyliner and use buses to get to other on-property locations.

> *unofficial* **TIP**
>
> If you plan to use Disney transportation to visit all four theme parks and one or both water parks, book a centrally located resort that has good transportation connections, such as the EPCOT resorts (page 126) or the **Polynesian Village, Caribbean Beach, Art of Animation, Pop Century,** or **Port Orleans Resorts.**

The resorts our readers rated as below average for transportation are the **Swan** and **Dolphin; Campsites at Fort Wilderness;** and **Shades of Green.** The bus service at Fort Wilderness is next-level difficult, with not just multiple stops, like at other resorts, but also totally separate internal bus loops, which increases the time it takes to get where you're going. The non-Disney bus service at the Swan and Dolphin runs less often than Disney's own buses and drops guests off at the Transportation and Ticket Center, not the Magic Kingdom park entrance. And Shades of Green recently lost its walking path to the Magic Kingdom, which makes a huge difference.

3. COST Hotel rooms start as low as $133 a night at the All-Stars and top out above $2,100 for many DVC villas. The table on page 91 shows the cost per night for various Disney hotel rooms.

Disney's **Value resorts** are the least expensive on-site hotels. Because they're popular, they have four separate, unofficial price categories:

- The **All-Star Resorts** are Disney's oldest and least expensive Value resorts.

- **Pop Century Resort** sits in the middle of the Value price range—about 20% per night more than the All-Stars. It's the most popular Disney World resort among *Unofficial Guide* readers.

- **Art of Animation Resort** has the largest rooms, best food court, and best pools in this category. Standard rooms cost about $100 per night more than those at the All-Stars.

- Two-room **Family Suites** are available at the All-Star Music and Art of Animation Resorts, from around $340 to $840 per night with tax.

While the All-Stars and Pop Century are older and less expensive than AOA, they've had extensive room renovations that make them among the most attractive and functional on-property. In terms of room quality, they're better and cheaper than AOA's standard rooms.

The next most expensive tier includes Disney's **Moderate resorts.** Like the Values, these have different price points:

- **Coronado Springs Resort** has the cheapest rooms in the Moderate category. It's large, with multiple bus stops, and has low-rated on-site dining.

- **Port Orleans Riverside** and **Port Orleans French Quarter** are only slightly more expensive. They are the favorite of many repeat visitors.

- **Caribbean Beach Resort** got a bump in popularity (and prices) when it got access to two Skyliner stations.

- **Gran Destino Tower** is the newest entry in the Moderate category. The 15-story tower is located on the grounds of Coronado Springs Resort. Its Club Level rooms are the least expensive of their type in Walt Disney World.

Rates at Disney's **Deluxe resorts** vary depending on room size and the hotel's location relative to the theme parks:

- The **Walt Disney World Swan, Walt Disney World Dolphin,** and **Swan Reserve** are usually the least expensive Deluxe hotel rooms on-property. They're not owned by Disney, and they cater to convention traffic as much as families, giving them a different feel from the other hotels. These hotels are within walking distance of EPCOT and Disney's Hollywood Studios.

- The smallest and least expensive Disney-owned Deluxe hotel rooms are found at **Wilderness Lodge** and **Animal Kingdom Lodge**. Both hotels have excellent theming; Animal Kingdom Lodge has excellent dining as well.

- The next tier of Deluxe prices applies to the EPCOT resorts: the **Yacht Club, Beach Club,** and **BoardWalk Inn**. These are arranged around Crescent Lake, with a short walk to EPCOT and a slightly longer walk (or Skyliner ride) to Disney's Hollywood Studios.

- Even more expensive are the **Polynesian Village** and **Contemporary Resorts**. Both opened in 1971 and are a short walk or monorail ride from the Magic Kingdom and EPCOT. The Polynesian Village has excellent theming. Along with its easy access to two theme parks, its location makes it easy to visit any hotel restaurant along the Magic Kingdom monorail loop.

- Finally, Disney's most expensive standard hotel rooms are found at the **Grand Floridian Resort & Spa**, Disney World's flagship hotel.

4. POOLS AND AMENITIES Disney's **Yacht & Beach Club Resorts** share the highest-rated pool in Walt Disney World. Called **Stormalong Bay,** it includes a lazy river with a sand bottom and an elaborate waterslide that begins from a pirate ship beached on Crescent Lake. Stormalong Bay is so popular that guests must show proof they're staying at the resort before being admitted to the pool area. *Note:* Stormalong Bay will be closed for refurbishment January–June 2025. Since this is such an important part of the resort's draw, you may want to consider booking elsewhere.

The **Riviera**'s pools also get top marks from readers. With two pools and a kids' water-play area, there's plenty of space for guests to relax. In the middle of the pools is **Bar Riva,** with shade and beverages for adults.

The pools at **Art of Animation** are also rated above average. These are well themed and have convenient bar and food options.

Readers rate the pools as below average at **Contemporary, All-Stars, Pop Century,** and **Fort Wilderness.** Our opinion is that all of these have relatively generic pools that are often crowded.

See the table on page 92 for specific resort pool ratings and the table on page 93 for a summary of the amenities at each resort.

5. LOCATION AND DISTANCE FROM THE THEME PARKS Once you've determined your budget, think about what you want to do at Walt Disney World. Will you go to all four theme parks or concentrate on one or two?

The resorts closest to the Magic Kingdom include the **Grand Floridian** and its **Villas;** the **Contemporary** and **Bay Lake Tower;** and the **Polynesian Village, Villas & Bungalows.** All are served by the monorail and walking paths, so staying at one of these resorts also gets you access to more dining options, many of which are among Disney World's best.

THE DISNEY RESORTS 91

2024 COST PER NIGHT OF DISNEY HOTEL ROOMS *(rack rates)*	
Rates are for standard rooms except as noted.	
ALL-STAR RESORTS	$133–$305
ALL-STAR MUSIC RESORT FAMILY SUITES	$336–$696
ANIMAL KINGDOM LODGE	$487–$1,195
ANIMAL KINGDOM VILLAS *(studio, Jambo House/Kidani Village)*	$458–$1,174
ART OF ANIMATION FAMILY SUITES	$478–$963
ART OF ANIMATION RESORT	$209–$413
BAY LAKE TOWER AT CONTEMPORARY RESORT *(studio)*	$672–$1,723
BEACH CLUB RESORT	$569–$1,252
BEACH CLUB VILLAS *(studio)*	$561–$1,036
BOARDWALK INN	$641–$1,199
BOARDWALK VILLAS *(studio)*	$620–$1,199
BOULDER RIDGE VILLAS *(studio)*	$475–$966
CARIBBEAN BEACH RESORT	$268–$582
CONTEMPORARY RESORT *(Garden Wing)*	$572–$1,190
COPPER CREEK VILLAS & CASCADE CABINS *(studio)*	$475–$966
CORONADO SPRINGS RESORT	$260–$539
DOLPHIN *(Sheraton)*	$202–$439
FORT WILDERNESS RESORT & CAMPGROUND *(cabins)*	$466–$920
GRAN DESTINO TOWER	$316–$664
GRAND FLORIDIAN RESORT & SPA	$824–$1,721
GRAND FLORIDIAN VILLAS *(studio)*	$816–$1,721
OLD KEY WEST RESORT *(studio)*	$474–$809
POLYNESIAN VILLAGE RESORT	$691–$1,645
POLYNESIAN VILLAS & BUNGALOWS *(studio)*	$691–$1,524
POP CENTURY RESORT	$183–$429
PORT ORLEANS RESORT FRENCH QUARTER AND RIVERSIDE	$289–$585
RIVIERA RESORT *(studio)*	$470–$1,326
SARATOGA SPRINGS RESORT & SPA *(studio)*	$448–$921
SHADES OF GREEN	$174–$239
SWAN *(Westin)*	$246–$507
SWAN RESERVE *(Autograph Collection)*	$364–$467
TREEHOUSE VILLAS	$1,152–$2,231
WILDERNESS LODGE	$524–$1,216
YACHT CLUB RESORT	$569–$1,180

Next closest to the Magic Kingdom, **Wilderness Lodge & Boulder Ridge/Copper Creek Villas,** along with **Fort Wilderness Resort & Campground,** are linked to the Magic Kingdom (and Contemporary) by boat and to everywhere else in Disney World by rather convoluted bus service.

The most centrally located hotels in Walt Disney World are the EPCOT resorts—**BoardWalk Inn, BoardWalk Villas, Yacht & Beach Club**

AUTHORS' RATINGS FOR THE DISNEY RESORT POOLS
1. YACHT & BEACH CLUB RESORTS & BEACH CLUB VILLAS* (*shared complex*) ★★★★★
2. GRAND FLORIDIAN RESORT & SPA, VILLAS ★★★★½
3. ANIMAL KINGDOM VILLAS (*Kidani Village*) ★★★★½
4. SARATOGA SPRINGS RESORT & SPA/TREEHOUSE VILLAS ★★★★½
5. WILDERNESS LODGE & BOULDER RIDGE/COPPER CREEK VILLAS ★★★★½
6. ANIMAL KINGDOM LODGE & VILLAS (*Jambo House*) ★★★★
7. PORT ORLEANS RESORT ★★★★
8. CORONADO SPRINGS RESORT/GRAN DESTINO TOWER ★★★★
9. DOLPHIN ★★★★
10. SWAN ★★★★
11. POLYNESIAN VILLAGE, VILLAS & BUNGALOWS ★★★★
12. BAY LAKE TOWER ★★★★
13. CARIBBEAN BEACH RESORT ★★★★
14. RIVIERA RESORT ★★★★
15. BOARDWALK INN & VILLAS ★★★½
16. CONTEMPORARY RESORT ★★★½
17. SWAN RESERVE ★★★½
18. ALL-STAR RESORTS ★★★
19. ART OF ANIMATION RESORT ★★★
20. OLD KEY WEST RESORT ★★★
21. FORT WILDERNESS RESORT & CAMPGROUND ★★★
22. POP CENTURY RESORT ★★★
23. SHADES OF GREEN ★★★

* *Closed January–June 2025*

unofficial **TIP**
If you stay at an EPCOT resort, you have more than 30 restaurants within a 5- to 12-minute walk.

Resorts, Beach Club Villas, Swan, Dolphin, and **Swan Reserve.** The EPCOT resorts are within easy walking distance of Disney's Hollywood Studios and EPCOT's International Gateway. Besides giving you easy theme park access, staying at one of these hotels gets you access to a wide variety of restaurants. EPCOT hotels are best for guests planning to spend most of their time in EPCOT or Hollywood Studios.

Caribbean Beach, Riviera, Pop Century, and **Art of Animation** are just south and east of EPCOT and Hollywood Studios. All are connected to EPCOT and DHS by the Skyliner and to everything else by bus.

The Disney resorts along Bonnet Creek, which offer quick access to Disney Springs and its top restaurants, include **Old Key West, Saratoga Springs** and its **Treehouse Villas,** and the two **Port Orleans Resorts.** On an adjacent 70-acre parcel of non-Disney land called **Bonnet Creek Resort** are the **Waldorf Astoria Orlando;** the **Signia by Hilton Orlando Bonnet Creek;** and two Wyndham properties, **Club Wyndham Bonnet Creek** and its more luxurious sibling, the **Wyndham Grand Orlando Resort Bonnet Creek.**

The Bonnet Creek Resort area walks the line between on- and off-property: The hotels are as close to the theme parks as Disney's own,

DISNEY RESORT AMENITIES					
RESORT	SUITES	CONCIERGE FLOOR	NUMBER OF ROOMS	ROOM SERVICE (full)	FITNESS CENTER
ALL-STAR RESORTS	•	—	5,406	—	—
ANIMAL KINGDOM LODGE	•	•	972	•	•
ANIMAL KINGDOM VILLAS	•	•*	458	•	•
ART OF ANIMATION RESORT	•	—	1,984	—	—
BAY LAKE TOWER	•	—	295	•	•
BEACH CLUB VILLAS	•	—	282	•	•
BOARDWALK INN	•	•	378	•	•
BOARDWALK VILLAS	•	—	532	•	•
CARIBBEAN BEACH RESORT	—	—	1,536	—	—
CONTEMPORARY RESORT	•	•	655	•	•
CORONADO SPRINGS RESORT	•	•	1,839	•	•
DOLPHIN	•	—	1,509	•	•
FORT WILDERNESS CABINS	—	—	409	—	—
GRAN DESTINO TOWER	•	•	545	•	—
GRAN FLORIDIAN RESORT & SPA, VILLAS	•	•	1,016	•	•
OLD KEY WEST RESORT	•	—	761	—	•
POLYNESIAN VILLAGE, VILLAS & BUNGALOWS	•	•	866	•	—
POP CENTURY RESORT	—	—	2,880	—	—
PORT ORLEANS RESORT	—	—	3,056	—	—
RIVIERA RESORT	—	—	300	•	•
SARATOGA SPRINGS RESORT & SPA	•	—	1,260	—	•
SHADES OF GREEN	•	—	586	•	•
SWAN	•	—	758	•	•
SWAN RESERVE	•	—	349	•	•
TREEHOUSE VILLAS	•	—	60	—	•
WILDERNESS LODGE, BOULDER RIDGE/COPPER CREEK VILLAS	•	•	889	•	•
YACHT & BEACH CLUB RESORTS	•	•	1,211	•	•

* Jambo House only

offer transportation to the parks and Disney Springs, and are every bit as good as Disney's best—often at around half the price. Further muddying the waters, guests of the Signia and Waldorf Astoria get Early Theme Park Entry privileges (as do guests of the **Four Seasons Resort Orlando,** adjacent to Fort Wilderness Resort).

6. THEME With a few exceptions, each Disney resort is designed to evoke a special place or period of history. Some resorts carry off their theming better than others, and some themes are more exciting. See the table on page 95 for a summary of each resort's theme.

Readers rate the resorts in the next four paragraphs tops for theming:

Animal Kingdom Lodge replicates grand safari lodges of Kenya and Tanzania and overlooks its own African-style game preserve. By far the most exotic Disney resort, the lodge and its villas are great for couples on romantic getaways and for families with children.

Wilderness Lodge is visually extraordinary, reminiscent of a grand early-20th-century national park lodge. The lobby opens eight stories to a timbered ceiling supported by giant columns of bundled logs. The lodge and its **Boulder Ridge Villas** and **Copper Creek Villas & Cabins** are a great choice for couples and seniors and are fun for children.

Likewise dramatic, the **Polynesian Village Resort** and **Polynesian Villas & Bungalows** convey the feeling of the Pacific Islands. They're great for couples and families. Many waterfront rooms on upper floors offer a perfect view of Cinderella Castle and the Magic Kingdom fireworks across Seven Seas Lagoon.

Port Orleans Resort–French Quarter does a good (albeit sanitized) job of capturing the architectural essence of its New Orleans inspiration. **Port Orleans Resort–Riverside** likewise succeeds with its early-19th-century Louisiana bayou setting.

Unofficial Guide readers rate the following resorts as below average for theming: the **All-Star Resorts; Pop Century; Saratoga Springs** and **Treehouse Villas;** the **Contemporary Resort** and **Bay Lake Tower;** and the **Swan, Swan Reserve,** and **Dolphin.**

The **All-Star Resorts** have 15 themed areas: 5 celebrate sports (surfing, basketball, tennis, football, and baseball), 5 relate to films, and 5 have musical motifs. The resort's design, with entrances shaped like giant Dalmatians, Coke cups, footballs, and the like, is somewhat adolescent, sacrificing grace and beauty for energy and novelty.

Pop Century Resort is pretty much a clone of the All-Star Resorts, only here the giant icons symbolize decades of the 20th century (Big Wheels, 45-rpm records, and such).

Saratoga Springs Resort & Spa, supposedly representative of an upstate New York country retreat, looks like what you'd get if you crossed the Beach Club with Wilderness Lodge. When it comes to the resorts inspired by Northeastern hotels (including the **Yacht and Beach Clubs**), thematic distinctions are subtle and thus difficult to differentiate.

The **Contemporary Resort** and its **Bay Lake Tower** and the **Swan, Swan Reserve,** and **Dolphin** are essentially themeless though architecturally interesting. The original Contemporary is a 15-story A-frame building with monorails running through the middle. An update in 2021 added characters from Pixar's *The Incredibles.* The Swan and Dolphin are massive yet whimsical; designed by Michael Graves, they're excellent examples of early-1990s "entertainment architecture," but they lack any references to Disney theme parks, films, or characters.

7. DINING OPTIONS If high-quality dining is a top priority for your Walt Disney World trip, **Animal Kingdom Lodge** and the **Grand Floridian** are excellent choices. Three of Walt Disney World's top sit-down restaurants are found in Animal Kingdom Lodge: **Jiko—The Cooking Place, Sanaa,** and **Boma—Flavors of Africa.** The Grand Floridian holds Walt Disney World's very best restaurant, **Victoria & Albert's,** and five of its other restaurants all place near the top of our reader surveys.

The best resorts for dining quality *and* selection are the EPCOT resorts: **BoardWalk Inn & Villas, Dolphin, Swan, Yacht and Beach Club Resorts,** and **Beach Club Villas.** Each has decent sit-down restaurants, and each is within easy walking distance of the others as well as the dining options available in World Showcase. However, on-site

THEMES AT THE DISNEY RESORTS	
ALL-STAR RESORTS Movies, music, and sports	
ANIMAL KINGDOM LODGE, VILLAS African game preserve	
ART OF ANIMATION RESORT Disney's animated films	
BAY LAKE TOWER Upscale, ultramodern urban hotel	
BEACH CLUB RESORT, VILLAS New England beach club of the 1870s	
BOARDWALK INN East Coast boardwalk hotel of the early 1900s	
BOARDWALK VILLAS East Coast beach cottage of the early 1900s	
CARIBBEAN BEACH RESORT Caribbean islands	
CONTEMPORARY RESORT The future as perceived by past and present generations	
CORONADO SPRINGS RESORT Northern Mexico and the American Southwest	
DOLPHIN "Modern" (early 1990s) Florida resort	
GRAN DESTINO TOWER Spanish/Moorish influences	
GRAND FLORIDIAN RESORT & SPA, VILLAS Turn-of-the-20th-century luxury hotel	
OLD KEY WEST RESORT Relaxed Florida Keys vibe	
POLYNESIAN VILLAGE RESORT, VILLAS & BUNGALOWS Hawaii–South Seas	
POP CENTURY RESORT Popular-culture icons from various decades of the 20th century	
PORT ORLEANS FRENCH QUARTER Turn-of-the-19th-century New Orleans	
PORT ORLEANS RIVERSIDE Old Louisiana bayou-side retreat	
RIVIERA RESORT Mediterranean beach resort in the South of France	
SARATOGA SPRINGS RESORT & SPA 1880s Victorian lake	
SWAN What modern looked like 30 years ago	
SWAN RESERVE Brand-new resort with a true 21st-century design aesthetic	
TREEHOUSE VILLAS Disney-rustic vacation homes with modern amenities	
WILDERNESS LODGE, VILLAS Grand national park lodge of the early 20th century	
YACHT CLUB RESORT New England seashore hotel of the 1880s	

quick-service options are limited, and readers rate these hotels below average for quick-service options. If quick, simple breakfasts and lunches are what you're after, stay elsewhere.

The only other hotels in Disney World with similar access to a concentrated area of good restaurants are in the **Disney Springs Resort Area.** In addition to restaurants in the hotels themselves, **DoubleTree Suites, Drury Plaza Hotel, Hilton Orlando Buena Vista Palace, Hilton Orlando Lake Buena Vista, Holiday Inn Orlando, Renaissance Orlando Resort and Spa,** and **Wyndham Garden Lake Buena Vista** are all within walking distance of restaurants in Disney Springs. As with the EPCOT resorts, though, many readers complain about the difficulty they have finding quick, tasty breakfast and lunch options at these hotels.

Hotels rated as below average for dining include **Fort Wilderness Resort & Campground,** all the **Value resorts, Coronado Springs,** and **Shades of Green.** Because Fort Wilderness caters primarily to guests who are cooking for themselves, on-site dining options are limited, and not just in terms of the menu selections: The restaurants' remote location, near the shore of Bay Lake, makes them a hassle to get to from most parts of the resort—so unless you've brought a car or you're renting a bike or golf cart, count on a *long* walk or bus ride to get something to eat. Coronado Springs probably needs a complete dining rethink—it's never been rated highly for food. Disney's opera-tion of the Value resort restaurants indicates that they want you to eat in the parks.

8. ROOM SIZE How much space you get inside a Disney hotel room almost always depends on how much you pay. The size of a standard (or studio) room at Disney's resorts varies from 260 square feet at the Value resorts to 440 square feet at the Deluxe **Grand Floridian Resort** to 460 square feet for a studio at the **Polynesian Villas** DVC resort. The diagrams on pages 97–101 show the size and layout of typical rooms at each Disney property.

It's no surprise that readers rate larger rooms better than smaller ones. At the top of this list are rooms at **Old Key West,** Disney's first DVC resort, which are larger than most. Also scoring well are the rooms at the **Grand Floridian Villas**—we're not kidding when we say that the showers here are large enough that you might consider sleep-ing in them to get away from a snoring partner. And although they don't score well in most other categories, the rooms at the **Cabins at Fort Wilderness Resort** and Saratoga Springs' **Treehouse Villas** are popular with readers in terms of sheer space.

There are two exceptions to the "more money, more space" mantra: Standard rooms in the main buildings of **Animal Kingdom Lodge** and **Wilderness Lodge** are 344 square feet—the smallest of any Deluxe resort, and closer in size to the rooms at many Moderate resorts than to those at Deluxes. Readers rate these among the lowest for space. The other rooms rated lowest for space are at the Value resorts.

Standard rooms at the **Riviera Resort** include a two-person, 225-square-foot Tower Studio that's so small that the only bed is a queen fold-down. They're almost certainly the worst rooms on Disney property, and we recommend skipping them.

STANDARD ROOMS THAT SLEEP FIVE (plus one child under age 3 in a crib) are found at the following resorts:

- **DELUXE** Beach Club, BoardWalk Inn, Contemporary, Grand Floridian, Polynesian Village, Yacht Club
- **MODERATE** Caribbean Beach, Port Orleans Riverside (Alligator Bayou only)

FAMILY SUITES sleep six people and are found exclusively at **All-Star Music** and **Art of Animation Resorts.** The All-Star versions are basically two Value rooms stuck together; those at Art of Animation, however, were designed from the ground up and are slightly larger (and nicer). Family Suites at both resorts have two bathrooms.

The **Cabins at Fort Wilderness Resort** also sleep six, but they have just one bathroom each.

HOW WE INSPECT HOTELS

WE EVALUATE SEVERAL HUNDRED hotels in the Walt Disney World area to compile the *Unofficial Guide*'s list of lodging choices. If a hotel has been renovated or has refurbished its guest rooms, we rein-spect it, along with any new hotels, for the next edition of the *Guide*. Hotels reporting no improvements are rechecked every two years. We

continued on page 101

DISNEY DELUXE RESORTS*

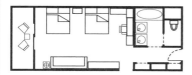

CONTEMPORARY RESORT
394 square feet; accommodates 5 guests
plus 1 child under age 3 in a crib

POLYNESIAN VILLAGE RESORT
415 square feet; accommodates
5 guests plus 1 child under age 3 in a crib

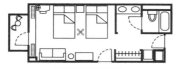

BOARDWALK INN
371 square feet; accommodates 5 guests
plus 1 child under age 3 in a crib

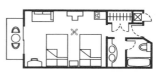

GRAND FLORIDIAN RESORT & SPA
440 square feet; accommodates
5 guests plus 1 child under age 3 in a crib

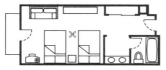

BEACH CLUB RESORT
381 square feet; accommodates 5 guests
plus 1 child under age 3 in a crib

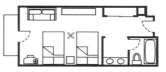

YACHT CLUB RESORT
381 square feet; accommodates
5 guests plus 1 child under age 3 in a crib

WILDERNESS LODGE
344 square feet; accommodates 4 guests
plus 1 child under age 3 in a crib

ANIMAL KINGDOM LODGE
344 square feet; accommodates
4 guests plus 1 child under age 3 in a crib

* Typical room

DVC RESORTS

**ANIMAL KINGDOM VILLAS–
JAMBO HOUSE**
Studio: 316–365 square feet (*gray area*)
1-bedroom: 629–710 sf
2-bedroom: 945–1,075 sf
Grand Villa: 2,349 square feet

**ANIMAL KINGDOM VILLAS–
KIDANI VILLAGE**
Studio: 366 square feet (*gray area*)
1-bedroom: 807 square feet
2-bedroom: 1,173 square feet
Grand Villa: 2,201 square feet

DVC RESORTS *(continued)*

BAY LAKE TOWER
Studio: 339 square feet (*gray area*);
1-bedroom: 803 sf; **2-bedroom:** 1,152 sf
Grand Villa: 2,044 square feet

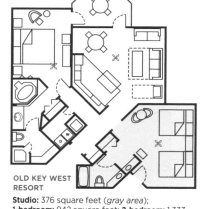

OLD KEY WEST RESORT
Studio: 376 square feet (*gray area*);
1-bedroom: 942 square feet; **2-bedroom:** 1,333
square feet; **Grand Villa:** 2,202 square feet

BEACH CLUB VILLAS
Studio: 356 square feet (*gray area*)
1-bedroom: 726 square feet
2-bedroom: 1,083 square feet

BOARDWALK VILLAS
Studio: 412 square feet (*gray area*);
1-bedroom: 814 square feet; **2-bedroom:** 1,236
square feet; **Grand Villa:** 2,491 square feet

GRAND FLORIDIAN VILLAS
Studio: 374 square feet (*gray area*)
1-bedroom: 844 square feet
2-bedroom lock-off: 1,232 square feet

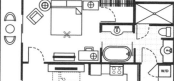

DVC GUEST-OCCUPANCY LIMITS

- **Studios:** 4 at all except: Boulder Ridge
  Villas (5), Grand Floridian (5), Polynesian
  (5), and Riviera (2 for Tower Studios,
  5 for Deluxe Studios)

- **1-bedroom villas:** 4 at Beach Club,
  Saratoga Springs, and Boulder Ridge;
  4 or 5 in Animal Kingdom Lodge
  (Jambo House); 5 everywhere else

- **2-bedroom villas and bungalows:**
  8 or 9 in Animal Kingdom Lodge & Villas
  (Jambo House); 9 in Animal Kingdom Villas
  (Kidani Village), Bay Lake Tower, Riviera,
  BoardWalk, and Old Key West; 9 or 10 at
  Grand Floridian; 8 everywhere else

- **3-bedroom and Grand Villas:**
  9 at Treehouse Villas; 12 everywhere else

  Note: To all these limits you may add
  1 child under age 3 in a crib.

DVC RESORTS *(continued)*

SARATOGA SPRINGS RESORT & SPA
Studio: 355 square feet *(gray area)*
1-bedroom: 714 square feet
2-bedroom: 1,075 square feet
Grand Villa: 2,113 square feet

TREEHOUSE VILLAS
3-bedroom:
1,074 square feet

**POLYNESIAN
BUNGALOWS**
1,650 square feet
(see next page
for villas)

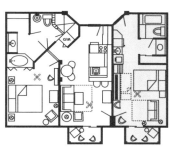

BOULDER RIDGE VILLAS
Studio: 356 square feet *(gray area)*
1-bedroom: 727 square feet
2-bedroom: 1,080 square feet

COPPER CREEK VILLAS & CABINS
Studio (sleeps 4): 345 square feet *(gray area)*
1-bedroom (sleeps 4): 761 square feet
2-bedroom (sleeps 8): 1,105 square feet
Cabin (2 bedrooms; sleeps 8): 1,737 square feet
Grand Villa (3 bedrooms; sleeps 12):
3,204 square feet

DVC RESORTS *(continued)*

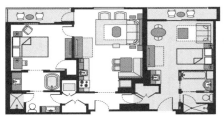

RIVIERA RESORT
Deluxe Studio:
423 square feet *(gray area)*
1-bedroom: 813 square feet
2-bedroom lock-off:
1,246 square feet
3-bedroom:
2,530 square feet

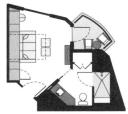

RIVIERA RESORT, TOWER STUDIO
225 square feet; accommodates 2 guests
plus 1 child under age 3 in a crib

POLYNESIAN VILLAS
Studio: 460 square feet

THE CABINS AT FORT WILDERNESS RESORT
504 square feet;
accommodate 6 guests
plus 1 child under age 3 in
a crib

DISNEY MODERATE RESORTS

CORONADO SPRINGS RESORT
Typical room, 314 square feet;
accommodates 4 guests
plus 1 child under age 3 in a crib

CARIBBEAN BEACH RESORT
Typical room, 314 square feet;
accommodates 5 guests
plus 1 child under age 3 in a crib

CORONADO SPRINGS RESORT, GRAN DESTINO TOWER
Typical room, 375 square feet;
accommodates 4 guests plus
1 child under age 3 in a crib

MODERATE RESORTS *(continued)*

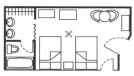

**PORT ORLEANS RESORT–
FRENCH QUARTER**
Typical room, 314 square feet;
accommodates 4 guests
plus 1 child under age 3 in a crib

PORT ORLEANS RESORT–RIVERSIDE
Typical room, 314 square feet;
accommodates 5 guests plus 1 child under
age 3 in a crib. Alligator Bayou has trundle
bed for child (54″ long) at no extra charge.

DISNEY VALUE RESORTS

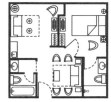

**ART OF ANIMATION RESORT,
FINDING NEMO FAMILY SUITE**
Typical suite, 565 square feet;
accommodates 6 guests plus
1 child under age 3 in a crib

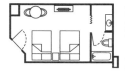

**ART OF ANIMATION
RESORT,
LITTLE MERMAID
STANDARD ROOM**
Typical room,
277 square feet;
accommodates
4 guests plus 1 child
under age 3 in a crib

**ALL-STAR RESORTS
(MUSIC AND
SPORTS)**
Typical room,
260 square feet;
accommodates
4 guests plus 1 child
under age 3 in a crib

ALL-STAR RESORTS FAMILY SUITE
Typical suite, 520 square feet;
accommodates 6 guests plus
1 child under age 3 in a crib

**ALL-STAR MOVIES
RESORT**
Typical room, 260
square feet;
accommodates
4 guests plus 1 child
under age 3 in a crib

**POP CENTURY
RESORT**
Typical room,
260 square feet;
accommodates
4 guests plus 1 child
under age 3 in a crib

continued from page 96

inspect most Disney-owned hotels every 6–12 months, and no less than
once every couple of years.

Pipe Down Out There!

The most common complaint that Walt Disney World–area hotel guests
make regarding their rooms is excessive noise. A well-designed room

Illustration: Chris Eliopoulos

blocks noise coming from both your neighbor's television and the pool across the resort.

The hotels with the best exterior sound-proofing are **Contemporary, Grand Floridian, Gran Destino Tower, Saratoga Springs, Riviera,** and **Yacht Club.** Hotels with the least exterior soundproofing are **All-Star Movies, Art of Animation**'s *Little Mermaid* rooms, **Caribbean Beach,** both **Port Orleans Resorts,** and **Polynesian Village** (but not the Polynesian Villas).

The **Riviera** and **Gran Destino Tower** are newer resorts, and it looks like Disney specifically addressed sound-proofing when installing those exterior doors. At the other end of the list, the **Polynesian Village** and **Port Orleans Resorts** have performed consistently poorly in our tests over the years. Your best bet here might be to ask for a remote corner room without a connecting interior door.

Room soundproofing, however, is only half of the story; the other half is location, particularly as it relates to people outside your room. A pool-view room at any resort, for instance, is likely to pick up a lot more noise than an upper-floor corner room.

With all these factors in mind, we set out to determine the amount of external noise affecting every single room at Walt Disney World. We took into account factors including the floor level, pedestrian traffic, proximity to public spaces, and number of nearby rooms.

Take the northwest-facing rooms in buildings 4 and 5 of Disney's **All-Star Music Resort:** They overlook the extreme end of a parking lot, well away from most public spaces. There's little pedestrian traffic here, and the rooms themselves are well soundproofed—a recipe for quiet, or so we thought. But as it turns out, the remoteness of this location isn't lost on Disney: It's where the diesel buses are warmed up in the morning before servicing the three All-Stars.

Our research indicates that quiet rooms can be found in almost any resort, regardless of price point. For readers who put peace and quiet at the top of their lists, we've listed the 12 quietest spots among all WDW resorts in the table on the opposite page.

Let There Be Light!

In addition to sound, we measure the amount of light available in three key areas of each hotel room: at the bathroom vanity or sink, at the desk or work area, and in bed. The good news is that Disney has been steadily improving the lighting throughout most of its resorts. The **Contemporary Resort** sets the standard: Light at the desk measures well above the recommended level for office or school work. Light at the bathroom vanity is brighter than normal daylight. Other resorts with good lighting include the **Riviera, Polynesian Village, Wilderness Lodge,** and **All-Stars.** Resorts that didn't do well in our lighting test include **BoardWalk Villas** (before its 2023 redo) and **Port Orleans Riverside.** If you think you'll

QUIETEST ROOMS AT WALT DISNEY WORLD	
ALL-STAR MUSIC Buildings 5 and 6, rooms facing west	
ALL-STAR SPORTS Building 3, rooms facing west; building 2, rooms facing north	
BAY LAKE TOWER Any room is good here—rooms are among the quietest in WDW	
BEACH CLUB Easternmost hallways, rooms facing east	
BEACH CLUB VILLAS Rooms facing southeast	
BOARDWALK INN All rooms facing courtyard, just east of main lobby	
BOULDER RIDGE VILLAS Southernmost part of the building, water-view rooms facing east	
CARIBBEAN BEACH Trinidad South, buildings 35 and 38, rooms facing lake	
PORT ORLEANS FRENCH QUARTER Building 1, rooms facing water; building 7, north wing, rooms facing water; building 6, north wing, rooms facing water	
PORT ORLEANS RIVERSIDE Alligator Bayou, buildings 26 and 28, rooms facing east; Acadian House, north wings, rooms facing west	
TREEHOUSE VILLAS Any room is good	
WILDERNESS LODGE/COPPER CREEK VILLAS Middle of northernmost wing, rooms facing northwest (woods)	

need to get work done while vacationing at Walt Disney World, consider staying at a hotel with good lighting.

Check-In and Checkout

Up to 60 days before you arrive, you can log on to mydisneyexperience .com to complete the check-in process. Depending on how much information you provide before your trip, your resort check-in can be eliminated or streamlined considerably.

DIRECT-TO-ROOM CHECK-IN If you provide the website with a credit card number, a PIN for purchases, and your arrival and departure times, Disney will send you an email or text confirmation that your check-in is complete. Next, Disney will email or text you with your room number when it is available, allowing you to go straight to your room without stopping at the front desk.

ONLINE CHECK-IN If you've checked in online but you haven't added a credit card or PIN to your account, you'll still be able to bypass the regular check-in desk and head for the Online Check-In Desk to finish the check-in process. *Note:* Online check-in should be completed at least 24 hours before you arrive.

unofficial **TIP**
Check the MDE app before you get in a long check-in line—sometimes the app will be updated with your room number even if you didn't get a text or email alert.

AT THE FRONT DESK At the Value resorts, such as All-Star Sports, Disney has separate check-in areas for large tour groups and sports teams, leaving the huge main check-in desk free for regular travelers. A cast member also roams the lobby and can issue an "all hands on deck" alert when lines develop. The arrival of a busload of guests can sometimes overwhelm the front desk of Deluxe resorts, which have smaller front desks and fewer agents, but this is the exception rather than the rule. If your room is unavailable when you arrive, Disney will offer to call or text you when it's ready.

On your checkout day, your bill will be prepared and emailed or made available in My Disney Experience. If everything is in order, you can simply pack up and depart. But beware—on a recent trip, our family left for breakfast at another resort but didn't check out. When we got back to our room to use bathrooms and grab a few snacks we left in the fridge, housekeeping was already cleaning the room! This isn't supposed to happen, but it's a possibility.

EARLY CHECK-IN Official check-in time is 3 p.m. at Disney hotels and 4 p.m. for DVC villas. Note that if you check in early and you ask for a room that's ready, that request will cancel out any previous one you've made.

HOUSEKEEPING SERVICE As of 2023, Disney's housekeeping service visits rooms every other day at Value and Moderate resorts and daily at the Deluxe resorts.

PARKING POLICIES Disney offers free parking at its resorts. Guests staying at the **Campsites at Fort Wilderness Resort** get a parking space for one vehicle. Day guests who visit the Disney resorts to eat, shop, use recreational facilities, and the like can park there for free (valet parking costs extra). Day parking in the theme parks is also free for guests staying on-property.

READERS' DISNEY RESORT REPORT CARD

EACH YEAR, SEVERAL THOUSAND READERS send in responses to our surveys. The Readers' 2024 Disney Resort Report Card, on pages 106–107, documents their opinions of the Walt Disney World resorts as well as the Swan, Dolphin, and Swan Reserve Resorts.

In the **% Stay Again** and **% Rec to Friends** columns, we list the percentage of readers responding "Definitely" to the questions "Would you stay at this hotel again?" and "Would you recommend this hotel to a friend?" For this edition, percentages of 95 or above in response to the first question and 79 or above in response to the second are considered **Above Average;** percentages of 88 or below in response to the first question and 63 or below in response to the second are considered **Below Average.** In the hotel profiles on the following pages, we include these two percentages, plus the overall reader rating expressed as a letter grade, from the Report Card.

Room Quality reflects readers' satisfaction with their rooms, while **Check-In Efficiency** rates the speed and ease of check-in. **Quietness of Room** measures how well, in the guests' perception, their rooms are insulated from external noise. **Shuttle Service** rates Disney bus, boat, Skyliner, and/or monorail service to and from the hotels. **Pool** reflects readers' satisfaction with the resorts' swimming pools. **Staff** measures the friendliness and helpfulness of the resort's employees, and **Dining** rates the overall food quality and value.

Off-site hotels are, on average, rated slightly lower than Disney hotels, with problems noted in food courts and transportation. As noted earlier in this chapter, we think these ratings justify the premium that Disney charges at many of its hotels.

UNOFFICIAL GUIDE PICKS FOR DISNEY RESORTS		
ADULTS		
VALUE: Pop Century For new room designs and Skyliner access		
MODERATE: Caribbean Beach For Skyliner access, redesigned rooms, and access to Riviera		
DELUXE: Wilderness Lodge For its just-right balance of location, amenities, and food		
GROUPS OF 5 OR MORE		
VALUE: All-Star Music Newest suites with two baths, and for 33% less than the suites at Art of Animation		
MODERATE: Caribbean Beach Book a fifth-sleeper room and request a location near a Skyliner station.		
DELUXE: Old Key West Two-bedroom villa (booked with DVC rental points)		
FAMILIES WITH YOUNG KIDS		
VALUE: Art of Animation Kids will delight in the architecture and themed pools.		
MODERATE: Caribbean Beach Fun colors and pool, plus Skyliner access to two parks		
DELUXE: Animal Kingdom Lodge Fantastic scenery and chances to see animals		
FAMILIES WITH OLDER KIDS		
VALUE: Pop Century A lively pool scene means meeting new friends. Very teen-friendly food court, with Art of Animation's within walking distance too.		
MODERATE: Port Orleans–Riverside There's plenty of opportunity to independently explore this large resort.		
DELUXE: Yacht & Beach Clubs For Stormalong Bay (closed January–June 2025) and easy access to EPCOT and Disney's Hollywood Studios		

Putting It All Together: Reader Picks for Best and Worst Resorts

Disney's **Wilderness Lodge** (and its DVC counterparts) takes top honors in this year's survey. It is highly rated in every category except food, where it scores just above average. Just behind Wilderness Lodge are **Port Orleans–French Quarter** and **Riviera Resort.**

The lowest-rated Disney resorts remain the **Swan** and **Dolphin** (but not the Swan Reserve). Both are rated low for transportation to the parks and for dining options. We think readers are spot-on with those assessments. And in a somewhat shocking development this year, the **Grand Floridian** is the third-lowest-rated resort, coming in just slightly above the Swan and Dolphin. Its quietness scores plummeted this year, perhaps due to the construction and retheming work being done.

WALT DISNEY WORLD HOTEL PROFILES

FOR MORE-DETAILED INFORMATION on the Disney resorts, including photos and videos, check out **TouringPlans.com.**

One of our readers' top concerns is getting to the parks quickly using Disney's transportation network. The simplest way to reduce your transportation wait is to walk—for example, from the Grand Floridian or Contemporary to the Magic Kingdom, or from any EPCOT resort to EPCOT or Disney's Hollywood Studios. The next-best alternative

continued on page 108

READERS' 2024 DISNEY RESORT REPORT CARD

RESORT	PAGE	NO. OF SURVEYS	% STAY AGAIN	% REC TO FRIENDS	
VALUE					
ALL-STAR MOVIES RESORT	158	91	87	57	
ALL-STAR MUSIC RESORT	158	99	93	62	
ALL-STAR SPORTS RESORT	158	65	93	63	
ART OF ANIMATION RESORT	164	158	89	67	
CAMPSITES AT FORT WILDERNESS	170	30	89	59	
POP CENTURY RESORT	162	488	95	70	
MODERATE					
CARIBBEAN BEACH RESORT	137	251	94	59	
CORONADO SPRINGS RESORT	155	160	94	76	
PORT ORLEANS FRENCH QUARTER	147	199	98	84	
PORT ORLEANS RIVERSIDE	149	161	88	59	
DELUXE					
ANIMAL KINGDOM LODGE	151	132	92	78	
BEACH CLUB RESORT	126	108	88	63	
BOARDWALK INN	130	73	87	61	
CONTEMPORARY RESORT	120	97	84	64	
GRAND FLORIDIAN RESORT & SPA	108	99	88	68	
POLYNESIAN VILLAGE RESORT	112	100	93	85	
WALT DISNEY WORLD DOLPHIN HOTEL	133	73	83	54	
WALT DISNEY WORLD SWAN HOTEL	133	65	88	63	
WALT DISNEY WORLD SWAN RESERVE	133	24	100	86	
WILDERNESS LODGE	116	114	95	79	
YACHT CLUB RESORT	126	125	89	76	
DELUXE VILLA (DVC)					
ANIMAL KINGDOM VILLAS–JAMBO HOUSE	151	54	96	78	
ANIMAL KINGDOM VILLAS–KIDANI VILLAGE	154	120	88	68	
BAY LAKE TOWER AT THE CONTEMPORARY	122	131	90	70	
BEACH CLUB VILLAS	129	75	97	70	
BOARDWALK VILLAS	133	112	92	68	
BOULDER RIDGE VILLAS	119	45	93	81	
CABINS AT FORT WILDERNESS	171	31	83	67	
COPPER CREEK VILLAS & CABINS AT WILDERNESS LODGE	119	53	98	86	
OLD KEY WEST RESORT	145	140	92	71	
POLYNESIAN VILLAS & BUNGALOWS	115	102	94	80	
RIVIERA RESORT	139	108	97	85	
SARATOGA SPRINGS RESORT & SPA	140	163	93	65	
SHADES OF GREEN	124	49	92	71	
VILLAS AT THE GRAND FLORIDIAN	110	43	98	80	
Average for Disney Hotels			**87**	**70**	
Average for Off-Site Hotels			**88**	**58**	

Treehouse Villas at Disney's Saratoga Springs Resort did not have enough surveys to rate for this editio

ROOM QUALITY	CHECK-IN EFFICIENCY	QUIETNESS OF ROOM	SHUTTLE SERVICE	POOL	STAFF	FOOD COURT	OVERALL
B-	A-	C	B	B	A-	D+	B+
B	A	B	B	B-	A-	C-	A-
B	A	C	B	B	A	C-	A
B	A-	C	B+	B	B+	D	A-
C+	B+	C	C-	C	B	D+	B
B-	A-	C	A-	B-	A-	D	A-
B	A-	B-	B	B-	A-	C	A-
B+	A	B-	B-	B-	A-	C	A
B	A	B	A-	B	A-	C-	A
B	B+	B	C+	B-	B	C-	B+
B	A-	B-	B-	B	A-	B	A
B	B+	C+	B	B+	A-	C	A-
B	A	C+	B+	B-	A	D	A-
B+	A-	B-	B	C	A-	C+	A-
B+	A-	C	B+	B-	A	C+	B+
B	B	C	A-	B	A-	C+	A
B-	B	B-	C-	B	B-	C-	B
B	B	B	D+	B	B	C	B+
A	B+	A	C+	B	A-	C+	A
B+	A-	B	B	B	A-	C+	A
B+	B+	C+	B	B+	A-	C	A
B	A	B-	C	B-	A	B	A-
A-	A-	A-	B-	B	A-	B-	A-
A-	A	A-	B	C+	A-	B-	A-
B	A-	B	B	B+	A-	C-	A-
B	A	B	B	B	A	D+	A-
A-	B+	A	B	B	A-	C	A
A-	A-	A	B-	C	A-	D+	A-
B+	A	B	B	B	A-	B-	A
A-	A-	B	B-	B	A-	C	A-
B	B+	C+	A-	B	A-	B-	A
A	B+	A-	B+	B	A	B	A
A-	A	A-	C	B	A-	C-	A-
A-	B+	B+	C	B	B+	C+	A
A-	A-	B	A-	B	A	B-	A
B	**A-**	**B-**	**B**	**B**	**A-**	**C**	**A-**
B	**A**	**B-**	**C-**	**D**	**B**	**C-**	**B+**

continued from page 105

is to get a taxi or ride-hailing service to drop you off at the closest resort to the park you're visiting and walk over. Driving your own car or taking a Disney bus is the next-best option. Boats, monorail, and the Skyliner are generally quick but susceptible to weather-related closures.

THE MAGIC KINGDOM RESORTS

Disney's Grand Floridian Resort & Spa

(See theugseries.com/grand-floridian *and* theugseries.com/gf-villas *for extended coverage.)*

STRENGTHS	WEAKNESSES
• High staff-to-guest ratio	• Most expensive WDW resort
• Excellent dining options for adults	• Public areas often blocked by wedding parties
• Large rooms with daybeds	
• Excellent on-site spa	• Noise from Magic Kingdom, boat horns, and whistles
• Fantastic kids' *Alice in Wonderland*–themed splash area	• Insanely crowded lobby during certain holidays
• Boat and monorail transportation to the Magic Kingdom, plus a pedestrian walkway	• Bus transportation may be shared by the other monorail resorts
• Diverse recreational options	
• Close to Palm, Magnolia, and Oak Trail Golf Courses	

Unofficial Guide **Reader-Survey Results**

Percentage of readers who'd stay here again	**88%** *(Below Average)*
Percentage of readers who'd recommend this resort to a friend	**68%** *(Average)*
Overall reader rating	**B+**

QUICK TAKE: *The Grand Floridian is the quintessential Walt Disney World resort. Unfortunately, the cost recognizes this demand. And during Christmas and Easter, crowds viewing the elaborate holiday displays in the lobby can negatively impact your experience.*

WALT DISNEY WORLD'S FLAGSHIP HOTEL is inspired by grand Victorian resorts such as the Hotel del Coronado in San Diego and Mount Washington Resort in New Hampshire. A complex of four- and five-story white-frame buildings, the Grand Floridian integrates verandas, intricate latticework, dormers, and turrets beneath a red-shingle roof to capture the feeling of a 19th-century ocean resort. Covering 40 acres along Seven Seas Lagoon, the Grand Floridian offers lovely pools, white-sand beaches, and a marina.

The 867 guest rooms have received a much-needed decorative refresh and now feature shades of blues, whites, and tans. Lighter furniture, hardwood floors, and wall paneling make the already large rooms seems lighter and more spacious than ever! The textured headboards and large rug add luxury without feeling stuffy. A typical room is 440 square feet (dormer rooms are smaller) and furnished with two queen beds, a daybed, and a small desk with chair. Many rooms have balconies. All rooms have a Keurig coffee maker, a large dresser with minifridge, and a wall-mounted TV.

Grand Floridian Resort & Spa and Grand Floridian Villas

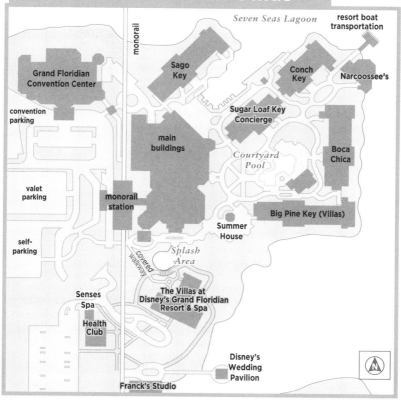

Bathrooms are large, with plenty of counter space and fluffy towels. Under-sink storage is lacking, but the fixtures are pretty. Water pressure in the shower is probably less than what you get at home but still enough to rinse out shampoo suds. The hotel is connected directly to the Magic Kingdom by monorail, boat, and a pedestrian walkway, and to other Disney World destinations by bus. Walking time to the monorail-, boat-, and bus-loading areas from the most remote guest rooms is about 7–10 minutes. It takes about 15–20 minutes on the pedestrian walkway to get to the Magic Kingdom tapstiles.

The resort has many highly rated table-service restaurants. Add to that everything accessible via the monorail, and you have very impressive dining selections. The main building displays life-size gingerbread houses at Christmas, which brings noise and crowds to the lobby. During this season, waits for the monorail can balloon up to 90 minutes.

The Grand Floridian's **Senses Spa,** modeled after the spas on the Disney Cruise Line ships, is one of the best in the Orlando area. In addition, the resort's pools are among the nicest on Disney property.

The **Courtyard Pool** has a zero-entry ramp for small children to splash in. An *Alice in Wonderland*–themed splash area sits between the main building and the Villas.

The grounds are a lovely place to walk around during the evening, with romantic light levels and charming background music.

Most of the reader comments we get about the Grand Floridian are positive. From a North Carolina mother of two preschoolers:

> *The Grand Floridian pool with the waterslide was a big hit with our kids. They also loved taking the boat across the lagoon to return from the Magic Kingdom.*

GOOD (AND NOT-SO-GOOD) ROOMS AT THE GRAND FLORIDIAN *(See* **theugseries.com/gf-views** *for photos.)* The resort is spread over a peninsula that juts into Seven Seas Lagoon. In addition to the main building, there are five rectangular outer buildings, one of which (**Big Pine Key**) contains the villas. Grand Floridian room numbers are coded. Take room 7213: 7 is the building number, 2 is the floor, and 13 is the room number. Most of the rooms have a balcony, and most balconies are enclosed by a rail that affords good visibility. Dormer rooms, just beneath the roof in each building, have smaller enclosed balconies that limit visibility when you're seated. Most dormer rooms, however, have vaulted ceilings and a coziness that compensates for the less-desirable balconies.

If you want to be near the bus and monorail, most of the restaurants, and shopping, ask for a room in the main building. It's the highest-rated building at this resort. The best rooms are **4322–4329** and **4422–4429,** which have full balconies and overlook the lagoon in the direction of the beach and the Polynesian Village. Other excellent main-building rooms are **4401–4409,** with full balconies overlooking the marina and an unobstructed view of Cinderella Castle across the lagoon.

Of the four outer guest-room buildings **Boca Chica** and **Conch Key** have one long side facing the lagoon and the other facing inner courtyards and swimming pools. At Conch Key, full-balcony rooms **7229–7231, 7328, 7329, 7331, 7425–7429,** and **7431** offer vistas across the lagoon to the Magic Kingdom and castle. Less-expensive rooms in the same building that offer good marina views are **7212, 7312, 7412–7415, 7417, 7419, 7421, 7513–7515,** and **7517.** In Boca Chica, ask for a lagoon-view room on the first, second, or third floor. Avoid garden-view rooms in this building if possible.

The other two guest-room buildings, **Sugar Loaf Key** (Club Level) and **Sago Key,** face each other across the marina. The opposite side of Sugar Loaf Key faces a courtyard, while the other side of Sago Key faces a finger of the lagoon and a forested area. These views are pleasant but not in the same league as those listed previously. Exceptions are end rooms in Sago Key that have a view of the lagoon and Cinderella Castle (rooms **5139, 5144, 5145, 5242–5245,** and **5342–5345**).

THE VILLAS AT DISNEY'S GRAND FLORIDIAN RESORT & SPA

Unofficial Guide Reader-Survey Results

Percentage of readers who'd stay here again	98% *(Above Average)*
Percentage of readers who'd recommend this resort to a friend	80% *(Above Average)*
Overall reader rating	A

THIS DISNEY VACATION CLUB PROPERTY opened in the fall of 2013. Readers consistently rate it as one of the best resorts in Walt Disney World, and it's the absolute favorite of many.

Decorated like close siblings to the new resort rooms, the villas are among the nicest at any DVC property. Most have vaulted living-room ceilings and faux-wood balconies or porches. Those balconies stretch the entire length of the room, giving everyone enough space for a good view.

Studios have a kitchenette with minifridge, sink, and drip coffee maker, while the larger rooms have full kitchens. Those feature a stainless steel oven range, with the dishwasher and refrigerator tucked behind white wood panels that match the glass-door cabinets. Other amenities in the full kitchens include a full-size coffee maker, a toaster, frying pans, and the usual set of plates, glasses, cups, and cutlery. Also in the kitchen are a banquette seat and a table with room for six.

The living room has a sofa that seats three comfortably, an upholstered chair and ottoman, a coffee table, and a large flat-screen TV. The sofa converts into a bed that sleeps two; a cabinet below the TV hides a small pull-down bed. We'd use these beds for kids, not adults.

Studio rooms have a queen bed in addition to the folding options listed above. One-bedroom villas have a king bed along with the folding options; two-bedroom villas have a king bed in one room and two queen beds in the other, plus the folding options; the Grand Villa's third bedroom has an additional two queen beds.

The one- and two-bedroom units and the Grand Villa bedrooms are outfitted with a large writing desk, a flat-screen TV with DVD player, two nightstands with convenient electric plugs, and a side chair. They also have large walk-in closets.

Bathrooms are large, with marble tile and flat-screen TVs built into the mirrors. Studio bathrooms have a separate toilet and shower area; in the one-bedroom configuration, a tub and dressing area sit adjacent to the bedroom. The bathroom and shower are connected by a pocket door, allowing two groups of people to get dressed at the same time. The tiled shower is so large that it could function as another bedroom if that was ever a need. It has a rain showerhead mounted in the ceiling in addition to a wall-mounted faucet.

The villas have their own well-located parking lot but no dining in their buildings. Within walking distance, however, are the restaurants of both the main Grand Floridian and Polynesian Village. Room service is available from the Grand Floridian's in-room dining menu.

GOOD (AND NOT-SO-GOOD) ROOMS AT THE GRAND FLORIDIAN VILLAS (See **theugseries.com/gf-villa-views** for photos.) Rooms **1X14, 1X16,** and **1X18** face the Magic Kingdom and have views of Space Mountain and the castle; **1X14** has probably the best views of any room in all of the villas. (X indicates a floor number.)

Even-numbered rooms **1X02–1X12** face west, toward the Polynesian Village and Seven Seas Lagoon, and afford a good view of the nightly water pageant as it floats by.

South-facing rooms in Big Pine Key look out over the Seven Seas Lagoon, although mature trees and landscaping partially block those views from many upper-floor rooms. Rooms **9X41–9X47** may have views of the Magic Kingdom fireworks.

Disney's Polynesian Village Resort, Villas & Bungalows

(See theugseries.com/ug-poly and theugseries.com/poly-villas for extended coverage.)

STRENGTHS	WEAKNESSES
• Walking distance to EPCOT monorail	• Close to Palm, Magnolia, and Oak Trail Golf Courses
• Most family-friendly dining on the monorail loop	**WEAKNESSES**
• Fun South Seas theme	• No spa or exercise facilities (guests can use those at the Grand Floridian)
• Boat and monorail transportation to the Magic Kingdom	• Noise from boat horns and whistles
• Among the best Club Levels of the Deluxe resorts	• Bus transportation to Hollywood Studios, Animal Kingdom, water parks, and Disney Springs

Unofficial Guide **Reader-Survey Results**
(resort only; see page 115 for villa/bungalow ratings)

Percentage of readers who'd stay here again	93% *(Average)*
Percentage of readers who'd recommend this resort to a friend	85% *(Above Average)*
Overall reader rating	A

SOUTH PACIFIC TROPICS ARE RE-CREATED at this Deluxe resort, which consists of two- and three-story Hawaiian longhouses situated around the four-story **Great Ceremonial House,** which contains restaurants, shops, and an atrium lobby with slate floors and tropical plants. Buildings feature wood accents, including exposed roof beams and tribal-inspired geometric inlays in the cornices.

Spread across 39 acres along Seven Seas Lagoon, the resort has fewer than 500 standard hotel rooms and three white-sand beaches. Its pool complex likewise captures the South Pacific theme. There is no dedicated fitness center, but guests are welcome to use the Grand Floridian's facilities, just a quarter-mile walk (bonus workout!) or 2-minute monorail ride away. Landscaping is superb—garden-view rooms are generally superior to equivalent rooms at other resorts.

The **Moorea, Pago Pago,** and **Tokelau** buildings—added after the rest of the resort opened, with the Magic Kingdom, in 1971—are part of the Disney Vacation Club. The most recent room refurbishments were completed in summer 2021, adding bright, island-themed murals and subtle references to characters from Disney's *Moana*. We're always suspicious when Disney adds characters to anything because we've had bad experiences with that in the past (RIP Maelstrom). But this is one of Disney's better room-renovation projects in recent memory (perhaps second only to the Grand Floridian redo), and the *Moana* additions work well with the resort's theme. Most rooms have two queen beds, a sofa, a reading chair, a large dresser with plenty of shelf space, and a wall-mounted TV. A minifridge and coffee maker sit between two large closets near the doorway and opposite the bathroom area. The closets are spacious and light. Lighting is good throughout the room, including by the desk and beds.

The Poly's bathrooms have two large sinks that offer plenty of counter space. A spacious, glass-enclosed shower provides good-to-excellent water pressure. The new bathroom layout includes a door

Polynesian Village Resort, Villas & Bungalows

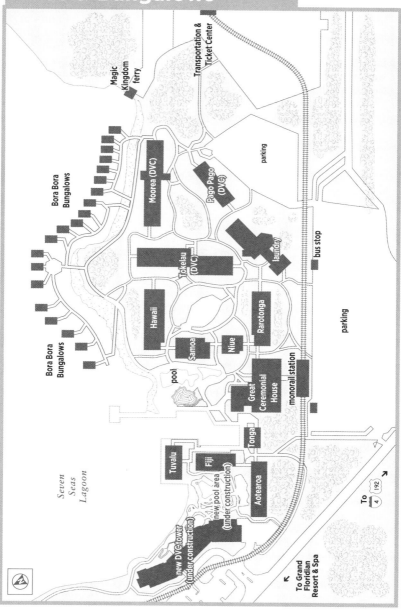

between the toilet and sink area, plus another separating the entire bathroom from the rest of the room. This allows three people to get dressed in privacy at once.

The resort has an on-site monorail station, and all rooms are within easy walking distance of the Transportation and Ticket Center, with access to the EPCOT monorail. Bus service is available to other Disney destinations, and boat service takes you to the Magic Kingdom. Walking time to the bus and on-site monorail stations is 8–11 minutes at most. The pedestrian walkway between the Poly and the Grand Floridian continues to the Magic Kingdom—it's about 1.5 miles from the farthest point at the Poly to the Magic Kingdom tapstiles. This walkway will remain closed until the opening of the new Polynesian DVC tower, which at the time of writing is scheduled to open in late 2024.

The Poly's transportation options are a major draw:

We stay at the Polynesian Village because it offers the best transportation. You can walk to a direct monorail to both the Magic Kingdom and EPCOT, the water taxi can be a fast option, and the bus service to other parks is fairly direct.

A Maryland family found the room soundproofing lacking, confirming our own research:

We took towels from the pool and stuffed them under the door to deaden the noise coming from the connecting room.

unofficial **TIP**
During busier times of the year, it can take several hours to get a table at Trader Sam's, so we don't recommend it.

The Polynesian Village has two lounges, with **Trader Sam's Grog Grotto** being the most popular. Modeled after the famed bar of the same name at the Disneyland Hotel, Trader Sam's serves whimsical (and potent) cocktails and tasty appetizers, along with interactive art and "artifacts" stuffed into every available inch of space. **Tambu Lounge** is less well known but rated better overall.

GOOD (AND NOT-SO-GOOD) ROOMS AT POLYNESIAN VILLAGE RESORT *(See* **theugseries.com/poly-views** *for photos.)* The Polynesian Village's 11 guest room buildings, or longhouses, are spread over a long strip of land bordered by the monorail on one side and Seven Seas Lagoon on the other. All buildings have first-floor patios and third-floor balconies. The older buildings, which contain about half of the resort's rooms, have faux balconies on their second floors. (The newer buildings offer full balconies on both the second and third floors, and patios on the first.) Mature vegetation blocks the views from some patios, but the patios are roomier than the balconies. If views are important, ask for a third-floor room.

The Great Ceremonial House contains most of the restaurants and shops, as well as the resort lobby, guest services, and bus and monorail stations. The longhouses most convenient to the Great Ceremonial House—**Fiji, Tonga, Rarotonga, Niue,** and **Samoa**—offer views of the swimming complex, a small marina, or inner gardens. There are no lagoon views from these except for oblique views from the upper floors of Fiji, Samoa, and Tuvalu; Aotearoa; and a tunnel view from Tonga. Samoa, however, because it's close to the main swimming complex, is a good choice for families who plan to spend time at the pool. The 22-room Niue is the highest-rated building at the Polynesian. You won't get views of the Magic Kingdom, but Niue is centrally located between both pools and the Great Ceremonial House.

You can specifically request a lagoon- or Magic Kingdom–view room at the Polynesian Village, if you're willing to pay extra. The best of these rooms are on the third floor in **Tuvalu** and, if you're staying in a Club Level (concierge) room, the third floor in **Hawaii.**

In addition to second-floor rooms with faux balconies, we also advise against booking the monorail-side (south-facing) rooms in **Rarotonga** and **Aotearoa.** The monorail runs within spitting distance.

Many first-floor rooms in **Hawaii (1501–1518)** are garden- or lagoon-view rooms; their scenery is blocked by the overwater bungalows. These rooms still offer a chance to see the evening fireworks, however, and are a little less expensive than similar rooms on higher floors.

POLYNESIAN VILLAS & BUNGALOWS

Unofficial Guide Reader-Survey Results

Percentage of readers who'd stay here again	94% (*Above Average*)
Percentage of readers who'd recommend this resort to a friend	80% (*Above Average*)
Overall reader rating	A

THE TOKELAU, MOOREA, AND PAGO PAGO longhouses hold DVC studio rooms that sleep five and are the largest studios in Walt Disney World's DVC inventory. They also have two bathrooms: The smaller bath has a small sink and step-in shower; the larger has a toilet, sink, and bath/shower combination. This allows three people to get ready simultaneously. The studios also include kitchenettes.

The Polynesian's 20 over-the-water **Bora Bora Bungalows** sit in front of Hawaii, Tokelau, and Moorea. Connected to land by a wood walkway, these two-bedroom bungalows offer stunning views of the Magic Kingdom fireworks and of Seven Seas Lagoon and its nightly Electrical Water Pageant. Not surprisingly, those stunning views come with stunning prices—up to $6,100 per night.

The bungalows are well built, with top-notch design elements from top to bottom. The bedrooms are spacious, the beds are the best on Disney property, the bathrooms are gorgeous, the showers are spectacular, and the open kitchen design works wonderfully. The doorbell even plays a different chime every time you ring it. And yeah, the views are spectacular.

However, the bungalows have two fatal flaws: price and noise. Regarding the first, they cost an average of 146 DVC points for a one-night stay, roughly equivalent to $2,920 at the time of this writing. Check-in is at 4 p.m. and checkout at 11 a.m., so a 19-hour stay costs about $154 an hour. That's assuming you get your room assigned on time and don't leave early.

And then there's the ferry horn. We were in room 7019, the second-closest bungalow to the Transportation and Ticket Center (TTC) ferry dock. A ferry leaves about every 12 minutes, from 30 minutes before Early Entry begins until an hour after the parks close. Every time a ferry departs, it sounds a warning horn. The sound is like an air-raid siren: loud enough to stop indoor conversation in its tracks. Reading, watching TV, getting a baby to nap, sleeping before one of those late-park-close nights? Forget it. If you're determined to stay here, shoot for **bungalows 7001–7005,** which are farthest from the TTC.

The Polynesian Villas have a separate parking lot close to their long-houses. Dining and transportation are shared with the main resort.

NEW DVC BUILDING Disney is in the midst of construction of a large new DVC building for the Polynesian. This new tower, which concept art suggests is at least eight stories high, will sit on the northwest side of the Polynesian's land, between the existing Aotearoa/Fiji buildings and Disney's Wedding Pavilion at the Grand Floridian. A new pool complex is also planned between those existing buildings and the new tower. The project has an aggressive construction schedule, with an expected opening in 2024.

GOOD (AND NOT-SO-GOOD) ROOMS AT THE POLYNESIAN VILLAS Because there are a few quirks in the way Disney categorizes room views here, it's possible to snag a Magic Kingdom view from a garden-view room. The second- and third-floor rooms in **Tokelau** (**2901–2928, 2939–2948, 3901–3928,** and **3939–3948**) offer the best shot at getting side views of Cinderella Castle and the fireworks, although palm trees may block many second-floor views. First-floor rooms also have landscaping blocking most views; on the upside, the patios provide room to move to find a better spot. Overall, Tokelau is the highest-rated DVC building at the Polynesian.

The second and third floors in **Moorea** have rooms with lagoon and Magic Kingdom views; those that face north see the Magic Kingdom. Avoid **Pago Pago**'s southeast-facing rooms (**1X01–1X12**)—these look onto the parking lot and monorail.

If you plan to spend a lot of time in EPCOT, **Moorea** and **Pago Pago** are good choices because they're within easy walking distance of the TTC and the EPCOT monorail. Even if you're going to the Magic Kingdom, it's a short walk from Moorea and Pago Pago to the TTC and its Magic Kingdom monorail.

Disney's Wilderness Lodge, Boulder Ridge Villas, and Copper Creek Villas & Cabins

(See theugseries.com/wilderness-lodge, theugseries.com/boulder, *and* theugseries.com/copper *for extended coverage.)*

STRENGTHS	WEAKNESSES
• National park lodge theme is beautiful and well executed	• Transportation to Magic Kingdom is by bus or boat only
• Along with Animal Kingdom Lodge, it's the least expensive Disney Deluxe resort	• Noise from main building's lobby can be heard inside nearby rooms
• Close to recreational options at Fort Wilderness	• Bus transportation to Magic Kingdom sometimes shared with Fort Wilderness
• Great views from guest rooms	• Smallest rooms and baths of Disney's Deluxe resorts
• Exceptionally peaceful location and public areas (Villas)	

Unofficial Guide **Reader-Survey Results** *(Wilderness Lodge only; see page 119 for Copper Creek Villas & Cabins and Boulder Ridge Villas)*

Percentage of readers who'd stay here again	95% *(Above Average)*
Percentage of readers who'd recommend this resort to a friend	79% *(Above Average)*
Overall reader rating	A

Wilderness Lodge, Boulder Ridge Villas, and Copper Creek Villas & Cabins

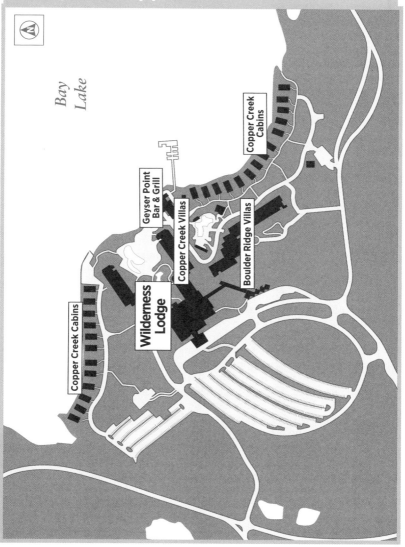

Bay Lake

Copper Creek Cabins

Geyser Point Bar & Grill

Copper Creek Villas

Boulder Ridge Villas

Wilderness Lodge

Copper Creek Cabins

QUICK TAKE: *With their recent renovations, the Boulder Ridge Villas are the new top pick here, followed by rooms in the main building.*

THIS DELUXE RESORT is inspired by grand, rustic Arts and Crafts lodges of the early 20th century—think The Ahwahnee in Yosemite National Park. Situated on the shore of Bay Lake, the lodge consists of an eight-story central building augmented by two seven-story guest wings, a wing of studio and one- and two-bedroom condominiums, and 26 lakeside cabins. The hotel features exposed timber columns, log cabin–style facades, and dormer windows, along with an 82-foot-tall stone fireplace in the lobby. Outside, there's a beach, a reliable geyser, and a pool complex modeled on a mountain stream.

We use the admittedly clunky "Wilderness Lodge, Boulder Ridge Villas, and Copper Creek Villas & Cabins" to refer to the entire complex, including its DVC units, which are available to the general public when not being used by DVC members. Here's what the various names mean:

- **Disney's Wilderness Lodge:** the resort component of the main building (the lodge), which opened in 1994
- **Boulder Ridge Villas:** DVC rooms in an adjacent building, opened in 2000
- **Copper Creek Villas & Cabins:** DVC rooms in the main building (Copper Creek Villas) and the lakeside cabins, both opened in 2017

The lodge's guest rooms were refurbished during the pandemic closures. More storage space, lots of outlets, and better lighting were added, and dark wood paneling was swapped out for soft headboards and lighter walls with woodsy Disney touches.

Typical rooms have two queen beds or a single king. All rooms have a table and chairs, a dresser, a TV, a double vanity just outside the bathroom, a minifridge, and a coffee maker. Rooms on the ground floor have patios; rooms above have balconies.

The pool area features a children's water-play area and a pool bar.

Dining choices consist of two full-service restaurants (Story Book Dining at Artist Point with Snow White and Whispering Canyon Cafe), plus the outdoor **Geyser Point Bar & Grill.** More dining is available via a short boat ride to the Contemporary or Fort Wilderness.

The resort is connected to the Magic Kingdom by boat and to other parks by bus. Your best bet for catching the first boat is to send someone out to the boat dock about 90 minutes before the Magic Kingdom's official opening time. If a line has started to form but has fewer than 30 people, get in line. If the line is longer than that, consider taking a bus or using a ride-hailing app. Boat service may be suspended during storms, so if it's raining or rain looks likely, Disney will provide buses. Walking time to buses and boats from the most remote rooms is 5–8 minutes. A mom from Oklahoma says that transportation is a big weakness:

> *During our most recent stay, transportation from Wilderness Lodge to the parks was the worst we have ever experienced in all our trips to WDW. We waited more than an hour for a boat to the Magic Kingdom; then, after it finally showed up and loaded, we made an unexplained trip to Fort Wilderness and loaded 26 more people. It took 90 minutes to get to the Magic Kingdom! The bus system wasn't much better—it's nearly impossible to get to the parks before opening.*

GOOD (AND NOT-SO-GOOD) ROOMS AT WILDERNESS LODGE *(See* theugseries.com/ug-wild-views *for photos.)* The lodge is shaped like a very blocky letter *U*. The main entrance and lobby are at the bottom of the *U*. Next are middle wings that connect the lobby to the parallel end sections, which extend to the open part of the *U*. The *U*'s open end flanks pools and gardens and overlooks Bay Lake directly or obliquely. Avoid rooms on the fourth, fifth, and sixth floors that end with numbers 67–99; these overlook the main lobby and pick up any noise there.

The better rooms are on floors four, five, and six, toward the *U*'s open end. Rooms **4000–4003, 5000–5003,** and **6000–6003** offer a direct frontal view of Bay Lake through some tall trees. Facing inward, odd-numbered rooms **4005–4023, 5005–5023,** and **6005–6023** face the courtyard but have excellent oblique lake views. Even-numbered rooms **5004–5034** and **6004–6034** face the Copper Creek Cabins; the woodlands northwest of the lodge; and the Magic Kingdom.

Odd-numbered rooms **5035–5041** and **6035–6041** offer a direct but distant view of the lake, with pools and gardens in the foreground.

COPPER CREEK VILLAS & CABINS

Unofficial Guide Reader-Survey Results

Percentage of readers who'd stay here again	98% (*Above Average*)
Percentage of readers who'd recommend this resort to a friend	86% (*Above Average*)
Overall reader rating	A

SOME ROOMS IN THE LODGE'S MAIN BUILDING are DVC units—Disney calls these Copper Creek Villas. Options include studios and one-, two-, and three-bedroom villas. The studios have kitchenettes, while most one- and two-bedroom villas have full kitchens. All rooms have vinyl plank flooring; modern furniture, including a table and chairs; a coffee maker; and a microwave. Bathrooms are spacious, although sink space is limited; storage is otherwise plentiful.

Copper Creek rooms have less theming than those in the rest of the lodge. They're still well appointed but now rank below the Boulder Ridge Villas after those received a more recent refurbishment.

The floor plan of the cabins is similar to that of the Bora Bora Bungalows at the Polynesian. Room quality and views are excellent— they'd better be, at around $5,100 per night in peak season.

We prefer the cabins to the bungalows, thanks to their slightly lower price and lack of ferry horns, as does this Iowa reader:

Loved the cabin at Copper Creek—better value than the Polynesian bungalows. Quiet and well arranged, but close to everything.

GOOD (AND NOT-SO-GOOD) ROOMS AT COPPER CREEK VILLAS AND CABINS *(See theugseries.com/copper-views for photos.)* Avoid rooms **X100–X106,** which overlook the lobby. Odd-numbered rooms **X107– X133** face the interior courtyard and pool. Studios **X119** have a view of the lake in the distance. Even-numbered rooms **X108–X134** face Boulder Ridge Villas, a garden area, and woods. Rooms on the sixth floor are high enough for you to see the lake past Boulder Ridge and the Copper Creek Cabins in the foreground.

Guests in cabins **8001–8006** get to watch boats glide to the Magic Kingdom, while cabins **8023–8026** offer excellent fireworks views.

BOULDER RIDGE VILLAS

Unofficial Guide Reader-Survey Results

Percentage of readers who'd stay here again	93% (*Average*)
Percentage of readers who'd recommend this resort to a friend	81% (*Above Average*)
Overall reader rating	A

ALSO PART OF DVC, the 136 Boulder Ridge Villas are studio and one- and two-bedroom units in a freestanding building to the right of the lodge.

Studios have kitchenettes; one- and two-bedroom villas have full kitchens. The recently updated décor is inspired by Native American design and makes the rooms feel lighter and larger than before. Boulder Ridge has its own pool but shares restaurants and other amenities with the main lodge.

The villas' studios have fold-down beds (other than the fifth floor, which has sleeper sofas). All villas have armoires and flat-screen TVs, and one- and two-bedroom units have stainless steel kitchen appliances. The renovated rooms are a perfect blend of inspiration from Disney characters, Native American art, and national parks. It sounds like a lot, but the integration is masterfully done.

GOOD (AND NOT-SO-GOOD) ROOMS AT BOULDER RIDGE VILLAS *See* **theugseries.com/boulder-views** *for photos.)* Except for a few rooms overlooking the pool, these rooms offer woodland views. The best are odd-numbered rooms **X531–X563** on floors three through five, which open to northeast side of the resort. Rooms on the opposite side of the same wing offer similar views, but with some roads and parking lots visible, and with traffic noise.

Disney's Contemporary Resort & Bay Lake Tower

(See **theugseries.com/ug-comtemporary** *and* **theugseries.com/ug-blt** *for extended coverage.)*

THIS 655-ROOM DELUXE RESORT'S A-frame design permits the Magic Kingdom monorail to pass through the structure's cavernous atrium. A 90-foot mosaic is a 1971 work by Disney animator and artist Mary Blair. The off-white central tower is augmented by a three-story **Garden Wing** fronting Bay Lake to the south and by **Bay Lake Tower,** a 295-room, 15-story DVC development, to the north.

STRENGTHS	WEAKNESSES
• The only hotel the monorail goes *through*	• Overpriced, especially "Magic Kingdom-view" rooms that mostly look out onto parking lots
• Large rooms with views of Bay Lake	
• Bay Lake Tower rooms are among the quietest in all of Walt Disney World	• Décor generally feels lazy and uninspired
• Easy walk to the Magic Kingdom	• Very small studios in Bay Lake Tower sleep no more than 2 people comfortably
• Excellent staff/service	
• Excellent lounge option (Top of the World in Bay Lake Tower)	• Bus transportation may be shared by the other monorail resorts
• Recreation options on Bay Lake	

Unofficial Guide **Reader-Survey Results** *(Contemporary Resort only; see page 122 for Bay Lake Tower ratings)*

Percentage of readers who'd stay here again	**84%** *(Below Average)*
Percentage of readers who'd recommend this resort to a friend	**64%** *(Below Average)*
Overall reader rating	**A-**

Standard rooms in the A-frame afford fantastic views of Bay Lake or the Magic Kingdom, and all have balconies. At 394 square feet each, they're only slightly smaller than equivalent rooms at the Grand Floridian Resort.

Rooms in the Contemporary's main building were refurbished in the summer of 2021, adding characters from Pixar's *The Incredibles* films. Off-white walls, bedspreads, and flooring are joined by carpets

Contemporary Resort & Bay Lake Tower

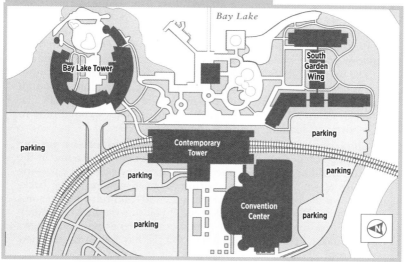

and couches in bold reds and other accent colors. All rooms include a minifridge and coffee maker. There's plenty of storage space and spots to plug in chargers. The beds are Sealy Posturepedic pillow-tops, which are very comfortable. The Contemporary's refurbishment also includes a new version of a foldout kids' bed. Soundproofing from outdoor noises has been improved.

Bathrooms have been remodeled, too, with a continuous countertop featuring two sinks and plenty of storage. The shower/tub combination is enclosed by glass sliders. It's quite possibly the best bathroom in any Disney Deluxe resort. Likewise, the bathroom door is a midcentury-appropriate (and space-saving) slider. References to *The Incredibles* are found around the room. If you're looking at photos of these rooms online, note that we think they look better in person.

Our main criticism of the Contemporary's look is that it's devoid of imagination. It's no secret that Disney tries to shoehorn characters into every available space, whether they're needed or not. It's also not a secret that Disney cuts corners by standardizing everything, like the same white bedspreads in every room in every resort. In some cases, like the new rooms at **Disney's Polynesian Village Resort** (see page 112), this can all still result in interesting rooms whose design melds with the resort's overall look and feel.

But at the Contemporary, Disney had the opportunity to transform it into one of America's great midcentury-themed hotels, and it didn't. Instead, it recycled the same generic ideas it has been putting into every recent hotel. Compare the look of the rooms themselves to the midcentury masterpiece Steakhouse 71 in the same building. That restaurant pops with a uniquely Disney but decidedly stylish feel. We wish the same vibe extended throughout the resort and the rooms.

What's the point of being a storytelling company if you're phoning it in at your flagship hotels?

Dining options abound at the Contemporary. On the first floor is **Steakhouse 71,** specializing in grilled meats. The counter-service **Contempo Café** on the fourth floor's Grand Canyon Concourse serves upscale sandwiches, salads, and flatbread pizzas. **Chef Mickey's,** also on the fourth floor, hosts a popular character buffet. On the 15th floor, **California Grill** serves sophisticated contemporary American cuisine.

The pool has slides for kids and cabanas for rent. The Contemporary is within easy walking distance of the Magic Kingdom; monorail transportation is available to both the Magic Kingdom and EPCOT. Other destinations can be accessed by bus or boat. Walking time to transportation loading areas is 6–9 minutes or less.

GOOD (AND NOT-SO-GOOD) ROOMS AT THE CONTEMPORARY RESORT *(See* theugseries.com/contemporary-views *for photos.)* Rooms in the A-frame building overlook either Bay Lake on one side or the parking lot, with Seven Seas Lagoon and the Magic Kingdom in the background, on the other. Except for most second- and third-floor rooms in the Garden Wing, all have balconies. If you stay on the Magic Kingdom side, ask for a room on the ninth floor or higher, where the views of the parking lot are less distracting. On the Bay Lake side, the view is fine from all floors, though higher floors are preferable.

In the Garden Wing, all ground-floor rooms have patios. Only end rooms on the second and third floors facing Bay Lake have full balconies; all other rooms have balconies that are just a foot deep. Keep in mind that the Garden Wing is a fair walk from the restaurants, shops, front desk, guest services, and monorail station in the A-frame. This makes them more peaceful but less convenient.

There's a lot of boat traffic in the lake and canal alongside the Garden Wing. Nearest the lake, and quietest, are rooms **6116–6123, 6216–6223,** and **6316–6323.** At the water's edge, but noisier, are rooms **6107–6115, 6207–6215,** and **6307–6315.** Flanking the canal connecting Bay Lake and Seven Seas Lagoon are rooms **5128–5151, 5228–5251,** and **5328–5351.** All of these have nice canal and lake views, which subject them to some daytime noise from passing watercraft, but the whole area is exceptionally quiet at night.

Avoid rooms ending with numbers **52–70;** almost all of these look directly onto a parking lot.

BAY LAKE TOWER AT DISNEY'S CONTEMPORARY RESORT

Unofficial Guide Reader-Survey Results

Percentage of readers who'd stay here again	90% *(Average)*
Percentage of readers who'd recommend this resort to a friend	70% *(Average)*
Overall reader rating	A–

OPENED IN 2009, this 15-story, 295-unit DVC resort consists of studios and one- and two-bedroom villas, as well as two-story, three-bedroom Grand Villas with views of Bay Lake and the Magic Kingdom. Laid out in a semicircle, Bay Lake Tower is connected to the Contemporary by an elevated, covered outdoor walkway and shares the main resort's monorail service.

Rooms have flat-screen TVs, minifridges, microwaves, and coffee makers. Brightly colored accessories, paintings, and accent walls complement an otherwise-neutral color scheme. Wood tables and granite countertops add a natural touch. Each room has a private balcony or patio. Rooms we've tested here rank as the quietest on Disney property.

Studios sleep up to four people and include one queen-size bed and one double sleeper sofa. The part of the studio with the bed, sofa, and TV measures about 170 square feet and feels small with even two people; four would be a squeeze.

One-bedroom villas sleep five people (the living room's chair and sofa fold out to sleep three) and provide a formal kitchen, a second bathroom, and a living room in addition to the studio bedroom.

The two-bedroom villas sleep nine and include all the kitchen amenities found in a one-bedroom, plus an extra bathroom. One of the baths is attached to a second bedroom with two queen beds or a queen plus a sleeper-size sofa. As with the one-bedrooms, a sofa bed and sleeper chair in the living room provide extra places to snooze, though they're best suited for small children. Bathrooms in the two-bedroom villas are a bit more spacious than those in the one-bedrooms.

The two-story Grand Villas sleep 12 and include four bathrooms, the same main-bedroom layout, and two bedrooms with two queen beds apiece. An upstairs seating area overlooking the main floor provides a sleeper sofa and chair. Two-story windows offer unparalleled views of Bay Lake or the Magic Kingdom—with prices to match.

Bay Lake Tower has its own check-in desk, as well as its own private pool and pool bar, plus a small fire pit on the beach. Its **Top of the World Lounge** is one of the best bars on Disney property, and it admits only DVC owners and their guests.

A 1-mile jogging path loops around Bay Lake Tower and the Contemporary's Garden Wing. Dining, transportation, and other recreational activities are shared with the Contemporary Resort.

Readers give Bay Lake an A rating for its room quality. This Minnesota family of four loved the views:

We had a studio with a Magic Kingdom view. The balcony was a private oasis where my husband and I would relax and watch the fireworks together after the kids were asleep. On our second night he looked at me and said, "We're always going to stay here."

GOOD (AND NOT-SO-GOOD) ROOMS AT BAY LAKE TOWER *(See* theug series.com/blt-views *for photos.)* If you're paying for a Magic Kingdom view, request a room on an upper level—above the seventh floor, at least—so you're not looking out at the parking lot. Even-numbered rooms **XX06–XX16** have the best viewing angle of the park. Rooms **XX24–XX30** may technically be described as having theme park views, but they're angled toward the Contemporary, and you have to turn the other way to see the park.

The rooms on the lake side of Bay Lake Tower have views of EPCOT's fireworks and more, as a reader from Washington found out:

I could watch the fireworks from our balcony (OK, the bed), and that was cool, but really the best part was being able to see Spaceship Earth lit up. Beautiful! More of this, please, Disney.

Shades of Green

(See theugseries.com/ug-shades for extended coverage.)

STRENGTHS	WEAKNESSES
• Large guest rooms	• No theming and nondescript room décor
• Discount tickets and rooms for military personnel with ID	• Limited on-site dining
• Quiet setting	• Limited bus service
• Views of golf course from guest rooms	• Daily parking fee ($17)
• Convenient self-parking	• No free parking at theme parks
• Swimming complex, fitness center	

Unofficial Guide **Reader-Survey Results**

Percentage of readers who'd stay here again	92% *(Average)*
Percentage of readers who'd recommend this resort to a friend	71% *(Average)*
Overall reader rating	A

ORIGINALLY OWNED BY DISNEY, Shades of Green was called The Golf Resort when it opened in 1973 and was renamed The Disney Inn in 1986. In 1994 Disney reached an agreement with the U.S. Army Family and Morale, Welfare, and Recreation Command (Army MWR) to lease the property as an official Armed Forces Recreation Center. In 1996 the Army MWR purchased the property outright; Disney still owns the land on which the resort is located.

Shades of Green is open to active and retired US service members (including reservists) and their families, among other qualifying groups. Civilians may accompany eligible military personnel as their guests. (For details, see shadesofgreen.org/about-shades-green /eligibility.) If you're planning a holiday visit or a long weekend here, book as early as possible—up to seven months in advance. Guests at Shades of Green are eligible for Disney's Early Theme Park Entry and Extended Evening Hours.

Shades of Green consists of one three-story and one five-story building nestled among three golf courses that are open to Disney guests. At 455 square feet each, the 586 guest rooms at Shades of Green are some of the largest on-property.

The resort's website states that Shades of Green is comparable to a Disney Deluxe resort. While the rooms are large and immaculately maintained—not to mention a great value for those who qualify to stay here—it lacks the wow factor found at many Deluxe resorts. The dining options and transportation are adequate. Service, on the other hand, is great—definitely up to the Deluxe standard.

Standard rooms have two queen-size beds, a single sleeper sofa, a minifridge, a table and two chairs, and a TV. Junior suites sleep six with three queen beds, one in the living area. Family suites sleep eight with three queen sleeper sofas and a king bed; these suites also have two bathrooms. All rooms have a patio or balcony.

A mom from Indiana makes the case for exploring all of your lodging options:

> *While it's true that SOG is often a good deal, military families should still do some comparison shopping. Room rates are tiered based on rank—the higher your rank, the higher the rate. Definitely check into*

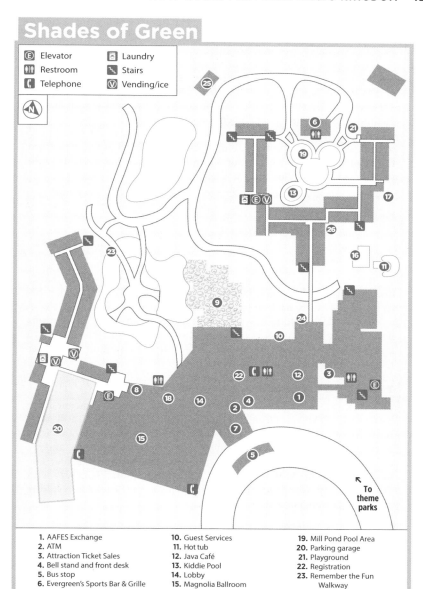

Shades of Green

E	Elevator	Laundry	Laundry
Restroom	Restroom	Stairs	Stairs
Telephone	Telephone	V	Vending/ice

1. AAFES Exchange
2. ATM
3. Attraction Ticket Sales
4. Bell stand and front desk
5. Bus stop
6. Evergreen's Sports Bar & Grille
7. Express Café
8. Fitness Center
9. The Garden Gallery Restaurant
10. Guest Services
11. Hot tub
12. Java Café
13. Kiddie Pool
14. Lobby
15. Magnolia Ballroom
16. Magnolia Pool Area
17. Magnolia Spa
18. Mangino's Bistro/Bistro To Go
19. Mill Pond Pool Area
20. Parking garage
21. Playground
22. Registration
23. Remember the Fun Walkway
24. Sales & Marketing
25. Tennis courts
26. Yoga room

military rates at Disney properties, and also check out the **Armed Forces Vacation Club** for condos near WDW [see afvclub.com for participating Orlando-area properties]. We rented a two-bedroom, two-bath condo with a full kitchen and pool for seven nights, and it cost us less than two nights at a Disney hotel.

Shades of Green has two pools. The **Mill Pond Pool** features a tiered waterslide, while the **Magnolia Pool** has a zero-entry feature as well as a splash-and-play area and hot tubs.

Restaurants include **Mangino's,** an Italian eatery; the **Garden Gallery** buffet; two quick-service options (**Express Café** and **Java Café**); and **Evergreen's,** a sports bar and grill. The **Army & Air Force Exchange Service** sells Disney merchandise in addition to snacks, soft drinks, alcohol, tobacco, and over-the-counter medicines.

Transportation to all theme parks is by bus; a transfer is required to almost all destinations. Walking time to the bus-loading area from the most remote rooms is about 5 minutes. Readers such as this Ohio woman report that bus service is a sore spot:

Please, please, please stress to your readers how awful the transportation system is—there is no direct access to the Magic Kingdom or EPCOT, and the buses that go directly to the other parks run only once an hour. If you want to go back to your room midday, plan for an hour to an hour and a half of travel time there and then back to the park.

Shades of Green used to have a walking path to the Magic Kingdom, but it has closed and is not expected to reopen. We consider this to be a major drawback in terms of transportation.

You don't have to worry much about bad room views or locations here: Except for a small percentage that overlook the entrance road and parking lot, most offer views of the surrounding golf courses or the swimming area.

THE EPCOT RESORTS

THE EPCOT RESORTS ARE POSITIONED around Crescent Lake between EPCOT and Disney's Hollywood Studios (closer to EPCOT). Both theme parks are accessible by boat, via Skyliner, and on foot. None of the resorts offer transportation to EPCOT's main entrance, and it's 0.7–1.1 miles to walk there, depending on the hotel and route. The **Skyliner** (see page 344) connects EPCOT's International Gateway with Disney's Hollywood Studios. If you're staying at the Beach Club, taking the Skyliner may be faster than walking.

Disney's Yacht & Beach Club Resorts and Beach Club Villas
(See **theugseries.com/ug-yacht, theugseries.com/ug-beach,** *and* **theugseries .com/bc-villas** *for extended coverage.)*

STRENGTHS	WEAKNESSES
• Best pool complex of any WDW resort	• Views and balcony size are hit-or-miss
• Walking distance to EPCOT's International Gateway	• Bus service to Magic Kingdom, Animal Kingdom, water parks, and Disney Springs is shared with other EPCOT resorts
• Boat and Skyliner transportation to DHS	• No three-bedroom Grand Villas
• Close to BoardWalk and EPCOT dining	• Villas have fewer baths per bedroom than newer DVC properties and no lake views
• Well-themed public spaces	
• Bright and attractive guest rooms	
• One- and two-bedroom villas offer laundry and kitchen facilities	

Yacht & Beach Club Resorts and Beach Club Villas

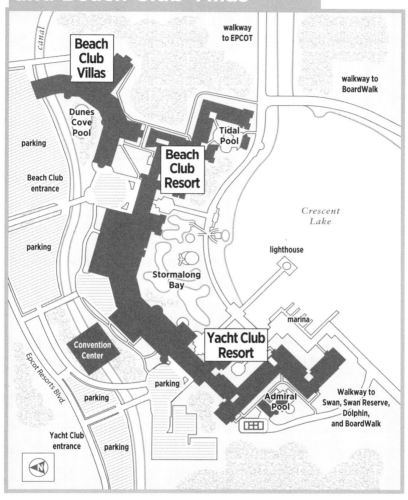

Unofficial Guide **Reader-Survey Results** *(resorts only; see page 129 for villa ratings)*

Percentage of readers who'd stay here again **Yacht: 89%; Beach: 88%** *(both Below Average)*
Percentage of readers who'd recommend to a friend **Yacht: 76%** *(Average)*; **Beach: 63%** *(Below Average)*
Overall reader rating **Yacht: A; Beach: A–**

THESE ADJOINING DELUXE RESORTS are very similar. Both have clapboard facades with whitewashed wood trim. The Yacht Club is painted a subdued gray, the Beach Club a brighter blue. The Yacht Club has a nautical theme with model ships and antique navigational instruments in public areas. The Beach Club has plenty of beach scenes in seafoam green and white. Both have themed lobbies, with a giant globe in the Yacht Club's and sea horse fixtures in the Beach Club's. The resorts face the 25-acre Crescent Lake and share an elaborate swimming complex.

There are 635 rooms and 21 suites at the Yacht Club and 576 rooms at the Beach Club, plus 282 studio and one- and two-bedroom DVC units at the Beach Club Villas. Most rooms are 381 square feet and have two queen-size beds, a sofa, a desk and chair, a dresser, a wall-mounted TV, a minifridge, and a coffee maker. The Yacht Club's rooms are decorated in white, with blue and brass accents and vinyl plank flooring, while the Beach Club's are decked out in summery tans and blues, with carpeted floors. Some rooms have full balconies; many rooms have mini balconies.

The Beach Club Villas evoke seaside Victorian cottages. Studio accommodations have kitchenettes; one- and two-bedroom villas have full kitchens. Like the Yacht Club, the villas have vinyl plank flooring, as well as updated bathrooms. Otherwise, the décor is like the Beach Club's. A reader from California appreciates the Yacht Club's rooms:

The rooms at Yacht Club are lovely. The [hard] floors are not noisy at all—if we had neighbors above us, we never heard them. Soundproofing on the balcony is good.

Both the Yacht Club and the Beach Club provide excellent service. Nine restaurants and lounges are within easy walking distance, and Beach Club has an expanded grab-and-go area for quick snacks.

Transportation from these resorts to other destinations is by bus, boat, or Skyliner. Walking time to the transportation loading areas from the most remote rooms is 7 minutes.

Although the Yacht & Beach Club are situated along Crescent Lake, opposite Disney's BoardWalk, only a relatively small percentage of rooms directly overlook the lake—many additional rooms have lake views from the side but actually face a courtyard or garden. To complicate matters, the resorts don't differentiate between a room with a lake view and one overlooking a swimming pool, pond, or canal. There's only one category for anything wet: water view. To see specific views from these rooms for yourself, go to theugseries.com/yacht-views or theugseries.com/beach-views.

The Beach Club consists of a long main building with several wings protruding toward Crescent Lake. The main building and the various wings range from three to five stories. Most rooms have full or mini balconies or, on the ground floor, patios. Full balconies are big enough for a couple of chairs, while mini balconies are about 6 inches deep. Top-floor rooms often have enclosed balconies set into the roof. Unless you're standing, visibility is somewhat limited from these dormer balconies.

We receive a lot of comments about the Yacht & Beach Club. First, from a Massachusetts mom:

This was the first time we stayed at the Beach Club, and for us, the amazing pool complex was worth the extra money. Several nights we climbed to the top of the waterslide as the sun was setting, and it was an incredible sight—truly a memorable experience!

Another family had a chillier experience, however:

Families with kids should not stay at the Beach Club during the winter. Based on an experience at the Polynesian Village in December, we anticipated that Stormalong Bay would be warm enough to swim in. It was not. This was a terrible disappointment to our kids. The resort's location is divine (I loved walking to France for breakfast), but the pool situation made me bitter about the cost of this place.

GOOD (AND NOT-SO-GOOD) ROOMS AT THE BEACH CLUB RESORT
(See theugseries.com/beach-views *for photos.)* The Beach Club's best views are from rooms that have full balconies and from those that overlook the lake. The woods-facing rooms are the resort's most peaceful accommodations. They are the nearest to EPCOT's International Gateway entrance if you're walking but the farthest from the resort's main pool area, lobby, and restaurants.

Of the remaining rooms, most face courtyards, with some providing oblique views of the lake and others overlooking parking lots and the resort's front entrance.

All room numbers are four digits, with the first digit specifying the floor and the remaining three digits specifying the room number.

Heads-up: The Beach Club will charge you for a water view if there's so much as a birdbath in sight. If you're going to spend the money, get a *real* water view.

- **Water-view rooms with full balconies facing the lake:** Odd-numbered rooms 2641–2645; suite 2647; rooms 3501–3507; odd-numbered rooms 4607–4623, and odd-numbered Club Level rooms 5699–5725

- **Standard-view rooms with full balconies facing the woods and EPCOT:** Even-numbered rooms 2528–2530, 2578–2596, 3512–3530, and 4532–4596

GOOD (AND NOT-SO-GOOD) ROOMS AT THE YACHT CLUB RESORT *(See* theugseries.com/yacht-views *for photos.)* All Yacht Club rooms offer full balconies or, on the ground floor, patios. Rooms with the best views are as follows (the higher the last three digits in the room number, the closer to the lobby, main pool area, and restaurants):

- **Rooms with full balconies facing the lake, with the BoardWalk Inn in the background:** Odd-numbered rooms 2001–2009, 2043–2065, 2123–2137, 2157–2163; 3001–3009, 3043–3065, 3123–3137, 3157–3163; 4057–4065, 4123–4137, 4157–4163; or Club Level rooms 5161, 5163, or 5241

- **Fifth-floor rooms directly facing EPCOT:** 5195–5199 or 5153

- **Standard-view fourth-floor rooms facing EPCOT:** 4195–4199 or 4153

BEACH CLUB VILLAS

Unofficial Guide **Reader-Survey Results**

Percentage of readers who'd stay here again	97% *(Above Average)*
Percentage of readers who'd recommend this resort to a friend	70% *(Average)*
Overall reader rating	A-

THIS DISNEY VACATION CLUB PROPERTY is supposedly inspired by grand Atlantic seaside homes of the early 20th century. But really, there's little to differentiate the Beach Club Villas from the Yacht & Beach Club Resorts, or from the parts of the BoardWalk Inn & Villas that aren't on the BoardWalk.

Configured roughly in the shape of a fat slingshot, the Beach Club Villas are set back away from the lake adjoining the front of the Beach Club Resort. Arrayed in connected four- and five-story taffy-blue sections topped with cupolas, the villas are adorned with white woodwork and slat-railed balconies. The effect is clean and breezy but not much else.

Studios have a kitchenette, a queen bed, a single pull-down bed, and a Murphy bed, and one- and two-bedroom villas have full kitchens. The rooms are a bit small but attractively decorated in blues and corals after a refurbishment completed in late 2023.

The Beach Club Villas have their own modest swimming pool but otherwise share the restaurants, facilities, and transportation options of the adjoining Yacht & Beach Club Resorts. The villas' biggest weakness is that they offer no lake views.

GOOD (AND NOT-SO-GOOD) ROOMS AT THE BEACH CLUB VILLAS *(See* **theugseries.com/bc-villas-views** *for photos.)* Although the studios and villas are attractive and livable, the location of the Beach Club Villas—between parking lots, roads, and canals—leaves much to be desired. Only southeast-facing rooms provide both a scenic landscape (woods) and relative relief from traffic noise. The noise probably won't bother you if you're indoors with the balcony door closed, but for the money you pay to stay at the villas, you can easily find nicer, quieter accommodations elsewhere on Disney property. If you choose to stay at the Beach Club Villas, go for odd-numbered rooms **225–251, 325–351, 425–451,** and **525–551.**

Disney's BoardWalk Inn & Villas
(See **theugseries.com/bw-inn** *and* **theugseries.com/bw-villas** *for extended coverage.)*

STRENGTHS	WEAKNESSES
• Walking distance to EPCOT's International Gateway and Disney's Hollywood Studios	• Long, confusing hallways
• Excellent staff/service	• Limited quick-service dining options suitable for kids
• Unique garden suites	• Not as many rooms overlook the BoardWalk as you might think
• Great dining options for adults	• Bus service to Magic Kingdom, Animal Kingdom, water parks, and Disney Springs is shared with other EPCOT resorts
• Large fitness center	
• Room refurbishment planned	• BoardWalk Villas have fewer baths per bedroom than newer DVC properties

Unofficial Guide **Reader-Survey Results** *(inn only; see page 133 for villa ratings)*

Percentage of readers who'd stay here again	87% *(Below Average)*
Percentage of readers who'd recommend this resort to a friend	61% *(Below Average)*
Overall reader rating	A–

ON CRESCENT LAKE ACROSS from the Yacht & Beach Club, the BoardWalk Inn is another of Disney's Deluxe resorts. The complex is a detailed replica of an early-20th-century East Coast beach boardwalk. Facades of hotels, diners, and shops create an inviting and exciting waterfront skyline.

In reality, the BoardWalk Inn & Villas comprise a single integrated structure behind the facades. Restaurants and shops occupy the

BoardWalk Inn & Villas

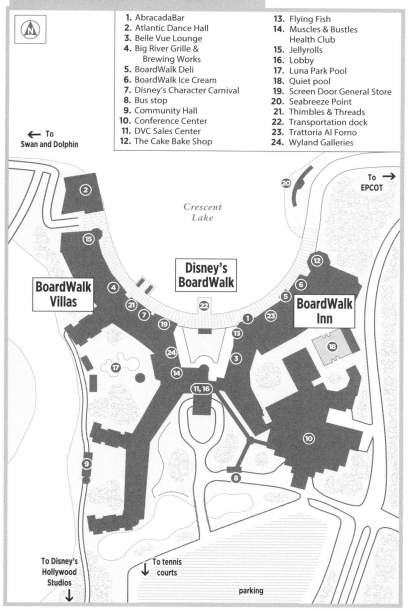

1. AbracadaBar
2. Atlantic Dance Hall
3. Belle Vue Lounge
4. Big River Grille & Brewing Works
5. BoardWalk Deli
6. BoardWalk Ice Cream
7. Disney's Character Carnival
8. Bus stop
9. Community Hall
10. Conference Center
11. DVC Sales Center
12. The Cake Bake Shop
13. Flying Fish
14. Muscles & Bustles Health Club
15. Jellyrolls
16. Lobby
17. Luna Park Pool
18. Quiet pool
19. Screen Door General Store
20. Seabreeze Point
21. Thimbles & Threads
22. Transportation dock
23. Trattoria Al Forno
24. Wyland Galleries

← To Swan and Dolphin

To → EPCOT

Crescent Lake

Disney's BoardWalk

BoardWalk Villas

BoardWalk Inn

To Disney's Hollywood Studios ↓

↓ To tennis courts

parking

boardwalk level, while accommodations rise to six stories above. The inn and villas share a pool featuring an old-fashioned amusement park theme; there are also two quiet pools for adults.

The inn's 378 Deluxe rooms measure 371 square feet each. Most have two queen beds, an upholstered daybed, a minifridge, a coffee maker, and a ceiling fan. The décor, updated in 2023, includes yellow wallpaper, vinyl plank flooring, and neutral curtains. Closet space exceeds that of rooms in other Deluxe resorts. Most rooms have balconies.

A new bakery, **The Cake Bake Shop** by Gwendolyn Rogers, will open in 2024 along the lakefront BoardWalk.

The complex is within walking distance of EPCOT and is connected to other destinations by bus and boat. Walking time to transportation loading areas from the most remote rooms is 5–6 minutes. It's about a 5-minute walk to the Skyliner's International Gateway station at EPCOT, if you'd rather use that to get to the Studios. If you're thinking about walking to the Studios, consider this tip from an Ontario reader:

When staying at BoardWalk, if you choose a room in the wing closest to the path to DHS, you have to walk back to the lobby to use the elevators. That negates the advantage of selecting a room close to DHS.

An Iowa family was surprised by the low number of rooms on the actual BoardWalk:

We were surprised that so relatively few rooms at the BoardWalk Inn have interesting views. The one couple in our group who actually had a view of the BoardWalk said it was noisy.

GOOD (AND NOT-SO-GOOD) ROOMS AT THE BOARDWALK INN *(See* theugseries.com/bw-inn-views *for photos.)* If you book a BoardWalk room through Disney's agents or website, *water view* means Crescent Lake and the BoardWalk area; views of the canal or pool are considered resort view. But if you book a villa through a DVC member or the DVC website, the same canal and pool are called standard, garden, or pool view, and the view of the BoardWalk is called BoardWalk view.

Most rooms have a balcony or patio, although balconies on the standard upper-floor rooms alternate between large and medium. The BoardWalk Inn & Villas each share about half the frontage on the promenade, which overlooks Crescent Lake. The promenade's clubs, stores, and attractions are spread about equally between the two sections, leading to similar levels of noise and commotion. However, the inn side is closer to EPCOT and the nearby access road; this means easier access to that theme park, but also more road noise. Otherwise, the inn is actually less noisy than the more expensive villas; there's one tranquil, enclosed courtyard and another half-enclosed area with a quiet pool (where BoardWalk's Garden Suites are located).

There are many rooms to avoid at the inn, starting with rooms overlooking the access roads and parking lots, and rooms looking down onto the roof of the resort's adjacent conference center. And although the aforementioned quiet rooms face courtyards, the views are pretty ho-hum. When you get right down to it, the only rooms with decent views are those fronting the promenade and lake, specifically odd-numbered rooms **3213–3259** and **4213–4259**. We're told by Disney insiders that most of these rooms are reserved more than 10 months ahead.

BOARDWALK VILLAS

Unofficial Guide Reader-Survey Results

Percentage of readers who'd stay here again	92% (*Average*)
Percentage of readers who'd recommend this resort to a friend	68% (*Average*)
Overall reader rating	A-

THE 532 BOARDWALK VILLAS are decorated in white, tan, and blue (popular colors along Crescent Lake), with white tile in the kitchens and baths. Villas measure 412–2,491 square feet (studio through three-bedroom) and sleep 4–12. Many villas have full kitchens, laundry rooms, and whirlpool tubs; most rooms have balconies. The studio and two-bedroom units tend to be pricier than similar accommodations at Old Key West and Saratoga Springs Resorts—you're paying for the location.

GOOD (AND NOT-SO-GOOD) ROOMS AT THE BOARDWALK VILLAS *(See* **theugseries.com/bw-villas-views** *for photos.)* As at the inn, the villas offer only a handful of rooms with good views. Odd-numbered rooms **3001–3047, 4001–4047,** and **5001–5047** afford dynamic views of the promenade and Crescent Lake, with EPCOT in the background. Rooms **X05, X07, X13, X15, X29,** and **X31** are studios. They're a little noisy if you open your balcony door but otherwise offer a glimpse of one of Walt Disney World's more happening places.

Promenade-facing villa rooms have the same noise issues as their inn counterparts. The midsection of the canal-facing villas looks out onto the **Luna Park Pool,** which gets extremely noisy during the day. Some quieter villas located away from the promenade have views of the canal and a partially enclosed quiet pool. Rooms on the opposite side of this wing are almost as quiet, but they face the parking lot.

Walt Disney World Swan, Dolphin, and Swan Reserve

(See **theugseries.com/swan** *and* **theugseries.com/dolphin,** *and* **theugseries .com/swan-reserve** *for extended coverage.)*

QUICK TAKE: *A respectable percentage of readers said they would stay here again; all things considered, however, these resorts rate below average among Disney resorts. If you're spending your own money versus using Marriott points, we recommend almost any other Moderate, Deluxe, or DVC resort over these.*

STRENGTHS	WEAKNESSES
• Best-priced location on Crescent Lake	• Presence of conventioneers may be off-putting to vacationing families
• The hotels participate in Marriott's loyalty program	• Daily resort fee ($45/night, plus tax) and parking fee ($35/night)
• Good on-site and nearby dining	• No Disney Dining Plan
• Only hotels within walking distance to minigolf (Fantasia Gardens)	• Non-Disney bus service runs less often than that of other resorts
• Large variety of upscale restaurants	• Architecture that was on the cutting edge decades ago now looks dated and cheesy (Swan, Dolphin)
• On-site car rental (Alamo, National)	
• Very nice pool complex	• Self-parking is quite distant from the hotels' entrances
• Impressive public spaces	• Tiny bathrooms (Swan)
• Walking distance to EPCOT's International Gateway and Disney's Hollywood Studios	• Spotty front-desk service and housekeeping (Swan)

Unofficial Guide Reader-Survey Results

Percentage of readers who'd stay here again **Swan: 88%** (*Below Average*); **Dolphin: 83%** (*Below Average*); **Swan Reserve: 100%** (*Above Average*)
Percentage of readers who'd recommend this resort to a friend **Swan: 63%** (*Below Average*); **Dolphin: 54%** (*Below Average*); **Swan Reserve: 86%** (*Above Average*)
Overall reader rating **Swan: B+; Dolphin: B; Swan Reserve: A+**

OPENED IN 1990, THE SWAN AND DOLPHIN face each other on either side of an inlet of Crescent Lake. The Swan Reserve is located across the street. Although they're inside Walt Disney World and Disney handles their reservations, they are independently managed and can also be booked directly at swandolphin.com or marriott.com. Because these hotels aren't run by Disney, service is less relentlessly "magical" than you'll find at other resorts.

All three resorts are served by bus transportation to the theme parks and participate in Early Entry and Extended Evening Hours, but they don't participate in the Disney Dining Plan.

The Dolphin's main building is a 27-story turquoise triangle. This central building, with large wings extending from both sides and four smaller arms from its rear, is attached to a large conference center. Perched on the roof, at the edge of each main wing, are two 56-foot-tall dolphins with their tails in the air. The Swan's gently arching main building rises 12 stories and is flanked by two 7-story towers, with two 47-foot-tall swans adorning its roof.

The last renovation of the hotels' guest rooms and lobby areas was completed in 2018, when the rooms received new bedding and carpets, more electrical outlets, new AC units, and new TVs. The Dolphin's lobby also got a larger bar area, **Phins,** and a grab-and-go restaurant, **Fuel.**

The Dolphin's rooms incorporate light wood, gray carpeting, and taupe draperies. Oversize upholstered headboards frame the plush Westin Heavenly Beds, and minimal art adorns the walls. A dresser and a desk with a chair round out the furnishings. Note that the Dolphin's beds are either doubles or kings (no queens). All rooms at the Dolphin have coffee makers, and some have balconies. The baths in most rooms have step-in showers.

The Swan's standard rooms are similar to but more attractive than the Dolphin's. Queen- or king-size Heavenly Beds make for ultra-comfy sleeping. A flat-screen TV sits on the dresser. The bathrooms—small for Disney—have step-in showers and limited counter space.

Be warned: Both resorts will nickel-and-dime you to death. Each tacks on a $45-per-day resort fee and another $35 per day for self-parking. Whatever rate you're quoted at either resort, count on another $100 per day in miscellaneous fees.

The two hotels collectively house more than a dozen restaurants and lounges and are within easy walking distance of EPCOT and the BoardWalk. They're also connected to other destinations by bus and boat. Walking time from the most remote rooms to the transportation loading areas is 7–9 minutes.

Regarding transportation, the Swan and Dolphin don't use Disney bus transportation between their hotels and Disney's theme parks and water parks. Buses going to the Magic Kingdom will drop you off

Swan, Swan Reserve & Dolphin

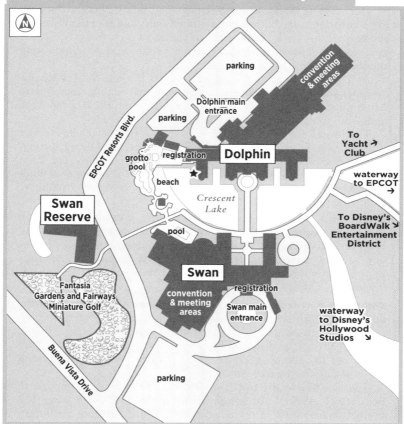

at the Transportation and Ticket Center, where you'll have to take a boat, monorail, or bus to get to the Magic Kingdom (Disney buses will drop you off right at the park entrance). These readers from Texas say the Swan is the slightly easier of the two to navigate:

> While the Dolphin is closer to EPCOT, we prefer the Swan because it's easier and more straightforward to walk from the hotel to the park and vice versa. The Dolphin has a very narrow, winding sidewalk that doesn't look like it gets much traffic.

This New Hampshire couple gives the pool complex high marks:

> Neither the Disney nor the Swan and Dolphin website depicts how great the pool complex is. Not only are there multiple pools, a waterslide, and maybe the best poolside bar in all of Disney World, there's also a wonderfully green, restful grotto-in-tropical-forest theme.

SWAN RESERVE This 14-story hotel opened in 2021 and is adjacent to Disney's Fantasia Gardens and Fairways minigolf course. It has 349 guest rooms and suites, some with views of either EPCOT or

Hollywood Studios. Standard rooms sleep four and are around 330 square feet, roughly the same as a Disney Moderate.

Our stays at the Swan Reserve have had mixed results. The beds are comfortable, the bathrooms are functional, and it's possible to see theme park fireworks from some of the rooms. However, we could hear normal-volume conversations from a room next door, indicating the soundproofing here isn't great.

As a smaller resort, the Swan Reserve has just one full-service restaurant, **Amare**. That can be a problem on busy nights, since Amare handles its own restaurant orders, plus those from the bar, the pool, and room service. Still, it gets stellar reviews from readers.

The Swan Reserve has a stylish pool and a fitness center. Bus service is provided to Disney's theme parks, water parks, and Disney Springs, and the Swan and Dolphin are a short walk across the street. Even though it's a slightly longer walk to the parks or the bigger pool complex, we love the newer rooms and smaller size of the Swan Reserve compared to the Swan or Dolphin.

GOOD (AND NOT-SO-GOOD) ROOMS AT THE SWAN AND DOLPHIN
Note: The Swan and Dolphin are configured very differently, and because of their irregular shapes, it's easier to discuss groups of rooms in relation to exterior landmarks and compass directions rather than by room numbers. When speaking with a reservationist, use the following tips and descriptions.

THE SWAN East-facing rooms offer prime views, particularly in the upper half of the seven-story wing above Il Mulino restaurant. From this vantage point, you overlook a canal and Disney's BoardWalk, with EPCOT in the distance. Balcony rooms on floors five, six, and seven cost an additional $50 or more per night. The best rooms with views of EPCOT are **626** and **726**.

The worst views are from the **west-facing rooms** above the fourth floor, which overlook the unsightly roof of the hotel's west wing. The northernmost rooms in the wing directly above Kimonos restaurant are an exception—their balconies overlook the pool and the beach on Crescent Lake's western shore. Rooms **680–691** offer nice pool views.

Above the Swan's main entrance, **south-facing rooms** overlook the parking lot, with forest and Hollywood Studios in the distance. However, the canal is also visible to the east. These rooms lack balconies.

THE DOLPHIN If you want a view of something besides a parking lot, your choices are relatively few. Rooms with pleasant views are in **the four arms on the rear of the building.** Rooms on all arms have balconies on floors one through four, and alternating balconies or windows on floors five through nine.

One of the Dolphin's best views overlooks the **Grotto Pool,** on the far west side of the building. An artificial beach with a small waterfall is visible from rooms at the very end of the large west wing. None of these rooms have a balcony.

The **Crescent Lake** side of arm four and the small jut of the large Dolphin wing perpendicular to it offer arguably the best views. You have an unobstructed view of the lake and EPCOT fireworks; a fine BoardWalk view for people-watching; and, from higher floors, a view of the beach at Beach Club. There's ferry noise, but these rooms still have the most going for them. The best of the best in this arm are rooms **8015, 7015, 5015, 4015,** and **3015.**

Disney's Caribbean Beach Resort

(See map on next page; see theugseries.com/caribbean *for extended coverage.)*

STRENGTHS	WEAKNESSES
• Colorful Caribbean theme	• Check-in is far from most of the resort
• Lakefront setting	• Dining gets low marks from readers
• Large food court	• Multiple bus stops make it slow to go to Disney Springs, Animal Kingdom, and Magic Kingdom
• Child-size Murphy beds in select rooms increase capacity to 5 people	• Some "villages" are a good distance from restaurants and shops
	• No elevators

Unofficial Guide **Reader-Survey Results**

Percentage of readers who'd stay here again	**94%** *(Average)*
Percentage of readers who'd recommend this resort to a friend	**59%** *(Below Average)*
Overall reader rating	**A−**

OPENED IN 1998, CARIBBEAN BEACH WAS DISNEY'S first Moderate resort. It has two dozen colorful, two-story motel-style buildings, separated into five areas named for Caribbean islands: **Aruba, Barbados, Jamaica, Martinique,** and **Trinidad.**

Most of the 1,536 guest rooms measure 314 square feet and are outfitted with two queen beds; a fold-down Murphy bed is also available in select rooms. In most rooms, décor is distinguished by neutral beach tones, bright tropical accent colors, and furnishings of dark wood and rattan. Sliding doors separate the vanity area from the main room, and the toilet and shower are behind another door, allowing three people to dress in privacy at once. All rooms have a dresser, a small table with chairs, a minifridge, a coffee maker, a TV, and plenty of storage. The rooms don't have private balconies because the front doors open to the outside.

Rooms in Trinidad (which used to be pirate-themed) have been more recently refurbished. These have lighter, brighter colors and a new room layout. Instead of two beds, these rooms have one fixed bed, one foldout sofa, and a fold-down child sleeper. This frees up space in the room during the day, making it appear larger (and making it easier to walk around in). Bathrooms, storage, and lighting have all been improved. If you're staying here, ask for an updated room.

The **Old Port Royale** building houses the check-in desk, restaurants, and shops. A food court has counter-service and grab-and-go options; **Sebastian's Bistro** is a sit-down restaurant with waterfront tables. Caribbean Beach's on-site dining remains a weakness with readers. But if you stay in sections near the Riviera Resort, you can walk to the highly rated dining there.

Caribbean Beach offers transportation to all Disney World destinations by bus and to EPCOT and the Studios by **Skyliner.** Caribbean Beach has access to two Skyliner stations: one south of Jamaica and one north of Aruba at the Riviera.

Caribbean Beach Resort & Riviera Resort

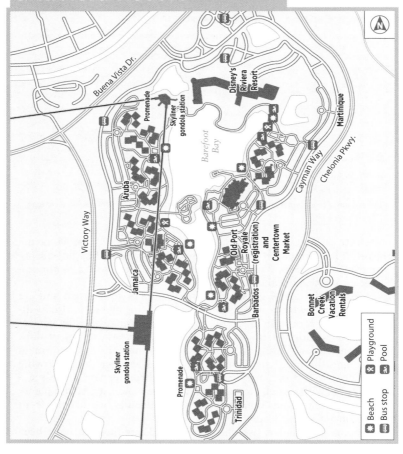

Walking time to the transportation-loading area from Caribbean Beach's most remote rooms is 7–9 minutes, and readers rate Disney bus service here as below average. Seriously consider bringing a car—this 20-something couple from Missouri wished they had:

> Caribbean Beach's bus service is horrendous. It often felt like there was only one bus running at a time, and we experienced several 30-plus-minute waits. The bus circled the entire resort—which is huge—before it headed out, so if you were unlucky enough to be at one of the last stops during a rush to the parks, the bus would pass right by if it was full. On multiple occasions, we arrived at the bus stop an hour or more before our dining reservations, but we still found ourselves running past the park gates to make it to the restaurant on time!

GOOD (AND NOT-SO-GOOD) ROOMS AT CARIBBEAN BEACH RESORT *(See* **theugseries.com/caribbean-views** *for photos.)* The five "islands," or groups of buildings clustered around Barefoot Bay, are identical. The two-story motel-style structures are arranged in various ways to face courtyards, pools, the bay, and so forth. The landscaping features lots of ferns and palm trees, especially in the courtyards.

In general, corner rooms are preferable because they have more windows. Beyond that, your choice depends on how close you want to be to Old Port Royale's check-in desk and restaurants, the Skyliner, pools, parking lots, or beaches on Barefoot Bay. Each island has direct access to at least one beach, playground, bus stop, and parking lot.

Martinique, next to the main pool and playground at Old Port Royale, is also close to the Riviera and its superior dining options.

Aruba and **Jamaica** are similar to Martinique, but guests must cross a footbridge from here to Old Port Royale. Aruba buildings 54, 55, and 56, along with Jamaica building 41, are closest to the two Skyliner stations. Jamaica building 43, also close to the Skyliner, is the highest-rated building at Caribbean Beach.

With just three buildings, **Barbados** gets noise from surrounding roads and from rambunctious kids at Old Port Royale next door.

The quietest island, and the farthest from resort facilities, is **Trinidad.** It has its own playground, and its beach looks across Barefoot Bay onto wild, undeveloped Florida forest—a rarity on Disney property.

When it comes to views, what you want is a **bay view.** Rooms that fill the bill are **4246–4252** in **Jamaica** or **5256–5260** and **5541–5548** (but not 5542 or 5545) in **Aruba.** If you don't mind the sun in your eyes during early evening, rooms **2254–2256, 2413–2416,** and **2445–2448** in Martinique are good bets, as are lake-facing rooms **3533–3534, 3853–3858,** and **3949** in Trinidad.

Disney's Riviera Resort
(See **theugseries.com/riviera** *for extended coverage.)*

STRENGTHS	WEAKNESSES
• Stylish, well-appointed rooms	• Expensive
• Skyliner to EPCOT and Hollywood Studios	• Tower studios are small and dark
• On-site dining and bar	
• Children's play area near main pool	

Unofficial Guide Reader-Survey Results

Percentage of readers who'd stay here again	97% *(Above Average)*
Percentage of readers who'd recommend this resort to a friend	85% *(Above Average)*
Overall reader rating	A

THE RIVIERA IS ONE OF THE TOP-RATED resorts in Walt Disney World. Themed like a glamorous beach resort in the South of France, it has 300 guest rooms, including studios and one-, two-, and three-bedroom villas, spread over nine floors. Although it's adjacent to Caribbean Beach, a Moderate resort, Disney has designed the Riviera to be as upscale as the Grand Floridian—with service, amenities, and prices to match.

Rooms at the Riviera are some of our favorites at Disney World, with white walls and off-white accents, beige carpets, and furniture in neutral tones. Vinyl plank flooring in a herringbone pattern covers the floors, except in the bedrooms, which have carpet. As is the case at other DVC resorts, deluxe studio accommodations have kitchenettes, while the one-, two-, and three-bedroom villas have full kitchens. The villas are bright, comfortable, and modern, even if the theme is understated.

The Riviera has a unique room type among DVC resorts that we don't recommend: the **tower studio,** which accommodates two guests. These rooms measure about 225 square feet—the smallest on Disney property—small enough that they require the bed to fold into the wall when not in use. These are just *too* small. If more than two people are staying in the room, one of you will feel the need to escape to the bathroom for some space. Tower studio rooms are also dim during the day and dismal at night. The most cheerful space is the bathroom because of the better lighting. There's little doubt that these are the worst rooms for the money in Walt Disney World.

The Riviera boasts easy access to EPCOT and Hollywood Studios. It sits about 1,500 feet from World Showcase, giving park-facing rooms on high floors excellent views of the evening entertainment at both EPCOT and the Studios. Its restaurants have similar views.

Disney charges a premium for these views: Depending on date and view, rates run $443–$814 per night for the undesirable tower studios; $665–$1,250 for deluxe studios; $934–$1,800 for one-bedroom villas; $1,477–$2,800 for two-bedroom units; and $2,956–$5,165 for three-bedroom villas.

The Riviera's restaurants include **Primo Piatto,** an excellent counter-service eatery with grab-and-go options; **Le Petit Café,** which serves coffee and pastries in the morning and wine in the evening; and **Bar Riva,** an upscale pool bar. **Topolino's Terrace,** the table-service restaurant, is a Disney Signature venue that serves fixed-price character breakfasts for kids (this is one of our family's favorites) and upscale dinners for grown-ups.

Other amenities include two pools and a fitness center. The main **Riviera Pool** offers play areas for children, while the **Beau Soleil Pool** is the quiet pool. Riviera Resort is connected to EPCOT and Disney's Hollywood Studios by **Skyliner** and to the rest of the World by bus.

THE BONNET CREEK RESORTS

Not to be confused with the Disney resorts that follow, the **Bonnet Creek Resort** *is a 70-acre hotel, golf, and convention complex located along Bonnet Creek. Although it's adjacent to and accessible from Walt Disney World, the resort is not owned by Disney.*

Disney's Saratoga Springs Resort & Spa and Treehouse Villas at Disney's Saratoga Springs Resort & Spa

(See map of Treehouse Villas on page 144; see **theugseries.com/saratoga** and **theugseries.com/treehouse** for extended coverage.)

SARATOGA SPRINGS, A DVC RESORT, has a theme described by Disney as recalling a Victorian-era retreat in upstate New York. Its 1,260 studio and one-, two-, and three-bedroom villas are located across the lake from Disney Springs. Most buildings were constructed around 2004, while the fitness center and check-in building are older. An

Saratoga Springs Resort & Spa

ACCOMMODATIONS
1. The Carousel (7101–7836)
2. Congress Park (1101–2836)
3. The Grandstand (8101–9836)
4. The Paddock (4501–6836)
5. The Springs (3101–4436)

AMENITIES
6. The Artist's Palette
7. Backstretch Pool Bar
8. BBQ Grill Area
9. On the Rocks Pool Bar
10. The Paddock Grill
11. Turf Club Bar & Grill

Boat dock
Bus stop

adjacent 60-unit DVC complex, **Treehouse Villas at Disney's Saratoga Springs Resort & Spa,** opened in 2009 (see page 143).

The color scheme of the villas' rooms tends toward neutral earth tones, with faux-teak vinyl flooring in the living rooms and dark-brown patterned carpets in the bedrooms. Kitchen cabinets are white, and appliances are stainless steel. Chairs, sofas, and tables are modern and not bulky, though you'd be hard-pressed to identify even the slightest bit of theming; this décor could be at any one of a dozen Disney hotels. A fold-down child's bed sits beneath the wall-mounted TV in the living room. Bathrooms, with color accent walls, are spacious in all but the studios, where they compare with those in any other hotel room.

Saratoga Springs guests can use Disney transportation, their cars, or an on-property walking path to get to Disney Springs.

Readers tend to be more critical of Saratoga Springs than other Disney resorts. The top reader complaints about Saratoga Springs have to do with transportation. A couple from Indiana had a variety of complaints:

Saratoga Springs is our least favorite resort. We didn't enjoy the theming, and unless you have a car, getting around by bus is a real hassle. The food court is very small and the food expensive. Also, checkout was very slow, and our room seemed smaller than comparable rooms at BoardWalk Villas and Old Key West.

The positive comments frequently mention the quiet rooms, proximity to Disney Springs, and quality of the fitness center. Those were enough for this reader:

We loved Saratoga Springs! It was comfortable, beautiful, and quiet, with a quick walk to the dock for the boat to Disney Springs.

The fitness center is by far the best at Disney World. Unfortunately, the highly rated **Senses Spa** remains closed, though its counterpart at the Grand Floridian has reopened.

Surrounded on three sides by a golf course, Saratoga Springs is the only Disney-owned resort that affords direct access to the links.

DISNEY'S SARATOGA SPRINGS RESORT & SPA

STRENGTHS	WEAKNESSES
• Often available at discounted rates or as a DVC rental	• On-site dining is limited for a resort of this size
• Attractive main pool; multiple well-themed quiet pools with snack bars	• Theme is dull compared with those of other Disney resorts
• Closest resort to Disney Springs	• Fewer baths per bedroom than newer DVC properties
• Convenient parking	• Bus service can take some time to get out of the (huge) resort
• Only WDW-owned resort with dedicated golf (Lake Buena Vista Golf Course)	
• Grocery options in gift shop	
• Very nice fitness center	

Unofficial Guide Reader-Survey Results *(resort & spa only)*

Percentage of readers who who'd stay here again	**93%** *(Average)*
Percentage of readers who'd recommend this resort to a friend	**65%** *(Below Average)*
Overall reader rating	**A−**

QUICK TAKE: *The key issue at Saratoga Springs is bus transportation, which is extremely inconvenient to use due to the spread-out nature of the resort.*

GOOD (AND NOT-SO-GOOD) ROOMS AT SARATOGA SPRINGS RESORT & SPA *(See* **theugseries.com/ss-views** *for photos.)* This resort's sprawling size puts some of its best rooms very far away from the main lobby, restaurants, and shops. If you don't have a car, the best rooms are those in **The Springs,** numbered **3101–3436** and **3501–3836.** Ask for a room toward the northeast side of these buildings (away from the lobby), as the southwest rooms border a well-traveled road. Avoid rooms **4101–4436**—a pedestrian walkway running behind the patios gets a lot of use in the early morning from guests who are heading to breakfast.

If you have a car or don't mind a longer walk to the lobby, rooms **1101–1436** and **2501–2836** in **Congress Park** offer quietness, a view of Disney Springs, and a relatively short walk to the bus stop. Also good are rooms **4501–4826, 6101–6436,** and **6501–6836** in **The Paddock.** Most of these rooms offer the shortest walks to Disney Springs. In The Paddock, avoid rooms on the northeast side of its **5101–5435** building, as well those as the northwest side of its **5501–5836** building—these border a swimming pool and bus stop.

If you're not concerned with the amenities of a specific room, ask for building 16 (**The Grandstand**). A short walk from the Carriage House, it's the top-rated building at Saratoga Springs.

TREEHOUSE VILLAS *(not enough surveys to rate)*

STRENGTHS	WEAKNESSES
• Spacious stand-alone three-bedroom villas	• Long distance from Saratoga Springs services such as check-in and dining
• Quiet location (but kids may find it boring)	
• Innovative round design feels more spacious than other villas with the same square footage	• Lackluster pool
	• Limited number of units makes them difficult to book
	• Only two baths per villa
	• Bus travelers connect through Saratoga Springs

THIS COMPLEX OF 60 THREE-BEDROOM VILLAS lies between Old Key West Resort and the Grandstand section of Saratoga Springs, with a separate entrance off Disney Vacation Club Way. The Treehouse Villas stand on stilts 10 feet off the ground, with ramps providing wheelchair access. Surrounded by a densely wooded landscape, each villa is a 1,072 square foot, eight-sided structure with three bedrooms and two full bathrooms.

Villas hold nine people, about the same number as comparably sized rooms at other DVC resorts. Two bedrooms have queen beds; the third bedroom has bunks; and the living room has a sofa bed and sleeper chair, both more appropriate for children than adults.

The interior is decorated with natural materials: stone floors in the kitchen, granite countertops, and stained-wood furniture. End tables, picture frames, and bunk beds are made from rustic logs. Bathrooms, outfitted in modern tile, have showers and tubs, along with a decent amount of counter space.

The three-bedroom treehouses usually cost about $70–$350 more per night than a comparable two-bedroom villa and $600–$700 *less* than a standard three-bedroom villa elsewhere at Saratoga Springs.

Treehouse Villas at Saratoga Springs Resort & Spa

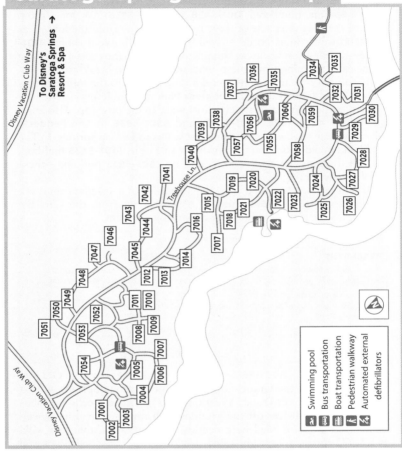

The trade-off for that third treehouse bedroom is giving up some space elsewhere. In particular, beware the primary-bath shower: Tilt down to grab a bottle of shampoo, and you could bang your head on the side of the tub. A New Jersey family thinks a stay at Treehouse Villas is money well spent:

> We give Treehouse Villas five stars for value. With nine people in our party, our villa saved us about $700–$1,000 per night. The three bedrooms and pullout couch comfortably slept our group. Plus, having a great eat-in kitchen helped us save money on breakfast.

A walking path connects the complex to the rest of Saratoga Springs. Two dedicated bus stops serve the villas, but transportation is nevertheless a weakness. This Rhode Island reader felt stranded:

> Transportation is abhorrent—and I actually had some idea what to expect (i.e., taking one bus at the villas to another bus at the main

resort). The treehouses are nice in and of themselves, but I would suggest not staying here if going to the parks is your main objective.

GOOD (AND NOT-SO-GOOD) ROOMS AT TREEHOUSE VILLAS *(See* **theugseries.com/th-views** *for photos.)* Numbers **7024–7034** and **7058–7060** are closest to one of the villas' two dedicated bus stops and the walkway to Saratoga Springs; **7026–7033** also have water views. Treehouses **7001–7011** and **7045–7054** are closest to the other bus stop; **7020–7023** are closest to the boat docks. Finally, treehouses **7035–7037, 7055, 7056,** and **7060** surround the pool.

Disney's Old Key West Resort

(See map on next page; see **theugseries.com/okw** *for extended coverage.)*

STRENGTHS	WEAKNESSES
• Largest villas of the DVC resorts	• Multiple bus stops
• Often available at discounted rates or as a DVC rental	• No elevators in most buildings
	• Highway noise
• Close to Lake Buena Vista Golf Course	• Fewer baths per bedroom than newer DVC properties
• Boat service to Disney Springs	
• Convenient parking	• Mediocre on-site dining

Unofficial Guide **Reader-Survey Results**

Percentage of readers who'd stay here again	92% *(Average)*
Percentage of readers who'd recommend this resort to a friend	71% *(Average)*
Overall reader rating	A-

OLD KEY WEST WAS THE FIRST Disney Vacation Club property. It's a favorite among readers and *Unofficial Guide* staff for its room quality and quiet surroundings. A Pennsylvania reader thinks it's Walt Disney World's best-kept secret:

> *Old Key West has the most spacious rooms and the easiest access to your car—right outside your door! There are a number of small, almost private pools, so you don't have to go to the main pool.*

The resort is a large collection of two- to three-story buildings modeled after homes and guesthouses of the Florida Keys. Set subdivision-style around a golf course and along Bonnet Creek, the buildings are arranged in small, neighborhood-like clusters and feature pastel facades, white trim, and shuttered windows. **Conch Flats Community Hall** houses the check-in area along with a full-service restaurant, fitness center, marina, and shop. Each cluster of accommodations has a quiet pool; Conch Flats is home to the main pool, featuring a waterslide in the shape of a giant sandcastle.

Old Key West boasts some of the roomiest accommodations at Walt Disney World, and all rooms were refurbished in 2018. Studios are 376 square feet; one-bedroom villas, 942; and two-bedroom villas, 1,333. Studios contain two queen beds, a table and two chairs, and an extra vanity outside the bathroom. One-bedroom villas have a king bed in the primary bedroom, a queen sleeper sofa in the living room, a laundry room, and a full kitchen with coffee maker. Two-bedroom villas feature a king bed in the first bedroom, a queen sleeper sofa and foldout chair in the living room, and two queens in the second bedroom. Closets are almost large enough to qualify as another bedroom.

Old Key West Resort

resort entrance

Disney Vacation Club Way

Miller's Rd.

15
64
63
17
16
14
19
18
62
20
13
12
21
11
22
23
24
registration and Olivia's Cafe
25
26
Peninsular Rd.
27
28
29
38 37
33 30
39 36
32 31
45
40
Old Turtle Pond Rd.
44
41
34
47
43
35
46
42
48
49
South Point Rd.
56 55
51 52
Buena Vista Dr.
53 54
50

Bonnet Creek Pkwy.

11 Building numbers

Villas have a light beach theme with some subtle Disney characters. One-bedroom and larger villas have wood flooring instead of carpet. Each villa has a private balcony that opens to views of the golf course, the landscape, or a waterway. The waterway views are among the best in Walt Disney World.

Transportation and lack of on-site dining options are Old Key West's main weaknesses with readers. Old Key West is connected by boat to Disney Springs (and by bus when the boat isn't running). Transportation to other Disney destinations is by bus. Walking time to the transportation loading areas from the most remote rooms is about

6 minutes. But there are multiple bus stops on the internal loop, which can add up to 15 minutes to your commute in any direction.

GOOD (AND NOT-SO-GOOD) ROOMS AT OLD KEY WEST RESORT *(See* **theugseries.com/okw-views** *for photos.)* Old Key West is huge, with 49 three-story villa buildings spread over about 100 acres. Views are nice from almost all villas; all multiroom villas and some studios have a large balcony furnished with a table and chairs.

Because the resort is bordered by busy Bonnet Creek Parkway and even busier Buena Vista Drive, the best villas are those located as far from the road noise as possible. For a lovely river view, ask for **building 45** or **46** (building 45 is the highest rated at Old Key West). For nice lake and golf-course views away from roads and close to restaurants, recreation, the marina, the main swimming complex, and shopping, ask for **building 13**. Nearby, **buildings 11** and **12** are likewise quiet and convenient; they offer primarily golf-course views. Avoid **buildings 19–22, 38, 39, 41, 42,** and **49–54,** which border Bonnet Creek Parkway and Buena Vista Drive.

Disney's Port Orleans Resort: French Quarter and Riverside
(See maps on pages 148 and 149; see **theugseries.com/riverside** *and* **theugseries .com/frq** *for extended coverage.)*

A MODERATE RESORT, Port Orleans is divided into two large sections. The smaller, southern part is called the **French Quarter;** the larger section is **Riverside.** French Quarter is this year's top Moderate, overall and in terms of readers who said they'd stay there again and readers who would recommend it to a friend.

PORT ORLEANS RESORT–FRENCH QUARTER

STRENGTHS	WEAKNESSES
• Excellent staff/service	• Boring pool
• Most compact of the Moderate resorts, with only one bus stop	• Shares bus service with Port Orleans Riverside during slower times of year
• Live entertainment in Scat Cat's Club	• No full-service dining
• Beignets!	
• Attractively themed lobby	

Unofficial Guide **Reader-Survey Results**
(French Quarter only; see page 149 for Riverside)

Percentage of readers who'd stay here again	98% *(Above Average)*
Percentage of readers who'd recommend this resort to a friend	84% *(Above Average)*
Overall reader rating	A

WITH SEVEN THREE-STORY GUEST-ROOM BUILDINGS next to Disney's artificial Sassagoula River, the 1,008-room French Quarter section is a Disney version of New Orleans's Vieux Carré. The prim pink-and-blue guest buildings boast wrought iron filigree, shutters, and old-fashioned iron lampposts. The centrally located **Mint** contains the registration area and food court. The registration desk features a vibrant Mardi Gras mural and old-fashioned bank-teller windows. **Doubloon Lagoon** surrounds a colorful sculpture depicting Neptune riding a sea serpent.

Rooms at Port Orleans French Quarter measure 314 square feet. Most are outfitted with two queen beds, a table and two chairs, a

Port Orleans Resort–French Quarter

dresser, a minifridge, a coffee maker, and a vanity outside the bathroom. With their hardwood floors, cherry headboards, and cherry credenzas, the rooms are themed but tasteful. A privacy curtain separates the bathroom area from the rest of the room, allowing three people to get dressed privately at once. No rooms have balconies, but accessways with iron railings provide a good (though less private) substitute.

Most readers really like Port Orleans French Quarter. Some, including this North Carolina family, rate it even higher than many Deluxe resorts:

> We stayed at the Polynesian Village in 2017, but we loved French Quarter! The updated rooms were great and the resort was so easy to navigate.

Note that there's no full-service restaurant—just a food court that can get overwhelmed. The closest full-service eatery is in the adjacent Riverside section, a 15-plus-minute walk away.

Disney buses link the French Quarter to all Disney World destinations. Walking time to bus-loading areas from the most remote French Quarter rooms is 5 minutes or less.

GOOD (AND NOT-SO-GOOD) ROOMS AT PORT ORLEANS RESORT–FRENCH QUARTER (See **theugseries.com/frq-views** for photos.) The best views are from rooms facing the river and a pine forest on the opposite bank. Below are the best river-view rooms in each building:

BUILDING 1: 1127–1132, 1227–1232 (a tree blocks some of the view in **1229** and **1230**), or **1327–1332**

BUILDING 2: 2227–2232 (landscaping blocks some of the view in **2129** and **2130**), or **2327–2332**

BUILDING 5: 5118–5123, 5218–5225, or 5318–5325

BUILDING 6: 6123–6129, 6138–6139, 6145–6148, 6223–6226, 6233–6240, 6245–6248, 6323–6329, 6335–6340, or 6345–6348

BUILDING 7: 7142–7147, 7242–7247, or 7342–7347

Port Orleans Resort–Riverside

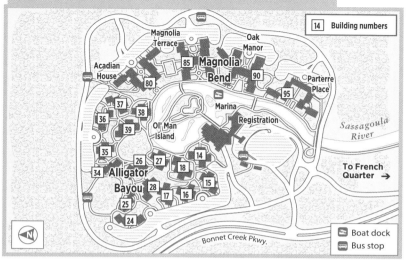

If you're not overly concerned with the specific room you get, the highest-rated building at French Quarter is building 6—in fact, it's the fourth-highest-rated building in Walt Disney World.

PORT ORLEANS RESORT–RIVERSIDE

STRENGTHS	
• Interesting narrative to theming	• Good place to walk or run for fitness
• Disney princess–themed rooms in Magnolia Bend	• Recreation options (bikes, boats)
	WEAKNESSES
• Live entertainment in River Roost Lounge	• Multiple bus stops; may share service with Port Orleans French Quarter during slower times of year
• Rooms at Alligator Bayou can sleep five, the fifth in a Murphy bed	
• Very nice feature pool	• This is a *large* resort, with many buildings very far from check-in and dining

Unofficial Guide Reader-Survey Results

Percentage of readers who'd stay here again	**88%** (*Below Average*)
Percentage of readers who'd recommend this resort to a friend	**59%** (*Below Average*)
Overall reader rating	**B+**

THIS SECTION DRAWS ON the lifestyle and architecture of Mississippi River communities in early-19th-century Louisiana. Spread along the Sassagoula River, which encircles **Ol' Man Island** (the main swimming area), Riverside is divided into two themed areas: **Magnolia Bend,** which features plantation-style architecture, and **Alligator Bayou,** featuring tin-roofed, rustic-looking buildings. Buildings in Magnolia Bend are three stories, while guesthouses in Alligator Bayou are two. The food court houses a working cotton press powered by a 32-foot waterwheel.

Each of Riverside's 2,048 rooms is 314 square feet. Most provide one king or two queen beds, a table and two chairs, a minifridge and coffee maker, and two pedestal sinks outside the bathroom.

Disney refurbished rooms in Alligator Bayou in 2019. These rooms sleep five people; the fifth bed is a Murphy-style fold-down, suitable for kids only. Rooms feature hickory-branch tables, and all have vinyl plank flooring. Bathrooms have increased shelf space and a curtain separator that allows three people to get dressed privately at once.

Rooms in Magnolia Bend are more conventional, with neutral walls, chestnut-colored wood furnishings, and vinyl plank flooring. Bathroom lighting seems to have been improved, and a small shelf above the dual-sink countertop provides additional storage space.

Oak Manor and **Parterre Place** in Magnolia Bend contain exclusively rooms themed to *The Princess and the Frog,* with appearances by Tiana's princess friends. These cost up to $75 more per night than standard rooms.

Disney buses link Riverside to all Disney World destinations. Walking time to bus-loading areas from the most remote rooms is 5 minutes or less. Unfortunately, bus service is one of readers' biggest gripes about Riverside. From a Delaware mom:

> Port Orleans Riverside has some of the worst bus service on-property. One day a bus to a park takes 20 minutes; two days later, going to the exact same park, you will experience a long, leisurely drive around the loop, then make a stopover at French Quarter, followed by finally getting to the park about 45 minutes later or more. Utter madness!

Additionally, the resort's size can be overwhelming to some guests, as this reader from Florida writes:

> It was our first extended stay at Port Orleans Riverside, and we found the resort to be too big and the pathways too confusing. We were situated half a mile from the lobby/food court, which made taking advantage of our refillable mugs a somewhat arduous task.

GOOD (AND NOT-SO-GOOD) ROOMS AT PORT ORLEANS RIVERSIDE RESORT *(See theugseries.com/riverside-views for photos.)* Riverside is so large that you may consider getting around via bicycle, if that's an option for your party. There are 20 guest-room buildings. The resort is arranged around two pine groves and Disney's Sassagoula River.

Magnolia Bend consists of four three-story, grand plantation–style complexes: **Acadian House, Magnolia Terrace, Oak Manor,** and **Parterre Place.** The best views are from the third-floor river side of Acadian House (building 80), which overlooks the river and Ol' Man Island: rooms **8414–8419.** Farther south, Parterre Place (building 95) has a number of rooms facing the river, but most views are blocked by trees or extend to the parking lot on the opposite shore. Try **9537–9540, 9573–9576, 9737–9739,** and **9773–9776.** In general, with the few previous exceptions, if you want a nice river view, opt for Port Orleans French Quarter.

Alligator Bayou, the other part of Port Orleans Riverside, forms an arch around the resort's northern half. These 16 smaller, two-story guest-room buildings, set among pine groves and abundant gardens, offer a cozy alternative to Magnolia Bend. If you want a river view, ask for a second-story water-view room in **building 27** or **38. Building 14** also offers some river-view rooms and is convenient to shops, the front desk, and the restaurant, but it's in a noisy, high-traffic area. A good compromise for families is **building 18.** It's insulated from traffic and noise by landscaping, but it's also next to a satellite swimming pool and within an easy walk of the lobby and restaurant.

Disney's official Riverside map shows two green areas north of the river bend in Alligator Bayou—these are dried-up lakes that are now richly forested with pine. Though out of sight of water, these offer the most peaceful and serene accommodations in the entire Port Orleans Resort. In this area, we recommend **buildings 26, 25,** and **39,** in that order. Note that these buildings are somewhat distant from the resort's central facilities, and there's no adjacent parking. In Alligator Bayou, avoid **buildings 15, 16, 17,** and **24,** all of which are subject to traffic noise from nearby Bonnet Creek Parkway.

THE ANIMAL KINGDOM RESORTS

Disney's Animal Kingdom Lodge & Villas: Jambo House and Kidani Village

(See map on next page; see theugseries.com/ak-lodge, theugseries.com/jambo -villas and theugseries.com/kidani-villas for extended coverage.)

ANIMAL KINGDOM LODGE AND VILLAS–JAMBO HOUSE

STRENGTHS	WEAKNESSES
• Magnificent lobby	• Few counter-service dining options
• Excellent on-site dining options	• Most villas here are smaller than those at Kidani Village
• Large, beautiful feature pool	
• On-site cultural and nature programs	• Rooms are among the smallest of the Deluxe resorts
• Best theming of any Disney hotel	• No direct non-bus transportation to any theme park

QUICK TAKE: *Jambo House is among the best Disney hotels. It has easy access to three of the table-service restaurants rated highest in our reader surveys. If it's in your budget, Animal Kingdom Lodge & Villas is the first on-property resort you should consider.*

IN THE SOUTHWESTERNMOST CORNER OF THE WORLD, adjacent to the Animal Kingdom theme park, Animal Kingdom Lodge opened in 2001. The resort is divided into **Jambo House,** which has regular rooms and DVC studios and villas, and the all-DVC studios and villas at **Kidani Village.**

Unofficial Guide Reader-Survey Results
(Jambo House only; see page 154 for Kidani Village)

Percentage of readers who'd stay here again	**Lodge: 92%** *(Average)* **Villas: 96%** *(Above Average)*
Percentage of readers who'd recommend this resort to a friend	**Lodge: 78%; Villas: 78%** *(both Above Average)*
Overall reader rating	**Lodge: A; Villas: A–**

DESIGNED BY PETER DOMINICK of Wilderness Lodge fame, Jambo House fuses African tribal architecture with the rugged style of grand African national park lodges. Five-story thatched-roof guest-room wings fan out from a vast central lobby. Public areas and about half of the rooms offer panoramic views of a private 21-acre wildlife preserve featuring streams and elevated *kopje* (rock outcrops) and inhabited by some 200 free-roaming hoofed animals and 130 birds.

Animal Kingdom Lodge & Villas

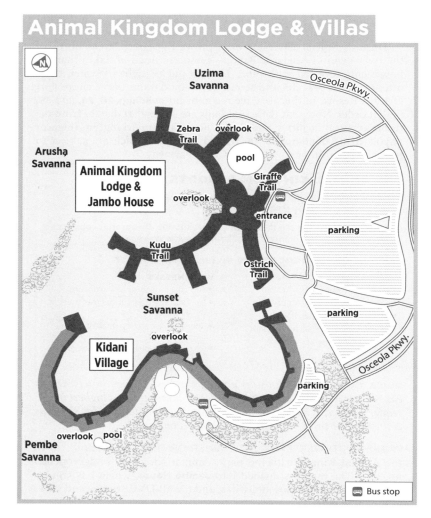

Most of the lodge's 972 guest rooms are 344 square feet and have hand-carved furnishings and richly colored soft goods. Amenities include a flat-screen TV, table with two chairs, ceiling fan, minifridge, and coffee maker. Bathrooms have light walls with textured fixtures, two sinks, and a large mirror. Almost all rooms have full balconies.

Jambo House also has DVC studios and one-, two-, and three-bedroom villas. Most are slightly smaller than at neighboring Kidani Village—anywhere from 50 square feet smaller for a studio to more than 200 square feet smaller for a two-bedroom villa. The three-bedroom Grand Villas at Jambo House are an exception, larger than those in Kidani by 148 square feet.

Jambo's lowest-priced one-bedroom rooms sleep four; standard, savanna, and Club Level rooms sleep five. A Tennessee mom loved everything but the room size:

We wanted to love staying in Animal Kingdom Lodge. We found the setting unique, the staff exceptional, and the common areas breathtakingly gorgeous. Loved all three table-service restaurants. Location wasn't an issue since we had a car, and the pool was fabulous. However, the rooms are really small for the price. We were especially dismayed at the commode/shower area—we had to sit on the commode in order to have room to shut the door. Unfortunately, the room size and bathrooms dropped us from "love" to "like."

Besides theming, another of Jambo House's strengths is its upscale dining: Readers place all 3 of the sit-down restaurants in Animal Kingdom Lodge near Walt Disney World's top 10 dining options. At the top of the list here is **Jiko—The Cooking Place.** Twin wood-burning ovens are the focal point of the restaurant, which serves upscale meals inspired by the cuisines of Africa. **Boma—Flavors of Africa** serves a buffet breakfast and dinner with food prepared in an exhibition kitchen featuring a wood-burning grill and rotisserie. Tables are under thatched roofs. (**Sanaa,** the third restaurant, is a short walk away at Kidani Village.) **Victoria Falls,** a delightful mezzanine lounge overlooking Boma, rounds out the hotel's sit-down service. **The Mara,** the lone quick-service place, can get crowded, even with extended hours. A family from Connecticut found the resort's restaurants a draw:

The restaurants in Animal Kingdom Lodge are great. We had lunch at Sanaa, which featured fantastic food and awesome views of the animals on the savanna. The Mara's counter-service options were way better than anything we found in the Magic Kingdom.

Uzima Springs serves drinks, salads, and snacks next to the resort's huge, elaborate pool. Other amenities include a village marketplace, outdoor movies shown nightly, and a nightly campfire.

The **Starlight Safari** wildlife tour is for guests age 8 and up and takes guests out onto the savanna at night to see its residents at their most active. The 1-hour tour costs $76–$89 per person and takes place nightly at 8:30 and 10 p.m.

Jambo House is connected to the rest of Walt Disney World by bus, but because of the resort's remote location, you should seriously consider having a car if you stay there.

GOOD (AND NOT-SO-GOOD) ROOMS AT JAMBO HOUSE *(See* theugseries.com/ak-views *for photos.)* A glance at the resort map tells you where the best rooms and villas are located. **Kudu Trail** and **Zebra Trail,** two wings branching from the rear of Jambo House, form a semicircle around the central wildlife savanna. Five buildings on each wing form the semicircle, while the remaining two buildings jut away from the center.

The best rooms—on floors three and four, facing into the circle—are high enough to overlook the entire savanna yet low enough to let you appreciate the ground-level detail of this amazing wildlife exhibit.

Second-floor rooms really can't take in the panorama, and fifth-floor rooms are a little too high for good views of the animals. Most of the fourth-floor rooms in Jambo House are reserved for Club Level guests, and the fifth and sixth floors house the DVC units. Rooms in the Zebra Trail section are rated higher by readers, on average, than those in any other section of Jambo House.

Less attractive are two smaller wings, **Ostrich Trail** and **Giraffe Trail,** branching from either side of the lodge near the main entrance. Some rooms on the left side of Ostrich Trail overlook a small savanna. Most rooms overlook the front entrance. Least desirable is Giraffe Trail, extending from the right side of the lobby: Its rooms overlook either the pool (water view) or the resort entrance (standard view).

ANIMAL KINGDOM VILLAS–KIDANI VILLAGE

STRENGTHS	
• Nice pool with excellent splash area	• Close to Jambo House amenities and restaurants
• Underground parking close to elevators	**WEAKNESSES**
• Beautiful, understated lobby	• Savanna views can be hit-or-miss
• Sanaa restaurant is an Unofficial Guide favorite	• Erratic bus service
• Great fitness room	• No quick-service dining options other than pool bar

Unofficial Guide Reader-Survey Results

Percentage of readers who'd stay here again	88% *(Below Average)*
Percentage of readers who'd recommend this resort to a friend	68% *(Below Average)*
Overall reader rating	A–

A SEPARATE BUILDING shaped like a backward 3, Kidani Village has 324 DVC units, a dedicated savanna, a well-themed pool and splash zone, and **Sanaa,** a top-rated table-service restaurant. Other amenities include a fitness center; an arcade; a gift shop; and tennis, shuffleboard, and basketball courts. Kidani Village is connected to Jambo House by a half-mile walking trail (or internal shuttle); DVC guests at either resort can use the facilities at both.

Kidani Village has studios and one-, two-, and three-bedroom villas. Except for the three-bedroom units, most rooms are larger than their counterparts at Jambo House. Kidani's villas also have one more bathroom for the one-, two-, and three-bedroom units. One-bedroom units in Kidani Village can accommodate up to five people, and two-bedroom units can hold up to nine guests with a sleeper chair in the living room. Kidani's rooms are scheduled for refurbishment in 2025.

Kidani Village is Becky's family's favorite resort. It's quiet and relaxed, and the lobby and rooms have a smaller, more personal feel than Jambo House's. Kidani's distance from Jambo House makes it feel especially remote.

GOOD (AND NOT-SO-GOOD) UNITS AT KIDANI VILLAGE *(See* **theug series.com/kidani-views** *for photos.)* The best views at Kidani Village are from the north-facing units near the bottom and middle of the backward 3. Try rooms **7X38–7X44, 7X46–7X52, 7X06–7X11, 7X68–7X82,** and **7X61–7X67.** These overlook the savanna next to Jambo House's Kudu Trail rooms and beyond into undeveloped woods. West- and south-facing units in the bottom half of Kidani Village overlook the parking lot; west-facing units in the top half have either pool or savanna views.

Disney's Coronado Springs Resort

(See map on next page; see **theugseries.com/coronado** *for extended coverage.)*

STRENGTHS	WEAKNESSES
• Most sophisticated room décor of the Moderate resorts	• Dining options rated low by readers
• Setting is beautiful at night	• Presence of conventioneers may be off-putting to vacationing families
• Themed swimming area with waterslides	• Some rooms are a long distance from check-in, lobby, and restaurants
• On-site business center	
• Best public Wi-Fi at any Disney resort	• Multiple bus stops

Unofficial Guide Reader-Survey Results

Percentage of readers who'd stay here again	**94%** *(Above Average)*
Percentage of readers who'd recommend this resort to a friend	**76%** *(Average)*
Overall reader rating	**A**

NEAR ANIMAL KINGDOM, Coronado Springs Resort is Disney's only midpriced convention property. Inspired by northern Mexico and the American Southwest, the resort is divided into four separately themed areas. The two- and three-story **Ranchos** call to mind Southwestern cattle ranches, while the two-story **Cabanas** are modeled after Mexican beach resorts. The multistory **Casitas** embody elements of Spanish architecture found in Mexico's great cities. **Gran Destino Tower** serves as the lobby for all of Coronado Springs, and the rooms in this 15-floor building are nicer than those in the rest of the resort. The vast resort, surrounding a 22-acre lake, has three small pools and one large swimming complex. The main pool features a reproduction of a Mayan step pyramid with a waterfall cascading down its side.

Most of the 1,839 rooms in the Ranchos, Cabanas, and Casitas measure 314 square feet and contain two queen beds, a desk with an excellent working area, a chair, a minifridge, a coffee maker, and a vanity outside the bathroom. Sliding doors divide the main living area from the sinks, allowing three people to get dressed privately at the same time. Bathrooms have plenty of storage. Rooms are decorated with a subtle Southwestern theme, in a desert-landscape palette. None of the rooms have balconies.

The 545 rooms in Gran Destino Tower range from very standard hotel rooms to deluxe, one-bedroom, and presidential suites. The public areas showcase a vibrant mix of Spanish and Moorish design, with bold colors and large, open spaces. Gran Destino's standard rooms are almost 20% larger than those in the rest of the resort. They have vinyl plank flooring, large windows, good lighting, and lots of desk and storage space; rooms are also equipped with a minifridge and a Keurig coffee maker. Bathrooms have plentiful lighting and shelf space, two sinks, a huge shower, and separate vanity and toilet areas, allowing three people to get dressed privately at the same time. But there's little theming: The rooms barely differ from those at other Disney resorts.

Our favorite thing about Gran Destino is the relatively low cost of Club Level rooms, which get you access to the **Chronos Club** lounge. Standard rates for these rooms run $100–$300 per night less than the next-cheapest Club Level room on-property. The Chronos Club has fantastic views, good food throughout the day, and a friendly staff. If

Coronado Springs Resort

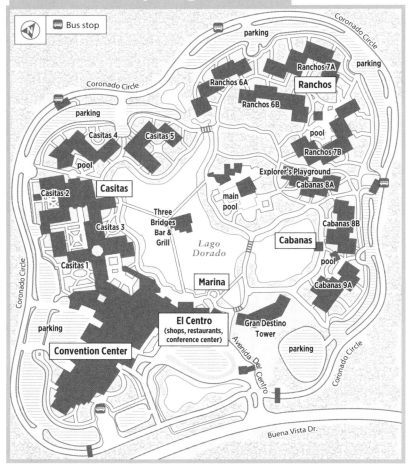

you're looking for pampering, Gran Destino's Club Level rooms are one of the best values in Walt Disney World.

Coronado Springs has four full-service restaurants and a food court, plus two bars. **Toledo—Tapas, Steak & Seafood** is in Gran Destino Tower and is featured in the *Michelin Guide*. An overwater bar called **Three Bridges Bar & Grill** sits in the middle of the lake, connected to the resort by—you guessed it—three bridges. Still, dining capacity, choices, quality, and value are not where they need to be for a resort this big. We suggest having a car to expand your options.

The resort is connected to other Disney destinations by bus only. Walking time from the most remote rooms to the bus stop is 8–10 minutes. Bus service is the other of Coronado Springs' weaknesses. This Oklahoma family's comments are representative:

The buses took at least 30–45 minutes to arrive at the parks and/or resort. The queues for the bus would be filled with guests, and they still wouldn't send another.

A Virginia mother had a different experience:

Coronado Springs was absolutely fabulous. The staff was friendly, the kids loved the pool, and we all loved the market. It was nice and quiet at night. There were many convention guests, but they didn't interfere with our trip.

Coronado Springs was the Disney Moderate resort of choice for this Kansas family:

On our previous three trips, we stayed at Pop Century, and I was curious if a Moderate resort was worth the extra money. At first the size of Coronado Springs was daunting, but we quickly settled into a routine and figured out the bus routes (bus service was really the only major drawback). The room was spacious, and the door separating the living area from the bath vanity was very useful because I was able to get ready in the morning without waking the kids. The kids really enjoyed the pool area, and I thought it was better themed than Pop Century. Overall, I thought the resort was worth the price difference.

GOOD (AND NOT-SO-GOOD) ROOMS AT CORONADO SPRINGS RESORT *(See* theugseries.com/csr-views *for photos.)* As convention hotels go, Coronado Springs is odd. At comparable hotels, everything is centrally located and the guest rooms are close to each other. Here, the rooms here are spread around a huge lake called **Lago Dorado.** If you're assigned a room on the opposite side of the lake from the meeting area and restaurants, plan on an 11- to 15-minute hike every time you leave your room.

Coronado Springs' main lobby is inside **Gran Destino Tower.** To its west is **El Centro**, which contains shops, restaurants, and a conference center. There are three accommodation "communities": **Casitas, Ranchos,** and **Cabanas.** If you think of Coronado Springs as a clock face, El Centro is at the 6 o'clock position. Moving clockwise around the lake, the Casitas are located near the lobby, in the 7–9 o'clock positions. For a good view of Lago Dorado, book one of these rooms:

3220–3223, 3241–3259, 3267–3273, or 3281–3287

3320–3383 (*except* 3324, 3330–3335, 3360–3365, 3374–3380, and 3384–3387)

3420–3423, 3425–3429, 3436–3459, 3466–3473, 3480–3482, or 3487

4461–4464

5202–5212

5303–5304 or 5311–5312

5400–5402, 5405–5410, 5413, or 5423–5463 (*except* 5450)

Next come the Ranchos, which are set back from the lake at the 11, 12, and 1 o'clock positions. The desert theme translates to lots of cactus and gravel, not much water or shade, and almost no good views. The Ranchos are a hike from everything but the main swimming area. We recommend avoiding this area.

The Cabanas are at 2, 3, and 4 o'clock. Lake-view rooms we recommend here include the following: **8129–8131** and **8142–8147; 8500– 8510, 8550–8553,** and **8573** (*except* 8505, 8507, and 8509). Specific rooms aside, Cabanas **building 8C** (rooms **8800–8993**) is the highest-rated building at the resort.

Finally, Gran Destino Tower is at 5 o'clock, close to El Centro. Even-numbered rooms face EPCOT and Hollywood Studios, and guests on upper floors can see those parks' fireworks shows. Odd-numbered rooms at Gran Destino have a view of the resort's lake.

Disney's All-Star Resorts: Movies, Music, and Sports

(See **theugseries.com/all-stars** *for extended coverage.)*

STRENGTHS	WEAKNESSES
• Least expensive of the Disney resorts	• Most likely Disney resorts to host large school groups
• Family suites at All-Star Music are less expensive than at Art of Animation	• Room soundproofing is poor; bring a white-noise machine
• Convenient parking	• No full-service dining; food courts often overwhelmed at mealtimes
• Lots of pools	• All three resorts share buses during slower times of year; bus stops often crowded

Unofficial Guide **Reader-Survey Results**
Percentage of readers who'd stay here again: **Movies: 87%** (*Below Average*); **Music: 93%** (*Average*); **Sports: 93%** (*Average*)
Percentage of readers who'd recommend this resort to a friend: **Movies: 57%** (*Below Average*); **Music: 62%** (*Below Average*); **Sports: 63%** (*Below Average*)
Overall reader rating: **Movies: B+; Music: A–; Sports: A**

DISNEY'S ORIGINAL VERSION of a budget resort features three distinct themes executed in the same hyperbolic style. The resorts' 30 three-story motel-style guest-room buildings are spread over a vast expanse. Although the three resorts are neighbors, each has its own lobby, food court, and registration area.

The facade of **All-Star Sports** features huge sports equipment: bright football helmets, tennis rackets, and baseball bats—all taller than the buildings they adorn. Similarly, **All-Star Music** features 40-foot guitars, maracas, and saxophones, while **All-Star Movies** showcases giant popcorn boxes and icons from Disney films.

The food courts function well for their size and purpose. Lobbies are loud (in both decibels and brightness) and cartoonish, with checkerboard walls; photographs of famous athletes, musicians, or film stars; and a dedicated area for kids to watch Disney shows and movies while parents are checking in.

Each resort has two main pools; Music's are shaped like musical instruments (the **Piano Pool** and the guitar-shaped **Calypso Pool**), and one of Movies' is star-shaped. All six pools feature plastic replicas of Disney characters, some shooting water pistols.

At 260 square feet, standard rooms at the All-Star Resorts are very small—the same size as those at Pop Century Resort and slightly smaller than Art of Animation's standard rooms. The All-Star rooms are so small, in fact, that a family of four attempting to stay in one room might question their life decisions by the end of a week.

All of the All-Star rooms have been recently refurbished. Each includes vinyl plank flooring, sleek modern storage units, queen beds, 10 USB outlets, and a coffee maker. One of the beds folds into the wall

All-Star Resorts

main entrance

W. Buena Vista Dr.

Stadium Blvd

parking

Sports

Hoops Hotel

Surf's Up!

laundry

check-in

Stadium Hall

pool

Dugout Dr.

play-ground

Touchdown!

Center Court

laundry

pool

Home Run Hotel

Hall of Fame Ln.

parking

W. Buena Vista Dr.

parking

Melody Ln.

parking

Rock Inn

Calypso

laundry

check-in

Music

pool

Melody Hall

Country Fair

pool

Jazz Inn

Stardust Dr.

laundry

Calypso

Melody Ln.

Director's Dr.

Broadway Hotel

playground

Show Biz Ln.

Mighty Ducks

pool

Melody Ln.

parking

laundry

parking

101 Dalmatians

Premiere Way

Love Bug

Fantasia

pool

check-in

Show Biz Ln.

laundry

Cinema Hall

W. Buena Vista Dr.

Movies

playground

Show Biz Ln.

Toy Story

when not being used, converting into a table; two chairs are included. Space is open under the bed for storage. The bathrooms have sliding glass doors, new showerheads, and tile walls. The vanity area is vastly improved, with modular shelving, better lighting, and increased counter space. Another sliding door separates the bath from the main living space, allowing three people to get ready in privacy at the same time.

While we think the refurbishments are a big improvement overall, there's always an unexpected miss or two in a renovation. This reader from New Hampshire found a couple:

The updated rooms have a couple of downsides. One is zero water pressure in the shower. And the thermostat is behind the coffee station, so it's impossible to see the temperature or which buttons you're hitting.

Due to the low staff-to-guest ratio, service is mediocre. Also, there are no full-service restaurants (there is, however, a McDonald's about a quarter mile away, with sidewalk access). Bus service to the theme and water parks is efficient. Walking time to the bus stop from the most remote guest rooms is about 8 minutes.

If space is an important consideration, you may want to budget enough for a bigger room at another resort—Art of Animation's standard rooms, at least. Also, All-Star Sports and Music are the noisiest Disney resorts; we use a white-noise app when we stay here. Be aware, however, that while the All-Stars suffer compared with other Disney properties, you're better off here than at most hotels you'll find in Kissimmee or Lake Buena Vista for $150 per night or less.

We receive a lot of letters commenting on the All-Star Resorts. An Indiana family loved their renovated room:

Our hotel room had so many storage shelves! Even though it was super small, we could be organized with our stuff for the week. I wish all hotels were like that! Shelves next to each bed (along with plenty of outlets), shelves inside the bathroom, shelves in the main bedroom. It was great. The fridge should be called a cooler. It didn't really keep stuff cold but cool.

A Canadian family had a not-so-positive experience:

The Guide didn't prepare us for the large groups of students who take over the resorts. They're very noisy and pushy when it comes to getting on buses. Our scariest experience was when we tried getting on a bus and got mobbed by about 100 students.

ALL-STAR MUSIC FAMILY SUITES In the Jazz and Calypso Buildings, the 192 suites measure roughly 520 square feet, slightly larger than the Fort Wilderness Cabins but slightly smaller than Art of Animation's Family Suites. Each suite, formed from the combination of two formerly separate rooms, includes a kitchenette with full-size fridge, microwave, and coffee maker. Sleeping accommodations include a fold-down queen bed in the bedroom, plus a pullout sleeper sofa. We don't recommend letting adults sleep on the sofa bed, but it's fine for kids. A hefty door separates the two rooms.

unofficial **TIP**

Music 5654 may be the best room at the All-Star Resorts. This third-floor corner room overlooks a small pond in a wooded area behind the resort. See theugseries.com/music-5654 to see the view.

The All-Star Music Family Suites have flat-screen TVs as well as two baths—one more than the Fort Wilderness Cabins. The suites cost up to 20% less than the cabins and about 15% less than Art of Animation's Family Suites, but they don't have the kitchen space or appliances to prepare anything more than rudimentary meals. If you're trying to save money by eating in your room, the cabins are your best bet. If you just want a little extra space and somewhere to nuke your Pop-Tarts in the morning, the All-Star suites are just fine.

Reader comments about the Family Suites are generally positive, albeit measured. From an Illinois family of five:

> We found the All-Star Music Family Suite to be very roomy. Our teenagers and preteen were quite comfortable on the pullout sofa. Having the two bathrooms was a must, and the kitchen area had lots of shelf space for the food we had delivered from Garden Grocer [see page 362]. Our only complaint is that from 7:30 a.m. until midnight there's music playing. The rooms are soundproofed but not enough; we had to use earplugs.

GOOD (AND NOT-SO-GOOD) ROOMS AT THE ALL-STAR RESORTS *(See* **theugseries.com/movies-views, theugseries.com/music-views,** *and* **theugseries.com/sports-views** *for photos.)* Although the layouts of the All-Star Resorts' Movies, Music, and Sports sections are different, the buildings are identical T-shaped, three-story, three-winged structures. The buildings are grouped into pairs, generally facing each other and sharing a common subtheme (for example, there's a *Toy Story* pair in the Movies section). In addition to being named by their theme, the buildings are numbered 1–10 in each section. Rooms are accessed via a motel-style outdoor walkway, but each building has an elevator.

Parking is plentiful, all of it in sprawling lots buffering the three sections. A room near a parking lot means easier loading and unloading but also unsightly views of the lot. The resort offers luggage service, but it often takes up to an hour for your bags to arrive.

To avoid a parking-lot view, you can request a room facing a courtyard or pool. The trade-off is noise—the sound of cars starting in the parking lot pales in comparison to shrieking children in the pool. The themed facade decorations are placed on the buildings' widest face—the top of the T—which is also the side facing the pool or courtyard. In some cases, as with the surfboards in the Sports section, these significantly obstruct the view. Floodlights are also trained on these facades, so if you step out of your room at night to view the action below, looking down may result in temporary blindness.

If you choose an All-Star Resort because you'd rather spend time and money at the parks, then you should book a room near the bus stop, your link to the rest of the World. Note that buses leave from the central public buildings of each section, which are near the larger, noisier pools. If you're planning to return to your room for an afternoon nap, request a room farther from the pools. Also consider an upper-story room to minimize foot traffic past your door. If you're only concerned with the highest-rated building in each resort (rather than the best rooms or specific amenities), here are the top-rated buildings at the All-Stars, according to our reader surveys:

- **All-Star Movies** 10 (*Toy Story*); 7 and 6 (*Love Bug*)
- **All-Star Music** 1 (Calypso)
- **All-Star Sports** 10 and 7 (Touchdown!)

On the other hand, if you choose an All-Star for its kid-friendliness, consider staying near the action. A bottom-floor room provides easy pool access, and a room looking out on a courtyard or pool allows you to keep an eye on children playing outside. Opt for a section and building with a theme that appeals to your kids. If you're staying in Home Run Hotel, for instance, don't forget the ball and gloves to maximize the experience. Older elementary- and middle-school children will probably want to spend hotel time in or near the bigger pools.

Playgrounds are tucked behind Cinema Hall, next to building 9, in **All-Star Movies;** between the backs of buildings 9 and 10 in **All-Star Music;** and between buildings 6 and 7 in **All-Star Sports.** Rooms facing these are ideal for families with children too young or timid for the often-chaotic larger pools. In All-Star Movies, the playground is nearer to the food court than to any rooms.

For travelers without young children, the best bets for privacy and quiet are rooms in buildings that overlook the forest behind the resort: **buildings 2** and **3** in **All-Star Sports** and **buildings 5** and **6** in **All-Star Music.**

The following tip from a former All-Star Resorts cast member from a Georgia illustrates just how big these resorts are:

Rooms at the far end of the Mighty Ducks building of All-Star Movies are closer to the All-Star Music food court, pool, and buses than to All-Star Movies' own facilities. Follow the walkway from the Ducks building north to All-Star Music's Melody Hall.

Disney's Pop Century Resort

(See map on page 164; see theugseries.com/pop for extended coverage.)

STRENGTHS	WEAKNESSES
• Theming is fun for anyone over 35	• Room soundproofing is poor; bring a white-noise machine
• Our favorite pool bar of the Value resorts	
• Just one bus stop	• Theming may be lost on kids and teens
• Skyliner connection to DHS and EPCOT	• Small rooms that are the same size as All-Stars' but slightly more expensive
• Stylish, modern room design	
• Convenient parking	

Unofficial Guide Reader-Survey Results

Percentage of readers who'd stay here again	**95%** *(Above Average)*
Percentage of readers who'd recommend this resort to a friend	**70%** *(Average)*
Overall reader rating	**A-**

NOTE: *More* Unofficial Guide *readers stay at Pop Century than any other Disney resort.*

ON CENTURY DRIVE, near the ESPN Wide World of Sports, is Pop Century Resort. A near-clone of the All-Star Resorts, it consists of four-story motel-style buildings arrayed around a central pool, food court, and registration area. Decorative touches make the difference: Pop Century features icons from 20th-century decades and their fads: building-size Big Wheels, Hula-Hoops, and the like, punctuated by silhouettes of folks doing the twist and other decade-specific dances.

Running $195–$367 per night, guest rooms at Pop Century are small, at 260 square feet. All feature vinyl plank flooring, IKEA-style storage nooks, and space-saving touches. A particular feature we love is that the second bed in the room folds up and becomes a desk when the bed is not in use, freeing floor space. Built-in shelving and a wall-mounted TV save even more space compared to a dresser. The bathrooms have lots of shelf space, plenty of storage, and a modern shower.

The public areas at Pop Century feature 20th-century furniture and décor with a nostalgic feel. A food court, bar, playground, pools, and so on emulate the All-Star versions in size and location. A lake separating Pop Century from Disney's Art of Animation Resort (AOA) offers water views.

Pop Century has a combination dining–shopping area featuring merchandise retailers and fast-food concessions. There's a bar but no full-service restaurant. AOA's food court is a short walk over a bridge from many Pop rooms; at press time, however, both food courts had the same selection. Because of the limited dining options, we recommend having a car.

unofficial **TIP**
We don't recommend Pop Century's so-called preferred rooms, which are closer to the main pool and lobby and cost about $15–$25 more than standard. They probably save only 5 minutes of walking per day and subject you to more noise from guests walking past your room.

Pop Century is connected to Walt Disney World by bus and **Skyliner.** Readers rate the bus service here relatively low. Pop Century shares a Skyliner station with AOA. The Skyliner connects Pop and AOA with the Caribbean Beach and Riviera Resorts, and it's the main Disney transportation to Hollywood Studios and EPCOT. (Disney adds bus service to EPCOT and DHS during busy times and when the Skyliner isn't running.) On average, the Skyliner is more efficient than the bus system for getting between these resorts and the theme parks.

We receive many complaints from readers about poor soundproofing between Pop Century's rooms. As with most hotel rooms, we recommend having a white-noise machine or app available. A Wisconsin family had this to say:

The remodeled room was very nice. We liked the Murphy bed and extra bathroom counter space. The only downside was when we left the parks in the afternoon to take a nap: The loudspeaker in the pool area made it hard to rest in our room nearby.

A reader from Georgia likes Pop for several reasons:

(1) There's a lake and a view of fireworks. (2) The courtyards have Twister and neat pools for little children. (3) Pop's dinner entrées are among the best bargains and the best food anywhere. (4) The layout is convenient to the food court. (5) Bus transportation is better than anywhere else, including Grand Floridian! (6) Where else do the cast members do the shag to oldies?

GOOD (AND NOT-SO-GOOD) ROOMS AT POP CENTURY RESORT *(See* theugseries.com/pop-views *for photos.)* The best rooms for both view and convenience are the lake-view rooms in **buildings 4** and **5** in the **1960s** area. Another option, though with a less compelling view, would be rooms in the same building facing east, toward the registration and food-court building. The next-best choices would be the east-facing rooms of **building 3** in the **1950s,** and of **building 6** in the **1970s.** Avoid

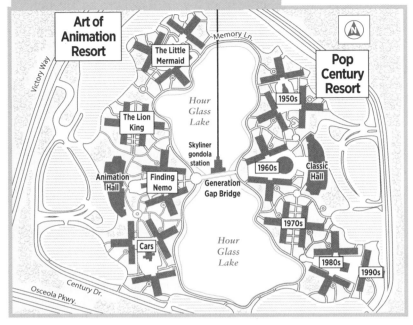

Pop Century Resort & Art of Animation Resort

Art of Animation Resort

The Little Mermaid

Memory Ln

Pop Century Resort

1950s

Victory Way

Hour Glass Lake

The Lion King

Skyliner gondola station

1960s

Classic Hall

Animation Hall

Finding Nemo

Generation Gap Bridge

1970s

Cars

Hour Glass Lake

1980s

1990s

Century Dr.

Osceola Pkwy.

south-facing rooms in the **1980s (building 7)** and the **1990s (building 8)**; both are echo chambers for noise from nearby Osceola Parkway.

Disney's Art of Animation Resort

*(See **theugseries.com/aoa** for extended coverage.)*

STRENGTHS	WEAKNESSES
• Exceptional theming, particularly *Cars* and *Lion King* areas	• Walking trail around Hour Glass Lake and connecting bridge to Pop Century
• Best pool of the Value resorts	**WEAKNESSES**
• Family Suites are innovatively designed and themed	• Most expensive Value resort
• Skyliner connection to DHS and EPCOT	• Terrible in-room cell reception
• Just one bus stop	• Standard rooms are rarely discounted
	• Poor soundproofing

Unofficial Guide **Reader-Survey Results**

Percentage of readers who'd stay here again	**89%** (*Below Average*)
Percentage of readers who'd recommend this resort to a friend	**67%** (*Average*)
Overall reader rating	**A–**

DISNEY'S ART OF ANIMATION is a Value resort across Hour Glass Lake from Pop Century. As at other Value resorts, standard rooms are housed in four-story buildings and exterior-facing walkups, with themed swimming pools and a food court. Most of the resort's accommodations, however, are family suites: There are 1,120 suites and 864 standard rooms. The suite buildings have interior hallways instead of exterior walkways.

Art of Animation's suites are around 565 square feet, about what you'd get by combining two standard rooms. Each suite has a main bedroom, a living room, two full bathrooms, and a kitchenette with minifridge, microwave, and coffee maker. Sleeping arrangements are a queen bed in the bedroom, a sleeper sofa, and a living room table that converts into a full-size bed. The bedroom and living room have flat-screen TVs.

This family from Texas appreciated that the suites' second bathroom sped things up in the morning:

With two teenagers, the extra space and second bathroom were absolutely worth the additional cost. Imagine being able to get ready for a park day twice as fast!

Slightly larger than comparable rooms at other Value resorts, standard rooms are 277 square feet and include one king bed or two doubles, a flat-screen TV, a minifridge, and a table and chairs.

The theming draws from four Disney animated films: *Cars, Finding Nemo, The Lion King,* and *The Little Mermaid.* All but the *Little Mermaid*–themed rooms are suites. Large, colorful icons stand in the middle of each group of buildings. Giant murals stretch the length of each exterior structure—the *Cars* buildings, for example, each display a four-story panoramic vista of the American desert, with the movie's iconic characters in the middle, while the *Lion King* buildings capture a single verdant jungle scene.

Readers complain, however, about the long walk from the *Little Mermaid*–themed buildings to the food court and front desk. A tired reader from Illinois offered this:

Only two reasons to stay in a Little Mermaid *room at Art of Animation: (1) There is a die-hard* Little Mermaid *fan in your party who will make your trip miserable if you don't get this room. (2) You don't feel you will walk enough in the parks and you want to add an extra-long trek to/from the bus, main pool, restaurant, gift shop, and front desk.*

Three of the four sets of themed buildings have pools. Like the other Value resorts, Art of Animation has a central building—here called **Animation Hall**—for check-in and bus transportation; it also houses the resort's food court, **Landscape of Flavors;** a gift shop; and a video-game arcade.

Most of the comments concerning Art of Animation are positive. A New Jersey reader says:

I was skeptical about Art of Animation. From pictures, it looked like it was going to be a child's dream but not necessarily an adult's. I was wrong—it's incredible! For a Value resort, it feels more like a Deluxe. The room was awesome—great layout, and having two bathrooms was so nice. The Big Blue Pool and the Cozy Cone Pool are great. Landscape of Flavors impressed me too—so many options for fresh, delicious comfort food as well as exotic fare.

The Skyliner is the main Disney transportation option from this resort to EPCOT and Disney's Hollywood Studios. In the morning, lines to get to Hollywood Studios can start around 90 minutes before park opening. (Disney adds bus service to EPCOT and DHS during busy times and when the Skyliner isn't running.) Access to the rest of Walt Disney World is via bus.

Another issue specific to Art of Animation is slow Wi-Fi speeds. This Texas reader ran some tests:

> *The Disney Wi-Fi speeds in the room (*Lion King *building 10) and by the pool were consistently around 25 Mbps download and 25 Mbps upload. When I stepped just outside our building, I got Disney Wi-Fi speeds of around 10 Mbps, but when I turned off Wi-Fi and used AT&T cellular, I actually got around 95 Mbps downloading.*

The reader is right to be concerned: Network speed and reliability are absolutely critical when you're competing with thousands of other guests to make Genie+ and Individual Lightning Lane reservations at exactly 7 a.m. We also get many comments about noise and sound-proofing issues here.

GOOD (AND NOT-SO-GOOD) ROOMS AT ART OF ANIMATION *(See* theug series.com/aoa-views *for photos.)* The quietest suites are south- and east-facing rooms in **buildings 3** (*Cars*), **4** (*Finding Nemo*), and **6** (*The Lion King*). The quietest standard rooms are east-facing rooms in **building 8** and south-facing rooms in **building 7** (both *The Little Mermaid*). Avoid northwest-facing rooms in **building 1** (*Cars*) and southwest-facing rooms in **building 10** (*The Lion King*), which face the Disney bus route and Art of Animation's bus stops.

The *Little Mermaid* buildings (7 and 8) are the lowest-rated at the resort, probably in part because they also have the smallest rooms. Ratings for the all-suite buildings tend to be very close, with the *Lion King* buildings (6 and 10) rated slightly higher than the others.

INDEPENDENT HOTELS OF THE DISNEY SPRINGS RESORT AREA

THE FIRST SIX HOTELS of the Disney Springs Resort Area (DSRA) were created back when Disney had far fewer of its own. These hotels— **DoubleTree Suites by Hilton Orlando–Disney Springs Area, Hilton Orlando Buena Vista Palace, Hilton Orlando Lake Buena Vista, Holiday Inn Orlando–Disney Springs Area, Renaissance Orlando Resort and Spa** (formerly B Resort & Spa), and **Wyndham Garden Lake Buena Vista**— are chains with minimal or nonexistent theming, though the Buena Vista Palace is fairly upscale. Several properties have shifted their focus to convention and business travelers. A seventh hotel, the **Drury Plaza Hotel Orlando,** opened in late 2022.

The main advantages to staying in the DSRA are as follows:

- The ability to pay for your stay with hotel rewards points
- The same Early Theme Park Entry benefits Disney resort guests get
- Being within walking distance of Disney Springs

The Wyndham Garden, Buena Vista Palace, and Holiday Inn are an easy 5- to 15-minute walk from the Marketplace, on the east end of

AMENITIES AT THE DSRA RESORTS					
HOTEL	CHILDREN'S PROGRAMS	DINING	KID-FRIENDLY	POOL(S)	RECREATION
DOUBLETREE SUITES	None	★★	★★★	★★½	★★½
DRURY PLAZA HOTEL ORLANDO	None	★★½	★★½	★★★	★★★
HILTON ORLANDO BUENA VISTA PALACE	★★★★	★★	★★★½	★★★½	★★★★
HILTON ORLANDO LBV	None	★★½	★★½	★★★	★★½
HOLIDAY INN ORLANDO	★★★	★★	★★	★★★	★★
WYNDHAM GARDEN LBV	★★½	★★½	★★★	★★★	★★★

* At press time, Renaissance Orlando Resort and Spa was under renovations in the building of the former B Resort & Spa and could not be rated for this edition.

WHAT IT COSTS TO STAY IN THE DSRA	
HOTEL	NIGHTLY RATE
DOUBLETREE SUITES BY HILTON ORLANDO	$124-$286
DRURY PLAZA HOTEL	$160-$375
HILTON ORLANDO BUENA VISTA PALACE	$270-$315
HILTON ORLANDO LAKE BUENA VISTA	$225-$290
HOLIDAY INN ORLANDO-DISNEY SPRINGS AREA	$145-$205
WYNDHAM GARDEN LAKE BUENA VISTA	$130-$210

* Rates for Renaissance Orlando were not available at press time.

ADDITIONAL FEES AT THE DSRA RESORTS (excludes tax)				
HOTEL	SELF-PARKING	RESORT FEE	INTERNET	TOTAL PER DAY
DOUBLETREE SUITES	$23	$25	Free*	$48
DRURY PLAZA HOTEL	$25	None	Free	$25
HILTON ORLANDO BUENA VISTA PALACE	$27	$44	Free	$71
HILTON ORLANDO LBV	Free	$39	Free	$39
HOLIDAY INN ORLANDO	$22	$43	Free	$65
RENAISSANCE ORLANDO	$30	Unknown	Free	Unknown
WYNDHAM GARDEN LBV	$23	$36	Free	$59

*After joining free Hilton Honors program

Disney Springs. Guests at DoubleTree Suites, Drury Plaza, and Renaissance Orlando Resort and Spa are about 10 minutes farther.

Although all of the DSRA hotels offer shuttles to the theme parks, the service is provided by private contractors and is inferior to Disney transportation in frequency of service, number of buses, and hours of operation. A Colorado family of five, for example, found that the Hilton Orlando Lake Buena Vista's shuttle service fell short:

> The transportation was unreliable. It did a better job of getting guests back to the hotel from the park than getting them to the park from the hotel. Shuttles from the hotel were randomly timed and went repeatedly to the same parks—skipping others and leaving guests to wait for up to an hour.

All the hotels are easily accessible by car and are only marginally farther from the Disney parks than several of the Disney resorts. And even the ones focused on business and convention travelers try to appeal to families. Some have pool complexes rivaling those at the Disney resorts, while others offer a food court or have all suites. A few have organized kids' activities; all have counters for buying Disney tickets, and most have Disney gift shops. On the downside, the rooms in several of the hotels are outdated.

The Value Proposition

The benefits that Disney extends to the DSRA hotels—such as Early Theme Park Entry—add to the value of staying in the DSRA. Some hotels, such as the **Drury,** offer free hot breakfast—a substantial savings for large families. That said, because of the lack of midday dining options and the poor shuttle service, many readers would be better off at **Disney's Pop Century.**

If you're using a hotel's rewards-program points to pay for your stay, you can save $600–$1,000 per week versus staying at Pop Century. Also, the **DoubleTree**'s 540-square-foot suites cost considerably less than comparable Disney suites, so if you can pay with points, the DoubleTree is a no-brainer.

Finally, when you're looking at room rates, note that they may not include tax or nightly self-parking and resort fees. These can add $25–$71 per night to the cost of your room (see table on previous page).

DoubleTree Suites by Hilton Orlando–Disney Springs Area
★★★½

2305 Hotel Plaza Blvd. | ☎ 407-934-1000 | doubletreeguestsuites.com

WITHIN WALKING DISTANCE OF DISNEY SPRINGS, this giant white bunker is the only all-suite resort on Disney property. What it lacks in atmosphere, it makes up for in convenience and comfort. The 229 suites are spacious for a family. Amenities include a safe, a hair dryer, a minifridge, a microwave, a coffee maker, a foldout sofa bed, and two TVs (in the bedroom and living room).

Children will enjoy a free chocolate-chip cookie and a small playground. The heated pool, children's pool, and whirlpool spa are moderate in size; traffic noise from I-4 can be heard faintly from the pool deck. The tiny fitness center, game room, four tennis courts, and outdoor bar are adjacent to the pool. The **EverGreen Cafe** serves breakfast, lunch, and dinner.

The DoubleTree is the farthest DSRA hotel from Disney Springs—a little over 0.5 mile to the closest entrance and a mile to its center, so figure on a 15- to 20-minute walk each way. If you're headed to the Magic Kingdom, the DoubleTree's bus service may drop you off at the Transportation and Ticket Center instead of the Magic Kingdom bus stop, adding another 10 minutes or so each way to your commute.

Drury Plaza Hotel Orlando *(not enough surveys to rate)*

2000 Hotel Plaza Blvd. | ☎ 407-560-6111 | druryplazahotelorlando.com

THE DRURY IS THE NEWEST HOTEL in Disney Springs, with 602 rooms. Amenities include a large pool area, two restaurants, a grab-and-go store, and a 24-hour fitness center. Room options include king beds, queen beds, and two-room suites. All rooms have a microwave, a minifridge, a coffee maker, and an iron and ironing board. The Drury is around a half-mile walk to Disney Springs and offers free transportation to the Disney parks and Disney Springs.

Hilton Orlando Buena Vista Palace ★ ★ ★

1900 E. Buena Vista Drive | ☎ 407-827-2727 | buenavistapalace.com

HILTON BOUGHT THIS PROPERTY in 2016 and has invested substantially in renovating it. Still, you should consider staying somewhere else. Rates approach $400 per night thanks to $71 in resort and parking fees; that's about the same as a Disney Moderate or Deluxe resort, and this Hilton isn't nearly as nice. The room layout and décor are dated, and the hotel's public-facing spaces show signs of wear and neglect. The resort's key strength is its outdoor recreation: a float lagoon and two heated pools, as well as private cabanas. Two restaurants and a minimarket are on-site.

Hilton Orlando Lake Buena Vista–Disney Springs Area ★ ★ ★ ★

1751 Hotel Plaza Blvd. | ☎ 407-827-4000 | hilton-wdwv.com

THE ROOMS HERE are clean, comfortable, and nicer overall than those at some other DSRA hotels. On-site dining includes **Benihana,** part of the Japanese steakhouse/sushi chain, as well as a grab-and-go market (open daily, 6 a.m.–1 a.m.) and a poolside café. Also on-site are two heated pools, a kids' spray pool, a fitness center, and a game room. Rates can approach $430 per night—within $25 per night of Disney's Coronado Springs Resort. If you're not paying with points, the Moderates are a better option.

Holiday Inn Orlando–Disney Springs Resort Area ★ ★ ★ ½

1805 Hotel Plaza Blvd. | ☎ 407-828-8888 | hiorlando.com

LAST RENOVATED IN 2018, the Holiday Inn's rooms are clean and comfortable. Disney Springs is a short walk away.

The totally upgraded 360-square-foot rooms feature pillow-top beds with firm or soft pillows. Each room has a 49- or 55-inch flat-screen TV and free high-speed internet. The bathrooms are the nicest in any DSRA resort—amenities include granite countertops and showerheads with a choice of comfort sprays. **Palm Breezes Restaurant** serves breakfast and dinner at reasonable prices. The grab-and-go in the lobby sells quick snacks and sandwiches. Other amenities include a large zero-entry pool and a whirlpool spa. If Disney's Value hotels are sold out, the Holiday Inn is worth considering.

Renaissance Orlando Resort and Spa
(formerly B Resort & Spa)

1905 Hotel Plaza Blvd. | ☎ 407-282-2828 | theugseries.com/renaissance-orlando

AT PRESS TIME, B Resort & Spa was undergoing renovations to reopen as a Renaissance, part of the Marriott brand. It will retain its walking distance to Disney Springs. We expect much of the rest of the resort will experience some changes, but all of them should be consistent with other Marriott locations. We'll update with more information in the next edition.

Wyndham Garden Lake Buena Vista ★ ★ ★ ½

1850-B Hotel Plaza Blvd. | ☎ 407-842-6644 | wyndhamlakebuenavista.com

THE MAIN REASON TO STAY at the Wyndham Garden is the short walk to Disney Springs. The lobby is bright and airy, and rooms are larger than most, with in-room refrigerators. Pool-facing rooms in the hotel's wings can be noisy during summer. Elevators are unusually slow—it's faster to walk to the second and third floors, if you can. As with most off-site resorts, transportation and quick-service dining options score low. Also, readers rate staff service at the Wyndham Garden lower than that at any other resort, Disney-owned or not.

CAMPING AT WALT DISNEY WORLD

Fort Wilderness Resort & Campground
(See map on pages 172–173.)

STRENGTHS	WEAKNESSES
• Children's play areas	• Isolated location
• Best recreational options at WDW	• Complicated bus service
• Special day and evening programs	• Confusing campground layout
• Campsite amenities	• Lack of privacy
• Shower and toilet facilities	• Very limited on-site dining options
• *Hoop-Dee-Doo Musical Revue* show	• Crowding at beaches and pools
• Convenient self-parking	• Extreme distance to store and
• Off-site dining via boat at the Magic Kingdom	restaurant facilities from many cabins and campsites

Unofficial Guide **Reader-Survey Results**

Percentage of readers who'd stay here again: **Cabins: 83%** (*Below Average*); **Campsites: 89%** (*Average*)
Percentage of readers who'd recommend this resort to a friend: **Cabins: 67%** (*Average*); **Campsites: 59%** (*Below Average*)
Overall reader rating: **Cabins: A–; Campsites: B**

DISNEY'S ONLY CAMPGROUND offers tent and RV camping, as well as fully equipped, air-conditioned cabins that can be rented through the Disney Vacation Club (DVC).

Tent/Pop-Up campsites provide water, electricity, and cable TV and run $76–$199 a night depending on season. **Full Hook-Up** campsites have all of the above amenities, accommodate large RVs, and run $116–$242 per night. **Preferred** campsites for tents and RVs add sewer connections and run $128–$270 per night. **Premium** campsites add an extra-large concrete parking pad and run $138–$280 a night. All campsites accommodate up to 10 people. Parking for one vehicle is included in the nightly rate.

Sites are level and include picnic tables, waste containers, grills, and free Wi-Fi. Fires are prohibited except in grills. Pets are permitted in some loops for a $5 fee per night.

Campsites are arranged on loops accessible from one of three main roads. There are 28 loops, with loops **100–2100** for tent and RV campers and loops **2200–2800** offering cabins rented through the DVC. The RV sites are roomy—Premium and Full Hook-Up campsites can accommodate RVs more than 45 feet long—but tent campers will probably feel a bit cramped. (Note that tent stakes cannot be used at the Premium sites due to the concrete.) On any given day, at least 90% of campers are in RVs.

Fort Wilderness offers arguably the widest variety of recreational facilities and activities of any Disney resort. Among them are two arcades; nightly campfire programs; Disney movies; a dinner theater; two swimming pools; a beach; walking paths; bike, boat, canoe, kayak, and golf-cart rentals; horseback riding; wagon rides; and tennis, basketball, and volleyball courts. There are multiple dining options, including a table-service restaurant, a food truck, and counter-service dining. Comfort stations with toilets, showers, pay phones, ice machines, and laundry facilities are within walking distance of all campsites.

Access to the Magic Kingdom is by boat from Fort Wilderness Landing and to EPCOT by bus, with a transfer at the Transportation and Ticket Center (TTC) to the EPCOT monorail. Boat service may be suspended during thunderstorms, in which case Disney will provide buses. An alternate route to the Magic Kingdom is by internal bus to the TTC, then by monorail or ferry to the park. You can also take a boat to Wilderness Lodge and the Contemporary Resort. Transportation to all other Disney destinations is by bus. Motor traffic within the campground is permitted only when entering or exiting. Get around within the campground by bus, golf cart, or bike—the latter two are available for rent.

For tent and RV campers, there's a trade-off between sites that are convenient to amenities and those that are scenic, shady, and quiet. RVers who prefer to be near guest services, the marina, the beach, and the restaurants should go for loops **100, 200, 700,** and **400** (in that order—loop 100 is the highest rated at Fort Wilderness). Loops near the campground's secondary facility area, with pool, trading post, bike and golf-cart rentals, and campfire program, are **1400, 1300, 600, 1000,** and **1500,** in order of preference.

If you're looking for a tranquil, scenic setting among mature trees, we recommend loops **1800, 1900, 1700,** and **1600,** in that order, and west-side sites on the **700** loop. The only loop offering both a lovely setting and proximity to key amenities is **300.** The best loops for tents and pop-up campers are **1500** and **2000,** with 1500 being nearest a swimming pool, a convenience store, and the campfire program.

Avoid most sites within 40 yards of the loop entrance—these are almost always near one of the main traffic paths. Sites on the outside of the loop are almost always preferable to those in the center. All sites are back-in, and the loop access roads are pretty tight and narrow.

Fort Wilderness Cabins

IN 2024, DISNEY CONVERTED the Fort Wilderness Cabins to a DVC resort. All 364 cabins were replaced. These new structures look more like modern tiny houses than log cabins, with lots of windows. The footprint stays about the same, with one bedroom, one bathroom, and sleeping accommodations for six.

Cabins offer a queen bed and bunk bed in the bedroom and a Murphy bed in the living room. The small bathroom has a shower and tub. All cabins have air-conditioning, TVs, full kitchens, and dining tables. Housekeeping is provided every other day. A New York family writes:

We stayed at Fort Wilderness in a cabin because (1) we wanted a separate bedroom area; (2) we wanted a kitchen; (3) our kids are very lively, and the cabins were apart from each other so we wouldn't disturb other guests; and (4) we thought the kids might

continued on page 174

Fort Wilderness Resort & Campground

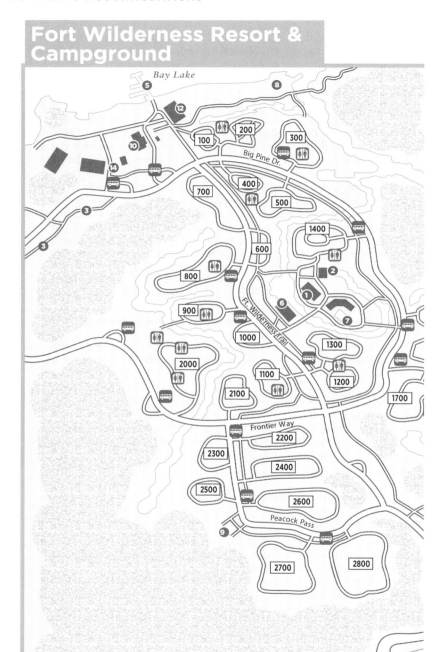

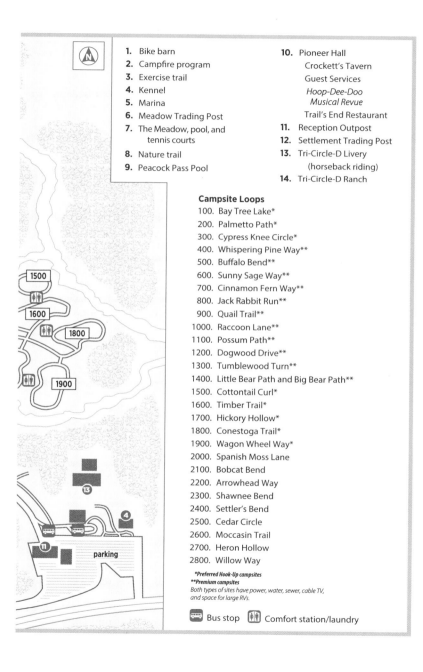

1. Bike barn
2. Campfire program
3. Exercise trail
4. Kennel
5. Marina
6. Meadow Trading Post
7. The Meadow, pool, and tennis courts
8. Nature trail
9. Peacock Pass Pool
10. Pioneer Hall
    Crockett's Tavern
    Guest Services
    Hoop-Dee-Doo Musical Revue
    Trail's End Restaurant
11. Reception Outpost
12. Settlement Trading Post
13. Tri-Circle-D Livery (horseback riding)
14. Tri-Circle-D Ranch

Campsite Loops

100. Bay Tree Lake*
200. Palmetto Path*
300. Cypress Knee Circle*
400. Whispering Pine Way**
500. Buffalo Bend**
600. Sunny Sage Way**
700. Cinnamon Fern Way**
800. Jack Rabbit Run**
900. Quail Trail**
1000. Raccoon Lane**
1100. Possum Path**
1200. Dogwood Drive**
1300. Tumblewood Turn**
1400. Little Bear Path and Big Bear Path**
1500. Cottontail Curl*
1600. Timber Trail*
1700. Hickory Hollow*
1800. Conestoga Trail*
1900. Wagon Wheel Way*
2000. Spanish Moss Lane
2100. Bobcat Bend
2200. Arrowhead Way
2300. Shawnee Bend
2400. Settler's Bend
2500. Cedar Circle
2600. Moccasin Trail
2700. Heron Hollow
2800. Willow Way

*Preferred Hook-Up campsites
**Premium campsites
Both types of sites have power, water, sewer, cable TV, and space for large RVs.

🚐 Bus stop   🚻 Comfort station/laundry

continued from page 171

> *meet other children to play with. The cabins worked out just right*
> *for us. The kids had a ball chasing the little lizards and frogs, kicking*
> *around pinecones, sitting on the deck to eat ice pops, and sleeping*
> *in bunk beds.*

A mother of two from Virginia is also a fan:

> *This is the only resort where you're encouraged to go outside and*
> *play! You can bike, swim, hike the nature trail, ride a horse, rent a*
> *boat, play volleyball, go to the beach, attend a character sing-along*
> *and marshmallow roast followed by a classic Disney movie, enjoy*
> *multiple playgrounds, play tennis, take a romantic carriage ride, take*
> *your first pony ride, and see a wild turkey. Don't forget the view*
> *of the fireworks from the beach or the up-close water light parade.*
> *With all of this stuff, much of it free or very affordable, who needs*
> *the parks?*

Bus service at Fort Wilderness leaves much to be desired—so much, in fact, that we wouldn't stay there unless we had a car. To go anywhere, you first have to catch an internal bus that makes many, many stops. If your destination is outside Fort Wilderness, you then must transfer to a second bus. To complicate things, buses serving destinations outside the campground depart from two locations, the **Reception Outpost** and **Pioneer Hall.** This means you must keep track of which destinations each transfer center serves. A Washington, D.C., family of five writes:

> *We generally enjoyed our cabin at Fort Wilderness. It was spacious,*
> *with bunk beds for the kids, a separate room for the parents to sleep,*
> *and a kitchen. We were very surprised and disappointed, though,*
> *when we figured out that we couldn't get anywhere in the resort in*
> *a timely fashion without either bikes or a golf cart—otherwise, you*
> *spend your day waiting for buses. A quick trip to the pool or the*
> *counter-service diner was impossible.*

HOW *to* EVALUATE *a* WALT DISNEY WORLD TRAVEL PACKAGE

HUNDREDS OF WALT DISNEY WORLD package vacations are offered each year. Some are created by the Walt Disney Travel Company, others by airlines, independent travel agents, and wholesalers. Almost all include lodging at or near Disney World, plus theme park tickets.

Prices vary seasonally; holiday periods and mid-February through Easter are the most expensive. Off-season, you can find great deals, especially at non-Disney hotels. Airfares and car rentals are cheaper off-peak too.

Almost all package ads are headlined something to the effect of "5 Days at Walt Disney World from $845." The key word is *from:* The rock-bottom price includes the least desirable options; if you want better or more-convenient digs, you'll pay more—often much more.

Packages offer a wide selection of hotels. Some, like the Disney resorts, are very dependable. Others vary in quality. Checking two or three independent sources is best. Also, before you book, ask how old the hotel is and when the guest rooms were last refurbished. Locate the hotel on a map to verify its proximity to Disney World. If you won't be driving a car, make sure the hotel has adequate shuttle service.

Because selling packages is efficient and the packager can often buy package components in bulk at a discount, the seller's savings in operating expenses can be passed on to the buyer. In practice, however, this rarely happens: Packages are sometimes loaded with extras that run the price sky-high.

Choose a package that includes features you're sure to use and minimizes features you probably won't. If the package price is less than the à la carte cost, the package is a good deal. If costs are about equal, the package is likely worth it for the convenience. Much of the time, you'll find you save money by buying the components individually.

WALT DISNEY TRAVEL COMPANY PACKAGES

DISNEY'S TRAVEL-PACKAGE PROGRAM mirrors the admission-ticket program. Here's how it works: You begin with a base package room and tickets. Tickets can be customized to match the number of days you intend to tour the theme parks and range in length from 2 to 10 days. (*Note:* The 1-Day Base Ticket isn't eligible for packages.) The package program offers strong financial incentives to book a longer stay. "The longer you play, the less you pay per day" is the way Disney puts it. An adult 1-Day Base Ticket costs $116–$201 (including tax), depending on the day of your visit, whereas if you buy a 7-Day Base Ticket, the average cost per day drops to $81–$119. You can purchase options to add to your Base Tickets, such as park-hopping or visiting the water parks. (see page 63 for more details on ticket pricing.)

unofficial **TIP**
Disney vacation packages may include dining plans as well as sweeteners such as a free round of minigolf and discounts on spa treatments, salon services, and recreational activities like water sports.

With Disney travel packages, you don't have to purchase a package with theme park tickets for the entire length of your stay. Rather, you can choose to purchase as many days of admission as you intend to use. For example, even if your Disney hotel stay is 7 days, you can buy admission tickets lasting anywhere from 2 to 10 days; the ticket length doesn't need to match your hotel-stay length. And if you don't normally park-hop, you don't have to purchase the Park Hopper add-on. Best of all, you can buy the various add-ons at any time during your vacation if you change your mind.

Let's start with the basic components of a Disney travel package:

- One or more nights of accommodation at your choice of any Disney resort. Rates vary with lodging choice.
- Base Ticket for the number of days you tour the theme parks (must be at least 2-Day Base Tickets for travel packages)
- Unlimited use of the Disney transportation system
- Free day parking at the theme parks

Booking Online vs. by Phone

It's much faster to book a Disney resort room online than it is to call Disney reservations (☎ 407-W-DISNEY [934-7639]). If you call, you'll be subjected to a minute or so of recordings covering recent park announcements—press 0 to skip this. Next, you'll go through about 5–10 minutes of answering more than a dozen recorded questions, asking you everything from your name and home address to the salutation you prefer. Slog on through, though, if you actually want to make a reservation. There doesn't seem to be a way to bypass these questions.

DOING THE MATH

COMPARING A DISNEY TRAVEL PACKAGE with purchasing the package components separately is a breeze.

1. Pick a Disney resort and decide how many nights you want to stay.

2. Next, work out a rough plan of what you want to do and see so you can determine the tickets you'll require.

3. When you're ready, go online or call the Disney Reservation Center (DRC) at ☎ 407-W-DISNEY (934-7639) and price a package *including tax* for your selected resort and dates. The package will include both admissions and lodging. It's also a good idea to get a quote from a Disney-savvy travel agent.

4. To calculate the costs of buying your accommodations and tickets separately, seek out those prices online separately or call the DRC a second time. This time, price a room-only rate for the same resort and dates. Be sure to ask about the availability of any special deals. While you're still on the line, obtain the prices, with tax, for the tickets you require. If you're not sure which of the various ticket options will best serve you, consult the free Ticket Calculator at **TouringPlans.com.**

5. Add the room-only rates and the ticket prices. Compare this sum to the DRC quote for the package.

6. Check for deals and discounts on packages and tickets.

THROW ME A LINE!

IF YOU BUY A PACKAGE FROM DISNEY, don't expect the reservationists to help you sort out your options. Generally, they respond only to your specific questions, ducking queries that require an opinion. A reader from Illinois complains:

> My wife made two phone calls, and the representatives from WDW were very courteous, but they answered only the questions posed and were not eager to give advice on what might be most cost-effective. I feel a person could spend 8 hours on the phone with WDW reps and not have any more input than you get from reading the literature.

HOTELS *outside* WALT DISNEY WORLD

SELECTING AND BOOKING A HOTEL OUTSIDE WALT DISNEY WORLD

LODGING COSTS OUTSIDE Disney World vary greatly. If you shop around, you can find a clean motel with a pool within 5–20 minutes of the World for as low as $70 a night with tax (but see our caveat on page 192). There are four primary out-of-the-World areas to consider (see pages 178, 185, 187, and 189 for maps):

1. INTERNATIONAL DRIVE AREA This area, located about 15–25 minutes northeast of the World, offers a wide selection of hotels and restaurants. Prices range from $55 to over $400 per night. The chief drawbacks are terribly congested roads and countless traffic signals. The mile between Kirkman and Sand Lake Roads on I-Drive is almost always gridlocked, which means you'll likely hit traffic going to a theme park in the morning, returning in the evening, or both. Regarding traffic on International Drive (known locally as I-Drive), a conventioneer from New York weighed in with this:

> When I visited Disney World last summer, we wasted huge chunks of time in traffic on I-Drive. Our hotel was in the section between the big McDonald's at Sand Lake Road and Volcano Bay at Universal Boulevard. There are practically no left-turn lanes in this section, so anyone turning left can hold up traffic for a long time.

I-Drive hotels are listed on the **Visit Orlando** website: visitorlando.com/places-to-stay (click "International Drive Area").

2. LAKE BUENA VISTA AND THE I-4 CORRIDOR A number of hotels are along FL 535 and west of I-4 between Disney World and I-4's intersection with Florida's Turnpike. They're easily reached from the interstate and are near many restaurants, including those on International Drive. The **Visit Orlando** website (visitorlando.com) lists most of them. This area includes Disney's value-priced **Flamingo Crossings** resort complex (see page 190).

3. US 192 (IRLO BRONSON MEMORIAL HIGHWAY) This is the highway to Kissimmee, southeast of Walt Disney World. In addition to large full-service hotels, some small, privately owned motels often offer a good value, and the number and variety of restaurants on US 192 is remarkable. Locally, US 192 is called **Irlo Bronson Memorial Highway;** though traffic is heavy on Irlo Bronson west of the Maingate, it doesn't compare with the congestion found east of the Maingate and I-4 between mile markers 8 and 13. That section can—and should—be avoided by using **Osceola Parkway,** a partial toll road that parallels Irlo Bronson to the north and ends in Disney World at the entrance to Animal Kingdom. No tolls are required to use Osceola Parkway while on Disney property.

Hotels on US 192 and in Kissimmee are listed at the **Experience Kissimmee** website (experiencekissimmee.com); you can also order a copy of its newsletter by calling ☎ 407-569-4800.

4. UNIVERSAL ORLANDO AREA In the triangular area bordered by I-4 on the southeast, Vineland Road on the north, and Turkey Lake Road on the west are Universal Orlando and the hotels most convenient to it. Running north–south through the middle of the triangle is **Kirkman Road,** which connects to I-4. On the east side of Kirkman are several independent hotels and restaurants. Universal hotels, theme parks, and CityWalk are west of Kirkman. Traffic in this area is not nearly as congested as on nearby International Drive, and there are good interstate connections in both directions.

Lodging Areas Around Walt Disney World

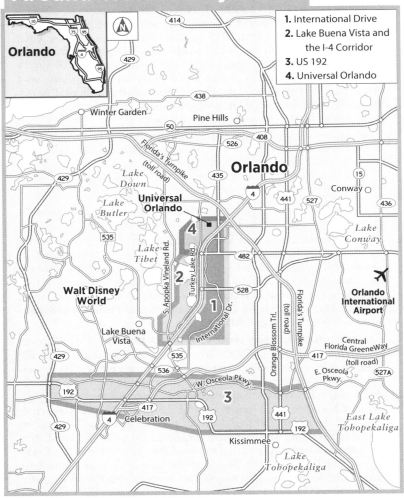

1. International Drive
2. Lake Buena Vista and the I-4 Corridor
3. US 192
4. Universal Orlando

DRIVING TIME TO THE PARKS

OUR HOTEL INFORMATION TABLE on pages 194–199 shows the commuting time to the Disney theme parks from each hotel listed. Those commuting times represent an average of several test runs. Your actual time may be shorter or longer depending on traffic, road construction (if any), and delays at traffic signals.

The commuting times in our Hotel Information Table clearly show that distance from the theme parks is not necessarily the biggest factor in determining commuting times. Among those we list, the hotels on Major Boulevard opposite the Kirkman Road entrance to Universal

Orlando, for example, are the most distant (in miles) from the Disney parks. But because they're only one traffic signal from easy access to I-4, commuting time to the parks is significantly less than for many closer hotels.

Note that times in the table differ from those in the Door-to-Door Commuting Times table (pages 338–339), which compares using the Disney transportation system with driving your own car *inside* Walt Disney World and includes actual transportation time plus tram, monorail, or other connections required to get from the parking lots to the entrance tapstiles. The Hotel Information Table's commuting times, in contrast, represent only the driving time to and from the entrance of the respective parking lot of each park, with no consideration for getting to and from the parking lot to the tapstiles.

Add to the commuting times in the Hotel Information Table a few minutes for paying your parking fee and parking. Once you park at the Transportation and Ticket Center (Magic Kingdom parking lot), it takes 20–30 minutes more to reach the Magic Kingdom via monorail or ferry, including security. To reach EPCOT from its parking lot, add 7–10 minutes. At Disney's Hollywood Studios and Animal Kingdom, the lot-to-gate transit is 5–15 minutes. If you haven't purchased your theme park admission in advance, tack on another 10–20 minutes.

HOTEL SHOPPING

OTAS Online travel agencies (**OTAs**) sell travel products from a wide assortment of suppliers, often at deep discounts. These sites include such familiar names as **Travelocity, Orbitz, Priceline, Expedia, Hotels.com,** and **Hotwire.**

More Hotel-Hunting Resources

NEW, INDEPENDENT, AND BOUTIQUE-HOTEL DEALS While chain hotels worry about sales costs and profit margins, independent and boutique hotels are concerned about making themselves known to the traveling public. The market is huge, and it's increasingly hard for such hotels to get noticed.

Independent and boutique hotels work on the premise that if they can get you through the front door, you'll become a loyal customer; thus, deep discounts are part of their marketing plan.

AIRBNB This service (airbnb.com) and the similar **vrbo.com** connect travelers with owner-hosted alternative lodging all over the world, from spare bedrooms in people's homes to private apartments and vacation homes. The incentives Disney offers for staying on-site are hard to beat. That said, Kissimmee is a rapidly growing market for rental services, and you can often find a two-bedroom condo that is a 10-minute drive from most Disney parks for roughly the same price as an on-site Value resort.

Be Careful Out There: Hotel Scams

In a very persuasive scam that has been hitting hotels all over the country, a guest receives a phone call from someone claiming that a computer glitch has occurred and that the hotel needs the guest's credit card information again to expedite checkout.

Here's what you need to know: A legit hotel won't ask you to provide sensitive information over the phone. If this happens to you, hang up and contact hotel security.

Another scam involves websites that look very polished and official and may even include the logos of well-known hotel brands. The scammers will happily sell you a room, paid for in advance with your credit card, and then email you credible-looking confirmation documents. Problem is, they never contacted the hotel to make the booking, *or* they made the booking but failed to pay the hotel.

CONDOMINIUMS AND VACATION HOMES

BECAUSE CONDOS TEND TO BE part of large developments (often time-shares), amenities such as swimming pools, playgrounds, game arcades, and fitness centers often rival those found in the best hotels. In a condo, if something goes wrong, someone will be on hand to fix the problem. Vacation homes rented from a property-management company likewise will have someone to come to the rescue, although responsiveness tends to vary vastly from company to company.

In a vacation home, all the amenities are self-contained. Depending on the specific home, you might find a small swimming pool, hot tub, two-car garage, family room, game room, and even a home theater. Features found in both condos and vacation homes include full kitchens, laundry rooms, TVs, and DVD players. Interestingly, though almost all freestanding vacation homes have private pools, very few have backyards. This means that, except for swimming, the kids are pretty much restricted to playing in the house.

Time-share condos are clones of each other when it comes to furniture and décor, but single-owner condos and vacation homes tend to be furnished and decorated in a style that reflects the owner's taste. Vacation homes, usually one- to two-story houses in a subdivision, very rarely provide interesting views (though some overlook lakes or natural areas), while condos, especially the high-rise variety, sometimes offer exceptional ones.

We frequently receive letters from readers extolling the virtues of renting a condo or vacation home. This endorsement by a New Jersey family of five is typical:

> *I cannot stress enough how important it is if you have a large family (more than two kids) to rent a house for your stay! We stayed at Windsor Hills Resort, 1.5 miles from the Disney Maingate. It took us about 10 minutes to drive there in the a.m., and we had no traffic issues at all.*

How the Vacation-Home Market Works

In the Walt Disney World area, there are more than 26,000 rental homes, including stand-alone homes, single-owner condos, and townhomes. Almost all the rental homes are occupied by their owners for at least a week or two each year; the rest of the year, owners make the homes available for rent. Some owners deal directly with renters, while others use a property-management company.

Incredibly, about 700 property-management companies operate in the Walt Disney World market. This suggests that the lowest rate of all can be obtained by dealing directly with owners, thus eliminating an intermediary. If you're interested in pursuing this route, try finding a condo association's Facebook page (such as Windsor Hills) and connecting with owners that way.

Location, Location, Location

The best vacation home is one that's within easy commuting distance of the theme parks (see map on pages 182–183). If you plan to spend most of your time in the World, the best selection of vacation homes is along **US 192,** south of the park.

To get the most from a vacation home, you need to be close enough to commute in 20 minutes or less to your Orlando destination. This will allow for naps, quiet time, swimming, and dollar-saving meals you prepare yourself.

Recommended Websites

After checking out dozens of sites, here are the ones we recommend.

Florida Dream Homes (floridadreamhomes.com) has a good reputation for customer service and has photos of and information about the homes in its online inventory.

Vrbo (Vacation Rentals by Owner; vrbo.com) is a nationwide vacation-home listing service that puts prospective renters in direct contact with owners. The site is straightforward and always lists a large number of rental properties.

Visit Orlando (visitorlando.com) is the website to check if you're interested in renting a condominium at one of the many time-share developments (click on "Places to Stay" at the site's home page). You can call the developments directly, but going through this site allows you to bypass sales departments and escape their high-pressure invitations to sit through sales presentations. The site also lists hotels, vacation homes, and campgrounds.

THE BEST OFF-SITE HOTELS FOR FAMILIES

WHAT MAKES A SUPER FAMILY HOTEL? For starters, you should look for spacious rooms, free breakfast, an in-room fridge, a great pool, and activities for kids.

Narrowed from hundreds of properties, the hotels profiled in the next section, listed by zone and alphabetically, are the best we've found in each area of Orlando. Some of our picks are expensive, others are more reasonable, and some are a bargain. All understand a family's needs.

The best square footage for your lodging dollar is often found in a suite. Suites have the advantage of separate bedrooms, allowing tired family members to rest while others stay up.

Unofficial Guide readers give low ratings to most off-site hotels' park-transportation options. Though all hotels profiled in the following pages offer some type of shuttle to the theme parks,

unofficial **TIP**
Check the resort's room photos to make sure you're booking an actual suite with multiple rooms. Some hotels with *suites* in their name or *all-suite* in their description are little more than slightly larger, single-space-for-everyone rooms with a microwave.

continued on page 184

Rental-Home Developments Near WDW

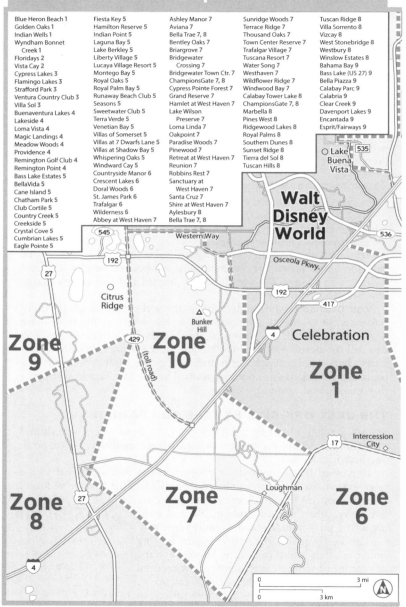

Blue Heron Beach 1
Golden Oaks 1
Indian Wells 1
Wyndham Bonnet
   Creek 1
Floridays 2
Vista Cay 2
Cypress Lakes 3
Flamingo Lakes 3
Strafford Park 3
Ventura Country Club 3
Villa Sol 3
Buenaventura Lakes 4
Lakeside 4
Loma Vista 4
Magic Landings 4
Meadow Woods 4
Providence 4
Remington Golf Club 4
Remington Point 4
Bass Lake Estates 5
BellaVida 5
Cane Island 5
Chatham Park 5
Club Cortile 5
Country Creek 5
Creekside 5
Crystal Cove 5
Cumbrian Lakes 5
Eagle Pointe 5

Fiesta Key 5
Hamilton Reserve 5
Indian Point 5
Laguna Bay 5
Lake Berkley 5
Liberty Village 5
Lucaya Village Resort 5
Montego Bay 5
Royal Oaks 5
Royal Palm Bay 5
Runaway Beach Club 5
Seasons 5
Sweetwater Club 5
Terra Verde 5
Venetian Bay 5
Villas of Somerset 5
Villas at 7 Dwarfs Lane 5
Villas at Shadow Bay 5
Whispering Oaks 5
Windward Cay 5
Countryside Manor 6
Crescent Lakes 6
Doral Woods 6
St. James Park 6
Trafalgar 6
Wilderness 6
Abbey at West Haven 7

Ashley Manor 7
Aviana 7
Bella Trae 7, 8
Bentley Oaks 7
Briargrove 7
Bridgewater
   Crossing 7
Bridgewater Town Ctr. 7
ChampionsGate 7, 8
Cypress Pointe Forest 7
Grand Reserve 7
Hamlet at West Haven 7
Lake Wilson
   Preserve 7
Loma Linda 7
Oakpoint 7
Paradise Woods 7
Pinewood 7
Retreat at West Haven 7
Reunion 7
Robbins Rest 7
Sanctuary at
   West Haven 7
Santa Cruz 7
Shire at West Haven 7
Aylesbury 8
Bella Trae 7, 8

Sunridge Woods 7
Terrace Ridge 7
Thousand Oaks 7
Town Center Reserve 7
Trafalgar Village 7
Tuscana Resort 7
Water Song 7
Westhaven 7
Wildflower Ridge 7
Windwood Bay 7
Calabay Tower Lake 8
ChampionsGate 7, 8
Marbella 8
Pines West 8
Ridgewood Lakes 8
Royal Palms 8
Southern Dunes 8
Sunset Ridge 8
Tierra del Sol 8
Tuscan Hills 8

Tuscan Ridge 8
Villa Sorrento 8
Vizcay 8
West Stonebridge 8
Westbury 8
Winslow Estates 8
Bahama Bay 9
Bass Lake (US 27) 9
Bella Piazza 9
Calabay Parc 9
Calabria 9
Clear Creek 9
Davenport Lakes 9
Encantada 9
Esprit/Fairways 9

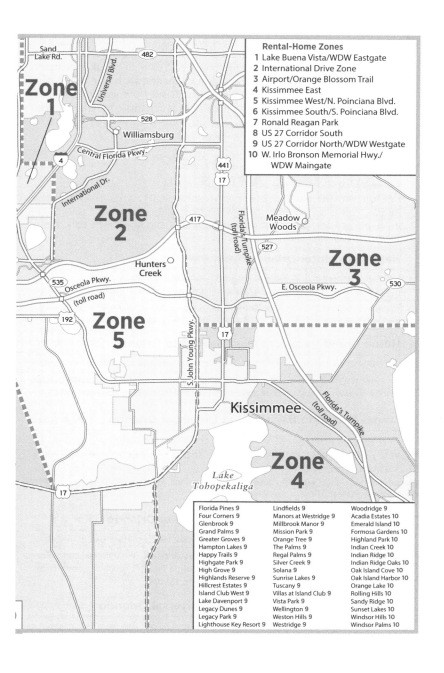

Rental-Home Zones
1 Lake Buena Vista/WDW Eastgate
2 International Drive Zone
3 Airport/Orange Blossom Trail
4 Kissimmee East
5 Kissimmee West/N. Poinciana Blvd.
6 Kissimmee South/S. Poinciana Blvd.
7 Ronald Reagan Park
8 US 27 Corridor South
9 US 27 Corridor North/WDW Westgate
10 W. Irlo Bronson Memorial Hwy./
    WDW Maingate

Florida Pines 9	Lindfields 9	Woodridge 9
Four Corners 9	Manors at Westridge 9	Acadia Estates 10
Glenbrook 9	Millbrook Manor 9	Emerald Island 10
Grand Palms 9	Mission Park 9	Formosa Gardens 10
Greater Groves 9	Orange Tree 9	Highland Park 10
Hampton Lakes 9	The Palms 9	Indian Creek 10
Happy Trails 9	Regal Palms 9	Indian Ridge 10
Highgate Park 9	Silver Creek 9	Indian Ridge Oaks 10
High Grove 9	Solana 9	Oak Island Cove 10
Highlands Reserve 9	Sunrise Lakes 9	Oak Island Harbor 10
Hillcrest Estates 9	Tuscany 9	Orange Lake 10
Island Club West 9	Villas at Island Club 9	Rolling Hills 10
Lake Davenport 9	Vista Park 9	Sandy Ridge 10
Legacy Dunes 9	Wellington 9	Sunset Lakes 10
Legacy Park 9	Weston Hills 9	Windsor Hills 10
Lighthouse Key Resort 9	Westridge 9	Windsor Palms 10

continued from page 181

some offer very limited service, so be sure to research the shuttle schedule before you book. Likewise, most off-site hotels' restaurants won't meet the needs of a family staying for a week, so plan to eat elsewhere.

For the hotels profiled on the following pages, we haven't included detailed descriptions like we have for the Disney-owned resorts. This is because experiences at off-site hotels are much more variable. If you choose to stay off-site, make sure to do your own research into these recommended options.

INTERNATIONAL DRIVE & UNIVERSAL AREAS

HELIOS GRAND HOTEL, STELLA NOVA RESORT, AND TERRA LUNA RESORT are all scheduled to open with Universal Epic Universe in early 2025. If you plan on spending most of your vacation at this new theme park, these should be your first choices.

Hard Rock Hotel Orlando ★★★★

5800 Universal Blvd. | ☎ 407-503-2000 | hardrockhotels.com/orlando

Rate per night $406–$711. **Pool ★★★★. Shuttle to parks** Yes (Universal parks, Sea-World). **Maximum number of occupants per room** 4 (king)/5 (double queen). **Comments** Pets welcome ($100 flat fee, 2 max). Parking $31/day.

Hilton Grand Vacations Club SeaWorld Orlando ★★★★★

6924 Grand Vacations Way | ☎ 407-239-0100 | theugseries.com/hilton-sea-world

Rate per night $210–$535. **Pool ★★★★. Shuttle to parks** Yes (Universal parks, Sea-World). **Maximum number of occupants per room** 2 (studio)/8 (3-bedroom suite).

Loews Portofino Bay Hotel at Universal Orlando ★★★★½

5601 Universal Blvd. | ☎ 407-503-1000 | loewshotels.com/portofino-bay-hotel

Rate per night $434–$762. **Pools ★★★★. Shuttle to parks** Yes (Universal parks, SeaWorld, Discovery Cove, Aquatica, Volcano Bay). **Maximum number of occupants per room** 3 (king)/5 (double queen). **Comments** Pets welcome ($100 flat fee, 2 max). Parking $31/day.

Loews Royal Pacific Resort at Universal Orlando ★★★★

6300 Hollywood Way | ☎ 407-503-3000 | loewshotels.com/royal-pacific-resort

Rate per night $406–$715. **Pools ★★★★. Shuttle to parks** Yes (Universal parks, Sea-World). **Maximum number of occupants per room** 3 (king)/5 (double queen). **Comments** Pets welcome ($100 flat fee, 2 max). Parking $31/day.

Loews Sapphire Falls Resort at Universal Orlando ★★★★

6601 Adventure Way | ☎ 407-503-5000 | loewshotels.com/sapphire-falls-resort

Rate per night $219–$535. **Pools ★★★★. Shuttle to parks** Yes (Universal parks, Sea-World). **Maximum number of occupants per room** 3 (king)/5 (double queen). **Comments** Pets welcome ($100 flat fee, 2 max). Parking $31/day.

Lodging Areas 1 & 4: I-Drive & Universal

Lake Cane

Peregrine Ave.
Windhover Dr.

Florida's Turnpike (toll road)

4 — East to Downtown Orlando

Vineland Road

435

77

Caravan Ct.

Orlando Premium Outlets

Universal Orlando

Universal Blvd.

Hollywood Way

Turkey Lake Road

Adventure Way

74B

75B

American Way

75A

75AB

W. Oak Ridge Road

Grand National Dr.

International Dr.

Del Verde Way

International Dr.

Carrier Dr.

Canada Ave.

Kirkman Road

482

Sand Lake Road

I-4 Exits

77	Florida's Turnpike
75A East	Universal Studios/ International Drive
75AB West	FL 435 North/South
75B East	Kirkman Road
74B	Universal Studios
74A	Sand Lake Road
72	FL 528 (Beachline Expressway)
71	Central Florida Parkway

Official Visitor Center

74A

Jamaican Ct.

Austrian Ct.

Austrian Row

International Dr.

Samoan Ct.

4

Universal Blvd.

Pointe Plaza Ave.

Universal Blvd.

Orange County Convention Center

Hawaiian Ct.

Destination Pkwy.

To Orlando International Airport →

528

Beachline Expy. (toll road)

72

Turkey Lake Road

(no toll)

(no toll)

Westwood Blvd.

Sea Harbor Dr.

Aquatica

International Dr.

Orangewood Blvd.

West to Walt Disney World Resort & Tampa

71

SeaWorld Orlando

Discovery Cove

Central Florida Parkway

Sheraton Vistana Villages Resort Villas, I-Drive/Orlando ★★★★½

12401 International Dr. | ☎ 407-238-5000 | theugseries.com/vistana-villages
Rate per night $159–$349. **Pool** ★★★★. **Shuttle to parks** No. **Maximum number of occupants per room** 6 (2-bedroom suite).

Universal's Aventura Hotel ★★★★

6725 Adventure Way | ☎ 407-503-6000 | loewshotels.com/universals-aventura-hotel
Rate per night Standard rooms, $174–$309; Kids' Suites, $299–$533. **Pools** ★★★½. **Shuttle to parks** Yes (Universal, SeaWorld). **Maximum number of occupants per room** 4 (double queen or king with pullout)/6 (Kids' Suites). **Comments** Parking $21/day.

Universal's Cabana Bay Beach Resort ★★★½

6550 Adventure Way | ☎ 407-503-4000 | loewshotels.com/cabana-bay-hotel
Rate per night Standard rooms, $158–$273; suites, $219–$369. **Pools** ★★★★. **Shuttle to parks** Yes (Universal, SeaWorld). **Maximum number of occupants per room** 4 (standard)/6 (suite). **Comments** Parking $21/day.

Universal's Endless Summer Resort ★★★★

Dockside Inn and Suites: 7125 Universal Blvd. | ☎ 407-503-8000
loewshotels.com/dockside-inn-and-suites
Surfside Inn and Suites: 7000 Universal Blvd. | ☎ 407-503-7000
loewshotels.com/surfside-inn-and-suites
Rate per night Standard rooms, $119–$229; suites, $171–$279. **Pool** ★★★. **Shuttle to parks** Yes (Universal, SeaWorld). **Maximum number of occupants per room** 4 (standard)/6 (suites). **Comments** Parking $17/day.

LAKE BUENA VISTA & I-4 CORRIDOR

Four Seasons Resort Orlando at Walt Disney World Resort ★★★★★

10100 Dream Tree Blvd. | ☎ 407-313-7777 | fourseasons.com/orlando
Rate per night $1,350–$2,715. **Pools** ★★★★★. **Shuttle to parks** Yes. **Maximum number of occupants per room** 4 (3 adults or 2 adults + 2 children). **Comments** The best deluxe hotel rooms, staff service, and pool complex in Walt Disney World, if not Orlando. Character breakfast on Thursday and Saturday (with reservation).

Evermore Orlando Resort ★★★★½

1590 Evermore Way | ☎ 407-239-4700 | evermoreresort.com
Rate per night $407–$1,102. **Pool** ★★★★★. **Shuttle to parks** Yes. **Maximum number of occupants per room** 4 (in the Conrad hotel on-site) to 32 (in the 11-bedroom homes). **Comments** This new resort near the Four Seasons aims to cater to a similar clientele. It has its own water park (Evermore Bay) and several lodging options: hotel rooms, flats, villas, and homes. $50/night resort fee.

Marriott's Harbour Lake ★★★★½

7102 Grand Horizons Blvd. | ☎ 407-465-6100 | theugseries.com/harbour-lake
Rate per night 1-bedroom villas, $229–$459; 2-bedroom villas, $259–$499. **Pool** ★★★★. **Shuttle to parks** No. **Max number of occupants per room** 4 (1-bedroom)/8 (2-bedroom). **Comments** Rated significantly higher than other suite hotels in the area.

Lodging Area 2: Lake Buena Vista & the I-4 Corridor

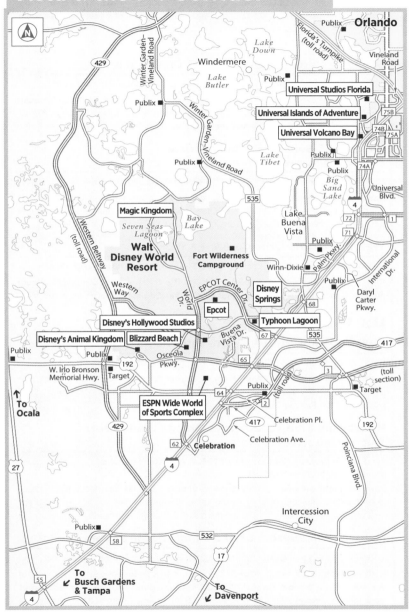

Sheraton Vistana Resort Villas ★★★★

8800 Vistana Centre Drive | ☎ 407-239-3100 | theugseries.com/sheraton-vistana

Rate per night 1-bedroom villas, $159–$329; 2-bedroom villas, $219–$389. **Pools** ★★★½. **Shuttle to parks** Yes (Disney). **Maximum number of occupants per room** 4 (1-bedroom)/8 (2-bedroom). **Comments** Though they're time-shares, the villas are rented nightly as well.

Signia by Hilton Orlando Bonnet Creek ★★★★

14100 Bonnet Creek Resort Ln. | ☎ 407-597-3600 | hiltonbonnetcreek.com

Rate per night $251–$454. **Pool** ★★★★½. **Shuttle to parks** Yes (Disney). **Maximum number of occupants per room** 4. **Comments** $50/night resort fee. Parking $36/day. Guests are eligible for Early Theme Park Entry benefits.

Sonesta ES Suites Lake Buena Vista
(not enough surveys to rate)

8751 Suiteside Drive | ☎ 407-238-0777 | theugseries.com/sonesta

Rate per night 1-bedroom suites, $163–$254; 2-bedroom suites, $189–$304. **Pool** ★★★. **Shuttle to parks** Yes (Disney, Universal); fee applies. **Maximum number of occupants per room** 4 (1-bedroom suites)/8 (2-bedroom suites). **Comments** Parking $15/day.

Waldorf Astoria Orlando ★★★★½

14200 Bonnet Creek Resort Ln. | ☎ 407-597-5500 | waldorfastoriaorlando.com

Rate per night $407–$854. **Pool** ★★★★. **Shuttle to parks** Yes (Disney). **Maximum number of occupants per room** 4 plus child in crib. **Comments** $50/night resort fee.

US 192 AREA

Gaylord Palms Resort & Convention Center ★★★½

6000 W. Osceola Pkwy. | ☎ 407-586-0000 | gaylordpalms.com

Rate per night $331–$854. **Pool** ★★★★. **Shuttle to parks** Yes (Disney, free; other parks, fee applies). **Maximum number of occupants per room** 4. **Comments** $38/night resort fee. Parking $38/day.

Holiday Inn Club Vacations at Orange Lake Resort
(not enough surveys to rate)

8505 W. Irlo Bronson Memorial Hwy. (US 192) | ☎ 407-477-7025 | theugseries.com/hi-orange-lake

Rate per night $149–$215. **Pools** ★★★★. **Shuttle to parks** Yes (fee applies). **Maximum number of occupants per room** Varies. **Comments** This is a time-share property, but you can rent directly through the resort. $30/night resort fee.

Margaritaville Resort Orlando *(not enough surveys to rate)*

8000 Fins Up Circle | ☎ 407-479-0950 | theugseries.com/margarita-orlando

Rate per night Hotel rooms, $201–$279; cottages (1–8 bedrooms), $249–$2,220. **Pool** ★★★★. **Fridge in room** Yes (full kitchen). **Shuttle to parks** No. **Maximum number of occupants per room** 2 for a standard room; 18 for an 8-bedroom cottage. **Comments** $50/night resort fee. $75/night pet fee (maximum charge of $300) in hotel, $40/night pet fee in Cottages.

Lodging Area 3: US 192

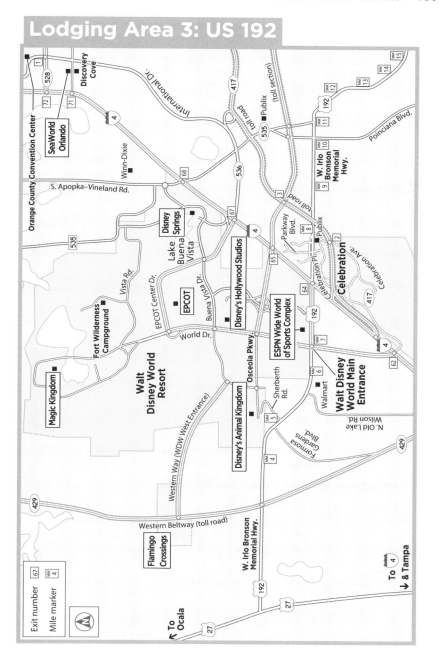

Polynesian Isles Resort (Diamond Resorts) ★★★★

3045 Polynesian Isles Blvd. | ☎ 407-396-1622 | polynesianisle.com

Rate per night 1-bedroom villas, $137–$306; 2-bedroom villas, $187–$364. **Pool** ★★★½. **Fridge in room** Yes (full kitchen). **Shuttle to parks** No. **Maximum number of occupants per room** 4 (1-bedroom)/6 (2-bedroom), plus child in crib. **Comments** $15/night resort fee.

FLAMINGO CROSSINGS

FLAMINGO CROSSINGS IS LOCATED at the intersection of US 429 and Western Way—less than 60 seconds from Disney property by car. Follow Western Way for a bit, and you'll end up at Coronado Springs Resort. There are five hotels in this area. Two are Hilton properties: **Home2Suites** and **Homewood Suites.** Three are Marriott brands: **Residence Inn**; **SpringHill Suites**; and the extended-stay **TownePlace Suites.** All have 220–300 rooms.

The brand-related hotels are adjacent and share parking, a huge pool complex, and gyms. Other amenities include practice fields and facilities—for the sports groups that participate in events at the ESPN Wide World of Sports Complex. The lobbies are constantly abuzz with color-coordinated teens either preparing for or unwinding from some event.

In addition to being close to Disney property, the Flamingo Crossings hotels are about a 10-minute drive to a wide variety of retailers on US 192, including a Publix, a Super Target, and tons of restaurants.

Home2Suites by Hilton *(not enough surveys to rate)*

341 Flagler Ave. | ☎ 407-993-3999 | theugseries.com/fc-home2

Rate per night $177–$280. **Pool** ★★★★. **Shuttle to parks** Yes (Magic Kingdom only, $5). **Maximum number of occupants per room** 6, plus child in crib.

Homewood Suites by Hilton ★★★★½

411 Flagler Ave. | ☎ 407-993-3011 | theugseries.com/fc-homewood

Rate per night $177–$280. **Pool** ★★★★. **Shuttle to parks** Yes (Magic Kingdom only, $5). **Maximum number of occupants per room** 4 (1-bedroom suite with king and pullout beds)–5 (1-bedroom suite with 2 queen and pullout beds), plus child in crib.

Residence Inn *(not enough surveys to rate)*

2111 Flagler Ave. | ☎ 407-993-3233 | theugseries.com/fc-res-inn

Rate per night Studios, $139–$209; 1-bedroom suites, $219–$343; 2-bedroom suites, $324–$433. **Pool** ★★★★. **Shuttle to parks** No. **Maximum number of occupants per room** 2 (studio)/6 (1-bedroom suite with pull-out sofa)/8 (2-bedroom suite with pull-out sofa).

SpringHill Suites ★★★★

13279 Hartzog Rd. | ☎ 407-507-1200 | theugseries.com/fc-springhill

Rate per night $141–$285. **Pool** ★★★★. **Shuttle to parks** Yes (Magic Kingdom only, $5). **Maximum number of occupants per room** 6, plus child in crib.

TownePlace Suites ★★★★

13295 Hartzog Rd. | ☎ 407-507-1300 | theugseries.com/fc-towne

Rate per night $114–$189. **Pool** ★★★★. **Shuttle to parks** Yes (Magic Kingdom only, $5). **Maximum number of occupants per room** 3 (1-bedroom suite)/5 (2-bedroom suite with 2 queen and pullout beds), plus child in crib.

HOTEL *and* MOTEL ROOMS:
Rated and Ranked

IN THIS SECTION, WE COMPARE HOTEL ROOMS in four main lodging areas outside Walt Disney World (see page 176) with those inside the World. Additional hotels can be found at the intersection of US 27 and I-4, on US 441 (Orange Blossom Trail), and in downtown Orlando. Most of these require more than 30 minutes of commuting to Disney World, so we don't recommend them. We also haven't rated lodging east of Siesta Lago Drive on US 192. If a hotel isn't listed in this section, the most likely reason is that the ones that *are* listed are better choices in terms of quality and price.

WHAT'S IN A ROOM?

OTHER THAN GENERAL CLEANLINESS, state of repair, and décor, many travelers pay little attention to hotel rooms. There is, of course, a certain standard of quality that differentiates Motel 6 from Holiday Inn, Holiday Inn from Marriott, and so on. But many guests don't fully appreciate that some rooms are better engineered than others. We have seen some beautifully appointed rooms that aren't very well designed. Making the room usable for its occupants is an art that combines both form and function. Even more than décor, your room's details and layout will make you feel comfortable and at home.

ROOM RATINGS

TO CATEGORIZE PROPERTIES by their quality, tastefulness, state of repair, cleanliness, and size of their standard rooms, we have assigned the hotels and motels an **overall star rating.** These ratings are based on expected levels of quality established by specific American hotel corporations (see table below) and don't necessarily correspond to ratings awarded by *Frommer's*, TripAdvisor, AAA, or other travel critics.

OVERALL STAR RATINGS		
★★★★★	Superior rooms	Tasteful and luxurious by any standard
★★★★	Extremely nice rooms	What you'd expect at a Hyatt Regency or Marriott
★★★	Nice rooms	Holiday Inn or comparable quality
★★	Adequate rooms	Clean, comfortable, and functional without frills—like a Motel 6
★	Super-budget	These exist but are not recommended

Overall star ratings apply only to room quality and describe the property's standard accommodations. For most hotels, a standard accommodation is a room with one king bed or two queen beds. In an all-suite property, a standard accommodation is either a studio or a one-bedroom suite. Ratings are assigned without regard to amenities such as restaurants, recreational facilities, and entertainment.

In addition to stars (which delineate broad categories), we use a numerical rating system—the **room-quality rating.** Our scale is 0–100, with 100 being the best possible rating and zero (0) the worst. Numerical ratings show the difference we perceive between one property and another.

The **location** column identifies the area around Walt Disney World where you'll find a particular property (key below).

LODGING AREAS *(see maps on pages 185, 187, and 189)*	
WDW Inside Walt Disney World	
1 On or near International Drive	**3** On or near US 192 (aka Irlo Bronson Memorial Highway, Vine Street, and Space Coast Parkway)
2 Lake Buena Vista, FL 535, and the I-4 corridor and vicinity	**4** Universal Orlando Area

The names of properties along US 192 also designate location (for example, the Holiday Inn Maingate West). The consensus in Orlando seems to be that the main entrance to Walt Disney World is the broad interstate-type road that runs off US 192. This is called the **Maingate.** Properties along US 192 call themselves Maingate East or West to differentiate their positions along the highway. So, driving southeast from Clermont or Florida's Turnpike, the properties before you reach the Maingate turnoff are called Maingate West, while the properties after you pass the Maingate turnoff are called Maingate East.

Cost estimates are based on the hotel's published rack rates for standard rooms. Each **$** represents $50; amounts over $200 are indicated by **$ x 5** and so on. We add new properties and change ratings and rankings annually, based on factors such as room renovations or a change in maintenance or housekeeping.

THE 20 BEST HOTEL VALUES

FOR THE TABLE ON THE OPPOSITE PAGE, we look at the best combinations of quality and value in a room. Rankings are calculated without consideration for location or the availability of restaurants, recreational facilities, entertainment, or amenities.

$120 IS THE NEW $70 One of our major research projects over the past few years has been to find hotels with clean, safe, functional rooms that we could recommend to you for around $70 per night with tax. Unfortunately, we found just one for this edition (the Rodeway Inn Maingate, which did not have enough surveys to rate). And we learned something along the way: At the $70 price point, we frequently had to make compromises in either safety or functionality, or both. At one motel on International Drive, we were greeted with a sign advising that copies of our driver's licenses would be shared with local police! At another motel, our door lock was made of plastic and didn't include a dead bolt—we had to pack our belongings into the car every time we left the room. At a third, our game of "spot the meth lab" became "spot the one that's *not* a meth lab." We were too scared to stay the night. Most of the rooms we checked at this price point also had some sort of mechanical problem, from balky toilets to water shooting out of the faucet whenever you turned it on. On the upside, the staff we met were uniformly helpful, and most were downright cheerful.

Ultimately, we decided that **$120 per night** (including tax) is the bare minimum you should expect to pay for a clean, safe hotel room near Disney property—the $70 room that made it into the guidebook is a rare exception to the rule and isn't really representative when it comes to quality.

If you find something cheaper than $100 per night that meets our criteria and isn't already listed here, please let us know.

THE TOP 20 BEST DEALS

	HOTEL	LODGING AREA	OVERALL QUALITY	ROOM QUALITY	COST ($ = $50)
1	Holiday Inn Orlando SW–Celebration Area	3	★★★★★	97	$$$+
2	Holiday Inn Resort Orlando–Lake Buena Vista	2	★★★★½	90	$$+
3	Mystic Dunes Resort & Golf Club (Diamond Resorts)	3	★★★★½	90	$$$+
4	Hilton Grand Vacations Club SeaWorld Orlando	1	★★★★★	97	$$$+
5	Homewood Suites by Hilton Orlando–International Drive/Convention Center	1	★★★★½	93	$$$
6	Best Western Plus Universal Inn	4	★★★★½	93	$$$
7	Holiday Inn Express & Suites/South Lake Buena Vista	2	★★★★½	90	$$$
8	Vacation Village at Parkway	3	★★★★	89	$$$-
9	Courtyard Orlando Lake Buena Vista at Vista Centre	2	★★★★	87	$$$-
10	Homewood Suites by Hilton Orlando Theme Parks	1	★★★★	87	$$$-
11	Galleria Palms Hotel	3	★★★★½	92	$$$+
12	Comfort Suites Maingate East	3	★★★★	87	$$$
13	Hilton Grand Vacations Club Tuscany Village	1	★★★★½	90	$$$+
14	Holiday Inn Orlando–Disney Springs Resort Area	WDW	★★★★½	90	$$$$-
15	Homewood Suites by Hilton Lake Buena Vista-Orlando	2	★★★★½	93	$$$$-
16	TownePlace Suites Orlando at Flamingo Crossings	2	★★★★	87	$$$
17	Marriott's Harbour Lake	2	★★★★½	94	$$$$-
18	Star Island Resort & Club	3	★★★★	82	$$$-
19	Homewood Suites by Hilton Orlando–Nearest to Universal Studios	1	★★★★	87	$$$
20	Extended Stay America Convention Center/Westwood	1	★★★★	87	$$

HOTEL INFORMATION TABLE

Bay Lake Tower at Disney's Contemporary Resort
(studios) ★ ★ ★ ★ ½
4600 N. World Dr.
Lake Buena Vista, FL 32830
☎ 407-824-1000
theugseries.com/wdw-bay

LOCATION	WDW
ROOM QUALITY	90
COST ($=$50)	$+ x 16
DAILY RESORT FEE	None
COMMUTING TIMES TO PARKS (in minutes):	
MAGIC KINGDOM	on monorail
EPCOT	11:00
ANIMAL KINGDOM	17:15
DHS	14:15

Boulder Ridge Villas at Disney's Wilderness Lodge (studios)
★ ★ ★ ★
901 Timberline Dr.
Lake Buena Vista, FL 32830
☎ 407-824-3200
theugseries.com/wdw-brv

LOCATION	WDW
ROOM QUALITY	83
COST ($=$50)	$- x 14
DAILY RESORT FEE	None
COMMUTING TIMES TO PARKS (in minutes):	
MAGIC KINGDOM	by ferry
EPCOT	10:00
ANIMAL KINGDOM	15:15
DHS	13:30

The Cabins at Disney's Fort Wilderness Resort ★ ★ ★ ★
4510 N. Fort Wilderness Trl.
Lake Buena Vista, FL 32830
☎ 407-824-2900
theugseries.com/wdw-cabin

LOCATION	WDW
ROOM QUALITY	88
COST ($=$50)	$- x 13
DAILY RESORT FEE	None
COMMUTING TIMES TO PARKS (in minutes):	
MAGIC KINGDOM	13:15
EPCOT	08:30
ANIMAL KINGDOM	20:00
DHS	14:00

Disney's All-Star Sports Resort
★ ★ ★ ★
1701 W. Buena Vista Dr.
Lake Buena Vista, FL 32830
☎ 407-939-5000
theugseries.com/wdw-assp

LOCATION	WDW
ROOM QUALITY	87
COST ($=$50)	$$$$+
DAILY RESORT FEE	None
COMMUTING TIMES TO PARKS (in minutes):	
MAGIC KINGDOM	19:00
EPCOT	04:00
ANIMAL KINGDOM	10:00
DHS	09:00

Disney's Animal Kingdom Lodge
★ ★ ★ ★
2901 W. Osceola Pkwy.
Lake Buena Vista, FL 32830
☎ 407-938-3000
theugseries.com/wdw-akl

LOCATION	WDW
ROOM QUALITY	88
COST ($=$50)	$ x 13
DAILY RESORT FEE	None
COMMUTING TIMES TO PARKS (in minutes):	
MAGIC KINGDOM	06:15
EPCOT	05:45
ANIMAL KINGDOM	04:15
DHS	05:15

Disney's Animal Kingdom Villas
(Jambo House, studios) ★ ★ ★ ★
2901 W. Osceola Pkwy.
Lake Buena Vista, FL 32830
☎ 407-938-3000
theugseries.com/wdw-jam

LOCATION	WDW
ROOM QUALITY	85
COST ($=$50)	$ x 13
DAILY RESORT FEE	None
COMMUTING TIMES TO PARKS (in minutes):	
MAGIC KINGDOM	08:15
EPCOT	06:15
ANIMAL KINGDOM	02:15
DHS	06:00

Disney's Beach Club Villas (studios)
★ ★ ★ ★
1800 EPCOT Resorts Blvd.
Lake Buena Vista, FL 32830
☎ 407-934-8000
theugseries.com/wdw-bcv

LOCATION	WDW
ROOM QUALITY	86
COST ($=$50)	$ x 15
DAILY RESORT FEE	None
COMMUTING TIMES TO PARKS (in minutes):	
MAGIC KINGDOM	07:15
EPCOT	05:15
ANIMAL KINGDOM	06:45
DHS	04:00

Disney's BoardWalk Inn ★ ★ ★ ★ ½
2101 N. EPCOT Resorts Blvd.
Lake Buena Vista, FL 32830
☎ 407-939-6200
theugseries.com/wdw-bwi

LOCATION	WDW
ROOM QUALITY	90
COST ($=$50)	$+ x 16
DAILY RESORT FEE	None
COMMUTING TIMES TO PARKS (in minutes):	
MAGIC KINGDOM	07:15
EPCOT	05:15
ANIMAL KINGDOM	06:45
DHS	04:00

Disney's BoardWalk Villas ★ ★ ★ ★
2101 N. EPCOT Resorts Blvd.
Lake Buena Vista, FL 32830
☎ 407-939-6200
theugseries.com/wdw-bwv

LOCATION	WDW
ROOM QUALITY	89
COST ($=$50)	$+ x 16
DAILY RESORT FEE	None
COMMUTING TIMES TO PARKS (in minutes):	
MAGIC KINGDOM	07:15
EPCOT	05:15
ANIMAL KINGDOM	06:45
DHS	04:00

Disney's Grand Floridian Resort & Spa ★ ★ ★ ★ ½
4401 Floridian Way
Lake Buena Vista, FL 32830
☎ 407-824-3000
theugseries.com/wdw-flo

LOCATION	WDW
ROOM QUALITY	90
COST ($=$50)	$- x 21
DAILY RESORT FEE	None
COMMUTING TIMES TO PARKS (in minutes):	
MAGIC KINGDOM	on monorail
EPCOT	04:45
ANIMAL KINGDOM	11:45
DHS	06:45

Disney's Old Key West Resort
★ ★ ★ ★ ½
1510 North Cove Rd.
Lake Buena Vista, FL 32830
☎ 407-827-7700
theugseries.com/wdw-okw

LOCATION	WDW
ROOM QUALITY	91
COST ($=$50)	$ x 12
DAILY RESORT FEE	None
COMMUTING TIMES TO PARKS (in minutes):	
MAGIC KINGDOM	10:45
EPCOT	06:00
ANIMAL KINGDOM	14:30
DHS	10:30

Disney's Polynesian Village Resort
★ ★ ★ ★ ½
1600 Seven Seas Dr.
Lake Buena Vista, FL 32830
☎ 407-824-2000
theugseries.com/wdw-poly

LOCATION	WDW
ROOM QUALITY	90
COST ($=$50)	$- x 19
DAILY RESORT FEE	None
COMMUTING TIMES TO PARKS (in minutes):	
MAGIC KINGDOM	on monorail
EPCOT	08:00
ANIMAL KINGDOM	16:15
DHS	12:30

---

* Irlo Bronson Memorial Highway   ** Not enough surveys or too new to rate

Copper Creek Villas & Cabins at Disney's Wilderness Lodge
(studios) ★ ★ ★ ★
901 Timberline Dr.
Lake Buena Vista, FL 32830
☎ 407-824-3200
theugseries.com/wdw-ccv

LOCATION	WDW
ROOM QUALITY	88
COST ($=$50)	$- x 14
DAILY RESORT FEE	None
COMMUTING TIMES TO PARKS (in minutes):	
MAGIC KINGDOM	17:45
EPCOT	13:15
ANIMAL KINGDOM	16:15
DHS	15:15

Disney's All-Star Movies Resort
★ ★ ★ ★
1901 W. Buena Vista Dr.
Lake Buena Vista, FL 32830
☎ 407-939-7000
theugseries.com/wdw-asmo

LOCATION	WDW
ROOM QUALITY	87
COST ($=$50)	$$$$+
DAILY RESORT FEE	None
COMMUTING TIMES TO PARKS (in minutes):	
MAGIC KINGDOM	19:00
EPCOT	04:00
ANIMAL KINGDOM	10:00
DHS	09:00

Disney's All-Star Music Resort
★ ★ ★ ★
1801 W. Buena Vista Dr.
Lake Buena Vista, FL 32830
☎ 407-939-6000
theugseries.com/wdw-asmu

LOCATION	WDW
ROOM QUALITY	87
COST ($=$50)	$$$$+
DAILY RESORT FEE	None
COMMUTING TIMES TO PARKS (in minutes):	
MAGIC KINGDOM	19:00
EPCOT	04:00
ANIMAL KINGDOM	10:00
DHS	09:00

Disney's Animal Kingdom Villas
(Kidani Village, studios) ★ ★ ★ ★
3701 W. Osceola Pkwy.
Bay Lake, FL 32830
☎ 407-938-7400
theugseries.com/wdw-kid

LOCATION	WDW
ROOM QUALITY	89
COST ($=$50)	$ x 13
DAILY RESORT FEE	None
COMMUTING TIMES TO PARKS (in minutes):	
MAGIC KINGDOM	08:15
EPCOT	06:15
ANIMAL KINGDOM	02:15
DHS	06:00

Disney's Art of Animation Resort
★ ★ ★ ½
1850 Animation Way
Lake Buena Vista, FL 32830
☎ 407-938-7000
theugseries.com/wdw-aoa

LOCATION	WDW
ROOM QUALITY	82
COST ($=$50)	$ x 6
DAILY RESORT FEE	None
COMMUTING TIMES TO PARKS (in minutes):	
MAGIC KINGDOM	08:15
EPCOT	06:15
ANIMAL KINGDOM	02:15
DHS	06:00

Disney's Beach Club Resort
★ ★ ★ ★
1800 EPCOT Resorts Blvd.
Lake Buena Vista, FL 32830
☎ 407-934-8000
theugseries.com/wdw-bcr

LOCATION	WDW
ROOM QUALITY	87
COST ($=$50)	$ x 15
DAILY RESORT FEE	None
COMMUTING TIMES TO PARKS (in minutes):	
MAGIC KINGDOM	12:00
EPCOT	10:00
ANIMAL KINGDOM	12:00
DHS	03:00

Disney's Caribbean Beach Resort
★ ★ ★ ★
1114 Cayman Way
Lake Buena Vista, FL 32830
☎ 407-934-3400
theugseries.com/wdw-cbr

LOCATION	WDW
ROOM QUALITY	88
COST ($=$50)	$- x 8
DAILY RESORT FEE	None
COMMUTING TIMES TO PARKS (in minutes):	
MAGIC KINGDOM	07:15
EPCOT	05:30
ANIMAL KINGDOM	07:00
DHS	03:00

Disney's Contemporary Resort
★ ★ ★ ★
4600 N. World Dr.
Lake Buena Vista, FL 32830
☎ 407-824-1000
theugseries.com/wdw-con

LOCATION	WDW
ROOM QUALITY	88
COST ($=$50)	$+ x 15
DAILY RESORT FEE	None
COMMUTING TIMES TO PARKS (in minutes):	
MAGIC KINGDOM	08:00
EPCOT	06:00
ANIMAL KINGDOM	07:15
DHS	04:15

Disney's Coronado Springs Resort ★ ★ ★ ★ ½
1000 W. Buena Vista Dr.
Lake Buena Vista, FL 32830
☎ 407-939-1000
theugseries.com/wdw-csr

LOCATION	WDW
ROOM QUALITY	90
COST ($=$50)	$+ x 7
DAILY RESORT FEE	None
COMMUTING TIMES TO PARKS (in minutes):	
MAGIC KINGDOM	on monorail
EPCOT	11:00
ANIMAL KINGDOM	17:15
DHS	14:15

Disney's Polynesian Villas & Bungalows (studios) ★ ★ ★ ★ ½
1600 Seven Seas Dr.
Lake Buena Vista, FL 32830
☎ 407-824-2000
theugseries.com/wdw-pvb

LOCATION	WDW
ROOM QUALITY	91
COST ($=$50)	$- x 19
DAILY RESORT FEE	None
COMMUTING TIMES TO PARKS (in minutes):	
MAGIC KINGDOM	on monorail
EPCOT	08:00
ANIMAL KINGDOM	16:15
DHS	12:30

Disney's Pop Century Resort
★ ★ ★ ★
1050 Century Dr.
Lake Buena Vista, FL 32830
☎ 407-938-4000
theugseries.com/wdw-pop

LOCATION	WDW
ROOM QUALITY	87
COST ($=$50)	$- x 6
DAILY RESORT FEE	None
COMMUTING TIMES TO PARKS (in minutes):	
MAGIC KINGDOM	08:30
EPCOT	06:30
ANIMAL KINGDOM	06:15
DHS	05:00

Disney's Port Orleans Resort– French Quarter ★ ★ ★ ★
2201 Orleans Dr.
Lake Buena Vista, FL 32830
☎ 407-934-5000
theugseries.com/wdw-frq

LOCATION	WDW
ROOM QUALITY	85
COST ($=$50)	$- x 8
DAILY RESORT FEE	None
COMMUTING TIMES TO PARKS (in minutes):	
MAGIC KINGDOM	12:00
EPCOT	08:00
ANIMAL KINGDOM	16:15
DHS	12:30

Note: Commuting times represent only the driving time to and from the parking lot entrance. You'll need to add some time (varies by park) for paying your parking fee and parking. See page 178 for details.

HOTEL INFORMATION TABLE (continued)

Disney's Port Orleans Resort–Riverside ★★★★
1251 Riverside Dr.
Lake Buena Vista, FL 32830
☎ 407-934-6000
theugseries.com/wdw-por

LOCATION	WDW
ROOM QUALITY	84
COST ($=$50)	$- x 8
DAILY RESORT FEE	None

COMMUTING TIMES TO PARKS (in minutes):

MAGIC KINGDOM	12:00
EPCOT	08:00
ANIMAL KINGDOM	16:15
DHS	12:30

Disney's Riviera Resort ★★★★½
1080 Esplanade Ave.
Lake Buena Vista, FL 32830
☎ 407-828-7030
theugseries.com/wdw-riv

LOCATION	WDW
ROOM QUALITY	93
COST ($=$50)	$- x 13
DAILY RESORT FEE	None

COMMUTING TIMES TO PARKS (in minutes):

MAGIC KINGDOM	08:00
EPCOT	06:00
ANIMAL KINGDOM	07:15
DHS	04:15

Disney's Saratoga Springs Resort & Spa ★★★★½
1960 Broadway
Lake Buena Vista, FL 32830
☎ 407-827-1100
theugseries.com/wdw-ssr

LOCATION	WDW
ROOM QUALITY	92
COST ($=$50)	$ x 12
DAILY RESORT FEE	None

COMMUTING TIMES TO PARKS (in minutes):

MAGIC KINGDOM	14:45
EPCOT	08:45
ANIMAL KINGDOM	18:15
DHS	14:30

Drury Plaza Hotel Orlando**
2000 Hotel Plaza Blvd.
Lake Buena Vista, FL 32830
☎ 407-560-6111
druryplazahotelorlando.com

LOCATION	WDW
ROOM QUALITY	-
COST ($=$50)	$$$$$+
DAILY RESORT FEE	None

COMMUTING TIMES TO PARKS (in minutes):

MAGIC KINGDOM	12:45
EPCOT	08:00
ANIMAL KINGDOM	11:00
DHS	10:30

Evermore Orlando Resort**
1590 Evermore Way
☎ 407-239-4700
evermoreresort.com

LOCATION	WDW
ROOM QUALITY	-
COST ($=$50)	$ x 8-22
DAILY RESORT FEE	$50

COMMUTING TIMES TO PARKS (in minutes):

MAGIC KINGDOM	16:00
EPCOT	15:00
ANIMAL KINGDOM	22:00
DHS	15:00

Four Seasons Resort Orlando at Walt Disney World Resort ★★★★★
10100 Dream Tree Blvd.
Lake Buena Vista, FL 32836
☎ 407-313-7777
fourseasons.com/orlando

LOCATION	WDW
ROOM QUALITY	100
COST ($=$50)	$ x 28
DAILY RESORT FEE	None

COMMUTING TIMES TO PARKS (in minutes):

MAGIC KINGDOM	09:00
EPCOT	08:00
ANIMAL KINGDOM	15:00
DHS	08:00

Hilton Orlando Buena Vista Palace ★★★★
1900 E. Buena Vista Dr.
Lake Buena Vista, FL 32830
☎ 407-827-2727
buenavistapalace.com

LOCATION	WDW
ROOM QUALITY	87
COST ($=$50)	$ x 6
DAILY RESORT FEE	$39

COMMUTING TIMES TO PARKS (in minutes):

MAGIC KINGDOM	08:00
EPCOT	06:00
ANIMAL KINGDOM	07:15
DHS	04:15

Hilton Orlando Lake Buena Vista–Disney Springs Area ★★★½
1751 Hotel Plaza Blvd.
Lake Buena Vista, FL 32830
☎ 407-827-4000
hilton-wdwv.com

LOCATION	WDW
ROOM QUALITY	79
COST ($=$50)	$$$$$
DAILY RESORT FEE	$35

COMMUTING TIMES TO PARKS (in minutes):

MAGIC KINGDOM	16:00
EPCOT	11:15
ANIMAL KINGDOM	15:15
DHS	13:00

Holiday Inn Club Vacations at Orange Lake Resort**
8505 W. US 192*
Kissimmee, FL 34747
☎ 407-477-7025
theugseries.com/hi-orange-lake

LOCATION	3
ROOM QUALITY	-
COST ($=$50)	$$$
DAILY RESORT FEE	$20

COMMUTING TIMES TO PARKS (in minutes):

MAGIC KINGDOM	19:00
EPCOT	14:15
ANIMAL KINGDOM	17:15
DHS	16:45

Loews Portofino Bay Hotel at Universal Orlando ★★★★½
5601 Universal Blvd.
Orlando, FL 32819
☎ 407-503-1000
loewshotels.com/portofino-bay-hotel

LOCATION	4
ROOM QUALITY	90
COST ($=$50)	$ x 12
DAILY RESORT FEE	None

COMMUTING TIMES TO PARKS (in minutes):

MAGIC KINGDOM	09:00
EPCOT	08:45
ANIMAL KINGDOM	05:15
DHS	08:15

Loews Royal Pacific Resort at Universal Orlando ★★★★
6300 Hollywood Way
Orlando, FL 32819
☎ 407-503-3000
loewshotels.com/royal-pacific-resort

LOCATION	4
ROOM QUALITY	86
COST ($=$50)	$ x 11
DAILY RESORT FEE	None

COMMUTING TIMES TO PARKS (in minutes):

MAGIC KINGDOM	21:45
EPCOT	17:15
ANIMAL KINGDOM	20:15
DHS	19:45

Loews Sapphire Falls Resort at Universal Orlando ★★★★
6601 Adventure Way
Orlando, FL 32819
☎ 407-503-5000
loewshotels.com/sapphire-falls-resort

LOCATION	4
ROOM QUALITY	86
COST ($=$50)	$- x 8
DAILY RESORT FEE	None

COMMUTING TIMES TO PARKS (in minutes):

MAGIC KINGDOM	20:00
EPCOT	15:15
ANIMAL KINGDOM	18:15
DHS	17:45

* Irlo Bronson Memorial Highway   ** Not enough surveys or too new to rate

Disney's Wilderness Lodge
★ ★ ★ ★
901 Timberline Dr.
Lake Buena Vista, FL 32830
☎ 407-824-3200
theugseries.com/wdw-wil

LOCATION	WDW
ROOM QUALITY	88
COST ($=$50)	$- x 14
DAILY RESORT FEE	None

COMMUTING TIMES TO PARKS
(in minutes):

MAGIC KINGDOM	by ferry
EPCOT	10:00
ANIMAL KINGDOM	15:15
DHS	13:30

Disney's Yacht Club Resort
★ ★ ★ ★
1700 EPCOT Resorts Blvd.
Lake Buena Vista, FL 32830
☎ 407-934-7000
theugseries.com/wdw-ycr

LOCATION	WDW
ROOM QUALITY	88
COST ($=$50)	$ x 15
DAILY RESORT FEE	None

COMMUTING TIMES TO PARKS
(in minutes):

MAGIC KINGDOM	07:15
EPCOT	05:15
ANIMAL KINGDOM	06:45
DHS	04:00

DoubleTree Suites by Hilton Orlando–Disney Springs Area
★ ★ ★ ★
2305 Hotel Plaza Blvd.
Lake Buena Vista, FL 32830
☎ 407-934-1000
doubletreeguestsuites.com

LOCATION	WDW
ROOM QUALITY	86
COST ($=$50)	$$$$
DAILY RESORT FEE	$23

COMMUTING TIMES TO PARKS
(in minutes):

MAGIC KINGDOM	13:00
EPCOT	08:30
ANIMAL KINGDOM	12:30
DHS	10:00

Gaylord Palms Resort & Convention Center ★ ★ ★ ½
6000 W. Osceola Pkwy.
Kissimmee, FL 34746
☎ 407-586-0000
gaylordpalms.com

LOCATION	3
ROOM QUALITY	80
COST ($=$50)	$+ x 8
DAILY RESORT FEE	$38

COMMUTING TIMES TO PARKS
(in minutes):

MAGIC KINGDOM	09:00
EPCOT	08:45
ANIMAL KINGDOM	07:00
DHS	08:15

Hard Rock Hotel Orlando ★ ★ ★ ★
5800 Universal Blvd.
Orlando, FL 32819
☎ 407-503-2000
hardrockhotels.com/orlando

LOCATION	4
ROOM QUALITY	87
COST ($=$50)	$ x 13
DAILY RESORT FEE	None

COMMUTING TIMES TO PARKS
(in minutes):

MAGIC KINGDOM	21:45
EPCOT	17:00
ANIMAL KINGDOM	20:00
DHS	19:30

Hilton Grand Vacations Club SeaWorld Orlando ★ ★ ★ ★ ★
6924 Grand Vacations Way
Orlando, FL 32821
☎ 407-239-0100
theugseries.com/hilton-sea-world

LOCATION	1
ROOM QUALITY	97
COST ($=$50)	$$$+
DAILY RESORT FEE	$25

COMMUTING TIMES TO PARKS
(in minutes):

MAGIC KINGDOM	17:00
EPCOT	12:30
ANIMAL KINGDOM	16:30
DHS	15:30

Holiday Inn Orlando–Disney Springs Resort Area ★ ★ ★ ½
1805 Hotel Plaza Blvd.
Lake Buena Vista, FL 32830
☎ 407-828-8888
hiorlando.com

LOCATION	WDW
ROOM QUALITY	90
COST ($=$50)	$$$$-
DAILY RESORT FEE	$30

COMMUTING TIMES TO PARKS
(in minutes):

MAGIC KINGDOM	12:15
EPCOT	12:00
ANIMAL KINGDOM	10:15
DHS	11:30

Home2Suites by Hilton Orlando at Flamingo Crossings Town Center**
341 Flagler Ave.
Winter Garden, FL 34787
☎ 407-993-3999
theugseries.com/fc-home2

LOCATION	2
ROOM QUALITY	–
COST ($=$50)	$$$$$-
DAILY RESORT FEE	None

COMMUTING TIMES TO PARKS
(in minutes):

MAGIC KINGDOM	10:45
EPCOT	06:00
ANIMAL KINGDOM	09:00
DHS	08:30

Homewood Suites by Hilton at Flamingo Crossings ★ ★ ★ ★ ½
411 Flagler Ave.
Winter Garden, FL 34787
☎ 407-993-3011
theugseries.com/fc-homewood

LOCATION	2
ROOM QUALITY	93
COST ($=$50)	$$$$$-
DAILY RESORT FEE	None

COMMUTING TIMES TO PARKS
(in minutes):

MAGIC KINGDOM	18:00
EPCOT	16:00
ANIMAL KINGDOM	10:00
DHS	15:00

Margaritaville Resort Orlando**
8000 Fins Up Circle
Kissimmee, FL 34747
☎ 407-479-0950
theugseries.com/margarita-orlando

LOCATION	3
ROOM QUALITY	–
COST ($=$50)	$$$$$-
DAILY RESORT FEE	None

COMMUTING TIMES TO PARKS
(in minutes):

MAGIC KINGDOM	20:00
EPCOT	15:00
ANIMAL KINGDOM	17:00
DHS	14:00

Marriott's Harbour Lake ★ ★ ★ ★ ½
7102 Grand Horizons Blvd.
Orlando, FL 32821
☎ 407-465-6100
theugseries.com/harbour-lake

LOCATION	2
ROOM QUALITY	94
COST ($=$50)	$$$$-
DAILY RESORT FEE	None

COMMUTING TIMES TO PARKS
(in minutes):

MAGIC KINGDOM	15:00
EPCOT	12:45
ANIMAL KINGDOM	15:45
DHS	15:15

Polynesian Isles Resort
(Diamond Resorts) ★ ★ ★ ★
3045 Polynesian Isles Blvd.
Kissimmee, FL 34746
☎ 407-396-1622
polynesianisle.com

LOCATION	3
ROOM QUALITY	88
COST ($=$50)	$$$$$+
DAILY RESORT FEE	$15

COMMUTING TIMES TO PARKS
(in minutes):

MAGIC KINGDOM	14:30
EPCOT	14:15
ANIMAL KINGDOM	12:30
DHS	14:00

Note: Commuting times represent only the driving time to and from the entrance of the parking lot. Add some time (varies by park) for paying your parking fee and parking. See page 178 for details.

HOTEL INFORMATION TABLE (continued)

Renaissance Orlando Resort & Spa (formerly B Resort & Spa)**
1905 Hotel Plaza Blvd.
Lake Buena Vista, FL 32830
☎ 407-828-2828
bresortlbv.com

LOCATION	WDW
ROOM QUALITY	–
COST ($=$50)	Unavailable
DAILY RESORT FEE	$30
COMMUTING TIMES TO PARKS (in minutes):	
MAGIC KINGDOM	15:45
EPCOT	11:00
ANIMAL KINGDOM	15:00
DHS	12:45

Residence Inn Orlando Flamingo Crossings Town Center**
2111 Flagler Ave.
Winter Garden, FL 34787
☎ 407-993-3233
theugseries.com/fc-res-inn

LOCATION	2
ROOM QUALITY	–
COST ($=$50)	$$$+
DAILY RESORT FEE	None
COMMUTING TIMES TO PARKS (in minutes):	
MAGIC KINGDOM	18:00
EPCOT	14:15
ANIMAL KINGDOM	18:00
DHS	16:00

Shades of Green ★ ★ ★ ★ ½
1950 W. Magnolia Palm Dr.
Lake Buena Vista, FL 32830
☎ 407-824-3400
shadesofgreen.org

LOCATION	WDW
ROOM QUALITY	92
COST ($=$50)	$$$+
DAILY RESORT FEE	None
COMMUTING TIMES TO PARKS (in minutes):	
MAGIC KINGDOM	03:30
EPCOT	04:45
ANIMAL KINGDOM	09:30
DHS	06:15

Sonesta ES Suites Lake Buena Vista**
8751 Suiteside Dr.
Orlando, FL 32836
☎ 407-238-0777
theugseries.com/sonesta

LOCATION	2
ROOM QUALITY	–
COST ($=$50)	$$$$
DAILY RESORT FEE	None
COMMUTING TIMES TO PARKS (in minutes):	
MAGIC KINGDOM	18:00
EPCOT	16:00
ANIMAL KINGDOM	10:00
DHS	15:00

SpringHill Suites Orlando at Flamingo Crossings ★ ★ ★ ★
13279 Hartzog Rd.
Winter Garden, FL 34787
☎ 407-507-1200
theugseries.com/fc-springhill

LOCATION	2
ROOM QUALITY	88
COST ($=$50)	$$$$+
DAILY RESORT FEE	None
COMMUTING TIMES TO PARKS (in minutes):	
MAGIC KINGDOM	22:00
EPCOT	09:00
ANIMAL KINGDOM	11:00
DHS	10:00

TownePlace Suites Orlando at Flamingo Crossings ★ ★ ★ ★
13295 Hartzog Rd.
Winter Garden, FL 34787
☎ 407-507-1300
theugseries.com/fc-towne

LOCATION	2
ROOM QUALITY	87
COST ($=$50)	$$$
DAILY RESORT FEE	None
COMMUTING TIMES TO PARKS (in minutes):	
MAGIC KINGDOM	18:00
EPCOT	16:00
ANIMAL KINGDOM	10:00
DHS	16:00

Universal's Endless Summer Resort: Dockside Inn & Suites ★ ★ ★ ★
7125 Universal Blvd.
Orlando, FL 32819
☎ 407-503-8000
loewshotels.com/dockside-inn -and-suites

LOCATION	4
ROOM QUALITY	85
COST ($=$50)	$$$+
DAILY RESORT FEE	None
COMMUTING TIMES TO PARKS (in minutes):	
MAGIC KINGDOM	19:00
EPCOT	17:00
ANIMAL KINGDOM	22:00
DHS	16:00

Universal's Endless Summer Resort: Surfside Inn & Suites ★ ★ ★ ★
7000 Universal Blvd.
Orlando, FL 32819
☎ 407-503-7000
loewshotels.com/surfside-inn -and-suites

LOCATION	4
ROOM QUALITY	86
COST ($=$50)	$$$+
DAILY RESORT FEE	None
COMMUTING TIMES TO PARKS (in minutes):	
MAGIC KINGDOM	19:00
EPCOT	17:00
ANIMAL KINGDOM	22:00
DHS	16:00

Vacation Village at Parkway ★ ★ ★ ★
2975 Arabian Nights Blvd.
Kissimmee, FL 34747
☎ 407-396-9086
theugseries.com/vv-pkwy

LOCATION	3
ROOM QUALITY	89
COST ($=$50)	$$$-
DAILY RESORT FEE	$30 (one-time)
COMMUTING TIMES TO PARKS (in minutes):	
MAGIC KINGDOM	08:30
EPCOT	08:15
ANIMAL KINGDOM	06:45
DHS	07:45

Walt Disney World Swan ★ ★ ★ ★
1200 EPCOT Resorts Blvd.
Lake Buena Vista, FL 32830
☎ 407-934-3000
swandolphin.com

LOCATION	WDW
ROOM QUALITY	86
COST ($=$50)	$ x 6
DAILY RESORT FEE	$40
COMMUTING TIMES TO PARKS (in minutes):	
MAGIC KINGDOM	06:30
EPCOT	04:45
ANIMAL KINGDOM	06:15
DHS	04:00

Walt Disney World Swan Reserve ★ ★ ★ ★
1255 EPCOT Resorts Blvd.
Lake Buena Vista, FL 32830
☎ 407-934-3000
swandolphin.com

LOCATION	WDW
ROOM QUALITY	86
COST ($=$50)	$ x 8
DAILY RESORT FEE	$40
COMMUTING TIMES TO PARKS (in minutes):	
MAGIC KINGDOM	06:30
EPCOT	04:30
ANIMAL KINGDOM	06:15
DHS	04:00

Westgate Lakes Resort & Spa ★ ★ ★ ★
9500 Turkey Lake Rd.
Orlando, FL 32819
☎ 407-345-0000
westgateresorts.com/lakes

LOCATION	2
ROOM QUALITY	89
COST ($=$50)	$$$$
DAILY RESORT FEE	$20
COMMUTING TIMES TO PARKS (in minutes):	
MAGIC KINGDOM	17:30
EPCOT	14:30
ANIMAL KINGDOM	19:15
DHS	18:00

* Irlo Bronson Memorial Highway   ** Not enough surveys or too new to rate

Sheraton Vistana Resort Villas, Lake Buena Vista ★★★★	
8800 Vistana Centre Dr.	
Orlando, FL 32821	
☎ 407-239-3100	
theugseries.com/sheraton-vistana	
LOCATION	2
ROOM QUALITY	88
COST ($=$50)	$$$$$
DAILY RESORT FEE	None
COMMUTING TIMES TO PARKS (in minutes):	
MAGIC KINGDOM	11:15
EPCOT	06:30
ANIMAL KINGDOM	09:30
DHS	09:00

Sheraton Vistana Villages Resort Villas, I-Drive/ Orlando ★★★★½	
12401 International Dr.	
Orlando, FL 32821	
☎ 407-238-5000	
theugseries.com/vistana-villages	
LOCATION	1
ROOM QUALITY	90
COST ($=$50)	$$$$$
DAILY RESORT FEE	None
COMMUTING TIMES TO PARKS (in minutes):	
MAGIC KINGDOM	11:15
EPCOT	06:30
ANIMAL KINGDOM	09:30
DHS	09:00

Signia by Hilton Orlando Bonnet Creek ★★★★	
14100 Bonnet Creek Resort Ln.	
Orlando, FL 32821	
☎ 407-597-3600	
hiltonbonnetcreek.com	
LOCATION	WDW
ROOM QUALITY	87
COST ($=$50)	$$$$+
DAILY RESORT FEE	$45
COMMUTING TIMES TO PARKS (in minutes):	
MAGIC KINGDOM	08:15
EPCOT	08:00
ANIMAL KINGDOM	04:30
DHS	07:30

Treehouse Villas at Disney's Saratoga Springs Resort & Spa ★★★★	
1960 Broadway	
Lake Buena Vista, FL 32830	
☎ 407-827-1100	
theugseries.com/wdw-ssr	
LOCATION	WDW
ROOM QUALITY	89
COST ($=$50)	$+ x 32
DAILY RESORT FEE	None
COMMUTING TIMES TO PARKS (in minutes):	
MAGIC KINGDOM	12:45
EPCOT	07:15
ANIMAL KINGDOM	16:45
DHS	12:30

Universal's Aventura Hotel ★★★★	
6725 Adventure Way	
Orlando, FL 32819	
☎ 407-503-6000	
loewshotels.com/universals -aventura-hotel	
LOCATION	4
ROOM QUALITY	88
COST ($=$50)	$$$$
DAILY RESORT FEE	None
COMMUTING TIMES TO PARKS (in minutes):	
MAGIC KINGDOM	20:00
EPCOT	15:00
ANIMAL KINGDOM	17:00
DHS	14:00

Universal's Cabana Bay Beach Resort ★★★½	
6550 Adventure Way	
Orlando, FL 32819	
☎ 407-503-4000	
loewshotels.com/cabana-bay -hotel	
LOCATION	4
ROOM QUALITY	82
COST ($=$50)	$$$$+
DAILY RESORT FEE	None
COMMUTING TIMES TO PARKS (in minutes):	
MAGIC KINGDOM	20:00
EPCOT	15:00
ANIMAL KINGDOM	17:00
DHS	14:00

The Villas at Disney's Grand Floridian Resort & Spa ★★★★½	
4401 Floridian Way	
Lake Buena Vista, FL 32830	
☎ 407-824-3000	
theugseries.com/wdw-gfv	
LOCATION	WDW
ROOM QUALITY	93
COST ($=$50)	$- x 21
DAILY RESORT FEE	None
COMMUTING TIMES TO PARKS (in minutes):	
MAGIC KINGDOM	on monorail
EPCOT	04:45
ANIMAL KINGDOM	11:45
DHS	06:45

Waldorf Astoria Orlando ★★★★½	
14200 Bonnet Creek Resort Ln.	
Orlando, FL 32821	
☎ 407-597-5500	
waldorfastoriaorlando.com	
LOCATION	WDW
ROOM QUALITY	90
COST ($=$50)	$ x 16
DAILY RESORT FEE	$45
COMMUTING TIMES TO PARKS (in minutes):	
MAGIC KINGDOM	08:00
EPCOT	06:00
ANIMAL KINGDOM	07:15
DHS	04:15

Walt Disney World Dolphin ★★★★	
1500 EPCOT Resorts Blvd.	
Lake Buena Vista, FL 32830	
☎ 407-934-4000	
swandolphin.com	
LOCATION	WDW
ROOM QUALITY	85
COST ($=$50)	$ x 6
DAILY RESORT FEE	$40
COMMUTING TIMES TO PARKS (in minutes):	
MAGIC KINGDOM	06:45
EPCOT	05:00
ANIMAL KINGDOM	06:15
DHS	04:00

Wyndham Garden Lake Buena Vista ★★★½	
1850-B Hotel Plaza Blvd.	
Lake Buena Vista, FL 32830	
☎ 407-842-6644	
wyndhamlakebuenavista.com	
LOCATION	WDW
ROOM QUALITY	80
COST ($=$50)	$$$$-
DAILY RESORT FEE	$34
COMMUTING TIMES TO PARKS (in minutes):	
MAGIC KINGDOM	15:15
EPCOT	10:45
ANIMAL KINGDOM	14:45
DHS	12:15

Wyndham Grand Orlando Resort Bonnet Creek ★★★★★	
14651 Chelonia Pkwy.	
Orlando, FL 32821	
☎ 407-390-2300	
theugseries.com/wyn-bc	
LOCATION	WDW
ROOM QUALITY	96
COST ($=$50)	$ x 6
DAILY RESORT FEE	$28
COMMUTING TIMES TO PARKS (in minutes):	
MAGIC KINGDOM	18:00
EPCOT	08:00
ANIMAL KINGDOM	15:00
DHS	10:00

Wyndham Orlando Resort International Drive ★★★½	
8001 International Dr.	
Orlando, FL 32819	
☎ 407-351-2420	
wyndhamorlandoresort.com	
LOCATION	1
ROOM QUALITY	77
COST ($=$50)	$$$+
DAILY RESORT FEE	$28
COMMUTING TIMES TO PARKS (in minutes):	
MAGIC KINGDOM	19:45
EPCOT	15:00
ANIMAL KINGDOM	18:15
DHS	17:30

Note: Commuting times represent only the driving time to and from the entrance of the parking lot. Add some time (varies by park) for paying your parking fee and parking. See page 178 for details.

DINING *in* AND *around* WALT DISNEY WORLD

READER SURVEYS *plus* EXPERT OPINIONS: *Our Approach to Dining*

WE'VE RECEIVED MORE THAN 60,000 SURVEYS about Walt Disney World restaurants in the past year, and more than 1 million since 2018. We think that's more than Yelp and TripAdvisor *combined*.

What makes the *Unofficial Guide* different from Yelp and Google is that we display the results of those surveys alongside objective reviews written by culinary experts. With both, you get a consistent evaluation of the entire range of Disney dining options from people who have tried every restaurant, kiosk, and food stand in the World. Here's how to use the reader surveys and critical reviews together:

If a restaurant has earned ratings of 90% or better in our reader surveys and at least four stars (table service) or a B or better (counter service) from our critics, make plans to visit. Chances are good that you'll enjoy your meal. In EPCOT, for example, France's counter-service **Les Halles Boulangerie–Pâtisserie** and Italy's table-service **Via Napoli Ristorante e Pizzeria** both fit this profile.

In general, avoid restaurants with ratings of 80% or less in our reader surveys and either three stars or less (table service) or a C or lower (counter service) from our critics. That said, you may need to bend this rule, depending on your tastes, for locations like EPCOT's **Akershus Royal Banquet Hall.** Akershus gets lower ratings overall, but if your kids adore princesses, it's a cheaper option than **Cinderella's Royal Table** and will save you time in line at other princess meets around the World. Similarly, **Roundup Rodeo BBQ** in Hollywood Studios doesn't get high overall scores, but families with young kids give it a 98% satisfaction rate.

When reader ratings disagree with our critical analysis, check the review for an explanation. An example is **Takumi-Tei** at EPCOT's Japan Pavilion. The food quality, presentation, and service of their kaiseki makes this one of the five best restaurants in Walt Disney World. Its low ratings are entirely due to its $250-per-person price, well beyond what many theme park guests are used to paying for Japanese food. But those "normal" experiences are typically hibachi, which doesn't compare to the quality at Takumi-Tei. Readers who are used to paying $125–$150 per person for omakase sushi have much higher opinions of Takumi-Tei.

SURVEY RESULTS DEMYSTIFIED

FOR BOTH COUNTER-SERVICE and full-service restaurants, we list reader-survey results for each restaurant profiled, expressed as a percentage of positive (+) responses.

The average positive rating for all Disney counter-service restaurants is **88.5%.** And we get so many surveys every year that we're 98% confident that average is between 88.45% and 88.55%. Statistically, that means these ratings are so accurate and representative that you can trust them when deciding whether a restaurant is worth trying.

We use the following categories to provide context for the percentages:

OUR DINING SURVEY RATINGS SYSTEM		
CATEGORY	**COUNTER-SERVICE RESTAURANTS** *(average positive rating)*	**TABLE-SERVICE RESTAURANTS** *(average positive rating)*
EXCEPTIONAL	96% or higher	95% or higher
MUCH ABOVE AVERAGE	94%–95%	93%–94%
ABOVE AVERAGE	92%–93%	90%–92%
AVERAGE	87%–91%	86%–89%
BELOW AVERAGE	82%–86%	81%–85%
MUCH BELOW AVERAGE	77%–81%	76%–80%
DO NOT VISIT	76% or lower	75% or lower

DINING *in* WALT DISNEY WORLD

THIS SECTION AIMS TO HELP YOU FIND good food worth the effort of getting a reservation and the money it costs. More than 200 restaurants—including around 90 full-service establishments, around 30 of which are in the theme parks—operate within the World. These restaurants offer exceptional variety, serving everything from

Moroccan lamb to Texas barbecue. Most are expensive, and many serve food that doesn't live up to the prices, but with our help you can find good choices in every area of Walt Disney World.

DINING OPTIONS AND EXPERIENCES

READER RATINGS FOR DISNEY RESTAURANTS have steadied after some low-rated years in 2021 and 2022. Restaurants run by third parties seem to be operating at very high levels: Five of the top 10 sit-down restaurants in Walt Disney World are operated by third parties at Disney Springs.

The rest of this chapter offers detailed advice on how to find the best Disney dining experiences. Here are a couple of quick tips to keep in mind, regardless of where you decide to eat:

- Place your counter-service restaurant order via the mobile app 30–45 minutes before you want to eat; that will allow the restaurant enough time to prepare your food before you arrive, and it will reduce your wait. During busier times of the year, you may need to submit orders 1–2 hours in advance, just to be safe.
- Consider eating before noon or after 1 p.m., when it will be easier to find open tables at counter-service restaurants.

GETTING IT RIGHT

ALTHOUGH WE WORK HARD to be fair, objective, and accurate, many readers, like this one from Pennsylvania, try to balance out our perspective:

> *Most of the food at Walt Disney World is OK. You pay more than you should, but it's more convenient to eat in Disney World than to try to find cheaper restaurants somewhere else.*

As you read, keep in mind that researching and reviewing restaurants is no straightforward endeavor—it's endlessly complicated by personal tastes and preferences. Take our reviews and read them through the lens of your own likes and dislikes.

The *Unofficial* Difference

How do we present the best possible dining coverage? At the *Unofficial Guide,* we begin with highly qualified culinary experts and then balance their opinions with those of our readers—which, by the way, don't always coincide. Our experts and authors don't get any invites from Disney for things like opening nights, and we pay for all of our own food. That keeps our opinions unbiased and a realistic representation of what you, too, might experience at these same locations.

In the spirit of democracy, we encourage you to fill out a reader survey at touringplans.com/walt-disney-world/survey. If you'd like to share your dining experiences in greater depth, we invite you to write us a letter or send us an email (see page 5).

WHERE TO FIND GOOD MEALS

THE BEST CONCENTRATIONS OF SIT-DOWN RESTAURANTS in Walt Disney World are found at **Disney's Animal Kingdom Lodge;**

Disney's **Grand Floridian Resort & Spa;** the **Contemporary Resort;** and the **Disney Springs** complex.

Animal Kingdom Lodge boasts 2 of the top 10 table-service restaurants in Walt Disney World: **Boma—Flavors of Africa** (No. 4 overall out of more than 110 sit-down restaurants), a beloved buffet favorite, and **Sanaa** (No. 3), serving delicious African–Indian fusion dishes. A third table-service restaurant at Animal Kingdom Lodge, **Jiko—The Cooking Place,** comes in just outside the top 10, in 11th place.

The Grand Floridian houses the best restaurant in Walt Disney World: **Victoria & Albert's,** which has won 20 consecutive AAA Five Diamond Awards and earned a Michelin star and a Michelin Special Service Award in 2024. The food and the service are both extraordinary. Beyond V&A's, you'll find **Cítricos, Narcoossee's,** the **Grand Floridian Cafe** and the **1900 Park Fare** character buffet. Within walking distance of the Grand Flo is the **Polynesian Village Resort**'s **Kona Cafe,** with excellent breakfast options, and **'Ohana,** with family-style dining at breakfast and dinner; the **Contemporary Resort**'s **California Grill** is a short monorail ride away too. If dining is an important part of your Disney World vacation and these resorts are within your budget, it's worth considering staying at one of them.

The next best concentration of restaurants is at the **Contemporary Resort.** Along with the California Grill, the resort has a sit-down restaurant called **Steakhouse 71** and character buffets at **Chef Mickey's.** The counter-service **Contempo Café** is convenient for simple meals.

Highlights at Disney Springs include **Chef Art Smith's Homecomin'** (No. 6), with excellent fried chicken, tasty cocktails, and rich desserts. The family-friendly **Raglan Road** is the new overall No. 1 for table-service dining and has an extensive menu with something for everyone. For seafood and steaks, try **The Boathouse** (No. 7). Disney Springs also has some of the World's top counter-service spots, including **The Polite Pig** barbecue joint (No. 1 in this category), **Earl of Sandwich** (No. 8), and **Blaze Fast-Fire'd Pizza.**

Disney Springs is also home to two of our favorite tapas restaurants. **Wine Bar George** is run by a master sommelier who partnered with a chef to create a menu that pairs food and wine. It's the perfect choice for a glass or two and some small bites. Our other tapas favorite is **Jaleo,** from celebrity chef José Andrés. Jaleo's menu of modern Spanish dishes is extensive and affordable. We'd willingly start a fight over the last bite of patatas bravas, and the Jamón Ibérico is the stuff of dreams.

If the dining at Disney Springs sounds good to you, you could consider a stay at **Disney's Saratoga Springs Resort & Spa.** Many of the buildings are a short walk to Disney Springs.

And if you're after in-park dining, the food in **Disney's Animal Kingdom** and **EPCOT** gets the highest marks.

DISNEY DINING 101

WALT DISNEY WORLD RESTAURANT CATEGORIES

IN GENERAL, food and beverage offerings at Walt Disney World are defined by service, price, and convenience:

FULL-SERVICE RESTAURANTS Full-service restaurants, also referred to as **table-service** and **sit-down** restaurants, are found in all the major theme parks, all Disney resorts except Value resorts and Port Orleans French Quarter, and Disney Springs. Disney operates most of the restaurants in the theme parks and its hotels, while contractors or franchisees operate the rest. **Advance Dining Reservations** (see page 208) are recommended for all full-service restaurants.

CHARACTER MEALS Thirteen WDW restaurants have Disney characters in attendance during meals. Seven are buffets, and six offer either a family-style fixed menu (all tables get the same food) or a limited menu. All fixed-menu locations have a kids' menu featuring items like hot dogs, burgers, chicken nuggets, pizza, and mac and cheese.

BUFFETS AND FAMILY-STYLE RESTAURANTS Disney buffets are self-serve and all-you-care-to-eat, and they include separate kid-friendly offerings such as chicken nuggets, pizza, and fries. There's no less food at Disney's family-style restaurants, such as EPCOT's Garden Grill. There, your party will be provided with several platters stacked high with meats, vegetables, and salads. You can ask for more (or less) of any item. We've tried all of Disney's family-style restaurants, and we've been pleasantly surprised at the food quality and quantity at most of them.

Advance Dining Reservations are strongly recommended for character meals and recommended for all other restaurants. Most credit cards are accepted. An automatic 18% gratuity is added to the bill for parties of six or more, but when the tipping is at *your* discretion, a North Carolina reader urges generosity with servers:

> *I've seen diners leave a dollar or two per person. I've also heard of people protesting Disney's prices by leaving a small tip or none at all. This is unacceptable—these servers keep your drinks full, keep your plates clean, and check on you constantly. They deserve at least 15%–18%. If you can't afford to tip, you shouldn't eat there.*

FOOD COURTS Featuring several counter-service eateries under one roof, food courts can be found at Disney's Moderate and Value resorts (see table on the opposite page). If you're staying at one of these resorts, you might eat once or twice a day at your hotel's food court. The closest thing to a food court at the theme parks is **Sunshine Seasons** in EPCOT (see page 235). Reservations are not available at these restaurants.

In recent years, Disney has simplified and standardized the food court menus across all its resorts. Reader satisfaction ratings have dropped considerably as a result.

COUNTER SERVICE Also called **quick service,** counter-service food, is plentiful at all the theme parks, the BoardWalk, and Disney Springs. You'll find hot dogs, hamburgers, chicken sandwiches, salads, and pizza almost everywhere. They're augmented by special items that relate to the part of the park you're touring. In EPCOT's Germany, for example, counter-service bratwurst and beer are sold; in Frontierland in the Magic Kingdom, vendors sell smoked turkey legs. Ordering meals ahead of time through the My Disney Experience app (mobile ordering) is strongly suggested at all locations that offer this service.

DISNEY RESORT FOOD COURTS: READER-SURVEY RATINGS		
RESORT	FOOD COURT	POSITIVE RATING
All-Star Movies	World Premier Food Court	81% (*Much Below Average*)
All-Star Music	Intermission Food Court	88% (*Average*)
All-Star Sports	End Zone Food Court	79% (*Much Below Average*)
Art of Animation	Landscape of Flavors	86% (*Below Average*)
Caribbean Beach	Centertown Market	84% (*Below Average*)
Coronado Springs	El Mercado de Coronado Food Court	70% (*Do Not Visit*)
Fort Wilderness	P & J's Southern Takeout	77% (*Much Below Average*)
Pop Century	Everything POP	87% (*Average*)
Port Orleans French Quarter	Sassagoula Floatworks & Food Factory	89% (*Average*)
Port Orleans Riverside	Riverside Mill Food Court	77% (*Much Below Average*)

Most counter-service restaurants serve combo meals, but you can order any meal without a side to save some money. Counter-service prices are fairly consistent from park to park. You can expect to pay the same for your coffee or hot dog in Disney's Animal Kingdom as you would in Disney's Hollywood Studios (see table on page 231).

FAST CASUAL Somewhere between quick burgers and formal dining are the establishments in Disney's fast casual category, including one in the theme parks: **Satu'li Canteen** (see page 236) in Animal Kingdom. Satu'li is one of the highest-rated options in the parks.

VENDOR FOOD Vendor carts abound at all the theme parks, Disney Springs, and the BoardWalk. Offerings include popcorn, ice-cream bars, churros, soft drinks, bottled water, and (in the theme parks) fresh fruit. Prices include tax; many vendors accept credit cards, charges to your room at a Disney resort, and the Disney Dining Plan (see below). A few may take cash only (look for a sign near the register).

DISNEY DINING PLANS

BEGINNING IN 2024, prepaid dining plans made their grand return as part of Walt Disney World vacation packages. There are two tiers of the Disney Dining Plan: the **Quick Service Disney Dining Plan** and the **Disney Dining Plan** (call it standard or regular or table service—I like *table service* as a differentiator). Both allow you to prepay for meals as part of your overall vacation cost. In exchange, you'll get a certain number of credits for each day of your vacation, which you can use to pay for meals and snacks. One important note is that gratuity is not included in the plan, which means that even if you use only credits to pay for meals, you still need to tip out of pocket.

Before we discuss what is included in each plan, we need to go over some definitions.

- A **counter-service meal** includes an entrée, a side, and a beverage (which may be alcoholic, where available).
- A **table-service meal** includes an entrée (with sides, if included in the menu item), a dessert, and a beverage (which may be alcoholic, where available). You can also substitute the dessert for a side salad, cup of soup, or fruit

plate, which is certainly healthier, but less fun—and almost always less cost-effective.

- A **snack** can include many items sold at snack carts, or even side items, hand-scooped ice cream, and many other options. All of these will be noted with a special symbol on the menus so you know what qualifies.

QUICK-SERVICE DINING PLAN This dining plan includes two counter-service meals per night, one snack per night, and a refillable drink mug per person on the room reservation. At the time we went to press, the plan cost $59.10 per adult per night, and $24.70 per child per night.

DISNEY DINING PLAN (AKA TABLE-SERVICE DINING PLAN) This dining plan includes one counter-service meal per night, one table-service meal per night, one snack per night, and a refillable drink mug per person on the room reservation. As we went to press, the plan cost $97.70 per adult per night, and $30.50 per child per night. Your eyes did not deceive you. That's almost $100 per adult per night.

Dining Plan Value

In order to decide whether the Dining Plan is worth the cost, we need to figure out the value of various credits. And to get started down that path, I'm going to make two assumptions up front:

1. Snacks are worth an average of $6.
2. The refillable mug is like a free throw-in. You might use it. You might not. It's a nice-to-have.

With those two assumptions, I can use some middle school algebra to figure out the value of an adult quick-service (QS) credit and an adult table-service (TS) credit. I'll spare you the equations, but the result is a quick-service credit is worth $26.50 (but we'll call it $27 to be nice), and a table-service credit is worth $65. That tells you exactly how much you're paying Disney into your "food account"—and exactly what you'll need your order to add up to, if you want to break even by using the dining plan.

Once we know what a credit is worth, we can look through all of the menu items at Walt Disney World to figure out how many of them will add up to be worth at least as much as you paid for your credits. Disney assumes no one is going to go through all that trouble . . . but we did, by figuring out average prices of desserts, different types of beverages, and every entrée on-property. The table on the opposite page walks you through the various chances you have of breaking even or "beating" Disney by using a dining plan.

For example, if you manage to find a quick-service breakfast cocktail with your meal (good luck with that), 20% of entrées will save you money with your QS credit. If you're fancy and prefer wine or beer with your breakfast (again, good luck), 1% of breakfast entrées will allow you to break even on the dining plan. If you prefer a specialty beverage (like coffee, juice, or milk) or soda with your breakfast, there is one single quick-service breakfast option that will save you money on the dining plan. In all of Walt Disney World. One option. And if you just want some tap water with your breakfast, there are no quick-service breakfast entrées that will allow you to break even. A 0% chance of saving money by using the dining plan in this scenario.

DRINK ORDERED	DINING PLAN/MEAL			
	COUNTER-SERVICE BREAKFAST	COUNTER-SERVICE LUNCH OR DINNER	TABLE-SERVICE BREAKFAST	TABLE-SERVICE LUNCH OR DINNER
COCKTAIL	20%	47%	1%	8%
WINE	1%	18%	1%	7%
BEER	1%	9%	1%	3%
SPECIALTY BEVERAGE* OR SODA	0%	1%	0%	1%
WATER	0%	0%	0%	1%

CHANCE OF SAVING MONEY WITH A DINING PLAN

* Includes artisanal milkshakes, fresh smoothies, premium hot chocolate, coffee, tea, juice, and milk

Look at all of those numbers together—not one of them is above 50%. You've probably heard the gambling term "the house always wins," and this is the Disney Dining Plan equivalent. The Mouse House always wins. If you just order randomly off of every menu at every meal, you will statistically lose money by paying for the dining plan instead of paying out of pocket. Can you come out ahead in Vegas? Sure, without too much alcohol and with a lot of skill. Can you come out ahead at Disney World? Sure, with a lot of alcohol and a lot of skill.

The people who should never use the dining plan are families with nondrinkers and anyone between the ages of 10 and 20—these folks have only a 1% chance of finding meals that make the dining plan worth what it costs.

Keep in mind that with the dining plan, you're ordering expensive drinks and meals to maximize the value of your plan. And the plan doesn't include gratuity, so you'll be paying a significant amount out of pocket, even if you're purchasing the dining plan for the convenience of prepaying and not worrying about costs when you eat.

Is it possible to "beat" Disney by using the dining plan? Absolutely. It requires a lot of planning, and getting reservations at the few locations on-property that will allow you to save money; plus, you'll be competing for those reservations with everyone else who is on the plan and has done just as much research as you.

Becky's Recommended Dining Plan Alternative

Want to prepay for your meals and save money but still retain all of your power of choice for what you want to eat and drink? The answer isn't the dining plan; it's Disney gift cards. My family frequently shops at Target, where you can save 5% on gift cards if you use the Target Red-Card. Many other stores offer similar deals. Once we've started planning a Disney vacation, we pick up a $50 or $100 Disney gift card during each Target run we make. By the time we go on our vacation, we've purchased enough in gift cards that we can pay for all of our meals with just that card. And that includes gratuity. All told, we have 100% chance of saving money on our food, and we can make whatever reservations we'd like, order whatever we'd like, and not feel forced to have a cocktail with every meal.

ADVANCE DINING RESERVATIONS
The Official Line

YOU CAN RESERVE THE FOLLOWING up to 60 days in advance:

- **AFTERNOON TEA AND CHILDREN'S PROGRAMS** at the Grand Floridian Resort & Spa *(closed at press time; no reopening date announced)*
- **ALL DISNEY TABLE-SERVICE RESTAURANTS** and character-dining venues
- *FANTASMIC!* **DINING PACKAGE** in Disney's Hollywood Studios
- *HOOP-DEE-DOO MUSICAL REVUE* at Fort Wilderness Resort & Campground
- **OGA'S CANTINA** at Star Wars: Galaxy's Edge, Disney's Hollywood Studios

Guests staying at Disney-owned resorts may make dining reservations for the entire length of their stay—up to 10 days—in a single booking up to 60 days in advance.

ADVANCE DINING RESERVATIONS

YOU CAN MAKE RESERVATIONS for Disney's table-service restaurants, including those in the theme parks (see table above). But making a reservation for dining at Disney World is more difficult than making a reservation at a restaurant elsewhere because hundreds of people are trying to get reservations at Disney's popular restaurants the instant they become available.

In fact, Disney's most popular restaurants can run out of reservations months in advance. And most Disney restaurants hold no tables at all—zero—for walk-in guests. That means it's important to book your dining reservations as soon as you're able (typically 60 days before your visit). This section explains how it all works, and why.

Behind the Scenes at Advance Dining Reservations

Disney reservations operate on what's known as a template system: Instead of an actual table at a restaurant, you're assigned to a time slot. The number of slots available is based on the average length of time that guests occupy a table at a particular restaurant, adjusted for seasonality.

Here's a rough example of how it works: Let's say Coral Reef Restaurant has 40 tables for four and 8 tables for six, and that the average length of time for a family to be seated, order, eat, pay, and depart is 70 minutes. Add 5 minutes to bus the table, and the table is turning every 75 minutes. The restaurant then provides Disney's central dining-reservations system (**CDRS**) with a computer template of its capacity, along with the average amount of time the table is occupied. Disney uses CDRS to process reservations both online and by phone.

Thus, when you use the website to make Advance Dining Reservations for four people at 6:15 p.m., CDRS removes one table for four from its overall capacity for 75 minutes. The system template indicates that the table will be unavailable for reassignment until 7:30 p.m. (75 minutes later). And so it goes for all tables in the restaurant.

CDRS tries to fill every time slot for every seat in the restaurant or come as close to filling every slot as possible; again, no seats are reserved for walk-ins. Templates are filled differently depending on the season and restaurant.

When you arrive at a restaurant with a reservation, your wait to be seated will usually be less than 20 minutes during peak hours and often less than 10. If you just show up without a reservation, expect to either wait 40–75 minutes or—more likely—be told that there are no tables available. You can sometimes get seated as a walk-in (see page 212), but you should never count on it.

NO-SHOW PENALTIES Disney restaurants charge a no-show fee of $10–$25 per person (or $100 per person in the case of **Monsieur Paul** at EPCOT and **Victoria & Albert's** at the Grand Floridian). This has reduced the no-show rate to virtually zero, and these restaurants are booked every day according to their actual capacity. Note the following, however:

- Only one person needs to dine at the restaurant for Disney to consider your reservation fulfilled, even if you have a reservation for more people.
- You can cancel up to 2 hours before your reservation time.

GETTING ADVANCE DINING RESERVATIONS AT POPULAR RESTAURANTS

TWO OF THE HARDEST RESERVATIONS TO GET in Walt Disney World these days are at EPCOT's **Space 220** and Hollywood Studios' **Oga's Cantina.** Why? Oga's capacity is very limited, and its theme makes it attractive to almost anyone visiting the *Star Wars* area of the park. Space 220 is, along with Coral Reef Restaurant, one of the most picturesque dining locations in EPCOT. You'll have to put in some effort to secure an Advance Dining Reservation at these places, especially during busier times of year. Also, keep in mind that readers who've eaten at Space 220 rate it poorly.

The easiest and fastest way to get a reservation is to go to disney world.disney.go.com/dining starting at 5:45 a.m. Eastern time, a full hour before phone reservations open. This is a major bummer if you live in California and have to get up at 2:45 a.m. But when demand exceeds supply, you do what you have to do.

To familiarize yourself with how the site works, try it out a couple of days before you actually make reservations. Be sure to read the directions below for some time-saving keyboard shortcuts—every millisecond counts. You'll also save time by setting up a **My Disney Experience** account online (see page 25) before your 60-day booking window, making sure to enter and save your credit card information to guarantee your reservations.

Early on the morning on which you want to make reservations, select your date, time, and party size on Disney's dining reservations page. Use the filters (such as dining type or location) to restrict the number of results returned to as few as possible; when the page returns results, you'll have less scrolling to find what you want, saving time. Next, start trying to search about 3 minutes before 5:45 a.m. The results returned will tell you whether your restaurant has a table available.

Note that while you're typing, other guests are also trying to make reservations, so you want the transaction to proceed as quickly as possible. Flexibility on your part counts—it's much harder to get seating for a large group, so consider breaking your group into numbers that can be accommodated at tables for four. Also make sure you have your credit card out where you can read it, if it's not already saved.

Advance Dining Reservations for **Cinderella's Royal Table,** other character meals, the *Fantasmic!* **Dining Package** and the *Hoop-Dee-Doo*

THE REALITY OF GETTING LAST-MINUTE DINING RESERVATIONS

IF YOUR VACATION is more than 60 days out and you want to dine at a popular venue, following our advice on pages 209–212 will get you the table you want more than 80% of the time. The longer you wait, the more effort you'll have to put in to find a reservation. The list below shows the restaurants where capacity and demand make finding a last-minute reservation more difficult.

- **AKERSHUS ROYAL BANQUET HALL** *(EPCOT)* Reservations are somewhat easier to get for lunch than dinner.

- **BEACHES & CREAM SODA SHOP** *(Beach Club)* It's not the food or the atmosphere but the limited seating that makes getting reservations difficult.

- **THE BOATHOUSE** *(Disney Springs)* Highly rated by readers. Dinner reservations from 5–9 p.m. are the most difficult to get.

- **CHEF ART SMITH'S HOMECOMIN'** *(Disney Springs)* One of Disney Springs' best restaurants. Your options might be lunch, or dinner after 10 p.m.

- **CHEF MICKEY'S** *(Contemporary Resort)* The food isn't anything special, and neither is the venue. The draw is the Disney characters.

- **OGA'S CANTINA** *(Disney's Hollywood Studios)* Tiny capacity and photogenic drinks make this the hardest place to get into at the Studios.

- **SPACE 220** *(EPCOT)* The draw here is the setting, inside a simulated space station, rather than the food.

- **T-REX** *(Disney Springs)* A popular venue for kids because of the theming and dinosaurs. If you can't get a reservation here, join Landry's Select Club (landrysselect .com) to get priority access instead.

Musical Revue require complete prepayment with a credit card at the time of the booking. The name on the booking can't be changed after the reservation is made. Reservations may be canceled, with the deposit refunded in full, by calling ☎ 407-WDW-DINE at least 48 hours before seating for these shows (versus 24 hours ahead for regular Advance Dining Reservations). Disney will work with you in the event of an emergency.

If you don't have access to a computer or smartphone at 5:45 a.m. on the morning you need to make reservations, then be ready to call ☎ 407-WDW-DINE at 6:45 a.m. Eastern and follow the prompts to speak to a live person. You may still get put on hold if call volume is higher than usual, and you'll be an hour behind the early birds with computers. Still, you'll be well ahead of those who couldn't wake up any earlier.

If you are planning to use the Disney Dining Plan to pay for a *Fantasmic!* package, Cinderella's Royal Table, or the *Hoop-Dee-Doo* dinner show, you may be better off reserving by phone anyway. The online system may not recognize your table-service credits, but you can book and pay with a credit card, then call ☎ 407-WDW-DINE after 6:45 a.m. and have them credit the charge for the meal back to your card. When you get to Walt Disney World, you'll use credits from your dining plan to "pay" for the meal. (Sometimes the online system has glitches and shows no availability; in this case, call after 6:45 a.m. to confirm whether the online system is correct.)

NEVER, NEVER, NEVER, NEVER GIVE UP Not getting what you want the first time you try doesn't mean the end of the story. A woman from Tennessee advises persistence:

RESTAURANT RECOMMENDATIONS BY TYPE OF DINING

From Bethany, Bella, and Colin at The Main St Dish *Podcast*

IF YOU'RE LOOKING FOR	TRY
CHARACTER DINING	• **Akershus Royal Banquet Hall** (Norway Pavilion, EPCOT) Princess dining at its finest. The menu is based on Norwegian cooking, but it also features some standard American dishes. • **Topolino's Terrace** (Riviera Resort) Elevated food on the top floor of the resort. Characters appear only during breakfast. This is easily one of the hardest dining reservations to get. • **Tusker House** (Animal Kingdom) A unique take on African-inspired dishes, with plenty for every picky eater on the buffet. Plus, you get to see classic Disney characters in safari gear.
BUFFET	• **Biergarten** (Germany Pavilion, EPCOT) A staple in EPCOT, especially if you love German food. In addition to the buffet, enjoy the live music and entertainment. • **Boma—Flavors of Africa** (Animal Kingdom Lodge) Escape from the crowds in the parks to enjoy this African-inspired buffet, one of the most underrated buffets in Walt Disney World, in our opinion.
ITALIAN	• **Ravello** (Four Seasons Orlando) A great spot for authentic Italian food. The menu is great and so customizable, from half-and-half pizzas to half orders of pasta. • **Trattoria al Forno** (BoardWalk Inn) Good, hearty Italian food. The open kitchen brings a wonderful feel to this restaurant, and the portions are large.
SEAFOOD	• **The Boathouse** (Disney Springs) The focus this waterside spot gives to fresh seafood is apparent. No matter the time of day you dine, there are always great options on the menu. • **Narcoossee's** (Grand Floridian) Excellent seafood in a great location right by the Magic Kingdom. The restaurant is light and airy, and the food is simply outstanding. The wraparound porch is also a great spot to watch fireworks after dinner.
FINE DINING	• **Capa** (Four Seasons Orlando) A Spanish-style steakhouse with slightly more casual fine dining. The A5 Wagyu is always a great option, and there are plenty of tapas and sides to accompany the meal. • **Victoria & Albert's** (Grand Floridian) The best of the best when it comes to dining at Disney World. No detail is missed, from the moment you walk in to your last drop of coffee. This is a dining experience.

I started trying to get a reservation at Be Our Guest Restaurant about a month out from our vacation. By checking the website whenever I thought of it—morning, noon, and night—I ended up getting not only a lunch reservation but a dinner reservation!

LAST-MINUTE DINING RESERVATIONS Because Advance Dining Reservations require a credit card, and because a fee is charged for failing to cancel in time, you can often score a last-minute reservation. Guests sometimes have to cancel their reservations due to sudden changes of plans, and as long as they cancel before midnight the day before, they won't be charged a no-show penalty (see page 209). So your best shot at picking up a canceled reservation is to repeatedly visit disneyworld.disney.go.com/dining as often as possible between 10 and 11 p.m.

WDW RESTAURANTS BOOKABLE WITH OPENTABLE *(subject to change)*
BONNET CREEK
• **Bull & Bear Steakhouse** Waldorf Astoria Orlando • **Illume** JW Marriott • **Sear & Sea** JW Marriott • **Unreserved** JW Marriott
DISNEY RESORTS
• **Flying Fish** BoardWalk • **Jiko—The Cooking Place** Animal Kingdom Lodge–Jambo House • **Toledo—Tapas, Steak & Seafood** Coronado Springs
DISNEY SPRINGS
• **The Edison** Town Center • **Enzo's Hideaway** The Landing • **Frontera Cocina** Town Center • **Jaleo** West Side • **Maria & Enzo's** The Landing • **Morimoto Asia** The Landing • **Paddlefish** The Landing • **Paradiso 37** The Landing • **Planet Hollywood** Town Center • **Raglan Road Irish Pub & Restaurant** The Landing • **Splitsville Dining Room** West Side • **STK Orlando** The Landing • **Terralina Crafted Italian** The Landing • **Wine Bar George** The Landing • **Wolfgang Puck Bar & Grill** Town Center
DOLPHIN, SWAN, AND SWAN RESERVE
• **Amare** Swan Reserve • **Il Mulino New York** Swan • **Rosa Mexicano** Dolphin • **Shula's Steak House** Dolphin • **Todd English's Bluezoo** Dolphin
FORT WILDERNESS AREA
• **Ravello** Four Seasons Resort Orlando

STILL **CAN'T GET A RESERVATION?** Go to the restaurant on the day you wish to dine, and try for a table as a walk-in. Yes, we've already told you this is a long shot—that said, you *may* be able to swing it between 2:30 and 4:30 p.m. Your chances of success increase during less-busy times of year or on cold or rainy days during busier seasons. If you don't mind eating late, you can also try to get a table during the restaurant's last hour of serving.

Full-service restaurants in the theme parks can be hard-nosed about walk-ins. Even if you walk up and see that the restaurant isn't busy, you may still need to use Disney's app or visit Guest Services to make a reservation. Alternatively, many restaurants now tell you their walk-up wait in the app, and you can join the walk-up list from that spot too.

Landing a reservation for Cinderella's Royal Table at dinner is somewhat easier than at lunch or breakfast, but the price is $84 for adults and $49 for children ages 3–9 during peak times of year. Throw in tax and gratuity, and you're looking at around $338 for one meal for a family of four. But if you're unable to lock up a table for breakfast or lunch, a dinner reservation will at least get your kids inside the castle.

ALSO TRY OPENTABLE Several Disney World restaurants take reservations through the popular online-booking service **OpenTable** (open table.com; mobile app available for iOS and Android). The participating restaurants (subject to change) are listed in the table above. If you're having trouble getting a dining reservation through the usual Disney channels, this option may be worth checking out. *A big bonus:* If you book through OpenTable, some restaurants won't subject you to the same no-show fee you'd have to pay through Disney if you missed your reservation without canceling. We should add, however, that OpenTable monitors no-shows and will chastise you by email if you fail to appear. Your account will be suspended if you no-show for four reservations within a year. Besides being the polite thing to do, it's a snap to cancel or change reservations on the website or app.

THEME PARK RESTAURANTS AND ADMISSION

SOME FIRST-TIME VISITORS to Walt Disney World are surprised when making their Advance Dining Reservations to learn that admission to a theme park is required to eat at the restaurants inside it. The lone exception is **Rainforest Cafe** in Animal Kingdom, which can be entered from the parking lot just outside of the theme park; you must have park tickets, however, if you want to enter Animal Kingdom.

If you're booking a meal for a day when you weren't expecting to visit the parks, be sure to check the restaurant's location to make sure it isn't in a theme park. Also, if you've visited a theme park earlier in the day that is different from the one in which your restaurant is located, you'll need to have purchased the **Park Hopper** option (see page 64) to dine inside the second theme park.

DRESS

DRESS IS INFORMAL at most theme park restaurants, but Disney has a business casual dress code for some of its resort restaurants: khakis, slacks, or dress shorts with a collared shirt for men, and capris, skirts, dresses, and dress shorts for women; jeans may be worn by men and women if in good condition. Restaurants with this dress code are **Jiko— The Cooking Place** in Animal Kingdom Lodge, **Flying Fish** at the Board-Walk, **California Grill** at the Contemporary Resort, **Monsieur Paul** at EPCOT's France Pavilion, **Takumi-Tei** at EPCOT's Japan Pavilion, **Cítricos** and **Narcoossee's** at the Grand Floridian, **Yachtsman Steakhouse** at the Yacht Club Resort, **Todd English's Bluezoo** and **Shula's Steak House** at the Dolphin, **Il Mulino** at the Swan, and **Topolino's Terrace** at the Riviera Resort. **Victoria & Albert's** at the Grand Floridian is the only Disney restaurant that requires men to wear a jacket to dinner (they'll provide one if needed).

FOOD ALLERGIES AND DIETARY NEEDS

IF YOU HAVE SPECIAL DIETARY NEEDS, make them known when you make reservations. For more information, see Part 8.

Healthful Food at Walt Disney World

Healthy choices such as fresh fruit are available at most fast-food counters and from vendors. Vegetarians, people who have diabetes, those requiring kosher meals, and anyone trying to eat healthfully should have no trouble finding something that meets their needs, but options may be limited.

*un*official **TIP**
Be aware that there is a charge for canceling a meal with kosher or other special requests, to cover the extra cost of ordering the individual meal components.

SIT-DOWN-RESTAURANT TIPS AND TRICKS

BEFORE YOU BEGIN EATING your way through the World, you need to know a few things:

1. Theme park restaurants often rush their customers to make room for the next group of diners. Dining at high speed may appeal to a family with young, restless children, but for people wanting to relax, it can be more like eating in a pressure chamber than fine dining.

2. Disney restaurants have comparatively few tables for parties of two. If you're a duo, you might have to wait longer to be seated.

3. At full-service Disney restaurants, an automatic gratuity of 18% is added to your tab for parties of six or more—even at buffets where you serve yourself.

While the inflation-adjusted peak cost of a one-day theme park ticket has increased about 105% since 2010, the average lunch entrée price at Le Cellier has gone from around $22 to around $55—an increase of 150%. For reference, the average meal cost in a US restaurant went up 51% during the same time, according to the Federal Reserve Bank of St. Louis. This comment from a Louisiana mom spells it out:

Disney keeps pushing prices up and up. For us, the sky is NOT the limit. We won't be back.

MOBILE ORDERING

DISNEY STRONGLY RECOMMENDS mobile ordering at almost all of its in-park counter-service restaurants. Using the My Disney Experience (MDE) app, you place an order, pay for your meal online, choose a time to pick up your food, and notify the restaurant when you've arrived for that pickup. The app will tell you when your food is ready, and you'll be directed to a specific window or line to collect your food. Be sure to keep your app updated to see the latest participating restaurants.

It can take restaurants 30 minutes or more to prepare your order once it's placed, and it may take another 5–10 minutes to pick it up. Plan to place your order 30–40 minutes before you want to eat during most times of the year, or 1–2 hours in advance during the holidays.

If you're unable to access the MDE app or use mobile ordering, speak with a cast member outside the restaurant. They'll usually provide a paper menu and individual access to a cashier for payment. You may still have to wait to be served.

TIPS FOR SAVING TIME AND MONEY

EVEN IF YOU CONFINE YOUR MEALS to counter-service fare, you lose a lot of time getting food in the parks—not to mention the costs can add up fast (see the table on page 231). Here are some ways to minimize the time you spend hunting and gathering:

1. Eat breakfast before you arrive, either at a restaurant outside the World or from a stocked fridge or cooler in your room. This will save you a ton of time and money.

2. After a good breakfast, bring your own snacks into the parks.

3. All theme park restaurants are busiest between 11:30 a.m. and 2:15 p.m. for lunch and between 6 and 9 p.m. for dinner. Avoid trying to eat during these hours, especially noon–1 p.m.

4. If you're short on time and the park is closing early, just stay until closing and eat dinner at your resort or Disney Springs. If the park stays open late, eat dinner at about 4:30 or 5 p.m. at the restaurant of your choice. You should sneak in just ahead of the dinner crowd.

This Missouri mom shares some of her own tips:

Each child had a belt bag of his own, which he filled from a special box of goodies each day with things like packages of crackers and cheese and packets of peanuts and raisins. Each child also had a small, rectangular plastic water bottle that could hang on the belt. We filled these at water fountains before getting into lines.

We left the park before noon; ate sandwiches, chips, and soda in the room; and napped. We purchased our evening meal in the park at a counter-service eatery. We budgeted for both morning and evening snacks from a vendor but often didn't need them.

CHARACTER DINING

CHARACTER DINING IS FOUND throughout Walt Disney World. At press time, 13 restaurants offer a chance to see Disney characters while you eat. There's enough demand for these character experiences that reservations for popular dining times can be hard to come by.

What's more, if you want to book a character meal, you must provide Disney with a credit card number. Your card will be charged $10 per person if you don't show or if you cancel your reservation less than 24 hours in advance; you may, however, reschedule with no penalty. See "Getting Advance Dining Reservations at Popular Restaurants" (page 209) for the full story.

WHAT TO EXPECT

CHARACTER BREAKFASTS TYPICALLY OFFER a fixed menu served family-style (in large skillets or platters at your table), buffet-style, or à la carte. The typical breakfast includes scrambled eggs; bacon and sausage; potato casserole; waffles, pancakes, or French toast; biscuits, rolls, or pastries; and fruit.

Character dinners range from buffets to family-style fixed menus to dishes ordered off the menu. Dinners, such as those at 1900 Park Fare at the Grand Floridian and Akershus Royal Banquet Hall at EPCOT, separate the kids' fare from the grown-ups', though everyone is free to eat from both menus. Typically, the kids' menu includes burgers, hot dogs, pizza, fish sticks, chicken nuggets, macaroni and cheese, and peanut-butter-and-jelly sandwiches. Selections from the buffet and adult menu usually include prime rib or another carved meat, baked or broiled seafood, pasta, chicken, a cultural dish or two, vegetables, potatoes, and salad.

At all meals, characters circulate around the room while you eat. During your meal, each of the three to five characters present will stop by your table, sign autographs, and pose for photos with your family. Characters move slowly, and it's unlikely you'll miss them when they swing by.

WHEN TO GO

ATTENDING A RESORT'S CHARACTER BREAKFAST usually prevents you from arriving at the theme parks in time for opening. Because early morning is best for touring and you don't want to burn daylight lingering over breakfast, we suggest the following strategies:

1. Go to a character dinner or lunch instead of breakfast. It will be a nice break.

2. Schedule the first seating for lunch, typically 11 or 11:30 a.m. Have a light breakfast before you head to the parks for opening, hit the most popular

attractions until 10:45–11:15 a.m., and then head for lunch. That should keep you fueled until dinnertime, especially if you eat another light snack in the afternoon.

3. Go on arrival or departure day. The day you arrive and check in is good for a character dinner—not only is it a good way to ease into your trip, but it can also help your children get acquainted with how they'll encounter characters in the parks. Similarly, scheduling a character breakfast on checkout day, before you head for the airport or begin your drive home, is a nice way to cap off the trip.

4. Go on a rest day. If you plan to stay five or more days, you'll probably take a day or a half day off from touring to rest or do something else. These are perfect days for a character meal.

If you book an in-park character breakfast, schedule yours for the first seating if the park opens at 8 a.m. or later. You'll be admitted to the park before other guests through a special line at the tapstiles (park tickets are still required; see page 213). Arrive early to be among the first parties seated.

HOW TO CHOOSE A CHARACTER MEAL

MANY READERS ASK FOR ADVICE about character meals. This question from an Iowa mom is typical:

Are all character meals pretty much the same or are some better than others? How should I go about choosing one?

In fact, some *are* better, sometimes much better. When we evaluate character meals, we look for the following:

1. THE CHARACTERS The meals feature a diverse assortment of characters. See our Character-Meal Hit Parade table on pages 218–219 to find out which characters are assigned to each meal.

2. ATTENTION FROM THE CHARACTERS At all character meals, Disney characters circulate among diners. How much time a character spends in camera range of you and your children depends primarily on the ratio of characters to guests. The more characters and fewer guests, the better. Because many character-meal venues never fill to capacity, the character-to-guest ratios in our table have been adjusted to reflect an average attendance. Even so, there's quite a range. The best ratio of currently open restaurants is at Garden Grill and Topolino's Terrace, where there's about one character to every 46 guests.

The worst ratio is theoretically at the Swan resort's **Garden Grove,** where there could be as few as 1 character for every 198 guests. (*Note:* At press time it's open, but no characters visit.) We say *theoretically*, however, because in practice there are far fewer guests at Garden Grove than at character meals in Disney-owned resorts, and often more characters. (During one meal, some friends of ours were the only guests in the restaurant for breakfast and had to ask the characters to leave them alone so they could eat.)

A Vermont mom gives the characters high marks:

My kids are all about the characters. I love that for them but sometimes hate skipping other attractions to stand in yet another character line. By paying for a few strategic character meals, we can knock out a bunch of important characters at once without waiting in multiple lines throughout our day.

3. THE SETTING Some character meals have exotic settings; for others, moving the event to an elementary-school cafeteria would be an improvement. Our table rates each meal's setting with the familiar scale of one (worst) to five (best) stars. **Garden Grill** in The Land in EPCOT deserves special mention; it's a revolving restaurant overlooking several scenes from the Living with the Land boat ride. Also in EPCOT, the popular **Princess Storybook Dining** is held in the castlelike Akershus Royal Banquet Hall. Though **Chef Mickey's** at the Contemporary Resort is rather sterile in appearance, it affords a great view of the monorail running through the hotel.

4. THE FOOD Although some food served at character meals is remarkably good, most is just average. To help you sort everything out, we rate the food at each character meal in the Character-Meal Hit Parade table using a five-star scale.

Most restaurants currently offer a buffet or family-style service in which all hot items are served from the same pot or skillet. A Texas mom notes:

The family-style meals are much better for character dining—at a buffet, you're scared to leave your table in case you miss a character or other action.

5. NOISE If you want to eat in peace, character meals are usually a bad choice. That said, some are much noisier than others. Our table gives you an idea of what to expect.

6. WHICH MEAL? Although breakfasts seem to be the most popular, character lunches and dinners are usually more practical because they don't interfere with early-morning touring. During hot weather, a character lunch can be a welcome break.

7. COST Dinners and lunches cost more than breakfasts. Meal prices vary considerably from the least expensive to the most expensive restaurant. Breakfasts run about $42–$65 for adults and $27–$39 for kids ages 3–9. For character lunches and dinners, expect to pay around $55–$84 for adults and $36–$49 for kids. Little ones age 2 years and younger eat free.

8. ADVANCE DINING RESERVATIONS (See "Advance Dining Reservations: The Official Line," page 208, for details.) If you don't get what you want at first, keep trying, advises a London mother of two:

When a booking window opens, many people overbook and then either get buyer's remorse or find alternative bookings and cancel. When my booking window first opened, I was able to book barely 20% of what I wanted, but within two to three weeks I had 100%.

9. "FRIENDS" Some character meals advertise a main character and a varying cast of "friends"—for example, "Pooh and friends," meaning Eeyore, Piglet, and Tigger, or some combination thereof, or "Mickey and friends" with some assortment chosen from among Minnie, Goofy, Pluto, Donald, Daisy, Chip, and Dale.

CHARACTER-MEAL HIT PARADE

1. AKERSHUS ROYAL BANQUET HALL   EPCOT

- MEALS SERVED Breakfast, lunch, and dinner • SETTING ★★★★
- CHARACTERS 4–6 Disney princesses chosen from among Ariel, Belle, Jasmine, Tiana, Snow White, Aurora, Mulan, and Cinderella
- TYPE OF SERVICE Family-style (all you care to eat)
- FOOD VARIETY & QUALITY ★★★½ • NOISE LEVEL Moderate
- CHARACTER–GUEST RATIO 1:54

2. ARTIST POINT   WILDERNESS LODGE

- MEAL SERVED Dinner • SETTING ★★★½
- CHARACTERS Snow White, Dopey, Grumpy, the Evil Queen
- TYPE OF SERVICE Fixed menu with several choices
- FOOD VARIETY & QUALITY ★★★★½
- NOISE LEVEL Moderate • CHARACTER–GUEST RATIO 1:35

3. CAPE MAY CAFE   BEACH CLUB RESORT

- MEAL SERVED Breakfast • SETTING ★★★
- CHARACTERS Goofy, Donald, Minnie, Daisy
- TYPE OF SERVICE Buffet • FOOD VARIETY & QUALITY ★★½
- NOISE LEVEL Moderate • CHARACTER–GUEST RATIO 1:67

4. CHEF MICKEY'S   CONTEMPORARY RESORT

- MEALS SERVED Breakfast and dinner • SETTING ★★★
- CHARACTERS Mickey, Minnie, Donald, Goofy, Pluto
- TYPE OF SERVICE Buffet • FOOD VARIETY & QUALITY ★★★
- NOISE LEVEL Very loud • CHARACTER–GUEST RATIO 1:56

5. CINDERELLA'S ROYAL TABLE   MAGIC KINGDOM

- MEALS SERVED Breakfast, lunch, and dinner • SETTING ★★★★
- CHARACTERS Some combination of Cinderella, Ariel, Aurora, Belle, Jasmine, Snow White, and Fairy Godmother
- TYPE OF SERVICE Fixed menu • FOOD VARIETY & QUALITY ★★★
- NOISE LEVEL Quiet • CHARACTER–GUEST RATIO 1:26

6. THE CRYSTAL PALACE   MAGIC KINGDOM

- MEALS SERVED Breakfast, lunch, and dinner • SETTING ★★★
- CHARACTERS Pooh, Eeyore, Piglet, Tigger • TYPE OF SERVICE Buffet
- FOOD VARIETY & QUALITY Breakfast ★★½ Lunch and dinner ★★★
- NOISE LEVEL Very loud
- CHARACTER–GUEST RATIO Breakfast, 1:67; lunch and dinner, 1:89

7. GARDEN GRILL RESTAURANT   EPCOT

- MEALS SERVED Breakfast, lunch, and dinner • SETTING ★★★★
- CHARACTERS Mickey, Pluto, Chip 'n' Dale • TYPE OF SERVICE Family-style
- FOOD VARIETY & QUALITY ★★★½ • NOISE LEVEL Very quiet
- CHARACTER–GUEST RATIO 1:46

Characters are subject to change, so check before you go.

10. CINDY'S ROYAL RUSH Most character meals are leisurely affairs, and you can usually stay as long as you want. However, because Cinderella's Royal Table in the Magic Kingdom is in such high demand, the restaurant does everything it can to move you through, as this European mother of a 5-year-old can attest:

CHARACTER-MEAL HIT PARADE

8. HOLLYWOOD & VINE   DISNEY'S HOLLYWOOD STUDIOS

- **MEALS SERVED** Breakfast, lunch, and dinner • **SETTING** ★★½
- **CHARACTERS** *Breakfast:* Disney Junior characters *Lunch and dinner:* Minnie, Mickey, Goofy, Pluto, Donald (and sometimes Daisy)
- **TYPE OF SERVICE** Buffet • **FOOD VARIETY & QUALITY** ★★★
- **NOISE LEVEL** Moderate • **CHARACTER-GUEST RATIO** 1:71

9. 'OHANA   POLYNESIAN VILLAGE RESORT

- **MEAL SERVED** Breakfast • **SETTING** ★★
- **CHARACTERS** Lilo and Stitch, Mickey, Pluto
- **TYPE OF SERVICE** Family-style
- **FOOD VARIETY & QUALITY** ★★½ • **NOISE LEVEL** Loud
- **CHARACTER-GUEST RATIO** 1:57

10. 1900 PARK FARE   GRAND FLORIDIAN RESORT

- **MEALS SERVED** Breakfast and dinner • **SETTING** ★★★
- **CHARACTERS** Cinderella, Aladdin as Prince Ali, Mirabel, and Tiana in her Bayou Adventure outfit
- **TYPE OF SERVICE** Buffet
- **FOOD VARIETY & QUALITY** Breakfast ★★★   Dinner ★★★½
- **NOISE LEVEL** Moderate • **CHARACTER-GUEST RATIO** 1:68

11. RAVELLO   FOUR SEASONS ORLANDO

- **MEAL SERVED** Breakfast • **SETTING** ★★★
- **CHARACTERS** Mickey, Minnie, Goofy • **TYPE OF SERVICE** Buffet
- **FOOD VARIETY & QUALITY** ★★★★ • **NOISE LEVEL** Quiet
- **CHARACTER-GUEST RATIO** 1:30

12. TUSKER HOUSE RESTAURANT   DISNEY'S ANIMAL KINGDOM

- **MEALS SERVED** Breakfast, lunch, and dinner • **SETTING** ★★★
- **CHARACTERS** Donald, Daisy, Mickey, Goofy, Pluto • **TYPE OF SERVICE** Buffet
- **FOOD VARIETY & QUALITY** ★★★ • **NOISE LEVEL** Very loud
- **CHARACTER-GUEST RATIO** 1:112

13. TOPOLINO'S TERRACE   RIVIERA RESORT

- **MEAL SERVED** Breakfast • **SETTING** ★★★★
- **CHARACTERS** Mickey, Minnie, Donald, Daisy
- **TYPE OF SERVICE** Fixed menu • **FOOD VARIETY & QUALITY** ★★★★
- **NOISE LEVEL** Moderate • **CHARACTER-GUEST RATIO** 1:45

14. TRATTORIA AL FORNO*   DISNEY'S BOARDWALK

- **MEAL SERVED** Breakfast • **SETTING** ★★★½
- **CHARACTERS** Rapunzel, Flynn Ryder, Ariel, Prince Eric
- **TYPE OF SERVICE** Fixed menu with several choices
- **FOOD VARIETY & QUALITY** ★★★½
- **NOISE LEVEL** Quiet • **CHARACTER-GUEST RATIO** 1:50

* Open but no characters at press time

We dined a lot, did three character meals and a few Signature restaurants, and every meal was awesome except for lunch with Cinderella. It was a rushed affair. We had barely sat down when the appetizers were thrown on our table, the princesses each spent just a few seconds with our daughter—almost no interaction—and the side dishes were cold. We were out of there within 40 minutes and felt very stressed. Considering the price, I cannot recommend it.

DISNEY DINING SUGGESTIONS

FOLLOWING ARE OUR SUGGESTIONS for dining at each of the major theme parks. If you want to minimize the impact on your park day, it's good to know that the restaurants continue to serve after the park's official closing time.

THE MAGIC KINGDOM

OF THE PARK'S full-time full-service restaurants, the best are **Liberty Tree Tavern** (92%/Above Average) in Liberty Square and **Jungle Navigation Co. Ltd. Skipper Canteen** (91%/Above Average) in Adventureland. Liberty Tree Tavern serves standard American family-style meals for lunch and dinner, while Skipper Canteen serves hearty food in a Jungle Cruise–themed environment.

The big draw at the pricey **Cinderella's Royal Table** (83%/Below Average) is the setting—the food is . . . not. **The Plaza Restaurant** (79%/Much Below Average) on Main Street serves passable meals at more moderate prices than the other sit-down restaurants.

unofficial **TIP**
All Magic Kingdom sit-down restaurants serve beer and wine with dinner.

The most in-demand restaurant in the Magic Kingdom is **Be Our Guest** (67%/Do Not Visit) in Fantasyland; unfortunately, the entire dining experience has declined substantially, even as the prices have increased. You're not missing anything—it's an especially poor value—and we hope Disney does something about it soon. Likewise, quality at **The Crystal Palace** (87%/Average) has dropped lately. Additionally, avoid **Tony's Town Square** (80%/Much Below Average) on Main Street and (if it's open) **The Diamond Horseshoe** (77%/Much Below Average)—these two are among the worst restaurants in Walt Disney World parks.

AUTHORS' FAVORITE MAGIC KINGDOM COUNTER-SERVICE RESTAURANTS

• Friar's Nook Fantasyland   • Columbia Harbour House Liberty Square

---

Columbia Harbour House (94%/Much Above Average) is the best counter-service restaurant in the Magic Kingdom. Its menu focuses on seafood, with a tasty lobster roll, grilled salmon, and grilled shrimp all worth ordering, plus solid options for kids, vegans, and vegetarians. Secret double bonus: If you go upstairs, you'll usually have almost the whole space to yourself! **Casey's Corner** (89%/Average), on Main Street, U.S.A., serves ballpark-style hot dogs and fries. It's one of the rare Disney restaurants to have improved its food quality over the past few years. **Liberty Square Market** (89%/Average) also serves tasty hot dogs, plus pretzels and other snacks.

If these places don't do it for you, be prepared to make some compromises at the Magic Kingdom's other counter-service restaurants, all of which struggle to achieve average levels of quality. The best is probably **Pecos Bill Tall Tale Inn and Cafe** (82%/Below Average) in Frontierland, serving healthy portions of burgers and Tex-Mex. Avoid

Cosmic Ray's Starlight Café (76%/Do Not Visit) in Tomorrowland and, if it's open, **Tortuga Tavern** (72%/Do Not Visit) in Adventureland.

EPCOT

SINCE THE BEGINNING, dining has been an integral part of EPCOT's identity. World Showcase has many more restaurants than attractions, and EPCOT has added bars, tapas-style eateries, and full-service restaurants faster than any other park. (See the table on next page for a list of all the park's full-service restaurants.)

EPCOT also features food festival booths almost every day. Its annual **Food & Wine Festival** runs from late August through mid-November; the **Festival of the Holidays** begins a few days later. The **Festival of the Arts** follows that in January and lasts through late February, and then it's time for the **Flower & Garden Festival** from March through May.

unofficial **TIP**
EPCOT has 20 full-service restaurants: 3 in Future World and 17 in World Showcase. With a couple of exceptions, these are among the best restaurants at Walt Disney World, in or out of the theme parks.

While it's not the same as sitting inside a well-themed World Showcase pavilion, the food booths have their pluses: There's a lot of variety, the food quality can be quite good, and it's generally faster than a full sit-down meal.

For the most part, EPCOT's restaurants serve decent food, although World Showcase spots can be timid when it comes to delivering authentic representations of their host nations' cuisine—the "spicy" items in China are nowhere close to their domestic intensity, for example. While it's true that the less adventurous diner can find steak and potatoes on virtually every menu, the same kitchens will happily serve up a more traditional preparation of any dish, if you ask. (We've had wonderful experiences by asking for our food to be prepared the way the chefs would make it for themselves.)

An EPCOT evening without dinner in the World Showcase is like a birthday without presents. Each pavilion except the American Adventure has a beautifully themed restaurant. To tour them and not eat at any of them is just silly. Still, some restaurants are better than others.

EPCOT restaurants that combine attractive ambience and well-prepared food with good value are **Teppan Edo** in Japan (92%/Above Average); **Via Napoli Ristorante e Pizzeria** in Italy (93%/Much Above Average); **Spice Road Table** in Morocco (90%/Above Average); and **Garden Grill Restaurant** in The Land (92%/Above Average). Those that *don't* provide good value for the money include **San Angel Inn Restaurante** in Mexico (88%/Average); **Rose & Crown Dining Room** in the United Kingdom (84%/Below Average); **Tutto Italia** in Italy (86%/Average); **Akershus Royal Banquet Hall** in Norway (84%/Below Average); and **Monsieur Paul** in France (81%/Below Average). For the record, the last time we were served bisque at Monsieur Paul, it had sat long enough to form a skin. A Tennessee woman who ate at Via Napoli found the leisurely service uncharacteristic—and not in a good way:

We waited 40 minutes for dessert, which we wouldn't have bothered to order had it not been included in our Candlelight Processional dining package. On one hand, this more closely resembled what we

FULL-SERVICE RESTAURANTS IN EPCOT
WORLD NATURE AND WORLD DISCOVERY (*formerly Future World*)
• Coral Reef Restaurant The Seas with Nemo & Friends • Garden Grill Restaurant The Land • Space 220 World Discovery
WORLD SHOWCASE
• Akershus Royal Banquet Hall Norway • Biergarten Restaurant Germany • Chefs de France France • La Crêperie de Paris France • La Hacienda de San Angel Mexico • Le Cellier Steakhouse Canada • Monsieur Paul France • Nine Dragons Restaurant China • Rose & Crown Dining Room United Kingdom • San Angel Inn Restaurante Mexico • Shiki-Sai Japan • Spice Road Table Morocco • Takumi-Tei Japan • Teppan Edo Japan • Tutto Italia Ristorante Italy • Via Napoli Ristorante e Pizzeria Italy

experienced on a trip to the actual country of Italy versus the typical in-and-out experience of WDW restaurants. On the other hand, I don't believe Via Napoli was particularly striving for authenticity—it was just bad service.

AUTHORS' FAVORITE EPCOT COUNTER-SERVICE RESTAURANTS
• Les Halles Boulangerie–Pâtisserie France • Kringla Bakeri og Kafe Norway • Connections Café and Eatery World Celebration

Les Halles Boulangerie–Pâtisserie (95%/Much Above Average) in France is one of the highest-rated counter-service restaurants in Walt Disney World. It sells pastries, sandwiches, and quiches. The bread and pastries are made on-site, and the sandwiches are as close to actual French street food as you'll get anywhere in EPCOT. Another favorite is the barbecue at **Regal Eagle Smokehouse** (91%/Average).

In addition to these, we recommend the United Kingdom's **Rose & Crown Pub** (97%/Exceptional) for Guinness, Harp, and Bass beers, and **Yorkshire County Fish Shop** (96%/Exceptional) for fresh fish-and-chips. And the relatively new **Connections Café and Eatery** (90%/Average) performs surprisingly well—enough to be a good bet if you don't want to make your way over to World Showcase at mealtime.

EPCOT FOOD FESTIVALS As mentioned on the previous page, EPCOT hosts four major festivals per year. No matter what season or theme the festival has, food and drinks are the main draw. For each festival, EPCOT runs small, semipermanent, themed booths around the park. The booths serve appetizer-size portions—and almost always beer and wine—that fit the stand's theme. These festivals give EPCOT's chefs a chance to experiment with new ingredients and flavor combinations. The food quality is generally very good, and sometimes amazing.

Readers rate the food quality of the booths at the Flower & Garden and Food & Wine Festivals as above average. Many guest favorites return year after year. On the opposite page, we share a list of the best food items you're likely to find at each festival.

Drinking Around the World (Showcase)

A popular adult pastime in EPCOT is to make a complete circuit of World Showcase, sampling the alcoholic drinks from each nation. Here's a list of the don't-miss places.

BEST FOOD AT EACH EPCOT FESTIVAL

From Bethany, Bella, and Colin at The Main St Dish Podcast

INTERNATIONAL FESTIVAL OF THE ARTS *January–February*

• **Deconstructed BLT** The Deconstructed Dish • **Cast Iron–Roasted P.E.I. Mussels** Cuisine Classique • **Red Wine–Braised Short Rib** and **Black Forest Cake** Pastoral Palate • **Hummingbird Cake** The Artist's Table • **Chorizo and Potato Empanada** Vibrante & Vívido Encanto Cocina • **Tomato Soup with Pimento Cheese, Bacon, and Fried Green Tomato Grilled Cheese** Pop Eats • **Carne Asada** El Artista Hambriento

INTERNATIONAL FLOWER & GARDEN FESTIVAL *March–May*

• **Chargrilled Bison Ribeye with Creamy Leek Fondue** Farmers Feast • **Boneless Impossible Korean Short Ribs** Trowel & Trellis • **Taco Vampiro** Jardin de Fiestas • **Potato Pancakes** Bauernmarkt: Farmer's Market • **Frushi** Hanami • **Seared Scallops** Northern Bloom

INTERNATIONAL FOOD & WINE FESTIVAL *August–November*

• **Oysters Rockefeller** Coastal Eats • **Crispy Paneer** India • **Kenyan Coffee Barbecued Beef** Kenya • **Schinkennudeln** Germany • **Charcuterie** Spain • **Griddled Cheese** Greece • **Warm Chocolate Pudding** Ireland • **Spam Musubi Nigiri** Hawai'i

INTERNATIONAL FESTIVAL OF THE HOLIDAYS *November–December*

• **Pork Schnitzel** Bavaria Holiday Kitchen • **Blackened Catfish** American Holiday Table • **Pastrami on Rye** L'Chaim! Holiday Kitchen • **Turkey Poutine** Refreshment Port • **Peanut Stew** Refreshment Outpost • **New Year Celebration Soba** Shi Wasu Holiday Kitchen

LA CAVA DEL TEQUILA, MEXICO (95%/Much Above Average) Located inside the pyramid of the Mexico Pavilion, this is one of the best bars in Walt Disney World and one of the best tequila bars in the country. Its ever-changing menu includes more than 200 kinds of tequila and mezcal, several margaritas, and various light appetizers. On most weekends and during special events such as the Food & Wine Festival, Cinco de Mayo, and National Tequila Day (July 24), expect a significant wait to get a drink.

Most days, La Cava has a tequila expert on hand to explain the different types and provide tasting notes. (Ask for Hilda or Humberto, both from Tequila in Jalisco, Mexico—tell them Len sent you.) If you happen to be in EPCOT during the fall Food & Wine Festival, sign up for a tequila tasting if they're offered. Done in small groups with flights of tequila, it will teach you how to appreciate this magical liquid.

ROSE & CROWN PUB, UNITED KINGDOM (97%/Exceptional) It's a little brighter than many British pubs we've seen elsewhere, but Rose & Crown serves a wide variety of ales, lagers, stouts, and ciders alongside traditional English pub fare such as fish-and-chips and sausage rolls. If you're wanting something stronger, the pub has Scotch whiskies and Irish whiskeys. Service is cheerful and fast.

SAKE BARS, JAPAN (93%/Above Average) There are two sake bars in Japan: One is an outdoor kiosk on the walking path toward the back of the pavilion, and the other is a small counter tucked into the back of the first floor of the Mitsukoshi Department Store. Both have decent, affordable selections of sakes. We're still amazed these haven't turned into a waterside bar.

WEINKELLER, GERMANY (91%/Average) If you love sweet white wines, this is the place to be. Decorated with stone, dark wood, and heavy chandeliers, Weinkeller serves wines by the glass (around $9). Selections usually include a couple of Rieslings, a Liebfraumilch, dessert wines, and ice wines. Becky highly recommends asking for a Mozart chocolate liqueur. It's pricey but worth every penny. The bar has no seating and wasn't serving food at press time, but the wine pours are generous.

TUTTO GUSTO WINE CELLAR, ITALY (89%/Average) Tucked away on the left side of the pavilion, this small bar looks like the inside of a small home (or cave). With a wide selection of Italian wines, cheeses, and meats, it's perfect for drinking and snacking around the world.

DISNEY'S ANIMAL KINGDOM

ALONG WITH EPCOT, Animal Kingdom has some of the best dining options of any Disney theme park. The food isn't particularly exotic, and a lot of it is counter-service, but the quality is superior to that found in the Magic Kingdom and Disney's Hollywood Studios.

The park's *Avatar*-themed **Satu'li Canteen** (97%/Exceptional) is Disney's answer to Chipotle's rice bowls—you pick a base of starch, grain, or lettuce and then add a protein and garnishes. The nearby **Pongu Pongu Lounge** (93%/Above Average) serves drinks inspired by *Avatar,* plus the best breakfast biscuits in the park. If you need a drink and a place to gather yourself before venturing into Flight of Passage's long wait, stop at the **Nomad Lounge** (97%/Exceptional), which is on the way to Pandora from Discovery Island. The drinks here are well balanced and flavorful, and the lounge's décor is pretty.

A California dad praises Satu'li Canteen:

Our favorite place to eat was, by far, Satu'li Canteen. I would honestly make a special trip just to eat there. First, the food was crazy good. Yes, they basically make a bowl of food and that's all they serve, but everything was so delicious I could mix and match my ingredients to create something new every time. Second, they make everything from scratch there on-site. I can't stress enough how important this was to us, especially considering that our son has special dietary needs.

Our choices for sit-down restaurants in the park include **Yak & Yeti Restaurant** (94%/Much Above Average) in Asia, serving familiar Asian and Indian dishes, and **Tusker House Restaurant** (91%/Above Average) in Africa, whose choices are much more interesting than most others at Disney. **Tiffins** (91%/Above Average) is too expensive for us to recommend it to everyone. Also skip the **Rainforest Cafe** (82%/Below Average), which is among the lowest-rated Disney restaurants.

AUTHORS' FAVORITE ANIMAL KINGDOM COUNTER-SERVICE RESTAURANTS

• Flame Tree Barbecue Discovery Island   • Harambe Market Africa
• Satu'li Canteen Pandora

Besides Satu'li Canteen, our two other favorite counter-service dining options in the park are **Flame Tree Barbecue** (94%/Much Above Average), serving house-made barbecue at waterfront dining pavilions with excellent views of flotillas and Everest, and **Harambe Market** (95%/Much Above Average) in Africa, serving rice bowls with chicken or ribs, plant-based "sausages," and salads.

DISNEY'S HOLLYWOOD STUDIOS

DINING QUALITY AT THE STUDIOS has improved over the past several years but remains spotty at best. Two of the three highest-rated counter-service restaurants are in Galaxy's Edge. **Docking Bay 7 Food and Cargo** (90%/Average) serves chicken, ribs, and a vegetarian kefta, and **Ronto Roasters** (94%/Much Above Average) serves a limited menu of sausage wraps. Along with these, **Woody's Lunch Box** (91%/Average) in Toy Story Land is also rated better than average, with very good sandwiches, including plant-based options. As far as the rest of the park goes, **ABC Commissary** (90%/Average) and **Backlot Express** (86%/Below Average) are both skippable.

If you're looking for something to beat the heat, **Baseline Taphouse** (97%/Exceptional) on Grand Avenue is one of the highest-rated bars in Walt Disney World. It's small and mostly unthemed, but service is quick, and there's a decent selection of beers, plus a few snacks.

Good table-service dining is a long-running weakness at Hollywood Studios. One (expensive) option for a good meal is the upscale **Hollywood Brown Derby** (90%/Above Average), which serves well-prepared steaks, chicken, and fish. Our recommendation would be **50's Prime Time Café** (88%/Average), a restaurant where you sit in Mom's 1950s kitchen and scarf down meat loaf while watching clips of classic sitcoms. However, readers rate the experience of counter-service restaurants, packaged foods, popcorn, and booze higher than anything found in an actual restaurant.

What we think our reader surveys are saying here is that there are few restaurants in the Studios that combine good food, good service, an entertaining atmosphere, *and* reasonable prices; almost every place has at least one major flaw. Recent menu updates have not improved the food quality at the **Sci-Fi Dine-In Theater** (84%/Below Average)—where you eat in little cars at a simulated drive-in movie—but you won't find a better-themed restaurant in the World. **Hollywood & Vine** (89%/Average) features characters such as Minnie Mouse and friends at lunch and dinner; kids will love it, and the food has been improving. For simple Italian food, including flatbread pizzas, **Mama Melrose's Ristorante Italiano** (81%/Below Average) is just OK; don't expect anything fancy. A newer sit-down restaurant, **Roundup Rodeo BBQ** (83%/Below Average), opened in early 2023. It's not a quiet meal option, but the food is plentiful and higher-quality than most other sit-down options in the park. Ratings are low because of all that noise.

**AUTHORS' FAVORITE HOLLYWOOD STUDIOS
COUNTER-SERVICE RESTAURANT**

• **Docking Bay 7 Food and Cargo** Galaxy's Edge

Oga's Cantina (80%/Much Below Average), reminiscent of the bar from *A New Hope,* serves exotic alcoholic and nonalcoholic cocktails. Oga's is the only Galaxy's Edge restaurant that offers reservations, but they're difficult to get. You can join the walk-up waiting list if you're nearby and it's still open. But be warned: This is the lowest-rated bar in Walt Disney World because it's always packed (90% of people have to stand), the drinks seem abnormal, and food is almost nonexistent.

Galaxy's Edge's two outdoor stands are **Kat Saka's Kettle** (86%/Below Average), which offers multiflavored popcorn, and **Milk Stand** (87%/ Average), which serves the films' famous blue and green "milks." Both are actually vegan, made from coconut and rice. Neither is very good.

Our general advice when it comes to the Studios is to eat a good breakfast before you get to the park. For lunch and dinner, try for a cheap counter-service meal and a table-service meal where you'll enjoy the theming.

FULL-SERVICE DINING FOR FAMILIES WITH YOUNG CHILDREN

DISNEY RESTAURANTS OFFER an excellent (though expensive) opportunity to introduce young children to the variety and excitement of food from different cultures. No matter how formal a restaurant appears, the staff is accustomed to fidgety, impatient, and loud children.

unofficial **TIP**
Look for the **Mickey Check** icon on healthy menu items such as fresh fruit and low-fat milk.

Almost all Disney restaurants offer kids' menus, and all have booster seats and high chairs. Servers understand how tough it is for children to sit still for an extended period, and they'll serve your dinner much faster than in comparable restaurants elsewhere. Reader letters suggest that being served too quickly is more common than waiting too long.

A New York dad says timing is key when dining with younger kids:

> *As a family with three girls all under the age of 10, we quickly discovered that no sit-down restaurant is worth dragging the family to after 8 p.m. We ended up with at least two children sleeping on the chairs after ordering chicken nuggets for the second time that day. I would rather eat at a quick-service restaurant if it gets my family in bed by 9 p.m.*

Good Restaurants for Children

Be Our Guest and **Cinderella's Royal Table** are hot tickets in the **Magic Kingdom,** and reservations at both are often difficult to get. (The only character at Be Our Guest is the Beast.) Be Our Guest's quality is substandard, it's overpriced, and you shouldn't eat there. We think the most kid-friendly fare is served at **Liberty Tree Tavern** in Liberty Square.

In **EPCOT,** preschoolers most enjoy **Biergarten Restaurant** in Germany, **Teppan Edo** in Japan, and **Coral Reef Restaurant** at The Seas with Nemo & Friends Pavilion in World Nature. Biergarten (91%/ Above Average) combines a rollicking and musical atmosphere with tasty, mostly familiar foods. A German oompah band entertains guests at both lunch and dinner. Teppan Edo (92%/Above Average) is on the upper floor of the Japan pavilion. Children can watch their food being cooked in front of them, along with the "show" elements of hibachi. Coral Reef (80%/Much Below Average), with tables beside windows looking into The Seas' aquarium, offers a satisfying mealtime diversion for all ages. For those who don't eat fish, it also serves beef, chicken, and vegetarian options, and with a new chef in 2023, we expect its scores to improve steadily.

The best table-service restaurants for kids in **Disney's Animal Kingdom** are **Yak & Yeti Restaurant** and **Tusker House.**

In **Disney's Hollywood Studios,** kids of all ages enjoy the atmosphere and entertainment at **Hollywood & Vine, Sci-Fi Dine-In Theater Restaurant,** and **50's Prime Time Café.**

NOISE AT RESTAURANTS

RESTAURANTS ARE NOISY all around the World. A Pennsylvania adult dining with one other adult shared this:

We ate four times at Signature restaurants. The food was always good, and the check, with wine and tip, was always at least $150. However, the noise, especially at Le Cellier and Il Mulino, was overwhelming. WDW seems to have really skimped on the acoustics, even at Cítricos and the California Grill.

QUIET, ROMANTIC PLACES TO EAT

RESTAURANTS WITH GOOD FOOD and a couple-friendly ambience are rare in the parks. Only the following satisfy both requirements: an alfresco table at **Tutto Italia Ristorante,** the terraces at **Rose & Crown Dining Room** and **Teppan Edo,** and the Japanese-themed **Takumi Tei,** all in EPCOT, the small and seemingly secluded **Tiffins** at Animal Kingdom, and the old-school-cool **Hollywood Brown Derby** in Disney's Hollywood Studios.

> **unofficial TIP**
> The **California Grill** at the Contemporary Resort and **Topolino's Terrace** at the Riviera have elevated views at Walt Disney World.

Victoria & Albert's at the Grand Floridian is Disney's showcase gourmet restaurant; the current menu starts at $295 per person. Other good choices for couples include **Jiko—The Cooking Place** and **Sanaa** in Animal Kingdom Lodge, along with **Cítricos** and **Narcoossee's** at the Grand Floridian.

Eating later in the evening and choosing a restaurant we've mentioned will improve your chances for intimate dining; nevertheless, children—well behaved or otherwise—are everywhere at Walt Disney World, and there will always be children no matter where you eat.

WALT DISNEY WORLD DINNER THEATERS

AS IS THE CASE with other Disney restaurant reservations, when you make a reservation for *Hoop-Dee-Doo Musical Revue* (the only dinner show currently offered), you'll receive a confirmation number, and your credit card will be charged the full amount unless you cancel your tickets at least 48 hours before your reservation time. Dinner-show reservations can be made 60 days in advance; book online or call ☎ 407-939-3463.

> **unofficial TIP**
> To make reservations for the *Hoop-Dee-Doo Musical Revue,* book online or call as soon as you know the dates of your visit. The earlier you call, the better selection of dates and times you'll have.

It's worth noting that obtaining reservations for *Hoop-Dee-Doo* during busy periods can be a trick of the first order. If you want to see a show but can't get reservations:

1. Call ☎ 407-939-3463 at 9 a.m. each morning while at Disney World to make a same-day reservation. There are two to three performances each night, and for each night, only 3–24 people total will be admitted with same-day reservations.

2. Arrive at the show 45 minutes before showtime (late shows are your best bets) and put your name on the standby list. If someone with reservations fails to show, you may be admitted.

Disney offers tiered seating for *Hoop-Dee-Doo*. The best seats are in **Category 1**. Next comes **Category 2,** with seats off to the side or behind Category 1. Finally, **Category 3** seats are farther still to the side or back, or on another level from the stage. Good views can be had from almost all seats, so you can decide if sitting closer to the action is worth the extra bucks.

Hoop-Dee-Doo Musical Revue

⊕ 96% (Exceptional)

Pioneer Hall, Fort Wilderness Campground ☎ 407-939-3463. **Showtimes** Nightly, 4, 6:15, and 8:30 p.m. **Cost** Category 1, $74 adults ($44 children ages 3–9); Category 2, $69 adults ($40 children); Category 3, $66 adults ($39 children). Prices include tax and gratuity. **Duration of show** 2 hours. **Menu** All-you-can-eat barbecue ribs, fried chicken, salad, baked beans, and cornbread; unlimited beer, wine, sangria, and soft drinks. Vegetarian, vegan, and gluten-free options available.

DESCRIPTION AND COMMENTS *Hoop-Dee-Doo* is the longest-running (and now only) dinner show at Walt Disney World and a nostalgic favorite for many families. If you've ever thought *Country Bear Jamboree* would benefit from free-flowing barbecue, beer, and wine, this is the show for you.

Audience participation includes sing-alongs, hand-clapping, and a finale where you may find yourself onstage. During the meal, the music continues (softly). The food itself is pretty good.

Think about transportation when planning your evening at Fort Wilderness; it'll take some time to get there and back. There is no parking at Pioneer Hall, which is accessible only by boat (the Magic Kingdom and the loop between Fort Wilderness, Wilderness Lodge, and the Contemporary), and the Fort Wilderness internal bus system. After the show, resort buses at the Pioneer Hall stop will take you back to your resort. The quickest and most convenient option may be to take a **Disney Minnie Van** (page 330).

MORE READER COMMENTS ABOUT WALT DISNEY WORLD DINING

EATING IS A POPULAR TOPIC among *Unofficial Guide* readers. In addition to participating in our annual restaurant survey, many readers share their thoughts. The following comments are representative.

Here's a 13-year-old from Nebraska who shares some wisdom beyond her years and recommends not getting bent out of shape over one bad meal:

Honestly, when was the last time you came home from Disney World and said, "Gosh, my vacation really sucked because I ate at a bad restaurant?"

Sanaa, in the Kidani Village section of Animal Kingdom Lodge, really impressed a Maryland family:

Sanaa is a beautiful restaurant with delicious and inexpensive (for Disney) food that you can't find anywhere else in Walt Disney World. We had a fabulous adults-only evening here, but I would bring children too, for an early dinner overlooking the savanna.

And Raglan Road at Disney Springs was a big hit with a mom of two from California:

> *Cannot say enough about this amazing Irish pub. The ambience, the food, and the entertainment were all absolutely top-notch.*

WALT DISNEY WORLD LOUNGES

IN THE *UNOFFICIAL GUIDE*, we have always provided overviews of counter-service and table-service restaurants. But some of the very best dining experiences we've had were at lounges. In an effort to bring more awareness to these often overlooked options, Bethany, Bella, and Colin of *The Main St Dish* podcast highlight some of their recommended lounges for you to try on your next visit.

WDW LOUNGE RECOMMENDATIONS
From Bethany, Bella, and Colin at The Main St Dish Podcast

LOCATION	LOUNGES
ANIMAL KINGDOM	• **Nomad Lounge** A wonderful spot to cool off, with indoor and outdoor lounge seating. The menu has unique cocktails, mocktails, great small plates, and rotating seasonal menu selections. We recommend trying the Hightower Rocks, Lamu Libation, and Jenn's Tattoo. It is also the home of one of the best hidden menu items in Disney: ask for the kids' chicken nuggets—some of the best nuggets in the parks!
DISNEY'S HOLLYWOOD STUDIOS	• **Baseline Tap House** This California-themed tap house is the perfect place to grab a beer and a light snack. There is plenty of seating outside, and it's a great place to people-watch. • **Tune-In Lounge** Flash back to the 1950s in this retro-themed lounge, where you can duck the crowds or grab some air-conditioning or a drink to go. Ask the bartenders about a Mozart Moment—if you love chocolate and sweet drinks, this one's for you.
EPCOT	• **La Cava del Tequila** This tequila cave is a must-stop in EPCOT. It's hidden in the pyramid of the Mexico Pavilion and has an impressive tequila list. The entire team here is incredibly knowledgeable when it comes to tequila and are happy to make recommendations for you. La Cava can get crowded, so we recommend being there when they open at 11 a.m.
RESORTS	• **Belle Vue Lounge** (BoardWalk Inn) Located off the main lobby, this quaint lounge has comfortable 1930s-style furnishings and is usually a very quiet spot. There is also a small outdoor patio with seating that overlooks the BoardWalk, ideal for sipping a cocktail and taking in the views! • **Dahlia Lounge** (Coronado Springs) Located on the top floor of the Gran Destino Tower, this beautiful, modern lounge inspired by the iconic architecture of Spain features a very large bar with lots of additional indoor and outdoor seating. The menu consists of amazing cocktails and delicious tapas-style small plates. • **Enchanted Rose** (Grand Floridian) Located on the second floor of the main lobby, this is a stunning lounge inspired by the live-action remake of *Beauty and the Beast*. The cocktails here are on the more expensive side, but the quality of all the drinks is outstanding.

COUNTER-SERVICE
Mini-Profiles

TO HELP YOU FIND TASTY FAST FOOD, we profile the counter-service restaurants in each theme park and Disney Springs. They are rated for quality, value, and portion size. All participate in the Disney Dining Plan, except where noted, though participating restaurants are subject to change; check theugseries.com/wdwupdates for the latest updates. Mobile ordering (page 214) is encouraged at almost all of these restaurants. Value ratings range from A to F, as follows:

A	Exceptional value; a real bargain
B	Good value
C	Fair value; you get exactly what you pay for
D	Somewhat overpriced
F	Extremely overpriced

See page 201 for how the reader-survey percentages break down.

THE MAGIC KINGDOM

Aloha Isle

QUALITY Excellent   **VALUE** B   **PORTION** Medium   **LOCATION** Adventureland
READER-SURVEY RESPONSES ✚ 99% (Exceptional)

Selections Soft-serve, ice-cream floats, pineapple juice.
Comments Located next to *Walt Disney's Enchanted Tiki Room.* The pineapple Dole Whip soft-serve is a world-famous Disney theme park treat.

Casey's Corner

QUALITY Good   **VALUE** C   **PORTION** Medium   **LOCATION** Main Street, U.S.A.
READER-SURVEY RESPONSES ✚ 89% (Average)

Selections Hot dogs, plant-based "sausage" dogs, corn dog nuggets, fries, Baseball Brownie.
Comments Casey's offers the best hot dogs in Walt Disney World—which isn't a hard competition. The quality rivals that of a good ballpark frank.

Columbia Harbour House

QUALITY Good   **VALUE** B   **PORTION** Medium   **LOCATION** Liberty Square
READER-SURVEY RESPONSES ✚ 94% (Much Above Average)

Selections Eat light with the grilled salmon with rice, indulge with fried shrimp and fish, or splurge on the lobster roll. Other choices: fried chicken, grilled shrimp, plant-based "crab" cake sandwich, salads, and hush puppies. For kids: shrimp skewer or grilled salmon.
Comments Columbia Harbour House is the highest-rated counter-service restaurant in the Magic Kingdom. The upstairs seating is quieter and often downright peaceful.

Cosmic Ray's Starlight Café

QUALITY Fair–Poor   **VALUE** C   **PORTION** Medium   **LOCATION** Tomorrowland
READER-SURVEY RESPONSES ✚ 76% (Do Not Visit)

Selections Burgers, hot dogs, Greek salad, chicken sandwich, chicken strips, hot dogs, plant-based burgers, seasonal dessert. Kosher choices available on request.
Comments This is a crowded, high-volume restaurant where food quality and ambience are sacrificed in the name of just getting something to eat.

COST OF COUNTER-SERVICE FOOD	
BAGEL OR MUFFIN $5	HOT DOG $10-$14
BROWNIE $5	ICE CREAM/FROZEN NOVELTIES $6-$13
BURRITO BOWL $12	NACHOS WITH CHEESE $12
CAKE OR PIE $6-$9	PB&J SANDWICH $8 (kids' meal)-$11
CEREAL WITH MILK $5-$6	PIZZA (personal) $12
CHEESEBURGER WITH FRIES $12-$14	POPCORN $5
CHICKEN BREAST SANDWICH $12-$14	PRETZEL $8
CHICKEN NUGGETS WITH FRIES $11-$12	SALAD (entrée) $9-$12
CHILDREN'S MEAL (various) $8-$11	SALAD (side) $9-$12
CHIPS $4	SMOKED TURKEY LEG $12-$15
COOKIE $4-$8	SOUP/CHILI $5-$7
FRIED-FISH BASKET (with fries) $14-$16	SUB/DELI SANDWICH $12-$14
FRIES $5	TACO SALAD $11-$13
FRUIT (whole) $2-$4	VEGGIE BURGER $13
FRUIT CUP/FRUIT SALAD $6	

COST OF COUNTER-SERVICE DRINKS	
BEER small $9 large $14	BOTTLED WATER $4 (one size)
COFFEE $4 (one size)	LATTE small $5 large $6
FRUIT JUICE small $5 large $7	HOT TEA AND COCOA $4 (one size)
MILK $2 (one size)	
FLOAT, MILKSHAKE, OR SUNDAE small $9 large $14	
SOFT DRINKS, ICED TEA, AND LEMONADE small $4 large $5	

Each person on a Disney Dining Plan gets a free mug, refillable at any Disney resort. If you're not on a dining plan, a refillable souvenir mug costs $20 including tax (free refills) at Disney resorts and around $12 at the water parks.

The Friar's Nook

QUALITY Good   **VALUE** B   **PORTION** Medium-Large   **LOCATION** Fantasyland
READER-SURVEY RESPONSES ☉ 90% (Average)

Selections Hot dogs; burgers; bacon mac and cheese. Also serves a bacon, egg, and cheese breakfast croissant with tots.

Comments A good place for a hearty snack or light meal, but it can be difficult to find seating, especially in the shade.

Gaston's Tavern

QUALITY Good   **VALUE** B   **PORTION** Medium   **LOCATION** Fantasyland
READER-SURVEY RESPONSES ☉ 95% (Much Above Average)

Selections Ham-and-Swiss sandwich, cinnamon rolls, the Grey Stuff, LeFou's Brew (frozen apple juice with toasted-marshmallow flavoring).

Comments Very popular throughout the day. The cinnamon rolls are roughly the size of a barge. You can ask for extra icing!

Golden Oak Outpost (seasonal)

QUALITY Fair   **VALUE** C   **PORTION** Medium   **LOCATION** Frontierland
READER-SURVEY RESPONSES ☉ 89% (Average)

Selections Fried-fish sandwiches, chicken strips, chili-cheese fries, and chocolate chip cookies.

Comments Bare-bones basic eats.

Liberty Square Market

QUALITY Good	VALUE C	PORTION Medium	LOCATION Liberty Square
READER-SURVEY RESPONSES ⊕ 89% (Average)			

Selections Tasty hot dogs, plus fruit, pretzels, packaged drinks and snacks.
Comments There's seating nearby, but none of it is covered.

The Lunching Pad

QUALITY Fair	VALUE C	PORTION Medium	LOCATION Tomorrowland
READER-SURVEY RESPONSES ⊕ 78% (Much Below Average)			

Selections Hot dogs, pretzels, and specialty frozen drinks.
Comments Unless you want a cream cheese pretzel, sprint away.

Main Street Bakery *(Starbucks)*

QUALITY Good	VALUE B	PORTION Medium	LOCATION Main Street, U.S.A.
READER-SURVEY RESPONSES ⊕ 89% (Average)			

Selections Coffees, pastries, breakfast sandwiches.
Comments Extremely busy throughout the day, but the lines move fast.

Pecos Bill Tall Tale Inn and Cafe

QUALITY Fair	VALUE C	PORTION Medium–Large	LOCATION Frontierland
READER-SURVEY RESPONSES ⊕ 82% (Below Average)			

Selections Pork carnitas and chicken fajita platter with rice and beans; beef nachos; rice-and-veggie bowl; salad; burgers.
Comments Pecos Bill was known for its toppings bar, but now even that meager reason for going is gone.

Pinocchio Village Haus

QUALITY Fair–Poor	VALUE D	PORTION Medium	LOCATION Fantasyland
READER-SURVEY RESPONSES ⊕ 78% (Much Below Average)			

Selections Flatbread pizzas; chicken strips; fries; Caesar salad.
Comments The only reason to eat here is if you can get a seat overlooking It's a Small World.

Tomorrowland Terrace Restaurant *(seasonal)*

QUALITY Fair	VALUE C–	PORTION Medium–Large	LOCATION Tomorrowland
READER-SURVEY RESPONSES ⊕ 91% (Average)			

Selections Varies.
Comments Rarely open. Benefits greatly from simply not being Cosmic Ray's or The Lunching Pad.

Tortuga Tavern *(seasonal)*

QUALITY Fair	VALUE B	PORTION Medium–Large	LOCATION Adventureland
READER-SURVEY RESPONSES ⊕ 72% (Do Not Visit)			

Selections Chicken strips, sandwiches, and hot dogs.
Comments The eating area is large and shaded. Disney changes up the menu here from time to time—but it's never high-quality.

EPCOT

L'Artisan des Glaces

QUALITY Excellent	VALUE B	PORTION Large	LOCATION France
READER-SURVEY RESPONSES ⊕ 93% (Above Average)	NOT ON DISNEY DINING PLAN		

Selections Ice-cream flavors change but include classics and some more-sophisticated options, as well as dairy-free sorbets. Adults over age 21 can enjoy two scoops in a martini glass, topped with Grand Marnier, rum, or whipped cream–flavored vodka.

Comments L'Artisan des Glaces serves some of the best ice cream at Disney World. Be fancy and get yours served in a macaron or brioche!

La Cantina de San Angel

QUALITY Good	VALUE B	PORTION Medium–Large	LOCATION Mexico
READER-SURVEY RESPONSES ⊕ 92% (Above Average)			

Selections Tacos with beef, chicken, or shrimp; fried cheese empanada; grilled chicken with cascabel pepper sauce; guacamole; churros; margaritas. For kids: chicken tacos, empanadas, chicken tenders, or mac and cheese.

Comments A popular spot for a quick meal, with 150 covered outdoor seats, some well shaded. When it's extra busy, the back of La Hacienda de San Angel's dining room is opened for air-conditioned seating.

Connections Café and Connections Eatery

QUALITY Good	VALUE B	PORTION Large	LOCATION World Celebration
READER-SURVEY RESPONSES ⊕ 90% (Average)			

Selections Burgers, pizza, and salads, with plant-based options.

Comments Spacious, bright, and cheerful seating areas, with open-kitchen views into the pizza-making process. The pizza is regularly cited as some of the best counter-service pizza on-property.

Fife & Drum Tavern

QUALITY Fair	VALUE C	PORTION Large	LOCATION United States
READER-SURVEY RESPONSES ⊕ 91% (Average)			

Selections Turkey legs, hot dogs, popcorn, soft-serve ice cream, slushies, beer, alcoholic lemonade, and root beer floats.

Comments Seating is available in and around the Regal Eagle Smokehouse, behind the Fife & Drum.

Les Halles Boulangerie–Pâtisserie

QUALITY Excellent	VALUE B	PORTION Small–Medium	LOCATION France
READER-SURVEY RESPONSES ⊕ 95% (Much Above Average)			

Selections The beautiful deli–bakery case is stocked with goodies such as sandwiches (ham and cheese; Brie, cranberry, and apple), quiches, soups, bread, and delicate pastries.

Comments Les Halles is consistently rated as one of the top counter-service restaurants in EPCOT. Breads and pastries are made on-site. For an authentic Parisian experience, grab a half baguette (ask for extra butter) and eat it while you walk around France. Split up your party between waiting in line to order and waiting for a table if you want any chance of finding a seat.

Katsura Grill

QUALITY Good	VALUE B	PORTION Medium	LOCATION Japan
READER-SURVEY RESPONSES ⊕ 90% (Average)			

Selections Basic sushi; udon noodle bowls (vegetarian or shrimp tempura); pork ramen; chicken, beef, or shrimp teriyaki; chicken curry; edamame; miso soup; yuzu tea cheesecake; teriyaki kids' plate; Kirin beer, sake, and plum wine.

Comments The food is just average, but this might be the loveliest spot to escape the EPCOT crowd and eat a quick meal outside.

Kringla Bakeri og Kafe

QUALITY Good–Excellent   **VALUE** B   **PORTION** Small–Medium   **LOCATION** Norway
READER-SURVEY RESPONSES ⊕ 95% (Much Above Average)

Selections Norwegian pastries and desserts, iced coffee, and imported beers and wines.

Comments Limited menu. The School Bread (a sweet roll filled with custard and dipped in coconut) is popular. Outdoor seating only.

Lotus Blossom Café

QUALITY Fair   **VALUE** C   **PORTION** Medium   **LOCATION** China
READER-SURVEY RESPONSES ⊕ 85% (Below Average)

Selections Pork and vegetable egg rolls, pot stickers, orange chicken, chicken fried rice, Mongolian beef with rice, caramel-ginger or lychee ice cream, plum wine, Tsingtao beer.

Comments The menu rarely changes, and the food is a snooze. Opt for a nearby festival booth instead.

Refreshment Outpost

QUALITY Good   **VALUE** C   **PORTION** Small   **LOCATION** Between Germany and China
READER-SURVEY RESPONSES ⊕ 94% (Much Above Average)

Selections All-beef hot dogs, soft-serve, slushies, sodas, draft beer.

Comments The hot dogs here aren't bad, but there are plenty of better dining options within a few minutes' walk. We think this is highly rated for its cool slushies and ice cream, plus its regular festival offerings. Try the githeri.

Refreshment Port

QUALITY Good   **VALUE** C   **PORTION** Medium   **LOCATION** Near Canada
READER-SURVEY RESPONSES ⊕ 94% (Much Above Average)

Selections Soft-serve, specialty cocktails, and beer.

Comments Ratings are greatly boosted by the various festival foods served.

Regal Eagle Smokehouse: Craft Drafts & Barbecue

QUALITY Good   **VALUE** B   **PORTION** Large   **LOCATION** United States
READER-SURVEY RESPONSES ⊕ 91% (Average)

Selections Regional barbecue specialties, including Memphis smoked ribs, Kansas City chicken, North Carolina chopped pork, and Texas brisket, plus burgers, salads, and vegetarian options. Plus beer, hard cider, wine, and specialty cocktails.

Comments Regal Eagle serves decent barbecue in hearty portions, with the Texas brisket (on garlic toast) being our favorite. If you're a BBQ fan, **The Polite Pig** at Disney Springs (see page 240) is where you really need to go.

Rose & Crown Pub

QUALITY Good   **VALUE** B   **PORTION** Medium   **LOCATION** United Kingdom
READER-SURVEY RESPONSES ⊕ 97% (Exceptional)   **NOT ON DISNEY DINING PLAN**

Selections Fish-and-chips; Scotch egg; Guinness, Harp, and Bass beers, along with other spirits.

Comments Authentic British pub with everything you'd expect.

Sommerfest

QUALITY Fair   **VALUE** C   **PORTION** Medium   **LOCATION** Germany
READER-SURVEY RESPONSES ⊕ 92% (Above Average)

Selections Bratwurst, pretzel bread pudding, jumbo pretzel, cold beer.

Comments Tables are set up in the courtyard. Much of the food looks better than it tastes.

Sunshine Seasons

QUALITY Good	VALUE B	PORTION Medium	LOCATION The Land
READER-SURVEY RESPONSES ⊕ 86% (Below Average)			

Selections Sunshine Seasons consists of the following three areas: (1) wood-fired grills and rotisserie; (2) sandwiches and flatbreads; and (3) the soup-and-salad shop, with soups made daily and featuring creations such as the Power Salad (quinoa, almonds, and chicken).

Comments Sunshine Seasons used to set the standard for good cafeteria-style fare, but options have become more limited, and crowds usually slow things down.

Tangierine Café

QUALITY Good	VALUE B	PORTION Medium	LOCATION Morocco
READER-SURVEY RESPONSES ⊕ 93% (Above Average)			

Selections Grilled kebabs, hummus, Moroccan wine and beer.

Comments Before the pandemic, Tangierine was run by a third party. Disney now runs the place and typically only uses it as a festival booth. Thankfully, when it's open the food remains much better than average.

Yorkshire County Fish Shop

QUALITY Good	VALUE A	PORTION Large	LOCATION United Kingdom
READER-SURVEY RESPONSES ⊕ 95% (Much Above Average)			

Selections Fish-and-chips, Bass Pale Ale draft, and Harp Lager.

Comments There's usually a line for the crisp, hot fish-and-chips at this convenient fast-food window. A tasty chicken-and-mushroom pie might be served during cooler months. Outdoor seating overlooks the lagoon.

DISNEY'S ANIMAL KINGDOM
Creature Comforts *(Starbucks)*

QUALITY Good	VALUE C	PORTION Small	LOCATION Discovery Island near Africa
READER-SURVEY RESPONSES ⊕ 95% (Much Above Average)			

Selections Coffee drinks and teas; sandwiches and pastries.

Comments The fare is largely the same as you'd find at any other Starbucks, plus the occasional Animal Kingdom–themed treat.

Flame Tree Barbecue

QUALITY Good	VALUE B	PORTION Large	LOCATION Discovery Island
READER-SURVEY RESPONSES ⊕ 94% (Much Above Average)			

Selections St. Louis–style ribs; smoked half chicken; pulled-pork sandwich; mac and cheese with pulled pork; plant-based "sausage" sandwich; Safari Amber beer, frozen mango-raspberry coconut rum drink.

Comments One of our favorites for lunch, mostly for the location. Keep walking down and toward the water. Few others will trek that far with a tray, and you'll be rewarded with beautiful views. Portions here are large enough that our family of four can order two or three entrées and not finish all the food.

Harambe Market

QUALITY Good	VALUE B	PORTION Medium	LOCATION Africa
READER-SURVEY RESPONSES ⊕ 95% (Much Above Average)			

Selections Grilled chicken or shrimp served over rice and salad greens, salads, plant-based "sausage." Kids' selections include PB&J, chicken nuggets, and chicken and rice bowl.

Comments Disney Imagineers modeled Harambe's marketplace setting after a typical real-life market in an African nation during the 1960s colonial era.

Kusafiri Coffee Shop and Bakery

QUALITY Good	VALUE B	PORTION Medium	LOCATION Africa
READER-SURVEY RESPONSES ✪ 93% (Above Average)		NOT ON DISNEY DINING PLAN	

Selections Impossible empanadas with plant-based picadillo filling; flatbreads; breakfast pastries; pistachio-honey croissants; cookies; sausage, egg, and cheese biscuit; coffee; beer.

Comments The cinnamon roll is a favorite. Kosher items are available.

Pizzafari

QUALITY Poor	VALUE C	PORTION Medium	LOCATION Discovery Island
READER-SURVEY RESPONSES ✪ 82% (Below Average)			

Selections Chicken Parmesan sandwich; personal pizzas; Caesar salad. For kids: mac and cheese, pasta with turkey marinara, cheese pizza, or PB&J. Cannoli cake for dessert.

Comments The menu is profoundly unimpressive. One of the worst dining options in the park.

Restaurantosaurus

QUALITY Fair	VALUE C	PORTION Medium-Large	LOCATION DinoLand U.S.A.
READER-SURVEY RESPONSES ✪ 88% (Average)			

Selections Angus bacon cheeseburger; chili-cheese hot dog; chicken sandwich; chicken nuggets; Cobb salad; breaded shrimp; plant-based spicy Southwestern burger; kids' chicken nuggets, cheeseburger, or PB&J.

Comments A wide variety of selections. There's plenty of seating, divided into rooms. A hard-to-find lounge next door serves adult beverages.

Royal Anandapur Tea Company

QUALITY Good	VALUE B	PORTION Medium	LOCATION Asia
READER-SURVEY RESPONSES ✪ 91% (Average)		NOT ON DISNEY DINING PLAN	

Selections Wide variety of hot and iced teas, hot chocolate, and coffees (fantastic frozen chai); lattes and espresso; pastries.

Comments This is the kind of small, eclectic, Animal Kingdom–specific food stand that you wish other parks had. Around 10 loose teas from Asia and Africa can be ordered hot or iced.

Satu'li Canteen

QUALITY Good-Excellent	VALUE A	PORTION Medium-Large	LOCATION Pandora
READER-SURVEY RESPONSES ✪ 97% (Exceptional)			

Selections The signature item is the customizable bowl. Start with a base of salad, red and sweet potato hash, rice and beans, or whole grains and rice. Add wood-grilled chicken, slow-roasted beef, chili-garlic shrimp, or chili-spiced fried tofu, and finish with a choice of sauces. The menu also offers steamed "pods": bao buns with a cheeseburger filling, served with root-vegetable chips and crunchy vegetable slaw.

Comments The top counter-service spot in the park—and one of the best in all of the World.

Yak & Yeti Local Food Cafes

QUALITY Fair	VALUE C	PORTION Large	LOCATION Asia
READER-SURVEY RESPONSES ⊕ 93% (Above Average)			

Selections Honey chicken with steamed rice, cheeseburger, teriyaki chicken salad, vegetarian tikka masala, Korean-style fried chicken sandwich with kimchi, sweet-and-sour tempura shrimp, egg rolls, and fried rice. Kids' menu: chicken tenders, PB&J, or cheeseburger with carrot sticks and fresh fruit. Breakfast is American-style fare such as breakfast bowls and English muffin breakfast sandwiches.

Comments For filling up with quality food when you're in a hurry. Expanded seating area behind the pickup windows.

DISNEY'S HOLLYWOOD STUDIOS

ABC Commissary

QUALITY Fair	VALUE C	PORTION Medium	LOCATION Commissary Lane
READER-SURVEY RESPONSES ⊕ 90% (Average)			

Selections Pork carnitas or shrimp tacos, Buffalo chicken grilled cheese, Mediterranean salad with or without chicken, chicken club sandwich, plant-based burger, beer. Some kosher.

Comments The Buffalo chicken grilled cheese and the shrimp tacos are the standout menu items.

Backlot Express

QUALITY Fair	VALUE C	PORTION Medium	LOCATION Echo Lake
READER-SURVEY RESPONSES ⊕ 86% (Below Average)			

Selections One-third-pound Angus bacon cheeseburger, chicken strips, Cuban sandwich, Southwest salad, teriyaki chicken or tofu bowl.

Comments Fun props, some used in movies, decorate this spacious eatery.

Catalina Eddie's

QUALITY Fair	VALUE D	PORTION Medium–Large	LOCATION Sunset Boulevard
READER-SURVEY RESPONSES ⊕ 77% (Much Below Average)			

Selections Cheese and pepperoni pizzas, Caesar salad with or without chicken. Kids' menu has the same pizzas.

Comments Almost anything in the park—even a lemon-and-water cleanse, for that matter—is a better option.

Docking Bay 7 Food and Cargo

QUALITY Excellent	VALUE A	PORTION Medium	LOCATION Galaxy's Edge
READER-SURVEY RESPONSES ⊕ 90% (Average)			

Selections Smoked Kaadu Ribs, named after the creature Jar Jar Binks rode in *Episode I* (but actually pork), are cut vertically to give them an alien appearance, then glazed with a sticky-sweet sauce and served with down-home blueberry corn muffins. Endorian Tip Yip (chicken) is roasted on a salad or compressed into cubes, deep-fried, and served with mac and cheese and roasted vegetables.

Comments This is our choice for the best quick service in Hollywood Studios. Most items here are above-average quality. The Tip Yip chicken is moist and flavorful, as are the vegetable kefta in the Felucian Garden Spread; the ribs, however, are difficult to eat. Also, note that the kids' menu isn't particularly kid-friendly: In keeping with the idea that you're on an alien planet, many of the foods come in unfamiliar shapes and colors.

Dockside Diner

QUALITY Fair	VALUE D	PORTION Small–Medium	LOCATION Echo Lake
READER-SURVEY RESPONSES ➕ 73% (Do Not Visit)			

Selections Hot dogs with over-the-top toppings. The menu goes for shock and awe . . . and succeeds, in a bad way.

Comments Limited seating at nearby picnic tables.

Fairfax Fare

QUALITY Fair	VALUE B	PORTION Medium	LOCATION Sunset Boulevard
READER-SURVEY RESPONSES ➕ 82% (Below Average)			

Selections Bunches of bowls that don't impress anyone who tries them.

Comments This is the best dining option on Sunset Boulevard—but you should still walk elsewhere.

Milk Stand

QUALITY Fair	VALUE F	PORTION Small	LOCATION Galaxy's Edge
READER-SURVEY RESPONSES ➕ 87% (Average)			

Selections Frozen nondairy drinks, with or without alcohol.

Comments These plant-based beverages have the consistency of a smoothie. Green milk, as seen in *The Last Jedi,* has floral flavors, while the blue drink from *A New Hope* tastes of melon and pineapple. These "milks" are expensive, so split one if you can. We recommend avoiding the optional splash of booze. It's not worth the upcharge.

Oga's Cantina

QUALITY Fair	VALUE D	PORTION Medium	LOCATION Galaxy's Edge
READER-SURVEY RESPONSES ➕ 80% (Much Below Average)			

Selections Alcoholic and nonalcoholic cocktails; a sampler platter with cured and roasted meats, cheese, and pork cracklings.

Comments This cantina will instantly remind fans of the Mos Eisley watering hole from *A New Hope.* A droid DJ—actually a recycled Captain Rex from the original Star Tours—spins an original '80s-style soundtrack. The signature cocktails and nonalcoholic beverages are all unique and delightful.

Although it's technically neither counter service nor table service, Oga's does take reservations, which are available up to 60 days in advance. Be ready at your 60-day mark to grab one—the place has stayed packed from the moment it opened. *Note:* Most of the cantina is standing room only.

PizzeRizzo

QUALITY Poor	VALUE C	PORTION Large	LOCATION Grand Avenue
READER-SURVEY RESPONSES ➕ 81% (Much Below Average)			

Selections Personal pizzas, meatball subs, and salads—none of them good.

Comments Rizzo's Deluxe Supreme Banquet Hall features an ongoing wedding reception, with a disco-heavy soundtrack. This upstairs area is the best part of the restaurant.

Ronto Roasters

QUALITY Good	VALUE B	PORTION Medium	LOCATION Galaxy's Edge
READER-SURVEY RESPONSES ➕ 94% (Much Above Average)			

Selections Ronto Wrap (pita bread filled with roasted pork, grilled pork sausage, and slaw); pork rinds; nonalcoholic fruit punch. Breakfast wraps available too.

Comments A disgruntled smelting droid named 8D-J8 does the cooking, turning alien meats on a rotating spit beneath a recycled podracing engine. The wraps are delicious and filling.

Rosie's All-American Cafe

QUALITY Fair   **VALUE** C   **PORTION** Medium   **LOCATION** Sunset Boulevard
READER-SURVEY RESPONSES ⊕ 80% (Much Below Average)

Selections Burgers, hot dogs, chicken nuggets, fries, plant-based "lobster" roll; child's chicken nuggets with a yogurt smoothie and fruit.

Comments It's close enough to The Twilight Zone Tower of Terror that you can hear the screams as you eat—an ominous soundtrack to what is likely a disappointing meal.

The Trolley Car Cafe *(Starbucks)*

QUALITY Good   **VALUE** C   **PORTION** Small   **LOCATION** Hollywood Boulevard
READER-SURVEY RESPONSES ⊕ 92% (Above Average)

Selections Coffee drinks and teas; breakfast sandwiches and pastries.

Comments The building is the real attraction: The pink-stucco Spanish Colonial exterior calls to mind Old Hollywood, and the industrial-style interior evokes a trolley-car switching station.

Woody's Lunch Box

QUALITY Excellent   **VALUE** A-   **PORTION** Medium–Large   **LOCATION** Toy Story Land
READER-SURVEY RESPONSES ⊕ 91% (Average)

Selections *Breakfast:* Lunch Box Tarts (think gourmet toaster pastries), breakfast bowl with scrambled eggs, potato barrels, and country gravy. *Lunch and dinner:* Sandwiches (barbecue brisket, smoked turkey, grilled three-cheese); tomato-basil soup; "totchos" (potato barrels smothered with chili, queso, and corn chips).

Comments Very limited seating and shade. Be prepared to hover and pounce!

DISNEY SPRINGS

Amorette's Patisserie

QUALITY Excellent   **VALUE** B   **PORTION** Small-Medium   **LOCATION** Town Center
READER-SURVEY RESPONSES ⊕ 93% (Above Average)   **NOT ON DISNEY DINING PLAN**

Selections Cakes and pastries made by talented Disney chefs; Disney-themed 11-layer dome cake; sandwiches; Champagne.

Comments Don't miss Amorette's Petit Cake, a smaller portion of its signature cake with 11 layers of red velvet and chocolate cakes, cherry and chocolate mousses, raspberry jelly, and Italian buttercream.

Blaze Fast-Fire'd Pizza

QUALITY Good   **VALUE** A   **PORTION** Large   **LOCATION** Town Center
READER-SURVEY RESPONSES ⊕ 93% (Above Average)

Selections Specialty and build-your-own 11-inch pizzas with a selection of 40-plus fresh toppings and sauces; salads.

Comments Each fast-fired pizza is prepared in around 3 minutes after you select your toppings, Chipotle-style. Ignore any long line—it moves quickly. The versatility of making your own pizza goes a long way with parties of varying tastes or dietary restrictions.

Chicken Guy!

QUALITY Fair   **VALUE** C   **PORTION** Large   **LOCATION** Town Center
READER-SURVEY RESPONSES ⊕ 85% (Below Average)

Selections Fried chicken tenders, fries, mac and cheese.

Comments *Guy* refers to the restaurant's creator, celebrity chef Guy Fieri. The only way to get adventurous here is with the sauces; there are dozens.

Cookes of Dublin

QUALITY Fair   **VALUE** C   **PORTION** Medium–Large   **LOCATION** The Landing
READER-SURVEY RESPONSES ➕ 91% (Average)

Selections Fried chicken tenders, burgers, fish-and-chips, and Irish cheese-and-bacon dip.

Comments Wait times can be on the high side, but even the pickiest eaters can dine here. Still, if you're in the area and can get a table at **Raglan Road** (see page 269) next door, do that instead.

D-Luxe Burger

QUALITY Good   **VALUE** C   **PORTION** Medium   **LOCATION** Town Center
READER-SURVEY RESPONSES ➕ 88% (Average)

Selections Specialty burgers; hand-cut fries with a variety of dipping sauces (curry ketchup and garlic ranch are zesty and unique); gelato shakes (spiked and nonalcoholic).

Comments The food takes a little longer than we'd like, but the specialty options are worth the wait. Mobile ordering available.

Earl of Sandwich

QUALITY Good   **VALUE** B–   **PORTION** Small–Medium   **LOCATION** Marketplace
READER-SURVEY RESPONSES ➕ 95% (Much Above Average)

Selections Sandwiches, salads, wraps, soups; brownies and cookies.

Comments There's always a long line here, but it tends to move quickly. Thanks to quality ingredients and plenty of options, Earl of Sandwich has been very highly rated by readers for many years.

Eet by Maneet Chauhan

QUALITY Good   **VALUE** B   **PORTION** Medium   **LOCATION** Marketplace
READER-SURVEY RESPONSES ➕ 95% (Much Above Average)

Selections Naan, naan pizza, tandoori poutine, salads, and bowls.

Comments This is a fascinating selection of Indian fusion cuisine! The flavors are all thought-through, and the naan is authentically made. This is also a great place if you're looking for dining with fewer kids because even the kids' menu is slightly more adventurous than normal.

Pepe by José Andrés

QUALITY Good   **VALUE** B   **PORTION** Small   **LOCATION** West Side
READER SURVEY RESPONSES ➕ 87% (Average)   **NOT ON DISNEY DINING PLAN**

Selections Spanish sandwiches such as bikinis (think an elevated grilled cheese), as well as gazpacho.

Comments Pepe is the first permanent location of José Andrés's popular food truck in Disney Springs.

Pizza Ponte

QUALITY Good   **VALUE** C   **PORTION** Medium   **LOCATION** The Landing
READER-SURVEY RESPONSES ➕ 91% (Average)

Selections Sandwiches, pizza by the slice, and Italian desserts such as cannoli and tiramisu.

Comments Pizza Ponte is above average, even for New York. The prices ($7–$8 per slice) are high, but the slices are large.

The Polite Pig

QUALITY Excellent   **VALUE** A   **PORTION** Medium   **LOCATION** Town Center
READER-SURVEY RESPONSES ➕ 98% (Exceptional)

Selections Southern barbecue staples (pulled pork, ribs, smoked chicken); specialty veggie sides (barbecue cauliflower, grilled corn, whiskey-caramel Brussels sprouts); bourbon bar; cocktails and local beers on tap; homemade cakes and pies for dessert.

Comments A hybrid fast-casual restaurant, The Polite Pig offers more than your standard quick service. Meat smoked on-site is the name of the game, but the side dishes are the real star. Split a few entrées (the pulled pork and ribs are our favorites) with sides; it's the best bang for your buck and offers a chance to try as many sides as possible.

Salt & Straw

QUALITY Excellent	VALUE B	PORTION Medium	LOCATION West Side
READER SURVEY RESPONSES ➕ 93% (Above Average)			

Selections Gourmet flavors made by people who really care about ice cream.

Comments Along with familiar flavors based around chocolate and vanilla, some favorites include the strawberry honey balsamic with black pepper; the Arbequina olive oil; and the salted, malted chocolate chip cookie dough.

Starbucks

QUALITY Good	VALUE C	PORTION Small	LOCATION Marketplace
READER-SURVEY RESPONSES ➕ 95% (Much Above Average)			

Selections Coffee drinks and teas; breakfast sandwiches and pastries.

Comments Your typical Starbucks. Why the high rating? People love coffee.

FULL-SERVICE RESTAURANTS
In Depth

THE RESTAURANT PROFILES IN THIS SECTION allow you to quickly check the cuisine, location, star rating, cost range, quality rating, and value rating of every full-service restaurant at WDW. Reservations for full-service restaurants are strongly recommended.

The profiles, including the reader ratings, reflect menus and prices as we went to press. The Disney Dining Plan information is based on the 2024 version of the plan and was up-to-date as of May 2024.

OVERALL RATING Ranging from one to five stars, this rating encompasses the entire dining experience: style, service, ambience, and food quality. Five stars is the highest rating attainable. Our star ratings don't correspond to those awarded by AAA, Mobil, Zagat, or other restaurant reviewers.

COST RANGE This tells you approximately how much you can expect to spend on a full-service entrée (not including appetizers, side dishes, soups and salads, desserts, drinks, and tips). Cost ranges are categorized as **inexpensive** (less than $15), **moderate** ($15–$25), or **expensive** ($25 and up).

QUALITY RATING Food quality is rated from one to five stars, five being the highest possible rating. The criteria are taste, freshness of ingredients, preparation, presentation, and the creativity of the food served. Price is no consideration.

continued on page 245

WDW RESTAURANTS BY CUISINE

CUISINE	LOCATION	OVERALL RATING	COST	QUALITY RATING	VALUE RATING
AFRICAN					
BOMA—FLAVORS OF AFRICA	Animal Kingdom Lodge-Jambo House	★★★★	Exp	★★★★	★★★★
JIKO—THE COOKING PLACE	Animal Kingdom Lodge-Jambo House	★★★★	Exp	★★★★	★★½
SANAA	Animal Kingdom Villas-Kidani Village	★★★★	Exp	★★★★	★★★★
JUNGLE NAVIGATION CO. LTD. SKIPPER CANTEEN	Magic Kingdom	★★★½	Exp	★★★½	★★★
TUSKER HOUSE RESTAURANT	Animal Kingdom	★★★	Exp	★★★	★★★
AMERICAN					
CÍTRICOS	Grand Floridian	★★★★	Exp	★★★★½	★★★
CALIFORNIA GRILL	Contemporary	★★★½	Exp	★★★★	★★
CHEF ART SMITH'S HOMECOMIN'	Disney Springs	★★★½	Mod-Exp	★★★★	★★★
THE HOLLYWOOD BROWN DERBY	DHS	★★★½	Exp	★★★★	★★½
LIBERTY TREE TAVERN	Magic Kingdom	★★★½	Exp	★★★	★★★½
STORY BOOK DINING AT ARTIST POINT WITH SNOW WHITE	Wilderness Lodge	★★★½	Exp	★★★★	★★★½
TIFFINS	Animal Kingdom	★★★½	Exp	★★★½	★★½
ALE & COMPASS	Yacht Club	★★★	Mod-Exp	★★★	★★★★
CAPE MAY CAFE	Beach Club	★★★	Exp	★★★	★★★
CINDERELLA'S ROYAL TABLE	Magic Kingdom	★★★	Exp	★★★	★★
CITY WORKS EATERY AND POUR HOUSE	Disney Springs	★★★	Mod	★★★	★★★
THE EDISON	Disney Springs	★★★	Exp	★★★½	★★★
50'S PRIME TIME CAFÉ	DHS	★★★	Mod	★★★	★★★
GARDEN GRILL RESTAURANT	The Land, EPCOT	★★★	Exp	★★★	★★★
GRAND FLORIDIAN CAFE	Grand Floridian	★★★	Mod-Exp	★★★½	★★★
HOLLYWOOD & VINE	DHS	★★★	Exp	★★★	★★★
HOUSE OF BLUES	Disney Springs	★★★	Mod	★★★½	★★★
1900 PARK FARE	Grand Floridian	★★★	Exp	★★★	★★½
OLIVIA'S CAFE	Old Key West	★★★	Exp	★★★	★★
ROUNDUP RODEO BBQ	Disney's Hollywood Studios	★★★	Exp	★★★	★★★
THREE BRIDGES	Coronado Springs	★★★	Exp	★★★	★★½
TUSKER HOUSE	Animal Kingdom	★★★	Exp	★★★	★★★
WHISPERING CANYON CAFE	Wilderness Lodge	★★★	Exp	★★½	★★★½
WOLFGANG PUCK BAR & GRILL	Disney Springs	★★★	Mod-Exp	★★★	★★★
BEACHES & CREAM SODA SHOP	Beach Club	★★½	Mod	★★½	★★
CHEF MICKEY'S	Contemporary	★★½	Exp	★★½	★★★
THE CRYSTAL PALACE	Magic Kingdom	★★½	Exp	★★½	★★★

CUISINE	LOCATION	OVERALL RATING	COST	QUALITY RATING	VALUE RATING
AMERICAN *(continued)*					
PADDLEFISH	Disney Springs	★★½	Exp	★★★	★★½
SPLITSVILLE	Disney Springs	★★½	Mod	★★½	★★
BE OUR GUEST RESTAURANT	Magic Kingdom	★★	Exp	★★	★★
BOATWRIGHT'S DINING HALL	Port Orleans Riverside	★★	Mod–Exp	★★	★★
THE FOUNTAIN	Dolphin	★★	Mod	★★	★★
GARDEN GROVE	Swan	★★	Mod	★★½	★★
THE PLAZA RESTAURANT	Magic Kingdom	★★	Mod	★★	★★
RAINFOREST CAFE	Animal Kingdom and Disney Springs	★★	Mod	★½	★★
SCI-FI DINE-IN THEATER RESTAURANT	DHS	★★	Mod	★★	★★
SPACE 220	World Discovery, EPCOT	★★	Exp	★★½	★½
T-REX	Disney Springs	★★	Exp	★★	★★
TURF CLUB BAR & GRILL	Saratoga Springs	★★	Exp	★★½	★★
PLANET HOLLYWOOD	Disney Springs	★½	Mod	★	★★
MAYA GRILL	Coronado Springs	★	Exp	★	★
BRITISH					
ROSE & CROWN DINING ROOM	UK, EPCOT	★★★	Mod	★★★½	★★★
BUFFET					
BOMA—FLAVORS OF AFRICA	Animal Kingdom Lodge–Jambo House	★★★★	Exp	★★★★	★★★★
AKERSHUS ROYAL BANQUET HALL	Norway, EPCOT	★★★	Exp	★★★	★★★★
BIERGARTEN	Germany, EPCOT	★★★	Exp	★★★	★★★★
CAPE MAY CAFE	Beach Club	★★★	Exp	★★★	★★★
HOLLYWOOD & VINE	DHS	★★★	Exp	★★	★★★
1900 PARK FARE	Grand Floridian	★★★	Exp	★★★	★★★½
CHEF MICKEY'S	Contemporary	★★½	Exp	★★½	★★★
THE CRYSTAL PALACE	Magic Kingdom	★★½	Exp	★★½	★★★
CAJUN					
BOATWRIGHT'S DINING HALL	Port Orleans Riverside	★★	Mod–Exp	★★	★★
CHINESE					
NINE DRAGONS	China, EPCOT	★★★	Mod	★★★	★★½
FRENCH					
LA CRÊPERIE DE PARIS	France, EPCOT	★★★½	Mod	★★★½	★★★
TOPOLINO'S TERRACE	Riviera	★★★½	Exp	★★★★	★★½
MONSIEUR PAUL	France, EPCOT	★★★	Exp	★★★	★★★
CHEFS DE FRANCE	France, EPCOT	★★½	Exp	★★½	★★★
BE OUR GUEST RESTAURANT	Magic Kingdom	★★	Exp	★★	★★

WDW RESTAURANTS BY CUISINE *(continued)*

CUISINE	LOCATION	OVERALL RATING	COST	QUALITY RATING	VALUE RATING
GERMAN					
BIERGARTEN	Germany, EPCOT	★★★	Exp	★★★	★★★★
GOURMET					
VICTORIA & ALBERT'S	Grand Floridian	★★★★★	Exp	★★★★★★	★★★★
INDIAN					
SANAA	Animal Kingdom Villas–Kidani Village	★★★★	Exp	★★★★	★★★★
IRISH					
RAGLAN ROAD	Disney Springs	★★★★	Mod	★★★★	★★★
ITALIAN					
TOPOLINO'S TERRACE	Riviera	★★★½	Exp	★★★★	★★½
VIA NAPOLI	Italy, EPCOT	★★★½	Exp	★★★½	★★★
IL MULINO	Swan	★★★	Exp	★★★	★★
TRATTORIA AL FORNO	BoardWalk	★★★	Mod	★★★½	★★
TUTTO ITALIA RISTORANTE	Italy, EPCOT	★★★	Exp	★★★★	★★
MAMA MELROSE'S RISTORANTE ITALIANO	DHS	★★½	Exp	★★★	★★
TERRALINA CRAFTED ITALIAN	Disney Springs	★★½	Exp	★★½	★★½
MARIA & ENZO'S RISTORANTE	Disney Springs	★★	Exp	★★	★★
TONY'S TOWN SQUARE	Magic Kingdom	★★	Mod–Exp	★★	★★
JAPANESE/SUSHI					
TAKUMI-TEI	Japan, EPCOT	★★★★½	Exp	★★★★★	★★★½
MORIMOTO ASIA	Disney Springs	★★★★	Exp	★★★★	★★★★
TEPPAN EDO	Japan, EPCOT	★★★½	Exp	★★★★	★★★
KIMONOS	Swan	★★★	Mod	★★★★	★★★
LATIN					
JUNGLE NAVIGATION CO. LTD. SKIPPER CANTEEN	Magic Kingdom	★★★½	Exp	★★★½	★★★
SEBASTIAN'S BISTRO	Caribbean Beach	★★½	Exp	★★	★★½
PARADISO 37	Disney Springs	★★	Exp	★★½	★★
MEDITERRANEAN					
CÍTRICOS	Grand Floridian	★★★★	Exp	★★★★½	★★★
MEXICAN					
LA HACIENDA DE SAN ANGEL	Mexico, EPCOT	★★★½	Exp	★★★½	★★★
SAN ANGEL INN RESTAURANTE	Mexico, EPCOT	★★★	Exp	★★★	★★
FRONTERA COCINA	Disney Springs	★★½	Exp	★★★	★★
MAYA GRILL	Coronado Springs	★	Exp	★	★
ROSA MEXICANO	Dolphin	Too new to rate			
MOROCCAN					
SPICE ROAD TABLE	Morocco, EPCOT	★★★★	Inexp	★★★★	★★★

CUISINE	LOCATION	OVERALL RATING	COST	QUALITY RATING	VALUE RATING
NORWEGIAN					
AKERSHUS ROYAL BANQUET HALL	Norway, EPCOT	★★★	Exp	★★★	★★★★
PAN-ASIAN/POLYNESIAN					
MORIMOTO ASIA	Disney Springs	★★★★	Exp	★★★★	★★★★
JUNGLE NAVIGATION CO. LTD. SKIPPER CANTEEN	Magic Kingdom	★★★½	Exp	★★★½	★★★
TIFFINS	Animal Kingdom	★★★½	Exp	★★★½	★★½
KONA CAFE	Polynesian Village	★★★	Mod	★★★	★★★½
'OHANA	Polynesian Village	★★★	Exp	★★★½	★★★
YAK & YETI RESTAURANT	Animal Kingdom	★★★	Exp	★★★	★★
SEAFOOD					
THE BOATHOUSE	Disney Springs	★★★½	Exp	★★★	★★
FLYING FISH	BoardWalk	★★★½	Exp	★★★	★★★
NARCOOSSEE'S	Grand Floridian	★★★½	Exp	★★★★	★★½
CORAL REEF RESTAURANT	The Seas, EPCOT	★★★	Exp	★★★	★★
TODD ENGLISH'S BLUEZOO	Dolphin	★★★	Exp	★★★	★★
PADDLEFISH	Disney Springs	★★½	Exp	★★★	★★½
SEBASTIAN'S BISTRO	Caribbean Beach	★★½	Exp	★★	★★½
SPANISH/TAPAS					
JALEO BY JOSÉ ANDRÉS	Disney Springs	★★★★	Mod	★★★★	★★★½
THREE BRIDGES BAR & GRILL	Coronado Springs	★★★	Exp	★★★	★★½
TOLEDO	Coronado Springs	★★★	Exp	★★★	★★½
STEAK					
STEAKHOUSE 71	Contemporary	★★★★	Exp	★★★★	★★★½
LE CELLIER STEAKHOUSE	Canada, EPCOT	★★★	Exp	★★★	★★★
SHULA'S STEAKHOUSE	Dolphin	★★★	Exp	★★★★	★★
STK ORLANDO	Disney Springs	★★★	Exp	★★★★	★★
YACHTSMAN STEAKHOUSE	Yacht Club	★★½	Exp	★★★½	★★
WINE/SMALL PLATES					
WINE BAR GEORGE	Disney Springs	★★★★	Mod–Exp	★★★★	★★★½

continued from page 241

VALUE RATING If, on the other hand, you're looking for both quality *and* value, then you should check this rating, which is also expressed as stars.

PAYMENT All Walt Disney World restaurants take the following credit cards: American Express, Diners Club, Discover, Japan Credit Bureau, MasterCard, and Visa. And, unless otherwise noted, all accept the Disney Dining Plan.

NEW IN 2023 AND 2024

Rosa Mexicano

Dolphin; ☎ 407-934-1609

SUMMARY AND COMMENTS Part of a national chain, this new Mexican spot replaces Fresh Mediterranean Market.

Shiki-Sai

Japan, World Showcase, EPCOT; ☎ 407-939-3463

SUMMARY AND COMMENTS Adjacent to Teppan Edo, with views over the World Showcase Lagoon, Shiki-Sai joins the Japan pavilion's already excellent dining scene. This location focuses on celebrating traditional Japanese seasonal festivals year-round, with an extensive menu. Pictures of every dish make the menu very first-time-diner friendly, and the entire meal is steeped in tradition. Request a seat at the counter surrounding the open kitchen to see the beautiful food being prepared.

Summer House on the Lake

West Side, Disney Springs; ☎ 407-598-8645

SUMMARY AND COMMENTS Lighter, California-style fare served lakeside. Locals also rave about The Cookie Bar, with house-made desserts and alcoholic beverages, all served to go.

FULL-SERVICE RESTAURANT PROFILES

Akershus Royal Banquet Hall ★★★

NORWEGIAN/BUFFET	EXPENSIVE	QUALITY ★★★	VALUE ★★★★
READER-SURVEY RESPONSES ● 84% (Below Average)			

Norway, World Showcase, EPCOT; ☎ 407-939-3463

Reservations Required. **Dining Plan credits** Breakfast 1 per person, per meal; lunch and dinner 2 per person, per meal. **When to go** Anytime. **Cost range** Breakfast $55 (child $35), lunch and dinner $67 (child $43). **Service** ★★★★. **Bar** Full service. **Character breakfast** 8:30 a.m.–12:10 p.m. **Character lunch** 12:15–4:40 p.m. **Character dinner** 5:25–8:05 p.m.

SETTING AND ATMOSPHERE The interior looks like a fairy-tale castle: high ceilings, stone archways, purple carpets, and regal banners.

HOUSE SPECIALTIES Norwegian meatballs, grilled salmon, chicken and dumplings, lefse, mashed potatoes, green beans. *For kids:* Macaroni and cheese, corn dogs.

OTHER RECOMMENDATIONS Aquavit cocktails.

SUMMARY AND COMMENTS If you have kids who love the Disney princesses, this is a great spot. There was a time when the Scandinavian-style buffet was noteworthy, but the kitchen focuses its attention on getting family-style food out fast. At almost $20 less per adult than what you'd pay at Cinderella's Royal Table, we'd opt for this princess meal every time.

Ale & Compass ★★★

AMERICAN	MODERATE-EXPENSIVE	QUALITY ★★★	VALUE ★★★
READER-SURVEY RESPONSES ● 92% (Above Average)			

Yacht Club Resort; ☎ 407-939-3463

Reservations Recommended. **Dining Plan credits** 1 per person, per meal. **When to go** Anytime. **Cost range** Breakfast buffet $23 per person; à la carte items $15–$35 for all meals **Service** ★★★½. **Bar** Full service. **Breakfast** Daily, 7:30 a.m.–11 a.m. **Lunch** Daily, 11:45 a.m.–2 p.m. **Dinner** Daily, 5–9 p.m.

SETTING AND ATMOSPHERE The large dining room is polished and pretty in a generic way, but with no real theming.

HOUSE SPECIALTIES The burger is excellent. The fries used to be better. End with the 12-layer chocolate cake.

OTHER RECOMMENDATIONS Breakfast selections include salted caramel–apple French toast, plus the usual eggs, bacon, pancakes, and waffles. Vegetarians have two full-fledged meal options: the Protein Bowl (with quinoa, vegan Italian "sausage," sweet potato, and Broccolini) and a pasta with mushrooms and other veggies.

KIDS' MENU Grilled chicken, baked fish, pasta Bolognese, or cheeseburger with many side and dessert options.

SUMMARY AND COMMENTS Solid EPCOT-area dining option not in the park.

Beaches & Cream Soda Shop ★★½

AMERICAN	MODERATE	QUALITY ★★½	VALUE ★★
READER-SURVEY RESPONSES ⊕ 91% (Above Average)			

Beach Club Resort; ☎ 407-939-3463

Reservations Strongly recommended. **Dining Plan credits** 1 per person, per meal. **When to go** Lunch or dinner. **Cost range** $16–$22. **Service** ★★★. **Bar** Beer, wine, hard floats. **Hours** Daily, 11 a.m.–11 p.m.

SETTING AND ATMOSPHERE Retro soda-fountain décor and servers.

HOUSE SPECIALTIES Burgers and fries; grilled cheese and soup; hand-scooped ice cream, including the gargantuan $38 Kitchen Sink dessert, featuring five flavors of ice cream drowning in toppings.

OTHER RECOMMENDATIONS Root beer float, the No Way José sundae.

KIDS' MENU Grilled chicken or turkey sandwich, mac and cheese, hot dog, cheeseburger with fruits and veggies.

SUMMARY AND COMMENTS Beaches & Cream is always popular, and the seating area is small. Make reservations!

Be Our Guest Restaurant ★★

FRENCH/AMERICAN	EXPENSIVE	QUALITY ★★	VALUE ★★
READER-SURVEY RESPONSES ⊕ 67% (Do Not Visit)			

Fantasyland, Magic Kingdom; ☎ 407-939-3463

Reservations Strongly recommended. **Dining Plan credits** 2 per person, per meal. **When to go** Lunch or dinner. **Cost range** $70 (child $41). **Service** ★★★. **Bar** Beer, solid selection of French wines **Lunch** Daily, 11 a.m.–2:55 p.m. **Dinner** Daily, 3–10 p.m.

SETTING AND ATMOSPHERE Be Our Guest re-creates Beast's Castle from *Beauty and the Beast* with three themed rooms: the Grand Ballroom, the mysterious West Wing, and the Castle Gallery. The rooms fill up, with a noise level to match the crowd (up to 550 seats).

HOUSE SPECIALTIES French onion soup, roasted pork tenderloin, Grey Stuff.

OTHER RECOMMENDATIONS Filet mignon with Robuchon potatoes; pan-seared scallops with risotto.

KIDS' MENU Pan-seared chicken breast or shrimp, chicken strips, steak, or mac and cheese, with appetizer, side, and dessert.

SUMMARY AND COMMENTS Be Our Guest has been the most popular restaurant in the Magic Kingdom since it opened in 2012. Unfortunately, with the conversion to a prix fixe menu, it's now regularly one of the worst-rated restaurants on-property and still trending downward. The menu is heavy and expensive, and it lacks enough choices to justify the cost. We've received quite a few reader comments about Be Our Guest with a common refrain of "just OK," like this one from Colorado:

I worked harder to get this reservation than any other one that I wanted. But then the food was so underwhelming for what we paid. It all felt so mass-produced. Still, I'm glad we went once for the atmosphere. But we won't be back.

If you're looking for good food nearby, **Liberty Tree Tavern** (see page 263) and **Jungle Navigation Co. Ltd. Skipper Canteen** (see page 262) are better choices. But **Columbia Harbour House** (see page 230) is the highest-rated indoor restaurant in the Magic Kingdom.

Biergarten Restaurant ★★★

GERMAN/BUFFET	EXPENSIVE	QUALITY ★★★	VALUE ★★★★
READER-SURVEY RESPONSES ➕ 91% (Above Average)			

Germany, World Showcase, EPCOT; ☎ 407-939-3463

Reservations Recommended. **Dining Plan credits** 1 per person, per meal. **When to go** Lunch or dinner. **Cost range** $49 (child $27). **Service** ★★★★. **Bar** Full service with German wine and beer. **Lunch** Daily, noon–3:55 p.m. **Dinner** Daily, 4–8 p.m.

SETTING AND ATMOSPHERE Biergarten is a German restaurant set inside a nighttime town square. You're seated at big tables lined up in rows emanating from a central dance floor and stage. A lederhosen-clad oompah band plays and encourages diners to sing along.

HOUSE SPECIALTIES Schnitzel, traditional German sausages, and homemade spaetzle. *For kids:* Mac and cheese, frankfurters

OTHER RECOMMENDATIONS Rotisserie chicken, braised red cabbage.

ENTERTAINMENT AND AMENITIES Oompah band and German dancers perform throughout the day.

SUMMARY AND COMMENTS The buffet is stacked with an astonishing amount of good-quality food. There are plenty of places in Walt Disney World where you could pay more for less. (If you leave here hungry, don't rule out tapeworms.) The lively 25-minute show (one every hour) and noisy dining room are part of the fun, especially for families. Kids seem to love the place.

The Boathouse ★★★½

SEAFOOD	EXPENSIVE	QUALITY ★★★	VALUE ★★
READER-SURVEY RESPONSES ➕ 94% (Much Above Average)			

The Landing, Disney Springs; ☎ 407-939-BOAT (2628)

Reservations Strongly recommended. **Dining Plan credits** 2 per person, per meal. **When to go** Lunch or dinner. **Cost range** $27–$75 (child $12). **Service** ★★★★. **Parking** Orange garage. **Bar** Full service. **Wine selection** Good. **Dress** Casual. **Hours** Daily, 11 a.m.–11 p.m. (until 11:30 p.m. on Friday and Saturday).

SETTING AND ATMOSPHERE The first things you notice about The Boathouse, on the waterfront, are the vintage American Amphicars (1960s-era amphibious cars) and the Italian water taxis floating next to the front door—the multimillion-dollar fleet features 19 rare boats from around the world. The airy restaurant seats up to 600 in nautically themed dining rooms (two private), as well as outdoors. There are three bars, including one built over the water.

HOUSE SPECIALTIES The menu changes daily, but there's seafood of every sort: a raw bar with fresh oysters, tuna, and wild-caught shrimp; lobster; fish and shellfish; and jumbo lump crab. There's also filet mignon, as well as a selection of desserts.

KIDS' MENU Salmon, popcorn shrimp, mac and cheese, burger, or chicken tenders, served with either red grapes or fries.

SUMMARY AND COMMENTS If you're not sure where to eat in Disney Springs, then go to The Boathouse. It's a solid choice with an extensive menu. While seafood is the star, the steaks are top-notch as well.

A North Carolina family advises readers to save room—lots of room—for dessert:

By far the best meal was at The Boathouse in Disney Springs. Everyone's meal was superb—we all ordered seafood entrées. We had a mile-high ice-cream dessert designed to serve two. It was delicious and easily served all four of us.

Boatwright's Dining Hall ★★

AMERICAN/CAJUN	MODERATE-EXPENSIVE	QUALITY ★★	VALUE ★★
READER-SURVEY RESPONSES ➕ 83% (Below Average)			

Port Orleans Resort–Riverside; ☎ 407-939-3463

Reservations Strongly recommended. **Dining Plan credits** 1 per person, per meal. **When to go** Early evening. **Cost range** $24–$38 (child $11–$14). **Service** ★★★★½. **Bar** Beer and liquor only. **Hours** Daily, 5–9 p.m.

SETTING AND ATMOSPHERE Always busy and a tad noisy, Boatwright's features a New Orleans–inspired dining room with a large boat frame serving as a focal point overhead.

HOUSE SPECIALTIES The Mardi Gras pimento cheese fritters are the best appetizers. The best entrées are the shrimp and grits and the Nashville hot chicken (it's not that hot).

OTHER RECOMMENDATIONS Blackened prime rib, slow-roasted and served with mashed potatoes and horseradish cream.

KIDS' MENU Grilled chicken or fish, mac and cheese, cheeseburger, or pasta with marinara, with a very large and kid-friendly selection of sides.

SUMMARY AND COMMENTS The kitchen struggles with consistency when the restaurant is full. Stick to the basics.

Boma—Flavors of Africa ★★★★

AFRICAN/BUFFET	EXPENSIVE	QUALITY ★★★★	VALUE ★★★★
READER-SURVEY RESPONSES ➕ 95% (Exceptional)			

Animal Kingdom Lodge & Villas–Jambo House; ☎ 407-939-3463

Reservations Strongly recommended. **Dining Plan credits** 1 per person, per meal. **When to go** Late breakfast or early dinner. **Cost range** Breakfast $37 (child $22), dinner $56 (child $33). **Service** ★★★★½. **Bar** Full service, with South African wines. **Breakfast** Daily, 7:30–11:30 a.m. **Dinner** Daily, 5–9:30 p.m.

SETTING AND ATMOSPHERE Boma's huge dining room mimics an African marketplace, complete with thatched-roof ceilings. With so many tables and buffet dining stations, plus the massive open kitchen where guests can observe all the goings-on, the dining room is always loud.

HOUSE SPECIALTIES Boma's buffet takes guests on an adventure full of rich flavors. Dishes represent regional cuisines from across Africa. Daily rotating entrées include carved African spice–crusted beef sirloin, whole-roasted salmon, and slow-roasted ribs. Side dishes include spiced sweet potatoes, couscous, peanut rice, and Zulu cabbage. Boma's signature dessert, the Zebra Dome—a thin layer of white cake supporting an orb of Amarula cream-liqueur mousse, smothered with white chocolate ganache and drizzled with dark chocolate—has a cult following.

OTHER RECOMMENDATIONS For breakfast, French toast bread pudding shines; made-to-order omelets and carved meats satisfy those in search of more-American options.

SUMMARY AND COMMENTS Boma is consistently rated as one of the best restaurants in Walt Disney World, but in recent months, wait times (even with reservations) have gone way up, and tales of empty or sparse food trays on the buffet have become more frequent. The food is as good as ever, but operational issues may affect your experience.

California Grill ★★★½

AMERICAN	EXPENSIVE	QUALITY ★★★★	VALUE ★★
READER-SURVEY RESPONSES ✪ 91% (Above Average)			

Contemporary Resort; ☎ 407-939-3463

Reservations Strongly recommended. **Dining Plan credits** 2 per person, per meal. **When to go** During evening fireworks. **Cost range** Dinner $89 (child $39). **Service** ★★★★½. **Bar** Full service, with a fantastic wine selection. **Dinner** Daily, 5–10 p.m.

SETTING AND ATMOSPHERE California Grill remains one of the most popular choices for Disney dining, both for its remarkable view from the 15th floor of the Contemporary Resort and for its bustling open kitchen. It can be crowded and noisy; book a table early or late for a quieter experience. If you don't have a reservation, ask for a seat at the sushi bar, where you can order appetizers but not entrées.

HOUSE SPECIALTIES For starters, try the pizza being offered or the raviolo. Stick to steak or fish for your entrée.

KIDS' MENU Spectacular and almost infinitely customizable, this is where the restaurant shines. Order a few sides, or just an entrée. Make a side your dessert or a dessert your side. Each kid is the master of their own destiny. The kids' steak was better than the one I received off of the adult menu.

ENTERTAINMENT AND AMENITIES Magic Kingdom fireworks are the star of the show; guests with dinner reservations can watch from the terrace.

SUMMARY AND COMMENTS California Grill uses its fixed-price menu to discourage large groups from splitting one pizza and staying 3 hours to watch the fireworks. But the expensive adult menu is a large collection of disappointment, which can't make up for the excellent kids' menu.

Cape May Cafe ★★★

AMERICAN/BUFFET	EXPENSIVE	QUALITY ★★★	VALUE ★★★
READER-SURVEY RESPONSES ✪ 89% (Average)			

Beach Club Resort; ☎ 407-934-3358

Reservations Strongly recommended. **Dining Plan credits** 1 per person, per meal. **When to go** Breakfast or dinner. **Cost range** Breakfast $47 (child $30), dinner $47 (child $27). **Service** ★★★★★. **Bar** Full service. **Character breakfast** Daily, 7:30–11:30 a.m. **Dinner** Daily, 5–9 p.m.

SETTING AND ATMOSPHERE Cape May Cafe features nautical New England décor in two dining rooms and lots of comfortable seating.

HOUSE SPECIALTIES Breakfast buffet includes made-to-order crepes and omelets, a carving station, and salted caramel "beach buns" for dessert. It might be the best breakfast in Walt Disney World for the money.

SUMMARY AND COMMENTS Breakfast is a character buffet with Mickey and friends, and dinner is a buffet without characters. None of the dinner entrées are memorable. Stick to breakfast. Better nearby dinner options include **Ale & Compass** (page 246) and **Trattoria al Forno** (page 280).

Le Cellier Steakhouse ★★★½

STEAK	EXPENSIVE	QUALITY ★★★★	VALUE ★★★½
READER-SURVEY RESPONSES ✪ 89% (Average)			

Canada, World Showcase, EPCOT; ☎ 407-939-3463

Reservations Required. **Dining Plan credits** 2 per person, per meal. **When to go** Before 6 p.m. **Cost range** $36–$62 (child $14–$19). **Service** ★★★★. **Bar** Full service, with Canadian wines. **Lunch** Daily, noon–3:55 p.m. **Dinner** Daily, 4–9 p.m.

SETTING AND ATMOSPHERE Walk past the Canada Pavilion's pretty gardens into this small, darkened dining room, intended to look and feel like a wine cellar. The heavy wooden tables have no linens, but the steaks make up for the lack of ambience. Service is "cheerful Canadian," meaning servers apologize to *you* if you spill something on *them*.

HOUSE SPECIALTIES AAA Canadian filet mignon, Canadian cheddar soup.

OTHER RECOMMENDATIONS For sides, share the mac and cheese, the loaded mashed potatoes, or the poutine. For dessert, try the chocolate tart. Excellent wine selection.

KIDS' MENU Grilled chicken or steak, salmon, or mac and cheese, served with an extensive selection of sides.

SUMMARY AND COMMENTS Le Cellier is still expensive, but the steaks are perfectly seasoned and cooked, with a beautiful char. Service is unrushed—it's possible for a full dinner to take 2 hours, so plan accordingly.

Chef Art Smith's Homecomin' ★★★½

AMERICAN	MODERATE-EXPENSIVE	QUALITY ★★★★	VALUE ★★★
READER-SURVEY RESPONSES ➊ 94% (Much Above Average)			

The Landing, Disney Springs; ☎ 407-560-0100

Reservations Strongly recommended. **Dining Plan credits** 1 per person, per meal. **When to go** Anytime. **Cost range** Brunch $18–$32 (child $12), lunch and dinner $15–$42 (child $10). **Service** ★★★★. **Bar** Full service. **Lunch** Daily, 11 a.m.–3:55 p.m. **Dinner** Daily, 4–11 p.m. **Brunch** Saturday and Sunday, 9:30 a.m.–1 p.m. (full menu available after 11 a.m.).

SETTING AND ATMOSPHERE Florida farm style with a reclaimed-wood-and-mason-jar vibe. Born and raised in Florida, Art Smith was formerly Oprah Winfrey's private chef and has appeared on *Top Chef Masters* and *Iron Chef America.*

HOUSE SPECIALTIES Fried chicken, optionally with iced house-made doughnuts. The Thigh High Chicken Biscuits appetizer may be one of the best food items on Disney property. The cocktails and desserts are fabulous.

OTHER RECOMMENDATIONS Beyond the fried chicken, the Art Burger is good; ask for the house-made pimento cheese instead of American. The barbecue pork doesn't meet our standards (Len's favorite is Stamey's in Greensboro, North Carolina).

KIDS' MENU Fish sticks, chicken tenders, fried chicken sandwich, or mac and cheese, served with a veggie and starch.

SUMMARY AND COMMENTS If you can't get a table, try the bar.

Chef Mickey's ★★½

AMERICAN/BUFFET	EXPENSIVE	QUALITY ★★½	VALUE ★★★
READER-SURVEY RESPONSES ➊ 84% (Below Average)			

Contemporary Resort; ☎ 407-939-3463

Reservations Required. **Dining Plan credits** 1 per person, per meal. **When to go** Breakfast. **Cost range** Breakfast $54 (child $34), dinner $66 (child $41). **Service** ★★★★. **Bar** Full service. **Character breakfast** Daily, 7:30 a.m.–12:30 p.m. **Character dinner** Daily, 5–9:30 p.m.

SETTING AND ATMOSPHERE This is what every parent imagines as their nightmare character meal. The big, open dining room with the monorail whizzing by overhead (inside the hotel) is a cacophony of children's and parents' voices. And everyone is hyped about seeing Mickey and his pals.

HOUSE SPECIALTIES Banana-bread French toast, potato-cheese casserole with bacon and chives. At dinner, the gratin potato and farro wheat fried rice are better than average.

OTHER RECOMMENDATIONS Breakfast buffet offers standard options, such as eggs, Mickey waffles, and bacon.

ENTERTAINMENT AND AMENITIES Mickey doesn't meet you until after the meal—his "friends" roam the restaurant.

SUMMARY AND COMMENTS Both breakfast and dinner are buffets. Nothing on the dinner menu is as good as at EPCOT's **Garden Grill Restaurant** (see page 257) or the Magic Kingdom's **Liberty Tree Tavern** (see page 263), but the kids' choices will satisfy picky eaters.

Chefs de France ★★½

FRENCH	EXPENSIVE	QUALITY ★★½	VALUE ★★★
READER-SURVEY RESPONSES ✪ 85% (Below Average)			

France, World Showcase, EPCOT; ☎ 407-827-8709

Reservations Strongly recommended. **Dining Plan credits** 1 per person, per meal. **When to go** Anytime. **Cost range** $26–$47 (child $12–$14), prix fixe meal $66. **Service** ★★★★. **Bar** Beer and cocktails, with a very good wine selection. **Lunch** Daily, noon–3 p.m. **Dinner** Daily, 4–8:55 p.m.

SETTING AND ATMOSPHERE The smells are delicious, with baguettes from the on-site bakery on every table. White cloth napkins and cushioned banquettes accentuate the classic bistro décor in the main dining room, where the tables by the window make for fun people-watching on the World Showcase Promenade.

HOUSE SPECIALTIES Dishes inspired by French chefs Paul Bocuse, Gaston Lenôtre, and Roger Vergé. For a classic meal, order the French onion soup with Gruyère cheese for your appetizer and the Boeuf Bourguignon for your entrée.

OTHER RECOMMENDATIONS The prix fixe menu can be a good value.

KIDS' MENU Grilled chicken, salmon, or French burger, each with only one side. Relatively poor selection.

SUMMARY AND COMMENTS The kitchen has struggled with the basics of food temperature and seasoning during our last couple of visits.

Cinderella's Royal Table ★★★

AMERICAN	EXPENSIVE	QUALITY ★★★	VALUE ★★
READER-SURVEY RESPONSES ✪ 83% (Below Average)			

Cinderella Castle, Fantasyland, Magic Kingdom; ☎ 407-939-3463

Reservations Required; must prepay in full. **Dining Plan credits** 2 per person, per meal. **When to go** Early. **Cost range** Breakfast $69 (child $42), lunch and dinner $84 (child $49). **Service** ★★★★. **Bar** Limited selection of sparkling wine. **Character breakfast** Daily, 8–10:15 a.m. **Character lunch** Daily, 11 a.m.–2:55 p.m. **Character dinner** Daily, 3–10 p.m.

SETTING AND ATMOSPHERE A medieval banquet hall located in Cinderella Castle! While the food is tasty, it's more about the location. Cinderella makes an appearance at all three meals, with plenty of time for photos. Other princesses include some combination of Ariel, Aurora, Snow White, Jasmine, and Rapunzel.

HOUSE SPECIALTIES Lunch and dinner have the same entrée selections: lamb chops, filet mignon, catch of the day, grilled chicken, or vegetarian gnocchi. For starters, try the braised beef or the Castle Salad. Ask your server if you can sample each of the three desserts.

KIDS' MENU Seared fish, grilled steak, chicken strips, or mac and cheese, each with two sides (out of four options) and an appetizer and dessert.

SUMMARY AND COMMENTS We think the food quality is better than average, despite the reader-survey ratings, and service is good, though rushed. For more on reserving a spot at the Royal Table, see page 209.

Cítricos ★★★★

AMERICAN/MEDITERRANEAN	EXPENSIVE	QUALITY ★★★★½	VALUE ★★★
READER-SURVEY RESPONSES ➕ 88% (Average)			

Grand Floridian Resort & Spa; ☎ 407-939-3463

Reservations Required. **Dining Plan credits** 2 per person, per meal. **When to go** Dinner. **Cost range** $36–$59 (child $13–$19). **Service** ★★★★★. **Bar** Full service. **Dress** Dressy casual. **Dinner** Daily, 5–9:30 p.m.

SETTING AND ATMOSPHERE Cítricos has a *Mary Poppins* theme, which feels upscale without being stuffy. The full-view show kitchen is on display.

HOUSE SPECIALTIES The roulade of chicken belongs with rainbows and puppies in the pantheon of things everyone should love. Other standouts: (seasonal) strawberry salad, house-made pasta.

OTHER RECOMMENDATIONS For starters, try the pork belly or the duck breast. The dessert menu changes too frequently for us to be able to make a recommendation.

KIDS' MENU Grilled chicken, steak, shrimp, pizza, mac and cheese, grilled cheese, or pasta with marinara, with a fair selection of sides.

SUMMARY AND COMMENTS This is an excellent choice for a nice dinner, with enough availability that you'll have a decent chance to get in. Expect the menu to change often, and ask your server for their recommendations. If you can't get a reservation at **Victoria & Albert's** next door (see page 283), this is the next-best place we've eaten at the Grand Floridian.

City Works Eatery and Pour House ★★★

AMERICAN	MODERATE	QUALITY ★★★	VALUE ★★★
READER-SURVEY RESPONSES ➕ 92% (Above Average)			

West Side, Disney Springs; ☎ 407-801-3730

Reservations Accepted. **Dining Plan credits** Not accepted. **When to go** Anytime. **Cost range** Brunch $12–$14, lunch and dinner $16–$39 (child $12). **Service** ★★★★. **Bar** Full service. **Wine selection** Good. **Lunch** Daily, 11 a.m.–2:55 p.m. **Dinner** Daily, 3–11 p.m. (until 11:30 p.m. on Friday and Saturday).

SETTING AND ATMOSPHERE Indoor seating may be available; the outdoor seats can be hot in the Florida sun.

HOUSE SPECIALTIES "A solid beer selection for brew nerds," says one of our resident beer experts. The fish tacos are a favorite.

KIDS' MENU Mini burgers, pizza, chicken tenders, or Kraft mac and cheese, all served with fries or a fruit cup. Too expensive for what you get.

SUMMARY AND COMMENTS City Works is a small chain of sports bars with an extensive list of beer taps. Its location near Cirque du Soleil means crowds before and after shows. The food is standard for a sports bar.

Coral Reef Restaurant ★★★

SEAFOOD	EXPENSIVE	QUALITY ★★★	VALUE ★★
READER-SURVEY RESPONSES ➕ 79% (Much Below Average)			

The Seas with Nemo & Friends, World Nature, EPCOT; ☎ 407-939-3463

Reservations Required. **Dining Plan credits** 1 per person, per meal. **When to go** Lunch. **Cost range** $29–$36 (child $13–$16). **Service** ★★★★. **Bar** Full service. **Lunch** Daily, 11:30 a.m.–3:30 p.m. **Dinner** Daily, 3:45–8:30 p.m.

SETTING AND ATMOSPHERE You can't beat the view in this dining room, which faces one of the world's largest saltwater aquariums. Tiered seating gives everyone a good view of the fish (and sometimes Mickey in a scuba suit). The entryway gives the impression that you're going under the sea; special light fixtures throw ripple patterns on the ceiling.

HOUSE SPECIALTIES 10-ounce slow-roasted prime rib, chocolate cake.

KIDS' MENU Grilled chicken, fish, or shrimp; prime rib; or mac and cheese, each served with a decent selection of sides.

SUMMARY AND COMMENTS Not the best restaurant in EPCOT but a great escape from the Florida sun. Coral Reef got a new chef in 2023, and we expect reader scores to start increasing as a result.

La Crêperie de Paris ★★★½

FRENCH	MODERATE	QUALITY ★★★½	VALUE ★★★
READER-SURVEY RESPONSES ⊕ 89% (Average)			

France, World Showcase, EPCOT; ☎ 407-939-3463

Reservations Strongly recommended. **Dining Plan credits** Not available. **When to go** Anytime. **Cost range** 3-course prix fixe $40 or $19 per crepe (child prix fixe $17). **Service** ★★★★. **Bar** Full service. **Hours** Daily, 11:30 a.m.–8:30 p.m.

SETTING AND ATMOSPHERE Found on the walk back to Remy's Ratatouille Adventure, La Crêperie de Paris looks from the outside like a streetside Parisian café. There's little theming inside—you could be anywhere from a Canadian poutine place to a nice Wendy's.

HOUSE SPECIALTIES Try the chèvre, spinach, and walnut savory crepe (galette) for dinner, with the banana-filled crepe for dessert. The fixed-price meal used to be a relative bargain for Walt Disney World, but recent price increases now make it too expensive.

KIDS' MENU Combo of one galette and one sweet crepe. Very limited options.

SUMMARY AND COMMENTS Generous portions. Walk-up window available.

The Crystal Palace ★★½

AMERICAN/BUFFET	EXPENSIVE	QUALITY ★★½	VALUE ★★★
READER-SURVEY RESPONSES ⊕ 87% (Average)			

Main Street, U.S.A., Magic Kingdom; ☎ 407-939-3463

Reservations Required. **Dining Plan credits** 1 per person, per meal. **When to go** Lunch and dinner. **Cost range** Breakfast $48 (child $30), lunch and dinner $61 (child $40). **Service** ★★★. **Bar** Full service. **Character breakfast** Daily, 8–10:45 a.m. **Character lunch** Daily, 11 a.m.–2:55 p.m. **Character dinner** Daily, 3–9 p.m.

SETTING AND ATMOSPHERE In the daytime, The Crystal Palace surrounds you with cool sunlight and decorative plants. The restaurant's white steel supports, arched ceilings, and glass roof (especially the atrium) are tributes to its namesake, built to house London's 1851 Great Exhibition—the first world's fair—and among the first structures to use plate glass in large quantities.

HOUSE SPECIALTIES Nothing is particularly good.

SUMMARY AND COMMENTS Pooh, Piglet, and friends are at all meals. The restaurant has trouble maintaining its food quality on the buffet. The fried chicken is greasy, and the prime rib is tough and overcooked. The best of the bunch might be the Southern Fried Cauliflower, but nobody should have to pay $61 for albino broccoli.

Reader ratings for The Crystal Palace remain low. For the same price, we recommend **Liberty Tree Tavern** (see page 263) in the Magic Kingdom or **Garden Grill Restaurant** (see page 257) in EPCOT instead.

The Edison   ★★★

AMERICAN	EXPENSIVE	QUALITY ★★★½	VALUE ★★★
READER-SURVEY RESPONSES ● 83% (Below Average)			

The Landing, Disney Springs; ☎ 407-560-WATT (9288)

Reservations Recommended. **Dining Plan credits** 1 per person, per meal. **When to go** Dinner. **Cost range** $18–$47 (child $15). **Service** ★★★½. **Bar** Full service. **Hours** Sunday–Thursday, 11:30 a.m.–10:30 p.m. (until 11 p.m. on Friday and Saturday).

SETTING AND ATMOSPHERE With its steampunk aesthetic and an abundance of gear imagery, the place has a distinct industrial vibe. Clips of black-and-white movies are projected onto some of the walls.

HOUSE SPECIALTIES The DB Clothesline Candied Bacon is the signature appetizer: four pieces of heavily smoked candied bacon and a few sprigs of rosemary clipped to a suspended string with clothespins. It's photogenic—and that's about it. The entrées are American comfort food: prime rib and burgers. The food is decent but not a good value.

OTHER RECOMMENDATIONS Drinks are where The Edison shines. In addition to signature cocktails such as the Time Turner, made with Bacardi light rum, Campari, lime, pineapple, and orgeat (almond-flavored flower-water syrup), there are about 10 draft beers, along with bottled and canned beers and ciders; substantial wine offerings by the bottle and glass; a dozen vodkas; and almost as many varieties of gin, tequila, whiskey, and rum.

KIDS' MENU Burgers, chicken strips, or grilled cheese, all with appetizer and dessert but all too expensive.

SUMMARY AND COMMENTS This is not in the first or second tier of restaurants we would recommend at Disney Springs. It's not bad for an after-dinner drink, but our experience in getting one is that service is terse.

50's Prime Time Café   ★★★

AMERICAN	MODERATE	QUALITY ★★★	VALUE ★★★
READER-SURVEY RESPONSES ● 88% (Average)			

Echo Lake, Disney's Hollywood Studios; ☎ 407-939-3463

Reservations Strongly recommended. **Dining Plan credits** 1 per person, per meal. **When to go** Lunch or dinner. **Cost range** $17–$30 (child $12–$14). **Service** ★★★★★. **Bar** Full service. **Lunch** Daily, 10:45 a.m.–3:55 p.m. **Dinner** Daily, 4–9 p.m.

SETTING AND ATMOSPHERE Dine in a 1950s kitchen stocked with antique fridges, laminate tabletops, and sunburst clocks. Black-and-white TVs play vintage sitcom clips while you wait for your meal.

HOUSE SPECIALTIES Pot roast, fried chicken, meat loaf, plus a sampler platter with some of each; PB&J milkshake and other retro fare. Desserts are a strong point, with warm apple crisp and a chocolate–peanut butter layer cake being the highlights. This is filling comfort food.

KIDS' MENU Salmon (our recommendation), sloppy Joe, grilled chicken, or chicken strips; a good selection of sides, but your kids might be put off by the "stained glass dessert." Servers describe it as a bowl of Jell-O, but it's mostly "whipped pineapple fluff."

SUMMARY AND COMMENTS The waitstaff makes this location worthwhile, admonishing you just like Mom did to "take your elbows off the table!" and making sure you eat your vegetables.

Flying Fish ★★★½

SEAFOOD	EXPENSIVE	QUALITY ★★★	VALUE ★★★
READER-SURVEY RESPONSES ✚ 92% (Above Average)			

BoardWalk; ☎ 407-939-3463

Reservations Strongly recommended. **Dining Plan credits** 2 per person, per meal. **When to go** Dinner. **Cost range** $38–$59 (child $14–$24). **Service** ★★★★. **Bar** Full service, with an extensive wine selection. **Dress** Dressy casual. **Dinner** Daily, 5–9:30 p.m.

SETTING AND ATMOSPHERE At the heart of the BoardWalk, Flying Fish gives diners an upscale modern seafood dinner enveloped by splashy blue-and-silver décor. The open kitchen and showcase bar entertain guests seated near the front of the bustling restaurant, with a more muted experience in the rear of the main dining room.

HOUSE SPECIALTIES The potato-wrapped red snapper has remained on the menu through several iterations of chefs and management. Bartenders craft specialty cocktails that pair with most meals, while a strong wine program complements every dish from start to finish.

OTHER RECOMMENDATIONS Plancha-seared scallops with savory grits shine on the seafood-dominant menu, though landlubbers will be perfectly content with the filet mignon. Soup and salad, rotating frequently throughout every season, are solid ways to start any meal here, and both highlight the freshest produce Florida has to offer.

KIDS' MENU Grilled chicken or steak, red snapper or "fish," or pasta with marinara; there are only a few sides to choose from, including the unexpected kid favorite . . . asparagus.

SUMMARY AND COMMENTS The kitchen can sometimes force a slower-paced meal here.

The Fountain ★★

AMERICAN	MODERATE	QUALITY ★★	VALUE ★★
READER-SURVEY RESPONSES ✚ 81% (Below Average)			

Dolphin Resort; ☎ 407-934-1609

Reservations Not accepted. **Dining Plan credits** Not accepted. **When to go** Lunch or dinner. **Cost range** $12–$20 (child $13). **Service** ★★★★. **Bar** Limited beer and wine. **Parking** Valet ($39) or hotel lot ($29), both free with validation. **Lunch and dinner** Daily, 11 a.m.–11 p.m.

SETTING AND ATMOSPHERE Informal soda-shop ambience.

HOUSE SPECIALTIES Hot dogs and burgers (including veggie and turkey burgers), milkshakes (we love the PB&J), and ice cream.

OTHER RECOMMENDATIONS Generous salads, including seared salmon and chicken Caesar.

KIDS' MENU Too many options to list, all relatively expensive. Every kid will find something to love.

SUMMARY AND COMMENTS The Fountain is one of the Dolphin's few casual-dining spots, none of which get high marks from readers.

Frontera Cocina ★★½

MEXICAN	EXPENSIVE	QUALITY ★★★	VALUE ★★
READER-SURVEY RESPONSES ✚ 80% (Much Below Average)			

Town Center, Disney Springs; ☎ 407-939-3463

Reservations Strongly recommended. **Dining Plan credits** 1 per person, per meal. **When to go** Dinner. **Cost range** $23–$58 (children $10–$13). **Service** ★★★★. **Parking** Lime garage. **Bar** Full service. **Hours** Daily, 11 a.m.–11 p.m.

SETTING AND ATMOSPHERE The outside has muted beige walls, but the interior is sleek and modern, with exposed ductwork, bright pops of color from the chandelier and bar, and cozy dark-wood furnishings. The open kitchen and Wall of Fame shelves, packed with specialty liquors and wines, are bathed in sunlight from the large windows on nearly every wall, showcasing the springs and the patio.

HOUSE SPECIALTIES Tacos with carne asada or chipotle chicken, chicken enchiladas in red sauce, plantains, margaritas and specialty tequila flights.

OTHER RECOMMENDATIONS Guacamole, coconut-lime cuatro leches cake. The dessert menu is small—get dessert elsewhere.

KIDS' MENU Quesadilla, shredded chicken, or tacos with inflexible side choices. Not for picky eaters.

SUMMARY AND COMMENTS The menu often spotlights the flavors and ingredients of a particular region of Mexico. **Frontera Cocina To Go,** a walk-up window, serves two kinds of tacos, soft drinks, beer, and margaritas.

Garden Grill Restaurant ★★★

AMERICAN	EXPENSIVE	QUALITY ★★★	VALUE ★★★
READER-SURVEY RESPONSES ➕ 92% (Above Average)			

The Land, World Nature, EPCOT; ☎ 407-939-3463

Reservations Required. **Dining Plan credits** 1 per person, per meal. **When to go** Anytime. **Cost range** Breakfast $47 (child $30), lunch and dinner $62 (child $40). **Service** ★★★★. **Bar** Wine, beer, and mixed drinks. **Character breakfast** Daily, 8:30–10:30 a.m. **Character lunch** Daily, 11:30 a.m.–3:40 p.m. **Character dinner** Daily, 3:45–8 p.m.

SETTING AND ATMOSPHERE The all-you-can-eat Garden Grill stays busy, even though the dining room has grown rather dated. The floor revolves slowly as you peer down into scenes from **Living with the Land,** The Land Pavilion's ride-through attraction (see page 417). During your meal, you complete one revolution, past scenes of a desert, a rainforest, and a farm.

Much more exciting for kids are the Disney characters. Mickey, Chip 'n' Dale, and Pluto stop at each table for autographs and photos.

HOUSE SPECIALTIES Grilled beef with chimichurri, turkey breast with stuffing and gravy, BBQ ribs, mashed potatoes, veggies, and salads made with ingredients from The Land's greenhouses. Dessert is a berry shortcake with whipped cream. Plant-based options available on request. Cinnamon rolls and Mickey waffles at breakfast.

ENTERTAINMENT AND AMENITIES The view into Living with the Land and character dining at all meals.

SUMMARY AND COMMENTS The food quality has been improving, and you won't beat the retro-EPCOT setting. A worthy character meal.

Garden Grove ★★

AMERICAN	MODERATE	QUALITY ★★½	VALUE ★★
READER-SURVEY RESPONSES ➕ 86% (Average)			

Swan Resort; ☎ 407-934-1609

Reservations Recommended. **Dining Plan credits** Not accepted. **When to go** Breakfast or brunch. **Cost range** $17–$23 (child $10). **Service** ★★★. **Parking** Valet ($39) or hotel lot ($29), both free with validation. **Bar** Full service. **Hours** Daily, 7 a.m.–11:30 a.m.

SETTING AND ATMOSPHERE A spacious dining room features a 25-foot faux oak tree in the center.

HOUSE SPECIALTIES Familiar breakfast combinations, including waffles, French toast, and eggs.

KIDS' MENU Waffles, pancakes, or American-style breakfast (eggs, potatoes, toast, and choice of bacon or sausage).

SUMMARY AND COMMENTS Garden Grove isn't worth a special trip if you aren't staying at the Swan. But the room is pretty, and the food is plentiful, if not highly rated.

Grand Floridian Cafe ★★★

AMERICAN	MODERATE-EXPENSIVE	QUALITY ★★★½	VALUE ★★★
READER-SURVEY RESPONSES ⊕ 86% (Average)			

Grand Floridian Resort & Spa; ☎ 407-939-3463

Reservations Recommended. **Dining Plan credits** 1 per person, per meal. **When to go** Anytime. **Cost range** Breakfast and lunch $16–$29 (child $10–$13), dinner $25–$36 (child $11–$16). **Service** ★★★★. **Bar** Full service. **Breakfast** Daily, 7:30–11 a.m. **Lunch** Daily, 11:05 a.m.–2 p.m. **Dinner** Daily, 5–9 p.m.

SETTING AND ATMOSPHERE Light and airy with lots of sunlight, servers dressed in Victorian costumes, and views of the pool and courtyard.

HOUSE SPECIALTIES The breakfast/lunch menu is extensive, ranging from eggs Benedict and buttermilk pancakes to tomato-and-feta quiche and miso-glazed salmon. Try the Signature Burger (with Brie, bacon-pepper jam, and roasted garlic aioli) or the buttermilk-fried chicken (which is outstanding) served with a waffle drizzled with sriracha honey. Dinner options include New York strip, vegetable curry with chicken or tofu, and fried chicken served with loaded mashed potatoes.

OTHER RECOMMENDATIONS Any dessert the kitchen recommends.

KIDS' MENU *Breakfast:* Grilled chicken, waffles, eggs, or pancake; *lunch and dinner:* Grilled salmon, steak or chicken or pizza; tiny selection of sides.

SUMMARY AND COMMENTS A quick place to grab a tasty bite in a pleasantly themed room.

La Hacienda de San Angel ★★★½

MEXICAN	EXPENSIVE	QUALITY ★★★½	VALUE ★★★
READER-SURVEY RESPONSES ⊕ 88% (Average)			

Mexico, World Showcase, EPCOT; ☎ 407-939-3463

Reservations Required. **Dining Plan credits** 1 per person, per meal. **When to go** Dinner. **Cost range** $29–$54 (child $12–$16). **Service** ★★★★. **Bar** Full service. **Hours** Daily, 3 p.m.–9 p.m.

SETTING AND ATMOSPHERE Right along the waterfront in Mexico, La Hacienda is a prime spot for watching fireworks through the tall windows. The interior has authentic touches of Mexico in its lighting and décor.

HOUSE SPECIALTIES Excellent guacamole; queso fundido; carne asada–style New York strip; tenderloin fajitas with bacon, poblano and bell peppers, cheese, and salsa; and fried-shrimp tacos with chipotle-lime aioli.

OTHER RECOMMENDATIONS For starters, try the flautas—fried tortillas with potato, chipotle chicken, cheese, and ranchero sauce. The margaritas are the real deal—or just go for a flight of fine tequila.

KIDS' MENU Tacos, quesadilla, chicken tenders, grilled chicken, or mac and cheese, all with limited side options.

SUMMARY AND COMMENTS The menu quality is first-rate. The Alambre de Res tenderloin fajitas are our favorite.

Hollywood & Vine ★★★

AMERICAN/BUFFET	EXPENSIVE	QUALITY ★★★	VALUE ★★★
READER-SURVEY RESPONSES ☺ 89% (Average)			

Echo Lake, Disney's Hollywood Studios; ☎ 407-939-3463

Reservations Strongly recommended. **Dining Plan credits** 1 per person, per meal. **When to go** Breakfast, lunch, or dinner. **Cost range** Breakfast $47 (child $30), lunch and dinner $63 (child $40). **Service** ★★★★. **Bar** Full service. **Character breakfast** Daily, 8:30–10:30 a.m. **Character lunch** Daily, 11:30 a.m.–3:55 p.m. **Character dinner** Daily, 4–8 p.m.

SETTING AND ATMOSPHERE Just off Hollywood Boulevard, this 1940s-era diner has a sleek Art Deco design (think chrome and tile) that gets lost amid all the Disney-character frenzy. Breakfast includes characters from Disney Junior, such as Doc McStuffins and Fancy Nancy, while seasonal lunches and dinners feature Minnie, Mickey, Goofy, Pluto, and Donald (and sometimes Daisy), usually in holiday- or Hollywood-themed outfits.

HOUSE SPECIALTIES *Breakfast:* Bananas Foster French toast, eggs benedict, chicken with Mickey waffles. *Dinner:* Beef tenderloin, roasted chicken, mac and cheese with shrimp, or roasted pork. There's also a plant-based option, most recently a mushroom risotto.

SUMMARY AND COMMENTS The food here is on the upswing, and the characters provide some of the highest-energy interactions you'll find in any park. Don't let old reviews fool you—this is a great character meal, and it's easier to get reservations for than many others.

The Hollywood Brown Derby ★★★½

AMERICAN	EXPENSIVE	QUALITY ★★★★	VALUE ★★½
READER-SURVEY RESPONSES ☺ 90% (Above Average)			

Hollywood Boulevard, Disney's Hollywood Studios; ☎ 407-939-3463

Reservations Strongly recommended. **Dining Plan credits** 2 per person, per meal. **When to go** Early evening. **Cost range** $25–$49 (child $9–$18). **Service** ★★★★★. **Bar** Full service. **Lunch** Daily, 11 a.m.–3:55 p.m. **Dinner** Daily, 4–8 p.m.

SETTING AND ATMOSPHERE This is a replica of the original Brown Derby on Vine Street in Hollywood (not the one shaped like a hat). The sunken dining room has a certain elegance, with tuxedoed waiters, curved booths, and white linen. Tall palm trees in huge pots stand in the center of the room. Ask for a seat on the second-level gallery; it's much quieter and affords good people-watching in the hectic main space.

HOUSE SPECIALTIES Cobb salad (named for Bob Cobb, owner of the original restaurant); the famous grapefruit cake made from the original Brown Derby recipe.

OTHER RECOMMENDATIONS The menu varies and the kitchen is unusually adept with pork and lamb—we'd recommend those if available.

KIDS' MENU Grilled chicken, fish, or beef filet; hot dog; or mac and cheese, all served with two sides from a good selection.

SUMMARY AND COMMENTS The Brown Derby is expensive, yes, but also the most relaxing restaurant you'll find inside Hollywood Studios. If you don't have reservations, the patio lounge opens at 11 a.m. and is first come, first served, with a menu of small plates and cocktails.

Drink choices are far more extensive than Disney's online menu might indicate and include various flights—martinis, margaritas, Champagnes, white and red wine, Scotches, and Grand Marnier vintages—along with wine by the bottle and by the glass, beer, and classic cocktails.

House of Blues Restaurant & Bar ★★★

AMERICAN	MODERATE	QUALITY ★★★½	VALUE ★★★
READER-SURVEY RESPONSES ● 83% (Below Average)			

West Side, Disney Springs; ☎ 407-934-2583

Reservations Recommended. **Dining Plan credits** 1 per person, per meal. **When to go** Lunch or early dinner; weekend brunch. **Cost range** Brunch $15–$19, lunch and dinner $17–$36 (child $10). **Service** ★★★★. **Parking** Orange garage. **Bar** Full service. **Brunch** Saturday–Sunday: 10 a.m.–1:55 p.m. **Lunch** Monday–Friday, 11:30 a.m.–3:55 p.m.; Saturday–Sunday, 2 p.m.–3:55 p.m. **Dinner** Daily, 4–11 p.m. (until 11:30 p.m. Friday–Sunday).

SETTING AND ATMOSPHERE Adjacent to the Cirque du Soleil theater, House of Blues has a ramshackle look, but it's a solid stop for lunch or dinner before or after a show. A separate concert hall hosts great live music, along with a lively Sunday gospel brunch. A quick-service window (the Smokehouse), along with the outdoor bar and seating, draws passersby. The fabulous folk art in the restaurant is worth a look.

HOUSE SPECIALTIES Barbecue sandwiches (pulled pork and brisket), ribs, steaks, burgers, and shrimp and grits.

OTHER RECOMMENDATIONS Jambalaya and jalapeño cornbread.

KIDS' MENU Pizza, burger, hot dog, chicken tenders, or mac and cheese, all served with a side of fruit.

SUMMARY AND COMMENTS Meat-centric menu on Disney Springs' West Side in a fun and casual setting.

Il Mulino ★★★

ITALIAN	EXPENSIVE	QUALITY ★★★	VALUE ★★
READER-SURVEY RESPONSES ● 86% (Average)			

Swan Resort; ☎ 407-939-3463

Reservations Recommended. **Dining Plan credits** Not accepted. **When to go** Dinner. **Cost range** $20–$71 (child $13–$17). **Service** ★★★. **Parking** Valet ($39) or hotel lot ($29), both free with validation. **Bar** Full service. **Dress** Dressy casual. **Hours** Daily, 5–11 p.m.

SETTING AND ATMOSPHERE A spin-off of the acclaimed Manhattan restaurant, Il Mulino takes an upscale-casual, downtown New York approach to Italian cuisine, with family-style platters for sharing. An open kitchen creates a bustle. You can request private dining in one of the smaller rooms.

HOUSE SPECIALTIES Try the spaghetti carbonara or the veal saltimbocca. The risottos are well made; the spaghetti with baby shrimp, scallops, clams, mussels, and calamari is also good, though overpriced.

OTHER RECOMMENDATIONS Charcuterie, mussels in white wine, pizzas, sautéed jumbo shrimp, rib eye with sautéed spinach.

KIDS' MENU Pizza, four pasta options, or chicken parmesan; no sides.

SUMMARY AND COMMENTS A predictable menu, with a little bit of everything you would expect in an Italian restaurant and nothing particularly adventurous. The kids' menu is comparatively overpriced.

Jaleo by José Andrés ★★★★

SPANISH/TAPAS	MODERATE	QUALITY ★★★★	VALUE ★★★½
READER-SURVEY RESPONSES ● 92% (Above Average)			

West Side, Disney Springs; ☎ 407-939-3463

Reservations Strongly recommended. **Dining Plan credits** 2 per person, per meal. **When to go** Dinner. **Cost range** Tapas $11–$32 (child $5–$14). **Service** ★★★★.

Parking Orange garage. **Bar** Full service with emphasis on Spanish drinks and wines. **Hours** Daily, 11:30 a.m.–11 p.m.

SETTING AND ATMOSPHERE Jaleo's entrance has tile mosaics and large-scale photo murals of iconic Spanish scenes. Warm colors from lighting in the kitchen and dining areas bathe the restaurant, reflecting off metal accents. The highlight is the paella pit and accompanying view into the kitchen—every time one of the massive paella dishes has finished cooking, the chefs ring a bell and the entire restaurant joins in the celebration.

HOUSE SPECIALTIES The restaurant serves Spain's famed Jamón Ibérico. A selection of Spanish cheeses and traditional pan de cristal con tomate are both good first courses. Garlic shrimp and grilled chicken with garlic sauce burst with flavor, highlighting incredibly fresh produce and tons of herbs. Our table nearly came to blows fighting over the last morsels of patatas bravas—fried potatoes topped with spicy tomato sauce and aioli. The paella is decent but maybe not worth all the hoopla . . . or the price.

OTHER RECOMMENDATIONS Drinks are on par with other Disney Springs restaurants in terms of pricing and quality. The wine menu is extensive.

KIDS' MENU Grilled steak or chicken, chicken fritters, or grilled cheese; very limited side selections. Leave the kids at home for this one.

SUMMARY AND COMMENTS This restaurant from celebrity chef José Andrés brings classic Spanish cuisine to Disney Springs' West Side neighborhood. We think Jaleo is one of the best restaurants in Disney Springs.

Jiko—The Cooking Place ★★★★

AFRICAN/FUSION	EXPENSIVE	QUALITY ★★★★	VALUE ★★½
READER-SURVEY RESPONSES ⊕ 92% (Above Average)			

Animal Kingdom Lodge & Villas–Jambo House; ☎ 407-939-3463

Reservations Required. **Dining Plan credits** 2 per person, per meal. **When to go** Dinner. **Cost range** $38–$59 (child $10–$18). **Service** ★★★★★. **Bar** Full service with South African. **Dress** Dressy casual. **Hours** Daily, 5–9:30 p.m.

SETTING AND ATMOSPHERE Bathed in a perpetual sunset, with metal birds soaring around, the main dining room is warm and inviting, accented by the central *jiko* ("cooking place" in Swahili), where chefs prepare many of the appetizers featured on the restaurant's seasonally rotating menu in view of a few lucky diners. As you enter, stop to gaze at the wine room. The bottles on display represent just a sample of the massive wine selection—the largest collection of South African wines available in any North American restaurant.

HOUSE SPECIALTIES Guests flock to Jiko for several dishes, among them the braised wild-boar tenderloin appetizer, African spice–infused flatbreads, seafood tagine, and oak-grilled filet mignon with South African red-wine sauce and bobotie mac and cheese. The seasonally updated malva (mallow) pudding dessert highlights traditional African flavors on the sweet spectrum.

OTHER RECOMMENDATIONS Botswanan-style beef short ribs and Moroccan lamb shank bring on the spices, while luscious seasonal soups start any meal off on the right foot. For those in search of vegan and vegetarian options, Jiko stands out as one of the few Disney Signature restaurants to offer dedicated options that are both satisfying and flavorful. A large selection of specialty teas and Kenyan press-pot coffee complement the excellent dessert selections.

KIDS' MENU Grilled chicken, fish, shrimp, or steak; cheese pizza; or mac and cheese, with many side options—but half of them are desserts!

SUMMARY AND COMMENTS Jiko is one of the true hidden gems of fine dining in Walt Disney World. It provides superb service in a nonfussy atmosphere, welcoming guests for a meal packed with truly unique flavors. Solo diners or small parties may want to take advantage of the jiko's seating for both dinner and a show. I ate solo at the jiko, and it is one of my favorite Disney dining experiences to this day.

Jungle Navigation Co. Ltd. Skipper Canteen ★★★½

AFRICAN/LATIN/PAN-ASIAN	EXPENSIVE	QUALITY ★★★½	VALUE ★★★
READER-SURVEY RESPONSES ➕ 91% (Above Average)			

Adventureland, Magic Kingdom; ☎ 407-939-3463

Reservations Strongly recommended. **Dining Plan credits** 1 per person, per meal. **When to go** Lunch or dinner. **Cost range** $23–$38 (child $11–$14). **Service** ★★★★. **Bar** Limited selection of beer and wine. **Hours** Daily, 11 a.m.–9 p.m.

SETTING AND ATMOSPHERE Themed as the home of off-duty Jungle Cruise skippers, Skipper Canteen offers guests an oasis from the theme park, with three distinct dining rooms (and a boatload of corny jokes). The crew's mess hall features high ceilings, dark wooden fixtures, and souvenirs collected from the skippers' travels, all bathed in stained glass–tinted natural light. Behind a hidden bookcase (with highly amusing titles), guests can visit the secret meeting room of the Society of Explorers and Adventurers, filled with posh fixtures, maps, and a beautiful collection of butterflies. The Jungle Room has intimate seating near intricately carved wood bookshelves and colorful stained glass lamps.

HOUSE SPECIALTIES The menu features flavors from several world cuisines, with Asian influences in the char siu pork (a house favorite) and Korean barbecue–inspired crispy fried chicken. Latin flavors make their way into the grilled steak with adobo, as well as the house-made corn pancakes topped with pork and avocado cream. The Kungaloosh! (chocolate cake with caramelized bananas) will close out any meal with a smile—and is the only dessert worth ordering here.

OTHER RECOMMENDATIONS Plant-based dining is well represented here, with an emphasis on vegetables instead of meat substitutes.

KIDS' MENU Grilled steak, crispy chicken, mac and cheese, or coconut-curry pineapple tofu. A large selection of unique and tasty sides.

SUMMARY AND COMMENTS Skipper Canteen has fresh flavors and fine service. The menu decidedly doesn't cater to simpler tastes, which means reservations are readily available.

Kimonos ★★★

JAPANESE	MODERATE	QUALITY ★★★★	VALUE ★★★
READER-SURVEY RESPONSES ➕ 87% (Average)			

Swan Resort; ☎ 407-934-1792

Reservations Not accepted. **Dining Plan credits** Not accepted. **When to go** Dinner. **Cost range** Sushi rolls and appetizers à la carte $10–$25. **Service** ★★★★★. **Parking** Valet or hotel lot; validated for customers. **Bar** Full service. **Hours** Daily, 5:30 p.m.–1 a.m.

SETTING AND ATMOSPHERE Sushi and nightly karaoke—what a combo! Go early if you want a zen experience with sushi and sake in the serene setting: dark teak tabletops and counters, tall pillars rising to bamboo rafters with rice-paper lanterns, and elegant kimonos that hang outstretched on the walls and between the dining sections. The chefs will greet you, and you'll be offered a hot towel to clean your hands.

HOUSE SPECIALTIES Both cooked and raw sushi and hot dishes. Classic rolls include California, tuna, and soft-shell crab; the Kimonos Roll features tuna, salmon, yellowtail, and wasabi mayo. Small plates include beef satay and chicken katsu.

KIDS' MENU None.

SUMMARY AND COMMENTS The skill of the sushi artists is as much a joy to watch as is eating the wonderfully fresh creations. Excellent sake choices. Karaoke starts at 9:30 p.m.

Kona Cafe ★★★

PAN-ASIAN/POLYNESIAN	MODERATE	QUALITY ★★★	VALUE ★★★½
READER-SURVEY RESPONSES ➕ 90% (Above Average)			

Polynesian Village Resort; ☎ 407-939-3463

Reservations Strongly recommended. **Dining Plan credits** 1 per person, per meal. **When to go** Anytime. **Cost range** Breakfast $15–$22 (child $6–$10), lunch $16–$31 (child $11–$13), dinner $18–$40 (child $10–$13). **Service** ★★★★. **Bar** Full service. **Breakfast** Daily, 7:30–11 a.m. **Lunch** Daily, 11:30 a.m.–2 p.m. **Dinner** Daily, 5–10 p.m.

SETTING AND ATMOSPHERE Open for three meals a day, Kona Cafe is a casual, open dining room in the heart of the Polynesian. Located right next to the monorail station, it is easy to get to from the Magic Kingdom by boat or monorail.

HOUSE SPECIALTIES *Breakfast:* Tonga Toast (French toast with bananas) is the most requested dish. *Lunch:* Turkey banh mi, chicken stir-fry, noodle bowls with pork belly or vegetables, duck fried rice, and sushi rolls. *Dinner:* Sushi, tuna poke, Kona coffee–braised short rib.

OTHER RECOMMENDATIONS The kids' sushi makes for a great adult snack. Desserts, served in small glasses, are cute but not much else; Kona coffee served in a press pot.

KIDS' MENU Sushi, chicken taco, cheeseburger, or mac and cheese; limited side selections.

SUMMARY AND COMMENTS The dining room isn't fancy, but the food is good quality.

Liberty Tree Tavern ★★★½

AMERICAN	EXPENSIVE	QUALITY ★★★	VALUE ★★★½
READER-SURVEY RESPONSES ➕ 92% (Above Average)			

Liberty Square, Magic Kingdom; ☎ 407-939-3463

Reservations Strongly recommended. **Dining Plan credits** 1 per person, per meal. **When to go** Lunch or dinner. **Cost range** $42 (child $23). **Service** ★★★★. **Bar** Limited selection of beer, wine, and hard cider. **Hours** Daily, 11 a.m.–8 p.m.

SETTING AND ATMOSPHERE With six rooms themed to key figures in early American history—Betsy Ross, Benjamin Franklin, Thomas Jefferson, John Paul Jones, Paul Revere, and George and Martha Washington—Liberty Tree Tavern feels like a quaint and cozy Colonial home. Appropriately creaky wooden staircases flank the busy central lobby.

HOUSE SPECIALTIES Most guests come to Liberty Tree for the All-You-Care-to-Enjoy Patriot's Platter, consisting of roasted turkey, carved pork roast, mashed potatoes, stuffing, seasonal vegetables, and house-made mac and cheese. Save room for the Ooey Gooey Toffee Cake.

OTHER RECOMMENDATIONS The Impossible Meatloaf, a plant-based dish served with mashed potatoes, seasonal vegetables, and mushroom gravy, is a tasty vegan option.

SUMMARY AND COMMENTS A solid standby for families in search of classic American fare, the tavern serves up high-quality food with good service at a quick pace. Liberty Tree Tavern regularly ranks as one of the top meals inside the Magic Kingdom.

Mama Melrose's Ristorante Italiano ★★½

ITALIAN	EXPENSIVE	QUALITY ★★★	VALUE ★★
READER-SURVEY RESPONSES ⊕ 81% (Below Average)			

Grand Avenue, Disney's Hollywood Studios; ☎ 407-939-3463

Reservations Strongly recommended. **Dining Plan credits** 1 per person, per meal. **When to go** Lunch or dinner. **Cost range** $21–$36 (child $12–$14). **Service** ★★★. **Bar** Full service. **Hours** Daily, 10:45 a.m.–9 p.m.

SETTING AND ATMOSPHERE This casual restaurant is inspired by red-sauce Italian joints as much as New York and LA movie scenes: twinkling lights, red vinyl booths, and grapevines hanging from the rafters. Thanks to its tucked-away location, it's generally quiet unless it's peak season.

HOUSE SPECIALTIES Fresh mozzarella, campanelle with shrimp, flatbread "pizzas," seasonal pastas.

OTHER RECOMMENDATIONS Charred strip steak; tiramisu, Ghirardelli chocolate and cherry torte, and cannoli for dessert.

KIDS' MENU Spaghetti three different ways, penne with meatballs, cheese pizza, or grilled chicken, all with sides that may be off-putting for most kids (like zucchini and whole-grain pilaf).

SUMMARY AND COMMENTS The food won't win any awards, but for basic Italian, it's fine.

Maria & Enzo's Ristorante ★★

ITALIAN	EXPENSIVE	QUALITY ★★	VALUE ★★
READER-SURVEY RESPONSES ⊕70% (Do Not Visit)			

The Landing, Disney Springs; ☎ 407-939-3463

Reservations Recommended. **Dining Plan credits** 1 per person, per meal. **When to go** Dinner. **Cost range** Brunch $23–$52, lunch $17–$23 (child $16), dinner $28–$52 (child $16). **Service** ★★★½. **Parking** Orange garage. **Bar** Full service; extensive wine selection. **Brunch** Saturday–Sunday, 11:30 a.m.–3:30 p.m. **Lunch** Monday–Friday, 11:30 a.m.–3:30 p.m. **Dinner** Daily, 4–10 p.m.

SETTING AND ATMOSPHERE This trattoria is housed in an elegant Art Deco replica of a 1930s airline terminal, with servers clad in spiffy period flight-attendant uniforms. A smaller seating area called the First Class Lounge offers dining in a quieter setting.

HOUSE SPECIALTIES The extensive bar menu features aperitivi, prosecco cocktails, and a variety of seasonal specialty drinks. The dishes consist primarily of Italian classics.

KIDS' MENU Chicken tenders, cheese pizza, or spaghetti with meatballs; all come with vanilla ice cream dessert.

SUMMARY AND COMMENTS Excellent setting, mediocre food, high prices.

Maya Grill ★

AMERICAN/MEXICAN	EXPENSIVE	QUALITY ★	VALUE ★
READER-SURVEY RESPONSES 74% (Do Not Visit)			

Coronado Springs Resort; ☎ 407-939-3463

Reservations Recommended. **Dining Plan credits** 1 per person, per meal. **When to go** Never. **Cost range** $22–$38 (child $12). **Service** ★★★. **Bar** Full service. **Hours** Daily, 5–10 p.m.

SETTING AND ATMOSPHERE The dated dining room is intended to evoke the ancient world of the Maya, but the idea misses the mark. The kitchen is open to view—but so is the barren walkway outside.

HOUSE SPECIALTIES Tex-Mex and Nuevo Latino dinner fare, including a fajita skillet and slow-cooked pork with corn tortillas.

KIDS' MENU Tacos, quesadilla, grilled chicken, chicken tenders, or mac and cheese; no sides listed.

SUMMARY AND COMMENTS Maya Grill is owned by the same folks who run the restaurants at the Mexico Pavilion in EPCOT. Go to any of those instead.

Monsieur Paul ★★★

FRENCH	EXPENSIVE	QUALITY ★★★	VALUE ★★★
READER-SURVEY RESPONSES ➕ 81% (Below Average)			

France, World Showcase, EPCOT; ☎ 407-939-3463

Reservations Required; a $100 no-show fee applies if you fail to cancel at least 72 hours before your meal. **Dining Plan credits** 2 per person, per meal. **When to go** Late dinner. **Cost range** $195 fixed-price menu. **Service** ★★★★★. **Bar** Full service. **Dress** Dressy casual (no swimwear). **Hours** Daily, 5:30–7:30 p.m.

SETTING AND ATMOSPHERE Light and modern, Monsieur Paul is tucked away at the France Pavilion, accessed by a stairway lined with photos of legendary chef Paul Bocuse, whose son, Jérôme, owns and runs both this restaurant and Chefs de France, located next door (see page 252). Request a table at the windows to watch the world go by on the World Showcase Lagoon.

HOUSE SPECIALTIES Chef Bocuse's black-truffle soup, black sea bass in potato "scales," and roasted duck.

KIDS' MENU None.

SUMMARY AND COMMENTS Disney's moving a number of fancy restaurants to fixed-price menus, and Monsieur Paul is a casualty. The food doesn't live up to the price. And few people want to get dressed up, pay $160 for theme park admission, and then pay another $250 per person (including tax and tip) for a heavy nine-course dinner.

Morimoto Asia ★★★★

JAPANESE/PAN-ASIAN	EXPENSIVE	QUALITY ★★★★	VALUE ★★★★
READER-SURVEY RESPONSES ➕ 88% (Average)			

The Landing, Disney Springs; ☎ 407-939-6686

Reservations Recommended. **Dining Plan credits** 2 per person, per meal. **When to go** Lunch or dinner. **Cost range** $16–$59 (child $16). **Service** ★★★★. **Parking** Lime garage. **Bar** Wide range of wine, beer, sake, and cocktails. **Lunch** Daily, 11:30 a.m.–3:30 p.m. **Dinner** Daily, 4:30–10 p.m. (until 10:30 p.m. on Friday and Saturday).

SETTING AND ATMOSPHERE Quirky takes on Chinese, Japanese, and Korean dishes join a substantial sushi menu from the kitchen and upstairs sushi bar, where Iron Chef Masaharu Morimoto makes appearances. Fishing baskets and steel beads form the chandeliers, and a continuous white engineered-stone ribbon runs from the "secret" entrance to the Forbidden Lounge upstairs, creating the handrail, bar, and seating areas throughout the building and framing the glass-bottle lighting upstairs.

HOUSE SPECIALTIES Pork dim sum; 24-hour-marinated, house-carved Peking duck; orange chicken; Morimoto spare ribs; Korean buri bop; lo mein and ramen noodles; sushi rolls and sashimi.

KIDS' MENU Orange chicken, lo mein, ramen, egg fried rice; all come with boba tea and ice cream/sorbet

SUMMARY AND COMMENTS Chef Morimoto is famously hands-on with this restaurant, and it's not uncommon to see him in the kitchen or behind the sushi counter. We think this is one of the top restaurants in Disney Springs. The food is both better and more expensive than at most hometown Asian restaurants. If you're ordering the Peking duck for yourself and the waitstaff says it serves two, the proper response is "Challenge accepted."

Narcoossee's ★★★½

SEAFOOD	EXPENSIVE	QUALITY ★★★★	VALUE ★★½
READER-SURVEY RESPONSES ✪ 88% (Average)			

Grand Floridian Resort & Spa; ☎ 407-939-3463

Reservations Required. **Dining Plan credits** 2 per person, per meal. **When to go** Early evening. **Cost range** $36–$87 (child $15–$18). **Service** ★★★★★. **Bar** Full service. **Dress** Dressy casual. **Hours** Daily, 5–9:30 p.m.

SETTING AND ATMOSPHERE Situated on the Seven Seas Lagoon at the far end of the Grand Floridian Resort, Narcoossee's completed an extended refurbishment in 2023.

HOUSE SPECIALTIES Anything with seafood or risotto, plus the almond-crusted cheesecake.

KIDS' MENU Grilled chicken or steak, seasonal fish, or chicken strips, all served with two sides from a moderate selection.

SUMMARY AND COMMENTS This is the perfect spot to dine on a sunny day when you can see the Magic Kingdom. Also makes a great date night with a fireworks view.

Nine Dragons Restaurant ★★★

CHINESE	MODERATE	QUALITY ★★★	VALUE ★★½
READER-SURVEY RESPONSES 75% (Do Not Visit)			

China, World Showcase, EPCOT; ☎ 407-939-3463

Reservations Recommended. **Dining Plan credits** 1 per person, per meal. **When to go** Lunch or dinner. **Cost range** $20–$30 (child $10–$13). **Service** ★★★. **Bar** Full service. **Hours** Daily, noon–9 p.m.

SETTING AND ATMOSPHERE An attractive interior—subdued wood tones, colorful lanterns, beautiful backlit glass sculptures from China—and efficient service create a respite from the bustle of World Showcase.

HOUSE SPECIALTIES Crispy duck bao buns, honey-sesame chicken, salt-and-pepper shrimp.

OTHER RECOMMENDATIONS Stick to the appetizers and put the chili oil on everything. It's made in-house and should be sold as a souvenir.

KIDS' MENU Honey chicken nuggets, shrimp with lo mein, The Deluxe (chicken, shrimp, carrots, and vegetable egg fried rice)

SUMMARY AND COMMENTS Nine Dragons gets a bum rap for being pricey, but we think the food and service are above average.

1900 Park Fare ★★★

BUFFET	EXPENSIVE	QUALITY ★★★	VALUE ★★★½
READER-SURVEY RESPONSES Too new to rate			

Grand Floridian Resort & Spa; ☎ 407-939-3463

Reservations Required. **Dining Plan credits** 1 per person, per meal. **When to go** Anytime. **Cost range** Breakfast $54 (child $34), dinner $66 (child $41). **Bar** Full service. **Breakfast** Daily, 8 a.m.–noon. **Dinner** Daily, 4–9 p.m.

SETTING AND ATMOSPHERE The interior of this newly refurbished restaurant features an old pipe organ and paintings of various Disney characters making a wish but is otherwise pretty unremarkable.

SUMMARY AND COMMENTS 1900 Park Fare reopened in April 2024 with the theme of "the power of a wish." Characters at breakfast and dinner host a "wishing ceremony" once an hour, which is unique—but the food borders on mediocre.

'Ohana ★★★

POLYNESIAN	EXPENSIVE	QUALITY ★★★½	VALUE ★★★
READER-SURVEY RESPONSES ➕ 86% (Average)			

Polynesian Village Resort; ☎ 407-939-3463

Reservations Strongly recommended. **Dining Plan credits** 1 per person, per meal. **When to go** Breakfast or dinner. **Cost range** Breakfast $49 (child $30), dinner $62 (child $40). **Service** ★★★★. **Bar** Full service. **Character breakfast** Daily, 7:30 a.m.– 12:15 p.m. **Dinner** Daily, 3:30–10 p.m.

SETTING AND ATMOSPHERE Columns of carved tiki gods support the raised thatched roof in the center of 'Ohana's main dining room, while the dining tables, arranged in rows, resemble long, segmented surfboards. Request a seat in the main dining room, where the fire pit is.

HOUSE SPECIALTIES The menu here is fixed—your only choice is between the regular meal and the plant-based meal. With that decided, the food starts arriving and doesn't stop until you've had enough. Breakfast, a character meal with Lilo and Stitch, starts with seasonal fruit and pineapple-coconut "breakfast bread" (a Danish). Standard breakfast skillets include scrambled eggs, sausage, ham, potatoes, Mickey-shaped waffles, and biscuits; plant-based options are available too. At dinner, starters include honey-glazed chicken wings, fried pork dumplings, mixed green salads, and coconut-papaya scones and cheddar-bacon biscuits. The main course features teriyaki beef, peel-and-eat shrimp, grilled chicken, noodles, and Broccolini.

SUMMARY AND COMMENTS 'Ohana means "family," and family-style certainly applies to the portions—it's an astounding amount of food that just keeps coming. That's great if you have a hungry crew, but be aware that the servers tend to bring out your food at warp speed. If you're dining with little ones, this is fabulous. If, however, you're a group of grown-ups looking for a relaxed meal, 'Ohana will probably feel more like competitive eating than dinner. Feel free to ask your server to space out your courses a bit.

Olivia's Cafe ★★★

AMERICAN	EXPENSIVE	QUALITY ★★★	VALUE ★★
READER-SURVEY RESPONSES ➕ 88% (Average)			

Old Key West Resort; ☎ 407-939-3463

Reservations Recommended. **Dining Plan credits** 1 per person, per meal. **When to go** Brunch. **Cost range** Brunch $11–$26 (child $9–$11), dinner $23–$36 (child $11–$13). **Service** ★★★★. **Bar** Full service. **Brunch** Daily, 7:30 a.m.–2 p.m. **Dinner** Daily, 5–9 p.m.

SETTING AND ATMOSPHERE Many Disney Vacation Club (DVC) members consider Olivia's their home restaurant, and their photos decorate the walls. The décor features pastels, mosaic-tile floors, potted palms, and tropical trees in the center of the room. Some outside seating looks out over the waterway. The tile, wood siding, and lack of tablecloths make for a noisy dining room.

HOUSE SPECIALTIES *Brunch:* Banana-bread French toast, omelets, waffles, pancakes. *Dinner:* Slow-cooked prime rib, shrimp pasta, fried chicken.

OTHER RECOMMENDATIONS Catch of the day, tofu and coconut curry, banana-bread pudding sundae, Key lime tart.

KIDS' MENU Grilled chicken or fish, chicken tenders, or pasta with marinara, all with a choice of two sides from a limited selection.

SUMMARY AND COMMENTS Brunch might be worth a special trip here. Service is super friendly, and the kitchen turns out tasty casual fare.

Paddlefish ★★½

AMERICAN/SEAFOOD	EXPENSIVE	QUALITY ★★★	VALUE ★★½
READER-SURVEY RESPONSES ➊ 78% (Much Below Average)			

The Landing, Disney Springs; ☎ 407-934-2628

Reservations Recommended. **Dining Plan credits** 2 per person, per meal. **When to go** Lunch or dinner. **Cost range** Lunch $15–$54 (child $8–$17), dinner $15–$70 (child $8–$17). **Service** ★★★★½. **Parking** Lime garage. **Bar** Full service. **Lunch** Daily, noon–3:55 p.m. **Dinner** Daily, 4–11 p.m.

SETTING AND ATMOSPHERE Paddlefish has a modern aesthetic, making the stationary "steamship" seem more like a classy yacht than a classic paddleboat. The interior's sleek design doesn't distract from the views offered from the large picture windows at the sides and rear of the ship, overlooking the iconic paddle wheel. Outdoor seating on the first and third decks offers prime views of the area, but the true star of the restaurant is the rooftop bar, where you can enjoy a Florida sunset with your cocktail.

HOUSE SPECIALTIES Crab guacamole. The crab fries (hand-cut and perfectly fried) are a solid choice for an appetizer. Ahi poke and ceviche will cool you down on hot summer days. That said, we don't think the food is good enough to justify the high prices.

OTHER RECOMMENDATIONS You can't go wrong with the lobster roll or the crab cakes.

KIDS' MENU An impressive 11 entrée options—everyone should be able to find something to eat.

SUMMARY AND COMMENTS Readers don't think much of Paddlefish, and we share the sentiment. Our recommendation is to go somewhere else, such as **The Boathouse** (see page 248), **Chef Art Smith's Homecomin'** (see page 251), or **Morimoto Asia** (see page 265).

Paradiso 37 ★★

GLOBAL	EXPENSIVE	QUALITY ★★½	VALUE ★★
READER-SURVEY RESPONSES ➊ 57% (Do Not Visit)			

The Landing, Disney Springs; ☎ 407-934-3700

Reservations Recommended. **Dining Plan credits** 1 per person, per meal. **When to go** Just don't. **Cost range** $22–$39 (child $14). **Service** ★★★. **Parking** Lime garage. **Bar** Full service. **Hours** Daily, 11 a.m.–11 p.m. (until 11:30 p.m. on Friday and Saturday).

SETTING AND ATMOSPHERE Paradiso's outdoor seating features elevated terrace dining and a stage along the waterfront for live music performances. The open kitchen keeps things festive and casual. The *37* in the name refers to the number of North, South, and Central American countries represented on the menu.

HOUSE SPECIALTIES Argentinean skirt steak, Patagonian seared salmon, burgers, and the P37 Swirl, a margarita–sangria combo.

OTHER RECOMMENDATIONS Baja fish tacos.

KIDS' MENU Chicken tenders, cheeseburger, pizza, or double dog (hot dog *and* mini corn dogs), all served with fries.

SUMMARY AND COMMENTS Readers rate this as one of the worst restaurants in Walt Disney World. It clearly does amazing bar business to stay in Disney Springs.

Planet Hollywood ★½

AMERICAN	MODERATE	QUALITY ★	VALUE ★★
READER-SURVEY RESPONSES ⊕ 61% (Do Not Visit)			

Town Center, Disney Springs; ☎ 407-827-7827

Reservations Recommended. **Dining Plan credits** 1 per person, per meal. **When to go** Lunch or dinner. **Cost range** $19–$50 (child $10). **Service** ★★★. **Parking** Orange garage. **Bar** Full service. **Hours** Daily, 11:30 a.m.–11 p.m. (until 11:30 p.m. on Friday and Saturday).

SETTING AND ATMOSPHERE The main dining room is exceptionally loud, but an outdoor patio offers seating with a view of Disney Springs in a much quieter atmosphere.

HOUSE SPECIALTIES Thanks to celebrity chef Guy Fieri, over-the-top burgers reign supreme. L.A. Lasagna, St. Louis–style barbecue ribs served on a mini picnic table, and the High Roller appetizer sampler served on a (nonfunctional) Ferris wheel round out the highlights.

OTHER RECOMMENDATIONS Food much like what you'd find at your neighborhood chain restaurant makes up much of the menu.

KIDS MENU Cheese pizza, mac and cheese, chicken tenders, or spaghetti with meatballs; all come with an unlisted dessert.

SUMMARY AND COMMENTS With higher-quality food just a few steps away at **Chef Art Smith's Homecomin'** (see page 251), **Blaze Fast-Fire'd Pizza** (see page 239), and **D-Luxe Burger** (see page 240), we don't think Planet Hollywood is worth your time or money.

The Plaza Restaurant ★★

AMERICAN	MODERATE	QUALITY ★★	VALUE ★★
READER-SURVEY RESPONSES ⊕ 80% (Much Below Average)			

Main Street, U.S.A., Magic Kingdom; ☎ 407-939-3463

Reservations Strongly recommended. **Dining Plan credits** 1 per person, per meal. **When to go** Lunch or dinner. **Cost range** $19–$26 (child $10–$12). **Service** ★★★★. **Bar** Wine and beer only. **Hours** Daily, 11 a.m.–9 p.m.

SETTING AND ATMOSPHERE The Plaza, a quaint and cozy spot tucked away on a side street at the end of Main Street as you head to Tomorrowland, embraces Art Nouveau touches. It's an air-conditioned heaven on a sweltering Florida day.

HOUSE SPECIALTIES Bacon cheeseburger, the Plaza Restaurant Sundae.

OTHER RECOMMENDATIONS Chicken sandwich.

KIDS' MENU Burgers, chicken strips, turkey sandwich, or PB&J, all with two sides from a small selection.

SUMMARY AND COMMENTS The Plaza isn't fine dining, but it was one of the first restaurants in the Magic Kingdom when the park opened in 1971. Go and enjoy an old-timey indulgence, like a hot-fudge sundae. It's a small space, so reservations are strongly suggested.

Raglan Road Irish Pub & Restaurant ★★★★

IRISH	MODERATE	QUALITY ★★★★	VALUE ★★★
READER-SURVEY RESPONSES ⊕ 96% (Exceptional)			

The Landing, Disney Springs; ☎ 407-938-0300

Reservations Strongly recommended. **Dining Plan credits** 1 per person, per meal. **When to go** Weeknights. **Cost range** Brunch $17–$33 (child $8–$12), lunch and dinner $22–$39 (child $9–$12). **Service** ★★★½. **Parking** Lime garage. **Bar** Irish whiskeys and beers. **Brunch** Saturday–Sunday, 10 a.m.–3 p.m. **Lunch** Monday–Friday, 11 a.m.–3 p.m. **Dinner** Daily, 3:05–11 p.m.

SETTING AND ATMOSPHERE Many of the elements of this pub, including the four bars, were handcrafted from hardwoods in Ireland. The venue is huge by Irish-pub standards, but the dark polished-wood paneling, along with the snugs (small, private cubbyholes), preserves the feel of the traditional pub. The pentagonal main room sits beneath an impressive dome. In the middle of the room is a high platform that's accessible to Celtic dancers via a short staircase. A modest bandstand is situated along the wall in front of a large pseudo-hearth. Branching from this cavernous domed center room are cozy dining areas and snugs.

HOUSE SPECIALTIES Branch out and try the Worth the Wait beef sandwich (made with slow-braised beef, garlic aioli, mushrooms, onions, and cheddar) or the Gnocchi Sea Gnocchi Do with above-average scallops.

Brunch options include the Now You're Talkin' Chicken Sandwich (buttermilk fried chicken breast with hot sauce and scallions); a vegan shepherd's pie; the Full Irish breakfast with Cheshire heritage pork Irish banger, bacon, black-and-white pudding, roasted tomato, mushrooms, fried eggs, and double-cooked chips; and Irish coffee.

KIDS' MENU Grilled chicken, fried chicken or fish, or mac and cheese, each served with salad, mashed potatoes, or a vegetable medley.

ENTERTAINMENT AND AMENITIES The real draw here is the Celtic music. A talented band plays daily. Celtic dancers fill the stage and dance on the aforementioned table to some of the numbers.

SUMMARY AND COMMENTS A night at Raglan Road is a joyous and uplifting experience. If you're traveling with kids, they'll almost certainly be inspired to dance. A quick fish-and-chips can be had around the corner at **Cookes of Dublin** (see page 240) if you're in a hurry.

Rainforest Cafe ★★

AMERICAN	MODERATE	QUALITY ★½	VALUE ★★
READER-SURVEY RESPONSES ➕ 80% (Much Below Average)			

Disney's Animal Kingdom; ☎ 407-938-9100
Marketplace, Disney Springs; ☎ 407-827-8500

Reservations Recommended. **Dining Plan credits** 1 per person, per meal. **When to go** After the lunch rush, late afternoon, or before dinner hour. **Cost range** Breakfast $13–$21 (child $9–$11), lunch and dinner $19–$43 (child $11). **Service** ★★★. **Bar** Full service. **Hours** *Animal Kingdom:* Daily, 8:30 a.m.–7:30 p.m. *Disney Springs Marketplace:* Daily, 11 a.m.–11 p.m. (until 11:30 p.m. on Friday and Saturday).

SETTING AND ATMOSPHERE Families flock to this familiar restaurant for big plates of food served in a noisy dining room with lots to keep the kids entertained. The dining room looks like a jungle, complete with animatronic elephants, bats, and monkeys—not the most realistic we've seen. There's occasional thunder and even some rainfall. At the Disney Springs location, look for the giant volcano that can be seen, and heard, erupting all over the Marketplace; the smoke coming from the volcano is nonpolluting, in accordance with the restaurant's conservation theme.

HOUSE SPECIALTIES Spinach-and-artichoke dip, Caribbean coconut shrimp, burgers, ribs, brownie cake with ice cream.

KIDS' MENU With 13 options, the problem will be deciding.

SUMMARY AND COMMENTS We've never been impressed by the Rainforest Cafes. People must go here when their kids demand it. If you're willing to pay to avoid the long wait, stop by the day before and buy a Landry's Select Club membership for $25 (you get a $25 Welcome Reward back for joining). Present your card on the day you want to dine, and you'll be seated much faster (and earn points and sometimes discounts).

Rose & Crown Dining Room ★★★

BRITISH	MODERATE	QUALITY ★★★½	VALUE ★★★
READER-SURVEY RESPONSES ⊕ 84% (Below Average)			

United Kingdom, World Showcase, EPCOT; ☎ 407-939-3463

Reservations Strongly recommended. **Dining Plan credits** 1 per person, per meal. **When to go** Dinner. **Cost range** $25–$28 (child $15). **Service** ★★★★★. **Bar** Full service with beers on tap. **Hours** Daily, 4–9 p.m.

SETTING AND ATMOSPHERE Pub in the front, dining room in the back. The pub hops with activity from open to close and has the look and feel of a traditional English watering hole: a large, cozy bar with rich wood appointments, beamed ceilings, and a hardwood floor. The adjoining dining room is rustic and simple.

HOUSE SPECIALTIES Fish-and-chips, bangers and mash, and shepherd's pie (the vegetarian version is delicious too), washed down with Bass ale.

OTHER RECOMMENDATIONS The Scotch egg (a hard-boiled egg with a deep-fried sausage coating) and the sticky toffee pudding for dessert.

KIDS' MENU Grilled chicken or fish-and-chips, both served with a house salad and dessert.

SUMMARY AND COMMENTS At dinnertime, the Rose & Crown is packed with folks staking tables for the EPCOT fireworks. The food is good, so branch out and try something new—you can always get fish-and-chips at the adjacent walk-up window, the **Yorkshire County Fish Shop** (page 235).

Roundup Rodeo BBQ ★★★

BARBECUE	EXPENSIVE	QUALITY ★★★	VALUE ★★★
READER-SURVEY RESPONSES ⊕ 83% (Below Average)			

Toy Story Land, Disney's Hollywood Studios; ☎ 407-939-3463

Reservations Strongly recommended. **Dining Plan credits** 1 per person, per meal. **When to go** Anytime. **Cost range** $45 (child $25). **Service** ★★★★½. **Bar** Full service. **Lunch** Daily, 10:45 a.m.–3:55 p.m. **Dinner** Daily, 4–9 p.m.

SETTING AND ATMOSPHERE Like the rest of Toy Story Land, you've been shrunk to toy size, and you're invited to dine in this rodeo setup that Andy made for all of his toys. Servers (some more than others) will refer to you as toys, you'll get to ride toy horses to your table, and more.

HOUSE SPECIALTIES Cheddar biscuits with sweet pepper jelly, salmon (by request only, but for no extra cost).

OTHER RECOMMENDATIONS Almost everything on the menu plays it safe to appeal to as many people as possible.

KIDS' MENU The same as the adults' menu, except kids have their own specialty cupcake dessert option!

SUMMARY AND COMMENTS Meats are of middling quality and cook at best. The Slinky Dooooooooog's Mac & Cheese, with spring-shaped pasta and Goldfish crackers on top, is clever, and the street corn and tots have bolder flavors than anything else on the table. Still, you'll forgive the boring food when the servers yell that Andy is coming and the entire restaurant freezes. Pure we're-all-in-this-together fun.

Sanaa ★★★★

AFRICAN/INDIAN	EXPENSIVE	QUALITY ★★★★	VALUE ★★★★
READER-SURVEY RESPONSES ✪ 96% (Exceptional)			

Animal Kingdom Lodge & Villas–Kidani Village; ☎ 407-939-3463

Reservations Strongly recommended. **Dining Plan credits** 1 per person, per meal. **When to go** Lunch or dinner. **Cost range** Lunch $20–$33 (child $11–$14), dinner $24–$36 (child $11–$14). **Service** ★★★★. **Bar** Full service. **Quick-service breakfast** Daily, 7:30–11 a.m. (reservations not necessary). **Lunch** Daily, 11:30 a.m.–3 p.m. **Dinner** Daily, 5–9:30 p.m.

SETTING AND ATMOSPHERE Sanaa's casual dining room is inspired by African outdoor markets, with baskets, beads, and art on the walls. It's a cozy space, with 9-foot-tall windows that look out on the resort's savanna—giraffes, zebras, and other animals wander right outside as you dine.

HOUSE SPECIALTIES The most famous dish here is the Indian-style bread service (naan, onion kulcha, and paneer paratha) served with an impressive array of sauces.

OTHER RECOMMENDATIONS Butter chicken, the burger (available at lunch only), African triple-chocolate mousse. Sanaa also serves a quick-service breakfast, with hot foods such as eggs, waffles, and bacon, as well as a limited array of grab-and-go cold foods.

KIDS' MENU Fish, butter chicken, cheese pizza, or cheeseburger, all served with two sides. My kids ask to come here mostly because of the Timon Grubs dessert, a creamy treat with gummy worms, graham cracker bugs, and chocolate rocks—the stuff kids' dreams are made of.

SUMMARY AND COMMENTS Sanaa (pronounced sah-NAH) is a favorite of Disney cast members and locals—the flavors are addicting. It's not as upscale as **Jiko,** the resort's fine-dining restaurant (see page 261), offering instead a casual take on African–Indian fusion cuisine.

San Angel Inn Restaurante ★★★

MEXICAN	EXPENSIVE	QUALITY ★★★	VALUE ★★
READER-SURVEY RESPONSES ✪ 88% (Average)			

Mexico, World Showcase, EPCOT; ☎ 407-939-3463

Reservations Strongly recommended. **Dining Plan credits** 1 per person, per meal. **When to go** Lunch or dinner. **Cost range** $18–$54 (child $12–$16). **Service** ★★★. **Bar** Full service. **Hours** Daily, 11:30 a.m.–9 p.m.

SETTING AND ATMOSPHERE Step inside the Mexico Pavilion, navigate the busy marketplace, and end up at San Angel Inn, which overlooks a starry sky and the Gran Fiesta Tour boat ride. Its décor is inspired by the original San Angel Inn in Mexico City and is incredibly atmospheric—it really does feel like you're dining in an outdoor Mexican square.

HOUSE SPECIALTIES For appetizers try the queso fundido (melted cheese with flour tortillas).

OTHER RECOMMENDATIONS Rib eye tacos should please almost anyone. Vegetarians can try the huarache vegetariano—fried corn masa with pinto beans, grilled queso fresco, and salsa verde. Try the sweet corn ice cream for dessert.

KIDS' MENU Tacos, quesadilla, chicken tenders, grilled chicken, or mac and cheese, all with limited side options.

SUMMARY AND COMMENTS The prices are steep (which affects reader ratings), but the menu goes beyond the typical tacos, offering regional dishes that are difficult to find in the States. The dining room is a cool respite from the theme park, but you might need a flashlight to read the menu.

Sci-Fi Dine-In Theater Restaurant ★★

AMERICAN	MODERATE	QUALITY ★★	VALUE ★★
READER-SURVEY RESPONSES ● 84% (Below Average)			

Commissary Lane, Disney's Hollywood Studios; ☎ 407-939-3463

Reservations Strongly recommended. Dining Plan credits 1 per person, per meal. When to go Lunch or dinner. Cost range $19–$30 (child $11–$13). Service ★★★. Bar Full service. Hours Daily, 10:30 a.m.–9 p.m. (until 9:30 p.m. on Friday and Saturday).

SETTING AND ATMOSPHERE Walk through the doors and around a corner into a set that resembles a drive-in from the 1950s, with faux classic cars instead of tables. Hop in, order, and watch campy black-and-white video clips. It's a blast.

HOUSE SPECIALTIES The milkshakes are expensive but worth it. Burgers are also expensive and only mediocre.

KIDS' MENU Burgers, chicken skewer or bites, or mac and cheese, all served with two sides from a small selection.

ENTERTAINMENT AND AMENITIES Clips of cartoons and vintage horror and sci-fi movies, such as *Attack of the 50 Foot Woman, Robot Monster,* and *The Blob.*

SUMMARY AND COMMENTS The kitsch is fun, but the food remains solidly below average. Stick with simple fare like one of the burgers. Or just fill up on an appetizer and dessert.

Sebastian's Bistro ★★½

LATIN/SEAFOOD	EXPENSIVE	QUALITY ★★	VALUE ★★½
READER-SURVEY RESPONSES ● 92% (Above Average)			

Caribbean Beach Resort; ☎ 407-939-3463

Reservations Recommended. Dining Plan credits 1 per person, per meal. When to go Dinner. Cost range $38 (child $20). Service ★★★½. Bar Full service. Hours Daily, 4:30–9:30 p.m.

SETTING AND ATMOSPHERE Sebastian's is remarkably understated for a Disney restaurant. White walls and tables are offset by blue-and-white chairs in two rooms with vaulted ceilings and plenty of windows to let in the sunlight.

HOUSE SPECIALTIES This family-style menu includes pull-apart rolls (warm bread with guava butter and caramelized onion jam), oven-roasted citrus chicken, slow-cooked mojo pork, grilled flank steak, cilantro rice and beans, vegetable curry, seasonal vegetables, and coconut-pineapple bread pudding with caramel sauce and vanilla ice cream. There's also a plant-based menu option.

SUMMARY AND COMMENTS The pull-apart rolls are probably adding 10 points to Sebastian's reader surveys by themselves. But we'd still choose to head over to the Riviera Resort for better restaurants.

Shula's Steak House ★★★

STEAK	EXPENSIVE	QUALITY ★★★★	VALUE ★★

READER-SURVEY RESPONSES ➕ 81% (Below Average)

Dolphin Resort; ☎ 407-934-1362

Reservations Strongly recommended. **Dining Plan credits** Not accepted. **When to go** Dinner. **Cost range** $40–$76 (child $8–$14). **Service** ★★★★. **Parking** Valet or hotel lot, both free with validation. **Bar** Full service. **Dress** Dressy. **Hours** Daily, 5–11 p.m.

SETTING AND ATMOSPHERE Shula's feels more like an old-school men's club than a resort restaurant: dark woods, even darker lighting, framed black-and-white photos of football players, and high prices that might get passed on to expense accounts.

HOUSE SPECIALTIES In a word, meat—really expensive but very high-quality meat. Only certified Angus beef is served: filet mignon, New York strip, cowboy rib eye, and porterhouse (including a 24-ounce cut).

OTHER RECOMMENDATIONS Prime rib, daily market fish.

KIDS' MENU Chicken breast or cheeseburger; mac and cheese and mashed potatoes sold separately (and expensively).

SUMMARY AND COMMENTS We had a fantastic rib eye here in early 2022—one of the best steaks we've had on Disney property in a long time. And then reader ratings dropped by 10 points. We still think it's worth trying.

Space 220 ★★

AMERICAN	EXPENSIVE	QUALITY ★★½	VALUE ★½

READER-SURVEY RESPONSES ➕ 81% (Below Average)

World Discovery, EPCOT; ☎ 407-939-3463

Reservations Strongly recommended. **Dining Plan credits** Not yet available. **When to go** Lunch or dinner. **Cost range** Lunch $55 (child $29), dinner $79 (child $35). **Service** ★★★. **Bar** Full service. **Wine selection** Fair. **Lunch** Daily, 11:30 a.m.–3:30 p.m. **Dinner** Daily, 4–9 p.m.

SETTING AND ATMOSPHERE The idea here is that you're transported from EPCOT to a space station orbit, where you dine in front of large windows (computer screens) that show the earth, moon, and stars, and various passersby, while you dine. Your journey includes a ride on a "space elevator" up to and back from the space station. Otherwise, it's a fairly generic, dark semicircle.

HOUSE SPECIALTIES The house's specialty is disappointment. Used liberally. In everything.

SUMMARY AND COMMENTS A hassle to get into, overpriced for what you get, and in need of new ideas. There's no possible way that a four-person dinner here is worth $320 before tax and tip. This place will only last as long as there are people interested in its theme.

Spice Road Table ★★★★

MOROCCAN	INEXPENSIVE	QUALITY ★★★★	VALUE ★★★

READER-SURVEY RESPONSES ➕ 90% (Above Average)

Morocco, World Showcase, EPCOT; ☎ 407-939-3463

Reservations Recommended. **Dining Plan credits** 1 per person, per meal. **When to go** During nightly fireworks. **Cost range** Small plates $9–$15. **Service** ★★★★. **Bar** Full service. **Lunch** Daily, 11:30–3:30 p.m. **Dinner** Daily, 3:45–9 p.m.

SETTING AND ATMOSPHERE Spice Road Table is situated directly along World Showcase Lagoon at the front of the Morocco Pavilion, making it perfect for watching fireworks. The covered patio features excellent dining in open air when Florida weather cooperates, with colorful pops of modern Moroccan décor inside too.

HOUSE SPECIALTIES Perfectly fried calamari and hummus fries stand out as favorites on the small-plates side of the menu.

OTHER RECOMMENDATIONS Lamb kefta with tzatziki offers a bit of punch and spice. Spiced shrimp and chicken may sound simple, but the accompanying sauces and sides elevate the otherwise pedestrian dish.

KIDS' MENU None.

SUMMARY AND COMMENTS Food quality and service are both good. The appetizers and desserts pair excellently with the extensive wine and cocktail lists. The service is attentive, and the casual atmosphere is relaxing.

Splitsville Dining Room ★★½

AMERICAN	MODERATE	QUALITY ★★½	VALUE ★★
READER-SURVEY RESPONSES ➕ 88% (Average)			

West Side, Disney Springs; ☎ 407-938-7467

Reservations Strongly recommended. **Dining Plan credits** 1 per person, per meal. **When to Go** Lunch or dinner. **Cost range** $14–$42 (child $10). **Service** ★★½. **Parking** Orange garage. **Bar** Full service. **Hours** Monday–Thursday, 11 a.m.–10 p.m.; Friday-Sunday, 10:30 a.m.–11 p.m.

SETTING AND ATMOSPHERE Part of a chain of combination restaurants and bowling alleys, Splitsville is loud, as you might expect, but there's plenty to see and room for rambunctious kids to roam while you wait for your food. Décor is vaguely midcentury modern, with Sputnik lamps and other space-age touches.

HOUSE SPECIALTIES The sushi—salmon, shrimp, tuna, crab, and various combinations thereof—is the best thing on the menu.

KIDS' MENU Burgers, chicken tenders, cheese pizza, hot dog, mac and cheese, or grilled cheese, most served with either applesauce, fries, or carrots.

SUMMARY AND COMMENTS The menu is more spread out than a 7/10 split: burgers, pizza, seafood, Asian, and Mexican are represented, along with assorted bar food. Readers seem to enjoy it, but the only thing we'd order again is the sushi.

Steakhouse 71 ★★★★

STEAK	EXPENSIVE	QUALITY ★★★★	VALUE ★★★½
READER-SURVEY RESPONSES ➕ 93% (Much Above Average)			

Contemporary Resort; ☎ 407-939-3463

Reservations Recommended. **Dining Plan credits** Not available. **When to go** Anytime. **Cost range** Breakfast $13–$21 (child $11), lunch $16–$26 (child $13–$15), dinner $26–$39 (child $13–$15). **Service** ★★★★. **Bar** Full service. **Breakfast** Daily, 7:30–11 a.m. **Lunch** Daily, 11:30 a.m.–2 p.m. **Dinner** Daily, 5–9 p.m.

SETTING AND ATMOSPHERE A midcentury modern vibe with bold colors and sleek design.

HOUSE SPECIALTIES For appetizers, the Fork & Knife Caesar Salad or the chef's "Bacon & Eggs"—maple-lacquered pork belly with smoky cheese grits and a poached egg. For mains, pick a cut of meat that sounds appealing. Plant-forward folks should absolutely try Chef Nik's vegan take on Beef Wellington, which may be the best thing on the menu.

KIDS' MENU Grilled steak, chicken breast, baked fish, or cheeseburger, all served with two sides from a decent selection.

SUMMARY AND COMMENTS Steakhouse 71 is designed to appeal to everyone, so it isn't very adventurous, but it is reliably good.

STK Orlando ★★★

STEAK	EXPENSIVE	QUALITY ★★★★	VALUE ★★½
READER-SURVEY RESPONSES ⊕ 73% (Do Not Visit)			

The Landing, Disney Springs; ☎ 407-917-7440

Reservations Strongly recommended. **Dining Plan credits** 2 per person, per meal. **When to go** Weekend brunch and dinner. **Cost range** Brunch $10–$160, lunch $10–$112, dinner $44–$160 **Parking** Orange garage. **Service** ★★★. **Bar** Full service. **Brunch** Saturday–Sunday, 11 a.m.–3 p.m. **Lunch** Monday–Friday, 11 a.m.–3 p.m. **Dinner** Daily, 4–10 p.m. (until 11 p.m. on Friday and Saturday).

SETTING AND ATMOSPHERE The turreted brick exterior couldn't be more different from the inside. The lower level houses a bar and seating area with a Las Vegas–ultralounge feel, complete with DJ and *lots* of noise. The quieter, less-glitzy upstairs has both indoor and outdoor seating.

HOUSE SPECIALTIES Steaks, ranging from a $49 filet mignon to a $122, 28-ounce dry-aged porterhouse. Sides include macaroni and cheese, sweet corn pudding, and Parmesan-truffle fries; all cost extra.

KIDS' MENU None.

SUMMARY AND COMMENTS Since it opened, STK has been rated as one of the worst dining experiences in Disney World. The steaks are good but overpriced, and the restaurant is too loud. Instead, we recommend **The Boathouse** (see page 248), **Chef Art Smith's Homecomin'** (see page 251), **Jaleo by José Andrés,** (see page 260), **Wine Bar George** (see page 284), or **Morimoto Asia** (see page 265), all in Disney Springs.

Story Book Dining at Artist Point with Snow White ★★★½

AMERICAN	EXPENSIVE	QUALITY ★★★★	VALUE ★★★½
READER SURVEY RESPONSES ⊕ 85% (Below Average)			

Wilderness Lodge, Boulder Ridge Villas, and Copper Creek Villas & Cabins; ☎ 407-939-3463

Reservations Recommended. **Dining Plan credits** 1 per person, per meal. **When to go** Dinner. **Cost range** $65 (child $39). **Service** ★★★½. **Bar** Full service. **Character dinner** Daily, 4–9:15 p.m.

SETTING AND ATMOSPHERE When Artist Point transformed from quiet Signature dining to loud character meals, the only décor change was the addition of many "enchanted" branches and leaves to the existing rustic décor. The branches sometimes dance and will twinkle after dark.

HOUSE SPECIALTIES The mushroom bisque appetizer is a holdover from the "old" Artist Point and is glorious. Entrées include prime rib, pork shank, roast chicken, a fish dish, and a vegetarian option. The pork shank is one of the best pork dishes I've ever eaten.

KIDS' MENU Grilled chicken or fish, or prime rib, all served with two sides from a decent selection.

ENTERTAINMENT AND AMENITIES The Evil Queen presides in the center of the restaurant with a decidedly chilly demeanor. Snow White, Grumpy, and Dopey frolic through the dining room, interacting with guests.

SUMMARY AND COMMENTS While the experience is loud and the character interactions short, the food here is some of the best you'll find at any character meal on-property.

Takumi-Tei ★★★★½

JAPANESE	EXPENSIVE	QUALITY ★★★★★	VALUE ★★★½
READER-SURVEY RESPONSES ➕ 79% (Much Below Average)			

Japan, World Showcase, EPCOT; ☎ 407-939-3463

Reservations Strongly recommended. **Dining Plan credits** Not offered. **When to go** Dinner. **Cost range** $150 or $250 (child $100). **Service** ★★★★★. **Bar** Full service. **Hours** Thursday–Monday, 4:30–7:30 p.m.

SETTING AND ATMOSPHERE In keeping with the restaurant's name, which means "house of the artisan," the décor celebrates five natural elements revered by Japanese craftsmen: water, wood, earth, stone, and washi (paper). The private dining room, home to traditional kaiseki dining, features a custom waterfall that looks like it's flowing straight into the dining table.

HOUSE SPECIALTIES The fixed-price menu rotates seasonally to reflect the freshest and most seasonal produce at the chef's disposal. A-5 Wagyu beef—the most prized in the world—anchors the main-course menu and makes for a meal unlike any other.

OTHER RECOMMENDATIONS Sashimi and nigiri with the freshest fish you'll ever taste; specialty desserts tailor-made for Instagramming.

KIDS' MENU Multicourse menu including soba, sushi, entrées, and appetizers plus dessert.

SUMMARY AND COMMENTS Filtering classical Japanese cookery through an upscale modern lens, Takumi-Tei treats diners to an indulgent retreat from the hustle and bustle of the theme park. Many readers confuse this with **Teppan Edo**—don't do that. If you're comfortable spending $135–$175 per person on a good omakase sushi meal, you'll love Takumi-Tei.

Teppan Edo ★★★½

JAPANESE	EXPENSIVE	QUALITY ★★★★	VALUE ★★★
READER-SURVEY RESPONSES ➕ 92% (Above Average)			

Japan, World Showcase, EPCOT; ☎ 407-939-3463

Reservations Strongly recommended. **Dining Plan credits** 1 per person, per meal. **When to go** Lunch or dinner. **Cost range** $17–$48 (child $18–$26). **Service** ★★★★★. **Bar** Full service. **Hours** Daily, noon–9 p.m.

SETTING AND ATMOSPHERE Six Japanese dining rooms with grills on tables and entertaining chefs chopping, slicing, and dicing.

HOUSE SPECIALTIES Chicken, shrimp, beef, scallops, and Asian vegetables stir-fried on a teppanyaki grill by a knife-juggling chef.

KIDS' MENU Steak, shrimp, salmon, chicken breast, or vegetables, all served with udon noodles, salad, and seasonal vegetables.

ENTERTAINMENT AND AMENITIES Watching the teppanyaki chefs.

SUMMARY AND COMMENTS A popular dining option for families, Teppan Edo has been one of the highest-rated restaurants in EPCOT for three years. The food quality is comparable to what you'd get at your hometown hibachi place. You'll get plenty to eat, plus entertainment. What's not to like?

Terralina Crafted Italian ★★½

ITALIAN	EXPENSIVE	QUALITY ★★½	VALUE ★★½
READER-SURVEY RESPONSES ➕ 74% (Do Not Visit)			

The Landing, Disney Springs; ☎ 407-934-8888

Reservations Recommended. **Dining Plan credits** 1 per person, per meal. **When to go** Lunch or dinner. **Cost range** Lunch and dinner $17–$46 (child $8–$13), brunch $16–$24.

Service ★★½. **Parking** Lime garage. **Bar** Full service. **Lunch and dinner** Daily, noon–11 p.m. **Brunch** Saturday–Sunday, 11:30–3 p.m.

SETTING AND ATMOSPHERE "Italian Lake District" is the theme, with stonework, exposed wood beams, and warm colors. The waiting area has a fireplace and leather chairs.

HOUSE SPECIALTIES Mozzarella-stuffed rice ball appetizer, gnocchi with pork ragù and shaved Parmesan, eggplant Parmesan, tiramisu.

KIDS' MENU With 10 entrées to choose from, kids have lots of options!

SUMMARY AND COMMENTS If you're in the mood for really good Italian, you won't find it here.

Three Bridges Bar & Grill at Villa del Lago   ★★★

AMERICAN/SPANISH	EXPENSIVE	QUALITY ★★★	VALUE ★★½
READER-SURVEY RESPONSES ➕ 89% (Average)			

Coronado Springs Resort; ☎ 407-939-3463

Reservations Not available. **Dining Plan credits** 1 per person, per meal. **When to go** Dinner. **Cost range** $18–$26 (child $10–$12). **Service** ★★★★. **Bar** Full service. **Hours** Daily, 4:30 p.m.–midnight.

SETTING AND ATMOSPHERE This bar and grill floats in the middle of picturesque Lago Dorado, reflecting sunsets nightly at the intersection of Coronado Spring's three commuter bridges and offering grand views of the complex's Gran Destino Tower. Three Bridges is a happening spot even in the late afternoon.

HOUSE SPECIALTIES Cheese dip with chorizo, a fantastic house burger, fresh tacos (with made-from-scratch tortillas). Portions aren't hefty, but they are enough to satisfy anyone looking to split a few snacks or grab a light meal. Specialty cocktails complement a hearty wine-and-beer selection.

OTHER RECOMMENDATIONS Filling salads and poke bowls are good main-dish choices.

KIDS' MENU Burger, grilled chicken, shrimp, chicken quesadilla, or Impossible tacos, all served with two sides from a small selection.

SUMMARY AND COMMENTS Taking waterside dining to the next level, Three Bridges unites traditional bar fare with Spanish flair. Dishes are well executed, and drinks are delightful at this beautiful island retreat.

Tiffins Restaurant   ★★★½

AMERICAN/PAN-ASIAN	EXPENSIVE	QUALITY ★★★½	VALUE ★★½
READER-SURVEY RESPONSES ➕ 91% (Above Average)			

Discovery Island, Animal Kingdom; ☎ 407-939-3463

Reservations Strongly recommended. **Dining Plan credits** 2 per person, per meal. **When to go** Lunch or dinner. **Cost range** $34–$68 (child $14–$19). **Service** ★★★★. **Bar** Full service. **Hours** Daily, 11:30 a.m.–7 p.m.

SETTING AND ATMOSPHERE Tiffins is found on a walking path to the land of Pandora. Inside are three relatively small, quiet dining rooms. The décor is said to be inspired by the travel adventures of the Imagineers who built Animal Kingdom. You'll see artifacts from Asia and Africa lining the walls of one room, and giant butterflies in another. The main dining room's centerpiece is carved-wood sculptures.

HOUSE SPECIALTIES Charred octopus and honey-glazed pork belly appetizers. For entrées, try the tamarind-braised short rib or the butter chicken.

OTHER RECOMMENDATIONS Skip the bread service and desserts.

KIDS' MENU Grilled steak, teriyaki chicken thigh, grilled shrimp, or Impossible "chow," each served with two sides from a small selection. Overpriced for the portions.

SUMMARY AND COMMENTS Despite the above-average reader ratings, we think the food here is overpriced and not as good as it used to be. The **Nomad Lounge** next door is undoubtedly the better option.

Todd English's Bluezoo ★★

SEAFOOD	EXPENSIVE	QUALITY ★★	VALUE ★★
READER-SURVEY RESPONSES ● 68% (Do Not Visit)			

Dolphin Resort; ☎ 407-934-1609

Reservations Recommended. **Dining Plan credits** Not accepted. **When to go** Dinner. **Cost range** $31–$95 (child $10–$12). **Service** ★★★. **Parking** Valet or hotel lot, both free with validation. **Bar** Full service. **Dress** Dressy casual. **Hours** Daily, 5–11 p.m.

SETTING AND ATMOSPHERE The name is courtesy of celebrity chef Todd English's son, who as a youngster saw an under-the-sea movie and said it looked like a "blue zoo." There is an open kitchen and a circular rotisserie that makes the fish being grilled on it seem to dance on the coals.

HOUSE SPECIALTIES Nightly fish selection (from the rotisserie), Angus filet.

OTHER RECOMMENDATIONS New England–style clam chowder with salt-cured bacon, teppan-seared jumbo sea scallops.

KIDS' MENU Burger, cheese pizza, grilled chicken, fish-and-chips, or pasta, all served with predetermined sides.

SUMMARY AND COMMENTS You could fashion a good meal from just the appetizers and desserts, which are above average.

Toledo—Tapas, Steak & Seafood ★★★

SPANISH	EXPENSIVE	QUALITY ★★★	VALUE ★★½
READER-SURVEY RESPONSES ● 85% (Below Average)			

Gran Destino Tower, Coronado Springs Resort; ☎ 407-939-3463

Reservations Recommended. **Dining Plan credits** 1 per person, per meal. **When to go** Dinner. **Cost range** $30–$38 (child $13–$16). **Service** ★★★★. **Bar** Full service. **Hours** Wednesday–Sunday, 5–10 p.m.

SETTING AND ATMOSPHERE High atop Gran Destino Tower, Toledo envelops diners in a Cubist cloud heaven, complete with color-changing ceiling and trees reaching to the sky right beside several tables. A showcase bar anchors one side of the restaurant, while an open tapas kitchen greets guests at the far end of the dining room. The real attraction, though, is the massive wall of windows, offering views of some of Walt Disney World's most popular attractions and nighttime spectaculars.

HOUSE SPECIALTIES None. Everything is unreliable—it can be great, and it can be terrible.

OTHER RECOMMENDATIONS Stick to the less expensive small plates and save your money for somewhere else. The blistered shishito peppers are more than enough to share.

KIDS' MENU Fish, shrimp, grilled steak or chicken breast, or meatballs, all served with two sides from a rather large selection.

SUMMARY AND COMMENTS **Jaleo by José Andrés** (see page 260) has better food for less money. Toledo caters to resort guests and conventioneers stuck at the resort. We're baffled that it made it into the *Michelin Guide*.

Tony's Town Square Restaurant ★★

ITALIAN	MODERATE-EXPENSIVE	QUALITY ★★	VALUE ★★
READER-SURVEY RESPONSES ✪ 80% (Much Below Average)			

Main Street, U.S.A., Magic Kingdom; ☎ 407-939-3463

Reservations Strongly recommended. **Dining Plan credits** 1 per person, per meal. **When to go** Late lunch or early dinner. **Cost range** $24–$33 (child $11–$12). **Service** ★★★. **Bar** Limited selection of beer and wine. **Hours** Daily, 11:30 a.m.–9 p.m.

SETTING AND ATMOSPHERE Just inside the Magic Kingdom on Main Street, with a glass-windowed porch that's wonderful for watching the action outside, Tony's Town Square doesn't have great food, but it's a rite of passage for Disney fans—one *must* have a plate of spaghetti in the restaurant that commemorates *Lady and the Tramp*.

HOUSE SPECIALTIES Spaghetti with meatballs (or Impossible meatballs), shrimp fettuccine Alfredo, chicken parmigiana, butcher's steak.

KIDS' MENU Spaghetti with turkey meatball, grilled chicken, or mac and cheese, all served with two sides from a kid-friendly selection.

SUMMARY AND COMMENTS Though it's consistently rated as one of the worst restaurants in the Magic Kingdom, Tony's does a decent job with simple pasta (multigrain and gluten-free options available). And ratings have been trending up, so maybe Tony's is onto something!

Topolino's Terrace—Flavors of the Riviera ★★★½

FRENCH/ITALIAN	EXPENSIVE	QUALITY ★★★★	VALUE ★★★
READER-SURVEY RESPONSES ✪ 94% (Much Above Average)			

Riviera Resort; ☎ 407-939-3463

Reservations Strongly recommended. **Dining Plan credits** 2 per person, per meal. **When to go** Breakfast or dinner. **Cost range** Breakfast $49 (child $30); dinner $37–$59 (child $11–$18). **Service** ★★★★★. **Bar** Full service. **Character breakfast** Daily, 7:30 a.m.–12:15 p.m. **Dinner** Daily, 5–9:30 p.m.

SETTING AND ATMOSPHERE This rooftop restaurant at the Riviera has a fantastic view of EPCOT and Disney's Hollywood Studios, especially at night when those parks run their fireworks spectaculars. Inside you'll find burgundy-and-cream carpets and dark wood tables and accents. In keeping with Disney's recent decorative trends, there's absolutely nothing here that's overtly tied to the Riviera.

HOUSE SPECIALTIES *Breakfast:* Sour cream waffle with roasted apples and orange-maple syrup; smoked salmon bagel. *Dinner:* French veal chop with potatoes; roasted eggplant with romesco sauce.

OTHER RECOMMENDATIONS Lobster linguini; rigatoni pasta with chicken, Broccolini, and wild mushrooms.

KIDS' MENU *Breakfast:* Waffle dippers, scrambled egg, or fruit and yogurt, all with sides. *Dinner:* Grilled steak or chicken or rigatoni, all served with two sides from a limited selection.

SUMMARY AND COMMENTS One of the most difficult reservations to get in Walt Disney World. There are seemingly no bad choices on this menu, and the service team is excellent. Breakfast features a parade of Disney characters including Mickey, Minnie, Donald, and Daisy. Breakfast has become a worse value, with no multi-entrée ordering and a significantly higher price than a year ago.

Trattoria al Forno ★★★

ITALIAN	MODERATE	QUALITY ★★★½	VALUE ★★
READER-SURVEY RESPONSES ✪ 89% (Average)			

BoardWalk; ☎407-939-3463

Reservations Strongly recommended. **Dining Plan credits** 1 per person, per meal. **When to go** Breakfast or dinner. **Cost range** Breakfast $13–$21 (child $7–$10), dinner $20–$39 (child $13–$16). **Service** ★★★★. **Bar** Full service, with all Italian wines. **Breakfast** Daily, 7:30–11:30 a.m. **Dinner** Daily, 5–10 p.m.

SETTING AND ATMOSPHERE The space contains three dining areas, a private room, and an open kitchen for watching the action. Our favorite spots are the informal dining room, right in front of the kitchen, or at a booth at the back.

HOUSE SPECIALTIES *Breakfast:* Poached egg over polenta with fennel sausage; pancakes; steak and eggs; breakfast pizza (scrambled eggs, bacon, ham, sausage, bell peppers, and cheese). *Dinner:* Rigatoni Bolognese, chicken parmigiana, tiramisu.

KIDS' MENU Breakfast and dinner both feature five entrée options and a bunch of sides that should be manageable for all eaters.

SUMMARY AND COMMENTS The kitchen makes mozzarella and fresh pasta daily. The wines represent Italy's major regions, with more than 30 available by the glass or quartino. The breakfast is one of the best on Disney property, even without the characters that used to appear here.

T-Rex ★★

AMERICAN	EXPENSIVE	QUALITY ★★	VALUE ★★
READER-SURVEY RESPONSES ➕ 78% (Much Below Average)			

Marketplace, Disney Springs; ☎ 407-828-8739

Reservations Strongly recommended. **Dining Plan credits** 1 per person, per meal. **When to go** Lunch or dinner. **Cost range** $20–$44 (child $11). **Service** ★★1/2. **Parking** Orange garage. **Bar** Full service. **Hours** Daily, 11 a.m.–11:05 p.m.

SETTING AND ATMOSPHERE Sensory overload in a cavernous dining room with life-size robotic dinosaurs, giant fish tanks, bubbling geysers, waterfalls, fossils in the bathrooms, and crystals in the walls. It's unbelievably loud.

HOUSE SPECIALTY Megasaurus Burger.

KIDS' MENU Extensive.

SUMMARY AND COMMENTS Expect a wait unless there's an empty seat at the bar. Nobody's here just for the ordinary, overpriced food—it's nonstop "eatertainment," with kid-friendly food served in huge portions.

The Turf Club Bar and Grill ★★

AMERICAN	EXPENSIVE	QUALITY ★★½	VALUE ★★
READER-SURVEY RESPONSES ➕ 67% (Do Not Visit)			

Saratoga Springs Resort & Spa; ☎ 407-939-3463

Reservations Accepted. **Dining Plan credits** 1 per person, per meal. **When to go** Dinner. **Cost range** $22–$38 (child $11–$13). **Service** ★★★. **Bar** Full service. **Hours** Wednesday–Sunday, 4:30–9 p.m.

SETTING AND ATMOSPHERE When the weather is nice, ask for an outdoor table; you can spot golfers on the adjacent Lake Buena Vista Golf Course and look across the way to Disney Springs. The dining room is equestrian themed.

HOUSE SPECIALTY Slow-roasted 10-ounce prime rib.

OTHER RECOMMENDATIONS Pan-seared salmon.

KIDS' MENU Chicken, prime rib, salmon, cheeseburger, or pasta with marinara, all served with two sides from a small selection.

SUMMARY AND COMMENTS Rarely crowded, but you'll find much better food at Disney Springs.

Tusker House Restaurant ★★★

AFRICAN/AMERICAN	EXPENSIVE	QUALITY ★★★	VALUE ★★★
READER-SURVEY RESPONSES ✪ 89% (Average)			

Africa, Animal Kingdom; ☎ 407-939-3463

Reservations Required. **Dining Plan credits** 1 per person, per meal. **When to go** Anytime. **Cost range** Breakfast $47 (child $30), lunch and dinner $62 (child $40). **Service** ★★★. **Bar** Full-service bar next door. **Character breakfast** Daily, 8–10:30 a.m. **Character lunch** Daily, 11 a.m.–3:30 p.m. **Character dinner** Daily, 3:35–7 p.m.

SETTING AND ATMOSPHERE Character meals feature Mickey, Donald, Daisy, and Goofy. The setting—inside the Harambe Village square—is pretty plain, especially after dark. The food, however, is surprisingly good, with spices and taste combinations you won't find at other character-dining spots.

HOUSE SPECIALTIES Roast pork, beef, and chicken.

SUMMARY AND COMMENTS Tusker House appeals not just to kids but also to grown-ups who appreciate more interesting dishes.

Tutto Italia Ristorante ★★★

ITALIAN	EXPENSIVE	QUALITY ★★★★	VALUE ★★
READER-SURVEY RESPONSES ✪ 86% (Average)			

Italy, World Showcase, EPCOT; ☎ 407-939-3463

Reservations Strongly recommended. **Dining Plan credits** 1 per person, per meal. **When to go** Midafternoon. **Cost range** $26–$48 (child $11). **Service** ★★★. **Bar** Beer and wine only, with all Italian wines. **Hours** Daily, 12:30–9 p.m.

SETTING AND ATMOSPHERE Tutto Italia feels like a big restaurant in Rome or Milan, with murals of a piazza along the wall behind upholstered banquettes. It can get noisy—if the weather is nice, request an outside table.

HOUSE SPECIALTIES It's hard to identify anything as being done particularly well.

OTHER RECOMMENDATIONS Stick to the least-expensive menu items.

KIDS' MENU Spaghetti, chicken tenders, mozzarella sticks, or pizza.

SUMMARY AND COMMENTS This *should* be one of the best Italian restaurants in Orlando, but it's not. Everything that happens inside Tutto Italia—from the cooking to the service—feels like it's done on autopilot. The food quality can't support the prices: $34 for chicken parm is nearly double what you'd pay in many neighborhood Italian joints. Everything here should be done better.

Via Napoli Ristorante e Pizzeria ★★★½

ITALIAN	EXPENSIVE	QUALITY ★★★½	VALUE ★★★
READER-SURVEY RESPONSES ✪ 93% (Much Above Average)			

Italy, World Showcase, EPCOT; ☎ 407-939-3463

Reservations Strongly recommended. **Dining Plan credits** 1 per person, per meal. **When to go** Lunch or dinner. **Cost range** Entrées $27–$49, individual pizzas $21–$26, pizzas (serves 2–5) $36–$60. **Service** ★★★. **Bar** Beer and wine only. **Hours** Daily, 11:30 a.m.–9 p.m.

SETTING AND ATMOSPHERE Three big pizza ovens, named after the three active Italian volcanoes—Etna, Vesuvio, and Stromboli—are the stars of the show in this loud, cavernous dining room.

HOUSE SPECIALTIES Some of the best pizza in Walt Disney World. Our favorites are the Carciofi (artichokes, fontina, and truffle oil) and Quattro Formaggi (four cheese).

KIDS' MENU Margherita pizza, chicken tenders, or spaghetti with meatball.

SUMMARY AND COMMENTS The main dining room is loud . . . but so is an Italian family.

Victoria & Albert's ★★★★★

GOURMET	EXPENSIVE	QUALITY ★★★★★	VALUE ★★★★
READER-SURVEY RESPONSES ➕ 87% (Average)			

Grand Floridian Resort & Spa; ☎ 407-939-3463

Reservations Required; call at least 60 days in advance to reserve; you must confirm special dietary needs by noon the day of your seating. A $100 no-show fee applies if you fail to cancel at least 5 days before your meal; if you cancel less than 24 hours before, you'll be charged the full price. **Dining Plan credits** Not accepted. **When to go** Dinner. **Cost range** Main dining room $295, Queen Victoria's Room $375, Chef's Table $425 (all menus fixed price; tax and gratuities extra). Optional wine pairings start at $155, zero-proof beverage pairings start at $115. **Service ★★★★★**. **Parking** Valet (free). **Wine selection** 700 on the menu, 4,200 more in the cellar. **Dress** Jacket required for men, evening wear for women. **Hours** Open Tuesday–Saturday. Main dining room: 5:30–8:05 p.m. Queen Victoria's Room: 5:30–7 p.m. Chef's Table: 1 seating at 5:30 p.m. (Seating times may vary.) *Note:* No children under age 10 admitted except at Chef's Table.

SETTING AND ATMOSPHERE With just 14 tables in the main dining room, Queen Victoria's Room with seating for up to eight, and the eight-seat Chef's Table, this is the top dining experience at Walt Disney World. A consecutive winner of AAA's Five Diamond Award since 2000—the only restaurant in Central Florida so honored—Victoria & Albert's is lavish and expensive, with Frette linens, Riedel crystal, Christofle silver, and a harp playing live music every night.

HOUSE SPECIALTIES Chef Matthew Sower's menu changes daily, but has included Minnesota elk tenderloin, Alaskan salmon, local free-range chicken, Florida sturgeon caviar, and Australian Kobe-style beef. Pastry chef Alessandra Roger's desserts are divine.

SUMMARY AND COMMENTS Sower and his team prepare modern American cuisine with the best of the best from around the world. The main dining room and Queen Victoria's Room are whisper-quiet, but the Chef's Table is convivial and relaxed.

V&A reopened in the fall of 2022 with a single, fixed-price menu and its usual excellent food and service. V&A made the *Michelin Guide* for the first time in 2023 and earned its first Michelin star in 2024. Low reader reviews almost all mention the high price.

Whispering Canyon Cafe ★★★

AMERICAN	EXPENSIVE	QUALITY ★★½	VALUE ★★★½
READER-SURVEY RESPONSES ➕ 90% (Above Average)			

Wilderness Lodge, Boulder Ridge Villas, and Copper Creek Villas & Cabins; ☎ 407-939-3463

Reservations Strongly recommended. **Dining Plan credits** 1 per person, per meal. **When to go** Anytime. **Cost range** Breakfast and lunch $11–$26 (child $6–$14), dinner $24–$40 (child $10–$17). **Service ★★★★**. **Bar** Full service. **Breakfast** Daily, 7:30–11:25 a.m. **Lunch** Daily, 11:30 a.m.–2 p.m. **Dinner** Daily, 5–10 p.m.

SETTING AND ATMOSPHERE A big, open dining room just off the lobby of Wilderness Lodge, with whimsical Wild West décor.

HOUSE SPECIALTIES For breakfast, the all-you-can-eat skillet offers bacon, sausage, scrambled eggs, waffles, and buttermilk biscuits and gravy. For lunch and dinner, a big skillet loaded with barbecue pulled pork or ribs, roasted chicken, mashed potatoes, green beans, and corn is a crowd-pleaser. Three other skillet options are also available at dinner.

KIDS' MENU One egg, Mickey waffles, oatmeal, cheeseburger, chicken tenders, grilled chicken, or mac and cheese, all served with two sides from a large selection.

SUMMARY AND COMMENTS The all-you-can-eat skillets give hungry folks their money's worth. Make sure you ask for ketchup!

Wine Bar George   ★★★★

WINE/SMALL PLATES	MODERATE-EXPENSIVE	QUALITY ★★★★	VALUE ★★★½
READER-SURVEY RESPONSES ➊ 90% (Above Average)			

The Landing, Disney Springs; ☎ 407-490-1800

Reservations Accepted. **Dining Plan credits** 1 per person, per meal. **When to go** Anytime. **Cost range** Brunch $17–$25, lunch $17–$23, dinner $38–$52 (child $10). Small plates $8–$18. **Parking** Lime garage. **Service** ★★★★½. **Bar** Full service. **Wine selection** Wide-ranging—more than 140 wines in all—with a focus on affordability. **Brunch** Saturday–Sunday, 10:30 a.m.–2 p.m. **Lunch** Monday–Friday, 11:30 a.m.–2:55 p.m. **Dinner** Daily, 3–11 p.m. (until 11:30 p.m. on Friday and Saturday).

SETTING AND ATMOSPHERE Décor is spare and industrial: exposed air vents, concrete floors, brick walls, and lots of windows. The focus of the ground floor is the central bar, with an elevated wine rack and seating for around 18 people; a dozen 6-person high-tops and four 4-person tables are also available. It's noisy here even before you add alcohol, but the second floor is much quieter, and it has outdoor as well as indoor seating.

HOUSE SPECIALTIES Tapas-style small bites made for sharing—we like the saganaki (cheese set on fire!). Entrées are limited—try the family-style skirt steak with roasted potatoes and seasonal vegetables.

OTHER RECOMMENDATIONS Many of the wines are available by the ounce, the glass, and the bottle, letting you create your own inexpensive wine-flight theme.

KIDS' MENU Chicken tenders, mac and cheese, meatballs, or hot dog, all served with applesauce and fresh fruit.

SUMMARY AND COMMENTS Owner and namesake George Miliotes is one of just 274 Master Sommeliers in the world. Miliotes is also committed to making great wines affordable: The wines we price-checked are offered at a much more reasonable markup than at other Disney restaurants.

   The Basket, a counter-service window beneath the second-story terrace, serves European-style sandwiches, cheese, olives, hummus, charcuterie, cookies, and wines on tap—served to-go by the glass or carafe.

Wolfgang Puck Bar & Grill   ★★★

AMERICAN	MODERATE-EXPENSIVE	QUALITY ★★★	VALUE ★★★
READER-SURVEY RESPONSES ➊ 96% (Exceptional)			

Town Center, Disney Springs; ☎ 407-939-3463

Reservations Recommended. **Dining Plan credits** 1 per person, per meal. **When to go** Anytime. **Cost range** Brunch $19–$42, lunch and dinner $18–$65 (child $6–$14). **Parking** Orange garage. **Service** ★★★. **Bar** Full service. **Brunch** Saturday–Sunday, 10 a.m.–3 p.m. **Lunch** Monday–Friday, 11 a.m.–4 p.m. **Dinner** Monday–Friday, 4:05–10 p.m. (until 11 p.m. on Friday); Saturday–Sunday, 3:05–11 p.m.

SETTING AND ATMOSPHERE The décor melds the sleek style of the surrounding garage and over-the-top retail locations with the Florida waterfront look of the rest of Town Center. As you enter, an open kitchen draws the eye, while exposed wood beams and a copper-accented pizza oven bring warmth to the restaurant's 250-seat interior, with an indoor bar offset from the main dining room. A slight outdoor seating area abuts one side of the restaurant's exterior, with the other side dedicated to a grab-and-go dessert and gelato window.

HOUSE SPECIALTIES The pizza is recommended. For dinner, the chicken Wiener schnitzel and roasted half chicken are both good.

OTHER RECOMMENDATIONS Nothing here is bad, but the meats are better than the pastas.

KIDS' MENU Chicken strips, grilled chicken, spaghetti, cheeseburger, or pizza, all served with predetermined sides.

SUMMARY AND COMMENTS Not the flashiest restaurant, but it has good food at decent prices (for Disney). It's also often easier to get into than other places in Disney Springs.

Yachtsman Steakhouse   ★★½

STEAK	EXPENSIVE	QUALITY ★★★½	VALUE ★★
READER-SURVEY RESPONSES ➕ 90% (Above Average)			

Yacht Club Resort; ☎ 407-939-3463

Reservations Strongly recommended. **Dining Plan credits** 2 per person, per meal. **When to go** Dinner. **Cost range** $38–$65 (child $12–$17). **Service** ★★★½. **Bar** Full service. **Dress** Dressy casual. **Hours** Daily, 5–9:30 p.m.

SETTING AND ATMOSPHERE Wooden beams, white linens, and a view of the Yacht Club's sandy lagoon make Yachtsman feel light and airy rather than dark and masculine like the typical steakhouse. Beef is the star, of course, but there are other options on the menu.

HOUSE SPECIALTIES Bread service with roasted sweet garlic.

KIDS' MENU Grilled chicken, steak, baked fish, or pasta with marinara, all served with two sides from a decent selection.

SUMMARY AND COMMENTS We're consistently disappointed by Yachtsman. The kitchen struggles with the basics of flavor and temperature, and the prices are simply too high for the quality of the food being served. Try **Shula's Steak House** (see page 274) over at the Dolphin instead.

Yak & Yeti Restaurant   ★★★

PAN-ASIAN	EXPENSIVE	QUALITY ★★★	VALUE ★★
READER-SURVEY RESPONSES ➕ 94% (Much Above Average)			

Asia, Animal Kingdom; ☎ 407-939-3463

Reservations Strongly recommended. **Dining Plan credits** 1 per person, per meal. **When to go** Dinner. **Cost range** $21–$38 (child $11). **Service** ★★★½. **Bar** Full service. **Hours** Daily, 10:30 a.m.–6:50 p.m.

SETTING AND ATMOSPHERE A rustic two-story Nepalese inn—with seating for hundreds. Windows on the second floor overlook the Asia section of the theme park.

HOUSE SPECIALTIES Lo mein bowls, coconut shrimp, chicken tikka masala.

OTHER RECOMMENDATIONS Try the Korean fried chicken tenders or the firecracker shrimp.

KIDS' MENU Kids have eight different entrée options—the most of any in-park restaurant. Each is served with two sides from a plentiful selection.

SUMMARY AND COMMENTS The food isn't groundbreaking, but Yak & Yeti is one of the highest-rated sit-down restaurants in a theme park. Sitting at the bar with a Pink Himalayan cocktail and a basket of egg rolls is the perfect escape from Animal Kingdom madness. Note the early closing time.

PART 7

WALT DISNEY WORLD *with* KIDS

KEY QUESTIONS ANSWERED IN THIS CHAPTER

- How important will naps and rest be during our trip? *(page 289)*
- What do kids like best in Walt Disney World? *(page 293)*
- Will we need a stroller? *(page 296)*
- Which rides are scary? *(page 300)*
- Which rides have height requirements? *(page 303)*
- How do we take turns riding something our child won't be riding? *(page 303)*
- Where can we meet the Disney characters? *(page 306)*

MANAGING *the* MAGIC

IT'S SAFE TO SAY that most of the *Guide*, and especially this chapter, is based on real-world experience: what we and our readers have learned through extensive firsthand experience and by making our own mistakes in Walt Disney World. Prepare the best you can and don't beat yourself up when something goes wrong. That's the key to Disney vacation magic.

The reality of a family vacation, especially at Disney, particularly if you chase perfection, can be closer to agony than to ecstasy. An Ohio mother who took her 5-year-old one summer recalls:

> I felt so happy and excited before we went, but when I look back, I think I should have had my head examined. The first day we went to the Magic Kingdom, it was packed. By 11 in the morning, we had walked so far and stood in so many lines that we were all exhausted. Kristy cried about going on anything that looked or even sounded scary and was frightened by all of the Disney characters (they're so big!) except Minnie and Snow White.
>
> We got hungry about the same time as everyone else, but the lines for food were too long and my husband said we'd have to wait. By 1 in the afternoon, we were just plugging along, not seeing anything we were really interested in, but picking rides because the lines were short or because it was air-conditioned. At around 2:30, we finally got something to eat, but by then we were so hot and tired that it felt

*like we had worked in the yard all day. At the end, we were so P.O.'d
and uncomfortable that we weren't having any fun.*

This family's experience is not unusual. Most young children are
as picky about rides as they are about what they eat (and where they
are willing to use the bathroom, but I digress),
and many preschoolers are intimidated by the
Disney characters. Few humans (of any age) are
mentally or physically equipped to march all
day in a throng of 60,000-plus people in the
Florida heat and humidity. Most preschoolers
will say the thing they liked best about their
Disney trip is the hotel swimming pool! And it's
not hard to imagine why—it's the one place the
whole family feel like they can relax and have fun without worrying
about lines, planning, or money.

unofficial **TIP**
When considering a trip
to Walt Disney World,
think about whether your
kids are prepared to enjoy
what can be a very fun
but exhausting trip.

Still, with some planning, an appropriate response when things
inevitably go wrong, and a sense of humor, you'll be emailing me messages like this one from a Virginia mom:

*I thought I knew how magical Disney was. And then I brought
my son for the first time. Nothing will ever beat seeing everything
through his eyes on that first trip.*

REALITY TESTING: WHOSE DREAM IS IT?

ASK YOURSELF A VERY IMPORTANT QUESTION about your vacation to Walt Disney World. Whose dream are you trying to make come
true: yours or your child's?

Young children have an uncanny ability to feed off their parents'
emotions. When you ask, "Honey, how would you like to go to Disney World?" your child will respond more to your smile and enthu-
siasm than to any thought of what Disney World is actually like. The
younger the child, the more this holds true. From many preschoolers,
you could get the same excited reaction by asking, "Sweetie, how
would you like to go to Cambodia on a dogsled?"

Follow up that first important question with a few others. For
example, will your child have sufficient endurance and patience to
cope with long lines and large crowds? Do they usually wilt in the
heat or power through if they're having fun? Do they need to stick to
a specific schedule to avoid melting down? Are they anxious or afraid
in new situations? None of the answers to these questions are deal-
breakers, but they are important to consider during your planning
and preparation.

RECOMMENDATIONS FOR
MAKING THE DREAM COME TRUE

WHEN YOU'RE PLANNING a Walt Disney World vacation with
young children, consider the following:

AGE Although Disney World's bright colors and overall activity excite
all children, and specific attractions delight toddlers and preschoolers, some entertainment and attractions are meant for older kids and
adults. Every member of our family enjoyed every park at Walt Disney

World when they were as young as 18 months old. But if this is a once-in-a-lifetime trip, or your kids aren't used to long days and traveling, then you should take that into consideration when timing your vacation. Readers continually debate how old a child should be or the ideal age to go to Disney World. But really, you need to know your kids and how to make a vacation successful for them.

A Georgia mother of two toddlers emphasizes the importance of maintaining your kids' regular schedule:

The first day, we tried your suggestion about an early start, so we woke the kids (ages 4 and 2) and hurried them to get going. BAD IDEA. This put them off-schedule for naps and meals for the rest of the day.

A Pennsylvania mom with two young kids recounts her experience:

Eighteen months is the absolute worst age to bring a child to Disney. They have no concept of waiting in lines, can't stand the heat, will not sit in a stroller, only want to be carried, and only want to go up and down the stairs outside of the attraction you want to ride. Expect lots of meltdowns, and good luck with the baby swap when they have to go to someone else. (Mom didn't get to do much.)

WHEN TO VISIT Avoid the exceedingly hot summer months, especially if you have preschoolers or your family isn't used to being outdoors in the heat. These times tend to be less crowded, but it's not worth melting a couple of hours into the day. Go in November (except Thanksgiving), early December, late January, or February (except Mardi Gras and Presidents' Day). If your children can't afford to miss school, try late August, before school starts; crowds and hotel rates are lower. We should warn you, however, that special events, festivals, and attraction breakdowns can combine to make the parks seem crowded no matter the time of year.

If you have children of varying ages and they're good students, you can consider taking them out of school and visiting during the cooler, less congested offseason. Most readers who have tried this at various times agree. A New Hampshire parent writes:

I took my grade-school children out of school for a few days to go during a slow time and highly recommend it. We communicated with the teachers about a month before traveling to seek their preference for whether classwork and homework should be completed before, during, or after our trip. It's so much more enjoyable to be at Disney when your children can experience rides, attractions, and all that is Disney rather than standing in line.

There's another side to this story, and we've received some well-considered letters from parents and teachers who don't think taking kids out of school is such a hot idea. A California teacher offers a compelling analogy:

There are a precious 180 days for us as teachers to instruct our students, and there are 185 days during the year for Disney World. I've seen countless students struggle to catch up the rest of the year due to a week of vacation. The analogy I use with my students' parents is that it's like walking out of a movie after watching the first 5 minutes, then returning for the last 5 minutes and trying to figure out what happened.

But a teacher from New York sees things differently:

As a teacher and a parent, I disagree that it's horrible for a parent to take a child out for a vacation. If a parent takes the time to let us know that a child is going to be out, we help them get ready for upcoming homework the best we can. If the child is a good student, why shouldn't they go have a wonderful experience with their family?

Only you and your teacher know your kid and how missing some days of school might affect them. If possible, ask your child's teacher for a list of topics they'll be covering while you're away. Have your child study these on the plane or in the car, while waiting for meals, or at night before bed. You can even provide the teacher with all of the "bonus" education your child received from touring the World Showcase, seeing animatronics in action, and more. We try to give teachers a couple of weeks advance notice so that if they choose to send work home, it's not a mad scramble of extra effort for them a day or two before we leave.

BUILD NAPS AND REST INTO YOUR ITINERARY By a wide margin, the thing most parents say they learned during their first Disney visit was the importance of daily breaks and naps or, more generically, vacationing at a pace they can maintain through the entire trip.

unofficial **TIP**
If you want to return to the hotel during the day for rest, prioritize a resort with easy transportation, or spend money to rent a car.

Why? The parks are huge and require a lot of walking, and crowds can make it even more difficult to navigate, so inevitably someone is going to run out of energy. And when that someone is little and developmentally can't be expected to keep a good handle on their emotions when they're exhausted, things happen—ugly things. Pushing the tired or discontented beyond their capacity will spoil the day for them *and* you. Go back to your hotel midday to rest and relax, then return to the park (or hop to another) in the late afternoon or early evening. If a midday break sounds like a waste of time, plan for an entire rest day after two full days in the parks so everyone can catch up on sleep and downtime.

Regarding naps, this mom doesn't mince words:

Take the book's advice—get out of the park, and take the nap, take the nap, TAKE THE NAP!

A mom from Illinois offers a suggestion:

With small children, two days on, one day off is helpful. We did three park days in a row, with travel days on either end, and our third day was a waste for the 5-year-old—she was tired and sick of walking, and she and I ended up only doing a few rides while everyone else went off and had fun. If I'd thought through that, we would have made one of the travel days a park day and had a pool day in the middle.

Be prepared for someone to get tired and irritable. When it happens, mentally pause and trust your instincts: What would be the best decision for the long-term sustainability of the day and the vacation—another ride, an ice-cream break, or going back to the room for a nap?

WHERE TO STAY If you're going to take midday breaks, you'll be making two trips per day to the theme parks, so you'll want to book a place to stay that's within a 20-minute drive. This doesn't necessarily mean you have to stay inside Disney World. Because the World is so spread out, some off-site hotels are closer to the parks than some Disney resorts (see our Hotel Information Table, pages 194–199, showing commuting times from Disney and non-Disney hotels).

If you want to stay in Walt Disney World, we recommend the **Crescent Lake, Skyliner,** and **monorail resorts**—in that order. Crescent Lake resorts provide walking access to EPCOT (great for parents looking for a high-quality bite later at night) and Skyliner or walking access to Hollywood Studios—no cars or buses to deal with for two parks. Other Skyliner resorts may not be walkable to any parks, but they get you quick access to EPCOT and Hollywood Studios—that's a win. Bonus: There are Moderate (**Caribbean Beach**) and Value (**Pop Century** and **Art of Animation**) resorts with Skyliner access, so there should be budget-friendly options for everyone. Monorail-loop resorts have walking, boat, and/or monorail access to the Magic Kingdom, but the resort loop can get *very* bogged down during busy seasons (for example, a 90-minute wait during the week before Christmas), and you have to transfer to get a monorail to EPCOT. These still avoid cars and buses for two parks, but the transportation is much less convenient.

BUILDING ENDURANCE Although most kids are active, their normal play usually doesn't condition them for all the walking required to tour a Disney park. Start family walks four to six weeks before your trip to get in shape. A mother from Pennsylvania reports:

> We had our 6-year-old begin walking with us a bit every day one month before leaving. When we arrived at Disney World, her little legs could carry her, and she had a lot of stamina.

From a Delaware mom:

> You recommended walking for six weeks prior to the trip, but we began months in advance, just because. My husband lost 10 pounds, my daughter never once complained, and we met a lot of neighbors!

At the very least, run a little test—say, a trip to your local zoo or other park where you do some activities—and walk a total of at least 6 miles together to establish your family's baseline level of fitness. Many find out the hard way that they're not as fit as they think. If your kids need incentives to "train" and build up that walking endurance, I recommend a set contribution to their souvenir budget for every mile walked in the weeks leading up to your trip. This doesn't have to be a large cost to the parents either—50 cents per mile does *wonders* as a motivator for our girls. As a postscript, be prepared to average something closer to 10 miles during each park day.

SETTING LIMITS AND MAKING PLANS To avoid arguments and disappointments, establish expectations for each day, and get everybody aligned. It's amazing what a difference just knowing the plan can make for a kid's attitude and reactions. Include the following:

1. Wake-up time and breakfast plans
2. When to depart for the park and what to take with you
3. A policy for splitting the group or for staying together, and what to do if the group gets separated or someone is lost
4. What you want to see, including plans in the event that an attraction is closed or too crowded

5. A policy on what you can afford for snacks
6. How long you plan to tour and what time you'll return to your hotel to rest (if applicable)
7. When you'll return to the park and how late you'll stay
8. Meal plans
9. A policy for buying souvenirs, including who pays (kids or parents)
10. Bedtimes

BE FLEXIBLE Any day at Disney World includes surprises, so be prepared to adjust your plan. Trust your own judgement.

MAINTAINING SOME SEMBLANCE OF ORDER

DISCIPLINE AND ORDER are more difficult to maintain when traveling than at home because everyone is "in and out"—in strange surroundings and out of the normal routine. For kids, it's hard to contain the excitement and anticipation that bubble to the surface in the form of fidgety hyperactivity (especially nerve-wracking for parents in large crowds where little limbs are flying), nervous energy, and (sometimes) acting out. Confinement in a car, plane, or hotel room only adds to the problem. Crowds, overstimulation, heat, and miles of walking, combined with inadequate rest, can all lead to meltdowns even for the most regularly well-behaved kids.

Remember that line about kids reading their parents' emotions well? That applies here too. It's amazing how easily they can pick up on the importance of this "big" trip and how they want it to go well—for themselves and for you. An incident that would hardly elicit a pouty lip at home will escalate to sobbing or screaming at Disney World. Before you depart on your trip, it's important to discuss the ground rules with your children and to explore their needs and expectations as well.

No one wants to discipline their kids at the most magical place on earth, but the most important thing you can do is to remain consistent. Behaviors that aren't allowed at home need to stay on the no-no list on vacation. If kids get a warning before a consequence at home, they should at Disney too.

I regularly have to remind myself that I'm the adult, and I'm the one expected to react to problems in the midst of exhaustion in a reasonable manner. My kids are still kids. They are going to make mistakes, and then they're going to make mistakes when reacting to and handling their mistakes. It's my job to offer an example—and not be the parent flying into a rage and creating a spectacle by yelling at my kids.

Active Listening and Communication

Whining, tantrums, defiance, and holding up the group aren't just things your kids do to drive you nuts; they're also methods your kids use to communicate with you. Taken at face value, a fit may *seem* to be about the ice cream you refused to buy because you ate lunch 30 minutes ago, but there's almost always something deeper just beneath the surface. And frequently, the root cause is simply a need for attention. Put the phone down (even if you have a Genie+ reservation to make), get physically to their level, and listen. Make memories together. Spend time connecting.

unofficial TIP
Teaching your kids to tell you clearly what they want or need will help make the trip more enjoyable for everyone.

Dealing with Negative Behaviors

Responding appropriately in a disciplinary situation requires thought and preparation, so keep the following in mind when your world blows up as you try to rope drop Slinky Dog Dash and you worry your whole day is going to be ruined:

1. BE THE ADULT. Most kids are experts at knowing how to push their parents' buttons. If you take the bait and respond with a tantrum of your own, you're no longer the adult in the room; worse, you suggest by your example that ranting and raving is acceptable behavior. No matter what happens, take a deep breath and remind yourself, "I'm the adult here." Unironically, I find that watching episodes of *Bluey* on repeat helps me to ask myself, "What would Chilli do?" in the middle of stressful situations.

2. FREEZE THE ACTION. Instead of responding to your kids' provocations in kind, and at a comparable maturity level, what you need to do is freeze the action. This usually means initiating a cool-down period where no one can talk about the negative situation. Find a place, preferably one that's private, to sit your child down, and refrain from talking until you've both cooled off.

3. SEPARATE THE CHILD FROM THE GROUP. Let the rest of the family go eat or explore without you, and arrange to meet up later. In addition to letting the others get on with their day, this relieves the child of the burden of being the focus of attention—and the object of the rest of the family's frustration. This step comes with an important caveat. If feeling like they're missing out on an exciting adventure makes things even more heated, then calmly give them the option of continuing with the group *if they're willing to talk calmly* about what is happening. Otherwise, the natural consequence is missing out for a bit.

4. REVIEW THE SITUATION AND TAKE ACTION. If, as we've recommended, you've made your expectations clear, stated the consequences of not complying, and issued a warning, then review the situation with the child and follow through with the discipline warranted.

5. BREAK THE CYCLE. Tantrums, of course, aren't always one-off events—kids often learn through experience that acting out will get them what they want. By scolding, admonishing, threatening, or negotiating, you actually continue the cycle and likely prolong the behavior, especially on vacation when your kid knows you want to avoid embarrassment and move on as quickly as possible.

To break the cycle, you must learn to speak calmly and not reward the behavior with your own escalating voice or mannerisms. If you don't think you're capable of maintaining that calm manner, or it's not working, then you need to take a break and disengage. A private place is ideal for a break, but it's not absolutely necessary. You can carve out space almost anywhere: on a bench, in your car, in a restroom, or even on a sidewalk. See the Touring Plan Companions, starting on page, for good rest stops in each theme park.

KIDS' FAVORITE MAGIC KINGDOM ATTRACTIONS (*2019–present*)

RANK	PRESCHOOL	GRADE SCHOOL
1	Christmas parade	Evening fireworks
2	Pete's Silly Sideshow meet and greet	Bibbidi Bobbidi Boutique
3	Afternoon parade	Big Thunder Mountain Railroad
4	Halloween/Christmas parades	Halloween/Christmas parades
5	Bibbidi Bobbidi Boutique	Seven Dwarfs Mine Train
6	Meet Mickey Mouse at Town Square Theater	Meet Mickey Mouse at Town Square Theater
7	Adventure Friends cavalcade	Tron Lightcycle/Run
8	Prince Charming Regal Carrousel	Cinderella Castle
9	Festival of Fantasy parade	Festival of Fantasy parade
10	Dumbo the Flying Elephant	Meet Ariel at Her Grotto

WHAT KIDS LIKE BEST IN WALT DISNEY WORLD

WHEN IT COMES TO DISNEY WORLD, what kids want is often different from what parents want: Kids consistently name their hotel's pool as one of their favorite activities, for example. Likewise, children prefer vastly different attractions than adults in Disney's theme parks.

While looking at our reader-survey responses for this, however, we noticed something else: Kids prefer almost any character greeting, parade, or fireworks show to any ride in Walt Disney World.

The table above lists the 10 most popular attractions in the Magic Kingdom for preschool and grade-school kids from 2023 to the present. The only two rides that appeared in the top 10 for preschoolers are **Dumbo the Flying Elephant** and **Prince Charming Regal Carrousel.** In fact, 16 of the top 20 attractions were parades, fireworks, or character greetings (the third and fourth rides were **Under the Sea: Journey of the Little Mermaid** and **The Magic Carpets of Aladdin**).

Grade-school kids enjoy Disney's thrill rides more, but 7 of their 10 favorite attractions were also parades, fireworks, and character greetings. While the touring plans in this edition include character greetings and parades, keep these survey results in mind if you don't expect to use a touring plan. Each theme park chapter contains an updated list of age-group favorites too. (For more on the Disney characters, see page 306.)

ABOUT THE *UNOFFICIAL GUIDE* TOURING PLANS

CHILDREN HAVE A SPECIAL SKILL for wreaking havoc on a schedule. If you're following a touring plan on the Lines app and something unexpected happens, just click "Optimize" when you're ready to get started again. Lines will redo your touring plan from that moment forward, based on current crowd conditions and Genie+ and Individual Lightning Lane availability. (See page 20 for more on Lines.)

If you're following a paper-based touring plan, here's what to expect regarding some common sources of interruptions:

1. CHARACTER GREETINGS CAN SLOW DOWN THE TOURING PLANS.
Lines at character greetings can be as long as those for major attractions. Consider using Genie+ for any character greetings that are offered, or prioritizing just one or two meet and greets in a day.

2. OUR TOURING PLANS CALL FOR VISITING ATTRACTIONS IN A CERTAIN ORDER, OFTEN SKIPPING ATTRACTIONS ALONG THE WAY. Typically, kids don't like to skip *anything* they want to do if they're walking by and it catches their eye. Some can be persuaded to skip attractions if parents explain their plans in advance, but other kids flip out at skipping something. Plan in advance for how you think your kid will react. I regularly detour my family onto a longer walking path to avoid an attraction I absolutely do not want to participate in—I'm looking at you, Tomorrowland Speedway.

3. IF YOU'RE USING A STROLLER, YOU WON'T BE ABLE TO TAKE IT INTO ATTRACTIONS OR ONTO RIDES. It takes time to park and retrieve a stroller outside each attraction. Also, cast members will often move and rearrange strollers to make space, which adds to the time it takes to find yours later. Make sure to have a very visible name tag or some other way to pick out your stroller in the sea of similar-looking child conveyance devices.

Magic Kingdom visitors can use the **Walt Disney World Railroad** to save on walking. The railroad, however, permits only folded strollers on board. If you're renting a Disney stroller, allow time to remove your stuff from it before boarding, and allow time at your destination to get another stroller. Read more stroller advice on page 296.

OTHER CONSIDERATIONS FOR KIDS

OVERHEATING, SUNBURN, AND DEHYDRATION are the most common problems that younger children have at Walt Disney World. Carry and use sunscreen. Apply it on children in strollers, even if the stroller has a canopy. To avoid overheating, stop for rest regularly—in the shade or in a restaurant or at a show with air-conditioning. Carry bottles of water (you can bring your own from home to save money or purchase them at the park).

BLISTERS AND SORE FEET are the next most common problem that First Aid treats. In addition to wearing comfortable shoes, bring along blister bandages if you or your children are susceptible to blisters. These bandages (also available at First Aid in more shapes than you can imagine) offer excellent protection, stick well, and won't sweat off. Remember that a preschooler may not say anything about a blister until it has already formed, so keep an eye on things during the day. See page 358 for more on blister prevention. As soon as one of my kids mentions something about a foot or toe hurting, we *immediately* stop to check out and address the situation. Even if it halts a very quick walk to Rise of the Resistance at the beginning of the day. Don't mess with foot issues.

GLASSES AND SUNGLASSES If your kids (or you) wear them, attach a strap or string to the frames so the glasses will stay on during rides and can hang from the child's neck while indoors. Check Lost and Found (see page 357) if they go missing.

THINGS YOU FORGOT OR RAN OUT OF The theme parks and Disney Springs sell raingear, diapers, baby formula, sunburn treatments, memory cards, and other sundries. The water parks sell towels and disposable waterproof cameras. If you don't see something you need, ask if it's in stock. And keep in mind that Walmart, Target, and other retailers are often only a 10-minute drive or rideshare away.

RUNNING OUT OF STEAM Battling heat, humidity, and crowds at Walt Disney World quickly contributes to exhaustion, especially with kids in the mix. Limiting calorie consumption to mealtimes just won't cut it. This is like a marathon where you need an almost constant intake of fluids, electrolytes, and calories. Our kids don't normally get sports drinks at home—we save them for things like recovering from immunizations and call them "medicine drinks." But most dining locations at Disney offer Powerade, so that bright-blue beverage full of electrolytes is a delightful treat that they gulp down happily, fueling their day. Keep close tabs on everyone's "hanger" levels and provide snacks accordingly.

WILD THINGS Alligators can be found in almost all bodies of fresh water in Florida, including those at Disney World, such as Seven Seas Lagoon and Bay Lake. Though attacks are very rare, adults and especially kids may become targets while swimming, wading, or sitting near the water's edge. Alligators are most active in the late afternoon and evening. If you happen to see one, put as much space between you and it as possible, and keep kids close by. (In case you're wondering, alligators can run 11 mph but only for a short distance.)

BABY CARE

IN EACH OF THE MAJOR THEME PARKS, the **First Aid** and **Baby Care Centers** are located next to each other. In the **Magic Kingdom,** they're at the end of Main Street on the left, by Casey's Corner and The Crystal Palace. At **EPCOT,** they're on the World Showcase side of Odyssey Center. In **Animal Kingdom,** they're in Discovery Island, on the left just before you cross the bridge to Africa, near Creature Comforts. In **Hollywood Studios,** they're at Guest Relations inside the main entrance.

Everything necessary for changing diapers, preparing formula, and warming bottles and food is available at the Baby Care Centers. A small shop at each center sells diapers, wipes, baby food, and other things you may need. Rockers and special chairs for nursing mothers are provided. Dads are welcome, too, and can use most services; in addition, many of the men's restrooms in the major parks have changing stations.

If your baby is on formula, this Wisconsin mom has a handy tip:

We got hot water from the food vendors and mixed the formula as needed. It eliminated having to keep bottles cold and then warm them up.

Infants and toddlers are allowed at any attraction that doesn't have minimum height or age restrictions. Prioritize attractions like boat rides, theater shows, and walk-throughs if you don't want to deal with wrangling you and the baby into and out of ride vehicles.

NURSING Let us state unequivocally that nursing mothers are free to feed their babies whenever and wherever in Walt Disney World they choose. If you are comfortable feeding your baby in line, on Main Street while waiting for a parade, or in a souvenir shop, no one around you gets to judge. They can leave if they're uncomfortable.

FIRST AID If your child or you need minor medical attention, go to a **First Aid Center.** Staffed by registered nurses, the centers treat everything from paper cuts to allergic reactions in addition to sunburns and blisters. Basic over-the-counter meds are often available free in small quantities too.

STROLLERS

THE NEED FOR STROLLERS at Walt Disney World is a hot topic among families with kids. Some parents, in fact, don't realize just how important strollers are until they take their first trip to the World.

Walt Disney World Stroller Policy

The size limit for strollers in the theme parks is **31 inches wide by 52 inches long.** Stroller wagons, both pull and push models, are prohibited. Don't try to skirt the rules.

Strollers for Older Kids

It's not just the parents of babies and toddlers who rent strollers in the parks: Many parents tell us that they use them with kids who are well past needing them at home. If that seems odd, consider that a typical day in the parks requires at least a few miles of walking, which most kids don't do regularly (see "Building Endurance," page 290). But you have to consider the trade-offs. Kids in strollers may be more exhausting for parents as you push them around the park and do extra walking to park and pick up the stroller. But kids without strollers and lacking physical endurance can be an emotional drain on parents or an even bigger physical drain when they demand to be carried to the next attraction. Everyone has different opinions, and you need to decide what works best for your family. We recommend the following method:

UNDER AGE 4 I would argue that anyone under the age of 4 needs a stroller (or parents blessed with an abundance of stamina and a baby sling or hip carrier). The littlest legs just can't do the miles of walking required in a Disney park day.

AGES 4–6 This is the transitional phase when you need to figure out what will work best for your kids. At these ages, we would start just bringing an umbrella stroller and taking it with us on a particularly busy day or leaving it in the room if we thought we could take it easy and not need it for a day.

AGE 6 AND UP At this point, the calculation was easy for us as parents. Once we stopped needing the umbrella stroller, we began traveling without a stroller altogether. Our youngest actually went without a stroller as young as age 4, but that was with weeks of "Disney walks" at home in preparation.

Stroller Options

You have three options for using a stroller in Walt Disney World: renting from Disney, bringing or buying your own, or renting from a third party. We discuss the pros and cons of each option next.

RENTING A STROLLER You can rent a Disney stroller at all four WDW theme parks and at Disney Springs, and improved stroller models were introduced in 2021. To see what these strollers look like, Google "rental strollers at Walt Disney World." A single stroller rents for $15 per day with no deposit, $13 per day for a multiday rental; double strollers cost $31 per day with no deposit, $27 per day for a multiday rental. Note that stroller rentals at Disney Springs require a $100 credit card deposit. Strollers are welcome at Blizzard Beach and Typhoon Lagoon, but no rentals are available.

With multiday rentals, you can skip the rental line completely after your first visit—simply head over to the stroller pickup area, present your receipt, and you'll be wheeling out of there in no time. If you rent a stroller in the Magic Kingdom and decide to go to EPCOT, Animal Kingdom, or Hollywood Studios, just turn in your Magic Kingdom stroller and present your receipt at the next park. You'll be issued another stroller at no additional charge.

Note that you can rent a stroller in advance; this allows you to bypass the payment line and go straight to the pickup line. Disney resort guests can pay ahead at their resort's gift shop, so hang on to your receipts.

Pick up strollers at the **Magic Kingdom** entrance; at **EPCOT**'s main and International Gateway entrances; and at **Oscar's Super Service,** just inside the entrance of **Disney's Hollywood Studios.** In **Animal Kingdom,** they're at **Garden Gate Gifts,** to the right just inside the entrance. Returning a stroller is a breeze—you can ditch it anywhere in the park when you get ready to leave.

Disney's strollers are too large and uncomfortable for infants and potentially small toddlers. If you want to rent one, bring blankets or towels for padding. On the plus side, because the strollers are large, they also provide a convenient place to stow water and snacks.

BRINGING OR BUYING A STROLLER Only collapsible strollers are permitted on monorails, the Walt Disney World Railroad, parking trams, and buses. Many Disney gift shops and local big-box stores like Walmart and Target sell umbrella strollers that you can use for the duration of the trip—potentially saving you money compared to renting every day.

THIRD-PARTY RENTAL Because Disney's stroller rentals are generally expensive and uncomfortable (especially in the heat), a few Orlando rental companies have sprung up that undercut Disney's prices, provide more comfortable strollers, and deliver them to your hotel or offer pickup and drop-off at the Orlando airport. Most of the larger companies offer the same stroller models (the Baby Jogger City Mini Single, for example), so the primary differences between the companies are price and service.

Regarding service, Disney no longer allows stroller companies to drop off and pick up at a Disney hotel without the guest being physically present. Guests must meet the delivery driver for all stroller and scooter rentals.

*un*official **TIP**
Always ask any stroller company if you have to be present when the stroller is delivered.

Kingdom Strollers (☎ 407-271-5301; kingdom strollers.com) is well reviewed for its easy-to-use website, along with its stroller selection and condition and overall customer service. The strollers it offers are much easier to use than Disney's plastic model, have more storage, and have an easier-to-use braking system. A rental of one to three nights costs $60; four to seven nights is $80. That's a five-day break-even point for choosing Kingdom Strollers over Disney's strollers.

Orlando Stroller Rentals, LLC (☎ 800-281-0884; orlandostroller rentals.com), offers similar prices ($55 for one to three nights and $75 for four to seven nights) and an excellent website that allows you to easily compare the features of the different strollers.

Scooterbug Rentals (☎ 800-726-8284; scooterbug.com/orlando) is the only rental company that officially partners with Walt Disney World to allow for drop-off and pickup of strollers from the bell services desk at your resort. All other companies have to meet you in the lobby or in a parking lot for you to receive and return your stroller. So if you're looking for flexibility, along with better stroller selection than Disney has, this is your best bet. You'll usually pay a little more for the convenience, though. A City Mini will cost $60 for up to three nights, and seven nights costs $90.

unofficial **TIP**
Do *not* try to lock your stroller to a fence, post, or anything else.

STROLLER WARS Sometimes your stroller will seem to disappear while you're enjoying a ride or watching a show. Cast members frequently rearrange strollers parked outside an attraction. This may be done to tidy up, clear a walkway, or make space for more parking. Don't assume that your stroller is stolen because it isn't where you left it. It may be neatly arranged a few feet away—or perhaps more than a few feet away.

Sometimes, however, strollers are taken by mistake or ripped off by people too lazy to rent their own. Don't be alarmed if your rental disappears: You won't have to buy it, and you'll be issued a new one at no charge. But while replacing a stroller is free, it's inconvenient.

In either case, it's a good idea to have some sort of very visible identifier on your stroller so you can pick it out from far away. Through our own experiments and readers' suggestions, we've come up with a way to distinguish a rented stroller: Affix something personal but expendable to the handle. We tried several items and concluded that a bright, inexpensive scarf or bandanna tied to the handle works well as identification.

LOST CHILDREN

ALTHOUGH IT'S EASY to lose a child in the theme parks, it usually isn't a serious problem: Cast members are schooled in handling the situation. If a cast member encounters a lost child, they will take the child immediately to the park's **Baby Care Center** (see page 295 for locations in each theme park). If you lose a child, let a cast member know, and then check at the Baby Care Center and at **Guest Relations/ City Hall** in the Magic Kingdom, where lost-children logs are kept. Paging isn't used except in an emergency, but a bulletin can be issued throughout the park(s) via internal communications.

One great way to try to avoid separation is to come up with a family "call." This shouldn't be "Mom" or "Dad." It should be some sort of unique noise or random word that can be yelled at the top of the kid's lungs in the middle of a crowded store, restaurant, or attraction where separations might occur. Your lost kid yelling "Mom" will get lost in the cacophony of the crowd. But as a parent, if you start yelling "AVOCADO" as loud as you can in the middle of a store, chances are everyone around you will get quiet and your kid will be able to follow your voice. Momentary embarrassment is infinitely better than the stress of losing a kid.

You could sew a label onto each child's shirt that states their name, your name, the name of your hotel, and your phone number. You can also purchase custom iron-on labels or write the information on a strip of masking tape so your kid doesn't have to try to remember all of that information.

An easier and trendier option is a **temporary tattoo** with the child's name and your phone number. Unlike labels, ID bracelets, or wristbands, the tattoos can't fall off or get lost. You can purchase customized tattoos online from **SafetyTat** (safetytat.com). Tattoos are available for children with nut allergies, asthma, diabetes, autism, or other medical conditions. Or you can purchase a **temporary tattoo marker,** such as **Bic BodyMark,** available from Amazon and at retailers such as CVS, Walmart, and Target. Cast members recommend the temporary tattoo method and are trained to look for phone numbers.

Another way to keep track of your family is to buy each person a Disney "uniform," such as matching brightly and distinctively colored T-shirts. An Arizona family tried this with great success:

We all got the same shirts (bright red) so that we could easily spot each other in case of separation (VERY easy to do). It was a lifesaver when our 18-month-old decided to get out of the stroller and wander off. No matter what precautions you may try, it seems there are always opportunities to lose a child, but the recognizable shirts helped tremendously.

HOW KIDS GET LOST

CHILDREN GET SEPARATED from their parents every day at Disney World under similar (and predictable) circumstances:

1. PREOCCUPIED SOLO PARENT The party's only adult is preoccupied with something like buying refreshments, booking a Genie+ reservation, or using the restroom. It's remarkably easy for a child to disappear into a crowd in just a second or two.

2. THE HIDDEN EXIT Sometimes parents wait on the sidelines while two or more children experience a ride together. Parents expect the kids to exit in one place, but they pop out elsewhere. Exits from some attractions are distant from entrances. Know exactly where your children will emerge before you send them to ride (or play) by themselves.

3. AFTER THE SHOW At the end of many shows and rides, a cast member announces, "Check for personal belongings and take small children by the hand." This is because when dozens, if not hundreds, of people leave an attraction simultaneously, it's easy for parents to lose their children in the shuffle unless they have direct contact.

4. RESTROOMS WITH MULTIPLE EXITS If you can't find a companion- or family-accessible restroom, make sure there's only one exit. One restroom in the Magic Kingdom, on a passageway between Frontier-land and Adventureland, is notorious for disorienting visitors. Children and adults alike have walked in from the Adventureland side and walked out into Frontierland (and vice versa). Adults realize quickly that something is wrong, but kids sometimes fail to recognize the problem. Designate an easy-to-remember meeting spot and provide clear instructions: "I'll meet you by this flagpole. If you get out first, stay right here." Have your child repeat the directions back to you.

5. PARADES There are many parades and shows at which the audience stands. Children tend to jockey for a better view. By moving a little this way and that, the child quickly puts distance between you and them before either of you notices.

6. MASS MOVEMENTS Be on guard when huge crowds disperse after a fireworks presentation or parade, or at park closing. With thousands of people at once in an area, it's very easy to get separated from a child or others in your party. Use extra caution after the evening fireworks or any other day-capping event. Make a plan for where to meet in case you get separated.

7. ANIMAL KINGDOM EXPLORATION It's especially easy to lose a child in this theme park, particularly in The Oasis, on the Maharajah Jungle Trek, and on the Gorilla Falls Exploration Trail: Mom and Dad will stop to observe an animal; Junior stays close for a minute or so and then, losing patience, wanders to the exhibit's other side or to a different exhibit. In the multipath Oasis, locating a lost child can be maddening, as a Florida mother describes:

> Manny wandered off in the paths that lead to the jungle village while we were looking at a bird. It reminded me of losing somebody in the supermarket, when you run back and forth looking down each aisle but can't find the person you're looking for because they're running around too. I was nutso before we even got to the first ride.

KIDS *and* SCARY STUFF

DISNEY RIDES AND SHOWS are adventures with universal themes: good and evil, life and death, beauty and ugliness, fellowship and enmity. As you sample the attractions at Walt Disney World, you'll experience not just the spinning and bouncing of midway rides but also emotionally powerful entertainment that is sometimes too much for the littlest members of your family.

The endings are happy ones, but given Disney's gift for special effects, these adventures often intimidate and occasionally scare young children. There are attractions with menacing witches, burning towns, skeletons, and ghouls popping out of their graves—all done with humor, provided you're old enough to understand the joke.

Most children take Disney's more intense moments in stride, and others are easily comforted by an arm around the shoulder or a squeeze of the hand. Parents who know that their children tend to become upset should take it slow and easy, sampling fun adventures like the Jungle Cruise, gauging reactions, and discussing with the children how they feel about what they've seen. Figure out what your kid will and will not enjoy and try to identify coping mechanisms that help them handle and enjoy more attractions. For example, my littler

unofficial TIP
Every kid has different scary triggers. Research attractions before you visit so that you'll know which ones you need to skip and which will be fine.

kid can ride just about anything as long as she covers her own ears so she's not surprised by loud noises. But we also mix in a bunch of her more "soothing" favorites like It's a Small World and Living with the Land so she gets some relaxation.

Sometimes kids will try to rise above their anxiety in an effort to please their parents or siblings. This doesn't mean they weren't afraid, or even that they enjoyed the attraction. If your child leaves a ride in apparently good shape, ask if they'd like to go on it again—not necessarily now, but sometime. Their response should tell you all you need to know.

Evaluating children's capacity to handle the visual and tactile effects of Walt Disney World requires patience and understanding. If your child balks at or is frightened by a ride, respond compassionately: Make clear that it's all right to be scared and that you won't think any less of your child for not wanting to ride.

What you definitely *don't* want to do is add to a child's fear and distress by coercing, belittling, or guilt-tripping. And don't let older siblings apply that pressure either.

THE FRIGHT FACTOR

WHILE EACH KID IS DIFFERENT, the following attraction elements, alone or combined, could push a child's buttons and indicate that a certain attraction isn't age appropriate for that child:

THE NAME It's only natural that young children will be apprehensive about something called, say, The Haunted Mansion or The Twilight Zone Tower of Terror. If you think your kid will enjoy the attraction but bristle at the name, feel free to call it something else.

THE VISUAL IMPACT OF THE RIDE FROM OUTSIDE Big Thunder Mountain Railroad, Tiana's Bayou Adventure, and the Tower of Terror look scary enough to give adults second thoughts, and they terrify many little kids. A Utah grandma reports the following:

At 5 years old, my granddaughter was willing to go on almost everything. The problem was with the preliminary introductions to The Haunted Mansion and the Tower of Terror. Walking through and learning the stories before the actual rides were what frightened her and made her opt out without going in. The rides themselves wouldn't have been bad—she loved Splash Mountain [now Tiana's Bayou Adventure] and Big Thunder Mountain, but she could SEE those before entering.

THE VISUAL IMPACT OF THE INDOOR-QUEUING AREA The caves at Pirates of the Caribbean and the dungeons and "stretch rooms" of The Haunted Mansion can frighten kids.

THE INTENSITY Some attractions overwhelm with sights, sounds, movements, and even smells. Animal Kingdom's *It's Tough to Be a Bug!* show, for example, combines loud sounds, lights, smoke, and animatronic insects with 3D cinematography to create a total sensory experience. An Iowa mom describes it well:

> *The 3D and 4D experiences are way too scary for even a very brave 5-year-old girl. The shows that blew things on her, shot smells in the air, had bugs flying, etc., scared the bejesus out of her. We escorted her crying from* It's Tough to Be a Bug! *and* Mickey's PhilharMagic.

THE VISUAL IMPACT OF THE ATTRACTION Sights in various attractions range from falling boulders and lurking buzzards to grazing dinosaurs and waltzing ghosts. What one child calmly watches may scare the pants off another who's the same age.

THE DARKNESS Many attractions operate indoors in the dark, which can be scary. A child who gets frightened on one dark ride (such as The Haunted Mansion) may be unwilling to try others.

THE PHYSICAL EXPERIENCE Some rides are wild enough to cause motion sickness, wrench backs, and discombobulate guests of any age.

A BIT OF PREPARATION

WE RECEIVE MANY TIPS from parents telling how they prepared their young children for the Disney experience. Common strategies include reading Disney books and watching Disney videos. A Kentucky mom suggests watching videos of the theme parks on **YouTube:**

> *My timid 7-year-old daughter and I watched ride and show videos on YouTube, and we cut out all the ones that looked too scary.*

You can also watch Walt Disney World specials produced by Disney and others on Disney+ and Netflix.

ATTRACTIONS THAT EAT ADULTS

ADULTS GET SCARED TOO. The attractions in the table below can cause motion sickness or other issues for older kids and adults.

POTENTIALLY PROBLEMATIC ATTRACTIONS FOR GROWN-UPS
THE MAGIC KINGDOM
• Mad Tea Party • Big Thunder Mountain Railroad • Tiana's Bayou Adventure (formerly Splash Mountain) • Space Mountain • Tron Lightcycle/Run
EPCOT
• Guardians of the Galaxy: Cosmic Rewind • Mission: Space • Test Track
DISNEY'S ANIMAL KINGDOM
• Expedition Everest • Kali River Rapids • Dinosaur • Avatar Flight of Passage
DISNEY'S HOLLYWOOD STUDIOS
• Star Tours—The Adventures Continue • Rock 'n' Roller Coaster • The Twilight Zone Tower of Terror • *Millennium Falcon:* Smugglers Run • Star Wars: Rise of the Resistance

HEIGHT REQUIREMENTS

A NUMBER OF ATTRACTIONS require children to meet minimum height or age requirements (see table on page 307 for details). All rides, regardless of height requirements, state that children under age 7 must have someone age 14 or older ride with them. That means kids under 7 can't use the single-rider line. If you have children who don't meet the posted requirements, you have several options, including Rider Switch (see below). If your group is headed to an attraction where some family members will not meet the minimum height requirement, consider planning on doing something nearby instead of just waiting at the exit. Take a look at the posted wait time and plan to busy yourself for that amount of time.

WAITING-LINE STRATEGIES *for* YOUNG CHILDREN

CHILDREN HOLD UP BETTER THROUGH THE DAY if you limit the time they spend *bored* in lines. Arriving early and using a touring plan are two ways to greatly reduce waiting. Here are other ways to reduce stress or boredom in lines for kids:

1. RIDER SWITCH (AKA SWITCHING OFF OR RIDER SWAP) Some of Disney's best rides have minimum height and/or age requirements. Couples with children too small or too young might either skip these attractions or take turns riding. Neither option is ideal: One is an unnecessary sacrifice, and the other is a tremendous waste of time. Disney's solution is a system called Rider Switch. There must be two to three adults in your party for this to work. Here's how to do it:

1. When you approach the queue, tell the first cast member you see that you want to use Rider Switch.
2. The cast member will ask who is riding first and who is riding second—that is, the adults who will be supervising the nonriding child (up to three can ride second).
3. The first group will enter the queue.
4. The cast member will scan the MagicBands or tickets of the group riding second—along with any repeat riders—who then wait or do other attractions with the nonriding child.
5. When the first group returns, they take over watching the nonriding child while the second group goes to the Alternate Access line—usually the Lightning Lane.
6. The cast member will scan the second group's MagicBands or tickets again, after which the group enters the Alternate Access line.
7. Both groups reunite after the second group finishes the ride.

Rider Switch passes—digital entitlements scanned into your MagicBand or ticket—must be used on the day they're issued. Guests may hold no more than one Rider Switch pass at a time—a pass must be redeemed before another one can be issued.

Cast members administering Rider Switch are very accommodating and will typically let you self-select who is in the first and second group, within reason. Don't plan on a 17-member party getting to ride

continued on page 306

SMALL-CHILD FRIGHT-POTENTIAL TABLE

THIS QUICK REFERENCE identifies attractions to be wary of if you have kids ages 3–7. Younger children are more likely to be frightened than older ones. Attractions not listed aren't typically frightening.

THE MAGIC KINGDOM

ADVENTURELAND

- **JUNGLE CRUISE** Moderately intense; some concerning situations. This is a good test attraction to see how your kids handle the fright factor.
- **THE MAGIC CARPETS OF ALADDIN** Could scare kids who don't like heights if you raise your ride vehicle high in the air.
- **PIRATES OF THE CARIBBEAN** Slightly intimidating queuing area; intense boat ride with some scary (though humorously presented) sights and a short, unexpected slide.
- **SWISS FAMILY TREEHOUSE** Anyone who's afraid of heights may want to skip it.
- **WALT DISNEY'S ENCHANTED TIKI ROOM** A thunderstorm, loud volume level, and simulated explosions frighten some preschoolers.

FRONTIERLAND

- **BIG THUNDER MOUNTAIN RAILROAD*** This is a moderate roller coaster, but it does have tight turns and some "threat" of explosion.
- **TIANA'S BAYOU ADVENTURE* (FORMERLY SPLASH MOUNTAIN)** Visually intimidating from the outside, the ride culminates in a 52-foot plunge down a steep chute.
- **TOM SAWYER ISLAND AND FORT LANGHORN** Some very young children are intimidated by dark and tight walk-through tunnels, but these can be easily avoided.

LIBERTY SQUARE

- **THE HAUNTED MANSION** Intense attraction with humorously presented ghostly sights. The name alone raises anxiety, as do the sounds and sights of the waiting area, but the ride itself is gentle.

FANTASYLAND

- **THE BARNSTORMER*** May frighten some preschoolers.
- **DUMBO THE FLYING ELEPHANT** Could scare kids who are afraid of heights if you raise your ride vehicle high in the air.
- **MAD TEA PARTY** Midway-type ride; can induce motion sickness in all ages.
- **THE MANY ADVENTURES OF WINNIE THE POOH** Frightens a few preschoolers with Heffalumps and Woozles.
- **SEVEN DWARFS MINE TRAIN*** May frighten some preschoolers—especially catching sight of the villain.
- **UNDER THE SEA: JOURNEY OF THE LITTLE MERMAID** Animatronic Ursula frightens some preschoolers.

TOMORROWLAND

- **ASTRO ORBITER** Could scare kids who are afraid of heights.
- **BUZZ LIGHTYEAR'S SPACE RANGER SPIN** Villain and (bright, goofy) aliens may frighten some preschoolers.
- **MONSTERS, INC. LAUGH FLOOR** May frighten some preschoolers.
- **SPACE MOUNTAIN*** Very intense roller coaster in the dark; the Magic Kingdom's wildest ride and a scary coaster by any standard.
- **TRON LIGHTCYCLE/RUN*** Intense indoor/outdoor coaster.

EPCOT

FUTURE WORLD

- **GUARDIANS OF THE GALAXY: COSMIC REWIND*** Intense coaster in the dark.
- **JOURNEY INTO IMAGINATION WITH FIGMENT** Loud noises and unexpected flashing lights startle younger children.

* Rider Switch option provided *(see page 303)*

SMALL-CHILD FRIGHT-POTENTIAL TABLE *(continued)*
EPCOT *(continued)*

FUTURE WORLD *(continued)*

- **MISSION: SPACE*** Extremely intense space-simulation ride that has been known to cause some anxiety for guests of all ages.
- **THE SEAS WITH NEMO & FRIENDS** Sharks and fish-chasing scenes may scare preschoolers not familiar with the movie's storyline.
- **SOARIN' AROUND THE WORLD*** May frighten anyone with a fear of heights. Otherwise gentle and enjoyable.
- **TEST TRACK*** Intense thrill ride that may frighten guests of any age.

WORLD SHOWCASE

- **FROZEN EVER AFTER*** Small drop at the end could scare little ones.
- **REMY'S RATATOUILLE ADVENTURE** May frighten some preschoolers.

DISNEY'S ANIMAL KINGDOM
DISCOVERY ISLAND

- **TREE OF LIFE/*IT'S TOUGH TO BE A BUG!*** Intense and loud, with special effects that startle viewers of all ages and potentially terrify little kids.

ASIA

- **EXPEDITION EVEREST*** The ride, especially the yeti, can frighten guests of all ages.
- ***FEATHERED FRIENDS IN FLIGHT!*** Swooping birds may frighten a few small children.
- **KALI RIVER RAPIDS*** Potentially frightening and certainly wet for guests of all ages.
- **MAHARAJAH JUNGLE TREK** Some children may balk at the bat exhibit.

DINOLAND U.S.A.

- **DINOSAUR*** High-tech thrill ride that rattles riders of all ages.
- **TRICERATOP SPIN** Could scare kids who are afraid of heights if you raise your vehicle high in the air.

PANDORA—THE WORLD OF AVATAR

- **AVATAR FLIGHT OF PASSAGE*** May frighten kids age 7 and younger, those with claustrophobia or a fear of heights, or those who are prone to motion sickness.
- **NA'VI RIVER JOURNEY*** Dark ride with imposing animatronic figures that frightens some preschoolers.

DISNEY'S HOLLYWOOD STUDIOS
SUNSET BOULEVARD

- ***FANTASMIC!*** Terrifies some preschoolers thanks to featured villains.
- **ROCK 'N' ROLLER COASTER*** The wildest coaster at Hollywood Studios. May frighten guests of any age.
- **THE TWILIGHT ZONE TOWER OF TERROR*** Visually intimidating to young kids; contains intense and realistic special effects. The plummeting elevator at the end frightens many adults as well as kids.

ECHO LAKE

- **STAR TOURS—THE ADVENTURES CONTINUE*** Less intense than Rise of the Resistance, but depending on scenes during the ride, may be scary for younger kids.

HOLLYWOOD BOULEVARD

- **MICKEY & MINNIE'S RUNAWAY RAILWAY** Track ride with wild twists and turns but benign visuals. May scare kids age 6 and under.

* Rider Switch option provided *(see page 303)*

continued on next page

SMALL-CHILD FRIGHT-POTENTIAL TABLE *(continued)*
DISNEY'S HOLLYWOOD STUDIOS *(continued)*
TOY STORY LAND
• SLINKY DOG DASH* Mild first roller coaster for most kids. May frighten preschoolers.
STAR WARS: GALAXY'S EDGE
• *MILLENNIUM FALCON:* SMUGGLERS RUN* Intense visual effects and movement.
• STAR WARS: RISE OF THE RESISTANCE Intense visual effects and movement.

* Rider Switch option provided *(see page 303)*

continued from page 303

Tron twice because the 18th person sits out with a nonriding child. But if you're a family of four and your older child wants to ride in the first *and* second groups, this will almost always be allowed.

2. LINE GAMES Anticipate that children will get restless in line, and plan activities to reduce the stress and boredom. In the morning, have waiting children discuss what they want to see and do during the day. Later, watch for and count Disney characters (or hidden Mickeys) or play simple games such as 20 Questions. Games requiring pen and paper are impractical in a fast-moving line, but you could pack a small notebook and a few crayons for places like theater shows or table-service meals.

3. PHONE FUN If games and coloring are likely to induce eye rolls, load some age-appropriate games on your or your kids' phones. Many Disney games exist (even educational ones), and these can be a special vacation "treat" so that your kids don't expect to keep playing at home.

4. LAST-MINUTE COLD FEET If your young child gets cold feet while you're waiting to board a ride where Rider Switch isn't offered (this happens frequently in Pirates of the Caribbean's dungeon waiting area), just alert an attendant and they will either 1) find a space for half of the party to wait while the other half rides, and then let you switch before you exit or 2) show you to the exit, whichever you prefer.

 The **DISNEY CHARACTERS**

THE LONGEST LEN HAS EVER WAITED in line at a theme park was 5 hours, with daughter Hannah to meet Anna and Elsa from *Frozen*. ("I've had relationships that didn't last that long," he muses.) Spontaneous group parenting took over, with adults taking turns buying food and drinks and running bathroom breaks for each other's kids.

But the thing that surprised Len most was how excited Anna was to see Hannah at the end of that 5-hour wait. Displaying the energy of a squirrel fed Cuban coffee, Anna jumped and danced around Hannah, hugging and talking to her as if it was Anna who'd been waiting to see her.

Hannah cried. Len cried. It was great.

ATTRACTION HEIGHT RESTRICTIONS

THE MAGIC KINGDOM

The Barnstormer* 35" minimum

Big Thunder Mountain Railroad* 40" minimum

Seven Dwarfs Mine Train* 38" minimum

Space Mountain* 44" minimum

Tiana's Bayou Adventure *(formerly Splash Mountain)** 40" minimum

Tomorrowland Speedway* 32" minimum to ride, 54" to drive unassisted

Tron Lightcycle/Run* 48" minimum

EPCOT

Guardians of the Galaxy: Cosmic Rewind* 42" minimum

Mission: Space* 40" minimum (Green); 44" minimum (Orange)

Soarin' Around the World* 40" minimum

Test Track* 40" minimum

DISNEY'S ANIMAL KINGDOM

Avatar Flight of Passage* 44" minimum

Dinosaur* 40" minimum

Expedition Everest* 44" minimum

Kali River Rapids* 38" minimum

DISNEY'S HOLLYWOOD STUDIOS

Alien Swirling Saucers* 32" minimum

Millennium Falcon: **Smugglers Run*** 38" minimum

Rock 'n' Roller Coaster* 48" minimum

Slinky Dog Dash* 38" minimum

Star Tours—The Adventures Continue* 40" minimum

Star Wars: Rise of the Resistance 40" minimum

The Twilight Zone Tower of Terror* 40" minimum

DISNEY SPRINGS

Marketplace Carousel 42" minimum

BLIZZARD BEACH WATER PARK

Downhill Double Dipper 48" minimum

Ski lift 32" minimum

Slush Gusher* 48" minimum

Summit Plummet 48" minimum

T-Bar zip line *(in Ski Patrol Training Camp)* 60" maximum

Tike's Peak children's area 48" maximum

TYPHOON LAGOON WATER PARK

Bay Slides 60" minimum

Crush 'n' Gusher 48" minimum

Humunga Kowabunga 48" minimum

Ketchakiddee Creek 48" maximum

Wave Pool *Adult supervision required*

* Rider Switch option provided *(see page 303)*

ATTRACTIONS OFFERING RIDER SWITCH
MAGIC KINGDOM
• The Barnstormer • Big Thunder Mountain Railroad • Seven Dwarfs Mine Train • Space Mountain • Tiana's Bayou Adventure *(formerly Splash Mountain)*
EPCOT
• Frozen Ever After • Guardians of the Galaxy: Cosmic Rewind • Mission: Space • Soarin' Around the World • Test Track
DISNEY'S ANIMAL KINGDOM
• Avatar Flight of Passage • Dinosaur • Expedition Everest • Kali River Rapids • Na'vi River Journey
DISNEY'S HOLLYWOOD STUDIOS
• Alien Swirling Saucers • *Millennium Falcon:* Smugglers Run • Rock 'n' Roller Coaster • Slinky Dog Dash • Star Tours—The Adventures Continue • The Twilight Zone Tower of Terror

Len's experience is repeated every day throughout Walt Disney World by cast members determined to be the Disney characters they're dressed as. We receive hundreds of reader comments telling us how much these cast members enhanced their theme park experience. This email from a Wisconsin mom is representative:

I can't say enough about the characters and how they react to the children and just people in general. They are highly trained in people skills and just add an extra dimension to the park.

As we've mentioned, meeting the Disney characters is one of the highest-rated activities among all age groups who visit Walt Disney World. To those who love them, the characters in Disney's films and TV shows are as real as family or friends; never mind that they were drawn by an animator or generated by a computer.

By extension, the theme park personifications of the Disney characters are just as real: It's not a guy in a mouse costume but Mickey himself; she's not a cast member in a sequined fish tail but Ariel, Princess of Atlantica. Meeting a Disney character is an encounter with a real celebrity, a memory to be treasured.

MEETING THE CHARACTERS

DISNEY MAKES ITS MOST POPULAR CHARACTERS available in dedicated meet-and-greet venues in each theme park (see the table on page 310 for the locations of specific characters) and at Disney Deluxe resorts that host character meals (see "Character Meals," page 311). Gone are the days of characters spontaneously wandering in parks. If you see one walking through the park, they are likely walking with a purpose and aren't stopping for interactions.

Some characters who don't have dedicated spaces appear only in parades or stage shows, and still others appear only in a location consistent with their starring role. The Fairy Godmother, for example, is often near Cinderella Castle in Fantasyland, while Stitch regularly pops up in Tomorrowland. Characters may visit the Disney resorts and water parks and occasionally appear at Disney Springs.

Illustration: Tami Knight

A New York dad was surprised at how much time his family was willing to spend meeting characters:

> The characters are now available practically all day long at different locations, according to a fixed schedule, which our son was old enough to read. We spent more time standing in line for autographs than we did for the most popular rides!

PREPARING YOUR CHILDREN TO MEET CHARACTERS There are two kinds of Disney characters: **fur characters,** whose costumes include face-covering headpieces (including animal characters and humanlike characters such as Captain Hook), and **face characters,** who wear no mask or headpiece, such as the Disney princesses and princes, Aladdin, Mary Poppins, and the like.

Only face characters speak. Because cast members couldn't possibly imitate the furs' distinctive voices, it's more effective for them to be silent. Nonetheless, fur characters are warm and responsive, and they communicate effectively with gestures. Most of the furs are quite large; a few, like Sully from *Monsters, Inc.,* are huge. Small children don't expect this, and preschoolers especially can be intimidated.

On first encounter, don't thrust your child at the character; rather, allow the little one to deal with this big thing from whatever distance feels safe. If two adults are present, one should stay near the youngster while the other approaches the character and demonstrates that it's safe and friendly.

Be aware that some character costumes are quite cumbersome and make it hard for the cast members inside to see well. (Eyeholes are frequently placed in the mouth of the costume or even on the neck or chest.) Children who approach the character from the back or side may not be noticed, even if the child touches the character.

A child should approach a character from the front, but occasionally not even this works—Donald and Daisy, for example, have to

CHARACTER-GREETING VENUES

MAGIC KINGDOM

MICKEY AND HIS POSSE

- **Mickey** Town Square Theater
- **Minnie, Daisy, Donald, and Goofy** Pete's Silly Sideshow

DISNEY ROYALTY *(Princesses, Princes, Suitors, and Such)*

- **Aladdin and Jasmine** Adventureland • **Ariel** Ariel's Grotto • **Belle** *Enchanted Tales with Belle* • **Cinderella, Elena of Avalor, Rapunzel, and Tiana** Princess Fairytale Hall • **Fairy Godmother and the Tremaines** Fantasyland near Cinderella's Castle • **Gaston** Fountain outside Gaston's Tavern • **Snow White** Next to City Hall

OTHER CHARACTERS

- **Alice** Mad Tea Party • **Captain Jack Sparrow** Adventureland • **Chip 'n' Dale** Tomorrowland • **Country Bears** Frontierland • **Mirabel** Fairytale Garden
- **Peter Pan** Fantasyland next to Peter Pan's Flight • **Pooh and Tigger** Fantasyland by The Many Adventures of Winnie the Pooh • **Stitch** Tomorrowland

EPCOT

MICKEY AND HIS POSSE

- **Donald** Mexico

DISNEY ROYALTY

- **Anna and Elsa** Norway • **Asha** International Gateway • **Aurora** France gazebo
- **Belle** France • **Jasmine** Morocco • **Mulan** China • **Snow White** Germany

OTHER CHARACTERS

- **Alice** United Kingdom • **Winnie the Pooh** United Kingdom
- **Joy** and **Figment** Inside the Imagination! Pavilion

DISNEY'S ANIMAL KINGDOM

MICKEY AND HIS POSSE

- **Mickey and Minnie** Adventurers Outpost on Discovery Island • **Daisy** DinoLand U.S.A., Lower Cretaceous Trail • **Donald** DinoLand U.S.A., Celebration Welcome Center

DISNEY ROYALTY

- **Moana** Discovery Island at Character Landing

OTHER CHARACTERS

- **Chip 'n' Dale** DinoLand U.S.A., Upper Cretaceous Trail • **Kevin** (*Up*) Discovery Island
- **Russell and Dug** Adventure Flotilla–*Up* on Discovery River • **Launchpad McQuack and Scrooge McDuck** Adventure Flotilla on Discovery River

DISNEY'S HOLLYWOOD STUDIOS

MICKEY AND HIS POSSE

- **Minnie and Sorcerer Mickey** *Red Carpet Dreams* on Commissary Lane
- **Chip 'n' Dale** and **Daisy** Outside Animation Courtyard • **Donald** Near Echo Lake
- **Pluto** Animation Courtyard

DISNEY JUNIOR STARS

- **Doc McStuffins, Fancy Nancy,** and **Vampirina** Animation Courtyard

OTHER CHARACTERS

- **Buzz, Jessie, Woody, and Green Army Men** Toy Story Land • **Chewbacca, Darth Vader, and BB-8** Star Wars Launch Bay • **Cruz Ramirez** Lightning McQueen's Racing Academy • **Edna Mode, Frozone, and the Incredibles** and **Sully** Pixar Place
- **Olaf** Celebrity Spotlight in Echo Lake • **Stormtroopers, Kylo Ren, Rey, Grogu, R2D2, and more from** *Star Wars* Galaxy's Edge

Characters are subject to change.

peer around their bills. If a character appears to be ignoring your child, the character's handler will get its attention.

It's OK for your child to touch, pat, or hug (but not hit or punch) the character. Understanding the unpredictability of children, characters will keep their feet still, particularly refraining from moving backward or sideways.

Most characters will pose for pictures or sign autographs, but note that costumes can make it difficult to wield a normal pen. Some can't sign autographs at all, but they are always glad to pose for photos.

Character-Greeting Venues

Walt Disney World has numerous character-greeting locations. The table at left lists some of them by park and character. *Note:* Characters are subject to change, so check before you head to the parks.

During these meet and greets, characters often engage in dialogue appropriate to their storylines, which catches many people by surprise. Characters in the parks will also know about the park's attractions that involve them, as this Canadian mom found out:

> *Immediately after watching* Mickey's PhilharMagic, *my daughter was so worried about Donald smashing through a wall [on film as part of the show] that we had to drop what we were going to do and stand in line just so she could kiss Donald and make sure he was OK. Fortunately, Donald knew what she was talking about and played along with the doctoring.*

CHARACTER MEALS

DISNEY CHARACTERS APPEAR at meals served in full-service restaurants at the theme parks and Deluxe resorts, among other locations. For more information, see page 215. At press time, character-dining experiences were available only at the following locations:

- AKERSHUS ROYAL BANQUET HALL Norway, World Showcase, EPCOT (see page 246)
- CAPE MAY CAFE Beach Club Resort (see page 250)
- CHEF MICKEY'S Contemporary Resort (see page 251)
- CINDERELLA'S ROYAL TABLE Magic Kingdom (see page 252)
- THE CRYSTAL PALACE Magic Kingdom (see page 254)
- GARDEN GRILL RESTAURANT EPCOT (see page 257)
- HOLLYWOOD & VINE Disney's Hollywood Studios (see page 259)
- 1900 PARK FARE Grand Floridian Resort (see page 266)
- 'OHANA Polynesian Village Resort (see page 267)
- RAVELLO Four Seasons Orlando (see page 211)
- STORY BOOK DINING AT ARTIST POINT Wilderness Lodge Resort (see page 276)
- TOPOLINO'S TERRACE—FLAVORS OF THE RIVIERA Riviera Resort (see page 280)
- TUSKER HOUSE RESTAURANT Animal Kingdom (see page 282)

CHILDCARE

IN-ROOM BABYSITTING Kid's Nite Out (☎ 877-761-3580; kidsniteout.com) provides in-room and

unofficial TIP
Childcare is unavailable at Walt Disney World resort hotels.

in-park childcare in the Walt Disney World/Universal area. Base hourly rates (4-hour minimum) are $30 for one child and $3 per hour for each additional child, plus a $15 travel fee. Sitters are security-checked, bonded, and trained in CPR. See the website for additional services and fees.

SPECIAL KIDS' PROGRAMS

FREE ACTIVITIES

MANY DISNEY DELUXE AND DVC RESORTS offer a continuous slate of free kids' activities from early morning through the evening, from storytelling and cookie decorating to hands-on activities themed to the resort. (Many of these activities are outdoors, too.) These programs offer an inexpensive alternative to the theme parks on your first or last day of travel, or whenever parents need a quiet break by the pool.

BIRTHDAYS *and* SPECIAL OCCASIONS

WHEN YOU CHECK IN TO A HOTEL or restaurant, Disney cast members will generally ask if you're celebrating something special, such as a birthday or anniversary. Don't expect anything to happen, but if you get a birthday or celebration button from your resort or the park, cast members will regularly comment as you pass. And if you note the special occasion when checking in for a table-service reservation, you may even be given a special dessert.

TIPS *for* VARIED CIRCUMSTANCES

WALT DISNEY WORLD *for* GUESTS *with* DISABILITIES

DISNEY WORLD IS EXCEPTIONALLY ACCOMMODATING to guests with physical and cognitive disabilities. If you have a disability, Disney is well prepared to meet your needs.

DISNEY RESORTS

WHEN BOOKING YOUR ROOM, inform the reservation agent of any particular accommodations you'll need. The following equipment, services, and facilities are available at most Disney resorts (note that not all resorts offer all items).

- Accessible vanities
- Bed and bathroom rails
- Braille on signs and elevators
- Closed-captioned TVs
- Double peepholes in doors
- Handheld showerheads
- Knock and phone alerts
- Lowered beds
- Phone amplifiers
- Portable commodes
- Refrigerators
- Roll-in showers
- Rubber bed padding
- Shower benches
- Strobe-light smoke detectors
- TTYs
- Wheelchairs for temporary use
- Widened bathroom doors

SERVICE ANIMALS

DISNEY WELCOMES DOGS AND MINIATURE HORSES that are trained to assist guests with disabilities. Service animals are permitted in most locations in all Disney resorts and theme parks, although they may not be admitted on certain theme park rides. Check disneyworld .disney.go.com/guest-services/service-animals for more information.

IN THE THEME PARKS

EACH THEME PARK OFFERS a free booklet describing services and accommodations for guests with disabilities. Find it at theugseries.com /disabilities-guide. You can also obtain this booklet when you enter the parks, at resort front desks, and at wheelchair-rental locations in the parks. For specific requests, call ☎ 407-560-2547 (voice). When the recorded menu comes up, press 1. Limit your questions and requests to those regarding your disability; address other questions to ☎ 407-824-4321 or 407-827-5141 (TTY).

DISNEY'S DISABILITY ACCESS SERVICE (DAS)

WE RECEIVE MANY LETTERS from readers whose traveling companion or child requires special assistance but who is not visibly disabled. Autism spectrum disorder, for example, can make it very difficult or impossible for someone to wait in line for more than a few minutes or in queues surrounded by a crowd. A trip to Disney World can nonetheless be a positive and rewarding for guests with autism. And while any Disney vacation requires planning, a little extra effort to accommodate the affected person will pay large dividends.

Disney's Disability Access Service (**DAS**) is designed to accommodate guests with developmental disabilities such as autism. **Amy Schinner,** a member of the TouringPlans team, explains how it works:

- DAS allows you to make a reservation at the attraction, then join the Lightning Lane at your arrival time, allowing you to spend most of your wait time in a more comfortable space. In May 2024, the policy was overhauled, and the Guest Services team is not involved with DAS unless you have a technical problem while using the My Disney Experience app. You can only request DAS using video chat. We strongly suggest doing this 30 days before your trip (see theugseries .com/wdw-das). There will be iPads dedicated to video chat in the park. There will not be an opportunity to speak to a cast member in person.

- DAS is valid for as many park days as your ticket, and the service carries over to each subsequent park you visit. If you have an Annual Pass, you will need to renew DAS every 120 days. The process is explained below. For clarity, we'll refer to the person signing up for DAS as the enrollee. *Note:* Guests whose disability requires only a wheelchair or mobility vehicle do not need (or qualify for) DAS.

unofficial **TIP**
For those in your group without MagicMobile (phones), the MagicBands or physical tickets are easier to use for tapping into the Lightning Lanes.

PREPARATION Before you sign up, make sure you have My Disney Experience (MDE) information, including an email address, mailing address, and phone number for each guest who will be joining you. DAS works for parties of up to four people. For parties of more than four, ask about them when you request DAS.

SIGNING UP FOR DAS During your video chat, you'll be asked to present identification and describe the enrollee's limitations. You don't have to share a diagnosis or provide documentation of a specific condition; what Disney is looking for is a description of how the disability affects the enrollee in the parks. The goal is to determine the right level of assistance, not to make you prove that the enrollee qualifies. The enrollee must be present during this call.

Be as detailed as possible in describing limitations. For instance, if your child has autism spectrum disorder and has trouble waiting in long lines or has sensory issues such as sensitivity to noise, let the cast member know each of these things specifically.

Finally, you must check a box that says you agree to Disney's DAS rules. While this seems like a formality, no video chat or any other assistance will happen until you accept those terms and conditions.

DAS ADVANCE Up until the beginning of 2024, guests with DAS were eligible to make two ride reservations per day. This would allow them to choose hour-long return windows (similar to Genie+) for two attractions in a day, in addition to using DAS throughout the day. With the revamping of the program in May 2024, DAS Advance was discontinued.

USING DAS ON THE DAY OF YOUR VISIT DAS is navigated using the MDE app. You can request return times for any attraction or character-greeting venue with a queue. Tap the hamburger menu on the app, tap "DAS," scroll to the attraction, tap the standby time, then tap the DAS time. Then click each participating guest, tap "Continue," then "Confirm," and finally "View My Day." Every guest who is linked to the enrollee will have access to the DAS times on their app and is able to request or modify return times.

The return time will be the current wait time minus 10 minutes: If, say, you tap on Seven Dwarfs Mine Train at 12:20 p.m. and the standby time is 40 minutes, your return time will be 30 minutes later, at 12:50 p.m. You may return at the specified time or anytime thereafter. When you return, the enrollee's MagicBand will be scanned first; the scanner will turn blue initially, a cast member will quickly and quietly confirm it's the right person, and the rest of the group will get green lights when they scan in. The whole group will use the Lightning Lane.

You can hold one DAS return time at a time. However, you can use Genie+ (where offered), Individual Lightning Lane, boarding groups, and DAS at the same time.

unofficial **TIP**
Bring an external battery for your phone.

WHAT HAPPENS IF I'M LATE FOR THE RETURN WINDOW? If you have a Genie+ or Lightning Lane reservation, try to arrive within the window. The cast members try to work with you, but their hands can be tied at some attractions or on days when an attraction has broken down a lot. A DAS is open-ended; you may not be early, but it remains available until the park closes.

For more information on facilities and services available to guests with cognitive disabilities, download Disney's guide to planning a trip at theugseries.com/wdw-cognitive-guide. (At press time, the guide had not been updated since 2021, but other than references to FastPass+ that should be Genie+, the information appears current.)

For a ride-by-ride chart of the sights, sounds, smells, and experiences you'll encounter on each ride, see Disney's guide to its attractions at theugseries.com/wdw-cognitive-matrix.

WHEELCHAIRS AND ELECTRIC VEHICLES

GUESTS MAY RENT WHEELCHAIRS or three-wheeled electric conveyance vehicles (ECVs), aka scooters. These give guests with limited mobility tremendous freedom. If you are in a park and need assistance with these devices, go to Guest Relations.

Wheelchairs rent for $12 per day at the theme parks (see Parts 11–14 for specific locations). Wheelchairs are also available for rent at the water parks and Disney Springs for $12 per day with a refundable $100 deposit. ECVs cost $65 per day, plus a $20 refundable deposit ($100 at Disney Springs and the water parks).

Your rental deposit slip is good for a replacement wheelchair in any park during the same day. You can rent a chair in the Magic Kingdom in the morning, return it, go to any other park, present your deposit slip, and get another chair at no additional charge.

Apple Scooter (☎ 321-726-6837, applescooter.com) rents scooters with a wide variety of options, and is by far the least expensive choice for rentals of three or more days. **Buena Vista Scooters** (☎ 407-331-9147, buenavistascooters.com) also rents scooters with many options but is much more expensive. Both companies include free delivery to and pickup from your Disney resort. You'll need to be present for delivery and pickup.

All Disney parking lots have close-up spots for visitors with disabilities; request directions when you pay your parking fee. Most (but not all) rides, shows, restrooms, and restaurants accommodate wheelchairs, as do monorails and buses, as outlined below.

Even if an attraction doesn't accommodate wheelchairs or ECVs, nonambulatory guests may ride if they can transfer from their wheelchair to the ride vehicle. Disney staff aren't trained or permitted to assist with transfers—guests must be able to board the ride unassisted or have a member of their party assist them. Members of the guest's party may ride with the guest.

Because the waiting areas of some attractions won't accommodate wheelchairs, nonambulatory guests and their parties should ask a cast member for boarding instructions as soon as they arrive at an attraction entrance.

Much of the Disney transportation system is accessible. Monorails can be accessed by ramp or elevator, the Skyliner has special gondolas for wheelchairs and scooters, and all bus routes are served by vehicles with wheelchair lifts, though unusually wide or long wheelchairs (or motorized chairs) may not fit the lift. Watercraft accommodations for wheelchairs are iffier.

A large number of Disney hotel guests use scooters. This affects commuting times by bus, as each Disney bus can accommodate only two or three scooters or wheelchairs. A Minnesota woman touring with her parents shared her experience:

I was stunned by the number of scooters this year. My parents each had one, and several times they had to wait to find a bus that had available space for scooters or wheelchairs. If people needing a scooter can make it to the bus stop on foot, they'd be better off waiting until they get to the park and renting a scooter there.

Food and merchandise locations at theme parks, Disney Springs, and hotels are generally accessible, but some fast-food queues and shop aisles are too narrow for wheelchairs. At these locations, ask a cast member or member of your party for assistance.

DIETARY RESTRICTIONS AND ALLERGIES

WALT DISNEY WORLD is one of the best places to eat for people with food allergies. The restaurants and culinary teams are very accommodating. Almost everything we've heard about dining with food allergies has been positive. **Bob Jacobs,** an author for the TouringPlans blog, shares his experience and things he's learned while navigating dietary restrictions at the World with members of his family:

- Make your needs known when booking your visit. Follow up with an email to the **Special Dietary Requests** team (special.diets@disneyworld .com). Based on the information you provide, they may send a link asking you to fill out the Special Dietary Request Form to be sent back no sooner than 14 days before your visit.

- After you send back the completed form, Disney will share it with the restaurants you've indicated. If their culinary teams have any questions about the information you've sent, they'll reach out to you before your visit. When you arrive at a restaurant, tell a food-and-beverage cast member about your special dietary requests and they can assist you. We have found that even quick-service culinary staff members are happy to discuss available options with you.

- With more than 200 dining locations, it would be impossible to share experiences at each. But at the following restaurants, the head chef has come to the table to discuss our needs and then prepared an off-menu meal free of allergens: **Biergarten Restaurant, Chefs de France, Tutto Italia Ristorante,** and **Narcoossee's.** We've also received excellent care at **Kona Cafe, Rose & Crown Dining Room;** and **Le Cellier Steakhouse.**

- Quick-service locations that have been especially accommodating include **Columbia Harbour House, Cosmic Ray's Starlight Café, Gasparilla Island Grill, D-Luxe Burger, PizzeRizzo, Docking Bay 7 Food and Cargo,** and **Capt. Cook's.** In every instance, a member of the culinary team has spoken with us directly before preparing our meal.

- There are a couple of caveats worth mentioning:
  1. While restaurants make reasonable efforts to accommodate dietary requests, they can't guarantee that they will be able to meet every request. Buffets may be susceptible to cross-contact due to their self-service approach. If there is a concern about cross-contact, you can speak to a special diets–trained cast member about having your meal prepared and delivered to you separately. (We have done that at the **Biergarten** buffet in the Germany Pavilion.)

2. Allergy-friendly offerings rely on supplier ingredient labels, so Disney can't guarantee the accuracy of the contents of each food item. And since there are no separate allergy-friendly kitchens, Disney can't guarantee that a menu item is completely free of allergens.

MEDICATIONS

FOR GUESTS WHO EXPERIENCE ALLERGIC REACTIONS that can be severe or life-threatening, Disney provides epinephrine injectors (**EpiPens**) at **First Aid Centers** and other locations throughout the parks (check your park guide maps for locations). Nurses and first responders are trained in EpiPen use, but guests with known conditions should always travel with their own supplies.

VISUALLY IMPAIRED, DEAF, OR
HARD-OF-HEARING GUESTS

GUEST RELATIONS PROVIDES FREE **assistive-technology devices** to guests who are visually impaired, deaf, or hard-of-hearing ($25 refundable deposit, depending on the device). Sight-impaired guests can customize the given information (such as architectural details, restroom locations, and descriptions of attractions and restaurants) through an interactive audio menu that is guided by a GPS in the device. For deaf or hard-of-hearing guests, amplified audio and closed-captioning for attractions can be loaded into the same device.

Braille guidebooks are available from Guest Relations at all parks ($25 refundable deposit), and **Braille menus** are available at some theme park restaurants. Some rides provide **closed-captioning;** many theater attractions provide **reflective captioning.**

Disney provides **sign language interpretations** of live shows at the theme parks on certain designated days of the week:

- **MAGIC KINGDOM** Mondays and Thursdays
- **EPCOT** Fridays
- **DISNEY'S ANIMAL KINGDOM** Tuesdays and Saturdays
- **DISNEY'S HOLLYWOOD STUDIOS** Sundays and Wednesdays

Get confirmation of the interpreted-performance schedule a minimum of one week in advance by calling Disney World information at ☎ 407-824-4321 (voice) or 407-827-5141 (TTY). You'll be contacted before your visit with a schedule of the interpreted performances.

WALT DISNEY WORLD
for PREGNANT GUESTS

WHEN IT COMES TO VISITING DISNEY WORLD while pregnant, a Colorado reader has some good advice. During her fifth month of pregnancy, **Debbie Grubbs** intrepidly explored the World, compiling observations and tips for expectant moms that she shares below.

MAGIC KINGDOM Splash Mountain [*now* **Tiana's Bayou Adventure**] *is a no-go, obviously, due to the drop—or so I thought. It turns out that the seat configuration in the logs has more to do with it than* *the drop. The seats are made so that your knees are higher than your rear, compressing the abdomen (when it's this large). This is potentially harmful to the baby.*

Big Thunder Mountain Railroad *is also out of the question. It's just not a good idea to ride roller coasters when pregnant.*

Mad Tea Party *may be OK if you don't spin the cups. We didn't ride this one because my doctor advised me to skip rides with centrifugal [or centripetal] force.* **Dumbo** *in Fantasyland and the* **Astro Orbiter** *in Tomorrowland are OK, though.*

Space Mountain *is one of my favorite rides . . . but a roller coaster nonetheless.*

Tomorrowland Speedway *isn't recommended due to the amount of rear-ending by overzealous younger drivers.*

We also think Debbie would have had to pass on **Seven Dwarfs Mine Train** and its swinging cars, as well as **Tron Lightcycle/Run.**

ANIMAL KINGDOM Dinosaur *is very jerky and should be avoided.*

We think Debbie would've avoided **Expedition Everest** too. **Na'vi River Journey** at Pandora might be fine, but **Avatar Flight of Passage** is probably too much.

EPCOT Mission: Space, Test Track, *and* Guardians of the Galaxy: Cosmic Rewind *are restricted, as are all simulator rides; they're way too rough and jerky. [Nonmoving seats are available in some simulation attractions—ask a cast member.]* **Soarin' Around the World** *is fine.*

HOLLYWOOD STUDIOS Tower of Terror *is out of the question for the drop alone, and* **Star Tours** *is restricted because it's a simulator.* **Rock 'n' Roller Coaster** *is clearly off-limits. In Toy Story Land,* **Slinky Dog Dash** *(the beginner coaster) is out, as are the* **Alien Swirling Saucers.**

Millennium Falcon: **Smugglers Run** at Star Wars: Galaxy's Edge is a no-go, and possibly **Star Wars: Rise of the Resistance** for its reentry segment at the end. **Mickey & Minnie's Runaway Railway** *might* be doable—there's one scene where the ride vehicle shakes side to side while you're doing the mambo (we're not making this up, we swear).

WATER PARKS Slides *are off-limits, but not the* **wave pools** *and* **floating creeks** *(great for getting the weight off your feet).*

A New Jersey woman advises:

Moms-to-be should be really mindful of the temperature, staying hydrated, and having realistic expectations for how much you'll be able to do. We averaged 5–7 miles of walking per day during our trip, which may have been a bit too much for me (I was six months pregnant at the time). Once the temperatures started approaching 90, I found it difficult to catch my breath and my feet began to swell. A midday nap or swim break was 100% required—I tried to skip it on a few days, and I was miserable as a result. I was most frustrated at EPCOT, where most of the headliner attractions are restricted for pregnant guests.

MORE TIPS FOR MOMS-TO-BE

IN ADDITION TO OUR READERS' TIPS, we also suggest discussing your Disney World plans with your OB-GYN before your trip and walking at home to build up your stamina for the parks. Once in the World, use in-park transportation as much as possible.

WALT DISNEY WORLD *for* LARGER GUESTS

WHEN YOU'RE SPENDING A SMALL FORTUNE on your vacation, you don't want to worry about whether you'll have trouble fitting into the ride vehicles. Fortunately, Disney realizes that its guests come in all shapes and sizes and is quite accommodating.

Deb Wills and **Debra Martin Koma,** authors of the 2005 guidebook *PassPorter's Walt Disney World for Your Special Needs,* offer the following suggestions.

- You'll be on your feet for hours at a time, so wear comfortable, broken-in shoes. If you feel a blister starting to form, take care of it quickly. (Each theme park has a **First Aid Center** with bandages and other necessities.)
- If you're prone to chafing, consider bringing an antifriction product designed to control or eliminate rubbing (such as **Body Glide**).
- In restaurants, look for chairs without arms. Check with a dining host if you don't see one.
- Request a hotel room with a king-size bed. The good sleep you'll get will be worth it.
- Attractions have different kinds of vehicles and seating. Some have bench seats, while others have individual seats; some have overhead harnesses, while others have seat belts or lap bars. Learn what type of seating or vehicle each attraction has before you go so you know what to expect (check out theugseries.com/allears-ride-gallery for details). If the attraction has a seat belt, pull it all the way out before you sit down, to make it easier to strap yourself in. Note that some attractions have seat-belt extenders—ask a cast member about these.
- Several attractions offer a sample ride vehicle for you to try before you get in line. These can be found at **Tron Lightcycle/Run** in the Magic Kingdom, **Test Track** in Epcot, **Avatar Flight of Passage** and **Expedition Everest** in Animal Kingdom, and **Star Wars: Rise of the Resistance** and **Rock 'n' Roller Coaster** in Disney's Hollywood Studios. Ask a cast member if the test seats aren't immediately visible.

Sometimes it isn't size in general but your particular build that can present a problem when it comes to ride vehicles. For example, Tron's leg restraints don't accommodate all guests with large calves, regardless of torso size. Likewise, a Connecticut reader relates her experience in Animal Kingdom:

Since I was a very young girl, I've dreamed of riding on a dragon, so I was extremely excited about the chance to experience Avatar Flight of Passage in Pandora. Unfortunately, though I was able to mount the ride's motorcycle-like seat without difficulty, the safety braces that came up behind would not lock due to my particular dimensions. The cast member in charge of checking the safeties was very kind and did try to coach me into a better fit, but in the end I had to get out and leave the ride as my husband and son looked on. I was absolutely mortified, though I was graciously offered two additional ride reservations as compensation.

Fast-forward to the next day at Disney's Hollywood Studios. I was determined not to repeat the experience, so when the time came to ride the Rock 'n' Roller Coaster, I asked if there were sample seats and restraints I could try before entering the line. I was ushered backstage by a cast member and was able to try out the exact seating configuration with success.

WALT DISNEY WORLD *for* OLDER GUESTS

OLDER VISITORS HAVE MANY OF THE SAME PROBLEMS and concerns as all Disney visitors ("Is Space Mountain too rough? How much walking will I have to do? Why isn't Figment featured in more rides?"). Pressure to endure the frantic pace set by their younger family members can cause older adults to concentrate on simply surviving Disney World rather than enjoying it. Instead, they should set their own pace or dispatch the younger folks to tour separately. A reader in Alabama writes:

> *Being a senior is not for wussies, particularly at Walt Disney World. Things that used to be easy take a lot of effort, and sometimes your brain has to wait for your body to catch up. Half the time, your grandchildren treat you like a crumbling ruin; then they turn around and trick you into getting on a roller coaster in the dark. Seniors must be alert and not trust anyone—not their children, not the Disney people, and especially not their grandchildren. Don't follow along blindly like a lamb to the slaughter.* He who hesitates is launched!

Most older people we interview enjoy Disney World much more when they tour with other people their age. But if you're considering visiting with your grandchildren, we recommend establishing limits, maintaining control of your own schedule and boundaries, and setting a comfortable pace. You could even take the grandkids to a local theme park, fair, or zoo before you extend the Walt Disney World invitation to see what you're getting yourself into.

When it comes to attractions, we feel that personal taste should trump age. We hate to see older folks pass up a full-blown adventure like Rise of the Resistance just because it's a so-called thrill ride—it gets its appeal more from the music and visual effects than from the thrill of the ride. Our attraction profiles in Parts 11–14 will help you make informed decisions.

GETTING AROUND

MANY OLDER PEOPLE LIKE TO WALK, but a 7-hour visit to a theme park can include up to 10 miles on foot. Consider renting a wheelchair or scooter (see page 316) if you're not up for that distance.

LOOK OUT FOR STROLLERS! Given the number of wheeled vehicles, pedestrians, and tight spaces, mishaps are inevitable. In response to a few incidents involving strollers taking up too much space or running into other guests, Disney has limited stroller sizes to **31 inches wide by 52 inches long.**

TIMING YOUR VISIT

RETIREES SHOULD MAKE THE MOST of their flexible schedules and go to Walt Disney World in the fall or spring (excluding holiday weeks), when the weather is nicest and the crowds are comparatively thinner. Crowds and weather are also generally reasonable from late January through early February. See page 27 for more information.

LODGING

IF YOU CAN AFFORD IT, STAY ON-PROPERTY. Rooms are among the area's nicest, and transportation is always available to any Disney destination at no additional cost.

Disney hotels reserve rooms close to restaurants and transportation for guests who can't tolerate much walking. They also provide golf carts to pick up and deliver guests at their rooms. Service can vary dramatically depending on the time of day and number of guests requesting carts. At check-in time, for example, the wait for a ride can be as long as 40 minutes.

Walt Disney World hotels are spread out—it's easy to avoid stairs, but it's often a long way to your room from parking lots or bus stops.

If you enjoy watching birds and animals, try **Animal Kingdom Lodge & Villas.** Try **Saratoga Springs Resort & Spa** for golf. RVers will find pleasant surroundings at **The Campsites at Disney's Fort Wilderness Resort.**

TRANSPORTATION

ROADS IN DISNEY WORLD CAN BE DAUNTING. Armed with a decent sense of direction and a great sense of humor, however, even the most timid driver can get around. Plus, you don't have to be very specific to use a mapping app on your smartphone—if you want to go to EPCOT for example, entering "EPCOT" or "EPCOT parking" will get the job done.

Parking for guests with disabilities is available near each theme park's entrance; toll-plaza attendants will provide a dashboard ticket and direct you to the reserved spaces. Disney requires that you be recognized officially as disabled to use this parking, but temporarily disabled persons are also permitted access.

DINING

EAT BREAKFAST AT YOUR HOTEL RESTAURANT or have juice and pastries in your room. Bring your own snacks into the park, and supplement them with fresh or dried fruit, fruit juice, and soft drinks purchased from vendors. To avoid the crowds, make Advance Dining Reservations for lunch before noon. Then you can have an early dinner and be out of the restaurants, ready for evening touring and fireworks, long before the main crowd even thinks about dinner.

WALT DISNEY WORLD *for* COUPLES

WEDDINGS, COMMITMENT CEREMONIES, AND VOW RENEWALS

SO MANY COUPLES TIE THE KNOT, get engaged, or honeymoon at Disney World that Disney has a dedicated department to help arrange the day or vacation of your dreams. **Disney's Fairy Tale Weddings & Honeymoons** (☎ 321-939-4610; disneyweddings.com) offers a range of in-park ceremony venues and services—including photographers, videographers, musicians, and floral designers—for any size or type of gathering. Have a fairy-tale wedding in front of Cinderella Castle or an intimate beach gathering at Crescent Cove. You can even request fireworks or Disney characters at your event.

You are responsible for obtaining an officiant and a marriage certificate. Disney maintains a list of officiants from which you can choose, or you can bring your own—if you do, the officiant counts as one of your guests.

unofficial **TIP**
Contact Disney as soon as you have a date in mind for your event—popular dates may not be available on short notice. If you wish to hold your ceremony inside a theme park, you're restricted to very early in the morning or late at night, when the park is closed to guests.

LEGALITIES

TO MARRY IN THE WORLD, you need a marriage license ($94), issued at any Florida county courthouse. Florida residents must complete a 4-hour premarital counseling session to marry less than 3 days after applying for their license; completing the course reduces the license fee to $61. There is no waiting period for residents of other states; all weddings must occur within 60 days of getting the license. Blood tests aren't required, but both parties must present valid identification and their Social Security numbers. Finally, if you're widowed or divorced, you must also present a certified copy of the deceased spouse's death certificate or your divorce decree.

HONEYMOONS AND HONEYMOON REGISTRIES

HONEYMOON PACKAGES are adaptations of regular Walt Disney World travel packages, though you may purchase add-ons such as flowers and in-room gifts to make your trip more special.

Some couples who honeymoon at Walt Disney World create a registry that allows friends and family to give them tours, spa packages, special dinners, and the like. For more information on Disney honeymoon registries, visit disney.honeymoonwishes.com.

CELEBRATE . . . EVERYTHING!

DISNEY WORLD IS ALL ABOUT CELEBRATING—marriages, birthdays, anniversaries, the works—but only if you let somebody know. A Missouri newlywed offers this advice:

> If you're celebrating, ask for Celebration Buttons when you check into your hotel or at any park's Guest Relations, then WEAR THEM! Cast members regularly congratulated us, and I'm relatively certain we were seated at better tables for dinner based solely on our buttons.

TIPS FOR VISITORS WHO NEED "ADULT TIME"

AS WE'VE NOTED, WALT DISNEY WORLD is a great destination for adults traveling without kids, either as solos, couples, or groups of friends. The self-contained Disney universe, with its easy transportation, security, and variety of dining, drinking, and entertainment options, makes it a fabulous place to vacation without children (don't tell ours!).

Naturally, anyone who visits The Most Magical Place on Earth is well advised to be prepared to see children—lots of them. It would be naive to think otherwise. But that doesn't mean you need to be around the little tykes every minute. Here are some tips.

- **Dine late.** Most families will try to eat dinner before 8 p.m. Have a late lunch and try for a reservation closer to the last seating at your restaurant. The exceptions to this are **California Grill** and **Topolino's Terrace,** where many people (families or not) will try to time their meals around the fireworks in the Magic Kingdom, EPCOT, and Disney's Hollywood Studios.
- **Dine at Victoria & Albert's.** V&A is the only on-property restaurant that bans guests under age 10 (except at the Chef's Table). Pricey? Yes. Worth it? You bet.
- **Go to the spa.**
- **Linger in World Showcase.** We could spend hours poring over the details of the World Showcase pavilions. Favorites include the **Bijutsu-kan Gallery** in Japan and the **Gallery of Arts and History** in Morocco.
- **Really take in the trails of Animal Kingdom.** The animal trails in Asia, Africa, and Discovery Island are peaceful and beautiful.
- **Stay up late.** Take a tip from Tom Bricker of the Disney Tourist Blog, and don't leave the park until well past closing. There's something magical about having all of Main Street or Sunset Boulevard to yourself with the lights and background music still playing. Don't miss the last bus to your resort, though, if you didn't drive.
- **Take a tour.** Many Walt Disney World tours have an age limit for how young a guest can be to experience them.
- **Spend the morning at the pool.** Most families hit the parks in the morning and come back to their hotels around lunch. Do the opposite and you'll frequently get your own private pool.
- **See page 103** for a list of the quietest rooms at Walt Disney World, or use the TouringPlans.com hotel room finder (touringplans.com/walt-disney-world/room-finder) to scope out the quietest rooms at any Disney resort.

ROMANTIC GETAWAYS

NOT ALL DISNEY HOTELS lend themselves to a couple's getaway: Some are too family-oriented, while others swarm with conventioneers. For romantic (though expensive) lodging, we recommend **Animal Kingdom Lodge & Villas, Bay Lake Tower** at the Contemporary, **BoardWalk Inn & Villas, Grand Floridian Resort & Spa** and its **Villas, Polynesian Village Resort** and **Polynesian Villas, Riviera Resort, Wilderness Lodge & Villas,** and the **Yacht & Beach Club Resorts.**

The Alligator Bayou section at **Port Orleans Riverside,** a Disney Moderate resort, also has secluded rooms.

WALT DISNEY WORLD *for* SINGLES

DISNEY WORLD IS GREAT FOR SINGLES. Safety and comfort are unsurpassed, especially for women traveling alone. Parking lots are well lit and constantly patrolled. And if you're looking for a place to relax without being hit on, the bars, lounges, and nightclubs are among the most laid-back and friendly you're likely to find. Between the BoardWalk and Disney Springs, nightlife abounds; virtually every type of entertainment is available at a reasonable price. If you over-imbibe and you're a Disney resort guest, Disney buses will return you safely to your hotel.

See "Tips for Going Solo," page 326, for more ways to enjoy Walt Disney World on your own.

WALT DISNEY WORLD *for* INTERNATIONAL VISITORS

AS OF MARCH 10, 2023, the United States rescinded its requirement that visitors from China, Hong Kong, and Macau be vaccinated against COVID-19 before entering the country. Visitors from these countries no longer need to get tested, show a negative test result, or show documentation of recovery from COVID-19 prior to boarding a flight to the U.S.

A mom from Spain offers advice to readers who are making the long haul to Walt Disney World:

> You cannot predict how the time difference is going to affect you or the little people. Coming from Spain, we were looking at a 9-hour flight from the UK and a 6-hour time difference, and we spent our first few days in a haze after trying to do too much too soon.

Londoner and *Unofficial* friend Andrew Dakoutros sent us this grab bag of tips and advice for other Disney-bound Brits:

> (1) Jellyrolls [the piano bar at Disney's BoardWalk] doesn't accept UK driving licences as ID for entry [they accept passports]; (2) many MouseSavers codes [see page 27] can't be used from the UK; (3) the Twinings tea at The Tea Caddy at EPCOT doesn't taste as good as in London.
>
> Additionally, you need to emphasise how hot Florida is and the importance of sunscreen. Most Britons holiday in Spain or Greece, where the sun is nowhere near as strong.

TRANSLATION SERVICES A wireless device called **Ears to the World** provides synchronized narration in French, German, Japanese, Portuguese, or Spanish for more than 30 attractions in the theme parks. The

TIPS FOR GOING SOLO

TRAVELING BY YOURSELF DOESN'T MEAN YOU CAN'T HAVE A GREAT TIME at Disney World. **Deb Wills,** creator of the all-things-Disney website AllEars.net, offers this advice.

- One of the best parts about traveling solo is that you can be your own boss. Sleep in, have leisurely morning coffee on the balcony, relax by the pool . . . or not. If you'd rather get up and go early, who's to stop you?

- Put some spontaneity into your day. If you're taking Disney transportation, get on the first park bus that arrives.

- Get on the resort monorail at the Magic Kingdom and visit each of the resorts it stops at. Each resort has its own theme and character, with lots to see and explore.

- Did you know you can walk through the queues and view the preshows of the thrill rides even if you don't ride? Wander through at your own pace, then tell the cast member before boarding that you don't wish to ride. You'll be shown to a nearby exit.

- If you *do* want to experience the thrill rides, take advantage of the **single-rider lines** (when available) for the **Rock 'n' Roller Coaster, Expedition Everest,** *Millennium Falcon:* **Smugglers Run,** and **Test Track.** They can cut your wait time significantly.

- If you encounter folks taking photos of each other, ask if they'd like to be in one photo, then offer to snap the picture. This is a great way to meet people.

- Get your favorite Disney snack, find a bench, and people-watch. You'll be amazed at what you see: a honeymooning couple wearing bride-and-groom mouse ears, toddlers seeing Mickey and the characters for the first time, grandparents smiling indulgently as their grandchildren smear ice cream all over their faces. If you're missing the smiles of your own children, buy a couple of balloons and give them away. You'll make the recipients very, very happy.

- Learn how some of the magic is created. Take a **behind-the-scenes tour** (see Part 16) or one of the Deluxe hotel tours.

- Visit **Animal Kingdom Lodge** and relax at an animal-viewing area. Find an animal keeper; they'll gladly discuss care of the wild animals at the resort.

- Don't hesitate to strike up conversations with cast members or guests in line with you. International cast members in EPCOT's World Showcase will be happy to share stories about their homelands.

- Enjoy a leisurely shopping adventure around the World. Some stores, such as **Arribas Brothers** in Disney Springs and **Mitsukoshi Department Store** in the Japan Pavilion in EPCOT, have really neat displays and exhibits.

- Go to a restaurant you've always wanted to try but your picky eater has always declined. You don't have to order a full meal; try several appetizers or, better yet, just dessert.

- Special fun can be had at a character meal (no waiting in long lines). Which one has characters you love? Make an early or late reservation for fewer people and more character time. **The Garden Grill** in The Land, for example, is a hidden gem!

- Check the calendar for special events. EPCOT's annual **Flower & Garden Festival** has lots of eye candy that you can enjoy at your own pace.

- Use common sense about your personal security. I feel very comfortable and safe traveling alone at Walt Disney World and have done so many times, but I still don't do things that I wouldn't do at home (like announce to anyone listening that I'm traveling solo). If you aren't comfortable walking to your room alone, ask at the front desk for a security escort. Use extra caution in the parking lots at night, just as you would at home.

wireless, lightweight headsets provide real-time translation and are available for a $25 refundable deposit at Guest Relations in all parks.

ODDS *and* ENDS

FRIENDS OF BILL W. For information on **Alcoholics Anonymous** meetings in the area, visit osceolacountyintergroup.org. For information on **Al-Anon** and **Alateen** meetings, visit al-anonorlando.org.

LOOSE ICE AND DRY ICE are prohibited in coolers inside the theme parks and water parks. Reusable ice packs are permitted.

SMOKING All Walt Disney World theme parks and water parks, along with the ESPN Wide World of Sports Complex, are smoke-free— *smoking is allowed only outside of the park entrances.* Disney resort guests may smoke only in designated areas; smoking in your room or on your balcony is prohibited.

For a full list of places where smoking is permitted, see disneyworld .disney.go.com/guest-services/designated-smoking-areas.

ARRIVING *and* GETTING AROUND

GETTING *to* WALT DISNEY WORLD

FROM ORLANDO INTERNATIONAL AIRPORT (MCO)

YOU HAVE SEVERAL OPTIONS for getting from MCO to Disney World. Because most readers stay at a Disney hotel, we cover the **Mears Connect** bus service first, followed by towncar services, ride-sharing apps, and car rentals. Driving directions conclude this section.

Getting Between Orlando International Airport and Walt Disney World

Until 2022, Disney offered free bus service, called **Magical Express,** between Orlando International Airport (MCO) and Disney's hotels. With that service discontinued, several alternatives are available.

Behind the scenes, Disney's Magical Express was operated by Mears Transportation, which also runs taxi, towncar, and shuttle services throughout Central Florida. Shortly after Disney announced it was discontinuing Magical Express, Mears announced a similar bus service, called **Mears Connect** (☎ 407-422-4561; mearsconnect.com), that runs between MCO and Walt Disney World–area hotels.

Mears Connect comes in two flavors: Standard and Express. **Standard** works almost exactly like Magical Express, with shared bus service between the airport and Disney's hotels, including the non-Disney-owned Disney Springs and Bonnet Creek hotels, plus the Four

MCO-TO-DISNEY RESORT TRANSPORTATION OPTIONS

RIDE-SHARING APP (LYFT, UBER)

ROUND-TRIP PRICE • $80–$160 plus gratuity (up to 3 adults)
PROS • Possibly the cheapest option for 3 or 4 people • Direct service to your resort
CONS • Price varies considerably based on demand • May be hard to find cars with child seats • Car quality ranges from basic to luxurious

MEARS CONNECT

ROUND-TRIP PRICE • *Standard:* $32/adult, $27/child plus small gratuity • *Express:* $500 for up to 4 adults
PROS • Cheapest option for 1 or 2 people • Mears ran Magical Express for years, so they know what they're doing • Child seats available
CONS • Standard is longest transportation time of any option • Standard service may drop off passengers at other resorts before yours • Express service is expensive

MEARS TOWNCAR SERVICE

ROUND-TRIP PRICE • $236 plus gratuity (up to 4 adults)
PROS • Likely the fastest way to get to your resort • Direct service to your resort • Child seats available • Driver will meet at baggage claim and assist with luggage
CONS • More expensive than other options

Seasons, Shades of Green, Swan, Swan Reserve, and Dolphin. Pricing is $32 per adult and $27 per child, round-trip; one-way fares are half that. As with Magical Express, the bus may drop off passengers at other hotels before you get to yours. If you're traveling alone or with one other adult and you don't mind the wait to drop off other guests at their resorts, Standard is the cheapest option to get between your hotel and Walt Disney World. The **Express** option will take you (and possibly other groups) directly to your hotel. The one-way cost is $250 for up to four people, then $55 for each additional passenger.

Towncar Service

If you're concerned about finding a ride using an app or having to wait on other people to fill a bus to your destination, a towncar service may be your best bet. **Happy Limousine** (☎ 407-856-1280; happylimo.com) provides towncar, minivan, and limo service between MCO (and Sanford International Airport) and Disney World–area hotels. Child seats and boosters are available, as are wheelchair-accessible options. One-way trips start at $118 for a 4-person luxury SUV or 5-person minivan, and $160 for a 10-person transit van. Other services exist, too, and are easy to research online.

One advantage of a towncar is that the driver will meet you at baggage claim with a placard showing your name and will assist with your luggage. Another advantage is that towncar services generally don't use surge pricing, so you know in advance how much your transportation will cost. If you're a group of five or more, and the direct service to your hotel and convenience of having your driver meet you at baggage claim are worth paying a little extra for, then towncar service might be the best option for you.

Ride-Sharing Apps

We generally recommend **Lyft** and **Uber** over taxis and shuttle services. They're often significantly less expensive, and while you can't pick the specific car you'll get, it's rare that we find ourselves thinking a taxi or shuttle van would've been cleaner or more comfortable.

Both services are cheaper than taxis when commuting within the World. On a recent trip from Saratoga Springs Resort to the Magic Kingdom via Fort Wilderness, we paid $12, while the return taxi ride along the same route, in the same traffic, was $25.

Lyft and Uber can also pick you up from and drop you off at the airport. The pickup location is on MCO's second level, where baggage claim is and where passengers are picked up by family and friends. The cost of a one-way ride from the airport varies greatly depending on the number of people in your party, the kind of car you request, and the time of day you need to travel. A basic Uber or Lyft vehicle for up to three people in low crowds runs around $40, plus gratuity. The same ride can be $80 or more, depending on surges in demand. Likewise, a vehicle with room for five costs around $55 midday but more during peak times. Fancy cars, such as Uber Black or Lyft Premier, cost $80–$90 one-way, about the same as a towncar service.

DISNEY MINNIE VANS Disney's own ride-sharing service, developed in partnership with Lyft, uses the Lyft app to summon a car driven by a Disney cast member. Minnie Vans operate only within Walt Disney World—they can't be used to get between Disney and anywhere else off-property.

Painted red with white dots, Minnie Vans are certainly nicer than your average Lyft ride and are driven by cast members. But they cost roughly three times as much as a standard Lyft. And because there are relatively few of them, you might wait longer to be picked up.

Taxis

Taxis carry four to eight passengers, depending on vehicle type. Rates vary according to distance. If your hotel is in the World, your fare will be about $70–$82, plus tip. For the US 192 Maingate area, it will cost about $55. To International Drive or downtown Orlando, expect to pay in the neighborhood of $50–$70.

Mears provides local cab service, shuttle service, and an exclusive partnership with Uber called **Uber Taxi.** Using the Uber app, customers can book Mears taxis just as they would regular Uber rides. Mears says Uber Taxi is intended to offer the convenience of Uber to customers who prefer and trust a traditional taxi service over a rideshare.

Renting a Car

Readers staying in Walt Disney World frequently ask us if they'll need a car. If your plans don't include regular visits to restaurants, attractions, or other destinations outside Disney World, then the answer is a qualified no. If you want (or need) a car, the good news is that Orlando is one of the least-expensive car-rental markets in the US, averaging under $44 per day. As we went to press, the lowest price for a weekly rental we could find for mid-2024 was $40 per day for a car at the airport.

Becky's rule of thumb is that she springs for a rental car if the cost works out to be within about $100 of what she'd pay for airport transfers anyway. If you have young kids who are going to be tired of

RENTAL COMPANY	PICKUP EFFICIENCY	CONDITION OF CAR	CLEANLINESS OF CAR	RETURN EFFICIENCY	OVERALL RATING	SURVEY RANK
NATIONAL	96	94	97	91	94	1
TURO *(car share)*	94	91	94	87	91	2 (tie)
ALAMO	92	91	94	87	91	2 (tie)
ENTERPRISE	90	89	93	87	90	4
HERTZ	85	88	92	87	88	5
SIXT	84	92	94	80	88	6
AVERAGE	83	89	91	84	87	NA
AVIS	81	86	88	81	84	7
THRIFTY	71	88	89	84	83	8 (tie)
FOX	78	85	86	82	83	8 (tie)
BUDGET	70	84	87	82	81	10 (tie)
DOLLAR	71	87	88	75	81	10 (tie)

Note: For any car-rental agency not shown, we didn't receive enough survey responses to analyze.

standing in lines all day, it's worth the extra money and the walk to a car at the end of the day to avoid waiting in "another line" for a bus.

A dad from Ohio adds:

> *Although we stayed at the Grand Floridian, we found the monorail convenient only for the Magic Kingdom. Of the six nights we stayed, we used our car five days.*

PLAN TO RENT A CAR IF

1. Your hotel is outside Walt Disney World.
2. Your hotel is in the World but you want to eat off-property or at other WDW resorts regularly.
3. You plan to return to your hotel for naps or swimming during the day.
4. You plan to visit other area theme parks or water parks.

*un*official **TIP**
MCO's new terminal C holds an intermodal facility that includes commuter and intercity rail stations, plus rental car, taxi, shuttle, and public bus operations.

At **MCO,** most car-rental counters are on **level 1** of the main terminal (with terminals A and B). Level 1 is also where you can catch a courtesy shuttle to an off-site rental location.

Orlando is the largest rental-car market in the world. At last count, 36 companies vie for your business. Ten—**Alamo, Avis, Budget, Dollar, Enterprise, Hertz, National, Payless, SixT,** and **Thrifty**—have counters at terminals A, B, and C. **Fox** and 25 other companies have locations near the airport and provide courtesy shuttles outside the Arrivals level at all terminals.

We prefer renting inside the airport for the following reasons:

1. You can complete your paperwork while you wait for your checked luggage to arrive at baggage claim.
2. It's just a short walk to the garage to pick up your car.
3. The extra time and effort it takes to use the shuttle usually isn't worth the money saved, especially when you're traveling with kids.

If you rent on-site, you'll return your car to the garage adjacent to the terminal where your airline is located. If you return your car to the wrong garage, you'll have to haul your luggage from one side of the airport to the other to reach your check-in.

Most rental companies charge about $5–$8 a gallon to fill the gas tank. If you plan to drive a lot, prepay for a fill-up so you can return the car empty, or fill up at the **7-11** on airport property at 10505 Jeff Fuqua Blvd.

HOW ORLANDO RENTAL-CAR COMPANIES STACK UP When it comes to renting a car, most *Unofficial Guide* readers are looking for the following, as reflected in the table on the previous page:

1. Quick, courteous, and efficient processing on pickup
2. A nice, well-maintained, late-model automobile
3. A car that is clean and odor-free
4. Quick, courteous, and efficient processing on return
5. If applicable, an efficient shuttle between the rental agency and airport

On a 0 (worst) to 100 (best) scale, the table shows how readers rate the Orlando operations of each company. Companies not listed didn't get enough surveys to analyze; we strongly recommend renting from a company listed in the table. To participate in our survey, visit touringplans.com/walt-disney-world/survey.

National Car Rental was named the top rental company for the 13th time in the past 14 years. If you prioritize service and car condition as much as getting a good deal, go with National. **Alamo,** the only other winner in the last 13 years, is almost always in the top two. **Turo** is new to the list—let us know your experience if you use them. They're a car-share company (like Airbnb for cars) rather than a regular rental company, but you can still pick up and drop off at the airport.

Most companies, in fact, deliver consistently good cars and service. If budget is a top priority, we're comfortable recommending any company in the top five that has the lowest price. In general, cars from less-expensive companies tend to have higher miles and fewer amenities, such as backup cameras and satellite navigation or radio.

Readers complain most about the hassle of off-site shuttles and the paperwork involved in picking up cars at the off-site locations. At **Fox,** be prepared for the staff to assume you're going to steal the car; the voluminous paperwork is to help the bounty hunters find you. Also, the pace is slow at **SixT,** even if the line is short—we suspect most of their customers are visiting from outside the US and the staff needs time to review differences in rental policies, insurance coverage, electronic tolls, and the like. Both companies' employees are fantastic at what they do.

INSURANCE AND FEES When renting a car, make sure you understand what your auto insurance does and doesn't cover. If you have the slightest question about your coverage, call your agent. Have a similar discussion with the credit card company you use for the rental fee: Usually, credit card coverage picks up deductibles and some ancillary charges that your auto-insurance policy doesn't cover.

A 6%–7% sales tax, a $2.50-per-day airport-facility surcharge, and a vehicle-license-recovery fee of 45¢ to $2.02 per day will be added to your rental car bill. Some companies, including Alamo, add fees for tire and battery wear, plus other cryptic fees.

OUR BEST RENTAL-CAR DISCOUNT TIP We've saved hundreds of dollars over the past couple of years with a website called **AutoSlash** (autoslash.com), which does two things very well:

1. If you haven't yet rented a car, Autoslash will help you find the lowest rates available, using every discount you're eligible for.

2. If you've already rented a car, tell AutoSlash the details, and it'll search continuously for a lower rate. If a lower rate turns up, AutoSlash will email you a link to rebook.

AutoSlash frequently finds multiple low-price deals through **Priceline.** In those cases, AutoSlash will list the car type, rental company, and price for every deal available. Use our list of the best rental companies, opposite, to weed out the ones that don't appeal to you, and book the cheapest one that does.

TOLLS If you're flying into Orlando and plan on driving extensively, consider picking up a **Visitor Toll Pass** (visitortollpass.com) when you arrive at the airport. You'll pick up a small Toll Pass device from a vending machine at terminal A on level 1 and link it to your credit card. The Toll Pass hangs from your rearview mirror, pays tolls automatically, and allows you to use the electronic toll and express lanes throughout Florida. If the Visitor Toll Pass program isn't working, you can pick up a regular toll transponder at most grocery stores and drugstores, such as Publix and CVS. Otherwise, go old school and be prepared for about $3 in tolls each way to/from Walt Disney World.

I-4

Regardless of how you navigate to Orlando, you'll almost certainly drive on I-4, its busiest highway and one that demands a great deal of a driver's concentration. I-4 in Orlando is more or less under constant construction: A four-year project that started in 2023 is adding lanes and interchanges between Exits 58 (Champions Gate) and 67 (Osceola Parkway, leading to EPCOT and Disney Springs).

WDW EXITS OFF I-4 East to west (in the direction of Orlando to Tampa), five I-4 exits serve Walt Disney World:

Exit 68 (FL 535/Lake Buena Vista) primarily serves the Disney Springs Resort Area and Disney Springs, including the Marketplace and the West Side. It also serves non-Disney hotels with a Lake Buena Vista address. This exit puts you on a road with lots of traffic signals, especially near I-4. Avoid this area unless you're headed to the Disney Springs area.

Exit 67 (FL 536/EPCOT/Disney Springs) delivers you to a four-lane expressway into the heart of Disney World. It's the fastest and most convenient way for westbound travelers to access almost all Disney destinations except Animal Kingdom and ESPN Wide World of Sports Complex. Be alert for road construction through 2027.

Exit 65 (Osceola Parkway) is the best exit for westbound travelers to access Disney's Animal Kingdom, Animal Kingdom Lodge, Pop Century Resort, Art of Animation Resort, the All-Star Resorts, and the ESPN Wide World of Sports Complex. Expect road construction through 2027.

Exit 64 (US 192/Magic Kingdom) is the best route for eastbound travelers to access all Disney destinations. If eastbound traffic is heavy, get off at **Exit 62** instead. Expect road construction through 2027.

Exit 62 (Disney World/Celebration) is the first Disney exit you'll encounter heading east. This four-lane, controlled-access highway

I-4 & Walt Disney World Area

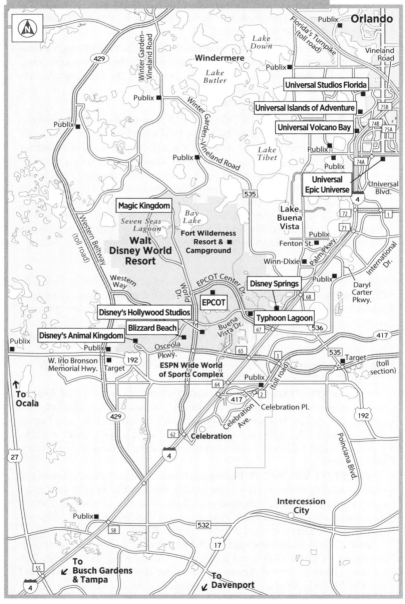

connects to the Walt Disney World Maingate. Accessing Disney World via the next exit, **Exit 64,** also routes you through the main entrance. Expect road construction through 2027.

I-4 DELAYS I-4 can be a mess anywhere in the Orlando area (and else-where). The greatest congestion is between the Universal Orlando–International Drive area and downtown Orlando, but the section to the southwest serving the Disney World exits can become a choke point at almost any time of day.

If you're going from Walt Disney World toward Orlando (east), the jam usually breaks up after you pass the FL 535 exit, but it gets congested again near Universal Orlando and northeast due to con-struction. As you head west toward Tampa, traffic eases up after the US 192 interchange.

If you're considering a hotel on or near I-Drive, try to find one toward the southern end. If I-4 traffic becomes intolerable, it's pretty easy to commute from the Universal Orlando–International Drive area to Walt Disney World on (1) **Turkey Lake Road,** connecting to Palm Parkway and FL 535 on the northwest side of I-4; (2) the south-ernmost section of **I-Drive,** connecting to FL 536 on the southeast side of the interstate; or (3) **Daryl Carter Parkway,** which bridges I-4 just northeast of FL 535, connecting Palm Parkway and International Drive near the Orlando International Premium Outlets.

AVOIDING THE I-4 BLUES Many mapping apps will automatically reroute you around delays from construction and traffic issues. For drivers without GPS, we provide the following alternative routes. Before you take any of these detours, however, use the websites men-tioned to verify whether the construction zones are still active.

If you're driving at low-traffic times, you might prefer to deal with I-4 construction rather than make a detour. During the day (6 a.m.–10 p.m.), most projects try to keep all lanes open, though traffic sometimes slows to a crawl (as it does in the WDW area even when no work is going on). From 10 p.m. to 6 a.m., however, there may be lane closures.

unofficial **TIP**
FL 417, aka the **Central Florida GreeneWay,** is a toll road, so make sure you have about $5 in cash or change to pay the toll.

Real-time road conditions are available online at the **Interstate 4 Exit Information Guide** (i4exitguide.com/i-4-traffic), and the **FDOT Interac-tive Project Map** (data.fdot.gov/road/projects) shows all active construc-tion projects in Florida. Information about construction in Orlando and the tourist areas is available at **Central Florida Roads** (cflroads.com). For info about and current conditions on area toll roads, visit the website for the **Central Florida Expressway Authority** (cfxway.com).

Traveling southwest on I-4, we recommend going around Orlando on FL 417/Central Florida GreeneWay (a toll road) and taking Exit 3 onto West Osceola Parkway into Walt Disney World. In addition to construction in Orlando and the Disney World area, there might also be construction between Daytona and DeLand. To avoid this part of I-4, take Exit 260C from southbound I-95 onto US 92 West, and turn south (left) onto US 17. When you hit I-4, take it west a short distance to FL 417, and bypass Orlando to the east.

From I-95 southbound, take Exit 260C onto US 92 westbound; then turn south (left) onto US 17. When you hit I-4, take it west a short distance to FL 417; bypass Orlando to the east, taking Exit 3 onto West Osceola Parkway and then into Walt Disney World.

From I-95 northbound, take Exit 249 onto FL 44 West toward DeLand. At I-4, go southwest, exiting onto Saxon Boulevard. Take Saxon Boulevard west to US 17, and turn south (left). When you hit I-4 again, take it west a short distance to FL 417. Take FL 417, and bypass Orlando to the east.

From MCO, exit the airport on Jeff Fuqua Boulevard and proceed south to the FL 417/Central Florida GreeneWay toll road. Turn right up the ramp and take FL 417 northwest. Take Exit 3 onto West Osceola Parkway and follow it to Walt Disney World.

From Sanford International Airport, take East Airport Boulevard west to the FL 417/Central Florida GreeneWay toll road and bypass Orlando to the east, taking Exit 3 onto West Osceola Parkway and continuing to Walt Disney World.

From Miami, Fort Lauderdale, and southeastern Florida, head north on Florida's Turnpike to Exit 249/Osceola Parkway West and follow the signs.

From Tampa and southwest Florida, take I-75 northbound to I-4; then drive east on I-4, take Exit 64 onto US 192 West and follow the signs.

ALTERNATIVE AIRPORTS

A SHORT DISTANCE northeast of Orlando is **Sanford International Airport** (**SFB;** orlandosanfordairport.com). Small, convenient, and easily accessible, it's low-hassle compared with the huge MCO and its mile-long security-checkpoint lines.

The primary domestic carrier at SFB is **Allegiant Air** (☎ 702-505-8888; allegiantair.com), with service throughout the East Coast and the Midwest. **Sun Country** (☎ 651-905-2737; suncountry.com) also serves SFB and dozens of US cities. Two low-cost Canadian airlines serve Sanford: **Flair Airlines** (flyflair.com) offers service between Canada and four other US cities, and **Swoop** (flyswoop.com) offers flights to Sanford from November through April, with twice-weekly return flights to Canada. An Uber or Lyft from Sanford to Disney property will run you $70–$150 or more one-way.

A reader from Virginia who frequently uses Sanford writes:

> *The 45-minute drive to WDW is more than made up for by avoiding the chaos at Orlando International, and it's stress-free.*

You could also fly into Tampa International Airport, but it's a 77-mile drive from there to the Magic Kingdom—about an hour and 15 minutes.

HOW *to* TRAVEL
around the WORLD

TRYING TO COMMUTE around Walt Disney World can be frustrating, simply because of the sheer number of transportation options available. Most times, your options include cars, boats, monorails, and elevated gondolas, plus walking.

Between any two points in Walt Disney World, there's almost always a free transportation option available. Some of the free options are slow enough, however, that paying for an alternative option often makes more sense. We'll walk you through those options right after some orientation.

FINDING YOUR WAY

WALT DISNEY WORLD IS HUGE—about the size of San Francisco. As with any big city, it's easy to get lost here. The easiest way to orient yourself is to think in terms of five major clusters:

1. **The Magic Kingdom area** encompasses all hotels and theme parks around Seven Seas Lagoon. This includes the Magic Kingdom; hotels connected by the monorail; Shades of Green resort; and the Palm, Magnolia, and Oak Trail Golf Courses.

2. **The Bay Lake area** includes developments on and around Bay Lake: Wilderness Lodge & Villas, Fort Wilderness campground, and the Four Seasons Resort Orlando and Tranquilo Golf Club.

3. **The EPCOT area** contains EPCOT and its resort hotels, Disney's Hollywood Studios, the BoardWalk, ESPN Wide World of Sports, Pop Century Resort, Art of Animation Resort, Caribbean Beach Resort, and Riviera Resort.

4. **The Disney Springs area** includes Disney Springs; Typhoon Lagoon water park; Lake Buena Vista Golf Course; the Disney Springs Resort Area; and the Port Orleans, Saratoga Springs, and Old Key West resorts.

5. **The Animal Kingdom area** includes Disney's Animal Kingdom, Animal Kingdom Lodge & Villas, the All-Star Resorts, Coronado Springs Resort and Blizzard Beach water park.

The following section covers how to get around Walt Disney World using the Disney transportation system. Tips using non-Disney hotel shuttles and for driving yourself begin on page 352.

THE DISNEY TRANSPORTATION SYSTEM (DTS)

THE DISNEY TRANSPORTATION SYSTEM is large, diverse, and generally efficient, but sometimes it gets overwhelmed, particularly at park opening and closing. If you could always be assured of getting on a bus, boat, monorail, or gondola at these critical times, we'd advise you to leave your car at home. In reality, delays are unavoidable when huge crowds want to go somewhere at once. In addition, some destinations are served directly, while many others require time-consuming transfers. Finally, it's sometimes difficult to figure out how Disney's various methods of transportation interconnect.

The DTS is a "hub and spoke" system. Hubs include the **Transportation and Ticket Center (TTC), Disney Springs,** and all four major **theme parks** (from about an hour before official opening time to 1 hour after closing). With some exceptions, direct service is available from Disney resorts to the major theme parks and Disney Springs, as well as between parks.

unofficial **TIP**
If a hotel offers boat or monorail service, its bus service will be limited—you'll have to transfer at a hub for many destinations.

If you're staying at a Magic Kingdom resort that's served by the monorail (**Contemporary** and **Bay Lake Tower, Grand Floridian Resort & Villas, Polynesian Village Resort & Villas**), you'll be able to commute

continued on page 341

COMMUTING TIMES BY CAR VS. THE

Average MAXIMUM time in minutes from	to MAGIC KINGDOM		to EPCOT		to DHS	
	YOUR CAR	DISNEY SYSTEM	YOUR CAR	DISNEY SYSTEM	YOUR CAR	DISNEY SYSTEM
ALL-STAR RESORTS	37 (47)	33 (50)	18 (23)	27 (50)	16 (20)	29 (49)
ANIMAL KINGDOM	37 (48)	26 (44)	16 (17)	38 (49)	16 (17)	24 (34)
ANIMAL KINGDOM LODGE & VILLAS	39 (50)	32 (44)	19 (21)	32 (45)	18 (19)	34 (50)
ART OF ANIMATION RESORT	40 (51)	33 (49)	23 (28)	27 (50)	20 (24)	34 (50)
BEACH CLUB RESORT & VILLAS	36 (46)	32 (49)	16 (21)	29 (36*)	14 (18)	29 (41*)
BLIZZARD BEACH	36 (46)	28 (39)	18 (23)	—	18 (22)	39 (54)
BOARDWALK INN & VILLAS	36 (46)	30 (46)	16 (21)	29 (46*)	14 (18)	23 (49*)
CARIBBEAN BEACH AND RIVIERA	37 (47)	31 (49)	18 (23)	***	15 (19)	***
CONTEMPORARY/ BAY LAKE TOWER	—	—	21 (26)	36 (49)	23 (27)	31 (49)
CORONADO SPRINGS	37 (47)	39 (44)	18 (23)	39 (45)	16 (20)	31 (44)
DHS	36 (46)	25 (35)	19 (24)	25 (35)	—	—
DISNEY SPRINGS	Bus service only back to your Disney resort					
DISNEY SPRINGS RESORT AREA	41 (51)	69 (91)	21 (26)	47 (62)	20 (24)	45 (60)
DOLPHIN	35 (45)	33 (65)	15 (20)	16 (44*)	15 (19)	16 (42*)
EPCOT	36 (46)	26 (37)	—	—	19 (23)	21 (30)
FORT WILDERNESS	37 (47)	28 (50)	18 (23)	34 (51*)	19 (23)	34 (50)
GRAND FLORIDIAN RESORT & VILLAS	—	—	18 (23)	38 (50*)	20 (24)	33 (50)
MAGIC KINGDOM	—	—	26 (39)	33 (45)	22 (29)	24 (34)
OLD KEY WEST	36 (46)	29 (50)	18 (23)	30 (50)	18 (22)	30 (50)
POLYNESIAN VILLAGE	—	—	17 (22)	33 (43**)	19 (23)	31 (50)
POP CENTURY	40 (51)	32 (50)	23 (28)	***	20 (24)	***
PORT ORLEANS FRENCH QUARTER	37 (47)	32 (50)	19 (24)	29 (50)	19 (23)	32 (50)
PORT ORLEANS RIVERSIDE	38 (48)	34 (50)	20 (25)	29 (50)	20 (24)	32 (50)
RIVIERA	37 (47)	32 (50)	18 (23)	***	15 (19)	***
SARATOGA SPRINGS	38 (48)	28 (49)	18 (23)	31 (47)	20 (24)	31 (47)
SHADES OF GREEN	28 (36)	35 (49)	18 (23)	33 (45)	20 (24)	20 (28)
SWAN/SWAN RESERVE	35 (45)	24 (61)	15 (20)	18 (42*)	15 (19)	14 (33*)
TREEHOUSE VILLAS AT SARATOGA SPRINGS	37 (47)	28 (49)	18 (23)	31 (47)	19 (23)	31 (47)
TYPHOON LAGOON	37 (47)	41 (56)	18 (23)	51 (70)	15 (19)	62 (85)
WILDERNESS LODGE	—	24 (63)	20 (25)	27 (50)	22 (26)	30 (50)
YACHT CLUB	36 (46)	33 (65)	16 (21)	16 (40*)	14 (18)	15 (35*)

Note: Before 4 p.m., all transportation between the theme parks and Disney Springs requires a transfer at a nearby resort. After 4 p.m., buses run directly from the theme parks to Disney Springs. There are no buses from Disney Springs directly to the theme parks.

† Driving time vs. time on DTS. Driving times include time in your car, stops to pay tolls, time to park, and any transfers on Disney trams and monorails.

DISNEY TRANSPORTATION SYSTEM†

to ANIMAL KINGDOM		to TYPHOON LAGOON		to DISNEY SPRINGS		to BLIZZARD BEACH	
YOUR CAR	DISNEY SYSTEM	YOUR CAR	DISNEY SYSTEM	YOUR CAR	DISNEY SYSTEM	YOUR CAR	DISNEY SYSTEM
11 (12)	26 (49)	12 (13)	27 (63)	13 (14)	31 (50)	6 (7)	26 (46)
—	—	17 (19)	65 (83)	19 (21)	—	10 (13)	41 (50)
9 (10)	26 (50)	19 (21)	26 (67)	22 (24)	33 (50)	11 (14)	23 (50)
14 (16)	29 (50)	12 (14)	19 (59)	15 (16)	22 (49)	10 (12)	29 (50)
17 (18)	31 (49)	9 (10)	23 (59)	10 (11)	32 (50)	12 (13)	22 (60)
10 (13)	—	13 (14)	80 (103)	14 (15)	—	—	—
17 (18)	33 (50)	9 (10)	25 (59)	10 (11)	31 (49)	12 (13)	22 (58)
17 (18)	32 (50)	6 (7)	23 (59)	7 (8)	31 (40)	12 (13)	25 (61)
20 (21)	35 (50)	17 (18)	27 (63)	16 (17)	34 (49)	15 (16)	25 (62)
11 (12)	32 (49)	12 (13)	6 (54)	13 (14)	28 (49)	6 (7)	30 (46)
16 (17)	20 (30)	8 (9)	77 (99)	9 (10)	—	11 (12)	56 (71)

Bus service only back to your Disney resort

to ANIMAL KINGDOM		to TYPHOON LAGOON		to DISNEY SPRINGS		to BLIZZARD BEACH	
YOUR CAR	DISNEY SYSTEM	YOUR CAR	DISNEY SYSTEM	YOUR CAR	DISNEY SYSTEM	YOUR CAR	DISNEY SYSTEM
21 (22)	48 (64)	9 (10)	26 (29)	6 (7)	—	16 (17)	66 (81)
16 (17)	36 (60)	10 (11)	21 (61)	11 (12)	25 (62)	11 (12)	22 (57)
16 (17)	33 (48)	12 (13)	50 (62)	13 (14)	—	11 (12)	51 (65)
29 (25)	35 (50)	10 (11)	26 (62)	11 (12)	33 (50)	19 (20)	30 (60)
18 (19)	34 (50)	15 (16)	26 (67)	16 (17)	33 (50)	13 (14)	24 (61)
17 (18)	45 (63)	23 (31)	59 (75)	27 (36)	—	12 (13)	61 (77)
19 (20)	28 (50)	8 (9)	20 (57)	9 (10)	32 (49)	14 (15)	20 (56)
17 (18)	32 (50)	14 (15)	25 (63)	15 (16)	32 (50)	12 (13)	18 (57)
14 (16)	30 (49)	12 (14)	23 (57)	15 (16)	32 (50)	10 (12)	20 (61)
19 (20)	28 (50)	9 (10)	20 (55)	10 (11)	29 (50)	14 (15)	23 (60)
20 (21)	30 (71)	10 (11)	19 (56)	11 (12)	31 (46)	15 (16)	24 (64)
15 (18)	29 (50)	5 (7)	24 (60)	7 (8)	28 (50)	10 (12)	25 (60)
21 (22)	28 (50)	9 (10)	23 (61)	6 (7)	36 (50)	16 (17)	24 (63)
18 (19)	22 (33)	15 (16)	59 (75)	18 (20)	57 (83)	13 (14)	50 (64)
16 (17)	35 (60)	10 (11)	21 (60)	11 (12)	24 (60)	11 (12)	21 (56)
17 (19)	28 (50)	9 (10)	22 (59)	6 (7)	36 (60)	13 (14)	24 (59)
20 (21)	28 (40)	—	—	8 (9)	—	15 (16)	55 (70)
20 (21)	32 (50)	17 (18)	28 (64)	18 (19)	33 (50)	15 (16)	24 (60)
17 (18)	31 (46)	8 (10)	24 (58)	10 (12)	31 (40)	12 (13)	21 (57)

*   This hotel is within walking distance of EPCOT; time given is for boat transportation to the International Gateway (EPCOT's rear entrance).

**   By foot to Transportation and Ticket Center and then by EPCOT monorail

***   Not enough data to calculate

continued from page 337

efficiently to the Magic Kingdom. If you want to visit EPCOT, you must take the monorail to the TTC and transfer to the EPCOT monorail. (Guests at the Polynesian Village & Villas can eliminate the transfer by walking 5–10 minutes to the TTC and catching the direct monorail to EPCOT.) Direct buses will deliver you to Animal Kingdom or Hollywood Studios.

If you're staying at an EPCOT resort (**BoardWalk Inn & Villas, Dolphin, Swan, Swan Reserve, Yacht & Beach Club Resorts**), you can walk or take a boat to EPCOT's International Gateway (rear) entrance. Direct buses link the EPCOT resorts to the Magic Kingdom and Disney's Animal Kingdom, but there is no direct bus to EPCOT's main entrance or Disney's Hollywood Studios. To reach the Studios from the EPCOT resorts, you must walk or take a boat or the Skyliner. Note that the Swan, Swan Reserve, and Dolphin use Mears Transportation, not Disney, for bus service—if you're headed to the Magic Kingdom, Mears will drop you off at the TTC, while Disney buses will drop you off at the park entrance. To get around this inconvenience, you can walk over to the Yacht Club bus stop when you want to go to the Magic Kingdom.

The **Caribbean Beach, Pop Century, Art of Animation, Saratoga Springs, Port Orleans, Coronado Springs, Old Key West, Animal Kingdom Lodge & Villas,** and **All-Star** resorts offer direct buses to all theme parks (though Pop and Animation may provide only the Skyliner to EPCOT and Hollywood Studios during slower times of the year). The rub is that you may have to walk a long way to bus stops or stop for more than half a dozen additional pickups before actually heading for the park(s). **Shades of Green** runs frequent shuttles from the resort to the TTC, where guests can transfer to their final destinations.

Hotels of the **Disney Springs Resort Area** (**DSRA**) provide shuttle service through an independent company. These shuttles are rated poorly by guests at these hotels—the service is substandard. Before you book a hotel, in this area, check its shuttle details and schedule.

Guests staying at **Fort Wilderness Resort & Campground** must use its buses to reach boat landings or the Settlement Depot and Reception Outpost bus stops. From these points, guests can travel directly by boat to the Magic Kingdom or by bus to other destinations. Other than going to the Magic Kingdom, the best way for Fort Wilderness guests to commute is in their own car.

DTS vs. Your Own Car

To help you assess your transportation options, we've developed a table comparing the approximate commuting times from the Disney resorts to various Walt Disney World destinations, using Disney transportation or your own car (see pages 338–339). The table represents more than 600,000 data points collected for this edition, all in 2022 and 2023. It includes bus, monorail, and boat options—the Skyliner system has its own table (see page 345).

DISNEY TRANSPORTATION The times in the "Disney System" columns represent average-case and worst-case scenarios. For example, if you want to go from the All-Star Resorts to the Magic Kingdom, the table indicates the times as "33 (50)." The first number, 33, indicates how many minutes your commute will take on an average day. It assumes that buses arrive every 20 minutes (see "Walt Disney World Bus Service," on page 341), that your average wait is half of that, that there are no major traffic delays, and that everything else is as usual. It represents the average time we observed during our research. For the pessimists, the number in parentheses (50) indicates the maximum trip time—the longest it should take for the next bus to show up, load, and deliver you to your destination. Use this number to plan for contingencies. (*Example:* The bus is pulling away as you arrive at the stop, and you must wait around 20 minutes for the next one. Once en route, the bus hits every red light on the way to the Magic Kingdom.)

Bus schedules are also adjusted based on demand and fuel costs. By far the biggest influence on your travel time between two points is the amount of time you have to wait for your bus to arrive. Once you hop on your bus, the travel time is pretty consistent—barring any unusual traffic problems—but your time waiting for the bus can vary greatly. Most cast members will tell you that buses run every 20 minutes. Our data indicates they run ever-so-slightly more often: about every 19 minutes. Also, the maximum bus travel time between any two destinations is frequently 50 minutes. That's either a policy that Disney works hard to enforce ("never make a guest wait more than 50 minutes to get to a destination") or something in the data feed ("never show a total transportation time above 50 minutes"). Surprisingly, service at the Value and Moderate resorts is about the same as at Deluxe resorts.

Walt Disney World Bus Service

unofficial TIP

If your Disney resort doesn't have direct bus service to the water parks, use Uber, Lyft, or a taxi instead.

Note: For an up-to-date look at what time buses start running at each resort, visit theugseries.com/wdw -bus-times.

Each Disney bus has an illuminated panel above its windshield that flashes the bus's destination. Theme parks also have designated waiting areas for each Disney destination. To catch the bus to the Old Key West Resort from Disney's Hollywood Studios, for example, go to the bus stop and wait in the area designated for passengers going that park. At the resorts, go to any bus stop and wait for the bus displaying your destination on the illuminated panel; the **My Disney Experience** app (see page 26) displays the approximate arrival time of the next bus to your destination. Directions to Disney destinations are available at check-in or at your hotel's Guest Relations desk. Guest Relations can also answer questions about the transportation system.

Service from resorts to major theme parks is fairly direct. You may have intermediate stops, but you won't have to transfer. Service to the water parks and other Disney resorts almost always requires transfers or extra stops.

To travel between your Disney hotel and Blizzard Beach, you must transfer at the Animal Kingdom. Traveling between your Disney hotel and **Typhoon Lagoon** will probably also require a stop (and possibly a bus transfer) at Disney Springs; if you're unlucky, this round-trip journey could take 2–3 hours. Our advice is to ask your hotel if direct service is available; if not, use a ride-sharing app.

The fastest way to commute among resorts by bus is to take a bus from your resort to one of the major theme parks and then transfer to a bus destined for your resort. This works, of course, only when the parks are open—actually, from 1 hour before the park opens for Early Theme Park Entry (ETPE) until 1 hour after closing. (Disney buses stop taking passengers *to* the theme parks when they close, but they'll take passengers *from* the parks for an hour afterward.) If the park is open late for Extended Evening Theme Park Hours, buses will continue to run for an hour after the end of that.

If the parks have already closed, you'll have to transfer at **Disney Springs**—which is clever of Disney, hoping you'll spend en route. If the theme park buses are running, though, you should head to the park closest to your resort, and then transfer to the bus going to the resort where you'll be dining.

Despite what Disney's official schedule says, bus service to the parks begins about 90 minutes before official park opening, which is 60 minutes before ETPE (that is, buses will start running around **7:30 a.m.** on days when ETPE is at 8:30 a.m. and official park opening is 9 a.m.). Buses to all four parks deliver you to the park entrance (except those from the Swan, Dolphin, and Swan Reserve, which deliver you to the TTC).

To be on time for ETPE, catch direct buses to the parks 60–90 minutes before official park opening. If you must transfer to reach your park, such as at Fort Wilderness, leave 15–20 minutes earlier.

For your return bus trip in the evening, leave the park 40–60 minutes before closing to avoid the rush. If you're caught in the exodus, travel might be slow, but you won't be stranded.

An Ohio family thinks Disney should work on its bus-tracking technology:

> *Several times at Saratoga Springs, we had to wait 45 minutes or more for a bus. Often two buses for the same park will arrive back-to-back, and then you may need to wait 45 minutes until they come again. They need to track how the buses are spaced—maybe have some buses close by that can jump in when needed, or track them with GPS.*

A reader who stayed at Port Orleans reports:

> *The DTS was wildly erratic, but we were lucky more often than not. For every time we had to wait half an hour at the bus stop, there were two or three times with no wait at all.*

If you're staying at a resort with multiple bus stops, the bus may be full or standing-room-only before it gets to your stop. It may be worth the extra time and effort to walk to the "first" bus pickup points for these resorts:

- **CARIBBEAN BEACH** Martinique
- **CORONADO SPRINGS** Gran Destino
- **OLD KEY WEST** Peninsular Road
- **PORT ORLEANS RIVERSIDE** West Depot
- **SARATOGA SPRINGS** The Grandstand

NOT ALL HUBS ARE CREATED EQUAL All major theme parks, Disney Springs, and the TTC are hubs on the bus system. If your route

WALT DISNEY WORLD BOAT ROUTES (ROUND-TRIP)
Magic Kingdom → Fort Wilderness → Magic Kingdom
Magic Kingdom → Grand Floridian Resort & Villas → Polynesian Village → Magic Kingdom
Fort Wilderness Campground → Wilderness Lodge → Contemporary Resort → Fort Wilderness **Note:** Walk or take the monorail from the Contemporary to the Magic Kingdom.
EPCOT → Boardwalk Inn & Villas → Beach Club → Yacht Club → Swan → Dolphin → EPCOT
Disney's Hollywood Studios → Boardwalk Inn & Villas → Beach Club Resort & Villas → Yacht Club → Swan → Dolphin → Disney's Hollywood Studios
Disney Springs → Saratoga Springs → Old Key West → Disney Springs
Disney Springs → Port Orleans French Quarter → Port Orleans Riverside → Disney Springs

requires you to transfer at a hub, transfer at the closest park, except at park closing. Avoid Disney Springs as a transfer point—traffic around there slows everything to a crawl.

Walt Disney World Monorail Service

Picture the monorail system as three loops. **Loop A** is an express route that runs counterclockwise connecting the Magic Kingdom with the TTC. **Loop B** runs clockwise alongside Loop A, making all stops, with service to (in order) the TTC, Polynesian Village & Villas, Grand Floridian Resort & Villas, the Magic Kingdom, Contemporary Resort and Bay Lake Tower, and back to the TTC. The long **Loop C** dips southeast, connecting the TTC with EPCOT. The hub for all loops is the TTC (where you usually park to visit the Magic Kingdom).

The monorail that serves the **Magic Kingdom** resorts usually starts running an hour or so before official park opening. If you're staying at a Magic Kingdom resort and want to be among the first into the park for Early Theme Park Entry when official opening is 9 a.m., board the monorail at these times:

- **FROM CONTEMPORARY RESORT AND BAY LAKE TOWER** 7:45–8 a.m.
- **FROM POLYNESIAN VILLAGE & VILLAS** 7:50–8:05 a.m.
- **FROM GRAND FLORIDIAN RESORT & VILLAS** 8–8:10 a.m.

If you're a day guest, you'll be allowed on the monorail at the TTC between 8 and 8:15 a.m. when official opening is 9 a.m. If you want to board earlier, walk from the TTC to the Polynesian Village Resort and board there.

If you bought Disney's Park Hopper pass, you might think that means you can flit among the parks; alas, it's more complicated. For example, you can't go directly from the Magic Kingdom to EPCOT— you must catch the express monorail (Loop A) to the TTC and then transfer to the Loop C monorail to EPCOT. If lines to board either monorail are short, you can usually reach EPCOT in 30–40 minutes, but if you want to go to EPCOT for dinner (as many do) and you're leaving the Magic Kingdom in the late afternoon, you may have to wait 30 minutes or longer to board the Loop A monorail. This delay boosts your commuting time to 50–60 minutes.

Disney frequently changes the monorail's operating hours to allow for daytime inspection of the track and vehicles. Rain and lightning, which happen frequently in Orlando, will also stop the monorails, as this Michigan reader found out:

> It would have helped to know that monorails shut down during thunderstorms and lightning. We got stuck at EPCOT trying to get back to our Magic Kingdom hotel at the end of the night due to a thunderstorm. There were thousands of people drenched with nowhere to go for hours. Had we known there was no bus service back, we would not have gambled with even a slight chance of rain.

When the monorail is closed, Disney is supposed to provide bus or boat transportation to get you where you're going. But as the reader above notes, that doesn't always happen. In that case, your best bet is a ride-sharing app or taxi. If you're going to book an expensive monorail resort, first call the resort and inquire about monorail maintenance or construction that might affect its operation.

Walt Disney World Boat Service

Boats are a popular, third transportation option between some theme parks and resorts, as a reader from Iowa reminds us:

> We stayed at Port Orleans French Quarter in December and took the ferry to Disney Springs several times. We also did a self-guided resort Christmas-decorations tour and had fun taking different boats around the Magic Kingdom and EPCOT resorts. These ferries were a much more pleasant option than buses for most legs of that tour.

The table on the previous page shows the routes served by boats. Note that most routes stop at several resorts and service may be suspended during thunderstorms or because of low water levels. Wheelchairs and scooters are permitted; strollers must be folded before you board and stowed while you're on the boat. Most routes run from about 45 minutes before park opening to 45 minutes after park closing.

Disney Skyliner

This elevated gondola connects the **Art of Animation, Pop Century, Caribbean Beach,** and **Riviera Resorts** with **Disney's Hollywood Studios** and **EPCOT**'s International Gateway. The Skyliner routes have been added to our Walt Disney World overview map on pages 12–13 and to the maps for the above Disney resorts in Part 5. Each gondola holds about 10 guests, and unless there is no line, you'll almost always be sharing your cab with another group. **Caribbean Beach Resort** serves as the hub for all Skyliner routes.

Our big initial concern with the Skyliner was that the gondolas lacked air-conditioning. However, their 17-mph speed and good ventilation keep passengers cool even on very warm days.

Our one minor gripe is that riders have to get off the gondolas at the Caribbean Beach hub, then reboard another line to get to the Studios, EPCOT, the Riviera, or Pop Century and the Art of Animation (AOA). Anyone who's ever had to change trains in a major metropolitan city's subway hub, however, will take this in stride.

SKYLINER TRAVEL TIMES (IN MINUTES)					
	POP CENTURY/ ART OF ANIMATION	CARIBBEAN BEACH	EPCOT	HOLLYWOOD STUDIOS	RIVIERA RESORT
POP CENTURY/ ART OF ANIMATION	–	9-18 (3)	31-45 (15)	22-40 (10)	19-37 (7)
CARIBBEAN BEACH RESORT	9-18 (3)	–	18-27 (12)	13-22 (7)	10-19 (4)
EPCOT	28-37 (15)	22 (12)	–	35-44 (19)	18 (8)
HOLLYWOOD STUDIOS	26-35 (10)	17 (7)	35-44 (19)	–	27-36 (11)
RIVIERA RESORT	16-25 (10)	7 (4)	11 (8)	20-29 (14)	–

The table above shows typical point-to-point transportation times between any two Skyliner stations. The first pair of numbers is the average trip time assuming normal crowds, and the number in parentheses is the trip time assuming no crowds.

For example, the time to get from the Pop Century/AOA station to EPCOT reads "31–45 (15)." Thus, you should expect the trip to EPCOT to take 31–45 minutes from the time you arrive at the Pop/ AOA station. The actual time in transit will be about 15 minutes, and the rest of the time will be spent in line(s). During off-peak hours and seasons, your times may be much shorter.

DRIVING TO AND AROUND WALT DISNEY WORLD

THE VAST MAJORITY of *Unofficial Guide* readers who drive to Orlando use GPS to get where they're going, either through their phone, their car, or a dedicated device. All GPS units and apps made in the last few years recognize location names such as Magic Kingdom and Pop Century. If you have an older unit, use the addresses in the table on the next page for the theme parks and in Part 5 for hotels.

The best GPS apps will get traffic updates and route you around delays. Our favorite is **Waze,** which provides real-time traffic updates along with navigation.

If you're driving without GPS, print out directions to Walt Disney World from **Google Maps** (maps.google.com) before you leave home; then, once you're in Orlando, use the overview maps in Part One (see pages 10–11) and in this chapter to find your way around. If you want to go primitive, the rental-car companies have free maps available (we like **Alamo Rent a Car**'s Walt Disney World road map, also available at the front desk or concierge desk of any Disney resort). Once you're inside the World, Disney's road signs are generally clear and easy to follow even without a map.

GPS Names and Addresses for the Theme Parks

Google Maps gives correct directions for the addresses and/or names shown in the table on the next page. Disney's road signs also direct you to parking as you get close. If you ever get lost, follow the signs to the Magic Kingdom parking lot (or theme park parking gate), or pull into the nearest Disney resort and ask for directions.

Driving to and from the Theme Parks

1. PARKING LOT LOCATIONS The **Animal Kingdom, EPCOT,** and **DHS** lots are adjacent to each park's entrance; the **Magic Kingdom** lot is adjacent to the TTC. From the TTC, take a ferry, monorail, or bus to the park's entrance (the bus is often fastest). Electronic displays will show you the estimated transit times for the ferry and monorail.

2. PAYING TO PARK Disney resort guests and Annual Pass holders park free; all others pay. If you paid to park and you move your car later that day, show your receipt and you won't have to pay again at the new lot. The daily parking rate for motorcycles and standard cars is $30; a preferred parking option, with spots closer to the park entrances, costs $45–$55 per day.

3. REMEMBERING WHERE YOUR CAR IS PARKED Jot down, text, or take a phone picture of the section and row where you've parked. If you're driving a rental, note the license-plate number.

4. HOW LONG IT TAKES TO PARK AND GET TO THE PARK ENTRANCE At the **Magic Kingdom,** it'll take 35–50 minutes to get to the TTC; go through the security screening; board a monorail, ferry, or bus; and reach the park entrance. At **EPCOT, Hollywood Studios,** and **Animal Kingdom,** figure about 15–20 minutes to pay, park, walk, or ride to the entrance and get through the security screening. At Disney's Hollywood Studios, allow 15–20 minutes.

5. COMMUTING FROM PARK TO PARK Using Disney transportation or your car, allow 45–60 minutes one-way, entrance to entrance. If you plan to park-hop, make sure your car is in the lot of the park where you'll finish the day.

6. LEAVING THE PARK AT THE END OF THE DAY If you stay at a park until closing, expect the parking-lot trams, monorails, Skyliner, and ferries to be mobbed. (The Magic Kingdom has wait-time displays showing the lines for the monorail and ferry.) If the tram is taking too long, walk to your car or walk to the first stop on the tram route and wait there for a tram. When someone gets off, you can get on.

DESTINATION PARKING LOT	NAME TO LOOK FOR IN GPS	ADDRESS
MAGIC KINGDOM	"Magic Kingdom Park" or "Magic Kingdom Toll Plaza" works better than the address.	3450 World Dr. Winter Garden, FL 34787
EPCOT	"EPCOT" (but not "EPCOT Parking Lot")	200 EPCOT Center Dr. Lake Buena Vista, FL 32830
ANIMAL KINGDOM	"Animal Kingdom" or "Disney's Animal Kingdom Theme Park"	2901 Osceola Pkwy. Lake Buena Vista, FL 32380
DHS	Try "Disney's Hollywood Studios–South Studio Drive" before using the address.	351 S. Studio Dr. Lake Buena Vista, FL 32830
BLIZZARD BEACH	"Blizzard Beach" should get you close, but the address works better.	1534 Blizzard Beach Dr. Lake Buena Vista, FL 32830
TYPHOON LAGOON	"Typhoon Lagoon" should work better than the address.	1145 E. Buena Vista Dr. Lake Buena Vista, FL 32830
DISNEY SPRINGS	"Disney Springs" should give a list of all parking lots to choose from.	1530 E. Buena Vista Dr. Lake Buena Vista, FL 32830

7. DINNER AND A QUICK EXIT One way to beat closing crowds in the Magic Kingdom is to arrange reservations for dinner at the **Contemporary Resort.** When you leave the Magic Kingdom for dinner, move your car from the TTC lot to the Contemporary lot. After dinner, walk (8–10 minutes) or take the monorail back to the Magic Kingdom. When the park closes and everyone else is fighting to board the monorail or ferry, you can stroll back to the Contemporary, claim your car, and get on your way. Use the same strategy in EPCOT by arranging a reservation at an EPCOT resort. When the park closes after the fireworks, exit via the International Gateway and walk to the resort where you parked.

8. CAR TROUBLE Parking lots have security patrols; if you have a dead battery or minor automotive problem, they can help. For more-serious trouble, go to the **Car Care Center** (☎ 407-824-0976), near the Magic Kingdom parking lot. Prices for most services are comparable to those at home. The facility stays busy, so expect to have to leave your car unless the fix is simple. Hours are Monday–Friday, 7 a.m.–7 p.m.; Saturday, 7:30 a.m.–2 p.m.; and closed Sunday.

9. SCORING A GREAT PARKING SPOT If you arrive at a park after noon or move your car from park to park, check for available parking spaces close to the park entrance; these will have been vacated by early guests who've left. Instead of following signs or being directed by staff to a distant space, drive straight to the front and start hunting, or use the approach of this Pennsylvania couple:

After leaving EPCOT for lunch, we returned to find a fullish parking lot. We were unhappy because we had left a third-row parking spot. My husband told the attendant that we had left just an hour ago and that there were lots of spaces up front. Without a word of protest, he waved us to the front and we got our same spot back!

Speeders Beware

Orange County law enforcement's jurisdiction extends to Disney World's roads. Many readers have written us surprised after receiving citations, assuming they'd be let off with a warning at worst. Remember, it's a speed limit, not a speed suggestion—even when other cars are zipping around.

Sneak Routes

We're constantly looking for ways to avoid traffic snarls. If you have a GPS that will route you around traffic delays, use that. If not, try these sneak routes we've discovered.

US 192 (IRLO BRONSON MEMORIAL HIGHWAY) Traffic on US 192 runs east–west south of Walt Disney World. The road is divided into east and west sections—west is from I-4 to Kissimmee, and east is from I-4 east to US 27. Traffic is bad both ways. If your hotel is along the west section, you can bypass most of the traffic by driving north on **International Drive** or **Poinciana Boulevard** (a right turn if you're driving on US 192 in the direction of I-4) and accessing **Osceola Parkway,** a four-lane toll road that dead-ends in Disney World. If your hotel is on the east side, take US 192 to **Sherberth Road** at mile marker 5 and turn north to enter the World near Animal Kingdom.

US 192–Kissimmee Resort Area Sneak Routes

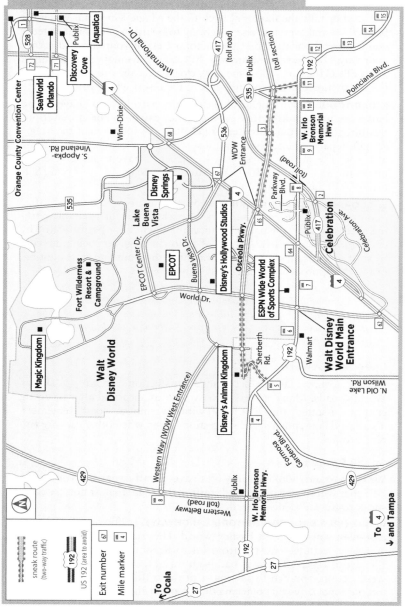

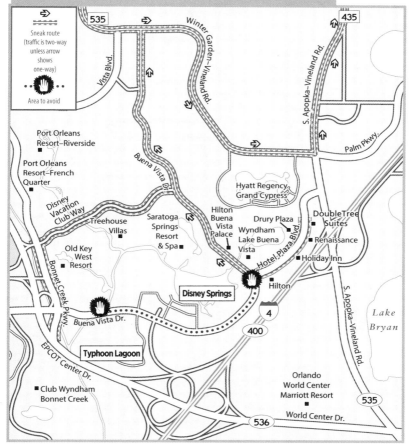

Disney Springs Sneak Routes

DISNEY SPRINGS The 3-mile stretch of **Buena Vista Drive** from Coronado Springs Resort to Disney Springs has 15 traffic signals—about one every 1,000 feet—making it a major traffic bottleneck from late afternoon through late evening. And it's not just around Disney Springs: Buena Vista Drive is one of Walt Disney World's most important roads, connecting the hotels of the Disney Springs Resort Area (DSRA), EPCOT, Disney's Hollywood Studios, the Magic Kingdom, Disney's Animal Kingdom, and Typhoon Lagoon.

The good news is that if you're coming by car from I-4 or on foot from the DSRA, it's easy to get to Disney Springs. Westbound **I-4** offers three exits to Disney Springs, including a direct exit to the Disney Springs parking garages—take **Exit 67** for EPCOT/Disney Springs. Guests staying at a DSRA hotel will find convenient pedestrian bridges linking Disney Springs to Hotel Plaza Boulevard and Buena Vista Drive.

I-4 Sneak Routes

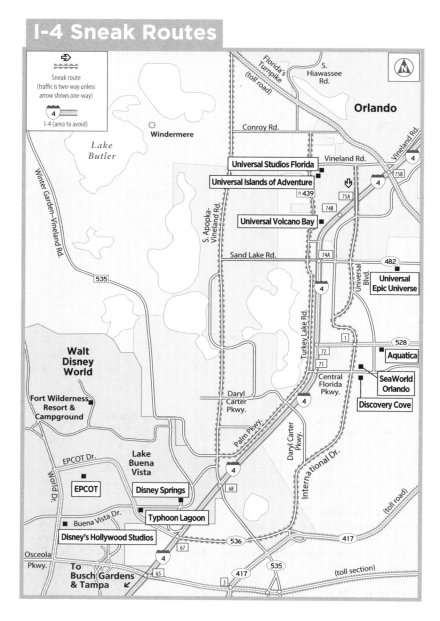

Coming from the theme parks, you can bypass the mess by taking **I-4** or alternatively by looping around on **Bonnet Creek Parkway** and **Disney Vacation Club Way**. If you're going back to an EPCOT or Magic Kingdom resort from Disney Springs, it may be faster to take I-4 West and follow the signs back to Disney property.

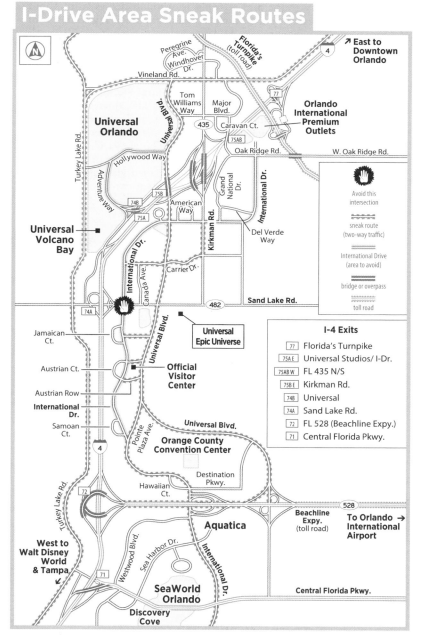

WESTBOUND EXIT 68 CONSTRUCTION A new off-ramp at Exit 68 is being constructed for westbound I-4 traffic to get to Disney Springs. This should open in 2024.

I-4 Expect heavy traffic and possible westbound delays from about 7 to 9:30 a.m.; eastbound toward Orlando, expect heavy traffic from 4 to 7 p.m. If you want to avoid I-4 altogether, check out our I-4 Sneak Routes map, on page 350.

INTERNATIONAL DRIVE The I-Drive area is by far the most difficult to navigate without long traffic delays. Most hotels on I-Drive are between **Kirkman Road** to the north and **FL 417 (Central Florida GreeneWay)** to the south. Between Kirkman Road and FL 417, three major roads cross I-Drive: From north to south on I-Drive (in the direction of Disney World), the first is **Universal Boulevard.** Next is **Sand Lake Road (FL 482),** pretty squarely in the middle of the hotel district. Finally, the **Beachline Expressway (FL 528)** connects I-4 and the airport.

The southern third of I-Drive can be accessed via **Central Florida Parkway,** which connects I-4 and Palm Parkway with the SeaWorld area of I-Drive, and by **Daryl Carter Parkway,** which connects Palm Parkway with the Orlando Vineland Premium Outlets.

I-Drive is a mess for a number of reasons: scarcity of left-turn lanes; long, multidirectional traffic signals; and, most critically, limited access to westbound I-4 (toward Disney). From the Orange County Convention Center south to the Beachline Expressway and FL 417/Central Florida GreeneWay, getting on westbound I-4 is easy, but in the stretch where the hotels are concentrated (from Kirkman to about a mile south of Sand Lake), the only way most visitors know to access I-4 westbound is to slog through the gridlock of the I-Drive–Sand Lake Road intersection en route to the I-4–Sand Lake Road interchange.

Since this is about as much fun as a root canal, the object is to access I-4 westbound without getting on Sand Lake Road. If your hotel is north of Sand Lake, access **Kirkman Road** by going north on I-Drive (in the opposite direction of the heaviest traffic) to Kirkman Road and turning left, or by cutting over to Kirkman via eastbound **Carrier Drive.** In either case, take Kirkman north over I-4 and make a U-turn at the first traffic signal (at the entrance to Universal Orlando). This puts you directly onto a westbound I-4 ramp. You can also go north on **Universal Boulevard,** which parallels I-Drive to the east; after you cross I-4 onto Universal property, stay left and follow the signs through two left turns to I-4—the signs are small, so stay alert.

unofficial **TIP**
Warning: Most off-site shuttles don't add vehicles at park opening or closing. In the morning, you may not get a seat.

If your hotel is south of Sand Lake Road but north of Austrian Court, use **Austrian Row** to cut over to Universal Boulevard. Turn right (south) on Universal and continue until you intersect the **Beachline Expressway (FL 528);** then take the Beachline west to I-4 (no toll).

TAKING A SHUTTLE BUS FROM YOUR OUT-OF-THE-WORLD HOTEL

MANY INDEPENDENT HOTELS near Disney World provide trams and buses. They're fairly hassle-free, depositing you near theme park entrances and saving you parking fees. The rub is that they might not get you there as early as you desire (a critical consideration if you take our touring advice) or be available quickly when you wish to return to your lodging.

Some shuttles go directly to Walt Disney World, while others stop at other hotels en route. This can be a problem if your hotel is the second or third stop on the route. During periods of high demand, buses frequently fill up at the first stop, leaving little or no room for passengers at subsequent stops. Before booking, ask how many hotels are on the route and the sequence of the stops.

The different hotels are often so close together that you can easily walk to the first hotel on the route and board there. Similarly, if there's a large hotel nearby, it might have its own bus service that's more efficient; you can use that instead of the service provided by your hotel. Most out-of-the-World shuttles work on a fixed schedule instead of arriving and departing somewhat randomly like the Disney buses do. Knowing exactly when a bus will depart makes it easier to plan your day.

A family from Washington shared their experience:

> *We stayed at a hotel off-site and it was fine, but I think next time we'll stay in the World. The shuttles weren't all that convenient or frequent, so we ended up taking taxis more than we thought we would.*

At closing or during a hard rain, more people will be waiting for the shuttle than it can hold, and some will be left behind. Most shuttles return for stranded guests, but those guests might have to wait 20 minutes to more than an hour.

If you're depending on non-Disney shuttles, leave the park at least 45 minutes before closing. If you stay until closing and don't want the hassle of the shuttle, take Uber, Lyft, or a taxi. If no cabs are on hand, a cast member will call one for you. If you're leaving the Magic Kingdom at closing, it's easier to walk or take the monorail to a hotel and hail a ride from there rather than at the TTC.

unofficial **TIP**
If you want to go from resort to resort or almost anywhere else, you'll have to transfer at a bus hub.

DEPARTING FROM ORLANDO INTERNATIONAL AIRPORT (MCO)

IF YOU'RE USING **Mears Connect** (see page 328), your bus will depart your hotel 3–4 hours before your flight, depending on how busy the airport is expected to be.

DRIVING Plan on leaving for the airport 2–3 hours before your flight, depending on whether you have to return a rental car, the route you take, and whether you have TSA PreCheck for security lines.

It takes about 35 minutes and around $5 in small bills and quarters to drive from Walt Disney World to MCO along the FL 417 or FL 528 toll roads. The same trip on I-4, FL 482 East, and Jeff Fuqua Boulevard is free but averages 50–60 minutes or even longer with traffic.

If you're returning a rental car, allow an extra 20 minutes to complete that process for on-site car rental companies; allow an extra 60 minutes to return a car to an off-site company and catch the airport shuttle to the terminal.

MCO handled over 50 million passengers in 2023. It's not unusual to see the security-checkpoint lines snaking out of the terminal and into the main shopping corridor and food court. A number of passengers have reported missing their flights even when they arrived at the airport 90 minutes before departure. System improvements have alleviated some, but by no means all, of the congestion. Most waits to clear security average 20 minutes or less, compared with 55 minutes or longer before the improvements.

Waits in the **TSA PreCheck** lines are almost always 5 minutes or less. If you fly frequently, PreCheck (tsa.gov/precheck) is good for five years and costs $78 per person. We don't fly without it, and it's especially helpful at MCO.

ELECTRIC-VEHICLE CHARGING

ECO-FRIENDLY READER Craig from Canada sent us this list of charging stations in and around the World.

In Walt Disney World

- **Animal Kingdom Parking Lot (2 chargers)** Follow the path to accessible parking, turn left after the shelter, go to the end of the row, and then double back.
- **Coronado Springs Resort (3 chargers)** In the parking lot adjacent to Gran Destino Tower
- **Disney's Fort Wilderness Resort** Campsites have 110V outlets plus 30-amp RV outlets
- **Disney's Hollywood Studios Parking Lot (2 chargers)** Just east of the main park entrance and northwest of the lots
- **Disney's Riviera Resort (1 charger)** West parking lot
- **Disney Springs Grapefruit Garage (2 chargers)** Level 3
- **Disney Springs Lime Garage (2 chargers)** Top level
- **Disney Springs Orange Garage (2 chargers)** Level 5
- **Disney's Wilderness Lodge (1 charger)** Halfway down the first row, near the taxi stand
- **EPCOT Parking Lot** At the front of the Journey lot
- **Shades of Green (1 generic charger plus 2 Tesla Destination Chargers)** Valet parking only
- **Transportation and Ticket Center (3 chargers)** Follow the blue lines on the right lane after paying for parking.

Tesla Superchargers (Off-Property)

- **Applebee's (10 chargers)** 6290 W. Irlo Bronson Memorial Hwy., just behind the restaurant
- **Wawa (6 chargers)** 7940 W. Irlo Bronson Memorial Hwy.

Craig adds, "There are Level 2 (midspeed) chargers in various places around Disney property; all are run by **ChargePoint** (chargepoint.com). Each charging station has two J-1772 charging ports to accommodate two cars at a time per station."

Finally, check **PlugShare** (plugshare.com) for the locations of other chargers near Walt Disney World.

KEY QUESTIONS ANSWERED IN THIS CHAPTER

▌ MONEY, *Etc.*

CREDIT CARDS, MOBILE PAYMENTS, AND DISNEY GIFT CARDS

CREDIT CARDS ACCEPTED throughout Disney World are **American Express, Diners Club, Discover, Japan Credit Bureau, MasterCard,** and **Visa.** Most shops and restaurants accept **Apple Pay** and **Google Pay** as well; however, some do not, so it's a good idea to carry a second form of payment. **Disney Gift Cards** can be used at most Disney-owned stores and restaurants, and for recreational activities, tickets, and parking (see disneygiftcard.com).

If you're staying at a Disney-owned resort, a **MagicBand** (see page 70) or your room key can be linked to the credit card you'll put on file for incidental hotel charges. This lets you use your MagicBand (or room key) as you would a credit card at most Disney-owned stores and restaurants on-property. This is useful if you're covering the expenses of others in your group, such as responsible teens or young adults who won't be with you all the time, don't have their own credit cards, or don't want to carry cash.

BANKING SERVICES

AT THE THEME PARKS, banking is limited to ATMs, which are marked on park maps and are plentiful throughout Walt Disney World; most MasterCard, Visa, Discover, Cirrus, Plus, Star, and Honor cards are also accepted. To get cash with an American Express card, you must sign an agreement with Amex before your trip. ATMs are also at every Disney resort and throughout Disney Springs.

CURRENCY EXCHANGE

EXCHANGE YOUR EUROS, KRONER, OR ZLOTY at **Guest Relations** in each theme park and at the **Welcome Center** Disney Springs. (See the "Services" sidebar and park map in Parts 11–14 and the Disney Springs map in Part 17 for locations.) All Disney resorts can do currency exchange at their front desks as well.

IN-PARK ISSUES

CELL PHONES

BRING YOUR CHARGING CABLE and an external battery pack to the parks. Your phone will likely get a lot of use in the parks, from guiding you around to taking pictures, checking wait times, using mobile ordering, and making Genie+ reservations. You'll probably want to increase your screen's brightness, too, for easier reading in the glaring Florida sun. All of that will drain your phone's battery faster than normal. We're fans of **Anker** batteries.

Charging stations are located near the *Tangled*-themed restrooms in Fantasyland in the Magic Kingdom; they're built into the faux-wood posts near the seating area. Also try the seating area behind Big Top Treats in Storybook Circus or the shopping area at the exit to Space Mountain. In EPCOT, look for outlets upstairs at The Land; near the restrooms at The Seas; and outside at Norway and Morocco.

Be aware that on very busy days, the park's cell towers and Wi-Fi may be overwhelmed, making it difficult to send or receive calls, texts, or data. A woman from Kansas spells out the problem:

In our group, we were using three different carriers, and we all had problems sending and receiving texts and making calls.

A Georgia woman adds:

I found the Wi-Fi horrible in all the parks. Dropped out continually, drained my battery, and wasn't strong enough to run Disney's own app. Very disappointing.

RAIN

LEN'S TWIN SISTER, LINDA, notes that when it comes to theme parks, "rain culls the weak from the herd." (She's the competitive one.) So go to the parks even in bad weather. Besides lighter crowds, most of the attractions and waiting areas are under cover. And rain showers, especially during warmer months, are short.

*un*official **TIP**
Raingear isn't always displayed in shops, so ask for it if you don't see it.

Ponchos and umbrellas cost about $13. Ponchos sold at Walt Disney World are made of semi-opaque clear plastic, which makes it tricky to pick out someone in your party on a rainy day. You can buy less expensive and more colorful ponchos to bring with you to help set your family apart in a plastic-covered sea of humanity.

A North Carolina mom recommends investing in good raingear:

We're outdoor-sports people, so we have good raincoats. It rained every day on this trip, driving many people out of the parks and leaving others looking miserable. Meanwhile, we hardly noticed the rain from inside our high-end jackets.

One *Unofficial Guide* researcher advises:

Wear a baseball cap under the poncho hood. Without it, the hood never covers your head properly, and your face always gets wet.

LOST AND FOUND

IF YOU LOSE (OR FIND) something in one of the theme parks, go to **Guest Relations**. See the "Services" sidebar and park map in each theme park chapter (Parts 11–14) for locations. If you discover that you've lost something 24 hours or more after you've left the parks, call ☎ 407-824-4245. The central Lost and Found is on the east side of the Transportation and Ticket Center. You can also report lost items at disneyworld.com/lostandfound.

It's unusual for readers to send us tips about Lost and Found, but a mom from Indiana sent two! Here's the first:

If you lose something on a ride and it has medication in it, Disney cast members will shut down the ride for 45 seconds to try to retrieve it. If they can't find it or it didn't contain meds, you have to come back to Lost and Found for it at the end of the day.

LOST MAGICBANDS AND TICKETS Duplicates can be made, usually at no cost, at Guest Relations at any theme park or resort. A replacement fee may be charged, depending on your situation.

Lost tickets are the subject of the second tip from our mom above:

If you've got plastic tickets, write down or take a picture of the serial numbers on the back. This way, a cast member can look up when the ticket was last used, giving you an idea of where it was lost.

LOST CARS Don't forget where you parked—snap a picture with your smartphone or camera or save the location in the MDE app, which has a new section for this purpose.

MEDICAL MATTERS

HEADACHE RELIEF Aspirin and other sundries are sold at the **Emporium** on Main Street, U.S.A., in the Magic Kingdom (behind the counter—you have to ask); at most retail shops in EPCOT's Future World and World Showcase, Disney's Hollywood Studios, and Disney's Animal Kingdom; and at each Disney resort's gift shop.

ILLNESSES REQUIRING MEDICAL ATTENTION For the locations of the **First Aid Centers** in the theme parks, see the "Services" sidebar and park map in each theme park chapter (Parts 11–14). Guests who use the first aid service are generally very positive about it. This North Carolina reader's experience is representative:

We visited First Aid a time or two in the parks (my wife needed her blood pressure checked because she was worried about the heat and her pregnancy). We found trained medical staff, no wait, and all the friendliness and knowledge you would expect from Disney.

Off-property, there's an **Advent Health Centra Care** walk-in clinic at 12500 S. Apopka–Vineland Road (☎ 407-934-CARE [2273]; open 24 hours).

A North Carolina family had a good experience at **Buena Vista Urgent Care** (8216 World Center Drive, Suite D; ☎ 407-465-1110):

We started day one needing medical care for our son, who has asthma and had developed croup. We found great care at Buena Vista Urgent Care. We waited 20 minutes, and then we were off to the parks.

The Medical Concierge (☎ 407-648-5252; themedicalconcierge .com) has board-certified physicians on call 24-7 to make in-person visits to your hotel room. Walk-in clinics are also available.

DENTAL NEEDS Call **Celebration Dental Group** (☎ 407-566-2222).

PRESCRIPTION MEDICINE Three drugstores located nearby are **CVS** (8242 World Center Drive; ☎ 407-239-1442), **Walgreens** (12100 S. Apopka–Vineland Road; ☎ 407-238-0600), and **Turner Drugs** (1530 Celebration Blvd., Ste. 105A; ☎ 407-828-8125; turnerdrug .com).

PREVENT BLISTERS IN FIVE EASY STEPS

1. PREPARE You can easily cover 5–12 miles a day at the parks, so get your feet and legs into shape before you leave home. Start with short walks around the neighborhood. Increase your distance gradually until you can do 6 miles in a day. Give kids an incentive to join you by adding to their souvenir fund for every half mile they walk.

2. PAY ATTENTION During your training program, your feet will tell you if you're wearing the right shoes. Choose well-constructed, broken-in running or hiking shoes. If you feel a hot spot coming on, a blister isn't far behind. If you develop a hot spot in the same place every time you walk, cover it with a blister bandage (such as Johnson & Johnson) or cushion before you set out.

Don't wear sandals, flip-flops, or slip-ons in the theme parks. Even if your feet don't blister, they'll get stepped on by other guests or run over by strollers.

3. SOCK IT UP Good socks are as important as good shoes. When you walk, your feet sweat, and the moisture increases friction. To avoid that, wear socks made from material such as Smartwool or CoolMax, which wicks perspiration away from your feet (Smartwool socks come in varying thicknesses). To further fight moisture, you can dust your feet with antifungal powder.

4. DON'T BE A HERO Take care of foot problems the minute you notice them. Carry a small foot-emergency kit or stop by a park **First Aid Center** (see page 357) as soon as you notice a hot spot forming.

5. CHECK THE KIDS Children might not say anything about blisters forming until it's too late. Stop several times a day and check their feet. If you find a blister, either treat it using the kit you're carrying or stop by a First Aid Center.

LODGING A COMPLAINT WITH DISNEY

COMPLAINING ABOUT A LEAKY FAUCET or not having enough towels is pretty straightforward, and you'll usually find Disney folks highly responsive. But for a complaint that goes beyond an on-site manager's ability to resolve, don't expect much—if anything.

Disney's unresponsiveness in fielding complaints is one of our readers' foremost gripes. A Rhode Island dad's remarks are typical:

It's all warm fuzzies and big smiles until you have a problem—then everybody plays hide-and-seek. The only thing you know for sure is it's never the responsibility of the Disney person you're talking to.

Disney prefers to receive complaints in writing. Address your letter to **Walt Disney World Guest Communications** at PO Box 10040, Lake Buena Vista, FL 32830, or email wdw.guest.communications@disney world.com. Be aware, though, that by the time you get home and draft a letter, it's often too late to correct the problem. And although Disney would have you believe they're a touchy-feely lot, they generally won't make things right for you after the fact. You *may* receive an acknowledgment ("we're sorry you *felt* inconvenienced"), but don't count on them actually offering to fix anything—even if you decide to take it up with Bob Iger himself.

SERVICES

PHOTOPASS AND MEMORY MAKER

DISNEY EMPLOYS roving photographers to take photos of guests as part of its **PhotoPass** service; guests may purchase these photos online. Use the **My Disney Experience** (**MDE**) app to find the locations of the photographers on the day of your visit.

*un*official **TIP**
If you're the trip planner and picture taker of your group, it's often worth it to purchase Memory Maker so that you're sure to receive a few pictures of your entire party.

PhotoPass images can be purchased at disneyphotopass.com. Prices range from $19 (plus tax and shipping) for two 4-by-6-inch prints or one 5-by-7-inch print to $21 for an 8-by-10-inch print. You can also buy personalized photo products such as mugs and smartphone cases.

Photographs are also sold in a package called **Memory Maker** (see disneyworld.disney.go.com/memory-maker) that includes not only PhotoPass pictures but also photos and videos taken by automated cameras on theme park rides (for the full list, see the table on the next page). Memory Maker costs $185 when purchased at least three days before your trip or $210 when purchased in the park. If you're planning to spend just one day in a park, you can buy a **Memory Maker One Day Entitlement** ($75), available exclusively through the MDE app. Disney Annual Pass holders can download photos at no charge if they purchase the PhotoPass supplement.

Because PhotoPass and Memory Maker are linked to your MDE account (see page 25), you can also see the photos of friends and family you've linked to there. Here's how to get started:

1. Find a PhotoPass photographer to take your first picture. Photographers roam throughout the theme parks and water parks, including near park entrances and around iconic attractions such as The Twilight Zone Tower of Terror.

2. The photographer will scan your RFID ticket, MagicBand, or your phone. This links your pictures to your MDE account. Onboard ride-photo systems should automatically detect your MagicBand and link the photos to your account.

3. Visit the MDE website within 45 days of your trip to view your photos. .

In some areas, such as the meet and greet with Anna and Elsa, Disney has replaced live photographers with automated cameras that capture your photos at select posing stations. Like the photos taken by live photographers, these images will be linked to your MDE account. If you're already logged in to MDE, your purchase will be automatically linked to your account. If not, you'll be asked to do so (or sign up for MDE) to complete the purchase.

ATTRACTIONS WHERE PHOTOS ARE AUTOMATICALLY LINKED TO YOUR MDE ACCOUNT
THE MAGIC KINGDOM • Big Thunder Mountain Railroad • Buzz Lightyear's Space Ranger Spin • *Enchanted Tales with Belle* • Pirates of the Caribbean • Seven Dwarfs Mine Train • Space Mountain • Tiana's Bayou Adventure
EPCOT • Frozen Ever After • Test Track
DISNEY'S ANIMAL KINGDOM • Dinosaur • Expedition Everest
DISNEY'S HOLLYWOOD STUDIOS • Rock 'n' Roller Coaster • Slinky Dog Dash • The Twilight Zone Tower of Terror

You can download Memory Maker photos as many times as you want, subject to a few restrictions: First, if you purchase Memory Maker at the advance-purchase price less than three days before your trip, note that photos taken within three days of the date of purchase are not included and must be bought separately. Next, each photo expires 45 days from the date it was taken, so you'll need to download them promptly once you return home (you can apply for a one-time 15-day extension). Disney grants you a limited license to reproduce Memory Maker photos for your personal use.

Because any two families can share a Memory Maker package via MDE, folks in the *Unofficial Guide* online community often split the cost with others traveling around the same time. It's a great way to get your photos at half price. Visit forum.touringplans.com and search "Memory Maker Share" to find a partner on our discussion boards.

unofficial **TIP**
Call beforehand to verify whether photographers will be at a particular character meal. Participating venues change, and otherwise reliable Disney websites, including Disney's own, don't always have up-to-date information.

We get a lot of reader comments about PhotoPass and Memory Maker, most of them positive. From an Ohio mom:

The PhotoPass option is awesome and so easy. Everywhere we went, we would find Disney photographers, and we got a lot of great pictures, which is nice since usually when you are on vacation you have part of your family missing as he/she is taking the photo.

A Maryland dad got an unexpected disappointment:

I advance-purchased Memory Maker largely because we were planning several character meals, under the apparently incorrect assumption that photographers would be there. There was no sign of any photographer at any of the four character meals we did.

Disney has installed automatic cameras at character meal and meet-and-greet venues. These cameras capture numerous moments throughout the meal or greeting and offer guests a variety of photos.

In addition to the in-park photographers, there is now a Memory Maker station at **Disney Springs.** There are no characters, but if you want a photographer to take a few snaps of your family, stop by. This can be a quick alternative to a formal posed photo session, and as a bonus, the pictures will be included in your existing photo package.

PET CARE

ACROSS FROM THE PORT ORLEANS RESORTS, the plush **Best Friends Pet Care** accommodates up to 270 dogs in its Doggy Village, which has standard and luxury suites, some with private outdoor patios and play yards; the Kitty City pavilion houses up to 24 cats in two- and four-story cat condos. There's also a separate area just for birds and "pocket pets" such as hamsters. Encompassing more than 17,000 square feet of air-conditioned indoor space plus 10,000 square feet of covered outdoor runs and play areas, the resort is open to both on-site and off-site guests. We sent Rosie, the *Unofficial Guide* research poodle, and it went great. The staff even emailed us photos of her during her stay. For more information, call ☎ 877-4-WDW-PETS (877-493-9738) or visit bestfriendspetcare.com. (*Note:* You must provide written proof of your pet's current vaccinations from a veterinarian, either at check-in or by fax at 203-840-5207.)

In addition, dogs are welcome at four hotels on Disney property: **Art of Animation, Port Orleans Riverside, Fort Wilderness Resort & Campground,** and **Yacht Club.** Additional fees of $50–$75 per night apply, along with a host of human- and animal-conduct rules; inquire when making your hotel reservation. This policy was met with skepticism by some, but we haven't seen a single complaint regarding dogs at Disney hotels in all the reader surveys we've received since the policy was enacted.

WHERE CAN I FIND . . .

RELIGIOUS SERVICES IN THE DISNEY WORLD AREA? Visit allears.net /btp/church.htm for a partial list.

A PLACE TO PUT ALL THESE PACKAGES? Lockers are located in each theme park (see the "Services" sidebar and park map in Parts 11–14). The cost is $10 per day for small lockers and $12 per day for large lockers at the theme parks. Lockers at the water parks cost $10 for small and $15 for large. Jumbo lockers, in EPCOT and the Magic Kingdom only, cost $15 per day. All lockers are now keyless.

Package Pickup remains temporarily suspended as of early 2024; when it's running, it's located near each theme park's entrance and closes 2 hours before the parks do (EPCOT has two Package Pickups, near the Future World and International Gateway entrances). Ask the salesperson to send your purchases to Package Pickup; when you leave the park, they'll be waiting for you. If you're staying at a Disney resort, you can also have packages delivered to your resort's gift shop for pickup the following day. If you're leaving within 24 hours, though, take them with you or use the in-park pickup location.

If you live in the United States, the gift shop at your Disney resort will ship your items to you via standard ground shipping. We're told that the maximum shipping cost is $40, so now is the time to buy souvenirs in bulk.

GROCERY DELIVERY If you don't have a car or don't want to take time to shop, you have a couple of options. Amazon Prime members can use **Amazon Pantry** to order prepackaged items, from boxed cereals and snacks to coffee, sunscreen, aspirin, and diapers, at very competitive prices and have them delivered to their resort.

If you're looking for a local option, various services such as **Instacart, Walmart+, Vacation Grocery Delivery,** and **Garden Grocer** all deliver to Disney resorts. Unless you order alcohol, most are able to drop off the order at bell services even if you are not present. Deliveries that include alcoholic beverages generally require ID at delivery.

WINE, BEER, AND LIQUOR? In Florida, wine and beer are sold in grocery stores; for the stronger stuff, you'll have to go to a state-licensed liquor store. The best range of booze in the Disney area is sold at **ABC Fine Wine & Spirits,** less than a mile north of the Crossroads shopping center (11951 S. Apopka–Vineland Road; ☎ 407-239-0775). We also like **Publix Liquors** in the Water Tower Shoppes (29 Blake Blvd., Celebration; ☎ 321-939-3109).

PART 11

The
MAGIC KINGDOM

KEY QUESTIONS ANSWERED IN THIS CHAPTER

▌ OVERVIEW

OPENED IN 1971, the Magic Kingdom was the first of Walt Disney World's four theme parks, much of it built by the same people who built Disneyland in California almost two decades earlier. The crown jewel of the World's parks, the Magic Kingdom is what springs to mind when most people think of Disney World. Its attractions, such as Cinderella Castle, Pirates of the Caribbean, and The Haunted Mansion, have helped set the standard for theme park attractions for over 50 years.

▌ ARRIVING

FROM INSIDE WALT DISNEY WORLD If you're staying at the **Contemporary, Bay Lake Tower, Grand Floridian Resort,** or **Polynesian Village,** you can commute to the Magic Kingdom by monorail or walk (though walking is harder from the Polynesian). If you're staying at **Wilderness Lodge, Boulder Ridge/Copper Creek Villas,** or **Fort Wilderness Resort & Campground,** you can take a boat or bus. (Note that monorails and boats don't run when lightning is in the area; Disney will provide

continued on page 366

The Magic Kingdom

G+ Offers Genie+

ILL Offers Individual Lightning Lane

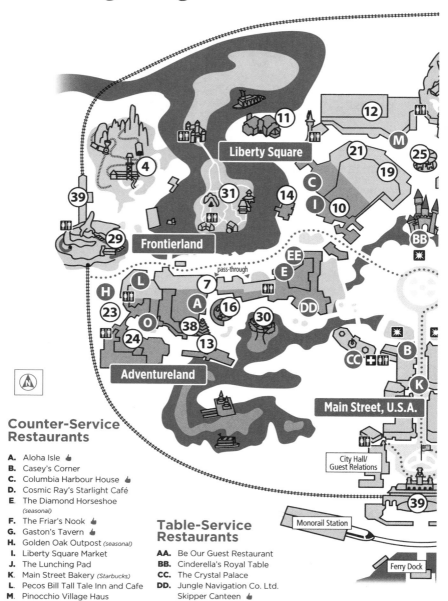

Counter-Service Restaurants

A. Aloha Isle 👍
B. Casey's Corner
C. Columbia Harbour House 👍
D. Cosmic Ray's Starlight Café
E. The Diamond Horseshoe *(seasonal)*
F. The Friar's Nook 👍
G. Gaston's Tavern 👍
H. Golden Oak Outpost *(seasonal)*
I. Liberty Square Market
J. The Lunching Pad
K. Main Street Bakery *(Starbucks)*
L. Pecos Bill Tall Tale Inn and Cafe
M. Pinocchio Village Haus
N. Tomorrowland Terrace Restaurant *(seasonal)*
O. Tortuga Tavern *(seasonal)*

Table-Service Restaurants

AA. Be Our Guest Restaurant
BB. Cinderella's Royal Table
CC. The Crystal Palace
DD. Jungle Navigation Co. Ltd. Skipper Canteen 👍
EE. Liberty Tree Tavern 👍
FF. The Plaza Restaurant
GG. Tony's Town Square Restaurant

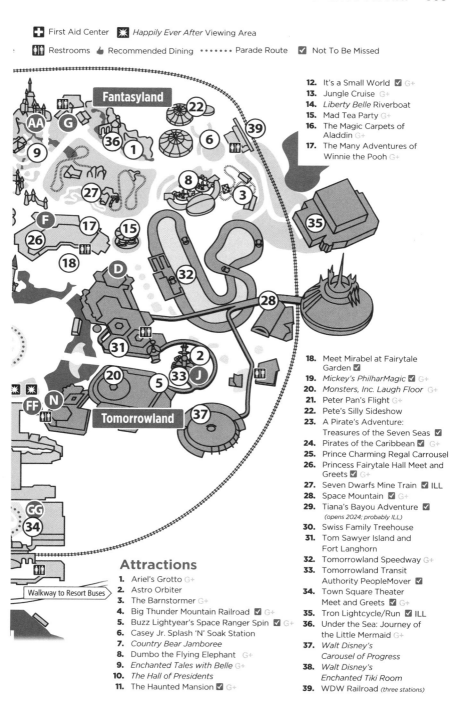

Legend:
- ➕ First Aid Center
- ✴ *Happily Ever After* Viewing Area
- 🚻 Restrooms
- 👍 Recommended Dining
- •••••• Parade Route
- ☑ Not To Be Missed

Attractions

1. Ariel's Grotto G+
2. Astro Orbiter
3. The Barnstormer G+
4. Big Thunder Mountain Railroad ☑ G+
5. Buzz Lightyear's Space Ranger Spin ☑ G+
6. Casey Jr. Splash 'N' Soak Station
7. *Country Bear Jamboree*
8. Dumbo the Flying Elephant G+
9. *Enchanted Tales with Belle* G+
10. *The Hall of Presidents*
11. The Haunted Mansion ☑ G+
12. It's a Small World ☑ G+
13. Jungle Cruise G+
14. *Liberty Belle* Riverboat
15. Mad Tea Party G+
16. The Magic Carpets of Aladdin G+
17. The Many Adventures of Winnie the Pooh G+
18. Meet Mirabel at Fairytale Garden ☑
19. *Mickey's PhilharMagic* ☑ G+
20. *Monsters, Inc. Laugh Floor* G+
21. Peter Pan's Flight G+
22. Pete's Silly Sideshow
23. A Pirate's Adventure: Treasures of the Seven Seas ☑
24. Pirates of the Caribbean ☑ G+
25. Prince Charming Regal Carrousel
26. Princess Fairytale Hall Meet and Greets ☑ G+
27. Seven Dwarfs Mine Train ☑ ILL
28. Space Mountain ☑ G+
29. Tiana's Bayou Adventure ☑ (opens 2024; probably ILL)
30. Swiss Family Treehouse
31. Tom Sawyer Island and Fort Langhorn
32. Tomorrowland Speedway G+
33. Tomorrowland Transit Authority PeopleMover ☑
34. Town Square Theater Meet and Greets ☑ G+
35. Tron Lightcycle/Run ☑ ILL
36. Under the Sea: Journey of the Little Mermaid G+
37. *Walt Disney's Carousel of Progress*
38. *Walt Disney's Enchanted Tiki Room*
39. WDW Railroad (three stations)

Walkway to Resort Buses ▷

continued from page 363

bus service instead.) Guests at other Walt Disney World resorts can reach the park by bus. All guests on Disney's transportation system are deposited directly at the park's entrance.

DRIVING If you're thinking about driving to the Magic Kingdom, you'll need to park at the Ticket and Transportation Center (TTC). Build in extra time for this process because you'll encounter lines to pay for parking, to board trams (or walk) to the TTC, to get through security, and to get on a monorail or ferry to take you to the actual park entrance. All of this can take an hour or more on busy days, or about 15–20 minutes if you breeze through.

You can also attempt to have a ride-sharing service drop you off at the **Contemporary** or **Grand Floridian** and walk from there. This costs more, and you may be turned away by security if they're checking for resort or dining reservations. When you're ready to leave the Magic Kingdom for the day, it's easy to head to the Contemporary or Grand Floridian and hail a ride, making sure to wait in front of the hotel. We've published this tip for a few years now, and it generally works pretty well. If security balks, your driver can drop you off on the street corner of the Contemporary's parking lot that's closest to the Magic Kingdom.

> *unofficial* **TIP**
> Getting dropped off at the Contemporary or Grand Floridian saves off-site guests the daily $30 Magic Kingdom parking fee and virtually all the waiting.

If driving is unavoidable and you're bringing a stroller, a New Jersey family recommends the ferry (which starts operating 30–90 minutes before official park opening):

The ferry to the Magic Kingdom is a must if you're using a stroller. You can drive the stroller right onto the ferry and then just head to the back to be the first ones off when it docks.

MAGIC KINGDOM OPENING PROCEDURES (ROPE DROP)

ARRIVING AT THE MAGIC KINGDOM **30–60 minutes before official opening** ensures the shortest possible waits for rides.

On-site guests who want to take advantage of Early Theme Park Entry (see page 30) should arrive at the park entrance 60 minutes before official opening (that is, 30 minutes before Early Entry) on all days. Off-site guests who aren't eligible for Early Theme Park Entry should arrive 30 minutes before official opening on all days.

> *unofficial* **TIP**
> *Rope drop* refers to cast members using a length of rope to hold back crowds until the park opens. After the rope is dropped— or rewound, to be precise—crowds race-walk to their first rides.

Once in the park, you'll find most of the rides in Fantasyland and Tomorrowland running, while rides in Adventureland, Frontierland, and Liberty Square start operations closer to the park's official opening time.

Main Street's larger shops, such as the **Emporium,** will be open when you're admitted into the park, in case you need sunscreen, rain ponchos, or ibuprofen. **Main Street Bakery (Starbucks)** will also be open for coffee and breakfast items.

Upon entering the park, most guests head for one of the headliners: **Seven Dwarfs Mine Train** in Fantasyland attracts families, and **Space Mountain** draws some of the secondary crowds. **Tiana's Bayou Adventure** is another big draw in this park for families with older children, along with many teens and adults. If/when **Tron Lightcycle/Run** stops using a virtual queue (see page 391), Tron will be the biggest rope-drop draw in the park. If you have young children, we recommend heading immediately to **Peter Pan's Flight** to get that quick attraction out of the way with minimal wait.

GETTING ORIENTED

IN THE MAGIC KINGDOM, **stroller, wheelchair, scooter, and locker rentals** are on the right, just inside the entrance. On your left as you enter **Main Street, U.S.A.,** is **City Hall,** the center for **Guest Relations,** lost and found, and guided tours.

Be sure to pick up a **guide map** at the park entrance or at City Hall. It shows all attractions, shops, and dining spots; provides information about first aid, baby care, and assistance for guests with disabilities; and provides tips for good photos. It also lists times for the day's special events, live entertainment, Disney-character parades, and concerts; plus, it tells you when and where to find Disney characters. It's a great backup if your phone battery is low or your **My Disney Experience** (**MDE**) app is misbehaving.

unofficial **TIP**
Because Cinderella Castle is so large, designate a specific meeting spot, such as the entrance to Cinderella's Royal Table restaurant at the rear of the castle.

The guide map is supplemented by a daily entertainment schedule, the *Times Guide.* In addition to performance times, the *Times Guide* contains info on Disney-character appearances and what Disney calls **Special Hours,** or operating hours for attractions and restaurants that open late or close early. The MDE app (see page 26) also contains this information, but—in a rare triumph of analog over digital—it's faster to use the *Times Guide.*

Main Street, U.S.A., ends at the **Central Plaza,** from which branch the entrances to five other "lands": (clockwise from the left) **Adventureland, Frontierland, Liberty Square, Fantasyland,** and **Tomorrowland.**

Cinderella Castle, at the entrance to Fantasyland, is the Magic Kingdom's visual anchor and is an excellent meeting place if your group decides to split up or gets separated.

NOT TO BE MISSED IN THE MAGIC KINGDOM
ADVENTURELAND • Pirates of the Caribbean
FANTASYLAND • Character meet and greets • It's a Small World • Seven Dwarfs Mine Train
FRONTIERLAND • Big Thunder Mountain Railroad • Tiana's Bayou Adventure
LIBERTY SQUARE • The Haunted Mansion
MAIN STREET, U.S.A. • Meet Mickey Mouse at Town Square Theater
PARADES AND FIREWORKS • Festival of Fantasy afternoon parade • *Happily Ever After* fireworks
TOMORROWLAND • Buzz Lightyear's Space Ranger Spin • Space Mountain • Tron Lightcycle/Run

MAGIC KINGDOM SERVICES

MOST PARK SERVICES are centered on Main Street, U.S.A., including:
ATMs Underneath the Main Street railroad station
Baby Care Center Next to The Crystal Palace, left around the Central Plaza (toward Adventureland)
Cell Phone Charging Space Mountain exit, behind Big Top Treats in Storybook Circus, and benches outside of *Tangled*-themed restrooms. Can drop at City Hall with cord for charging.
First Aid Center Next to The Crystal Palace, left around the Central Plaza (toward Adventureland)
Live Entertainment and Parade Information In the *Times Guide,* available at City Hall/Guest Relations, at the railroad-station end of Main Street
Lost and Found City Hall/Guest Relations
Lost Persons City Hall/Guest Relations
Storage Lockers Inside the tapstiles, to the right as you face the train station
Walt Disney World and Local Attraction Information City Hall/Guest Relations
Wheelchair, ECV, and Stroller Rentals Inside the tapstiles, to the right as you face the train station

FAVORITE ATTRACTIONS BY AGE GROUP

THERE ARE ALMOST 80 INDIVIDUAL ATTRACTIONS (rides, shows, and other entertainment) in the Magic Kingdom. The table on the opposite page lists the 10 most popular attractions by age group.

Parades and fireworks appear in the top 10 for every age group. Character greetings are especially popular with preschool and grade-school children, and meeting Mickey Mouse ranked in the top 20 park experiences for every age group.

These top attractions form the core of our Magic Kingdom touring plans. If you're looking for step-by-step instructions on where to go and when, start with these (see page 549). Many of the attractions offer Lightning Lane to reduce waits in line (see next section).

ATTRACTION RATINGS The attractions profiled in this book have two sets of ratings: an overall rating next to the attraction's name, which reflects the authors' opinions, and reader ratings broken down by age group. Both use a five-star scale, with five stars being best.

Appeal by Age ratings are rounded to the nearest half star. To help put them in context, we also provide a label, such as Above Average, showing how that attraction stacks up to others in the park. Labels are assigned using the attraction's average number of reader ratings and incorporate a 95% confidence interval (sort of like a margin of error), similar to our restaurant ratings (see page 201). As with restaurants, authors' ratings for attractions don't always match readers'.

The average reader ratings for all Magic Kingdom attractions by age group are as follows, based on the 92,000 attraction ratings we received over the past year:

PRESCHOOL	GRADE SCHOOL	TEENS	YOUNG ADULTS	OVER 30	OVER 65
4.2 stars	4.2 stars	4.0 stars	4.1 stars	4.1 stars	4.2 stars

GENIE+, INDIVIDUAL LIGHTNING LANE, AND THE TOURING PLANS

NOTE: See page 49 for detailed information and strategy suggestions for Genie+ and Individual Lightning Lane.

The big questions addressed in this section are:

MAGIC KINGDOM MOST POPULAR ATTRACTIONS BY AGE GROUP

PRESCHOOL	GRADE SCHOOL	TEENS	YOUNG ADULTS	OVER 30	OVER 65
Christmas parade	*Happily Ever After* fireworks	Tron Lightcycle/Run	Big Thunder Mountain Railroad	Halloween/Christmas parades	Dapper Dans barbershop quartet
Meet Mickey and Minnie at Pete's Silly Sideshow	Bibbidi Bobbidi Boutique	Big Thunder Mountain Railroad	*Happily Ever After* fireworks	*Happily Ever After* fireworks	The Haunted Mansion
Festival of Fantasy parade	Big Thunder Mountain Railroad	Space Mountain	Tron Lightcycle/Run	Big Thunder Mountain Railroad	*Happily Ever After* fireworks
Bibbidi Bobbidi Boutique	Halloween/Christmas parades	Halloween/Christmas parades	Halloween/Christmas parades	Dapper Dans barbershop quartet	Halloween/Christmas parades
Meet Mickey Mouse at Town Square Theater	Seven Dwarfs Mine Train	*Happily Ever After* fireworks	Dapper Dans barbershop quartet	Haunted Mansion	Meet Mickey Mouse at Town Square Theater
Meet Donald and Goofy at Pete's Silly Sideshow	Meet Mickey Mouse at Town Square Theater	Haunted Mansion	Space Mountain	Cinderella Princess Meet and Greet	Casey's Corner pianist
Adventure Friends cavalcade	Tron Lightcycle/Run	Pirates of the Caribbean	Pirates of the Caribbean	Tron Lightcycle/Run	Tomorrowland Transit Authority PeopleMover
Prince Charming Regal Carrousel	Cinderella Princess Meet and Greet	Cinderella Princess Meet and Greet	Cinderella Princess Meet and Greet	Pirates of the Caribbean	Walt Disney World Railroad
Dumbo the Flying Elephant	Festival of Fantasy parade	Meet Mickey Mouse at Town Square Theater	Haunted Mansion	Cadaver Dans barbershop quartet	Pirates of the Caribbean
Meet Ariel at Her Grotto	Meet Ariel at Her Grotto	Festival of Fantasy parade	Casey's Corner pianist	Casey's Corner pianist	*Mickey's PhilharMagic*

1. Are Genie+ and Individual Lightning Lane worth paying for in the Magic Kingdom?
2. If they're worth the cost, which attractions benefit most?
3. How can you avoid paying for Individual Lightning Lane?
4. How do Genie+ and Individual Lightning Lane work with the touring plans?

Are Genie+ and Individual Lightning Lane Worth Paying For in the Magic Kingdom?

The Magic Kingdom is the easiest park to recommend using Genie+ for. It's also the most expensive. We think Genie+ is worth the cost here if you meet any of these criteria:

- You'll arrive at the park after Early Theme Park Entry begins (that is, you won't be at the park as soon as it opens). This includes off-site guests who aren't eligible for Early Theme Park Entry and on-site guests who want to sleep in.
- You won't be using a touring plan.
- You're visiting at a time of year when crowds are moderate to high.

The other consideration with Genie+ is the number of Genie+ ride reservations you'll be able to get in a given day. On the next page, we break down how much time we think you can save using Genie+, based on data models showing how to optimize the number of time-saving reservations throughout the day.

GENIE+ AND INDIVIDUAL LIGHTNING LANE (ILL) RESERVATIONS IN THE MAGIC KINGDOM
ADVENTURELAND • Jungle Cruise • The Magic Carpets of Aladdin • Pirates of the Caribbean
FANTASYLAND • The Barnstormer • Dumbo the Flying Elephant • It's a Small World • Mad Tea Party • The Many Adventures of Winnie the Pooh • *Mickey's PhilharMagic* • Peter Pan's Flight • Meet Tiana and Cinderella at Princess Fairytale Hall • Seven Dwarfs Mine Train *(ILL)* • Under the Sea: Journey of the Little Mermaid
FRONTIERLAND • Big Thunder Mountain Railroad • Tiana's Bayou Adventure
LIBERTY SQUARE • The Haunted Mansion
MAIN STREET, U.S.A. • Festival of Fantasy Parade • Meet Mickey Mouse at Town Square Theater
TOMORROWLAND • Buzz Lightyear's Space Ranger Spin • *Monsters, Inc. Laugh Floor* • Space Mountain • Tomorrowland Speedway • Tron Lightcycle/Run *(ILL)*

The **Typical Use** scenario assumes you'll be able to obtain Genie+ reservations for roughly three or four attractions in your touring plan, provided you haven't already experienced those rides, the reservations don't conflict with any meals or breaks you've already planned, and the standby lines are long enough to justify obtaining the reservation. The **Optimistic Use** scenario assumes all the preceding *and* that Genie+ reservations are available at almost exactly the pace at which you'll visit the attractions, plus you'll get another reservation or two. The **Perfect Use** scenario assumes you're able to get Genie+ reservations, one by one, with a nearly immediate return time, for every eligible ride on your touring plan. We think that's exceedingly unlikely to happen; we mention it here to estimate the upper limit on what might be possible. Finally, remember that attractions that offer Individual Lightning Lane are not part of Genie+; there's a separate cost to use Lightning Lane at those attractions.

ESTIMATED TIME SAVINGS USING GENIE+ BY CROWD LEVEL			
CROWD LEVEL	**TYPICAL USE (3 RESERVATIONS PER DAY)**	**OPTIMISTIC USE (5 RESERVATIONS PER DAY)**	**PERFECT USE (8 RESERVATIONS PER DAY)**
LOW	40 minutes	80 minutes	95 minutes
MEDIUM	50 minutes	90 minutes	150 minutes
HIGH	80 minutes	120 minutes	180 minutes

Which Attractions Benefit Most from Genie+ and Individual Lightning Lane?

For Genie+, the table on page 372 shows the attractions that might benefit most from using Genie+, based on the data we've collected in 2023 and 2024. The chart does *not* assume use of a touring plan.

Whether Individual Lightning Lanes will be worth the cost will depend on what Disney is charging for them and how that lines up with your personal time-versus-money spectrum.

When Do Genie+ and Individual Lightning Lane Reservations Run Out in the Magic Kingdom?

The table on the opposite page shows the approximate time at which the Magic Kingdom's attractions run out of Genie+ or Individual

WHEN GENIE+ AND INDIVIDUAL LIGHTNING LANE RESERVATIONS RUN OUT BY ATTENDANCE LEVEL*

ATTRACTION	LOW ATTENDANCE	MODERATE ATTENDANCE	HIGH ATTENDANCE
THE BARNSTORMER	10 p.m.	10 p.m.	10 p.m.
BIG THUNDER MOUNTAIN RAILROAD	10 p.m.	9 p.m.	8 p.m.
BUZZ LIGHTYEAR'S SPACE RANGER SPIN	10 p.m.	10 p.m.	10 p.m.
DUMBO THE FLYING ELEPHANT	10 p.m.	10 p.m.	10 p.m.
FESTIVAL OF FANTASY PARADE	2 p.m.	2 p.m.	1 p.m.
THE HAUNTED MANSION	10 p.m.	8 p.m.	7 p.m.
IT'S A SMALL WORLD	10 p.m.	10 p.m.	10 p.m.
JUNGLE CRUISE	8 p.m.	6 p.m.	5 p.m.
MAD TEA PARTY	10 p.m.	10 p.m.	10 p.m.
THE MAGIC CARPETS OF ALADDIN	10 p.m.	10 p.m.	10 p.m.
THE MANY ADVENTURES OF WINNIE THE POOH	9 p.m.	8 p.m.	7 p.m.
MEET CINDERELLA AT PRINCESS FAIRYTALE HALL	9 p.m.	6 p.m.	5 p.m.
MEET MICKEY MOUSE AT TOWN SQUARE THEATER	8 p.m.	6 p.m.	6 p.m.
MEET TIANA AT PRINCESS FAIRYTALE HALL	9 p.m.	7 p.m.	6 p.m.
MICKEY'S PHILHARMAGIC	10 p.m.	10 p.m.	10 p.m.
MONSTERS, INC. LAUGH FLOOR	10 p.m.	10 p.m.	10 p.m.
PETER PAN'S FLIGHT	9 p.m.	7 p.m.	5 p.m.
PIRATES OF THE CARIBBEAN	10 p.m.	9 p.m.	9 p.m.
SEVEN DWARFS MINE TRAIN (ILL)	9 p.m.	8 p.m.	4 p.m.
SPACE MOUNTAIN	10 p.m.	9 p.m.	7 p.m.
TOMORROWLAND SPEEDWAY	10 p.m.	9 p.m.	9 p.m.
UNDER THE SEA: JOURNEY OF THE LITTLE MERMAID	10 p.m.	10 p.m.	10 p.m.

*Information is applicable until July 24, 2024.

At press time, Tron Lightcycle/Run had sell-outs that were too variable to predict, and Tiana's Bayou Adventure had not opened.

LOW ATTENDANCE Crowd levels 1–3 on the TouringPlans.com crowd calendar

MODERATE ATTENDANCE Crowd levels 4–7   HIGH ATTENDANCE Crowd levels 8–10

Lightning Lane capacity, by crowd level. Use this table in conjunction with the "Attractions That Benefit Most" table on the next page to determine which reservations to get first.

How Can You Avoid Paying for Individual Lightning Lane?

There are a few strategies to avoid paying for Individual Lightning Lane. Several of them involve additional cost:

1. Stay at a Disney resort, use Early Theme Park Entry over multiple days, and head to each attraction as soon as the park opens or right before it closes. For popular attractions, such as Seven Dwarfs Mine Train, this is likely to be the strategy recommended by the touring plan software.

2. Stay at a Disney Deluxe or DVC resort and visit the attractions during Extended Evening Theme Park Hours.

3. Visit the attraction during an After Hours event or the Halloween or Christmas parties.

4. Visit the attraction in the last 30 minutes the park is open. The time posted at the entrance will be significantly higher than your actual wait.

MAGIC KINGDOM ATTRACTIONS THAT BENEFIT MOST FROM GENIE+ AND INDIVIDUAL LIGHTNING LANE (ILL) *(Highest Priority to Lowest)*			
ATTRACTION	AVG. TIME IN LINE SAVED (IN MINUTES)	**ATTRACTION**	AVG. TIME IN LINE SAVED (IN MINUTES)
SEVEN DWARFS MINE TRAIN (ILL)	50	THE MANY ADVENTURES OF WINNIE THE POOH	20
TRON LIGHTCYCLE/RUN (ILL)	37	BUZZ LIGHTYEAR'S SPACE RANGER SPIN	20
SPACE MOUNTAIN	37	UNDER THE SEA: JOURNEY OF THE LITTLE MERMAID	19
JUNGLE CRUISE	35	MEET ARIEL AT HER GROTTO	18
PETER PAN'S FLIGHT	32	TOMORROWLAND SPEEDWAY	16
BIG THUNDER MOUNTAIN RAILROAD	30	THE MAGIC CARPETS OF ALADDIN	14
MEET MICKEY MOUSE AT TOWN SQUARE THEATER	24	THE BARNSTORMER	12
PIRATES OF THE CARIBBEAN	22	*ENCHANTED TALES WITH BELLE*	11
THE HAUNTED MANSION	21	IT'S A SMALL WORLD	10
PRINCESS FAIRYTALE HALL MEET AND GREETS	20	DUMBO THE FLYING ELEPHANT	9

At press time, Tiana's Bayou Adventure had not opened.

How Do Genie+ and Individual Lightning Lane Work with the Touring Plans?

FOR INDIVIDUAL LIGHTNING LANE First, obtain an ILL return time from My Disney Experience. Next:

If you're using one of the touring plans from this book, follow the plan step by step until it's time to use your reservation. Suspend the touring plan while riding the attraction, then pick up the plan where you left off. If the plan recommends visiting the attraction before or after your return time, skip that step.

If you're using the Lines app, enter the reservation return time into the software. The software will organize your plan so that you return to the attraction at your designated return time.

FOR GENIE+ If you're using one of the touring plans in this book, keep track of the next two or three steps in your plan as you go through the park. Get the first available reservation for any of those three attractions, and fit that return-time window into the plan.

For example, suppose the next three steps in your touring plan are Jungle Cruise, Pirates of the Caribbean, and Big Thunder Mountain Railroad. Upon checking Genie+ for the next available return time for those three attractions, you find that they are 10:45 a.m. for Big Thunder, 11 a.m. for Jungle Cruise, and 11:30 a.m. for Pirates. In this case, you'd select Big Thunder because it's the next available return time from among the three. Once in line for Big Thunder, check Genie+ availability for the next three attractions in your plan. If none of the next three steps in your plan participate in Genie+, then get a reservation for the next attraction in your plan that does participate.

If you're using the Lines app, the software will recommend which attraction to obtain a Genie+ reservation for next by analyzing your touring plan, the current Genie+ reservation distribution rate, and likely wait times for the rest of the day. When you obtain that reservation, simply enter the return time into the software, and the software will redo your touring plan to use it.

DINING IN THE MAGIC KINGDOM

HERE'S A QUICK RECAP of the Magic Kingdom's major restaurants, rated by readers from highest to lowest. See Part 6 for details.

MAGIC KINGDOM RESTAURANT REFRESHER	
COUNTER SERVICE	**TABLE SERVICE**
• **Aloha Isle** (🔼 99%/E), Adventureland • **Columbia Harbour House** (🔼 94%/MAA), Liberty Square • **Gaston's Tavern** (🔼 95%/MAA), Fantasyland	• **Jungle Navigation Co. Ltd. Skipper Canteen** (🔼 91%/AA), Adventureland • **Liberty Tree Tavern** (🔼 92%/AA), Liberty Square

Restaurants not shown are rated as average or below.

▌ MAIN STREET, U.S.A.

YOU'LL BEGIN AND END YOUR VISIT on Main Street, which opens and closes about an hour before/after the rest of the park. A Disneyfied version of a turn-of-the-20th-century small-town American thoroughfare, it's lined with shops, character-greeting venues, places to eat, City Hall, and a fire station displaying an old fire engine. In the morning, old-timey vehicles also transport visitors along Main Street. You'll regularly hear live music throughout the day, from the Dapper Dans, the Main Street Philharmonic, or invited marching bands from around the country.

The circular area around the Central Plaza is a paved, landscaped viewing spot for the large crowds that watch the parades and evening fireworks. To disperse heavy crowds during these events, the areas behind the shops on either side of Main Street can become pedestrian walkways on which guests can exit and enter the park.

unofficial **TIP**
The pedestrian walkway most frequently used during parades and fireworks runs from just past **Tony's Town Square Restaurant** to the Tomorrowland side of **The Plaza Restaurant.** The other walkway runs from near the **First Aid Center,** next to The Crystal Palace, to the Main Street fire station (**Engine Co. 71**), near City Hall.

The **Walt Disney World Railroad** (see next page) stops at Main Street Station; get on to tour the park or ride to Frontierland or Fantasyland. It's not faster than walking, but it's easier on the feet.

KEY TO ABBREVIATIONS In the attraction profiles that follow, each Appeal by Age rating is accompanied by a category label in parentheses (see page 368). E means **Exceptional,** MAA means **Much Above Average,** AA means **Above Average,** A means **Average,** BA means **Below Average,** and MBA means **Much Below Average.**

Main Street Vehicles

DESCRIPTION AND COMMENTS Trolleys, buses, and the like.
TOURING TIPS Fun and saves footsteps but not worth a wait.

Meet Mickey Mouse at Town Square Theater ★★★★

PRESCHOOL ★★★★★ (E)　　GRADE SCHOOL ★★★★★ (E)　　TEENS ★★★★ (AA)
YOUNG ADULTS ★★★★ (AA)　　OVER 30 ★★★★½ (AA)　　OVER 65 ★★★★½ (E)

What it is Character-greeting venue. **Scope and scale** Minor attraction. **When to go**
Early or late. **Duration** 2 minutes. **Probable waiting time** 30 minutes. **Queue speed**
Slow. **ECV/wheelchair access** May remain in wheelchair. **Participates in Genie+** Yes.
Early Theme Park Entry No. **Extended Evening Hours** No.

DESCRIPTION AND COMMENTS Children and teenagers rate character
greetings among the highest of any Disney attractions, and there's no bigger celebrity than Mickey Mouse. Meet Mickey throughout the day at Town
Square Theater on Main Street, to your right as you enter the park.

TOURING TIPS Lines tend to die down after dinner, but if you want fresh-
looking family pictures, you may want to go near park opening time.

Walt Disney World Railroad ★★★

PRESCHOOL ★★★★ (A)　　GRADE SCHOOL ★★★★ (A)　　TEENS ★★½ (A)
YOUNG ADULTS ★★½ (A)　　OVER 30 ★★★★ (AA)　　OVER 65 ★★★★½ (MAA)

What it is Scenic railroad ride around the Magic Kingdom. **Scope and scale** Minor
attraction. **When to go** Anytime. **Comment** This is usually the least congested station.
Duration 20 minutes for round-trip. **Loading speed** Moderate. **ECV/wheelchair access**
At the Frontierland and Fantasyland stations; must transfer from ECV to provided
wheelchair. **Participates in Genie+** No. **Early Theme Park Entry** No. **Extended Evening Hours** No.

DESCRIPTION AND COMMENTS View the Magic Kingdom from aboard a
steam-powered locomotive, with stops in Frontierland and Fantasyland.
The most scenic portion is between the Frontierland and Fantasyland stations. If you're in Frontierland and headed out of the park, it's a nice way
to end your visit.

TOURING TIPS We suggest saving the train until after you have seen the
major attractions. On busy days, lines form at the Frontierland station but
rarely at the Main Street station. Only folded strollers are permitted on the
train, so you can't board with your Disney stroller, but you can get a
replacement if you keep your stroller name card and receipt with you.

A dad from New Jersey points out that all stations are not equal:

*Tell your readers that if they ride the railroad, they should go to the Main
Street station. We tried to get on [at another station], and it was a zoo—there
were people shoving past other people and rolling over other people with
strollers and wheelchairs. The Main Street station is much more organized,
efficient, and relaxing because of the extra cast members working there.*

Finally, note that the railroad shuts down immediately before and during parades and fireworks; check your park map or *Times Guide* for times.
This is not the time to get in line.

▮ ADVENTURELAND

ADVENTURELAND, WITH A TROPICAL ISLAND ATMOSPHERE,
is the first land to the left of Main Street, U.S.A. Many of its attractions

are theme park classics and are among the oldest in the park, so crowds don't usually build here until late morning.

Jungle Cruise ★★★½

PRESCHOOL ★★★½ (BA)	GRADE SCHOOL ★★★★ (BA)	TEENS ★★★★ (AA)
YOUNG ADULTS ★★★★ (AA)	OVER 30 ★★★★ (A)	OVER 65 ★★★★ (A)

What it is Outdoor comedic boat ride. **Scope and scale** Major attraction. **When to go** Early or late. **Duration** 8–9 minutes. **Loading speed** Moderate. **ECV/wheelchair access** May remain in ECV/wheelchair and wait for specially configured boats. **Participates in Genie+** Yes. **Early Theme Park Entry** No. **Extended Evening Hours** No.

DESCRIPTION AND COMMENTS On this outdoor group boat ride through tropical waterways, you'll pass through forest and jungle populated by animatronic animals and natives.

Jungle Cruise was the park's signature ride when it opened at Disneyland. This now seems silly since you can go on a safari in Animal Kingdom and see the real thing. But the skippers do *the* cheesiest, most groaninducing stand-up you've ever heard. If you dig that sort of thing (or just want to admire the excellent animatronics), it's glorious.

Jungle Cruise is one of the rare attractions where a pause in operations may be a good thing. That's when the skippers can go (more) off-script and run through a bunch of jokes that don't feel as stale or predictable.

TOURING TIPS We think the ride is better at night.

The Magic Carpets of Aladdin ★★

PRESCHOOL ★★★★½ (AA)	GRADE SCHOOL ★★★★½ (AA)	TEENS ★★★ (BA)
YOUNG ADULTS ★★★ (BA)	OVER 30 ★★★ (MBA)	OVER 65 ★★★½ (MBA)

What it is Themed spinner ride. **Scope and scale** Minor attraction. **When to go** Before noon or after dark. **Duration** 1½ minutes. **Loading speed** Slow. **ECV/wheelchair access** Must transfer from ECV to provided wheelchair. **Participates in Genie+** Yes. **Early Theme Park Entry** No. **Extended Evening Hours** Yes.

DESCRIPTION AND COMMENTS This ride is like Dumbo (see page 382) with magic carpets instead of elephants. A spitting camel sprays jets of water on carpet riders. Riders can maneuver their carpets up and down and tilt. The front seat controls vehicle height, while the back seat controls tilt.

TOURING TIPS This ride has great eye appeal but an extremely slow loading time—slower than Dumbo because there is only one spinner. That means its line moves surprisingly slow. The whole queue is visible, so you'll be able to tell if you're in for a long wait.

A Pirate's Adventure: Treasure of the Seven Seas ★★½

PRESCHOOL ★★★★ (A)	GRADE SCHOOL ★★★★ (A)	TEENS ★★★★ (A)
YOUNG ADULTS ★★★★ (A)	OVER 30 ★★★★ (A)	OVER 65 ★★★½ (MBA)

What it is Interactive game. **Scope and scale** Diversion. **When to go** Afternoon. **Duration** About 20 minutes to play the entire game. **ECV/wheelchair access** May remain in ECV/wheelchair. **Participates in Genie+** No. **Early Theme Park Entry** No. **Extended Evening Hours** No.

DESCRIPTION AND COMMENTS A Pirate's Adventure features interactive areas with physical props and narrations that lead guests through a quest to help Captain Jack Sparrow find lost treasure, all within Adventureland.

Guests begin their journey at The Crow's Nest. Your group of up to six people chooses a leader; the leader's MagicBand (or ticket) activates a video screen that assigns the group to one of five missions. Your group is given a map and sent off to the first location.

Once at the location, the leader of the party touches their MagicBand to the symbol at the station, and the animation begins. Each adventure has four or five stops throughout Adventureland; each stop contains 30–45 seconds of activity. No strategy or action is required: Simply watch what unfolds on the screen, get your next destination, and head off.

A Maryland mom writes:

The very best thing we did with our 4-year-old was A Pirate's Adventure. It was incredible. We did all five scavenger hunts, and it took 2 hours—our most fun 2 hours at the park! It's high-tech, magical, imaginative, active, and individualized. And you can keep the beautiful maps!

TOURING TIPS A good way to spend time on a busy afternoon if you want to avoid lines, but not a must-do.

Pirates of the Caribbean ★★★★

**PRESCHOOL ★★★½ (BA)   GRADE SCHOOL ★★★½ (BA)   TEENS ★★★★½ (MAA)
YOUNG ADULTS ★★★★½ (MAA)   OVER 30 ★★★★½ (MAA)   OVER 65 ★★★★½ (MAA)**

What it is Indoor pirate-themed boat ride. **Scope and scale** Headliner. **When to go** Anytime. **Duration** About 7½ minutes. **Loading speed** Fast. **ECV/wheelchair access** Must transfer from ECV to provided wheelchair and then from wheelchair to the ride vehicle. **Participates in Genie+** Yes. **Early Theme Park Entry** No. **Extended Evening Hours** Yes.

DESCRIPTION AND COMMENTS This cruise through a series of scenes that depict a pirate raid on an island settlement is one of the most influential theme park attractions ever created. The Magic Kingdom's version retains the elaborate queuing area, grand scale, and detailed sets that have awed audiences since the ride's debut in Disneyland in 1967.

As one of the theme park's most popular rides, Pirates is scrutinized and revised often. The successful *Pirates of the Caribbean* movies led to the addition of animatronic figures of Captain Jack Sparrow and Captain Barbossa. These additions, however, makes the ride's story confusing. Why did the raid stop for a chicken auction? Why is Jack randomly appearing and hiding in the middle of all of this? Still, if you don't attempt to find a storyline, the sets are fun.

TOURING TIPS Pirates moves large crowds in a hurry. There are some dark scenes that could scare younger children.

Swiss Family Treehouse ★★

**PRESCHOOL ★★★½ (BA)   GRADE SCHOOL ★★★½ (BA)   TEENS ★★★ (BA)
YOUNG ADULTS ★★★ (BA)   OVER 30 ★★★½ (MBA)   OVER 65 ★★★½ (MBA)**

What it is Outdoor walk-through treehouse. **Scope and scale** Diversion. **When to go** Anytime. **Duration** 10-15 minutes. **Probable waiting time** None. **ECV/wheelchair access** Must be ambulatory. **Participates in Genie+** No. **Early Theme Park Entry** No. **Extended Evening Hours** Yes.

DESCRIPTION AND COMMENTS An immense replica of the Swiss Family Robinson's treetop home. It's the queen of all treehouses.

TOURING TIPS A self-guided walk-through tour involves a lot of stairs but no ropes, ladders, or anything crazy. Folks who must pay attention to every small detail or people stopping to rest sometimes create bottlenecks that slow things down.

Walt Disney's Enchanted Tiki Room   ★★★

PRESCHOOL ★★★★ (BA)   **GRADE SCHOOL** ★★★★ (BA)   **TEENS** ★★★ (BA)
YOUNG ADULTS ★★★½ (BA)   **OVER 30** ★★★★ (A)   **OVER 65** ★★★★ (A)

What it is Audio-Animatronic musical show. **Scope and scale** Minor attraction. **When to go** Anytime. **Duration** 15½ minutes. **Probable waiting time** 15 minutes. **ECV/wheelchair access** May remain in ECV/wheelchair. **Participates in Genie+** No. **Early Theme Park Entry** No. **Extended Evening Hours** Yes.

DESCRIPTION AND COMMENTS This show, conceived by Walt Disney himself, stars four singing, wisecracking mechanical parrots: José, Fritz, Michael, and Pierre (aka the Tiki Birds). The quartet performs songs arranged in styles from the 1940s to the 1960s, accompanied by dozens of other birds, plants, and tikis that come to life all around you.

The show was an engineering marvel when it opened in Disneyland in 1963. Most kids today don't get it. It remains a favorite of many fans of classic Disney, including us, who enjoy the period-appropriate musical references and direct link back to Walt.

TOURING TIPS Go in the late afternoon, when you will most appreciate the air-conditioning.

If you have young kids, be prepared for a dark and stormy scene that may startle some.

FRONTIERLAND

THIS "LAND" FOLLOWS ADVENTURELAND as you move clockwise around the Magic Kingdom. Frontierland's theme is 19th-century America, with pioneer roots. If you start at Big Thunder Mountain and walk toward The Haunted Mansion in Liberty Square, you'll also be walking back in time: The different rides and buildings represent distinct eras in US history, from the settling of the frontier through the California gold rush to the early-19th-century South.

Big Thunder Mountain Railroad   ★★★★

PRESCHOOL ★★★★ (BA) **GRADE SCHOOL** ★★★★ (BA)   **TEENS** ★★★★½ (E)
YOUNG ADULTS ★★★★½ (E)   **OVER 30** ★★★★½ (E)   **OVER 65** ★★★★½ (AA)

What it is Western-themed roller coaster. **Scope and scale** Headliner. **When to go** Early or late. **Comments** Must be 40" tall to ride; Rider Switch option provided (see page 303). **Duration** About 3½ minutes. **Loading speed** Moderate-fast. **ECV/wheelchair access** Must transfer to the ride vehicle. **Participates in Genie+** Yes. **Early Theme Park Entry** No. **Extended Evening Hours** Yes.

DESCRIPTION AND COMMENTS Not only is Big Thunder well themed, but it also has a moderately long duration. It doesn't leave you wanting more, unlike some of the other coasters in the park. On this attraction, you're on a runaway mine train careening through a gold rush frontier town. Big Thunder contains first-rate examples of Disney Imagineering at work: caverns, an earthquake, swinging opossums, and the like. Seats in the back offer the best experience.

In terms of intensity, we put this coaster at about a 5 on a scary scale of 10—it has tight turns rather than big hills, drops, and upside-down parts. Because it's outdoors and kids can see most of the ride, it's a much better introduction to "real" roller coasters for first-timers than Space Mountain.

But because of all the tight turns, it rates higher on the motion-sickness scale than you might expect.

TOURING TIPS Nearby **Tiana's Bayou Adventure** (see page 378) will affect traffic flow to Big Thunder Mountain Railroad—guests who ride one usually ride both. This translates to large crowds in Frontierland all day and longer waits for Big Thunder. A good one-day schedule might be Big Thunder and Tiana's Bayou Adventure in the morning, Space Mountain and Seven Dwarfs Mine Train in the evening, and Tron whenever you can get a spot in the virtual queue.

Country Bear Jamboree ★★★

PRESCHOOL ★★★★ (BA)	GRADE SCHOOL ★★★★ (BA)	TEENS ★★★ (MBA)
YOUNG ADULTS ★★★ (MBA)	OVER 30 ★★★½ (BA)	OVER 65 ★★★★ (BA)

What it is Corny Audio-Animatronic hoedown. **Scope and scale** Minor attraction. **When to go** Anytime. **Duration** 11 minutes. **Probable waiting time** Less than one show. **ECV/wheelchair access** May remain in wheelchair. **Participates in Genie+** No. **Early Theme Park Entry** No. **Extended Evening Hours** Yes.

DESCRIPTION AND COMMENTS A charming cast of animatronic bears sings and stomps through a series of country and Western songs. It's an air-conditioned refuge on hot days, and the remix of "The Ballad of Davy Crockett" and "Ole Slew Foot" is genius. As we were going to press, a new, revamped version of the show was being developed and was set to debut in 2024.

TOURING TIPS On hot and rainy days, the *Jamboree* draws crowds looking for an indoor haven. You may see a relative surge of interest in early 2025, depending on the success of the revamp, but probably nothing too crazy.

Tiana's Bayou Adventure
(formerly Splash Mountain)

TOO NEW TO RATE

What it is Water-flume adventure. **Scope and scale** Super-headliner. **When to go** Immediately at park opening or use Genie+. **Comments** Must be 40" tall to ride; Rider Switch option provided (see page 303). **Duration** About 10 minutes. **Loading speed** Moderate. **ECV/wheelchair access** Must transfer to the ride vehicle; transfer device available. **Participates in Genie+** Yes. **Early Theme Park Entry** No. **Extended Evening Hours** Yes.

Wet

DESCRIPTION AND COMMENTS Tiana's Bayou Adventure is a welcome retheming of Frontierland's controversial Splash Mountain ride. At press time, Disney had revealed that the new story follows Tiana as she expands her culinary empire from restaurant to farms, salt mines, and cooking schools. Tiana's will keep Splash Mountain's architecture, including its pacing, small drops, and big drop near the end.

From a thematic perspective, the Disneyland version is straightforward: Tiana's is adjacent to The Haunted Mansion in New Orleans Square, where Tiana's post-1927 New Orleans story fits in just fine. But Frontierland is solidly in the 1800s. It'll be interesting to see how Tiana fits in.

TOURING TIPS If you ride in the front seat, you'll almost certainly get wet; riders elsewhere get at least splashed. Be prepared—on a cool day, bring a poncho or a plastic garbage bag with holes in the bottom and sides for your head and arms. Or store a change of clothes in a rental locker.

Leave your camera or phone with a nonriding member of your group, or put it in a ziplock bag. Find a way to waterproof your shoes, or store a second pair in your locker for after the ride.

Tom Sawyer Island and Fort Langhorn   ★★★

PRESCHOOL ★★★★ (A)	GRADE SCHOOL ★★★★ (A)	TEENS ★★★½ (BA)
YOUNG ADULTS ★★★½ (BA)	OVER 30 ★★★½ (BA)	OVER 65 ★★★½ (MBA)

What it is Outdoor walk-through. **Scope and scale** Minor attraction. **When to go** Afternoon. **Comments** Closes at dusk. **ECV/wheelchair access** Must be ambulatory. **Participates in Genie+** No. **Early Theme Park Entry** No. **Extended Evening Hours** No.

DESCRIPTION AND COMMENTS A great midafternoon getaway from the crowds. Tom Sawyer Island has hills to climb; a cave, windmill, and pioneer stockade (Fort Langhorn) to explore; paths to follow; and even an escape tunnel. Tom Sawyer Island is underrated—we think it's one of the Magic Kingdom's better-conceived areas. It's almost a must for families with children; it's perfect for safer, unstructured exploring without fear of getting lost in large crowds. Get those wiggles out!

TOURING TIPS Plan on about 30 minutes here. Access is by raft from Frontierland; two rafts operate simultaneously, and while the trip itself is quick, you may have to stand in line to board both ways.

A Michigan family made an unplanned visit:

My 5-year-old son needed to run off some energy, so we veered from the touring plan and took the raft to Tom Sawyer Island. I thought it was a playground (we never bothered to head there before), but it was the coolest area to explore for our whole family! Very few people were there, which meant I got amazing pictures of my kids without strangers in the background, and the buildings, tunnels, and fort were so fun to explore! My kids asked to go back here the next day, and we did!

Walt Disney World Railroad

DESCRIPTION AND COMMENTS The railroad stops in Frontierland on its park tour. See page 374 for additional details.

TOURING TIPS It's a pleasant, feet-saving link to Main Street and Fantasyland, but the Frontierland station is more congested than the others.

■ LIBERTY SQUARE

LIBERTY SQUARE re-creates the United States at the time of the Revolutionary War. The **Liberty Tree,** a live oak more than 150 years old, lends dignity and grace to the patriotic setting.

The Hall of Presidents   ★★★

PRESCHOOL ★★ (MBA)*	GRADE SCHOOL ★★ (MBA)*	TEENS ★★★ (BA)*
YOUNG ADULTS ★★★ (BA)	OVER 30 ★★★★ (A)	OVER 65 ★★★★½ (AA)

* Hall of Presidents is the lowest-rated Magic Kingdom attraction among preschoolers and grade-schoolers.

What it is Audio-Animatronic historical presentation. **Scope and scale** Minor attraction. **When to go** Anytime. **Duration** Almost 23 minutes. **Probable waiting time** Less than one show. **ECV/wheelchair access** May remain in wheelchair. **Participates in Genie+** No. **Early Theme Park Entry** No. **Extended Evening Hours** No.

DESCRIPTION AND COMMENTS *The Hall of Presidents* combines a wide-screen theater presentation of key highlights and milestones in the political history of the United States with a short stage show featuring life-size animatronic replicas of every US president. Their physical resemblances and costumes are masterful.

Abraham Lincoln and George Washington have speaking roles, and the current president recites the oath of office. Regardless of who speaks, the inspirational, patriotic tone is a constant.

The current version of the show reiterates many of the same social and political points as EPCOT's *The American Adventure,* so it's probably not worthwhile to see both. Of the two, *The American Adventure* is better.

Many visitors comment that they appreciate this spot more for the cool, dark space it provides for naps or snacking than for the show itself.

TOURING TIPS In the last decade or so, it's become commonplace for some members of the audience to cheer or jeer as the current president and his contemporaries are named. Skip *The Hall of Presidents* if you'd rather not be reminded of politics on vacation.

The Haunted Mansion ★★★★½

PRESCHOOL ★★★ (MBA)   GRADE SCHOOL ★★★ (MBA)   TEENS ★★★★½ (MAA)
YOUNG ADULTS ★★★★½ (MAA)   OVER 30 ★★★★½ (E)   OVER 65 ★★★★½ (E)

What it is Haunted-house dark ride. **Scope and scale** Major attraction. **When to go** Early or late. **Duration** 7 minutes. **Loading speed** Fast. **ECV/wheelchair access** Must transfer to the ride vehicle. **Participates in Genie+** Yes. **Early Theme Park Entry** No. **Extended Evening Hours** Yes.

DESCRIPTION AND COMMENTS The Haunted Mansion—which opened with the rest of the World in 1971—proves that top-notch special effects don't always require 21st-century technology. "Doom Buggies" on a conveyor belt transport you through the house and graveyard. The effects range from generally spooky to totally laughable. Some kids get anxious about what they think they'll see, but almost nobody over the age of 6 actually gets scared. Below that age, you'll have a lot more explaining to do or sight lines to avoid. A Texas mom points out that your personal evaluation of the fright level may differ from the *Unofficial Guide's*:

You say the actual sights aren't really frightening—but what isn't *frightening about a hanging corpse, a coffin escapee, and an axe-wielding skeleton bride?*

Interactive elements in the outdoor queue occupy guests when lines are long. These include an interactive musical monument and a ship captain's tomb that squirts water.

TOURING TIPS When admitted to the Mansion, you'll first enter a foyer with a fireplace, then be guided quickly into a second, wood-paneled preshow room with four paintings above you. Keep close to the wall, find the wall panel with a small red light at about eye level, and stand with your back to that panel while you watch the preshow.

Liberty Belle Riverboat ★★½

PRESCHOOL ★★★ (MBA)   GRADE SCHOOL ★★★ (MBA)   TEENS ★★★ (MBA)
YOUNG ADULTS ★★★ (MBA)   OVER 30 ★★★½ (BA)   OVER 65 ★★★★ (A)

What it is Scenic boat ride. **Scope and scale** Minor attraction. **When to go** Anytime. **Duration of ride** About 16 minutes. **ECV/wheelchair access** May remain in ECV/wheelchair. **Participates in Genie+** No. **Early Theme Park Entry** No. **Extended Evening Hours** No.

DESCRIPTION AND COMMENTS This large paddle wheel riverboat navigates the waters around Tom Sawyer Island, passing settler cabins, old mining paraphernalia, an American Indian village, and a small menagerie of animatronic wildlife. The *Liberty Belle* provides a lofty view of Frontierland and Liberty Square.

TOURING TIPS The riverboat, which departs roughly every half hour, is a good attraction for the busy middle of the day. If it's hot outside, find a spot in the shade on the bottom deck.

FANTASYLAND

FANTASYLAND IS THE HEART of the Magic Kingdom, spread gracefully like a small Alpine village beneath the towers of **Cinderella Castle.** It is divided into several distinct sections. Directly behind Cinderella Castle and set upon a snowcapped mountain is **Beast's Castle,** part of a *Beauty and the Beast*–themed area. Most of this section holds dining and shopping, such as **Be Our Guest Restaurant** (see page 247); **Gaston's Tavern,** a small quick-service restaurant; and a gift shop. The far-right corner of Fantasyland—including **Dumbo the Flying Elephant, The Barnstormer** kiddie coaster, and the Fantasyland train station—is called **Storybook Circus** as an homage to the *Dumbo* films. A covered seating area with plush chairs, electrical outlets, and USB phone chargers is located behind **Big Top Souvenirs.**

The middle of Fantasyland holds the headliner, **Seven Dwarfs Mine Train,** and a secondary attraction, **Under the Sea: Journey of the Little Mermaid.** The placement of these two attractions allows good traffic flow either to the left (toward Beast's Castle) for dining, to the right for attractions geared to smaller children, or back to the original part of Fantasyland for Disney classics such as **Peter Pan's Flight** and **The Many Adventures of Winnie the Pooh.**

The original section, behind Cinderella Castle, holds **Princess Fairytale Hall,** *Mickey's PhilharMagic,* and the restored antique **Prince Charming Regal Carrousel.** Finally, the *Tangled*-**themed restrooms and outdoor seating** are a can't-miss section. We're not kidding. People have photo shoots in this restroom area, and we applaud them.

Ariel's Grotto ★★★

PRESCHOOL ★★★★½ (MAA) GRADE SCHOOL ★★★★½ (MAA) TEENS ★★★ (MBA)
YOUNG ADULTS ★★★ (MBA) OVER 30 ★★★½ (BA) OVER 65 ★★★★ (BA)

What it is Character-greeting venue. **Scope and scale** Minor attraction. **When to go** Early or late. **Duration of experience** A minute. **Probable waiting time** 45 minutes. **Queue speed** Slow. **ECV/wheelchair access** May remain in wheelchair. **Participates in Genie+** Yes. **Early Theme Park Entry** No. **Extended Evening Hours** No.

DESCRIPTION AND COMMENTS This is Ariel's home turf, next to her signature ride (see page 387). She greets guests from a seashell throne. The line for this one is slower than many other meet and greets, so be prepared for a wait. Kids love this meet and greet, but others in their party rate it poorly, generally because the long wait catches them by surprise.

TOURING TIPS The greeting area is set up almost as if to encourage guests to linger, which keeps the line long—and the queue isn't air-conditioned.

The Barnstormer ★½

PRESCHOOL ★★★★ (BA) GRADE SCHOOL ★★★★ (BA) TEENS ★★★ (MBA)
YOUNG ADULTS ★★★ (MBA) OVER 30 ★★★ (MBA) OVER 65 ★★★ (MBA)

What it is Small roller coaster. **Scope and scale** Minor attraction. **When to go** Early or late. **Comment** Must be 35" tall to ride. **Duration of ride** 53 seconds. **Loading speed**

Slow. **ECV/wheelchair access** Must transfer to the ride vehicle. **Participates in Genie+** Yes. **Early Theme Park Entry** Yes. **Extended Evening Hours** Yes.

DESCRIPTION AND COMMENTS The Barnstormer is a dinky little coaster with a zippy ride lasting only 53 seconds, 32 of which are spent starting and stopping. Actual time zooming around the track: 21 seconds. It's a good introduction to roller coasters for the littlest kids but should be avoided by all others.

TOURING TIPS The cars are too small for most adults and tend to give taller people whiplash. If The Barnstormer is high on your children's must-do list, try to ride within the first 2 hours Fantasyland is open.

Casey Jr. Splash 'N' Soak Station ★★½

PRESCHOOL ★★★★½ (AA)	GRADE SCHOOL ★★★★½ (AA)	TEENS ★★★ (MBA)
YOUNG ADULTS ★★ (MBA)	OVER 30 ★★½ (MBA)	OVER 65 ★★½ (MBA)

What it is Elaborate water-play area. **Scope and scale** Diversion. **When to go** When it's hot. **ECV/wheelchair access** May remain in wheelchair. **Participates in Genie+** No. **Early Theme Park Entry** No. **Extended Evening Hours** No.

 DESCRIPTION AND COMMENTS Casey Jr., the circus train from *Dumbo,* plays host to an absolutely drenching play area in the Storybook Circus area. Cars of captive circus beasts spray water on kids and parents. So. Much. Water.

TOURING TIPS Bring a change of clothes and a big towel. Note that it doesn't run during cooler weather. A mom from Kansas suggests another way to handle this attraction:

Casey Jr. is like a bright lamp, and toddlers are like moths. I almost wish we had skipped [Storybook Circus] just so I didn't have to keep dragging my child away from this spot that would leave him soggy for the rest of the day.

Dumbo the Flying Elephant ★★½

PRESCHOOL ★★★★½ (MAA)	GRADE SCHOOL ★★★★ (MAA)	TEENS ★★★ (BA)
YOUNG ADULTS ★★★½ (BA)	OVER 30 ★★★½ (BA)	OVER 65 ★★★★ (BA)

What it is Disneyfied spinner ride. **Scope and scale** Minor attraction. **When to go** Early or late. **Duration of ride** 1½ minutes. **Loading speed** Slow. **ECV/wheelchair access** Must transfer to the ride vehicle. **Participates in Genie+** Yes. **Early Theme Park Entry** Yes. **Extended Evening Hours** Yes.

DESCRIPTION AND COMMENTS A sweet ride based on the classic movie. Parents and kids sit in small elephants mounted on long metal arms that spin around a central axis. Controls inside each vehicle allow you to spin higher off the ground. Dumbo is the favorite Magic Kingdom attraction of many very young children.

TOURING TIPS If Dumbo is essential, ride after dinner; not only are the crowds smaller at night, but the lighting and effects make the ride much prettier. There is a covered play area mid-queue. You'll frequently be able to walk right past, but you can take advantage of the space if your little ones need some unstructured play.

Enchanted Tales with Belle ★★★★

PRESCHOOL ★★★★½ (A)	GRADE SCHOOL ★★★★ (A)	TEENS ★★★ (MA)
YOUNG ADULTS ★★★ (BA)	OVER 30 ★★★★ (A)	OVER 65 ★★★★ (AA)

What it is Interactive live character show. **Scope and scale** Minor attraction. **When to go** Early or late. **Duration of presentation** Approximately 20 minutes. **Queue speed**

Slow. **ECV/wheelchair access** Must transfer from ECV to provided wheelchair. **Participates in Genie+** No. **Early Theme Park Entry** No. **Extended Evening Hours** No.

DESCRIPTION AND COMMENTS This multiscene *Beauty and the Beast* experience begins in the cottage and workshop of Belle's father, Maurice, which happens to feature a magic mirror.

No spoilers here, but you'll eventually enter a room with The Wardrobe. Once there, cast members explain: You're here to reenact the story of *Beauty and the Beast* for Belle on her birthday. Guests are chosen to act out key parts in the play.

Next, everyone walks into the library and takes a seat. Cast members explain how the play will take place and introduce Belle. The play is acted out within a few minutes, and all of the actors get a chance to take photos with Belle and receive a small bookmark as a gift.

During our visits, only guests who chose to act in the play got to take photos with Belle. Those photos are accessed with a separate Memory Maker card. If you have a small child who is too shy to take part, cast members will usually allow them to take a picture with Belle if you ask nicely.

Enchanted Tales with Belle is the most interactive meet and greet in Walt Disney World. For those who get to act in the play, it's also a chance to interact with Belle in a way that isn't possible in other character encounters. Here's an enthusiastic review from a Texas mom:

Enchanted Tales with Belle *surprised us with how well it was done. My husband was a knight, my daughter was Mrs. Potts, and my son was silverware. It was so much fun, and the kids were so proud.*

TOURING TIPS Because the line moves slowly, see *Enchanted Tales* early in the morning or try to visit during the last 2 hours the attraction is open.

It's a Small World ★★★½

| PRESCHOOL ★★★★½ (A) | GRADE SCHOOL ★★★★½ (A) | TEENS ★★★ (MBA) |
| YOUNG ADULTS ★★★½ (BA) | OVER 30 ★★★★ (BA) | OVER 65 ★★★★ (B) |

What it is World harmony–themed indoor boat ride. **Scope and scale** Major attraction. **When to go** Early or late. **Duration of ride** About 11 minutes. **Loading speed** Fast. **ECV/wheelchair access** Must transfer from ECV to provided wheelchair. **Participates in Genie+** Yes. **Early Theme Park Entry** Yes. **Extended Evening Hours** Yes.

DESCRIPTION AND COMMENTS Happy and upbeat to an almost unsettling degree, It's a Small World is guaranteed to leave you humming its song for the rest of the day. Small boats carry you on a tour around the world, with singing and dancing dolls showcasing the dress and culture of each nation represented. One of Disney's oldest entertainment offerings, Small World first unleashed its mind-numbing theme song and unbearable cuteness at the 1964 New York World's Fair; the original exhibit was moved to Disneyland afterward, and a duplicate was created for Disney World when it opened in 1971. Almost everyone enjoys It's a Small World. It stands as a monument to a bygone age of entertainment.

Mad Tea Party ★★

| PRESCHOOL ★★★★½ (AA) | GRADE SCHOOL ★★★★½ (AA) | TEENS ★★★★ (AA) |
| YOUNG ADULTS ★★★★ (AA) | OVER 30 ★★★½ (MBA) | OVER 65 ★★★ (MBA) |

What it is Spinning ride. **Scope and scale** Minor attraction. **When to go** Anytime. **Comment** The teacup spins faster when you turn the wheel in the center. We're not sure if that's a good thing or not. **Duration of ride** 1½ minutes. **Loading speed** Slow.

ECV/wheelchair access Must transfer to the ride vehicle; transfer device available. **Participates in Genie+** Yes. **Early Theme Park Entry** Yes. **Extended Evening Hours** Yes.

DESCRIPTION AND COMMENTS Riders whirl around in big teacups. *Alice in Wonderland*'s Mad Hatter provides the theme. Kids like to lure adults onto the teacups and then turn the wheel in the middle—making the cup spin faster—until the adults are plastered helplessly against the sides and on the verge of tossing their tacos.

TOURING TIPS Mad Tea Party is notoriously slow-loading, especially if someone before you lost their lunch.

The Many Adventures of Winnie the Pooh ★★★½

PRESCHOOL ★★★★ (A)   **GRADE SCHOOL ★★★★** (A)   **TEENS ★★★½** (A)
YOUNG ADULTS ★★★½ (A)   **OVER 30 ★★★½** (BA)   **OVER 65 ★★★★** (BA)

What it is Indoor track ride. **Scope and scale** Minor attraction. **When to go** Early or late. **Duration of ride** About 4 minutes. **Loading speed** Moderate. **ECV/wheelchair access** Must transfer from ECV to provided wheelchair. **Participates in Genie+** Yes. **Early Theme Park Entry** Yes. **Extended Evening Hours** Yes.

DESCRIPTION AND COMMENTS Ride a Hunny Pot through the pages of a huge picture book into the Hundred Acre Wood, where you encounter all the familiar faces as they contend with a blustery day. There's even a dream sequence with Heffalumps and Woozles.

This is another attraction where Genie+ has slowed the standby line to a crawl. If the Lightning Lane looks backed up, your standby wait will move at a snail's pace. An Indiana mom loved Pooh's interactive queue:

The queue for The Many Adventures of Winnie the Pooh was amazing! There were so many things for little kids to do, and consequently fewer meltdowns! I wish there were more queues like that.

TOURING TIPS Sunny, happy, and upbeat, Pooh is a good choice if you have small children or if you've ever wanted to bounce like Tigger. Beware that they may fall in love with the characters and you'll have a hard time peeling them away from the gift shop.

Meet Mirabel at Fairytale Garden ★★★½

TOO NEW TO RATE

What it is Character meet and greet. **Scope and scale** Diversion. **When to go** Early or late. **Duration of experience** About 3 minutes. **Queue speed** Slow. **ECV/wheelchair access** May remain in wheelchair. **Participates in Genie+** No. **Early Theme Park Entry** No. **Extended Evening Hours** No.

DESCRIPTION AND COMMENTS Mirabel, of *Encanto* fame, takes over this spot from Merida (who now infrequently wanders Fantasyland instead). You'll find the Fairytale Garden in front of Cinderella Castle on the Tomorrowland side, between the castle and Cosmic Ray's Starlight Café.

TOURING TIPS This meet and greet tends to be exceedingly popular, so expect long lines. If meeting Mirabel is a must, get in line about 15 minutes before her character location opens for the day.

Mickey's PhilharMagic ★★★½

PRESCHOOL ★★★★ (A)   **GRADE SCHOOL ★★★★½** (A)   **TEENS ★★★★** (A)
YOUNG ADULTS ★★★★ (A)   **OVER 30 ★★★★** (AA)   **OVER 65 ★★★★½** (MAA)

What it is 3D movie. **Scope and scale** Minor attraction. **When to go** Anytime. **Duration of presentation** About 12 minutes. **Probable waiting time** Less than one show.

ECV/wheelchair access May remain in wheelchair. **Participates in Genie+** Yes. **Early Theme Park Entry** Yes. **Extended Evening Hours** Yes.

DESCRIPTION AND COMMENTS *Mickey's PhilharMagic* is a 3D film with a fun collection of Disney characters, mixing Mickey and Donald with Simba and Ariel, as well as Jasmine, Aladdin, and characters from *Coco.*

Presented in a theater large enough to accommodate a 150-foot-wide screen—huge by 3D standards—the movie is augmented by a variety of special effects built into the theater. The plot involves Donald attempting to take charge of Mickey's symphony, with disastrous results.

Mickey's PhilharMagic will leave you grinning. And where other Disney 3D movies are loud, in-your-face affairs, this one is softer and cuddlier. Things pop out of the screen, but they're really not scary. It's the rare child who's frightened.

TOURING TIPS Provides a nice midday air-conditioning break.

Peter Pan's Flight ★★★★

PRESCHOOL ★★★★ (A)	GRADE SCHOOL ★★★★ (A)	TEENS ★★★½ (A)
YOUNG ADULTS ★★★½ (MAA)	OVER 30 ★★★★ (A)	OVER 65 ★★★★½ (AA)

What it is Indoor flying track ride. **Scope and scale** Major attraction. **When to go** First or last 30 minutes the park is open. **Duration of ride** About 3 minutes. **Loading speed** Moderate-slow. **ECV/wheelchair access** Must be ambulatory. **Participates in Genie+** Yes. **Early Theme Park Entry** Yes. **Extended Evening Hours** Yes.

DESCRIPTION AND COMMENTS Peter Pan's Flight combines beloved characters, beautiful effects, and charming music. The ride begins in the Darling family's house before embarking on a relaxing trip in a "flying pirate ship" over old London and then to Never Land. Nothing here will frighten young children.

A themed queue has air-conditioning and features a walk through the Darlings' home, where you'll see various rooms, play a few games, and get sprinkled with a bit of (virtual) pixie dust.

TOURING TIPS Count on long lines all day. Fortunately, the queue is out of direct sun and rain and has tons of art and interactive games to help pass the time. Ride in the first 30 minutes the park is open, during a parade, or just before the park closes. Peter Pan's Flight is one of the most helpful Genie+ reservations you can get in the Magic Kingdom. Because its Lightning Lane is so popular, even a deceptively short-looking standby line will take eight forevers to load. That's been scientifically measured.

Pete's Silly Sideshow ★★★½

PRESCHOOL ★★★★★ (E)	GRADE SCHOOL ★★★★½ (MAA)	TEENS ★★★½ (A)
YOUNG ADULTS ★★★½ (A)	OVER 30 ★★★★ (A)	OVER 65 ★★★½ (BA)

What it is Character-greeting venue. **Scope and scale** Minor attraction. **When to go** Early or late. **Duration of experience** 3 minutes per character. **Queue speed** Slow. **ECV/wheelchair access** May remain in wheelchair. **Participates in Genie+** No. **Early Theme Park Entry** No. **Extended Evening Hours** No.

DESCRIPTION AND COMMENTS Pete's Silly Sideshow is a circus-themed character-greeting area. The characters' costumes are unique to this location. Characters include Goofy as The Great Goofini, Donald Duck as The Astounding Donaldo, Daisy Duck as Madame Daisy Fortuna, and Minnie Mouse as Minnie Magnifique.

TOURING TIPS The queue is indoors and air-conditioned. There's one queue for Goofy and Donald and a second queue for Minnie and Daisy; you can meet two characters at once, but you have to line up twice to meet all four. If you or your kids feel like character meet and greets are awkward, you'll appreciate the unique backdrops and costumes that make for easy conversation and interactions here.

Prince Charming Regal Carrousel ★★★

PRESCHOOL ★★★★½ (MAA)   **GRADE SCHOOL ★★★★½ (MAA)**   **TEENS ★★★ (BA)**
YOUNG ADULTS ★★★½ (BA)   **OVER 30 ★★★½ (BA)**   **OVER 65 ★★★½ (BA)**

What it is Merry-go-round. **Scope and scale** Minor attraction. **When to go** Anytime. **Duration of ride** About 2 minutes. **Loading speed** Slow. **ECV/wheelchair access** Must transfer from ECV to provided wheelchair. **Participates in Genie+** No. **Early Theme Park Entry** Yes. **Extended Evening Hours** Yes.

DESCRIPTION AND COMMENTS One of the most elaborate and beautiful merry-go-rounds you'll ever have the pleasure of seeing, especially when its lights are on.

TOURING TIPS Unless young children in your party insist on riding, appreciate the carousel from the sidelines—it loads and unloads very slowly.

Princess Fairytale Hall ★★★

PRESCHOOL ★★★★½ (AA)   **GRADE SCHOOL ★★★★½ (AA)**   **TEENS ★★★½ (A)**
YOUNG ADULTS ★★★½ (A)   **OVER 30 ★★★★ (A)**   **OVER 65 ★★★★ (BA)**

What it is Character-greeting venue. **Scope and scale** Minor attraction. **When to go** Early or late. **Duration of experience** 6-7 minutes. **Queue speed** Slow. **ECV/wheelchair access** May remain in wheelchair. **Participates in Genie+** Yes. **Early Theme Park Entry** No. **Extended Evening Hours** No.

DESCRIPTION AND COMMENTS Fairytale Hall is Princess Central in the Magic Kingdom. Inside are two greeting venues, with each holding a small reception area for two princesses. Thus, there are four princesses meeting and greeting at any time, and you can see two of them at once. Signs outside tell you which line leads to which princess pair. Tiana usually leads one side, typically paired with Rapunzel. Cinderella and Elena of Avalor (a Disney Channel character) are the usual pair on the other. Around 5–10 guests at a time are admitted to each greeting area, where there's plenty of time for small talk and a photo with each princess.

TOURING TIPS These lines can be substantial when new princesses are introduced. If your kids love princesses, get Fairytale Hall out of the way early, or use Genie+. The two queues are identical and almost always move at similar speeds, so if you're going standby, you'll be able to see which pair of princesses has a shorter wait, regardless of what the posted wait says.

Seven Dwarfs Mine Train ★★★★

PRESCHOOL ★★★★ (BA)   **GRADE SCHOOL ★★★★ (BA)**   **TEENS ★★★★½ (MAA)**
YOUNG ADULTS ★★★★½ (MAA)   **OVER 30 ★★★★½ (MAA)**   **OVER 65 ★★★★½ (AA)**

What it is Themed roller coaster. **Scope and scale** Super-headliner. **When to go** As soon as the park opens. **Comment** Must be 38″ tall to ride. **Duration of ride** About 2 minutes. **Loading speed** Fast. **ECV/wheelchair access** Must transfer to the ride vehicle. **Participates in Genie+** No (it offers Individual Lightning Lane). **Early Theme Park Entry** Yes. **Extended Evening Hours** Yes.

DESCRIPTION AND COMMENTS Seven Dwarfs Mine Train is geared to older grade-school kids who've been on amusement park rides before. There are no upside-down sections and no massive hills or steep drops. It's a curvy track with steep turns, and your ride vehicle's seats swing side-to-side as you go through the turns. An elaborate indoor section shows the dwarfs' underground mining operation.

The exterior design includes waterfalls, forests, and landscaping. The swinging effect is more noticeable the farther back you're seated in the train. The duration is almost jarringly short, so take that into consideration when deciding how long you're willing to wait.

A Virginia mom offers a little cost–benefit analysis:

Seven Dwarfs Mine Train was a great ride but not worth a 90-minute wait.

A woman from Saskatchewan, Canada, felt let down:

One-and-a-half hours of my time for one-and-a-half minutes of disappointment.

TOURING TIPS If you have children who might be interested in riding this but not Space Mountain, head for Seven Dwarfs as soon as the park opens. Depending on how they do here, try Big Thunder Mountain Railroad or Tiana's Bayou Adventure next.

Under the Sea: Journey of the Little Mermaid   ★ ★ ★

PRESCHOOL ★ ★ ★ ½ (AA)   **GRADE SCHOOL** ★ ★ ★ ½ (A)   **TEENS** ★ ★ ½ (A)
YOUNG ADULTS ★ ★ ★ ½ (A)   **OVER 30** ★ ★ ★ ½ (BA)   **OVER 65** ★ ★ ★ ★ (A)

What it is Story-retelling dark ride. **Scope and scale** Minor attraction. **When to go** Early or late. **Duration of ride** About 5½ minutes. **Loading speed** Fast. **ECV/wheelchair access** Must transfer from ECV to provided wheelchair. **Participates in Genie+** Yes. **Early Theme Park Entry** Yes. **Extended Evening Hours** Yes.

DESCRIPTION AND COMMENTS Under the Sea takes riders through almost a dozen scenes retelling the story of *The Little Mermaid* with animatronics, video effects, and a vibrant set. Guests board a clamshell-shaped ride vehicle running along a continuously moving track (similar to The Haunted Mansion's), then descend "underwater" past Ariel's grotto to King Triton's undersea kingdom. Ursula is the most impressive animatronic.

The attraction's exterior is attractive, with detailed rockwork and water elements. Our favorite effect is a hidden Mickey, created by the alignment of the sun's shadow and the rockwork, that appears only at noon on November 18, Mickey's birthday.

This ride isn't Disney's most ambitious, but it's cute. Most of the effects are simple and unimaginative, and almost the whole second half of the story is crammed into a few small scenes at the end, as if the budget ran out before the ride could be finished properly.

Walt Disney World Railroad

DESCRIPTION AND COMMENTS The railroad stops in Fantasyland on its circuit of the park. See the description under Main Street, U.S.A. (see page 374), for additional details.

TOURING TIPS Pleasant, feet-saving link to Main Street and Frontierland.

TOMORROWLAND

AT VARIOUS POINTS IN ITS HISTORY, Tomorrowland's attractions presented life's possibilities, ranging from present-day adventures (such as the 1970s ride If You Had Wings, which simulated round-the-world travel) to those imagining the distant future (such as Mission to Mars, which ran from 1975 to 1992). The problem that Disney repeatedly ran up against was that the future came faster and looked different than it had predicted, which made this land constantly feel outdated.

Today, Tomorrowland's theme makes the least sense of any Disney park land. Its current attractions are based on gas-powered race cars, rocket travel (two rides), a look back at 20th-century technology, a ride with aliens and lasers, a comedy show with monsters, and a motorcycle race inside a computer. It's less a vision of the future and more a collection of attractions that don't fit anywhere else.

Astro Orbiter ★★

PRESCHOOL ★★★★ (BA)	GRADE SCHOOL ★★★★ (BA)	TEENS ★★★ (BA)
YOUNG ADULTS ★★★ (BA)	OVER 30 ★★★ (MBA)	OVER 65 ★★★ (MBA)

What it is Retro rocket spinner. **Scope and scale** Minor attraction. **When to go** Before 11 a.m. or before park closing. **Duration of ride** 1½ minutes. **Loading speed** Slow. **ECV/wheelchair access** Must transfer to the ride vehicle. **Participates in Genie+** No. **Early Theme Park Entry** Yes. **Extended Evening Hours** Yes.

DESCRIPTION AND COMMENTS Though visually appealing, the Astro Orbiter is a slow-loading carnival ride, with little rocket ships flying in circles. The best thing about it is the nice view while you're aloft.

TOURING TIPS Easily skippable. If you ride with preschoolers, seat them first. The Astro Orbiter flies higher and faster than Dumbo and frightens some young children. Even if you are capable of riding stable spinners, consider the combination of spinning and heights before deciding to ride.

Buzz Lightyear's Space Ranger Spin ★★★★

PRESCHOOL ★★★★ (A)	GRADE SCHOOL ★★★★ (A)	TEENS ★★★★ (AA)
YOUNG ADULTS ★★★★ (A)	OVER 30 ★★★★ (A)	OVER 65 ★★★★ (A)

What it is Space-themed indoor blaster ride. **Scope and scale** Minor attraction. **When to go** First or last hour the park is open. **Duration of ride** About 4½ minutes. **Loading speed** Fast. **ECV/wheelchair access** Must transfer from ECV to provided wheelchair. **Participates in Genie+** Yes. **Early Theme Park Entry** Yes. **Extended Evening Hours** Yes.

DESCRIPTION AND COMMENTS This indoor attraction is based on Buzz Lightyear from the *Toy Story* film series. You and Buzz try to save the universe from the evil Emperor Zurg by shooting lasers at Zurg and his minions. Each car is equipped with two laser cannons and two scorekeeping displays, enabling you to compete with your riding partner. A joystick allows you to spin the car to line up the various targets. Each time you pull the trigger, you release a red laser beam that you can see hitting or missing the target—if you can distinguish it from all the other red dots.

TOURING TIPS The standby queue, like a few other Magic Kingdom attractions, gets remarkably slowed down by the prioritization of Lightning Lane riders. If the line is outside the door and not moving, you will have at least a 20-minute wait from that point.

Most folks spend their first ride learning how to use the equipment and figuring out how the targets work. (Hint: Keep the trigger depressed instead of firing individual shots—you get an automatic 100 points every few seconds even without aiming.) On the next ride, you'll be surprised by how much better you do.

The first room's mechanical claw and red robot contain high-value targets, so aim for these. If you're hopeless at games of skill, see our tips at theugseries.com/beating-buzz. *Unofficial* readers praise Buzz Lightyear. In fact, many ride until they reach the elusive title of Galactic Hero.

Monsters, Inc. Laugh Floor ★★★

PRESCHOOL ★★★½ MBA)   GRADE SCHOOL ★★★★ (BA)   TEENS ★★★★ (AA)
YOUNG ADULTS ★★★★ (AA)   OVER 30 ★★★★ (A)   OVER 65 ★★★★½ (AA)

What it is Interactive animated comedy show. **Scope and scale** Minor attraction. **When to go** Anytime. **Duration of presentation** About 15 minutes. **ECV/wheelchair access** May remain in wheelchair. **Participates in Genie+** Yes. **Early Theme Park Entry** No. **Extended Evening Hours** Yes.

DESCRIPTION AND COMMENTS In the movie *Monsters, Inc.*, monsters discovered that kids' laughter worked even better than kids' screams as an energy source, so in this attraction they've set up a comedy club to capture as many laughs as possible.

Mike Wazowski, the one-eyed green monster, emcees the club's three comedy acts. Each act consists of an animated monster trying out various bad jokes. Using technological wizardry, behind-the-scenes Disney employees voice the characters and often interact with audience members during the skits. Disney has shown a willingness to experiment with new routines and jokes. If you enjoy entertainment where the whole crowd is laughing together, you will enjoy the *Laugh Floor*.

A South Dakota mom is a big fan:

Laugh Floor was great—it's amazing how the characters interact with the audience. I got picked on twice without trying. Plus, kids can text jokes to Roz.

TOURING TIPS The theater holds several hundred people, so there's no need to rush here first thing in the morning.

Space Mountain ★★★★

PRESCHOOL ★★½* (MBA)   GRADE SCHOOL ★★★ (MBA)   TEENS ★★★★½ (E)
YOUNG ADULTS ★★★★½ (E)   OVER 30 ★★★★ (AA)   OVER 65 ★★★½ (BA)

* *Some preschoolers and grade-schoolers love Space Mountain; others are terrified by it.*

What it is Dark roller coaster. **Scope and scale** Super-headliner. **When to go** At park opening or the last hour before closing. Must be 44" tall to ride; Rider Switch option provided (see page 303). **Duration of ride** Almost 3 minutes. **Loading speed** Moderate–fast. **ECV/wheelchair access** Must transfer from ECV to provided wheelchair then to the ride vehicle. **Participates in Genie+** Yes. **Early Theme Park Entry** Yes. **Extended Evening Hours** Yes.

DESCRIPTION AND COMMENTS Space Mountain has long been one of the Magic Kingdom's most popular attractions. Themed as a space flight through dark recesses of the galaxy, the ride is one of the fastest, darkest, and wildest in the Magic Kingdom: It's zippier than Big Thunder Mountain Railroad but slower than Tron next door, Rock 'n' Roller Coaster in Hollywood Studios, or Expedition Everest in Animal Kingdom. There are no long drops or swooping hills—only quick, unexpected turns and small drops. The coaster is a classic midway ride design called a Wild Mouse; Disney just added a space theme and put it in the dark.

People who can handle a fairly wild coaster ride will take Space Mountain in stride. What sets Space Mountain apart is the darkness. Half the fun is not knowing where the car will go next.

TOURING TIPS Most guests head to Seven Dwarfs Mine Train first, then visit Space Mountain. Space Mountain has a lot of unexpected downtime—more than any other attraction in the Magic Kingdom. If it isn't running when you're in Tomorrowland, keep an eye on the MDE app. If you happen to notice when the ride opens (a posted wait time will appear instead of a star), you'll have the shortest wait of the day.

Seats are one behind another, as opposed to side by side, which means that parents can't sit next to their kids who might get scared.

Tomorrowland Speedway ★★

PRESCHOOL ★★★★ (A)	GRADE SCHOOL ★★★★ (A)	TEENS ★★★ (BA)
YOUNG ADULTS ★★★½ (BA)	OVER 30 ★★★ (MBA)	OVER 65 ★★½ (MBA)

What it is Drive-'em-yourself minicars. **Scope and scale** Minor attraction. **When to go** Not in the hot sun. **Comment** Kids must be 54″ tall to drive unassisted, 32″ with a person age 14 or older. **Duration of ride** About 4¼ minutes. **Loading speed** Slow. **ECV/wheelchair access** Must transfer to the ride vehicle; transfer device available. **Participates in Genie+** Yes. **Early Theme Park Entry** Yes. **Extended Evening Hours** Yes.

DESCRIPTION AND COMMENTS A mini raceway with gas-powered cars that travel up to 7 mph. Any small child that passes will want to drive. That's why some families (including mine) attempt to bypass the area entirely. The cars poke along on a guide rail, leaving drivers little to do. A woman from Minnesota had this to say:

I'm all about keeping classic Disney attractions, but this is one that needs to go. I really hope our "Tomorrow" doesn't involve cars full of fumes.

TOURING TIPS This ride is visually appealing (except for the puffs of fumes), and the 9-and-under set loves it. If your child is too short to drive, let them steer the car while you work the pedal.

The line for the speedway snakes across a pedestrian bridge to the loading areas. For a shorter wait, turn right off the bridge, then head to the first loading area rather than continuing to the second one.

Tomorrowland Transit Authority PeopleMover ★★★½

PRESCHOOL ★★★★ (BA)	GRADE SCHOOL ★★★★ (BA)	TEENS ★★★★ (AA)
YOUNG ADULTS ★★★★ (AA)	OVER 30 ★★★★½ (MAA)	OVER 65 ★★★★½ (MAA)

What it is Scenic tour of Tomorrowland. **Scope and scale** Minor attraction. **When to go** Anytime. **Duration of ride** 10 minutes. **Loading speed** Fast. **ECV/wheelchair access** Must be ambulatory. **Participates in Genie+** No. **Early Theme Park Entry** Yes. **Extended Evening Hours** Yes.

DESCRIPTION AND COMMENTS An early prototype of a linear induction–powered mass-transit system carries riders on a leisurely tour of Tomorrowland, including a peek inside Space Mountain.

A family from Georgia shares a perspective similar to Becky's:

The PeopleMover is one we recommend to every family that asks us for Disney advice. The line moves quickly, it offers a great overview of the land, and it has unbeatable views at night..

TOURING TIPS This is a great choice during busier times of day or to keep littles entertained while others experience Tron or Space Mountain.

Tron Lightcycle/Run ★★★★

PRESCHOOL ★★ (MBA)	GRADE SCHOOL ★★ (MBA)	TEENS ★★★★½ (E)
YOUNG ADULTS ★★★★½ (E)	OVER 30 ★★★★½ (E)	OVER 65 ★★★★ (MAA)

What it is High-speed indoor-outdoor roller coaster. **Scope and scale** Super-headliner. **When to go** When your boarding group is called. **Comments** Must be 48" tall to ride. Seating arrangement may prove uncomfortable for some. **Duration of ride** 1 minute. **Loading speed** Fast. **ECV/wheelchair access** Must transfer from wheelchair to the ride vehicle. **Participates in Genie+** No (it offers Individual Lightning Lane). **Early Theme Park Entry** Yes. **Extended Evening Hours** Yes.

DESCRIPTION AND COMMENTS Riders sit as if on a motorcycle while they rocket through dark scenes with neon lighting. The ride vehicles are set up as 14 semidetached "lightcycles," with seven rows of two cycles each. Riders must lift one leg up and over to board and must lean forward slightly to hold onto the cycle's handlebars. They are then launched from zero to super speed in no time into the first set of turns.

Tron is most like Hollywood Studios' Rock 'n' Roller Coaster (see page 469), which has a similar launch. Tron is by far the most intense coaster in the Magic Kingdom, but it doesn't have any loops or inversions. If Seven Dwarfs Mine Train or Space Mountain gives you pause, skip Tron.

Tron has safety restraints that may not fit every body type. Disney has two solutions for this: (1) a more traditional, seated car at the end of the motorcycle-like train of ride vehicles and (2) a test vehicle with test restraints, located just before you enter the ride's main building.

TOURING TIPS Tron is one of the Magic Kingdom's hottest rides. Expect Individual Lightning Lane (ILL) reservations to sell out daily within minutes of being offered and boarding groups (if offered) to be booked up within seconds. If you're using the virtual queue, expect waits of 45–50 minutes after you join the physical line. The wait will be shortest earlier in the day. The ILL wait should be much shorter.

This attraction is even more impressive at night!

BOARDING GROUPS These function like mandatory Genie+ reservations without a specific return time. You obtain a boarding group for everyone in your party through the MDE app at exactly 7 a.m. or exactly 1 p.m. on the day of your visit. If you're lucky, you'll get a boarding group number. MDE will then tell you which boarding groups are currently eligible to ride or give you an estimate of how long your wait will be. If your phone is set up to receive alerts from MDE, you'll get one when your group is ready. Disney is usually reasonably flexible with return times—but not at Tron. Return within an hour, or you'll have to show a receipt from another experience that explains why you're late; otherwise, you're out of luck. This keeps the lines at night shorter, as it discourages people from showing up late just so they can experience the lights.

You don't have to be in the park to request a boarding group at 7 a.m., but you must be in the park to request one at 1 p.m. For newly opened rides, all boarding groups will be snapped up within a few seconds of 7 a.m., so there's no room for delay or error. And that's a problem because neither MDE nor Disney's Wi-Fi are completely reliable.

The fast but unreliable nature of Disney's Wi-Fi means you should have as many people as possible try to obtain boarding groups for your entire party at 7 a.m. or at 1 p.m. If you're in the park, half of you should be on Disney's Wi-Fi and half should be on a cellular network.

Disney's implementation of boarding groups is essentially a lottery—some people win and some people lose, through no fault of their own. The second supply of boarding groups, handed out at 1 p.m., is generally considered a backup batch that gets used only if the attraction has run reliably and on time throughout the day.

Walt Disney's Carousel of Progress ★★★

What it is Audio-Animatronic theater show. **Scope and scale** Major attraction. **When to go** Anytime. **Duration of presentation** 21 minutes. **Probable waiting time** Less than 10 minutes. **ECV/wheelchair access** May remain in wheelchair. **Participates in Genie+** No. **Early Theme Park Entry** Yes. **Extended Evening Hours** No.

DESCRIPTION AND COMMENTS *Carousel of Progress* is a four-act play offering a nostalgic look at how electricity and technology changed the lives of an animatronic family. General Electric sponsored the first version of the show for the 1964 World's Fair in New York. The first scene is set in 1901; the second, around 1927; and the third, in the late 1940s. The fourth scene is allegedly contemporary, but your mileage may vary.

Carousel of Progress is the only attraction in the park that displays Walt's optimistic vision of a better future through technology. If you're interested in the man behind the mouse, this show is a must-see.

TOURING TIPS The show handles big crowds effectively and is a good choice during busier times of day.

MAGIC KINGDOM ENTERTAINMENT

LIVE ENTERTAINMENT

FOR SPECIFIC EVENTS the day you visit, check the schedule in the My Disney Experience app or in the *Times Guide*, available along with the guide map. Walt Disney World live-entertainment expert Steve Soares usually posts the Magic Kingdom's performance schedule about a week in advance at wdwent.com.

unofficial **TIP**
Note: If you're short on time, keep in mind that it's impossible to see all of Magic Kingdom's feature attractions and live performances.

CHARACTER CAVALCADES In addition to the main parade, Disney runs a small one- or two-float cavalcade on some days, usually in the afternoon. The route is the same as the parade route: from Frontierland near Tiana's Bayou Adventure, through Liberty Square, and then around the central hub and down Main Street. The cavalcade, called Disney Adventure Friends, is more of a random smattering of characters, from Miguel (of *Coco*), Baloo, and Mirabel to Stitch and Mary Poppins. Check MDE for times.

FLAG RETREAT Taking place at 5 p.m. daily at Town Square (the Walt Disney World Railroad end of Main Street), this ceremony honoring veterans is sometimes performed with large college marching bands and sometimes with a smaller Disney band.

FIREWORKS AND OTHER NIGHTTIME ENTERTAINMENT

LIKE ITS PARADES, the Magic Kingdom's dazzling nighttime spectaculars are highly rated and not to be missed.

BAY LAKE AND SEVEN SEAS LAGOON ELECTRICAL WATER PAGEANT ★★★★ Usually performed at nightfall (8:50 at the Polynesian Village

Resort, 9 at the Grand Floridian Resort, and 10:15 at the Contemporary Resort) on Seven Seas Lagoon and Bay Lake, this is one of our favorites among the Disney extras, but you must leave the Magic Kingdom to view it. The pageant is a stunning electric-light show set to nifty electronic music. Leave the Magic Kingdom and take the monorail to the Polynesian Village, Grand Floridian, or Contemporary.

HAPPILY EVER AFTER FIREWORKS SHOW ★★★★½ This multisensory show of fireworks, music, and video projections with the theme of Happily Ever After is one of the highest-rated attractions in Walt Disney World, across all age groups.

The show is not only about princesses and romance but also includes messages about work and determination as part of a path to . . . happily ever after. Images projected onto the castle include snippets from the usual suspects of *Frozen* and *Cinderella*, as well as *Hunchback of Notre Dame, Monsters, Inc., Cars,* and *Wreck-It Ralph,* among others. *Happily Ever After*'s fireworks can be enjoyed from outside the park. However, due to the strong integration of the castle projections into the performance, be aware that you'll be missing a substantial portion of the show if you're not viewing from the central hub or Main Street area inside the Magic Kingdom.

TINKER BELL'S FLIGHT Look for this quintessentially Disney special effect in the sky above Cinderella Castle during the nighttime fireworks shows.

Fireworks Dessert Parties and Cruises

FIREWORKS DESSERT PARTIES Disney reserves the **Plaza Gardens** and **Tomorrowland Terrace** restaurant for three paid fireworks-viewing opportunities:

1. **Happily Ever After Pre-Party** begins approximately 90 minutes before the show. It costs $99–$109 per adult and $59 per child. You'll be served desserts, beer, wine, and sodas until just before the fireworks begin, when you'll be escorted to a special, standing-room-only viewing spot.

2. **Happily Ever After Fireworks Dessert Parties (Seats & Sweets)** run before, during, and after the show inside Tomorrowland Terrace. They cost $119–$129 per adult and $69 per child. Note that the view of the castle is blocked at many seats, and the sound quality is poor inside the all-concrete echo chamber of the restaurant. The big advantage here is that you get actual seats for the show.

3. **Happily Ever After Post-Party** You'll be escorted to a special, standing-room-only viewing location approximately 30 minutes before the fireworks begin. After the fireworks, you'll be admitted to Tomorrowland Terrace for desserts, beer, wine, and sodas, for the next hour. The cost is $99–$109 per adult and $59 per child.

Reservations can be made 60 days in advance online or by calling ☎ 407-WDW-DINE (939-3463).

A Missouri reader who went to the dessert party declared it meh:

We did the fireworks dessert party at Tomorrowland Terrace against my better judgment. While the vantage point was pretty good and the desserts were tasty, it was definitely not worth the price.

FIREWORKS CRUISE For a different view, you can watch the fireworks from Seven Seas Lagoon aboard a pontoon boat. The cost is $449 (plus tax) for up to 10 people. Bottled sodas, water, and a selection of sweet and savory snacks are provided; sandwiches and other more substantial food items may be arranged through reservations. Your Disney captain will take you for a little cruise and then position the boat in a perfect place to watch the fireworks. (A major indirect benefit of the charter is that you can enjoy the fireworks without fighting the mob afterward.)

Because this is a private charter, only your group will be aboard. Life jackets are provided, but wearing them is at your discretion. To reserve a charter, call ☎ 407-WDW-PLAY (939-7529) at exactly 7 a.m. Eastern time about 180 days before the day you want to cruise.

VIEWING AND EXIT STRATEGIES FOR PARADES AND FIREWORKS

Vantage Points for Parades

Magic Kingdom parades begin in **Frontierland** by Tiana's Bayou Adventure and follow the waterfront through **Liberty Square.** From there, they cross the bridge to the **Central Plaza,** circle it, then head down **Main Street.** A quick trip around **Town Square** follows before they head offstage behind the Main Street fire station.

Because most spectators pack Main Street and the Central Plaza, we recommend watching the parade from **Liberty Square** or **Frontierland** instead. Great vantage points that are frequently overlooked are:

1. **Sleepy Hollow snack-and-beverage shop, immediately to your right as you cross the bridge into Liberty Square.** If you arrive early, buy refreshments and claim a table closest to the rail. You'll have a perfect view of the parade as it crosses Liberty Square Bridge.

2. **The pathway on the Liberty Square side of the moat from Sleepy Hollow snack-and-beverage shop to Cinderella Castle.** Any point along the way offers an unobstructed view as the parade crosses Liberty Square Bridge.

3. **The covered walkway between Liberty Tree Tavern and The Diamond Horseshoe.** This elevated vantage point is perfect (particularly on rainy days) and usually goes unnoticed until just before the parade starts.

4. **Elevated platforms in front of Frontier Trading Post and the building with the sign reading FRONTIER MERCANTILE.** These spots usually get picked off 10–12 minutes before parade time.

5. **Benches on the perimeter of the Central Plaza, between the entrances to Liberty Square and Adventureland,** offer a comfortable resting place and an unobstructed (though somewhat distant) view of the parade as it crosses Liberty Square Bridge.

6. **Liberty Square and Frontierland dockside areas.** Spots here usually go early.

7. **The porch of Tony's Town Square Restaurant,** on Main Street, provides an elevated viewing platform and an easy exit path when the fireworks are over.

Assuming it starts in Frontierland, the parade takes 16–20 minutes to reach the end of Main Street nearest the hub.

Vantage Points for Fireworks

As noted on page 392, the nightly fireworks show includes a dazzling video-projection display on the front of Cinderella Castle and down Main Street. The best viewing spots for the entire presentation are **between the Central Plaza and the castle,** offering up-close views of the castle projections.

The next-best spots are in **Plaza Gardens East and West** nearest the castle. These gardens are specifically constructed for fireworks viewing. We prefer Plaza Gardens East (the Tomorrowland side) because

Illustration: Tami Knight

the configuration of light/audio poles is slightly less obtrusive when you're viewing the castle.

If those spots are already taken, your next-best alternatives are on Main Street, where you'll get to see the (smaller) projections closer. Watching from the train-station end of Main Street is the easiest way to leave the park quickly, but you won't recognize most of the castle's images.

If we're staying in the park and trying to avoid the crowds on Main Street, our two favorite spots to see just the fireworks are:

1. **In Fantasyland between Seven Dwarfs Mine Train and _Enchanted Tales with Belle._**
   Some of the minor fireworks that float above the castle will be behind you, but all of the major effects will be right in front of you.

2. **On the bridge between the Central Plaza and Tomorrowland.** A few trees block some of the castle, but if Tinker Bell does her fireworks flight from the castle, she'll fly directly over this area.

Leaving the Park Before or During Fireworks

If you're trying to exit the park just before or during the fireworks, you'll need to walk down the passageways behind the east and west sides of Main Street to get out, or use the Tomorrowland Main Street passageways (see next page) if they're open. (If you're facing the train station, with Cinderella Castle behind you, east is on your left.)

Leaving the Park After Fireworks

With armies of guests leaving the park after fireworks, the Disney transportation system gets overwhelmed, causing long waits in boarding areas. (Similar situations occur during special holiday parades and fireworks.) An Oklahoma dad offers this advice:

> *Never, never leave the Magic Kingdom just after the evening fireworks. Go for another ride—no lines because everyone else is trying to get out!*

Congestion persists from the end of the fireworks until closing time. If you're parked at the Transportation and Ticket Center (TTC) and are intent on beating the crowd, view the fireworks from the Town Square end of Main Street, leaving the park as soon as the show ends and hustling to your transportation as quickly as possible.

MAIN STREET PASSAGEWAYS The Magic Kingdom has two pedestrian walkways behind the shops on either side of Main Street, specifically for guests who want to get in or out of the park without walking down the middle of the street. If you're on the Tomorrowland side, look for a passageway that runs from between **The Plaza Restaurant** and **Tomorrowland Terrace,** back behind the east side of Main Street, to **Tony's Town Square Restaurant** near the park exit. If you're on the Adventureland side, the passageway runs from the **First Aid Center** to the **Main Street fire station** near the park exit. These passageways aren't used every night, so there's no guarantee that they'll be available.

unofficial **TIP**
Instead of walking outside, you can cut through the Main Street shops—they have interior doors that let you pass from one shop to the next.

If the passageways aren't open and you're on the Tomorrowland side, cut through Tomorrowland Terrace, and then work your way down Main Street until you're past Main Street Bakery (Starbucks) and have crossed a small cul-de-sac. Bear left into the side door of that corner shop. Work your way from shop to shop until you reach Town Square—easy, because people will be outside watching the fireworks. At Town Square, bear left to reach the train station and park exit.

This also works if you're on the Adventureland side of the park. You can make your way through **Casey's Corner** to Main Street and then work your way through the shops, and when you pop out of the **Emporium** at Town Square, you can bolt for the exit.

If your car is parked at the TTC lot, you could line up for the ferry; one will depart about every 8–10 minutes. You could even leave before the fireworks and try to catch the ferry that will be crossing Seven Seas Lagoon while the fireworks show is in progress. The best vantage point is on the top deck to the right of the pilothouse as you face the Magic Kingdom—the sight of fireworks silhouetting the castle and reflecting off the lagoon is unforgettable.

While there's no guarantee that a ferry will load and depart within 3 or 4 minutes of the fireworks, your chances are about 50–50 of timing it just right. If you're in the front of the line for the ferry and don't want to board the boat that's loading, stop at the gate and let people pass you. You'll be the first to board the next boat.

Strollers, wheelchairs, and ECVs make navigating crowds even more difficult. If you have one of these, or if you're staying at a Disney hotel that is not served by the monorail, and you have to depend on Disney transportation, watch the fireworks; then enjoy the attractions or a rapidly emptying park until the crowds disperse. Then catch the Disney bus or boat back to your hotel.

MAGIC KINGDOM HARD-TICKET EVENTS

THE MAGIC KINGDOM HOSTS several **holiday-themed After Hours events** from mid-August through December. Celebrating Halloween and Christmas, they require separate paid admission and almost always sell out. Space doesn't permit us to cover them with more than a brief mention (see "The Walt Disney World Calendar," page 32). That said, ride wait times during these events are as low as they can be, making them a plausible alternative to, say, paying for a second day (and another hotel night) to finish seeing the Magic Kingdom. But we provide full details, including photos, best days to go, touring advice, and more, at **TouringPlans.com:** Go to blog.touringplans.com and search "Halloween party" and "Christmas party."

TRAFFIC PATTERNS *in the* MAGIC KINGDOM

WHEN WE RESEARCH THE MAGIC KINGDOM, we study its traffic patterns, asking:

1. WHICH SECTIONS OF THE PARK AND WHICH ATTRACTIONS DO GUESTS VISIT FIRST? When the park opens, guest traffic is heaviest going to Fantasyland and Tomorrowland, followed by Frontierland, after Early Entry. Seven Dwarfs Mine Train pulls people to Fantasyland, at the back of the park, while Space Mountain pulls a few to Tomorrowland, on the right side. Tiana's Bayou Adventure draws large crowds to Frontierland, on the left side.

2. HOW LONG DOES IT TAKE FOR THE PARK TO FILL UP? HOW ARE VISITORS DISPERSED IN THE PARK? A surge of early birds arrives before or around Early Entry, but they are quickly dispersed throughout the empty park. After this initial wave is absorbed, there's a lull lasting about an hour after opening. Then the park is inundated for about 2 hours, peaking between 10 a.m. and noon. Arrivals continue in a steady but diminishing stream until around 2 p.m. The lines we sampled were longest between 1 and 2 p.m., indicating more arrivals than departures into the early afternoon. For touring purposes, most attractions develop long lines between 10 and 11:30 a.m.

unofficial **TIP**
As the park fills up, visitors head for the top attractions before lines get long. This, more than anything else, determines morning traffic patterns.

From late morning until early afternoon, guests are evenly distributed among all the lands. However, guests concentrate in **Fantasyland, Liberty Square,** and **Frontierland** in late afternoon, with a decrease of visitors in Adventureland and Tomorrowland. Adventureland's **Jungle Cruise** and Tomorrowland's **Space Mountain** continue to be crowded, but most other attractions in those lands are readily accessible.

3. HOW DO MOST VISITORS TOUR THE PARK? Many **first-time visitors** are guided by friends or relatives familiar with the Magic Kingdom; these groups may or may not follow an orderly sequence. First-timers without personal guides tend to be more orderly in their touring, but they also tend to be drawn to Cinderella Castle upon entering the park and thus begin their rotation from Fantasyland. **Repeat visitors** usually head straight to their favorite attractions.

4. WILL GOING LEFT (OR RIGHT) HELP AVOID CROWDS? We tested a frequent claim that most people turn right into Tomorrowland and tour the Magic Kingdom counterclockwise. The claim is baseless. Neither do most people turn left and start in Adventureland.

Here's why: Magic Kingdom headliner attractions are located intentionally at opposite points around the park to distribute crowds evenly: **Space Mountain** and **Tron** on the east side, **Tiana's Bayou Adventure** and **Big Thunder Mountain Railroad** on the west, **Seven Dwarfs Mine Train** to the north, and so on.

If, therefore, you were to start touring by heading left, you'd have low crowds in Adventureland and moderate crowds in Frontierland—but by the time you got to Fantasyland and Tomorrowland, you'd run into the largest crowds of the day. A similar scenario would await you if you started by bearing right into Tomorrowland: packed crowds in the rest of the lands you visit.

Avoiding the biggest crowds in the Magic Kingdom requires:

1. Knowing which attractions to visit and when.
2. Knowing how to make the best use of Genie+ and Individual Lightning Lane (if you're willing to pay for them).
3. Being willing to cross the park to save time.

5. HOW DO SPECIAL EVENTS, SUCH AS PARADES AND LIVE SHOWS, AFFECT TRAFFIC PATTERNS? Parades pull huge numbers of guests away from attractions and provide a window of opportunity for experiencing the more popular attractions with less of a wait. (Character cavalcades don't have this effect.) Castle Stage shows also attract crowds but barely affect lines.

6. WHAT ARE THE TRAFFIC PATTERNS NEAR AND AT CLOSING TIME? On our sample days, in busy times and off-season, departures outnumbered arrivals beginning in midafternoon. Many visitors left in late afternoon as dinnertime approached. When the park closed early, guests departed steadily during the 2 hours before closing, with a huge exodus at closing. When the park closed late, the exodus began immediately after the fireworks, continuing until closing.

Because Main Street and transportation services remain open after the other lands close, crowds at closing mainly congregate on Main Street and at the monorail-, ferry-, and bus-boarding areas. In the hour before closing, the other lands are normally not crowded.

To get a complete view of actual traffic patterns while you're in the park, use our mobile app, **Lines.** It gives you current wait times and estimates in half-hour increments for the rest of the day. A quick glance shows how traffic patterns affect wait times throughout the day.

MAGIC KINGDOM TOURING PLANS

STARTING ON PAGE 549, our step-by-step touring plans are field-tested for seeing *as much as possible* in one day with a minimum of time wasted in lines. They're designed to help you avoid crowds and bottlenecks on days of moderate to heavy attendance. You should understand, however, that there's more to see in the Magic Kingdom than can be experienced in one day.

On days of lighter attendance (see "Selecting the Time of Year for Your Visit," page 27), our plans save you time but aren't as critical to successful touring as they are on busier days.

*un**official* TIP**
Don't worry that other people will be following the touring plans, rendering them useless. Fewer than 4 in every 100 people in the park will have been exposed to this info.

Each Magic Kingdom touring plan has two versions: one for Disney resort guests and one for off-site guests. The former uses Early Theme Park Entry to minimize waits in line. Because Early Entry means thousands of guests will already be in lines and on rides before off-site guests set foot in the park, the touring strategy for off-site guests must be different. Even with a perfect touring plan, Early Entry means off-site guests may wait up to an hour more in lines per day in the Magic Kingdom.

The touring plans do *not* require you to use Genie+ or Individual Lightning Lane. If you opt for either (or both) of these offerings, simply tell the free touring plan software which reservation times you have, and the software will adjust the plan (see page 46 for details).

CHOOSING THE APPROPRIATE TOURING PLAN

WE PRESENT FOUR MAGIC KINGDOM touring plans:

1. **One-Day Touring Plan for Adults**
2. **One-Day Touring Plan for Parents with Small Children**
3. **Dumbo-or-Die-in-a-Day Touring Plan for Parents with Small Children**
4. **Two-Day Touring Plan for Adults**

If you have two days (or two mornings) in the Magic Kingdom, the **Two-Day Touring Plan** is *by far* the most relaxed and efficient. It takes advantage of early morning, when lines are short and the park hasn't filled up with guests. This plan works well year-round and eliminates much of the extra walking required by the one-day plans. No matter when the park closes, our two-day plan guarantees the most efficient touring and the least time waiting in lines. The plan is perfect for guests who want to sample both the attractions and the atmosphere of the Magic Kingdom.

If you have just a single day to visit but you want to see as much as possible, then use the **One-Day Touring Plan for Adults.** Yes, it's a bear, but it gives you maximum bang for your buck.

If you have children younger than age 8, choose the **One-Day Touring Plan for Parents with Small Children.** A compromise that blends the preferences of younger children with those of older siblings and adults, this plan includes many children's rides in Fantasyland but omits the more intense rides and other attractions that may frighten young children or are off-limits because of height requirements. You could also use the One-Day Touring Plan for Adults and take advantage of **Rider Switch** on rides with age and height requirements; this option enables one adult to wait in the loading area with the child while another adult rides, and then switch off so the other adult can ride without having to wait in line twice (see page 303).

unofficial **TIP**
Rider Switch allows adults to enjoy the more adventurous attractions while keeping the group together.

The **Dumbo-or-Die-in-a-Day Touring Plan for Parents with Small Children** is designed for parents who are happy to self-sacrificially stand around, sweat, wipe noses, pay for stuff, and watch the kids enjoy themselves. *You'll love it!*

"Not a Touring Plan" Strategies

For the type-B reader, these strategies (see page 546) avoid detailed step-by-step plans for saving every last minute in line. To paraphrase one of our favorite movies, they're more guidelines than actual rules. Use them to avoid the longest waits in line while having maximum flexibility to see whatever interests you in a particular part of the park.

For the Magic Kingdom, these strategies include advice for adults and parents with one day in the park, for anyone with two days, and for anyone with an afternoon and a full day to tour.

Two-Day Touring Plan for Families with Small Children

If you have young children and are looking for a two-day itinerary, combine the **Magic Kingdom One-Day Touring Plan for Parents with Small Children** with the second day of the **Magic Kingdom Two-Day Touring Plan.**

Alternate Two-Day Touring Plan: Sleep In on Day Two

Many of us enjoy an early start in the Magic Kingdom on one day, followed by a second day with a lazy sleep-in morning, resuming touring in the afternoon and/or evening. If this appeals to you, use the **Magic Kingdom One-Day Touring Plan for Adults** or the **Magic Kingdom One-Day Touring Plan for Parents with Small Children** on your early day. Stick to the plan for as long as it feels comfortable (many folks leave after the afternoon parade). On the second day, pick up where you left off. Customize the rest of the plan to incorporate parades, fireworks, and other live performances according to your preferences.

TOURING PLAN COMPANIONS

WE'VE CONSOLIDATED A GREAT DEAL of information about the theme parks in the Touring Plan Companions, which start on page 565, just after the touring plans. Like the touring plans, the companions are designed to be clipped out and taken with you to the parks. The companions recap key information: the best times to visit each attraction, the authors' ratings, attraction height requirements and fright potential, and quick-reference info on dining and places to take a break.

THE SINGLE-DAY TOURING CONUNDRUM

TOURING THE MAGIC KINGDOM in a single day is complicated by two facts:

1. The park's average day is shorter than it was a few years ago.
2. The premier attractions are at opposite ends of the park.

Tiana's Bayou Adventure and **Big Thunder Mountain Railroad** are in Frontierland, **Space Mountain** and **Tron** are in **Tomorrowland,** and **Seven Dwarfs Mine Train** is in **Fantasyland.** It's virtually impossible to ride all five without encountering lines at one or the other.

If, for example, you hit Tron and Space Mountain right as the park opens, you won't have too bad of a wait, but by the time you get to Fantasyland, the line for Seven Dwarfs Mine Train will already be substantial. Likewise, you can ride Seven Dwarfs without a problem first thing in the morning, but by the time you get to Tomorrowland, Space Mountain and Tron will already have fair-size lines. See the profile of Tiana's Bayou Adventure on page 378 for our recommended strategy for these attractions.

PRELIMINARY INSTRUCTIONS
FOR USING THE TOURING PLANS

BECOME FAMILIAR WITH THE MAGIC KINGDOM'S **opening procedures** (see page 366). On days of moderate to heavy attendance, follow your chosen touring plan exactly, deviating from it only as follows:

1. **When you're not interested in an attraction in the plan.** Simply skip it and proceed to the next attraction.
2. **When you encounter a very long line at an attraction.** In this case, skip to the next attraction and try again later.

Before You Go

1. Check disneyworld.disney.go.com or the MDE app the day before you go to verify official opening time.
2. Purchase tickets before you arrive.
3. Get familiar with park-opening procedures (see page 366) and reread the plan you've chosen so you know what you're likely to encounter.
4. At 7 a.m. on the day of your visit, make Genie+ and/or Individual Lightning Lane reservations if you bought them.

MAGIC KINGDOM TOURING PLANS AT A GLANCE

Magic Kingdom One-Day Touring Plan for Adults
(see pages 549–550)

FOR Adults without young children.

ASSUMES Willingness to experience all major rides (including roller coasters) and shows that were operating at press time. Does not assume the use of Genie+ or Individual Lightning Lane.

THIS PLAN INCLUDES the attractions we think best represent the Magic Kingdom, from its newest roller coasters to those created by Walt Disney himself. It requires a lot of walking and some backtracking to avoid lines. Extra walking and morning hustling will spare you hours of standing in line. How far you get depends on how quickly you move from ride to ride, how many times you rest or eat, how quickly the park fills, and what time the park closes.

Magic Kingdom One-Day Touring Plan for Parents with Small Children   *(see pages 551–552)*

FOR Parents with children younger than age 8.

ASSUMES Periodic stops for rest, restrooms, and refreshments.

THIS PLAN INCLUDES the park's highest-rated attractions for younger children, plus many of the ones for adults and older kids. It also includes the evening fireworks.

The plan has a slower pace, with plenty of free time throughout the day. If more time is needed, though, the overall ratings of It's a Small World and The Many Adventures of Winnie the Pooh make them the most expendable in the plan.

Magic Kingdom Dumbo-or-Die-in-a-Day Touring Plan for Parents with Small Children   *(see pages 553–554)*

FOR Adults compelled to devote every waking moment to the pleasure and entertainment of their young children.

ASSUMES Frequent stops for rest, restrooms, and refreshments.

NAME ASIDE, this plan is no joke, y'all. Whether you're loving, masochistic, selfless, or just unhinged, this itinerary will provide a youngster with about as perfect a day as possible in the Magic Kingdom. Families using this plan should review the Magic Kingdom attractions in our **Small-Child Fright-Potential Table** on pages 304–306.

Magic Kingdom Two-Day Touring Plan for Adults *(see pages 555–556)*

FOR Those wishing to spread their Magic Kingdom visit over two days.

ASSUMES Willingness to experience all major rides and shows.

THIS TWO-DAY TOURING PLAN takes advantage of early-morning touring. Each day, you should complete the structured part of the plan by about 4 p.m. This leaves plenty of time for live entertainment or for a break at your hotel before deciding what to do in the evening.

PART 12

EPCOT

- How do I get to EPCOT? *(page 406)*
- How does park opening (rope drop) work? *(page 407)*
- What are the don't-miss rides? *(page 406)*
- What's the best way to use Genie+ and Individual Lightning Lane in EPCOT? *(page 408)*
- Where are the best spots for watching fireworks? *(page 429)*
- What's the easiest way to leave the park at the end of the day? *(page 430)*

■ OVERVIEW

WALT DISNEY'S ORIGINAL 1960s-era vision for EPCOT was a design for American cities of the future. Back then, **EPCOT** was an acronym meaning "Experimental Prototype Community of Tomorrow." Among Walt's ideas for future city planning were self-driving electric cars, prefab solar-powered homes electronically connected to a network of information services; and an entire city center enclosed in a giant air-conditioned dome.

After Walt Disney died in 1966, the people who took over his company considered his ideas too risky to build. When EPCOT Center opened at Walt Disney World 16 years later, it was a theme park with a split personality: Half of it—called **Future World**—was based on a futuristic, semi-educational look at the world, while the other half—**World Showcase**—was a kind of permanent world's fair (another of Walt's passions).

IS EPCOT WORTH VISITING NOW?

EPCOT IS EXPERIENCING something of a renaissance, having gone through a lot of changes in just the past few years. Two new headliners have opened: The **Guardians of the Galaxy: Cosmic Rewind** roller coaster opened in 2022, and **Remy's Ratatouille Adventure**, a family-friendly

continued on page 406

EPCOT

Attractions

1. *The American Adventure*
2. *Awesome Planet*
3. *Canada Far and Wide*
4. Club Cool
5. Disney & Pixar Short Film Festival G+
6. Frozen Ever After ☑ G+
7. Gran Fiesta Tour Starring the Three Caballeros
8. Guardians of the Galaxy: Cosmic Rewind ☑ ILL
9. *Impressions de France/ Beauty and the Beast Sing-Along*
10. Journey into Imagination with Figment G+
11. Journey of Water, Inspired by Moana
12. Living with the Land ☑ G+
13. Mission: Space G+
14. *Reflections of China*
15. Remy's Ratatouille Adventure ☑ G+
16. The Seas Main Tank and Exhibits ☑
17. The Seas with Nemo & Friends G+
18. Meet Anna and Elsa at Royal Sommerhus
19. Soarin' Around the World ☑ G+
20. Spaceship Earth ☑ G+
21. Test Track ☑ G+
22. *Turtle Talk with Crush* ☑ G+

Outpost

J

China

13

I   JJ

Norway

6   AA

14   18   H

HH

7   B

LL   ✳

Mexico

Odyssey Center   ✛

MM

21

13

World Discovery

8

4

C

World Celebration

20

11

✳

Bag Check

The Seas

17

EE   22

16

2

G+ Offers Genie+

ILL Offers Individual Lightning Lane

☑ Not To Be Missed

👍 Recommended Dining

✛ First Aid Center

✳ Fireworks Top Viewing Spot

🚻 Restrooms

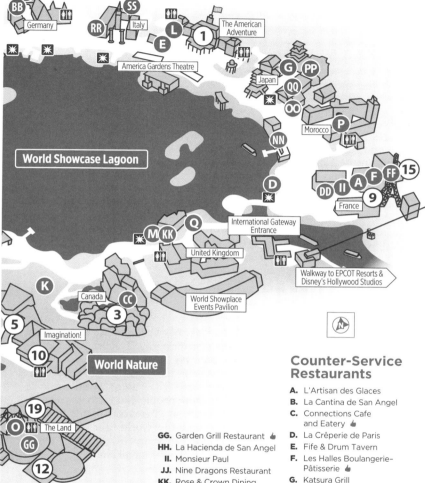

World Showcase Lagoon

World Nature

Germany
Italy
The American Adventure
America Gardens Theatre
Japan
Morocco
France
International Gateway Entrance
United Kingdom
Walkway to EPCOT Resorts & Disney's Hollywood Studios
World Showplace Events Pavilion
Canada
Imagination!
The Land

Counter-Service Restaurants

A. L'Artisan des Glaces
B. La Cantina de San Angel
C. Connections Cafe and Eatery
D. La Crêperie de Paris
E. Fife & Drum Tavern
F. Les Halles Boulangerie–Pâtisserie
G. Katsura Grill
H. Kringla Bakeri og Kafe
I. Lotus Blossom Café
J. Refreshment Outpost
K. Refreshment Port
L. Regal Eagle Smokehouse
M. Rose & Crown Pub
N. Sommerfest
O. Sunshine Seasons
P. Tangierine Café
Q. Yorkshire County Fish Shop

Table-Service Restaurants

AA. Akershus Royal Banquet Hall
BB. Biergarten Restaurant
CC. Le Cellier Steakhouse
DD. Chefs de France
EE. Coral Reef Restaurant
FF. La Crêperie de Paris

GG. Garden Grill Restaurant
HH. La Hacienda de San Angel
II. Monsieur Paul
JJ. Nine Dragons Restaurant
KK. Rose & Crown Dining Room
LL. San Angel Inn Restaurante
MM. Space 220
NN. Spice Road Table
OO. Takumi-Tei
PP. Teppan Edo
QQ. Shiki-Sai
RR. Tutto Italia Ristorante
SS. Via Napoli Ristorante e Pizzeria

continued from page 403

ride through a French kitchen, opened in the France Pavilion in 2021. **Journey of Water, Inspired by Moana** (an interactive walk-through) and a new fireworks show, *Luminous,* both debuted in late 2023.

NOT TO BE MISSED IN EPCOT
FUTURE WORLD • Guardians of the Galaxy: Cosmic Rewind • Living with the Land • The Seas Main Tank and Exhibits • Soarin' Around the World • Spaceship Earth • Test Track • *Turtle Talk with Crush*
WORLD SHOWCASE • Frozen Ever After • Japan and Mexico Pavilions • Meet Anna and Elsa at Royal Sommerhus • Remy's Ratatouille Adventure • Voices of Liberty

EPCOT LANDS

THE FRONT HALF OF EPCOT is subdivided into three "lands." **World Discovery** covers the east side (left if you enter from the main entrance) and includes the Test Track, Mission: Space, and Guardians of the Galaxy Pavilions. **World Nature** is on the west (right) side and includes the Imagination!, Land, and Seas Pavilions. The central part, including Spaceship Earth, is known as **World Celebration.** The **World Showcase** Pavilion is the "back" half of the park.

We'll use the older term "Future World" to generally refer to the front half of the park (everything but World Showcase), and we'll use the new land names when discussing the specific lands.

ARRIVING

ENTRANCES EPCOT has two entrances. The larger one is in Future World, at the front of the park, and it's the one you'll use if you arrive by car, bus, or monorail. The other, the **International Gateway** (**IG**), is in the rear of the park, between France and United Kingdom in World Showcase. The Future World entrance can handle more people and is closer to headliner rides such as Guardians of the Galaxy, Soarin' Around the World, and Test Track, while the IG entrance will put you closer to Remy's Ratatouille Adventure, which is important if you're touring with small children.

unofficial **TIP**
Arriving at EPCOT 30–60 minutes before official opening ensures the shortest possible waits for rides.

ARRIVING FROM INSIDE DISNEY WORLD If you're staying at an EPCOT resort, it will take you about 10–20 minutes to walk the mile or so from your hotel to the IG. **Boat service** is also available from the EPCOT resorts to the IG. You could also take a 10- to 20-minute ride (20–40 minutes with crowds) on the **Skyliner** (see page 344), which links the IG with Disney's Hollywood Studios and Disney's Caribbean Beach, Riviera, Pop Century, and Art of Animation Resorts. Add another 5–8 minutes to walk to Future World from the IG if that's your final destination.

DRIVING Arriving by car is easy and direct (see page 345 for GPS names and addresses). EPCOT has its own parking lot, and you can take a tram or walk from the parking lot to the front gate. Monorail service connects EPCOT with the Magic Kingdom (transfer required),

EPCOT SERVICES

EPCOT'S SERVICE FACILITIES, most located in Future World, include:

ATMs Outside the main entrance, on the Future World bridge, and in World Showcase at The American Adventure Pavilion and International Gateway entrance

Baby Care Center On the World Showcase side of the Odyssey Center (right of Test Track)

Cell Phone Charging Outlets available in The Seas with Nemo & Friends Pavilion, upstairs near the women's restroom; in The Land Pavilion, upstairs near Garden Grill; and possibly a few open outlets in the Test Track postshow, depending on how displays are arranged

Dining Reservations At Guest Relations, to the left of Spaceship Earth, or through the My Disney Experience app

First Aid Center On the World Showcase side of the Odyssey Center, next door to the Baby Care Center

Live-Entertainment Information In the *Times Guide,* available at Guest Relations

Lost and Found At the main entrance at the gift shop or Guest Relations

Lost Persons At Guest Relations and the Baby Care Center

Walt Disney World and Local Attraction Information At Guest Relations

Wheelchair, ECV, and Stroller Rentals Inside the main entrance and to the left, toward the rear of the Entrance Plaza; also at the International Gateway entrance

the Magic Kingdom resorts (transfer required), and the Transportation and Ticket Center.

If you want to drive and use the IG entrance, you'll need to pay for parking at a resort close to EPCOT: the **Swan, Dolphin,** or **Swan Reserve.** It may be cheaper and/or easier to use a ride-sharing app.

EPCOT OPENING PROCEDURES (ROPE DROP)

FUTURE WORLD AND WORLD SHOWCASE both typically open at 9 a.m. and close at 9 p.m. On-site guests who want to take advantage of Early Theme Park Entry (see page 30) should arrive 60 minutes before official opening (that is, 30 minutes before Early Entry) on all days. Off-site guests who aren't eligible for Early Theme Park Entry should arrive 30 minutes before official opening on all days.

WHICH EPCOT ENTRANCE SHOULD YOU USE? The IG entrance is about 10 minutes closer to the family-friendly **Remy's Ratatouille Adventure,** located in World Showcase's France Pavilion, than the Future World entrance is, and that's a huge head start. But if the rat ride isn't a priority, then enter at Future World instead for easier access to **Soarin' Around the World, Test Track,** and **Guardians of the Galaxy: Cosmic Rewind.** If you're heading for **Frozen Ever After,** both entrances are about equidistant.

▮ GETTING ORIENTED

EPCOT'S THEMED AREAS are markedly different: World Showcase features the landmarks, cuisine, and culture of almost a dozen nations and is meant to be a sort of permanent World's Fair. Future World is in flux: Its older attractions examine where mankind has come from and where it's going, while its newer attractions are themed to various Disney characters.

EPCOT is visually open, unlike the very visually siloed Magic Kingdom. And while it might seem odd to see a Japanese pagoda and the Eiffel Tower on the same horizon, getting around is fairly simple. An exception is Future World, where construction walls can make everything a bit of a mess.

The park's architectural anchor is **Spaceship Earth,** a shiny 180-foot geosphere that's visible from almost everywhere in the park. Like Cinderella Castle in the Magic Kingdom, Spaceship Earth can help you keep track of where you are in EPCOT. But it's in a high-traffic area, and it's not centrally located, so it's not a good meeting place.

Any World Showcase pavilion makes a good meeting place, but specifics matter. Each pavilion is a town in miniature, with buildings, gardens, and plazas. So instead of just saying "Let's meet in Japan," pick a specific place.

FAVORITE ATTRACTIONS BY AGE GROUP

EPCOT'S LINEUP INCLUDES more than 50 attractions, shows, live performers, and festival and seasonal entertainment. The table on the opposite page shows the park's 10 most popular attractions by age group. EPCOT's live entertainers are popular across all age groups. Those should be part of your day in EPCOT when they're available and convenient. The average reader ratings for all EPCOT attractions by age group are as follows, based on the 48,000 attraction ratings we received over the past 13 months:

PRESCHOOL	GRADE SCHOOL	TEENS	YOUNG ADULTS	OVER 30	OVER 65
3.9 stars	4.1 stars	3.9 stars	4.1 stars	4.1 stars	4.2 stars

RIDER SWITCH IN EPCOT At all Disney parks, select attractions allow one parent to ride while the other stays with a nonriding child. The parents then switch roles so that the other can ride using the Alternate Access (Lightning Lane) line. (See page 303 for complete details.)

unofficial **TIP**
If you plan to use Rider Switch in EPCOT, plan for extra time in line for the second rider.

In EPCOT, however, long waits in the Alternate Access line may complicate Rider Switch, requiring families to spend inordinate amounts of time in line so that both parents can ride. It's still better than waiting twice in the standby line but requires more planning for what to do with all the nonriding time. An Oklahoma dad who experienced a particularly bad day elaborates:

Rider Switch worked out really well on every ride in every park except EPCOT. The Alternate Access lines plus ride times for Test Track (45 minutes), Soarin' Around the World (30 minutes), and Mission: Space (30 minutes) were so long that it made Rider Switch very frustrating.

GENIE+, INDIVIDUAL LIGHTNING LANE, AND THE TOURING PLANS

NOTE: See page 49 for detailed information and strategy suggestions for Genie+ and Individual Lightning Lane.

The four big questions for Genie+ at EPCOT are as follows:

1. Is Genie+ worth paying for in EPCOT?

EPCOT MOST POPULAR ATTRACTIONS BY AGE GROUP

PRESCHOOL	GRADE SCHOOL	TEENS	YOUNG ADULTS	OVER 30	OVER 65
Meet Anna and Elsa at Royal Sommerhus	Journey of Water	Guardians of the Galaxy	Guardians of the Galaxy	Guardians of the Galaxy	Candlelight Processional
Journey of Water	Meet Anna and Elsa at Royal Sommerhus	Test Track	Journey of Water	Voices of Liberty	Voices of Liberty
Frozen Ever After	Test Track	Sergio	Test Track	Mariachi Cobre	Mariachi Cobre
The Seas with Nemo & Friends	Guardians of the Galaxy	Soarin' Around the World	Soarin' Around the World	Candlelight Processional	Sergio
Turtle Talk with Crush	Remy's Ratatouille Adventure	Japan Pavilion	Disney & Pixar Short Film Festival	Soarin' Around the World	Soarin' Around the World
Remy's Ratatouille Adventure	Soarin' Around the World	Remy's Ratatouille Adventure	JAMMitors	Matsuriza	JAMMitors
The Seas Main Tank and Exhibits	Turtle Talk with Crush	JAMMitors	Mariachi Cobre	Journey of Water	Matsuriza
Gran Fiesta Tour	Luminous	Mexico Pavilion	Japan Pavilion	JAMMitors	Living with the Land
JAMMitors	Frozen Ever After	Mariachi Cobre	Remy's Ratatouille Adventure	Sergio	Remy's Ratatouille Adventure
Imagination Pavilion	JAMMitors	Club Cool	Mexico Pavilion	Japan Pavilion	The American Adventure

2. If it's worth the cost, which attractions benefit most from Genie+ or Individual Lightning Lane?

3. How can you avoid paying for Individual Lightning Lane?

4. How do Genie+ and Individual Lightning Lane work with the touring plans?

Are Genie+ and Individual Lightning Lane Worth Paying For in EPCOT?

Individual Lightning Lane, potentially; Genie+, almost certainly not. Why? Several reasons:

1. An Individual Lightning Lane for Guardians of the Galaxy: Cosmic Rewind will save you about 40 minutes, and it also guarantees you a return time of your choosing.

2. Three attractions on Genie+ will save you significant time compared to standby. But under all crowd conditions, you will likely be able to use only one or two of them. Instead, avoid those one or two waits by taking advantage of Early Entry.

3. Can't do Early Entry? That's the one situation in which you may want to consider Genie+ at EPCOT.

GENIE+ AND INDIVIDUAL LIGHTNING LANE (ILL) SELECTIONS IN EPCOT

FUTURE WORLD • Disney and Pixar Short Film Festival • Guardians of the Galaxy: Cosmic Rewind (*ILL*) • Journey into Imagination with Figment • Living with the Land • Mission: Space • The Seas with Nemo & Friends • Soarin' Around the World • Spaceship Earth • Test Track • *Turtle Talk with Crush*

WORLD SHOWCASE • Frozen Ever After • Remy's Ratatouille Adventure

Regardless of the time of year you visit, arriving during Early Entry (or even at opening) should allow you to see at least one of EPCOT's headliner attractions without significant waits. Using Genie+ saves a decent amount of time at only three attractions. All others are a wash. And a bunch of people are competing for return times at those three attractions, which means they book up quickly. The table below shows how much time we estimate you'll be able to save using Genie+, at various crowd and Genie+ usage levels (see page 370 for an explanation of the usage levels):

ESTIMATED TIME SAVINGS USING GENIE+ BY CROWD LEVEL			
CROWD LEVEL	TYPICAL USE (3 GENIE+ RESERVATIONS PER DAY)	OPTIMISTIC USE (5 GENIE+ RESERVATIONS PER DAY)	PERFECT USE (7 GENIE+ RESERVATIONS PER DAY)
LOW	50 minutes	60 minutes	75 minutes
MODERATE	60 minutes	75 minutes	100 minutes
HIGH	75 minutes	115 minutes	145 minutes

Which EPCOT Attractions Benefit Most from Genie+ and Individual Lightning Lane?

The table below shows the top attractions that might benefit most from using Genie+, based on current wait times and historical Genie+ wait times. Regarding Individual Lightning Lane, we think Guardians of the Galaxy is not worth the cost, based on wait times alone.

EPCOT ATTRACTIONS THAT BENEFIT MOST FROM GENIE+ AND INDIVIDUAL LIGHTNING LANE (Highest Priority to Lowest)			
ATTRACTION	AVG. TIME IN LINE SAVED (IN MINUTES)	ATTRACTION	AVG. TIME IN LINE SAVED (IN MINUTES)
REMY'S RATATOUILLE ADVENTURE	45	SPACESHIP EARTH	12
FROZEN EVER AFTER	43	MISSION: SPACE (Orange/Green)	12/4
GUARDIANS OF THE GALAXY: COSMIC REWIND	39	THE SEAS WITH NEMO & FRIENDS	9
TEST TRACK	32	LIVING WITH THE LAND	7
SOARIN' AROUND THE WORLD	16	JOURNEY INTO IMAGINATION WITH FIGMENT	5

When Do Genie+ and Individual Lightning Lane Reservations Run Out in EPCOT?

The table on the opposite page shows the approximate time at which EPCOT attractions run out of Genie+ or Individual Lightning Lane capacity, by crowd level. Use this along with the "Which Attractions Benefit Most" table, above, to determine which reservations to get first.

How Can You Avoid Paying for Individual Lightning Lane?

At EPCOT, all you have to do is participate in the virtual queue for Guardians of the Galaxy: Cosmic Rewind. If you're successful at 7 a.m., or will be in the park at 1 p.m., you can just go after your boarding group is called instead of paying for Individual Lightning Lane. If the ride reverts to a standard standby queue, this advice would change.

WHEN GENIE+ AND INDIVIDUAL LIGHTNING LANE RESERVATIONS RUN OUT BY ATTENDANCE LEVEL*

ATTRACTION	LOW ATTENDANCE	MODERATE ATTENDANCE	HIGH ATTENDANCE
DISNEY & PIXAR SHORT FILM FESTIVAL	9 p.m.	9 p.m.	9 p.m.
FROZEN EVER AFTER	3 p.m.	1 p.m.	11 a.m.
GUARDIANS OF THE GALAXY: COSMIC REWIND (ILL)	5 p.m.	Noon	9 a.m.
JOURNEY INTO IMAGINATION WITH FIGMENT	9 p.m.	9 p.m.	9 p.m.
LIVING WITH THE LAND	9 p.m.	9 p.m.	8 p.m.
MISSION: SPACE	9 p.m.	9 p.m.	8 p.m.
REMY'S RATATOUILLE ADVENTURE	3 p.m.	Noon	9 a.m.
THE SEAS WITH NEMO AND FRIENDS	9 p.m.	9 p.m.	9 p.m.
SOARIN' AROUND THE WORLD	9 p.m.	9 p.m.	7 p.m.
SPACESHIP EARTH	9 p.m.	9 p.m.	8 p.m.
TEST TRACK	3 p.m.	1 p.m.	11 a.m.
TURTLE TALK WITH CRUSH	8 p.m.	8 p.m.	8 p.m.

*Information is applicable until July 24, 2024.
LOW ATTENDANCE Crowd levels 1–3 on the TouringPlans.com crowd calendar
MODERATE ATTENDANCE Crowd levels 4–7   HIGH ATTENDANCE Crowd levels 8–10

How Do Genie+ and Individual Lightning Lane Work with the Touring Plans?

See our advice on page 372.

DINING IN EPCOT

BELOW IS A RECAP of EPCOT's top restaurants, rated by readers, starting with the highest. There are too many restaurants rated average or better to list here. See Part 6 for details.

EPCOT RESTAURANT REFRESHER

COUNTER SERVICE	FULL SERVICE
Rose & Crown Pub (⊕ 97%/E) United Kingdom, World Showcase	**Via Napoli Ristorante e Pizzeria** (L, D) (⊕ 93%/MAA) Italy, World Showcase
Les Halles Boulangerie–Pâtisserie (⊕ 95%/MAA) France, World Showcase	**Garden Grill Restaurant** (L, D) (⊕ 92%/AA) The Land, World Nature
Kringla Bakeri og Kafe (⊕ 95%/MAA) Norway, World Showcase	**Teppan Edo** (L, D) (⊕ 92%/AA) Japan, World Showcase
Yorkshire County Fish Shop (⊕ 95%/MAA) United Kingdom, World Showcase	**Biergarten Restaurant** (L, D) (⊕ 91%/AA) Germany, World Showcase
Restaurant Outpost (⊕ 94%/MAA) Between Germany and China, World Showcase	**Spice Road Table** (L, D) (⊕ 90%/AA) Morocco, World Showcase
Restaurant Port (⊕ 94%/MAA) Near Canada, World Showcase	

Counter-service restaurants not listed are rated above average or below. Full-service restaurants not listed are rated average or below.

FUTURE WORLD

IMMENSE, GLEAMING FUTURISTIC STRUCTURES define the first themed area just beyond EPCOT's main entrance. Broad thoroughfares are punctuated with futuristic statues; generally some advertisements for the current festival; and, most recently, a bunch of construction walls. Front and center is the **Spaceship Earth** geosphere. Pavilions to the east (left as you enter from the Future World entrance) are dedicated to technological achievements; those to the right celebrate human imagination and the natural world.

Future World consists of three main "lands": **World Discovery, World Celebration,** and **World Nature.** Attractions are grouped together in pavilions within these areas. The pavilions and their attractions are described on the following pages.

KEY TO ABBREVIATIONS In the attraction profiles that follow, each star rating is accompanied by a category label in parentheses (see page 368 for details). **E** means **Exceptional, MAA** means **Much Above Average, AA** means **Above Average, A** means **Average, BA** means **Below Average,** and **MBA** means **Much Below Average.**

WORLD DISCOVERY

Guardians of the Galaxy: Cosmic Rewind
★★★★★

PRESCHOOL ★★★ (BA)   GRADE SCHOOL ★★★★½ (E)
TEENS, YOUNG ADULTS, OVER 30, AND OVER 65 ★★★★★ (E)

What it is Massive indoor roller coaster. **Scope and scale** Super-headliner. **When to go** When your boarding group is called. **Comments** Must be 42″ tall to ride. Audio descriptions and assistive-listening devices are available. **ECV/wheelchair access** Must transfer to the ride vehicle. **Participates in Genie+** No (it offers Individual Lightning Lane). **Early Theme Park Entry** No. **Extended Evening Hours** Yes.

DESCRIPTION AND COMMENTS Guardians of the Galaxy is one of the highest-rated attractions in Walt Disney World. The premise of the ride is that it's EPCOT's newest technology showcase . . . except you have to get out into space to view the new tech.

You'll start your interplanetary voyage at the Guardians of the Galaxy building near EPCOT's main entrance, in World Discovery. Once inside, the preshow area consists of numerous walkways curved around various display items that explain the history and culture of the planet Xandar and introduce the *Guardians of the Galaxy* cast for those who haven't seen the movies. The queue is set up to incorporate several holding areas—small preshow rooms through which guests are "pulsed" in regular intervals. The theory is that by switching you from lines to rooms to lines again, you'll feel better about the wait than if you were just in one long, uninterrupted line. Eventually, you make it to the final preshow room, where the ride's actual plot is revealed. In this case, a villain steals some very important equipment. Actor Terry Crews delivers the bad news—and his acting is definitely one of the highlights of the ride. He tells you to join the Guardians of the Galaxy to get the equipment back.

From this last preshow, you enter the ride's loading area. It's a large room with two identical loading platforms to the left and right. Having two loading areas helps keep wait times down. The ride begins with a backward launch. Then, at the exact moment you're supposed to enter deep space, your vehicle turns around to face forward. This might be the best effect in the entire ride. Disney has programmed the ride vehicle to spin and tilt down just a bit as you enter a massive room that's pitch black other than some simulated stars and planets. On our first ride, we felt like we were floating in space—an actual wow moment.

Much of the rest of the ride continues that feeling of soaring through space, with turns past a few scenic objects and a rock-and-roll soundtrack to accompany your ride (songs include A Flock of Seagulls' "I Ran"; Earth, Wind, and Fire's "September"; and Blondie's "One Way or Another"). The ride doesn't ever go upside down. The whole onboard experience takes just under 3 minutes. That gives Guardians a potential hourly capacity of around 2,500–2,800 riders per hour, which is very good.

TOURING TIPS Guardians of the Galaxy is one of EPCOT's three thrill rides. Disney calls it a "family thrill ride." In practice, it's about as intense as Space Mountain or Expedition Everest—with the addition of spinning cars, which ups the motion sickness factor.

At press time, Guardians of the Galaxy was requiring guests to obtain a boarding group reservation or pay to ride using Individual Lightning Lane (you can't just show up and wait in a standby line). Boarding groups were available at 7 a.m. and 1 p.m. for all guests, with a special 6 p.m. boarding group for guests staying at Disney Deluxe and DVC resorts on nights when EPCOT hosted Extended Evening Theme Park Hours. See page 49 for an explanation of how boarding groups work and how to obtain a boarding group reservation. We're surprised that Guardians still uses boarding groups more than three years after opening. It's only because of the limited indoor queueing space at this point.

Mission: Space ★★★

PRESCHOOL ★★★½ (BA/Green) GRADE SCHOOL ★★★★ (AA/Both) TEENS ★★★★ (AA/Orange)
YOUNG ADULTS ★★★★ (A/Orange)   OVER 30 AND OVER 65 ★★★½ (MBA/Both)

What it is Space-flight simulator ride. **Scope and scale** Major attraction. **When to go** Anytime. **Comments** Orange version not recommended for pregnant guests or anyone prone to motion sickness or claustrophobia; must be 40" tall to ride the Green (non-spinning) version, and 44" to ride the Orange version. **Duration** About 5 minutes plus preshow. **Loading speed** Moderate-fast. **ECV/wheelchair access** Must transfer to the ride vehicle. **Participates in Genie+** Yes. **Early Theme Park Entry** Yes. **Extended Evening Hours** Yes.

Motion Sickness

DESCRIPTION AND COMMENTS Mission: Space is a centrifuge-based space simulator that spins riders around a central axis to simulate the g-forces of rocket liftoff and, eventually, a moment of weightlessness. There is also a tamer nonspinning version.

Even before you walk into the building, you're asked whether you want your ride with or without spin. Choose the spinning version and you're on the **Orange** team; the **Green** team trains on the non-spinning side. Either way, you're immediately handed the appropriate "launch ticket" containing the first of myriad warnings that scare many riders into switching to the tamer version.

Mission: Space's Orange version is a journey to Mars. The Green version, which takes you orbiting around Earth, is comparatively smooth and mild enough for first-time astronauts—my child rode it at age 4. This Texas reader says you don't give up much by choosing the Green option:

I am 65 and have ridden the Orange version a number of times. On our latest trip, we went on the Orange version again and felt a little uncomfortable. My wife suggested that we try the Green version, which I mistakenly believed was some sort of boring mission-control exercise where we would sit behind a computer. The Green version gave us a great experience, including the feeling of lift-off and zero gravity, without the nausea.

Guests for both versions are strapped into space capsules for a simulated flight with—shockingly—unexpected results. Each capsule accommodates a crew consisting of a group commander, a pilot, a navigator, and an engineer, with a guest in each role. The crews' execution of their respective responsibilities has no effect on the outcome of the flight.

The capsules are small (if you have any sort of claustrophobia, you *will* be uncomfortable), and both ride versions are amazingly realistic. The nonspinning (Green) version doesn't subject your body to g-forces, but it does bounce and toss you around in a manner roughly comparable to other Disney motion simulators.

TOURING TIPS We're told that the posted wait time for the Orange version is always higher than the Green one to give those on the fence about riding a nudge toward trying the tamer version.

Your bladder will be shaken up and squished on this ride—hit the bathroom before you ride.

A space-themed restaurant, **Space 220,** opened between Mission: Space and Test Track in 2021 (see page 274). Its "dine on a space station" theme includes video displays of Earth from orbit.

TEST TRACK PAVILION

SPONSORED BY CHEVROLET, this pavilion (the last on the left before World Showcase) consists of the **Test Track** ride and some postshow multimedia presentations and interactive exhibits. All age groups except preschoolers rate Test Track highly. Grade-schoolers, teens, and young adults rate the postshow exhibits as above average. Promotional hype is more heavy-handed here than in most other sponsored attractions. Nonetheless, Test Track is one of the most creatively conceived attractions in Disney World.

Test Track ★★★★

PRESCHOOL ★★★½ (A)   GRADE SCHOOL ★★★★½ (E)   TEENS ★★★★½ (E)
YOUNG ADULTS ★★★★½ (E)   OVER 30 ★★★★½ (AA)   OVER 65 ★★★★½ (AA)

What it is Auto-test simulator ride. **Scope and scale** Super-headliner. **When to go** The first 30 minutes the park is open or just before closing, or use the single-rider line. **Comment** Must be 40" to ride. **Duration** About 4 minutes. **Loading speed** Moderate-fast. **ECV/wheelchair access** Must transfer to the ride vehicle. **Participates in Genie+** Yes. **Early Theme Park Entry** Yes. **Extended Evening Hours** Yes.

DESCRIPTION AND COMMENTS Test Track began a lengthy refurbishment in June 2024. We expect that this refurbishment will end in 2025. Disney is calling it a "reimagining" that draws inspiration from the original EPCOT attraction, World of Motion. When it reopens, we expect that it will join Guardians of the Galaxy as an Individual Lightning Lane option at EPCOT.

TOURING TIPS Test Track breaks down more often than almost any other ride in Walt Disney World—it's down for about an hour per day, on average. It's also one of the attractions most likely to be down at park opening. Ask if it's operating before you trek to this corner of the park.

When it's working properly, it's one of the park's better attractions—but for this Ohio dad, that never happened:

During one trip, despite being at EPCOT on several different days, we never saw Test Track open. I guess that's one of the hazards of traveling in September with its rain.

Because most groups are unwilling to split up, the **single-rider line** is frequently a walk-on, even with hour-long waits in the standby queue.

WORLD CELEBRATION

Club Cool

PRESCHOOL ★★★½ (A)   GRADE SCHOOL ★★★★ (AA)   TEENS ★★★★ (MAA)
YOUNG ADULTS ★★★★ (AA)   OVER 30 ★★★★ (BA)   OVER 65 ★★★★ (BA)

DESCRIPTION AND COMMENTS Attached to the Creations Shop in the center of Future World, this Coca-Cola–sponsored retail space and soda fountain provides free, unlimited samples of soft drinks from around the world. Some of the flavors will taste strange to Americans (such as bitter-tasting **Beverly** from Italy). Perhaps because it's free and refreshing on a hot day, many age groups rate Club Cool higher than most EPCOT attractions.

TOURING TIPS Club Cool can get crowded, so you may have to wait a bit before dispensing your drink during busier times. But don't worry—people don't usually spend a lot of time inside. Don't come in expecting to fill a Big Gulp–size cup of free soda—the cups hold just an ounce or two at a time. Watch out for sticky floors!

Spaceship Earth ★★★★

PRESCHOOL ★★★½ (A)   GRADE SCHOOL ★★★★ (A)   TEENS ★★★½ (A)
YOUNG ADULTS ★★★★ (AA)   OVER 30 ★★★★ (A)   OVER 65 ★★★★ (A)

What it is Educational dark ride. **Scope and scale** Headliner. **When to go** Midday. **Duration** About 16 minutes. **Loading speed** Fast. **ECV/wheelchair access** Must transfer to provided wheelchair, then to the ride vehicle. **Participates in Genie+** Yes. **Early Theme Park Entry** Yes. **Extended Evening Hours** Yes.

DESCRIPTION AND COMMENTS EPCOT's signature landmark, Spaceship Earth spirals through an 18-story geosphere, taking visitors past animatronic scenes depicting humankind's developments in communications, from cave painting to printing to television computer networks. The ride is a remarkably efficient use of the geosphere's interior.

Interactive screens (if they're working) in the vehicles let you customize the ending animated video. A postshow area with interactive exhibits rounds out the attraction.

TOURING TIPS Because it's located near EPCOT's main entrance, Spaceship Earth attracts arriving guests soon after the park opens. Your time is better spent on other Future World attractions, such as Soarin' Around the World or Test Track. Wait times usually fall after 4 p.m., so you could see it on the way out of the park.

Spaceship Earth has regular pauses and slowdowns. Be prepared for lots of stops throughout the dark attraction.

WORLD NATURE

IMAGINATION! PAVILION

THIS MULTI-ATTRACTION PAVILION is on the south side of World Nature. Outside are an "upside-down" waterfall and a fountain that "hops" over the heads of unsuspecting passersby.

Disney & Pixar Short Film Festival ★★½

PRESCHOOL ★★★★ (AA)   **GRADE SCHOOL ★★★★½** (MAA)   **TEENS ★★★★** (AA)
YOUNG ADULTS ★★★★½ (MAA)   **OVER 30 ★★★★** (A)   **OVER 65 ★★★★** (A)

What it is Short films from Disney and Pixar. **Scope and scale** Diversion. **When to go** Anytime. **Duration** About 20 minutes. **Probable waiting time** Less than one show. **ECV/wheelchair access** May remain in wheelchair. **Participates in Genie+** Yes. **Early Theme Park Entry** No. **Extended Evening Hours** No.

DESCRIPTION AND COMMENTS This theater screens three 3D shorts— Pixar's *Feast* and *Piper* and Disney's *Get a Horse*—all of which can be easily found online. The only reason to go here is to get out of the sun (or rain) and sit in the air-conditioning for a few minutes.

TOURING TIPS The shorts are cute, but watch them at home unless you need a place to cool down.

Journey into Imagination with Figment ★★½

PRESCHOOL ★★★★ (AA)   **GRADE SCHOOL ★★★½** (A)   **TEENS ★★★** (BA)
YOUNG ADULTS ★★★ (MBA)   **OVER 30 ★★★** (MBA)   **OVER 65 ★★★** (MBA)

What it is Fantasy dark ride. **Scope and scale** Minor attraction. **When to go** Anytime. **Duration** About 6 minutes. **Loading speed** Fast. **ECV/wheelchair access** May remain in wheelchair. **Participates in Genie+** Yes. **Early Theme Park Entry** No. **Extended Evening Hours** No.

DESCRIPTION AND COMMENTS The story takes you on a tour of a fictitious research lab dedicated to studying human imagination. Sometimes you're a passive observer and sometimes you're a test subject of the lab's inner workings. You will encounter optical illusions, a room that defies gravity, and other brain teasers. All along the way, Figment (a purple dragon) makes surprise appearances. After the ride, you can visit an interactive-exhibit area with fun meet and greets.

Reader responses to Figment and company are pretty consistent—and negative. It's one of the lowest-rated attractions in EPCOT. From a Tennessee family of three:

Journey into Imagination should be experienced only if you're a HUGE Figment fan. We, on the other hand, hated it.

TOURING TIPS You can do any of the meet and greets without the ride if you'd like. Scent-sensitive souls beware: You will get skunked on the ride.

JOURNEY OF WATER, INSPIRED BY MOANA ★★★★

PRESCHOOL ★★★★½ (E)   **GRADE SCHOOL ★★★★½** (E)   **TEENS ★★★★½** (E)
YOUNG ADULTS ★★★★★ (E)   **OVER 30 ★★★★½** (MAA)   **OVER 65 ★★★★½** (MAA)

BUILT TO SIMULATE THE LUSH LANDSCAPES of waterfalls and streams, this walk-through exhibit sits on the walk from the center of Future World to The Seas with Nemo & Friends Pavilion and can be toured at any time. The attraction offers some of the best nuanced Imagineering in any of Disney World's theme parks. With no frightening aspects and no hours-long lines, it offers interactive elements that guests of any age can enjoy. Not surprisingly, it has quickly made its way toward the top of many of the age-specific top 10 lists for the park.

Journey of Water takes about 10 minutes to tour and is accessible for guests using wheelchairs or scooters. It does not participate in Genie+, Early Entry, or Extended Evening Hours.

THE LAND PAVILION

THIS HUGE, ENVIRONMENT-THEMED PAVILION contains three attractions and two restaurants. Strollers aren't allowed inside and the stroller-parking area is a decent walk away—those with babies might want to bring a carrier.

Awesome Planet ★★½

NOT ENOUGH SURVEYS TO RATE

What it is Indoor film about the environment. **Scope and scale** Diversion. **When to go** Anytime. **Comments** The film is on the pavilion's upper level. **Duration** About 15 minutes. **Probable waiting time** Less than one show. **ECV/wheelchair access** May remain in wheelchair. **Participates in Genie+** No. **Early Theme Park Entry** No. **Extended Evening Hours** No.

DESCRIPTION AND COMMENTS *Awesome Planet* is a gorgeous short film that reviews the planet's animals and biomes. Where the film falls short is that the script has narrator Ty Burrell mimicking his role as real estate agent Phil Dunphy from the ABC-Disney TV show *Modern Family*. The film's premise is that you're looking for a planet to buy and Phil is walking you through the benefits of Earth—at this point an unnecessary and outdated gimmick.

TOURING TIPS The theater is large enough to accommodate everyone who wants to see the film, at any time of year. We suspect that most people who go into the theater only do so because they feel sorry for the lonely cast member standing outside.

Living with the Land ★★★★

| PRESCHOOL ★★★½ (A) | GRADE SCHOOL ★★★½ (BA) | TEENS ★★★½ (BA) |
| YOUNG ADULTS ★★★★ (A) | OVER 30 ★★★★ (AA) | OVER 65 ★★★★ (AA) |

What it is Indoor boat ride chronicling farming and agricultural history. **Scope and scale** Minor attraction. **When to go** Anytime. **Duration** About 14 minutes. **Loading speed** Moderate. **ECV/wheelchair access** Must transfer from ECV to provided wheelchair. **Participates in Genie+** Yes. **Early Theme Park Entry** No. **Extended Evening Hours** No.

DESCRIPTION AND COMMENTS The boat ride takes you through simulated swamps and farm environments, and then a futuristic greenhouse where real crops are grown using the latest agricultural technologies. The greenhouse exhibits change constantly: Along with familiar fruits and grains such as tomatoes, corn, and rice, recent plantings include Mickey-shaped pumpkins, hot peppers, Malabar nuts, pandan, caimito, and amaranth. This produce is used in restaurants throughout Walt Disney World.

Don't assume that Living with the Land will be too dry and educational. A woman from Texas writes:

I had a bad attitude about Living with the Land—I just didn't think I was up for a movie about wheat farming. Wow, was I surprised!

TOURING TIPS If you have an interest in the agricultural techniques being demonstrated, take the **Behind the Seeds at EPCOT** tour (see page 495).

Soarin' Around the World ★★★★½

| PRESCHOOL ★★★★ (AA) | GRADE SCHOOL ★★★★½ (MAA) | TEENS ★★★★½ (E) |
| YOUNG ADULTS ★★★★½ (MAA) | OVER 30 ★★★★½ (E) | OVER 65 ★★★★½ (E) |

What it is Flight simulator ride. **Scope and scale** Super-headliner. **When to go** First 2 hours the park is open or after 4 p.m. **Comments** Must be 40″ tall to ride; Rider Switch option provided (see page 303). **Duration** 5½ minutes. **Loading speed** Moderate. **ECV/wheelchair access** Must transfer to the ride vehicle. **Participates in Genie+** Yes. **Early Theme Park Entry** Yes. **Extended Evening Hours** Yes.

DESCRIPTION AND COMMENTS Soarin' Around the World is a ride for all ages, as exhilarating as being a hawk in the sky and as mellow as swinging in a hammock. If you have ever experienced flying dreams, that's how Soarin' feels.

Once you enter the main theater, you're secured in a seat hanging from a "hang glider." Then the rows of seats swing into position, making you feel as if the floor has dropped away, and you're suspended with your legs dangling. You embark on a simulated hang-glider tour, with images projected all around you and with the flight simulator moving in sync with the movie. Special effects include wind, sound, and even smell. The ride itself is exciting but perfectly smooth.

The film travels the globe, from the Matterhorn and an Arctic glacier to the Taj Mahal and the Great Wall of China. The visuals are stunningly sharp thanks to laser IMAX projectors, but computer-animated animals are regularly distracting. Soarin' is a must for anyone who meets the height requirement, thanks to its smooth glide and stunning visuals. A Maine dad gives it a hearty thumbs-up:

Soarin' is amazing! Even if the "trip around the world" doesn't make a lot of sense, it's still stunning.

TOURING TIPS The film's display of vertical landmarks appears comically distorted from seats on the left or right side of the screen. To avoid this, once you're directed to one of the three concourses, politely request to wait for seats in row B1 for an ideal view.

With three theaters operating, Soarin' Around the World can almost always keep up with its crowds. But if a special event, like a limited-time showing of the original Soarin', happens or a theater goes down, then lines get long quickly and can stay that way all day.

THE SEAS WITH NEMO & FRIENDS PAVILION

FEATURING CHARACTERS from Disney/Pixar's *Finding Nemo* and *Finding Dory,* The Seas encompasses what was once one of America's largest aquariums, a ride that tunnels through the aquarium, an interactive animated film, and a number of walk-through exhibits. The tank alone makes the pavilion a must-visit.

The Seas Main Tank and Exhibits ★★★½

PRESCHOOL ★★★★½ (MAA) GRADE SCHOOL ★★★★½ (MAA) TEENS ★★★★ (AA)
YOUNG ADULTS ★★★★ (AA)   OVER 30 ★★★★ (A)   OVER 65 ★★★★ (A)

What it is A huge saltwater aquarium, plus exhibits. **Scope and scale** Major attraction. **When to go** When you need a break from the heat, sun, or rain. **ECV/wheelchair access** May remain in wheelchair. **Participates in Genie+** No. **Early Theme Park Entry** Yes. **Extended Evening Hours** Yes.

DESCRIPTION AND COMMENTS The Seas is among Future World's most ambitious offerings, housed in a 200-foot-diameter, 27-foot-deep tank containing fish, marine mammals, and crustaceans. Visitors can watch the activity through 8-inch-thick windows below the surface (including some at **Coral Reef Restaurant;** see page 253).

About two-thirds of the aquarium is home to reef species, including sharks, rays, and many fish. The other third houses bottlenose dolphins and sea turtles. As you face the aquarium, the most glare-free viewing windows for the dolphins are on the ground floor to the left by the escalators. For the reef species, it's the same floor on the right by the escalators.

TOURING TIPS If you see a cast member standing near the tank's windows, ask them what kind of fish you're looking at and whether they have names. Kids enjoy an interactive booklet with stickers that they can fill out while touring the tanks.

The Seas with Nemo & Friends ★★★

PRESCHOOL ★★★½ (MAA)   GRADE SCHOOL ★★★★ (A)   TEENS ★★★ (BA)
YOUNG ADULTS ★★★½ (MBA)   OVER 30 ★★★½ (MBA)   OVER 65 ★★★½ (MBA)

What it is Ride through a tunnel in the main tank. **Scope and scale** Minor attraction. **When to go** Anytime. **Duration** 4 minutes. **Loading speed** Fast. **ECV/wheelchair access** Must transfer to the ride vehicle. **Participates in Genie+** Yes. **Early Theme Park Entry** Yes. **Extended Evening Hours** Yes.

DESCRIPTION AND COMMENTS This ride features characters from *Finding Nemo* and deposits you at the heart of the pavilion, where you'll find the exhibits, the interactive animated film *Turtle Talk with Crush,* and viewing platforms for the main aquarium.

You'll be ushered to the loading area and seated in a "clamobile" for your journey through the aquarium. The attraction features technology that makes it seem like the animated characters are swimming with live fish. It quickly retells the basic plot of *Finding Nemo.* Unlike the film, however, the ride ends with a musical finale that might be even more catchy than "It's a Small World." If you have small kids who are unfamiliar with the film, the anglerfish and shark scenes may be scary.

TOURING TIPS The ride is a fun way to enter the tanks, but if the wait is too long, it's not a necessary experience—you can head straight for the exhibits by going through the pavilion's exit, around back, and to the left of the main entrance.

Turtle Talk with Crush ★★★★

PRESCHOOL ★★★★½ (MAA)   GRADE SCHOOL ★★★★½ (MAA)   TEENS ★★★★ (A)
YOUNG ADULTS ★★★★ (A)   OVER 30 ★★★★ (A)   OVER 65 ★★★★ (A)

What it is Interactive animated film. **Scope and scale** Minor attraction. **When to go** Anytime. **Duration** 15 minutes. **Probable waiting time** One or two shows. **ECV/wheelchair access** May remain in wheelchair. **Participates in Genie+** Yes. **Early Theme Park Entry** No. **Extended Evening Hours** No.

DESCRIPTION AND COMMENTS *Turtle Talk with Crush* is a theater show starring the 153-year-old surfer-dude turtle from *Finding Nemo* and characters from *Finding Dory.* Breaking the fourth wall, the on-screen Crush begins to have conversations with guests in the audience. Real-time computer graphics are used to accurately move Crush's mouth as he forms words. A mom from Colorado has a crush on *Turtle Talk:*

Turtle Talk with Crush is a must-see. Our 4-year-old was picked out of the crowd by Crush, and we were just amazed by the technology. It was adorable and enjoyed by everyone from Grammy and Papa to the 4-year-old!

TOURING TIPS It's unusual to wait more than one or two shows to get in. If you find long lines at park opening, try back after 3 p.m. when more of the crowd has moved on to World Showcase.

WORLD SHOWCASE

EPCOT'S OTHER THEMED AREA, World Showcase, is an ongoing world's fair encircling a 40-acre lagoon. The cuisine, culture, history, and architecture of almost a dozen countries are permanently displayed in individual national pavilions spaced along a 1.2-mile promenade. The pavilions replicate familiar landmarks and feature representative street scenes from the host countries.

World Showcase has some of the most beautiful gardens anywhere in the United States. In Germany; Japan; France; the United Kingdom; Canada; and, to a lesser extent, China, they're sometimes tucked away and out of sight on the **World Showcase Promenade.**

In addition to the gardens, World Showcase's live entertainers are some of the most highly rated attractions in EPCOT, for all age groups. The section starting on page 428 calls out those that are especially popular. Check the *Times Guide* for performances and schedules.

To make World Showcase even more fun for kids, you can take them to the **Kidcot Fun Stop** in each pavilion. There, you'll find a table staffed with a cast member or two who hand out postcards, informational cards, or stamps for their country. It's a great way to learn and to get kids into a "gotta visit them all" mood. If they collect a card from every country, they'll be rewarded with a bonus card at their last stop.

Drinking Around the World (see page 222), an adult version of passport-stamp collecting, is enthusiastically endorsed by a woman from Louisiana:

We drank a beer in each country at EPCOT—Dad was the designated driver—and posed for photos in each, and it quickly became hilarious, as were the progression-of-drunkenness photos that followed.

There's another side to Drinking Around the World, as this reader from New York points out:

I had not been to EPCOT since 2018, and I was wholly unprepared for the HERDS OF DRUNK PEOPLE circling World Showcase in the evening. I counted at least five groups of 10+ people, in matching shirts that said stuff like "Let's Get Sheet-Faced," behaving very irresponsibly, acting out, and generally causing misery for people around them.

For this reason, we avoid EPCOT on the opening weekends of all of the park's festivals and try to avoid World Showcase with kids after dark on all weekends.

World Showcase also offers some of the most diverse and interesting shopping in Walt Disney World. See Part 17 for details.

DuckTales World Showcase Adventure ★★★

PRESCHOOL ★★★ (BA)	GRADE SCHOOL ★★★★ (AA)	TEENS ★★★½ (A)
YOUNG ADULTS ★★★½ (A)	OVER 30 ★★★½ (BA)	OVER 65 ★★★½ (BA)

What it is Interactive scavenger hunt. **Scope and scale** Diversion. **When to go** Anytime. **Duration** Allow 30 minutes per adventure. **Probable waiting time** None. **ECV/Wheelchair access** May remain in wheelchair.

DESCRIPTION AND COMMENTS In DuckTales World Showcase Adventure, you help Scrooge McDuck find valuable artifacts located in and around select World Showcase pavilions. DuckTales requires a smartphone and the Play Disney Parks app to play; download it before you leave home.

Once you arrive at a pavilion, you'll be assigned a "mission" to find an artifact. Your phone provides clues to help solve a set of simple puzzles to find the artifacts. As you discover each clue, you'll find special effects in the pavilions that physically animate some of the story you're following, leading people around you to ask, "How did you make that happen?"

Playing the game is completely free, and there are more than 35 different "missions." DuckTales makes the World Showcase pavilions even more interactive and kid-friendly. The adventures have simple clues and fast pacing. Don't be surprised if, having completed one pavilion's missions, your child wants to do more.

WORLD SHOWCASE PAVILIONS

MOVING CLOCKWISE AROUND World Showcase Promenade, here are the nations represented and their attractions.

For World Showcase, we list Appeal by Age ratings not just for the attractions but for the pavilions themselves. In addition to rides and films, they offer peaceful gardens; unique architecture; interesting places to eat, drink, and rest; stellar live entertainment; and more. Not every pavilion has a dedicated attraction.

MEXICO PAVILION

PRESCHOOL ★★★★ (BA)   GRADE SCHOOL ★★★★ (A)   TEENS ★★★★ (MAA)
YOUNG ADULTS ★★★★½ (MAA)   OVER 30 ★★★★½ (AA)   OVER 65 ★★★★½ (AA)

PRE-COLUMBIAN PYRAMIDS dominate Mexico's architecture. One pyramid forms the pavilion's facade; the other overlooks the restaurant and plaza alongside the **Gran Fiesta Tour** indoor boat ride.

Readers rate Mexico as one of the best pavilions in World Showcase. The village scene inside the pavilion is beautiful and exquisitely detailed. A retail shop occupies most of the inner pavilion, including Mexico's **Kidcot Fun Stop,** on the left side of the plaza. On the opposite side of the main floor is **La Cava del Tequila,** a bar serving more than 200 tequilas, as well as cocktails, Mexican beer, wine, and mescal.

The pyramids contain many authentic and valuable artifacts. Take the time to stop and see these treasures.

Gran Fiesta Tour Starring the Three Caballeros   ★★½

PRESCHOOL ★★★★½ (MAA)   GRADE SCHOOL ★★★★ (A)   TEENS ★★★½ (BA)
YOUNG ADULTS ★★★½ (BA)   OVER 30 ★★★½ (BA)   OVER 65 ★★★½ (BA)

What it is Scenic indoor boat ride. **Scope and scale** Minor attraction. **When to go** Anytime. **Duration** About 7 minutes. **Loading speed** Moderate. **ECV/wheelchair access** Must transfer from ECV to provided wheelchair. **Participates in Genie+** No. **Early Theme Park Entry** No. **Extended Evening Hours** Yes.

DESCRIPTION AND COMMENTS This ride incorporates animated versions of Donald Duck, José Carioca, and Panchito Pistoles from Disney's 1944 animated musical film *The Three Caballeros.*

The storyline has the Caballeros scheduled to perform at a fiesta when Donald suddenly goes missing; large video screens show him enjoying Mexico's sights and sounds while José and Panchito try to track him down. Everyone is reunited in time for a rousing concert near the end of the ride.

TOURING TIPS More of the ride's visuals seem to be on the left side of the boat, so have small children sit nearer the left to keep their attention and listen for Donald's humorous monologue as you wait to disembark.

If the line is still contained within the center of the pavilion, you shouldn't wait more than 5 minutes, no matter what the MDE app tells you. There's no Lightning Lane slowing the standby queue down.

NORWAY PAVILION

PRESCHOOL ★★★½ (A)	GRADE SCHOOL ★★★★ (A)	TEENS ★★★½ (A)
YOUNG ADULTS ★★★★ (A)	OVER 30 ★★★★ (A)	OVER 65 ★★★★ (A)

THIS PAVILION ENCAPSULATES both everything we love about EPCOT and everything we dislike about corporate Disney. Parts of the pavilion—that is, those based on the actual country of Norway—are complex, beautiful, and diverse. Highlights include replicas of the 14th-century **Akershus Castle** in Oslo; a miniature version of a **stave church** built in 1212 in Gol (go inside—the doors open!); and other buildings that accurately represent traditional Scandinavian architecture.

However, when Disney released 2013's *Frozen*, set in the mythical Scandinavian-ish kingdom of Arendelle, the fate of the Norway Pavilion was set. In an unprecedented (and, we hope, never repeated) move, Disney replaced the main attraction in the Norway Pavilion with **Frozen Ever After,** a boat ride about a fictional place in an animated movie.

Nothing against *Frozen*—it is one of the best Disney movies ever made and deserves to be celebrated in the parks. We just wish it wasn't a shot at the very heart of EPCOT's original purpose.

Frozen Ever After   ★★★★

PRESCHOOL ★★★★½ (E)	GRADE SCHOOL ★★★★½ (MAA)	TEENS ★★★★ (MBA)
YOUNG ADULTS ★★★★ (A)	OVER 30 ★★★★ (A)	OVER 65 ★★★★ (A)

What it is Indoor boat ride. **Scope and scale** Headliner. **When to go** Before noon or after 7 p.m. **Duration** Almost 5 minutes. **Loading speed** Fast. **ECV/wheelchair access** Must transfer to the ride vehicle. **Participates in Genie+** Yes. **Early Theme Park Entry** Yes. **Extended Evening Hours** Yes.

DESCRIPTION AND COMMENTS The premise of this boat ride through Arendelle is that you've arrived in time for the Winter in Summer celebration, in which Elsa will use her magical powers to make it snow during the hottest part of the year. Nearly every character from the film is represented, along with many of the film's songs.

Be aware that there's a short, mild section where you're propelled backward for a few seconds, followed by a short downhill and small splash that most kids should take in stride. The ride's detailed sets are augmented with digital projection mapping and more than a dozen animatronics sporting somewhat jarring video-screen faces.

TOURING TIPS Along with Test Track and Remy's Ratatouille Adventure, Frozen Ever After is one of the attractions that most guests head to first.

The ride experiences more breakdowns than most Walt Disney World attractions—it's down for over half an hour per day on average. If you plan to see Frozen Ever After first thing in the morning, ask a cast member if it's running before you hike all the way to Norway.

The opening of Remy's Ratatouille Adventure has diverted a large portion of the park-opening crowd away from Frozen Ever After. We recommend starting the day at the International Gateway, heading to Remy and then to Frozen to start your day.

Meet Anna and Elsa at Royal Sommerhus ★★★★

PRESCHOOL ★★★★½ (E)	GRADE SCHOOL ★★★★½ (E)	TEENS ★★★★ (A)
YOUNG ADULTS ★★★½ (MBA)	OVER 30 ★★★★ (BA)	OVER 65 ★★★★ (BA)

What it is Meet and greet. **Scope and scale** Minor attraction. **When to go** At opening, at lunch or dinner, or in the last hour the park is open. **Duration** About 3 minutes. **Probable waiting time** 15–25 minutes. **ECV/wheelchair access** May remain in wheelchair. **Participates in Genie+** No. **Early Theme Park Entry** No. **Extended Evening Hours** No.

DESCRIPTION AND COMMENTS Royal Sommerhus is a character-greeting venue for Anna and Elsa. They both meet in their *Frozen 2* outfits, in case that matters to the kids in your group. In a nod to its host pavilion, the meet and greet features traditional Norwegian architecture and crafts.

TOURING TIPS During times of peak meet and greet, Royal Sommerhus has multiple rooms with multiple Annas and Elsas receiving guests. If you're visiting World Showcase in the afternoon, waits tend to be shortest around lunchtime, 4 p.m., and 6–7 p.m.

CHINA PAVILION

PRESCHOOL ★★½ (MBA)	GRADE SCHOOL ★★★½ (BA)	TEENS ★★★½ (A)
YOUNG ADULTS ★★★½ (BA)	OVER 30 ★★★★ (A)	OVER 65 ★★★★ (BA)

A HALF-SIZE REPLICA of the **Temple of Heaven** in Beijing identifies this pavilion. Gardens and reflecting ponds simulate those found in Suzhou, and an art gallery features a lotus-blossom gate and formal saddle roofline. There are also exhibits on Chinese history and culture.

Reflections of China ★★★½

PRESCHOOL ★★ (MBA)	GRADE SCHOOL ★★★ (MBA)	TEENS ★★★ (MBA)
YOUNG ADULTS ★★★ (MBA)	OVER 30 ★★★½ (BA)	OVER 65 ★★★½ (BA)

What it is Film about the Chinese people and culture. **Scope and scale** Minor attraction. **When to go** Anytime. **Comment** Audience stands throughout performance. **Duration** About 14 minutes. **Probable waiting time** Less than one show. **ECV/wheelchair access** May remain in wheelchair. **Participates in Genie+** No. **Early Theme Park Entry** No. **Extended Evening Hours** No.

DESCRIPTION AND COMMENTS Pass through the Hall of Prayer for Good Harvest to view this Circle-Vision 360° film. Warm and appealing (albeit politically sanitized), it's a brilliant introduction to the people and natural beauty of China. We think the film's relatively low marks are due to the theater's lack of seats, not its cinematic quality. My kids even enjoyed this one when they were 5 and 3, so don't feel like you have to skip it for the littles.

TOURING TIPS *Reflections of China* can usually be enjoyed anytime without much waiting.

GERMANY PAVILION

PRESCHOOL ★★★ (BA)	GRADE SCHOOL ★★★½ (BA)	TEENS ★★★½ (A)
YOUNG ADULTS ★★★★ (A)	OVER 30 ★★★★ (AA)	OVER 65 ★★★★ (A)

GERMANY'S *PLATZ* (PLAZA), dominated by a clock tower and a fountain depicting St. George's victory over the dragon, is encircled by buildings in traditional architectural styles. The main attraction is **Biergarten Restaurant** (see page 248), which serves hearty German food and beer. Yodeling, folk dancing, and oompah-band music are part of the festivities, courtesy of the band **Oktoberfest Musikanten.**

The biggest draw here may be **Karamell-Küche** ("Caramel Kitchen"), offering small caramel-covered sweets, including apples and cupcakes. The large and elaborate model railroad, just beyond the restrooms as you walk from Germany toward Italy, is a true treasure, with enough detail to keep you discovering something new for hours. The display even changes periodically thanks to the attention of very dedicated cast members.

ITALY PAVILION

PRESCHOOL ★★★ (BA)	GRADE SCHOOL ★★★½ (BA)	TEENS ★★★½ (BA)
YOUNG ADULTS ★★★½ (BA)	OVER 30 ★★★★ (BA)	OVER 65 ★★★★ (BA)

THE ENTRANCE TO ITALY is marked by an 83-foot-tall campanile (bell tower) modeled after the tower in St. Mark's Square in Venice. Left of the campanile is a replica of the 14th-century Doge's Palace, also in the famous square. The pavilion has a waterfront on the lagoon where gondolas are tied to striped moorings.

Streets and courtyards in Italy are among the most realistic in World Showcase. **Via Napoli** has some of the best pizza in Walt Disney World; **Tutto Gusto Wine Cellar** serves small plates along with libations. There's no film or ride in the pavilion.

THE AMERICAN ADVENTURE PAVILION

PRESCHOOL ★★½ (MBA)	GRADE SCHOOL ★★★ (MBA)	TEENS ★★★ (MBA)
YOUNG ADULTS ★★★½ (BA)	OVER 30 ★★★★ (BA)	OVER 65 ★★★★ (BA)

THE AMERICAN ADVENTURE (UNITED STATES) PAVILION consists of a decent barbecue place (**Regal Eagle**), a preshow gallery of rotating exhibits on American history (the **American Heritage Gallery**), and a patriotic show called *The American Adventure.*

Voices of Liberty is a wildly talented and popular singing group that performs American and Disney classics either inside the pavilion or at the America Gardens Theatre stage opposite the pavilion. Anyone who is a teen or older rates the performances highly, and my kids were in awe of the group even at young ages.

The American Adventure ★★★½

PRESCHOOL ★★ (MBA)	GRADE SCHOOL ★★★ (MBA)	TEENS ★★★ (BA)
YOUNG ADULTS ★★★½ (BA)	OVER 30 ★★★★ (A)	OVER 65 ★★★★ (A)

What it is Mixed-media and Audio-Animatronic US history presentation. **Scope and scale** Minor attraction. **When to go** Anytime. **Duration** About 29 minutes. **Probable waiting time** Less than one show. **ECV/wheelchair access** May remain in wheelchair. **Participates in Genie+** No. **Early Theme Park Entry** No. **Extended Evening Hours** No.

DESCRIPTION AND COMMENTS *The American Adventure* demonstrates how good Disney theater presentations can be. Housed in an imposing brick structure reminiscent of Colonial Philadelphia, the 29-minute show is a stirring, albeit sanitized, rendition of American history, narrated by an animatronic Mark Twain (who carries a burning cigar) and Ben Franklin. Behind a stage almost half the size of a football field is a 72-foot screen on which motion picture images are interwoven with onstage action.

The American Adventure's scale is both its strength and its weakness: It takes a lot of time and money to mount a presentation this big, which explains why no new stage scenes have been added or updated since the show opened more than 40 years ago. In the meantime, our understanding of America's history and its role in the world has evolved, but the show hasn't kept pace: Topics such as racism, gender equality, labor relations, and the environment are treated as solved problems instead of the ongoing challenges they are.

I'll be honest and say it's past time for this attraction to be updated. This pavilion would do well to focus on the natural beauty of our country; the unique benefits we have as a nation full of people from diverse backgrounds; and the challenges we continue to face as we work to appreciate, embrace, and empower those different voices.

TOURING TIPS *The American Adventure* is (still) Disney's best patriotic attraction, and because of the theater's large capacity, it's highly unusual not to be admitted to the next performance.

JAPAN PAVILION

PRESCHOOL ★★★½ (A) GRADE SCHOOL ★★★★ (AA) TEENS ★★★★½ (E)
YOUNG ADULTS ★★★★½ (MAA) OVER 30 ★★★★½ (AA) OVER 65 ★★★★½ (AA)

A FIVE-STORY, BLUE-ROOFED PAGODA, inspired by an eighth-century shrine in Nara, sets this pavilion apart. A hill garden behind it features waterfalls, rocks, flowers, lanterns, paths, and rustic bridges. On the right as you face the entrance, a building inspired by the ceremonial and coronation hall at Kyoto's Imperial Palace contains restaurants and a branch of Japan's **Mitsukoshi** department store (in business since 1673). Through the center entrance and to the left, **Bijutsu-kan Gallery** exhibits colorful displays on Japanese pop culture.

Japan blends simplicity, architectural grandeur, and natural beauty. The second floor of the Japan Pavilion is also a decent viewing spot for EPCOT's fireworks show.

MOROCCO PAVILION

PRESCHOOL ★★★ (BA) GRADE SCHOOL ★★★½ (BA) TEENS ★★★½ (A)
YOUNG ADULTS ★★★½ (BA) OVER 30 ★★★★ (BA) OVER 65 ★★★★ (BA)

A BUSTLING MARKET, WINDING STREETS, lofty minarets, and stuccoed archways re-create the romance and intrigue of Marrakesh and Casablanca. The pavilion also has a museum of Moorish art and two restaurants, including one that mostly operates as a festival booth. A Minnesota mother exploring Morocco found, of all things, peace and quiet:

We found an awesome resting place in Morocco—an empty, air-conditioned gallery with padded benches. No one came in during the 15 minutes that we rested, which was quite a difference from the rest of the park! Look for the red doors on your left when you enter.

FRANCE PAVILION

PRESCHOOL ★★★ (BA) GRADE SCHOOL ★★★½ (BA) TEENS ★★★★ (AA)
YOUNG ADULTS ★★★★ (AA) OVER 30 ★★★★½ (AA) OVER 65 ★★★★½ (AA)

A REPLICA OF THE EIFFEL TOWER is, *naturellement,* this pavilion's centerpiece. The restaurants, along with the bakery and ice-cream shop, are very popular. The pavilion hosts two films: the ***Beauty and the***

Beast Sing-Along, which plays from 9:30 a.m. to 7 p.m. in the same theater as *Impressions de France,* which plays from 8:30 to 9:30 a.m. and again from 7 p.m. to just before park closing

Beauty and the Beast Sing-Along ★★

PRESCHOOL ★★★★ (AA)	GRADE SCHOOL ★★★½ (BA)	TEENS ★★★ (BA)
YOUNG ADULTS ★★★ (MBA)	OVER 30 ★★★½ (MBA)	OVER 65 ★★★½ (MBA)

What it is Film retelling of the story. **Scope and scale** Diversion. **When to go** 11 a.m.–6 p.m. **Duration** About 15 minutes. **Probable waiting time** Less than one show. **ECV/wheelchair access** May remain in wheelchair. **Participates in Genie+** No. **Early Theme Park Entry** No. **Extended Evening Hours** No.

DESCRIPTION AND COMMENTS This is the third current Walt Disney World attraction to tell the *Beauty and the Beast* story, along with the Magic Kingdom's *Enchanted Tales with Belle* and Hollywood Studios' *Beauty and the Beast—Live on Stage.* It's also the lowest-rated version.

For this show, Disney's script writers threw a small twist into the original *Beauty* story—supposedly, LeFou, Gaston's sidekick during the film, was secretly working behind the scenes the whole time to bring Belle and Beast together. This new twist might be confusing to kids (and discerning adults) because it just doesn't fit with LeFou's behavior in the movie.

What's even more confusing is that Mrs. Potts starts the film by saying that this is the true story of Beauty and the Beast, leaving viewers wondering whether everything they thought they knew was wrong or if the trusty teapot is lying.

Sadly, Disney doesn't take advantage of the full screen capacity in this theater—the entire film plays on just one of the five screens.

TOURING TIPS Stop by anytime, if you or your kids like sing-alongs.

Impressions de France ★★★

PRESCHOOL ★★ (MBA)	GRADE SCHOOL ★★★ (MBA)	TEENS ★★★ (BA)
YOUNG ADULTS ★★★½ (BA)	OVER 30 ★★★★ (A)	OVER 65 ★★★★ (A)

What it is Film essay on France and its people. **Scope and scale** Diversion. **When to go** 7–8.45 p.m. **Duration** About 18 minutes. **Probable waiting time** Less than one show. **ECV/wheelchair access** May remain in wheelchair. **Participates in Genie+** No. **Early Theme Park Entry** Yes. **Extended Evening Hours** No.

DESCRIPTION AND COMMENTS *Impressions de France* is an 18-minute movie with beautiful scenery, beautiful music, and beautiful towns, all projected over 200 degrees onto five screens. Unlike at China and Canada, the audience sits to view the film.

While we think this is the best film in World Showcase, it was outdated way before the Notre Dame fire in the spring of 2019. Disney definitely needs to update the film.

TOURING TIPS Usually begins on the half hour.

Remy's Ratatouille Adventure ★★★★

PRESCHOOL, GRADE SCHOOL, AND YOUNG ADULTS ★★★★½ (MAA)		
TEENS ★★★★ (MAA)	OVER 30 ★★★★½ (AA)	OVER 65 ★★★★½ (AA)

What it is Indoor dark ride. **Scope and scale** Major attraction. **When to go** As soon as the park opens. **Duration** About 4½ minutes. **Loading speed** Moderate. **ECV/wheelchair access** Must transfer to the ride vehicle. **Participates in Genie+** Yes. **Early Theme Park Entry** Yes. **Extended Evening Hours** Yes.

DESCRIPTION AND COMMENTS In Remy's Ratatouille Adventure, you're shrunk to the size of a rat and whisked through Paris for a quick retelling of the *Ratatouille* film's story.

Remy's storytelling combines 3D films on room-size screens with large, detailed ride-through sets that include water and heat effects. A couple of frenetic scenes, such as one in which Remy is chased with a cleaver, may frighten small children.

TOURING TIPS Remy's is the first all-new major attraction in World Showcase since 1988. It's family-friendly, with good theming and a lead character who's as lovable and cute as any rodent could hope to be.

Because it's located in a far corner of the park, Remy is difficult to work into any touring plan that doesn't start at the International Gateway. From anywhere else, it's a hike.

Your best bet to experience Remy without paying for Lightning Lane is to arrive at the International Gateway entrance about an hour before opening. That gives you a 10-minute head start on folks walking from the front entrance. If you have small children, head next to Frozen Ever After in Norway, about 0.5 mile either way around World Showcase. After experiencing Frozen Ever After, you'll have completed two of the park's five big rides, with Guardians of the Galaxy, Test Track, and Soarin' Around the World remaining.

UNITED KINGDOM PAVILION

PRESCHOOL ★★★½ (BA)   **GRADE SCHOOL** ★★★½ (A)   **TEENS** ★★★★ (AA)
YOUNG ADULTS ★★★★ (AA)   **OVER 30** ★★★★ (AA)   **OVER 65** ★★★★ (AA)

A HODGEPODGE OF PERIOD ARCHITECTURE attempts to depict Britain's urban and rural sides. One street has a thatched-roof cottage, a four-story Tudor half-timber building, a pre-Georgian plaster building, a formal Palladian facade of dressed stone, and a city square with a Hyde Park bandstand (whew!). The pavilion consists mostly of shops. The **Rose & Crown Pub** and **Rose & Crown Dining Room** offer dining on the water side of the promenade. For fish and chips to go, try **Yorkshire County Fish Shop.** Reservations aren't required for the Rose & Crown Pub, making it a nice place to stop for a beer.

There are no attractions here. We prefer to visit when the house band plays sets of British rock classics, generally between 3 and 8 p.m. daily.

CANADA PAVILION

PRESCHOOL ★★½ (MBA)   **GRADE SCHOOL** ★★★ (MBA)   **TEENS** ★★★ (BA)
YOUNG ADULTS ★★★½ (BA)   **OVER 30** ★★★★ (BA)   **OVER 65** ★★★★ (BA)

THE DIVERSITY OF CANADA—cultural, natural, and architectural—is reflected in this large, impressive pavilion. Thirty-foot-tall totem poles embellish a native village at the foot of a replica of a magnificent château-style hotel. **Le Cellier Steakhouse** is on Canada's lower level (see page 250 for our review).

Canada Far and Wide   ★★★

PRESCHOOL ★★½ (MBA)   **GRADE SCHOOL** ★★★ (MBA)   **TEENS** ★★★ (MBA)
YOUNG ADULTS ★★★½ (MBA)   **OVER 30** ★★★½ (BA)   **OVER 65** ★★★½ (BA)

What it is Film essay on Canada and its people. **Scope and scale** Minor attraction. **When to go** Anytime. **Comment** Audience stands for the show. **Duration** About 14 minutes. **Probable waiting time** Less than one show. **ECV/wheelchair access** May remain in wheelchair. **Participates in Genie+** No. **Early Theme Park Entry** No. **Extended Evening Hours** No.

DESCRIPTION AND COMMENTS *Canada Far and Wide* combines all of the visual majesty that you'd want in a 360-degree film, with a fast, modern script that works its way from one end of the country to the other. Montreal, Calgary, and Vancouver get their own segments. The film has additional clips of Canada's capital, Ottawa, and specifically mentions its three territories—Yukon, Northwest Territories, and Nunavut—and highlights their Indigenous Peoples and cultures.

EPCOT ENTERTAINMENT

LIVE ENTERTAINMENT IN EPCOT is incredibly diverse. In World Showcase, it reflects the nations represented. Future World provides a perfect setting for new and experimental offerings. Offerings on the day you visit can be found in the EPCOT guide map, often supplemented by a *Times Guide*. WDW live-entertainment expert Steve Soares usually posts EPCOT's performance schedule about a week in advance at wdwent.com. Here are some of the venues, performers, and performances you'll encounter:

AMERICA GARDENS THEATRE This large amphitheater, near The American Adventure Pavilion, faces World Showcase Lagoon. It hosts pop and oldies musical acts throughout much of the year, EPCOT's popular **Candlelight Processional** for the Christmas holidays, and sometimes **Voices of Liberty.** The special concerts hosted here are some of the top-rated entertainment acts in the park.

AROUND WORLD SHOWCASE Scheduled performances take place in and around the pavilions. Among the acts are a strolling mariachi group in Mexico (**Mariachi Cobre**); a juggler in Italy (**Sergio**); a singing group (**Voices of Liberty**) at The American Adventure Pavilion; traditional songs, drums, and dances (**Matsuriza**) in Japan; more traditional music in Morocco and the UK pub; and a band in Canada. Performances occur about every half hour.

FUTURE WORLD The **JAMMitors,** a crew of drumming janitors, work near the front entrance and around the rest of Future World, according to the daily entertainment schedule.

Luminous ★★★½

PRESCHOOL ★★★★ (MAA)	GRADE SCHOOL ★★★★ (MAA)	TEENS ★★★★ (AA)
YOUNG ADULTS ★★½ (A)	OVER 30 ★★★★ (A)	OVER 65 ★★★★ (A)

DESCRIPTION AND COMMENTS *Luminous* is Disney's attempt at a new classic nighttime show at EPCOT, following the ill-fated *Harmonious* and temporary *EPCOT Forever.*

Luminous tells the story of various stages of life, set to music—some original, but mostly songs from Disney and Pixar films. The show doesn't skimp on pyrotechnics or light and water features. But telling the story of a life obviously involves a lot of growing, learning, and heartbreak. All of these are captured in songs like "You'll Be in My Heart" from *Tarzan,* "When She Loved Me" from *Toy Story 2,* "Remember Me" from *Coco,* and "So Close" from *Enchanted.* If you're familiar with those movies and their soundtracks, you know those are all slow numbers—good for tugging at the heartstrings, not great for a rousing fireworks spectacular. I personally prefer the light and music shows at Spaceship Earth after dark for a better balance of emotional and uplifting vibes.

TOURING TIPS Fireworks dining packages let you see the show at the **Rose & Crown Dining Room** in the United Kingdom ($89 per adult, $39 per child) or **Spice Road Table** in Morocco ($79 per adult, $29 per child). Check-in starts 45 minutes before the show begins, meaning your meal should end around the same time the show ends. Otherwise, you can get a decent view of the show from anywhere around the lagoon. Spots fill up on the northern end (between Canada and Mexico) long before they do on the southern side.

VIEWING AND EXIT STRATEGIES FOR EPCOT'S FIREWORKS

AS NOTED ABOVE, EPCOT debuted a new fireworks show called *Luminous* in late 2023. One of *Harmonious*' many flaws was that it couldn't be viewed properly from anywhere except two spots around World Showcase Lagoon. In contrast, *Luminous* has at least decent views from all around the lagoon.

The best viewing location for fireworks is in **Showcase Plaza**—the area where Future World meets World Showcase—between the Disney Traders and Port of Entry shops.

The best place for viewing fireworks on the south side of World Showcase Lagoon is around Japan. Come early—at least 60 minutes before the show during busy seasons—and relax with a cold drink or a snack while you wait for the show.

La Hacienda de San Angel in Mexico, **Rose & Crown Pub** in the United Kingdom, and **Spice Road Table** in Morocco also offer lagoon views. The views at Spice Road Table are better than those at the other restaurants. If you want to combine dinner at these sit-down locations with viewing the show, make a reservation for about 1 hour and 15 minutes before showtime. Report a few minutes early for your seating, and tell the host that you want a table outside where you can watch the show. Our experience is that the staff will do their very best to accommodate you.

Because most guests run for the exits after a presentation and islands in the southern (American Adventure) half of the lagoon block the view from some places, the most popular spectator positions are along the **northern waterfront,** from Norway and Mexico to Canada and the UK. Although this half of the lagoon offers good views, you usually must claim a spot 60–90 minutes before the show begins.

For those who are late finishing dinner or don't want to spend an hour or more standing by a rail, here are some good viewing spots along the **southern perimeter** (moving counterclockwise from the United Kingdom to Germany) that often go unnoticed until 10–30 minutes before showtime:

1. **International Gateway Island.** The pedestrian bridge across the canal near the International Gateway spans an island that offers great viewing. This island normally fills 30 minutes or more before showtime.

2. **Second-floor (restaurant-level) deck of the Mitsukoshi building in Japan.** A Torii gate slightly blocks your sight line, but this covered deck offers a great vantage point,

especially if the weather is iffy. If you take up a position on the Mitsukoshi deck and find the wind blowing directly at you, you can be reasonably sure that the smoke from the fireworks won't be far behind. May be reserved by Disney for private viewings.

3. **Gondola landing at Italy.** An elaborate waterfront promenade offers decent viewing of all but the central barge. Claim a spot at least 30 minutes before showtime.

4. **Boat dock opposite Germany.** Another good vantage point, the dock generally fills 30 minutes before the show. Note that this area may be exposed to more smoke from the fireworks because of EPCOT's prevailing winds.

5. **Waterfront promenade by Germany.** Views are good from the 90-foot-long lagoonside walkway between Germany and China.

None of these viewing locations are reservable (except by Disney), and the best spots get snapped up early on busy nights. Most nights, you can still find an acceptable vantage point 15–30 minutes before the show. Don't position yourself under a tree, an awning, or anything that blocks your overhead view.

Getting Out of EPCOT After the Fireworks

EPCOT's fireworks show ends the day—when it's over, everyone leaves at once. It's important, then, to not only decide how quickly you want to flee the park after the show but also to pick a vantage point that will help you exit efficiently if a quick departure is your priority.

The **Skyliner** gondola system connects EPCOT with Disney's Hollywood Studios as well as the **Caribbean Beach, Riviera, Pop Century,** and **Art of Animation Resorts.** EPCOT's Skyliner station is just beyond the International Gateway exit. Waits can be an hour or more on busy nights. Also note that the Skyliner doesn't operate during thunderstorms or when lightning is in the area. If you want to be quick on the Skyliner ride back to your resort, watch the show from as close to the International Gateway as possible. You'll notice crowds of people starting to walk out about 5 minutes before the show ends. You can decide if you want to stay or if you want to join the exodus.

If you're staying at (or you parked at) one of the EPCOT resorts (**Swan, Dolphin, Swan Reserve, Yacht & Beach Club Resorts,** or **Board-Walk Inn & Villas**), watch the show from somewhere on the southern (American Adventure) half of World Showcase Lagoon, then leave through the **International Gateway** between France and the United Kingdom. You can walk or take a boat back to your hotel from the International Gateway.

If you're staying at any other Disney hotel and you don't have a car, the fastest way home is to join the mass exodus through **the main (Future World) entrance** and catch a bus or the monorail.

Those who've left a car parked in the EPCOT lot have a stickier situation. To beat the crowds, find a viewing spot at **the end of World Showcase Lagoon nearest Future World** (and the exits). Leave as soon as the show wraps up, trying to exit ahead of the crowd (noting that thousands of people will be doing the same thing).

More groups get separated and more kids get lost following the evening fireworks than at any other time. In summer, you'll be walking in a throng of up to 30,000 people. If you're heading for the parking lot, anticipate this congestion and pick a spot in the main EPCOT entrance area where you can meet if someone gets separated from the group.

For those with a car, the hardest part is reaching the parking lot: Once you've made it there, you're more or less home free. If you've paid close attention to where you parked, consider skipping the tram and walking. But if you do, watch your children closely and hang on to them if they're squirrelly—the parking lot can get dicey at this time of night, with hundreds of moving cars.

This Utah mom has an even quicker suggestion if you're willing to pay for transportation:

> We watched the fireworks from the bridge at the International Gateway by the United Kingdom; then we just walked straight to the BoardWalk Inn and got a ride from Lyft. It took us 10 minutes from leaving the fireworks to getting to our ride to getting dropped off at our hotel. Super convenient, and we didn't have to leave with the 30,000 people exiting EPCOT in the front of the park!

I have to say, though, if you don't have kids who have to immediately get back for bedtime, a slow post-park-closing stroll around World Showcase not only gives the transportation system time to deal with the crush of crowds and get back to normal, but it's also just about the most spectacular way to spend a night at Walt Disney World. Within 20 minutes of the end of the fireworks, you'll have entire pavilions to yourself, still beautifully lit. Minute-for-minute, it's my favorite way to spend time in any Disney park.

TRAFFIC PATTERNS *in* EPCOT

WITH REMY'S RATATOUILLE ADVENTURE, Frozen Ever After, and Test Track as the biggest rope-drop draws, crowds head for two opposite ends of EPCOT when it opens. Frozen Ever After in Norway is the second stop for many of the guests who headed to Remy first, while guests who headed to Test Track disperse among the other attractions in Future World, with Soarin' Around the World being the usual second choice.

EPCOT TOURING PLAN

TOURING EPCOT is much more strenuous than touring the other theme parks. EPCOT requires about twice as much walking and, unlike the Magic Kingdom, has no efficient in-park transportation—wherever you want to go, it's always quicker to walk. The sea of construction walls adds to the walking even more, forcing you to traipse big loops around Future World.

Our **One-Day Touring Plan** will help you avoid crowds and bottlenecks on days of moderate to heavy attendance, but it can't shorten the distance you have to cover. (Wear comfortable shoes.) On days of lighter attendance, when crowds aren't a critical factor, the touring plan will help you organize your day.

The plan packs as much as possible into one long day and requires a lot of hustle and stamina. It has two versions: one for Disney resort guests and one for off-site guests; the former uses Early Theme Park

Entry to minimize waits in line. Because Early Entry means thousands of guests will already be in lines and on rides before off-site guests set foot in the park, the touring strategy for off-site guests must be different. The plan does not assume use of Genie+ or Individual Lightning Lane. If you opt for either (or both) of these, you can use the free touring plan software to enter your return times.

To convert the one-day plan to a two-day plan, see the attractions on the east side of the park on your first day, and those on the west side on the second. Alternatively, tour Future World's attractions on one day and World Showcase's on the other. That strategy has a couple of disadvantages: One is that Future World has three headliner attractions, while World Showcase has two; the second is that World Showcase has better restaurant choices for dinner.

"Not a Touring Plan" Touring Plans

For the type-B reader, these touring plans (starting on page 546) dispense with detailed step-by-step strategies for saving every last minute in line. For EPCOT, these "not" touring plans include advice for adults and parents with one day in the park, for anyone with two days, and for anyone with an afternoon and a full day to tour.

PRELIMINARY INSTRUCTIONS FOR USING THE TOURING PLANS

BECOME FAMILIAR WITH EPCOT'S **opening procedures** (see page 407). On days of moderate to heavy attendance, follow the touring plan exactly, deviating from it only as follows:

1. **When you're not interested in an attraction in the plan.** In this case, simply skip it and proceed to the next attraction.

2. **When you encounter a very long line at an attraction.** In this case, skip to the next attraction and try again later at the one with the line.

Before You Go

1. Check disneyworld.disney.go.com or the MDE app the day before to verify the official opening time.

2. Make reservations at the EPCOT table-service restaurant(s) of your choice 60 days before your visit.

3. At 7 a.m. on the day of your visit, make Genie+ and/or Individual Lightning Lane reservations, if you bought them.

EPCOT TOURING PLAN AT A GLANCE
EPCOT One-Day Touring Plan   *(see pages 557–558)*

FOR Adults and children age 8 or older.
ASSUMES Willingness to experience all major rides and shows.

THIS PLAN INCLUDES **Frozen Ever After, Guardians of the Galaxy: Cosmic Rewind, Remy's Ratatouille Adventure, Soarin' Around the World,** and **Test Track.**

DISNEY'S ANIMAL KINGDOM

▌ OVERVIEW

WITH ITS LUSH VEGETATION, winding streams, meandering paths, and exotic settings, Animal Kingdom is stunningly beautiful. The landscaping alone transports you to rainforest, veldt, and formal gardens. Soothing, mysterious, and exciting, every vista is a feast for the eyes. Add to this loveliness a population of some 1,700 animals, replicas of Africa's and Asia's most intriguing architecture, and an impressive array of attractions, and you have Disney's most distinctive theme park.

Animal Kingdom is made up of six "lands" (**Africa, Asia, Discovery Island, DinoLand U.S.A., The Oasis,** and **Pandora—The World of Avatar**) but it offers relatively few attractions in its sprawling 500 acres: eight rides, several walk-through trails and exhibits, an indoor theater, three amphitheaters, a conservation station, and a children's playground.

unofficial **TIP**
Disney's Animal Kingdom is four times the size of the Magic Kingdom and almost twice the size of EPCOT, but most of it is accessible only on guided tours or as part of attractions.

Once upon a time, Disney's idea of animals in theme parks was limited to cartoon characters and Audio-Animatronic figures (think Jungle Cruise). But 84 miles away in Tampa, **Busch Gardens** had been slowly building on a successful combination of natural-habitat zoological exhibits and thrill rides.

continued on page 436

Disney's Animal Kingdom

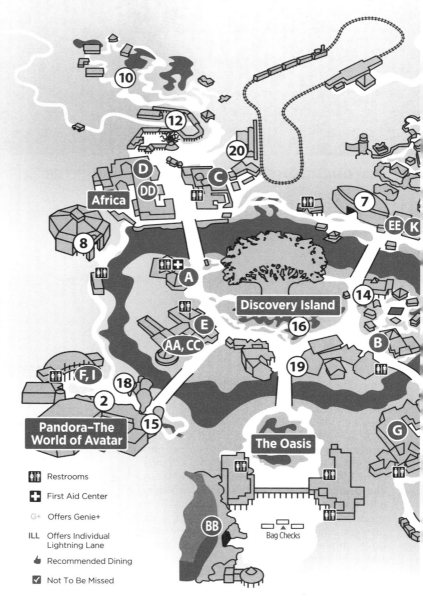

Legend:

| Restrooms |
| First Aid Center |
| G+ Offers Genie+ |
| ILL Offers Individual Lightning Lane |
| Recommended Dining |
| ✓ Not To Be Missed |

Bag Checks

Attractions

1. The Animation Experience at Conservation Station G+
2. Avatar Flight of Passage ☑ ILL
3. The Boneyard
4. Conservation Station and Affection Section
5. Dinosaur ☑ G+
6. Expedition Everest ☑ G+
7. Feathered Friends in Flight ☑ G+
8. Festival of the Lion King ☑ G+
9. Finding Nemo: The Big Blue . . . and Beyond! ☑ G+
10. Gorilla Falls Exploration Trail
11. Kali River Rapids G+
12. Kilimanjaro Safaris ☑ G+
13. Maharajah Jungle Trek
14. Meet Favorite Disney Pals at Adventurers Outpost G+
15. Na'vi River Journey ☑ G+
16. Tree of Life ☑ / Awakenings/ It's Tough to Be a Bug! G+
17. TriceraTop Spin
18. Valley of Mo'ara
19. Wilderness Explorers ☑
20. Wildlife Express Train

Rafiki's Planet Watch

Asia

DinoLand U.S.A.

Counter-Service Restaurants

A. Creature Comforts *(Starbucks)* 🍴
B. Flame Tree Barbecue 🍴
C. Harambe Market 🍴
D. Kusafiri Coffee Shop & Bakery 🍴
E. Pizzafari
F. Pongu Pongu
G. Restaurantosaurus
H. Royal Anandapur Tea Company 🍴
I. Satu'li Canteen 🍴
J. Thirsty River Bar & Trek Snacks
K. Yak & Yeti Local Food Cafes 🍴

Table-Service Restaurants

AA. Nomad Lounge
BB. Rainforest Cafe
CC. Tiffins 🍴
DD. Tusker House Restaurant 🍴
EE. Yak & Yeti Restaurant 🍴

ANIMAL KINGDOM SERVICES

MOST PARK SERVICES are inside the main entrance and on Discovery Island, including:

ATMs At the main entrance, by the tapstiles, and near Dinosaur in DinoLand U.S.A.	
Baby Care Center On Discovery Island	
Cell Phone Charging Outlets available at Pizzafari, Restaurantosaurus, Tusker House, and Conservation Station	
Entertainment Information In the *Times Guide,* available at Guest Relations	
First Aid Center On Discovery Island	
Guest Relations/Information Inside the main entrance, to the left	
Lost and Found Inside the main entrance, to the left	
Lost Persons Can be reported at Guest Relations and the Baby Care Center	
MagicBands Just inside the main entrance, at Garden Gate Gifts; in Africa at Mombasa Marketplace; and at other retail shops throughout the park	
Storage Lockers Inside the main entrance to the left	
Wheelchair, ECV (Scooter), and Stroller Rentals Inside the main entrance, to the right	

continued from page 433

There's nothing like competition to make Disney innovate and evolve. Disney announced its plans for Animal Kingdom in 1995, and the park opened in 1998 (that's less time than it took to build Tron Lightcycle/Run, but I digress).

Animal Kingdom is different than any other theme park, Disney or not. For starters, there's lots of space, allowing for sweeping vistas worthy of *National Geographic* or the Discovery Channel. And there are the enclosures—natural in appearance, with few or no apparent barriers between you and the animals. The operative word, of course, is *apparent:* That flimsy stand of bamboo separating you from a gorilla is actually a neatly disguised set of steel rods embedded in concrete.

Animal Kingdom gets mixed reviews from readers. The animal exhibits, along with the architecture and the landscaping, consistently draw praise, but guests also complain about the park's layout, as well as its congested walkways and lack of shade.

In spite of its weaknesses, Animal Kingdom works. It's a place to linger in, to explore. Of course, Disney, with its crowds, lines, and regimentation, has conditioned guests to do just the opposite of that; nevertheless, many visitors understand instinctively that Animal Kingdom must be approached differently.

A mother of three (ages 5, 7, and 9) from New York writes:

> *To enjoy Animal Kingdom, you must have the right attitude. It's an educational experience, not a thrill park. We spoke to a cast member who played games with the kids—my daughter found a drawer full of butterflies, and the boys located a hidden ostrich egg and lion skull.*

We agree: Animal Kingdom's best features are its animals, nature trails, and cast members. The **Wilderness Explorers** scavenger hunt (see page 445) ties together all of the park's best elements, and it's part of our Animal Kingdom touring plan, described on page 457. It's a lot of fun to play, and you're sure to learn something along the way.

Pandora—The World of Avatar is Animal Kingdom's newest land, themed to the James Cameron films. Pandora has two attractions: **Avatar Flight of Passage,** a state-of-the-art flight simulator, and **Na'vi River Journey,** a slow-moving boat ride through colorful forests and swamps. Readers rate Flight of Passage as one of the best attractions at any theme park in the United States.

unofficial **TIP**
If you want to beat the lines in Pandora, arrive well before opening or wait until the last hour the park is open.

ARRIVING

FROM INSIDE WALT DISNEY WORLD, Disney buses are the only free option for getting to Animal Kingdom from on-property resorts, but service from many resorts can be erratic.

DRIVING Animal Kingdom is in the southwest corner of Walt Disney World; from I-4, take **Exit 65** for Osceola Parkway. (For GPS address, see page 345.) **Animal Kingdom Lodge** is about a mile from the park on its west side; **Blizzard Beach** water park, **Coronado Springs Resort,** and the **All-Star Resorts** are also in the vicinity.

Animal Kingdom has its own vast paid parking lot with closer parking for guests with disabilities. Disney usually opens the parking lot about 60–75 minutes before official park opening. Once parked, you can walk or catch a tram to the entrance.

ANIMAL KINGDOM OPENING PROCEDURES (ROPE DROP)

ANIMAL KINGDOM is usually the first Disney World park to open in the morning and the first to close. Expect it to open at 8 a.m. daily, and possibly earlier during holidays and other times of peak attendance.

Disney resort guests eligible for Early Theme Park Entry should arrive at the entrance 60 minutes before official opening (30 minutes before Early Entry). Off-site guests who are not eligible for Early Entry should arrive 30 minutes before official opening.

unofficial **TIP**
To confirm the official park-opening time, check online the night before you go. To stay abreast of ride closures, delays, and the like, also check the daily *Times Guide,* the My Disney Experience app, or the **Lines** app.

Once you're in the park, you'll usually find all of Pandora, along with *It's Tough to be a Bug!,* **Expedition Everest, Dinosaur,** and **Tricera-Top Spin,** already open.

Avatar Flight of Passage remains among the hottest tickets in all of Walt Disney World. As a result, Animal Kingdom adjusts its opening procedures based on crowd levels, catching some guests by surprise. Here's what an Indiana reader experienced while trying to beat the morning crush:

unofficial **TIP**
During summer and holidays, your best chance to avoid a long wait in line at Avatar Flight of Passage (without paying for Individual Lightning Lane) is to stay at a Disney hotel and arrive at the Animal Kingdom entrance 1 hour before official opening.

> *We arrived at 7:20 expecting to be in the crowd for rope drop [for 7:30 a.m. Early Entry], but the crowd had already been admitted and we immediately had a 90-minute wait—before 7:40 a.m.—for Avatar Flight of Passage.*

ANIMAL KINGDOM MOST POPULAR ATTRACTIONS BY AGE GROUP

PRESCHOOL	GRADE SCHOOL	TEENS	YOUNG ADULTS	OVER 30	OVER 65
The Boneyard	Avatar Flight of Passage	Avatar Flight of Passage	Avatar Flight of Passage	Avatar Flight of Passage	Kilimanjaro Safaris
Meet Favorite Disney Pals at Adventurers Outpost	Kilimanjaro Safaris	Expedition Everest	Expedition Everest	Kora Tinga Tinga	*Festival of the Lion King*
Kilimanjaro Safaris	*Festival of the Lion King*	Kilimanjaro Safaris	Kilimanjaro Safaris	Expedition Everest	Avatar Flight of Passage
Festival of the Lion King	Expedition Everest	*Festival of the Lion King*	African Village Band	Kilimanjaro Safaris	Expedition Everest
Finding Nemo: The Big Blue . . . and Beyond	The Boneyard	The Animation Experience	*Festival of the Lion King*	*Festival of the Lion King*	Tam Tam Drummers of Harambe
TriceraTop Spin	*Feathered Friends in Flight*	Tree of Life/ *Awakenings*	*Winged Encounters— The Kingdom Takes Flight*	DiVine	DiVine
Wilderness Explorers	Wilderness Explorers	*Feathered Friends in Flight*	*Feathered Friends in Flight*	Harambe Village Acrobats	Harambe Village Acrobats
Tam Tam Drummers of Harambe	Meet Favorite Disney Pals at Adventurers Outpost	Tam Tam Drummers of Harambe	Tree of Life/ *Awakenings*	Tam Tam Drummers of Harambe	African Village Band
Affection Station	*Finding Nemo: The Big Blue . . . and Beyond*	Kali River Rapids	Wilderness Explorers	*Winged Encounters— The Kingdom Takes Flight*	*Winged Encounters— The Kingdom Takes Flight*
Maharajah Jungle Trek	Kali River Rapids	Gorilla Falls Exploration Trail	Gorilla Falls Exploration Trail	African Village Band	*Feathered Friends in Flight*

Because the park has relatively few attractions, most guests who arrive at park opening have left by midafternoon, leading to shorter waits in the late afternoon and evening. However, the lack of attractions also results in long waits in the middle of the day during busy holidays.

During slower or colder periods, the park may delay opening its secondary attractions: **Kali River Rapids** and **Maharajah Jungle Trek** in Asia, as well as **The Boneyard** in DinoLand U.S.A. The **Wildlife Express Train** and **Conservation Station** may either open late or remain closed for the day.

GETTING ORIENTED

AT THE ENTRANCE PLAZA, the security checkpoint and ticket kiosks are in front of the main entrance. After you pass through the tapstiles, **wheelchair and stroller rentals** are to your right. **Guest Relations** is to the left. Nearby are **restrooms and lockers.** Beyond the entrance plaza, you enter **The Oasis,** a network of converging pathways winding through a landscape punctuated with streams, waterfalls, and misty glades and inhabited by what Disney calls "colorful and unusual animals."

Animal Kingdom is arranged somewhat like the Magic Kingdom, in a hub-and-spoke configuration. Similar to Main Street, U.S.A.,

NOT TO BE MISSED IN ANIMAL KINGDOM
AFRICA • *Festival of the Lion King* • Kilimanjaro Safaris
ASIA • Expedition Everest • *Feathered Friends in Flight*
DINOLAND U.S.A. • Dinosaur • *Finding Nemo: The Big Blue . . . and Beyond!*
DISCOVERY ISLAND • Tree of Life/*Awakenings* • Wilderness Explorers
PANDORA—THE WORLD OF AVATAR • Avatar Flight of Passage

GENIE+ AND INDIVIDUAL LIGHTNING LANE (ILL) SELECTIONS IN ANIMAL KINGDOM
AFRICA • Kilimanjaro Safaris • The Animation Experience at Conservation Station • *Festival of the Lion King*
ASIA • Expedition Everest • *Feathered Friends in Flight* • Kali River Rapids
DINOLAND U.S.A. • Dinosaur • *Finding Nemo: The Big Blue . . . and Beyond!*
DISCOVERY ISLAND • *It's Tough to Be a Bug!* • Meet Favorite Disney Pals at Adventurers Outpost
PANDORA—THE WORLD OF AVATAR • Avatar Flight of Passage (*ILL*) • Na'vi River Journey

ESTIMATED TIME SAVINGS USING GENIE+ BY CROWD LEVEL			
CROWD LEVEL	**TYPICAL USE (2 GENIE+ RESERVATIONS PER DAY)**	**OPTIMISTIC USE (4 GENIE+ RESERVATIONS PER DAY)**	**PERFECT USE (6 GENIE+ RESERVATIONS PER DAY)**
LOW	25 minutes	40 minutes	50 minutes
MODERATE	50 minutes	75 minutes	90 minutes
HIGH	60 minutes	90 minutes	120 minutes

The Oasis funnels visitors to **Discovery Island.** Dominated by the park's central icon—the 14-story hand-carved **Tree of Life**—Discovery Island is the park's retail and dining center. From here, guests fan out to access the themed areas: **Africa, Asia, DinoLand U.S.A.,** and **Pandora.** Discovery Island also hosts a theater attraction in the Tree of Life, along with several short nature trails. You should be able to take in all of Animal Kingdom in one day—but we implore you to take your time.

FAVORITE ATTRACTIONS BY AGE GROUP

ANIMAL KINGDOM HAS about two dozen rides, shows, performers, and seasonal entertainment. The table on the opposite page shows the most popular attractions in the park by age group. All groups except preschoolers and adults over 65 put **Avatar Flight of Passage** first, and all but preschoolers include **Kilimanjaro Safaris** and **Expedition Everest** in their top attractions. Every age group's list includes at least one animal-centered attraction.

The average reader ratings for all Animal Kingdom attractions by age group are as follows, based on the 41,000 attraction ratings we received over the past year:

PRESCHOOL	GRADE SCHOOL	TEENS	YOUNG ADULTS	OVER 30	OVER 65
4.1 stars	4.2 stars	4.2 stars	4.3 stars	4.2 stars	4.3 stars

GENIE+, INDIVIDUAL LIGHTNING LANE, AND THE TOURING PLANS

N O T E : See page 49 for detailed information and strategy suggestions for Genie+ and Individual Lightning Lane. The big questions we're trying to answer are:

1. Is Genie+ worth paying for in Animal Kingdom?
2. Which attractions benefit most from Genie+ and Individual Lightning Lane?
3. How can you avoid paying for Individual Lightning Lane?
4. How do Genie+ and Individual Lightning Lane work with the touring plans?

Is Genie+ Worth Paying For in Animal Kingdom?

We think Genie+ is rarely worth the cost at Animal Kingdom because of the limited options and the ability to avoid significant waits in other ways. That being said, you should at least consider purchasing it if you meet any of these criteria:

- You won't be at the park for Early Entry. This includes off-site guests who aren't eligible for Early Theme Park Entry and on-site guests who want to sleep in.
- You're visiting during a peak season and don't want to use a touring plan.

Regardless of the time of year you visit, arriving at park opening should allow you to see at least two headliner attractions without significant waits. Since only 11 Animal Kingdom attractions participate in Genie+, it's unlikely you'd actually need more than three or four reservations per day. On days of heavy attendance, though, the lack of attractions means you'll be competing with lots of people, which pushes out return times and limits how many you can obtain. On the previous page, we break down how much time we think you can save using Genie+ with a touring plan, based on different assumptions about how many reservations it's possible to obtain in a day. See page 370 for more on the different usage levels.

Which Attractions Benefit Most from Genie+ and Individual Lightning Lane?

The table below shows the top attractions that benefit most from using Genie+ and Individual Lightning Lane, based on historical wait times over the past year.

ANIMAL KINGDOM ATTRACTIONS THAT BENEFIT MOST FROM GENIE+ AND INDIVIDUAL LIGHTNING LANE (ILL) *(Highest Priority to Lowest)*	
ATTRACTION	**AVERAGE TIME IN LINE SAVED (IN MINUTES)**
AVATAR FLIGHT OF PASSAGE (ILL)	58
NA'VI RIVER JOURNEY	39
KILIMANJARO SAFARIS	36
KALI RIVER RAPIDS	25
EXPEDITION EVEREST	23
MEET FAVORITE DISNEY PALS AT ADVENTURERS OUTPOST	15
DINOSAUR	11

Note: We haven't observed any time savings using Genie+ at the Animal Kingdom's live shows, *It's Tough to Be a Bug!,* or The Animation Experience at Conservation Station.

Regarding Individual Lightning Lane, we think Avatar Flight of Passage is worth the cost at almost any time of year, unless you can arrive at the park around 20 minutes before Early Entry or you're staying at Animal Kingdom into the evening.

As for Genie+, it seems to be useful at only a handful of attractions, most notably Na'vi River Journey and Kilimanjaro Safaris. These two should be your priorities if you're using Genie+ here. But really, there is almost no reason to purchase Genie+ for Animal Kingdom unless you're traveling at the busiest time of year.

When Do Genie+ and Individual Lightning Lane Reservations Run Out in Animal Kingdom?

The table below shows the approximate time at which Animal Kingdom's attractions run out of Genie+ or Individual Lightning Lane capacity, by crowd level. Use this table in conjunction with the "Attractions That Benefit Most" table, on the opposite page, to determine which reservations to get first.

WHEN GENIE+ AND INDIVIDUAL LIGHTNING LANE (ILL) RESERVATIONS RUN OUT BY ATTENDANCE LEVEL*			
ATTRACTION	LOW ATTENDANCE	MODERATE ATTENDANCE	HIGH ATTENDANCE
THE ANIMATION EXPERIENCE AT CONSERVATION STATION	4 p.m.	4 p.m.	3 p.m.
AVATAR FLIGHT OF PASSAGE (ILL)	2 p.m.	10 a.m.	8 a.m.
FESTIVAL OF THE LION KING	5 p.m.	5 p.m.	3 p.m.
DINOSAUR	7 p.m.	6 p.m.	4 p.m.
EXPEDITION EVEREST	5 p.m.	5 p.m.	3 p.m.
FEATHERED FRIENDS IN FLIGHT	3 p.m.	3 p.m.	3 p.m.
IT'S TOUGH TO BE A BUG!	7 p.m.	7 p.m.	7 p.m.
KALI RIVER RAPIDS	6 p.m.	6 p.m.	5 p.m.
KILIMANJARO SAFARIS	5 p.m.	5 p.m.	2 p.m.
NA'VI RIVER JOURNEY	6 p.m.	5 p.m.	1 p.m.

*Information is applicable until July 24, 2024.
LOW ATTENDANCE Crowd levels 1–3 on the TouringPlans crowd calendar
MODERATE ATTENDANCE Crowd levels 4–7   HIGH ATTENDANCE Crowd levels 8–10

How Can You Avoid Paying for Individual Lightning Lane?

Animal Kingdom doesn't regularly participate in Disney's Extended Evening Theme Park Hours program (it did on just four dates in late 2023, and the park was empty for those), so your best option to see Flight of Passage is to stay at a Disney resort and use Early Theme Park Entry: Head to Flight of Passage as soon as the park opens. Otherwise, wait until as late in the evening as possible, when most people have left for other parks or their resorts.

How Do Genie+ and Individual Lightning Lane Work with the Touring Plans?

See our advice on page 372.

DINING IN ANIMAL KINGDOM

HERE'S A QUICK RECAP of Animal Kingdom's top restaurants, rated by readers, starting with the highest rated. See Part 6 for details.

ANIMAL KINGDOM RESTAURANT REFRESHER	
COUNTER SERVICE	
Satu'li Canteen (⊕ 97%/E), Pandora	**Kusafiri Coffee Shop and Bakery** (⊕ 93%/AA), Africa
Creature Comforts (Starbucks) (⊕ 95%/MAA), Discovery island	**Yak & Yeti Local Food Cafes** (⊕ 93%/AA), Asia
Harambe Market (⊕ 95%/MAA), Africa	
Flame Tree Barbecue (⊕ 94%/MAA), Discovery Island	
TABLE SERVICE	
Yak & Yeti Restaurant (⊕ 94%/MAA), Asia	**Tusker House Restaurant** (⊕ 89%/AA), Africa
Tiffins (⊕ 91%/AA), Discovery Island	

Restaurants not shown are rated average or below. See opposite page for key to abbreviations.

The OASIS

THOUGH THE FUNCTION OF THE OASIS is the same as that of Magic Kingdom's Main Street—to direct guests to the center of the park—it also serves as what Disney calls a transitional experience, meaning it sets the stage and gets you in the right mood for enjoying Animal Kingdom. The minute you pass through the tapstiles, however, you'll know that this isn't just another central hub.

Rather than consisting of a single broad thoroughfare, The Oasis has multiple paths. Whereas Main Street and Hollywood Boulevard at the Studios direct you like an arrow straight into the heart of their respective parks, The Oasis immediately envelops you in an environment filled with choices. Nothing obvious hints at where you're going. Instead, you'll find a lush, green, canopied landscape dotted with streams, grottoes, and waterfalls.

The zoological exhibits in The Oasis are representative of those throughout Animal Kingdom. A sign identifies the animal(s) in each exhibit, but be aware that there's no guarantee they'll be immediately visible. Because most of the habitats are large and provide their occupants ample places to hide, you must linger and concentrate, looking for small movements in the vegetation. When you do spot the animal, you may make out only a shadowy figure, or perhaps only a leg or a tail.

The Oasis is a place to explore and appreciate—if you're used to blitzing at warp speed to queue up for the big attractions, plan to spend some time here, on your way into or out of the park. The Oasis usually closes 30–60 minutes after the rest of Animal Kingdom.

DISCOVERY ISLAND

DISCOVERY ISLAND COMBINES TROPICAL GREENERY with whimsical equatorial African architecture. Connected to the other lands by bridges, the island is the hub from which guests can access the park's various themed areas. A village is arrayed in a crescent around the base of Animal Kingdom's iconic landmark, the **Tree of Life**. Towering 14 stories above the village, it's flanked by pools, meadows, and exotic gardens populated by a diversity of birds and animals. It also houses a 4D theater attraction inspired by Disney/Pixar's *A Bug's Life*.

As you enter Discovery Island over the bridge from The Oasis and the park entrance, you'll see the Tree of Life directly ahead, at 12 o'clock. The bridge to **Asia** is to the right at 2 o'clock, with the bridge to **DinoLand U.S.A.** at roughly 4 o'clock. The bridge connecting The Oasis to Discovery Island is at 6 o'clock, the bridge to **Pandora—The World of Avatar** is at 8 o'clock, and the bridge to **Africa** is at 11 o'clock.

Discovery Island is also the park's central headquarters for shopping and services. Here you'll find the **First Aid** and **Baby Care Centers**. For Disney merchandise, try **Island Mercantile**. Counter-service food and snacks are available, as is upscale table-service dining at **Tiffins**.

KEY TO ABBREVIATIONS In the attraction profiles that follow, each star rating is accompanied by a category label in parentheses (see page 368 for details). E means **Exceptional**, MAA means **Much Above Average**, AA means **Above Average**, A means **Average**, BA means **Below Average**, and MBA means **Much Below Average**.

Discovery Island Trails ★★★

| PRESCHOOL ★★★★ (A) | GRADE SCHOOL ★★★★ (BA) | TEENS ★★★★ (A) |
| YOUNG ADULTS ★★★★ (BA) | OVER 30 ★★★★ (A) | OVER 65 ★★★★ (A) |

What it is Scenic walking trails. **Scope and scale** Diversion. **When to go** Anytime. **ECV/wheelchair access** May remain in wheelchair. **Participates in Genie+** No. **Early Theme Park Entry** Yes. **Extended Evening Hours** No.

DESCRIPTION AND COMMENTS A network of walking trails wind around and behind the tree, with around a dozen animal-viewing opportunities, from otters and tortoises to lemurs, storks, and porcupines. One end of the path begins just before the bridge from Discovery Island to Africa, on the right side of the walkway; the other is to the right of the entrance to the Tree of Life. In addition to the animals, you'll find verdant landscaping, waterfalls, and quiet spots to sit and reflect. Or play "I spy" using all of the animals—both real and carved—as subjects.

Meet Favorite Disney Pals at Adventurers Outpost   ★★★½

| PRESCHOOL ★★★★★ (E) | GRADE SCHOOL ★★★★½ (AA) | TEENS ★★★½ (BA) |
| YOUNG ADULTS ★★★★ (BA) | OVER 30 ★★★★ (A) | OVER 65 ★★★★ (A) |

What it is Character-greeting venue. **Scope and scale** Minor attraction. **When to go** First thing in the morning or after 5 p.m. **Duration** About 2 minutes. **Probable waiting time** About 25 minutes. **Queue speed** Moderate. **ECV/wheelchair access** May remain in wheelchair. **Participates in Genie+** Yes. **Early Theme Park Entry** No. **Extended Evening Hours** No.

DESCRIPTION AND COMMENTS This air-conditioned greeting location for Mickey and Minnie is decorated with photos and other memorabilia from the Mouses' world travels. The Outpost has two greeting rooms with two identical sets of characters in cute safari gear.

TREE OF LIFE

THE TREE OF LIFE, APART FROM ITS SIZE, IS A WORK OF ART—the most visually compelling structure in any Disney theme park. Although it's magnificent from afar, it's not until you get up close that you can truly appreciate the tree's rich detail. What appears from a distance to be ancient, gnarled bark is, in fact, hundreds of carvings depicting all manner of wildlife, each integrated seamlessly into the tree's trunk, roots, and limbs. Look for these carvings on the front left side of the tree, along the Discovery Island walkway to Africa. We find new animals every time we visit.

It's Tough to Be a Bug! ★★½

PRESCHOOL ★★★ (MBA)	GRADE SCHOOL ★★★½ (BA)	TEENS ★★★½ (BA)
YOUNG ADULTS ★★★★ (BA)	OVER 30 ★★★½ (BA)	OVER 65 ★★★★ (BA)

What it is 4D theater show. **Scope and scale** Minor attraction. **When to go** Anytime. **Duration** About 8 minutes. **Probable waiting time** Less than one show. **ECV/wheelchair access** May remain in wheelchair. **Participates in Genie+** Yes. **Early Theme Park Entry** Yes. **Extended Evening Hours** No.

DESCRIPTION AND COMMENTS In sharp contrast to the grandeur of the tree itself is the attraction housed within its trunk. This 4D presentation is somehow simultaneously humorous and frightening, as it presents the difficulties of being small and creepy-crawly. The show is similar to *Mickey's PhilharMagic* in the Magic Kingdom in that it combines a 3D film with an arsenal of tactile and visual special effects. Beware: *It's Tough to Be a Bug!* can do a number on anybody, young or old, who's squeamish about insects. A mom of two from New York shared this experience:

It's Tough to Be a Bug! was my girls' first Disney experience, and almost their last. The storyline was difficult to follow—all they were aware of was the torture of sitting in a darkened theater being overrun with bugs. A constant stream of parents headed to the exits with terrorized children. Those who were left behind were screaming and crying as well. The 11-year-old refused to talk for 20 minutes after the fiasco, and the 3½-year-old wanted to go home. Not back to the hotel, but home.

TOURING TIPS *It's Tough to Be a Bug!* is rarely crowded even on the busiest days. Go in the morning after the Pandora attractions, Kilimanjaro Safaris, Kali River Rapids, Expedition Everest, and Dinosaur. Or skip it for a nap—every age group rates it as below average.

Awakenings ★★★½

PRESCHOOL ★★★★ (A)	GRADE SCHOOL ★★★★ (A)	TEENS ★★★½ (AA)
YOUNG ADULTS ★★★★½ (AA)	OVER 30 ★★★★½ (A)	OVER 65 ★★★★½ (AA)

What it is Nighttime projection show. **Scope and scale** Minor attraction. **When to go** Anytime. **Duration** 3 minutes. **ECV/wheelchair access** May remain in wheelchair. **Participates in Genie+** No. **Early Theme Park Entry** Yes. **Extended Evening Hours** Yes (when they're offered).

DESCRIPTION AND COMMENTS The Tree of Life also hosts *Awakenings,* a child-friendly nighttime show projected onto the tree's trunk and canopy. Shown several times a night (when the park is open after dark), *Awakenings* combines digital video projections with music and special effects. Several shows rotate; in each, special projection effects make it appear that some animals carved into the tree trunk have come alive. Other special effects happen in the leaves and branches. We rate *Awakenings* as not to be missed if you're in the park after dark.

TOURING TIPS The best viewing spots are directly in front of the tree on Discovery Island, across from Island Mercantile.

Wilderness Explorers ★★★★

PRESCHOOL ★★★★½ (AA)	GRADE SCHOOL ★★★★½ (AA)	TEENS ★★★½ (BA)
YOUNG ADULTS ★★★★½ (AA)	OVER 30 ★★★★ (A)	OVER 65 ★★★½ (MBA)

What it is Parkwide educational scavenger hunt. **Scope and scale** Diversion. **When to go** Sign up in the morning and complete activities throughout the day. **ECV/wheelchair access** May remain in wheelchair. **Participates in Genie+** No. **Early Theme Park Entry** No. **Extended Evening Hours** No.

DESCRIPTION AND COMMENTS Walt Disney World offers several interactive games in its theme parks, and Wilderness Explorers is the best one—an educational and fun scavenger hunt based on Russell's Scout-like troop from the movie *Up*. Players earn "badges" (stickers given out by cast members) for completing predefined activities throughout the park. For example, to earn the Gorilla Badge, you might walk the Gorilla Falls Exploration Trail to observe how the primates behave, then mimic that behavior back to a cast member to show what you've seen.

Sign up near the bridge from The Oasis to Discovery Island or at other stations throughout the park as you come across them. You'll be given an instruction book and a map showing the park location for each badge to be earned.

Cast members have been specially trained for this game and can tailor the activities based on the age of the child playing: Small children might get an explanation about what deforestation means, for example, while older kids may have to figure out why tigers have stripes. It's tons of fun for kids and adults, and we participate every time we're in the park.

The program is a big hit with kids, as an Australian mom relates:

Wilderness Explorers was the highlight of my son's day. Much time is spent collecting badges, but it is well worth the investment of time!

TOURING TIPS Activities are spread throughout the park, including areas to which many guests never venture.

▌■ AFRICA

THE LARGEST OF ANIMAL KINGDOM'S LANDS, Africa is entered through **Harambe,** a Disneyfied take on a modern rural African town. A market is equipped with modern cash registers, and dining options consist of a sit-down buffet, a few counter-service options, and snack stands. What distinguishes Harambe is its understatement: The buildings, while interesting, are architecturally simple. Though better maintained and more idealized than the real thing, Disney's Harambe would be a lot more at home in Kenya than the Magic Kingdom's Main Street would be in Missouri.

Harambe serves as the gateway to Animal Kingdom's largest and most ambitious environment: the African veldt habitat. Guests access the veldt via the **Kilimanjaro Safaris** attraction, at the end of Harambe's main drag near the fat-trunked baobab tree. Harambe is also the departure point for the train to **Rafiki's Planet Watch** and

Conservation Station (the park's veterinary headquarters), and is the home of *Festival of the Lion King,* a popular and long-running live show. A walkway by the theater connects Africa with Pandora.

Festival of the Lion King ★★★★

PRESCHOOL ★★★★½ (MAA)   GRADE SCHOOL ★★★★½ (E)   TEENS ★★★★ (MAA)
YOUNG ADULTS ★★★★½ (MAA)   OVER 30 ★★★★½ (MAA)   OVER 65 ★★★★★ (E)

What it is Theater-in-the-round stage show. **Scope and scale** Major attraction. **When to go** Earlier or later showtimes. **Duration** 30 minutes. **Comment** Arrive 15–20 minutes before showtime. **ECV/wheelchair access** May remain in wheelchair. **Participates in Genie+** Yes. **Early Theme Park Entry** No. **Extended Evening Hours** No.

DESCRIPTION AND COMMENTS Inspired by Disney's 1994 animated feature *The Lion King, Festival of the Lion King* is part stage show and part parade. Guests sit in four sets of bleachers surrounding the stage and organized into cheering sections that are called on to make elephant, warthog, giraffe, and lion noises. (You won't be alone if you don't know what a giraffe sounds like.) There's a great deal of strutting around and a lot of singing and dancing. By my count, every tune from *The Lion King* is belted out—some more than once. Kids will adore being involved in the action, and parents might get teary-eyed watching them participate in the magic (not that I know from experience).

Unofficial Guide readers are almost unanimous in their praise of the show. This take from a Florida mom is typical:

> Festival of the Lion King *was the best thing we experienced at Animal Kingdom. The singers, dancers, fire twirlers, acrobats, and sets were spectacular.*

TOURING TIPS *Festival of the Lion King* is a big draw, so try to see the first show in the morning or one of the last two shows at night. For midday performances, you'll need to queue up at least 20–30 minutes before showtime. The bleachers can make viewing difficult for shorter folks—if you have small children or short adults in your party, snag a seat higher up. Despite its popularity, using Genie+ here doesn't actually save much time.

Gorilla Falls Exploration Trail ★★★★

PRESCHOOL ★★★★ (BA)   GRADE SCHOOL ★★★★ (A)   TEENS ★★★★ (A)
YOUNG ADULTS ★★★★½ (AA)   OVER 30 ★★★★ (A)   OVER 65 ★★★★ (A)

What it is Walk-through zoological exhibit. **Scope and scale** Major attraction. **When to go** Before or after Kilimanjaro Safaris. **Duration** About 20–30 minutes. **ECV/wheelchair access** May remain in wheelchair. **Participates in Genie+** No. **Early Theme Park Entry** No. **Extended Evening Hours** No.

DESCRIPTION AND COMMENTS On this beautiful trail winding between the domain of two troops of lowland gorillas, it's hard to see what, if anything, separates you from the primates. Other highlights are a naked-mole-rat exhibit, a hippo pool with an underwater viewing area, and an exotic-bird aviary so craftily designed that you can barely tell you're in an enclosure.

TOURING TIPS The Gorilla Falls Exploration Trail is filled with people much of the time. Guests exiting Kilimanjaro Safaris can choose between returning to Harambe or walking the Gorilla Falls Exploration Trail. Many opt for the trail. Thus, when Kilimanjaro Safaris is operating at full tilt, it spews hundreds of guests onto the Exploration Trail every couple of minutes.

The trail's hours are cut during fall and winter, when it closes as early as 4:30 p.m. Check the *Times Guide* for the schedule.

Kilimanjaro Safaris ★★★★★

PRESCHOOL ★★★½ (MAA)   **GRADE SCHOOL ★★★★½ (E)**   **TEENS ★★★★½ (E)**
YOUNG ADULTS ★★★★★ (MAA)   **OVER 30 ★★★★½ (E)**   **OVER 65 ★★★★★ (E)**

What it is Simulated ride through an African wildlife reservation. **Scope and scale** Super-headliner. **When to go** As soon as the park opens or after 3 p.m. **Duration** About 20 minutes. **Loading speed** Fast. **ECV/wheelchair access** Must transfer from ECV to provided wheelchair. **Participates in Genie+** Yes. **Early Theme Park Entry** No. **Extended Evening Hours** No.

DESCRIPTION AND COMMENTS As Animal Kingdom's premier zoological attraction, Kilimanjaro Safaris offers an exceptionally realistic, albeit brief, imitation of an actual African photo safari. Thirty-two guests at a time board tall, open vehicles and are dispatched into a simulated African veldt habitat. Animals such as zebras, wildebeests, impalas, Thomson's gazelles, giraffes, and even rhinos roam seemingly free, while predators such as lions, as well as potentially dangerous large animals like hippos, are separated from both prey and guests by nearly invisible, natural-looking barriers. Although the animals have more than 100 acres of savanna, woodland, streams, and rocky hills to call home, careful placement of watering holes, forage, and salt licks ensures that the critters are hanging out by the road when safari vehicles roll by.

Having traveled in Kenya and Tanzania, Bob can tell you that Disney has done an amazing job of replicating the sub-Saharan East African landscape. As on a real African safari, what animals you see, and how many, is pretty much a matter of luck. We've experienced Kilimanjaro Safaris more than 100 times and had a different experience on each trip.

TOURING TIPS Kilimanjaro Safaris is one of Animal Kingdom's busiest attractions, along with Expedition Everest and the two Pandora attractions. From a touring standpoint, this is a good thing: By distributing guests evenly throughout the park, those other attractions make it unnecessary to run to Kilimanjaro Safaris first thing in the morning. You can do Pandora first, then Safaris and still have lower waits and active animals.

RAFIKI'S PLANET WATCH

NOT A TRUE "LAND" IN SCOPE OR SCALE, this section of Animal Kingdom—named for a beloved *Lion King* character—consists of the park's animal-care center (**Conservation Station**), a petting zoo, an animation class, and educational exhibits, all accessible from Harambe via the **Wildlife Express Train.**

The Animation Experience at Conservation Station ★★★

PRESCHOOL ★★★★ (BA)   **GRADE SCHOOL ★★★★ (A)**   **TEENS ★★★★ (AA)**
YOUNG ADULTS ★★★★ (A)   **OVER 30 ★★★★½ (AA)**   **OVER 65 ★★★★ (A)**

What it is Character-drawing class. **Scope and scale** Minor attraction. **When to go** Check *Times Guide*. **Duration** 30 minutes. **Comments** Accessible only by the Wildlife Express Train. **Participates in Genie+** Yes. **Early Theme Park Entry** No. **Extended Evening Hours** No.

DESCRIPTION AND COMMENTS This experience provides insight into the history of Disney animation and gives participants of any skill level a chance to draw Disney characters with the help of an instructor, using real-life animals as inspiration. When a 5-year-old, 35-year-old, and 65-year-old can all follow the same instruction and end up with a recognizable Disney character, you've got yourself a winning activity.

TOURING TIPS Board the Wildlife Express Train 45 minutes prior to the experience start time. Don't use Genie+ for this.

Conservation Station and Affection Section ★★★

PRESCHOOL ★★★★ (A)   **GRADE SCHOOL ★★★★ (A)**   **TEENS ★★★½ (MBA)**
YOUNG ADULTS ★★★ (MBA)   **OVER 30 ★★★½ (BA)**   **OVER 65 ★★★½ (BA)**

What it is Behind-the-scenes educational exhibit and petting zoo. **Scope and scale** Minor attraction. **When to go** Anytime. **Comments** Check *Times Guide* for hours. Accessible only by the Wildlife Express Train. **ECV/wheelchair access** May remain in wheelchair. **Participates in Genie+** No. **Early Theme Park Entry** No. **Extended Evening Hours** No.

DESCRIPTION AND COMMENTS Conservation Station is Animal Kingdom's veterinary and conservation headquarters. Here, guests can meet wildlife experts, learn about the behind-the-scenes operations of the park, and observe ongoing projects.

While there are several permanent exhibits, including Affection Section (an animal-petting area), what you see at Conservation Station will largely depend on what's going on when you arrive. On most days, almost all veterinary and food-preparation activity happens before lunch.

A reader from England was amused by both the goings-on and the other guests:

The most memorable part of Animal Kingdom for me was watching a veterinary surgeon and his team at Conservation Station perform an operation on a rat snake that had inadvertently swallowed a golf ball, presumably believing it to be an egg! This operation caused at least one onlooker to pass out.

TOURING TIPS Because Conservation Station is so removed from the rest of the park, you won't see it unless you take the train.

Wildlife Express Train ★★

PRESCHOOL ★★★★ (A)   **GRADE SCHOOL ★★★½ (BA)**   **TEENS ★★★½ (BA)**
YOUNG ADULTS ★★★½ (MBA)   **OVER 30 ★★★½ (BA)**   **OVER 65 ★★★★ (BA)**

What it is Scenic railroad ride to Rafiki's Planet Watch. **Scope and scale** Minor attraction. **When to go** Anytime. **Comments** Last train departs at 4:30 p.m. **Duration** About 7 minutes one-way. **Loading speed** Moderate. **ECV/wheelchair access** May remain in wheelchair. **Participates in Genie+** No. **Early Theme Park Entry** No. **Extended Evening Hours** No.

DESCRIPTION AND COMMENTS This ride winds behind the African wildlife reserve as it connects Harambe to Rafiki's Planet Watch. En route, you see the barns for the animals that populate Kilimanjaro Safaris, and on the way back to Harambe, you see the backstage areas of Asia. None of the sights are especially stunning.

TOURING TIPS The train tends to get crowded only when people exit the Safaris and flood the loading area.

ASIA

CROSSING THE BRIDGE from Discovery Island, you enter Asia through the village of **Anandapur,** inspired by the architecture and ruins of India, Indonesia, Nepal, and Thailand. Situated near the bank of the Discovery River and surrounded by mature vegetation, Anandapur is home to a gibbon exhibit and Asia's two feature attractions: the **Kali River Rapids** raft ride and **Expedition Everest.**

Expedition Everest—at 200 feet, the tallest mountain in Florida—is a great roller coaster. You board an old railway destined for the base camp of Mount Everest and end up racing both forward and backward through caverns and frigid canyons en route to paying a call to the Abominable Snowman.

Expedition Everest ★★★★½

PRESCHOOL ★★★ (MBA)　　GRADE SCHOOL ★★★★½ (MAA)　　TEENS ★★★★★ (E)
YOUNG ADULTS ★★★★★ (E)　　OVER 30 ★★★★½ (E)　　OVER 65 ★★★★½ (MAA)

What it is High-speed roller coaster. **Scope and scale** Super-headliner. **When to go** Early or late. **Comments** Must be 44″ tall to ride; Rider Switch option provided (see page 303); single-rider line available. **Duration** 4 minutes. **Loading speed** Moderate–fast. **ECV/wheelchair access** Must transfer to the ride vehicle. **Participates in Genie+** Yes. **Early Theme Park Entry** Yes. **Extended Evening Hours** No.

Motion Sickness

DESCRIPTION AND COMMENTS Expedition Everest is the only roller coaster in Animal Kingdom. Your journey begins in a heavily themed queue modeled after a Nepalese village; then you board an old train headed for the base camp of Mount Everest. Notes from previous expeditions are posted throughout the waiting area, some with cryptic observations regarding a mysterious creature said to guard the mountain. These ominous signs are ignored (as if you have a choice!), resulting in an encounter with the yeti.

This coaster consists of tight turns (some while traveling backward), hills, and dips but no loops or inversions. After your departure at the loading station, you'll see some of the most spectacular panoramas in Walt Disney World. The final drop and last few turns are among Disney's very best coaster elements.

Disney bills Expedition Everest as a "family thrill ride"—more like Big Thunder Mountain Railroad than Rock 'n' Roller Coaster—but it's an exciting experience nonetheless. A Washington family of four gives Expedition Everest a thumbs-up:

Expedition Everest is tremendous. It has enough surprises and runaway speed to make it one of the more enjoyable thrill rides in the whole Orlando area.

A Georgia teen successfully recruited Grandma to ride:

Expedition Everest was so smooooth! I went right out and brought my granny back to ride it. She didn't throw up or anything!

TOURING TIPS Expedition Everest reaches a top speed of around 50 mph, about twice that of Space Mountain. Ask to be seated up front—the first few rows offer the best front-seat experience of any Disney coaster.

Feathered Friends in Flight ★★★★

PRESCHOOL ★★★★★ (A)　　GRADE SCHOOL ★★★★½ (MAA)　　TEENS ★★★★ (AA)
YOUNG ADULTS ★★★½ (AA)　　OVER 30 ★★★★½ (AA)　　OVER 65 ★★★★½ (AA)

What it is Stadium show about birds. **Scope and scale** Minor attraction. **When to go** Anytime; check *Times Guide* for performance times. **Comment** Arrive 10 minutes before showtime. **Duration** 30 minutes. **ECV/wheelchair access** May remain in wheelchair. **Participates in Genie+** Yes. **Early Theme Park Entry** No. **Extended Evening Hours** No.

DESCRIPTION AND COMMENTS Asia's theater has presented a show featuring live birds for years. *Feathered Friends in Flight* is the best version ever. The show's hosts are some of Disney's animal trainers, who explain different bird species' habitats and characteristics. The show is fast-paced, informative, and entertaining for everyone, with birds literally flying over-head. We rate this show as not to be missed.

Feathered Friends focuses on the birds' natural talents and character-istics, which far surpass any tricks they might have learned from humans—don't expect parrots riding bikes or cockatoos playing tiny pianos. A reader from Vermont appreciated learning about the natural skills of the talented stars of the show:

The birds are thrilling, and we especially appreciated the fact that their antics were not the results of training against the grain but actual survival tech-niques that the birds use in the wild.

TOURING TIPS *Feathered Friends* plays at the stadium near the bridge on the walkway into Asia. Although the stadium is covered, it is not air-conditioned; therefore, early-morning and late-afternoon performances are more comfortable.

Kali River Rapids ★★★½

PRESCHOOL ★★★★ (BA)	GRADE SCHOOL ★★★★ (A)	TEENS ★★★★ (A)
YOUNG ADULTS ★★★★ (BA)	OVER 30 ★★★★ (BA)	OVER 65 ★★★★ (BA)

What it is Whitewater raft ride. **Scope and scale** Major attraction. **When to go** Before 11 a.m. or the last hour the park is open. **Comments** You're likely to get wet; must be 38″ tall to ride; Rider Switch option provided (see page 303). **Duration** About 5 min-utes. **Loading speed** Moderate. **ECV/wheelchair access** Must transfer to the ride vehi-cle; transfer device available. **Participates in Genie+** Yes. **Early Theme Park Entry** No. **Extended Evening Hours** No.

Wet

DESCRIPTION AND COMMENTS Kali River Rapids takes you on a trip down an artificial river in a circular rubber raft with a top-mounted platform that seats 12 people. Because the river is fairly wide, with various waves, currents, eddies, and obstacles, each trip is different and exciting.

What distinguishes Kali River Rapids from other theme park raft rides is Disney's trademark attention to visual detail. Kali River Rapids flows through a dense rainforest and past waterfalls, temple ruins, and bamboo thickets, emerging into a cleared area where greedy loggers have ravaged the forest and finally drifting back under the tropical canopy as the river returns to Anandapur. Along the way, your raft runs a gauntlet of raging cataracts, logjams, and other dangers. That said, you get only about 3½ minutes on the water, and it's not a thrill ride. Yes, you get wet, but the drops and rapids aren't scary.

The queuing area, which winds through an ancient Southeast Asian temple, is one of the most striking and visually interesting settings of any Disney attraction.

TOURING TIPS Kali River Rapids is hugely popular on hot summer days. Plan accordingly! You won't get totally soaked, but you'll still get pretty wet; therefore, we recommend wearing shorts and sport sandals (such as Tevas) on the ride and/or putting anything you want to stay dry into a plastic bag.

Kali River Rapids offers free 2-hour locker rentals to the left of the attraction entrance, near the restrooms. You could store a change of dry clothes here or, alternatively, wear as little as the law and Disney will allow. If you're wearing closed shoes, prop up your feet above the bottom of the raft to keep them from getting completely soaked—slogging around in wet shoes is a surefire ticket to Blisterville.

Maharajah Jungle Trek ★★★★

| PRESCHOOL ★★★★ (A) | GRADE SCHOOL ★★★★ (BA) | TEENS ★★★★ (A) |
| YOUNG ADULTS ★★★★ (A) | OVER 30 ★★★★ (A) | OVER 65 ★★★★ (A) |

What it is Walk-through zoological exhibit. **Scope and scale** Major attraction. **When to go** Anytime. **Duration** About 20–30 minutes. **ECV/wheelchair access** May remain in wheelchair. **Participates in Genie+** No. **Early Theme Park Entry** No. **Extended Evening Hours** No.

DESCRIPTION AND COMMENTS This walk is similar to the **Gorilla Falls Exploration Trail** (see page 446) but with a Southeast Asian setting. Animals you might see range from Komodo dragons to large fruit bats. Ruins of the maharajah's palace provide the setting for Bengal tigers. The trek concludes with an aviary.

Labyrinthine, overgrown, and elaborately detailed, the ruins would be a compelling attraction even without the animals. Look for a plaster triptych just after the tiger exhibit that shows (right to left) a parable about humans living in harmony with nature. Most readers, like this Washington, D.C., couple, agree:

The Maharajah Jungle Trek was absolutely amazing. We were able to see all the animals, which were awake by that time (9:30 a.m.), including the elusive tigers. The part with the birds was fabulous; you could spot hundreds, some of which were eating on the ground a mere 3 feet away from us.

TOURING TIPS The Maharajah Jungle Trek doesn't get as jammed up as the Gorilla Falls Exploration Trail and is a good choice for midday touring when most other attractions are crowded. The downside, of course, is that the exhibit showcases tigers, bats, and other creatures that might not be very active in the heat of the day.

DINOLAND U.S.A.

THIS LEAST LOVED of Animal Kingdom's lands crosses an anthropological dig with a quirky roadside attraction. Accessible via the bridge from Discovery Island, DinoLand U.S.A. is home to a children's play area; a nature trail; a 1,500-seat amphitheater; and **Dinosaur,** one of Animal Kingdom's three thrill rides.

The Boneyard ★★★½

| PRESCHOOL ★★★★★ (E) | GRADE SCHOOL ★★★★½ (MAA) | TEENS ★★ (MBA) |
| YOUNG ADULTS ★★ (MBA) | OVER 30 ★★★ (MBA) | OVER 65 ★★★½ (MBA) |

What it is Elaborate playground. **Scope and scale** Diversion. **When to go** Anytime. **ECV/wheelchair access** May remain in wheelchair. **Participates in Genie+** No. **Early Theme Park Entry** No. **Extended Evening Hours** No.

DESCRIPTION AND COMMENTS Centered around an open-air "dig site," this elaborately themed playground appeals to kids age 10 and younger, but all ages will find it fun to explore. The dig site is a gravel pit where kids can scrounge for bones and fossils. There's also a ropes course, as well as slides, swings, climbing areas, and caves to play in. As a Michigan family attests, kids love The Boneyard:

The highlight for our kids was The Boneyard, especially the dig site. They just kept digging and digging to uncover the bones of the woolly mammoth.

TOURING TIPS This is certainly a space where younger kids will want to spend some time. It gets incredibly hot in the Florida sun, so keep your kids well hydrated, and drag them into the shade from time to time. Try to save this until after you've experienced the main attractions.

Be aware: The Boneyard rambles over about 0.5 acre and has multiple stories, making it easy to lose sight of a small child. Fortunately, there's only one entrance and exit, and it's guarded by a cast member who won't let solo children escape. From the mother of a 3-year-old:

If your child is quite young, make sure you have two people in The Boneyard— one to help them up all the stairs, the other to stay at the bottom and watch them as they exit the slide. By the time you get from the top of the structure to the bottom, they're off who-knows-where getting into mischief of one kind or another without adult supervision.

Dinosaur ★★★½

PRESCHOOL ★★★ (MBA)   **GRADE SCHOOL ★★★½ (MBA)**   **TEENS ★★★★ (BA)**
YOUNG ADULTS ★★★★ (BA)   **OVER 30 ★★★½ (BA)**   **OVER 65 ★★★½ (MBA)**

What it is Motion-simulator dark ride. **Scope and scale** Major attraction. **When to go** Early or late. **Comment** Must be 40″ tall to ride; Rider Switch option provided (see page 303). **Duration** 3½ minutes. **Loading speed** Fast. **ECV/wheelchair access** Must transfer to the ride vehicle. **Participates in Genie+** Yes. **Early Theme Park Entry** Yes. **Extended Evening Hours** No.

DESCRIPTION AND COMMENTS Dinosaur is a combination track ride and motion simulator. In addition to moving along a cleverly hidden track, the ride vehicle bucks and pitches in sync with the visuals and special effects.

The plot has you traveling back in time on a conservation mission. Your objective: to rescue a living dinosaur before the species becomes extinct. You arrive on the prehistoric scene just as a giant asteroid is hurtling toward Earth. Mayhem ensues as you evade carnivorous predators, catch the beast, and get out before the asteroid hits.

The menacing dinosaurs and the intensity of the experience make Dinosaur a no-go for most younger kids, as this Michigan family discovered:

Our 7-year-old son withstood every ride Disney threw at him, from Space Mountain to Tower of Terror. Dinosaur, however, did him in. By the end, he was riding with his head down, scared to look around.

TOURING TIPS Disney stuck Dinosaur in such a remote corner of the park that you have to poke around to find it. This, in conjunction with the overwhelming popularity of Pandora's rides, makes it Walt Disney World's easiest major attraction to get on. Lines should be relatively light through midmorning, but keep in mind that every age group rates it poorly.

Finding Nemo: The Big Blue . . . and Beyond! ★★★★

PRESCHOOL ★★★★½ (MAA)   **GRADE SCHOOL ★★★★½ (AA)**   **TEENS ★★★★ (AA)**
YOUNG ADULTS ★★★★ (A)   **OVER 30 ★★★★½ (AA)**   **OVER 65 ★★★★ (A)**

What it is Live stage show. **Scope and scale** Major attraction. **When to go** Check *Times Guide* for showtimes. **Duration** About 24 minutes. **When to arrive** 30 minutes before showtime. **ECV/wheelchair access** May remain in wheelchair. **Participates in Genie+** Yes. **Early Theme Park Entry** No. **Extended Evening Hours** No.

DESCRIPTION AND COMMENTS Along with *Festival of the Lion King* (see page 446), *Finding Nemo* is arguably the most elaborate live show in any of the Disney World theme parks. Incorporating sophisticated digital backdrops of the undersea world, dancing, and special effects, it features onstage human performers retelling Nemo's story with colorful, larger-than-life puppets. To be fair, *puppets* doesn't adequately convey the size or detail of these props, many of which are as big as a car and require two people to manipulate.

TOURING TIPS Access to the theater is via a relatively narrow pedestrian path—if you arrive as the previous show is letting out, you'll feel like a salmon swimming upstream. Never a good use of Genie+.

TriceraTop Spin ★★

PRESCHOOL ★★★½ (MAA)	GRADE SCHOOL ★★★★ (A)	TEENS ★★★ (MBA)
YOUNG ADULTS ★★★ (MBA)	OVER 30 ★★★ (MBA)	OVER 65 ★★★ (MBA)

What it is Spinner ride. **Scope and scale** Minor attraction. **When to go** Anytime. **Duration** 1½ minutes. **Loading speed** Slow. **ECV/wheelchair access** Must transfer from ECV to provided wheelchair. **Participates in Genie+** No. **Early Theme Park Entry** Yes. **Extended Evening Hours** No.

DESCRIPTION AND COMMENTS On this Dumbo-like ride, you spin around until a dinosaur pops out of the top of the hub.

TOURING TIPS Come back later if the posted wait exceeds 20 minutes.

▌PANDORA—*The World of Avatar*

DISNEY SIGNED DIRECTOR JAMES CAMERON to a theme park development deal in 2011 based on his blockbuster 2009 film *Avatar.* Pandora's headliner attraction, **Avatar Flight of Passage,** opened as (and is still) one of the highest-rated attractions in any Disney or Universal theme park in the United States. In addition, Pandora boasts an awe-inspiringly immersive setting, called the **Valley of Mo'ara.**

Rather than tie this Pandora to *Avatar* characters or storylines, Disney chose to set the scene a generation after the events in the first movie: The Indigenous Na'vi have made peace with the humans who had exploited Pandora for its natural resources, and Pandora is now an ecotourism destination and a center for scientific research. We'll see how this gels with new movies now being released.

What Disney has built in Pandora is a world more beautiful than nature produces on its own. The colors are more vibrant, the sounds more alive, the landscaping entirely more interesting, and the details more, well, detailed than what you can probably see out your window right now. It's intersected by perfectly placed waterfalls, and in the middle of it all is a giant floating mountain.

Avatar Flight of Passage ★★★★½

PRESCHOOL ★★★½ (MBA)	GRADE SCHOOL ★★★★½ (E)	TEENS ★★★★★ (E)
YOUNG ADULTS ★★★★★ (E)	OVER 30 ★★★★★ (E)	OVER 65 ★★★★½ (E)

What it is Flight simulator. **Scope and scale** Super-headliner. **When to go** As soon as the park opens or after 3 p.m. **Comments** One of Disney's most advanced rides; must be 44" to ride. **Duration** About 6 minutes. **Loading speed** Moderate. **ECV/wheelchair access** Must transfer from ECV to provided wheelchair, then to the ride vehicle; transfer device available. **Participates in Genie+** No (it offers Individual Lightning Lane). **Early Theme Park Entry** Yes. **Extended Evening Hours** No.

DESCRIPTION AND COMMENTS Avatar Flight of Passage is one of the most technologically advanced rides Disney has ever produced: a flight simulator in which you hop on the back of a Pandora banshee (a winged, dragonlike creature) for a flight through the planet's scenery.

The queue takes you from the base of Pandora, up into abandoned cave dwellings, and then to the research laboratory of the humans who have settled on Pandora and are studying the planet's wildlife. The laboratory's star exhibit is a Na'vi avatar that is floating gently in suspended animation, with occasional finger twitches or leg movements.

Once through the queue, you're brought to a 16-person chamber to prepare for your flight. Your preparation includes several quasi-scientific processes, mainly to help pass the time until your ride vehicles are ready.

When it's time to ride, you're led into a small room holding what looks like 16 stationary bicycles without pedals. You're handed 3D goggles and told to mount the "bike" and scoot as far forward as you can. Once you're seated, padded restraints are deployed along your calves and lower back. The snugness of the restraints, coupled with the somewhat confined space holding the vehicles, makes some claustrophobic guests exit before riding.

During the ride, you soar over plains, through mountains, and across seas, all through a high-definition video projected onto a giant screen in front of you. As you fly, airbags at your legs inflate and deflate to simulate the banshee's breathing below you.

The technology at work here is similar to that used at EPCOT's **Soarin' Around the World,** with the individual "bikes" replacing the grouped seats. The video is clear and well synchronized with the ride vehicles, and we've heard very few reports of motion sickness—which is unusual for screen-based motion simulators.

All that being said, Flight of Passage is starting to show its age. After more than seven years in operation, the preshow screens have some images burnt in, the misting effects are especially unreliable (not that I'm complaining), and your banshee's breathing may be more of a whack in the calf than a gentle inflation. I'm hoping this excellent attraction gets the love and attention it needs soon, even though taking it down for a refurbishment will be a big blow to the park.

The word *rave* hardly does justice to how Flight of Passage has been received. From an Indiana family of four:

Our favorite ride in all of Walt Disney World is Avatar Flight of Passage. The experience is magical. It really does feel like you're flying because of the wind, smells, and movement of the banshee. A lot of people compare it to Soarin', but after riding Flight of Passage first, Soarin' was a letdown.

TOURING TIPS Flight of Passage is the first ride most people head for in Animal Kingdom. The good news is that when the park opens by 8 a.m., most guests leave well before closing. Thus, lines for Flight of Passage drop considerably near park closing. If you can't arrive before park opening or stay until closing, we think purchasing Individual Lightning Lane is worth the cost. It's one of the best cost-per-minute-saved line-skipping options at Walt Disney World.

Na'vi River Journey ★★★½

PRESCHOOL ★★★★ (A)	GRADE SCHOOL ★★★★ (BA)	TEENS ★★★½ (BA)
YOUNG ADULTS ★★★½ (BA)	OVER 30 ★★★★ (BA)	OVER 65 ★★★★ (BA)

What it is Boat ride. **Scope and scale** Major attraction. **When to go** Before 9:30 a.m. or during the last 2 hours before closing. **Duration** 5 minutes. **Loading speed** Moderate. **ECV/wheelchair access** Must transfer to the ride vehicle; transfer device available. **Participates in Genie+** Yes. **Early Theme Park Entry** Yes. **Extended Evening Hours** No.

DESCRIPTION AND COMMENTS Na'vi River Journey is a 4½-minute boat ride through the Pandora jungle. You begin by boarding a small, hewn raft. Each raft has two rows of seats, so six people can go in each boat.

Off you go into the nighttime jungle, past glowing plants and exotic animals. Disney has used traditional physical sets for the flora, coupled with video screens showing the movement of the fauna. These video screens are semitransparent, though. What's past them are more screens, with background scenes that also move. That means you're seeing action in the foreground and background simultaneously, all surrounded by densely packed landscaping.

The big star, however, is displayed in the ride's culminating scene: the Shaman of Songs, the most lifelike animatronic figure Disney has ever created. The shaman's arms move with astonishing grace—we certainly don't know any real people who are that coordinated.

The main problem with Na'vi River Journey has to do with storytelling: You go into it not knowing anything about the character, and not enough story unfolds during the ride to get you excited about meeting the shaman. It's like Pirates of the Caribbean, with even prettier scenery but with absolutely no storyline.

TOURING TIPS It's not worth waiting longer than 30 minutes or standing in any unshaded part of the queue.

ANIMAL KINGDOM ENTERTAINMENT

ANIMAL ENCOUNTERS Throughout the day, Animal Kingdom cast members conduct short, impromptu lessons on specific animals at the park. Look for a cast member in safari garb holding a bird, reptile, or small mammal.

Winged Encounters—The Kingdom Takes Flight (★★★½), a small, interactive event featuring macaws and their handlers, takes place on Discovery Island in front of the Tree of Life. Guests can talk to the animals' trainers and see the birds fly around the middle of the park.

CHARACTER CAVALCADES In place of parades, small boats carry Disney characters on the waterway around Discovery Island, each to its own soundtrack. The characters don't appear at specific times, but they appear regularly starting about an hour after park opening. The spot where you can see the characters closest is from the bridge on the walkway between Pandora and Africa.

DONALD'S DINO-BASH! ★★½ Regular character greetings are a welcome addition to DinoLand U.S.A. In this case, Donald has discovered that birds are evolutionary descendants of dinosaurs, so he's brought out his friends to celebrate. Characters usually appear intermittently starting at 10 a.m. as follows: **Chip 'n' Dale** across from TriceraTop Spin until 4:30 p.m.; **Daisy, Donald,** and **Goofy** until 7 p.m. at Chester and Hester's Dino-Rama; and **Launchpad McQuack** and **Scrooge McDuck** at The Boneyard until 5 p.m. Because the venues are outdoors, the Dino-Bash may shut down temporarily if it's raining.

STREET PERFORMERS The park's most popular live performers are found in Africa, including the **Tam Tam Drummers of Harambe** (★★★★)

and a harp-playing act called **Kora Tinga Tinga** (★★★★). The **Harambe Village Acrobats** (★★★★) dance, vault, and climb through sets around the Dawa Bar. Over on Discovery Island, the **Viva Gaia Street Band** (★★★★) plays high-energy music across from Flame Tree Barbecue.

Far and away the most intriguing of these performers, though, is a stilt walker named **DiVine** (★★★★). Bedecked in foliage and vines, she blends so completely with Animal Kingdom's vegetation that you don't notice her until she moves. We've seen guests standing less than a foot away gasp in amazement as DiVine brushes them with a leafy tendril. Found near the park entrance or on the path between Asia and Africa, DiVine is a must-see.

TRAFFIC PATTERNS
in ANIMAL KINGDOM

THIS THEME PARK'S MAIN DRAWS are the **Pandora** attractions and **Kilimanjaro Safaris** in Africa, with **Expedition Everest** in Asia as a distant fourth.

During busy times of year, guests will start lining up outside the Animal Kingdom entrance 30 minutes to an hour before opening to be close to the front of the standby line for Flight of Passage. Plan on arriving 60 minutes before park opening.

Most rope drop crowds head straight for Pandora at opening, or to the Safaris when they open. Waits at Dinosaur remain low until 10:30 or 11 a.m. Likewise, crowds don't peak at Expedition Everest until about an hour after park opening, and even later than that at Kali River Rapids. As the day wears on, guests who've experienced the headliners turn their attention to other rides, animal exhibits, and shows, further distributing crowds across the entire park.

unofficial **TIP**
Wait times at the Pandora attractions often peak in the 2 hours after park opening. Less popular attractions generally don't get high traffic until 11 a.m.

Many guests who arrive at opening will leave by late afternoon, having completed their tour of the park. Wait times at the headliners historically dip as the afternoon wears on, usually bottoming out between 3 and 6 p.m. The main exception is the Pandora's attractions as guests stay to see the land's "bioluminescent" landscaping.

ANIMAL KINGDOM
TOURING PLAN

OUR ANIMAL KINGDOM TOURING PLAN has two versions: one for Disney resort guests and one for off-site guests; the former uses Early Theme Park Entry (see page 30) to minimize waits in line. Because Early Entry means thousands of guests will already be in lines and on rides before off-site guests set foot in the park, the touring strategy for off-site guests must be different.

The plan does not assume use of Genie+ or Individual Lightning Lane. If you opt for either (or both) of these, just use our free touring plan software (see page 46) to enter your return times.

"Not a Touring Plan" Touring Plans

For the type-B reader, these "not" touring plans (see page 546) dispense with detailed step-by-step strategies for saving every last minute in line. For Animal Kingdom, these plans include advice for adults and parents with one day to tour the park, arriving either at park opening or later in the morning.

PRELIMINARY INSTRUCTIONS FOR USING THE TOURING PLAN

BECOME FAMILIAR WITH Animal Kingdom's **opening procedures** (see page 437). On days of moderate to heavy attendance, follow the touring plan exactly, deviating from it only as follows:

1. **When you're not interested in an attraction in the plan.** In this case, simply skip it and proceed to the next attraction.
2. **When you encounter a very long line at an attraction.** In this case, skip to the next attraction and try again later.

Before You Go

1. Check disneyworld.disney.go.com or the MDE app the day before to verify the opening time.
2. Make reservations at the Animal Kingdom table-service restaurant(s) of your choice 60 days before your visit.

ANIMAL KINGDOM TOURING PLAN AT A GLANCE

Disney's Animal Kingdom One-Day Touring Plan
(see pages 559–560)

THIS TOURING PLAN ASSUMES a willingness to experience all major rides and shows. If you have children under age 8, refer to the **Small-Child Fright-Potential Table** on pages 304–306.

PART 14

DISNEY'S HOLLYWOOD STUDIOS

KEY QUESTIONS ANSWERED IN THIS CHAPTER

- How do I get to Disney's Hollywood Studios? *(opposite page)*
- How does park opening (rope drop) work? *(opposite page)*
- What are the don't-miss rides? *(opposite page)*
- What's the best way to use Genie+ and Individual Lightning Lane in the Studios? *(page 463)*
- How do I experience Star Wars: Rise of the Resistance with minimal waits in line? *(page 478)*

OVERVIEW

WITH THE OPENING OF TOY STORY LAND (in 2018) and **Star Wars: Galaxy's Edge** (in 2019) and the launch of **Mickey & Minnie's Runaway Railway** (in 2020) all well in the past now, Disney's Hollywood Studios has reached something of an equilibrium as a park. But it's also the park with the highest average wait times and the worst problems with unexpected downtime. You might have the best day of your trip here, or you might end the day in a huff of frustration. It all depends on a lot of planning and a little luck.

WHO SHOULD SEE THE STUDIOS

SEVERAL OF THE STUDIOS' attractions are among Disney's best and most popular for older children, teens, and adults. **Star Wars: Rise of the Resistance** is arguably the best ride Disney has made in decades, while Mickey & Minnie's Runaway Railway is so immersive, colorful, and full of Mickey's personality that it's impossible to leave it without a smile on your face.

Parents with small children may want to look through the attractions and entertainment before deciding on a full day in this park. The Studios has relatively few child-friendly rides and entertainment options—but the immersive lands appeal to everyone.

ARRIVING

ARRIVING FROM INSIDE DISNEY WORLD If you're staying at an EPCOT resort, it'll take you 20–30 minutes to walk the mile or so from your hotel to the Studios' entrance. **Boat service** is also available from the EPCOT resorts to the Studios, and it's about a 15- or 20-minute ride on the **Skyliner** (see page 344), which links EPCOT's International Gateway with Hollywood Studios and Disney's **Caribbean Beach, Riviera, Pop Century,** and **Art of Animation Resorts.** In addition to the Skyliner, Disney may offer bus service to the Studios from these hotels on days of high attendance. Guests at other Disney resorts access Hollywood Studios by **bus.**

DRIVING The Hollywood Studios parking lot is adjacent to the park (for GPS names and addresses, see page 345). The parking lots open about an hour before official park opening. Take a tram or walk from the parking lot to the front gate. Anticipate traffic delays in the morning while everyone waits for the lot to open.

HOLLYWOOD STUDIOS OPENING PROCEDURES (ROPE DROP)

SOME RIDES WILL BEGIN OPERATION as soon as guests are admitted into the park, while others won't start operating until Early Theme Park Entry officially begins. Shows normally begin running an hour or more after the rest of the park opens. Disney resort guests wishing to use Early Entry should arrive at the Studios entrance 60 minutes before official opening on off-peak days and 90 minutes before official opening on days of high attendance. Off-site guests who are not eligible for Early Entry should arrive 30 minutes before official opening on all days.

HOW MUCH TIME TO ALLOCATE

DEPENDING ON WHEN YOU ARRIVE, the time of year you tour, and how big of a *Star Wars* fan you are, a comprehensive tour of the park takes 8–10 hours with lunch and breaks. Allow more time if you want to enjoy the lightsaber- or droid-building experiences in Galaxy's Edge. Hollywood Studios also offers After Hours events where you can experience attractions at night with lower wait times—this is a separately ticketed event (see page 73).

NOT TO BE MISSED IN DISNEY'S HOLLYWOOD STUDIOS
COMMISSARY LANE • Meet Disney Stars at *Red Carpet Dreams*
ECHO LAKE • Star Tours—The Adventures Continue • Meet Olaf at Celebrity Spotlight • *For the First Time in Forever: A Frozen Sing-Along Celebration*
HOLLYWOOD AND SUNSET BOULEVARDS • *Fantasmic!* • Mickey & Minnie's Runaway Railway • Rock 'n' Roller Coaster • The Twilight Zone Tower of Terror
TOY STORY LAND • Slinky Dog Dash • Toy Story Mania!
STAR WARS: GALAXY'S EDGE • *Millennium Falcon:* Smugglers Run • Star Wars: Rise of the Resistance

continued on page 462

Disney's Hollywood Studios

G+ Offers Genie+

ILL Offers Individual
Lightning Lane

☑ Not To Be Missed

👍 Recommended Dining

🚹🚺 Restrooms

✚ First Aid Center

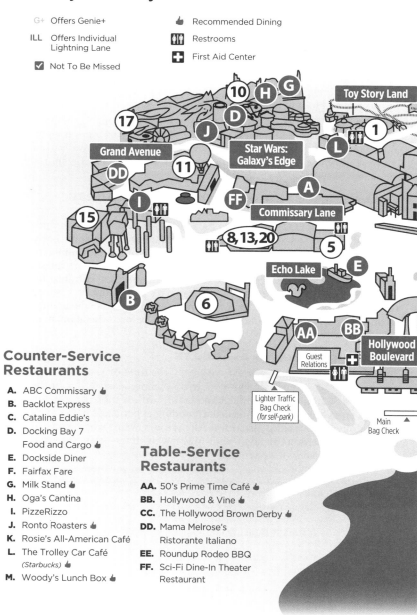

Counter-Service Restaurants

A. ABC Commissary 👍
B. Backlot Express
C. Catalina Eddie's
D. Docking Bay 7 Food and Cargo 👍
E. Dockside Diner
F. Fairfax Fare
G. Milk Stand 👍
H. Oga's Cantina
I. PizzeRizzo
J. Ronto Roasters 👍
K. Rosie's All-American Café
L. The Trolley Car Café
   (Starbucks) 👍
M. Woody's Lunch Box 👍

Table-Service Restaurants

AA. 50's Prime Time Café 👍
BB. Hollywood & Vine 👍
CC. The Hollywood Brown Derby 👍
DD. Mama Melrose's Ristorante Italiano
EE. Roundup Rodeo BBQ
FF. Sci-Fi Dine-In Theater Restaurant

Attractions

1. Alien Swirling Saucers G+
2. *Beauty and the Beast—Live on Stage/* Theater of the Stars G+
3. *Disney Junior Play and Dance!* G+
4. *Fantasmic!* ☑
5. *For the First Time in Forever: A Frozen Sing-Along Celebration* G+
6. *Indiana Jones Epic Stunt Spectacular!* G+
7. *Lightning McQueen's Racing Academy*
8. Meet Olaf at Celebrity Spotlight ☑ G+
9. Mickey & Minnie's Runaway Railway ☑ ILL G+
10. *Millennium Falcon:* Smugglers Run ☑ G+
11. *Muppet*Vision 3D* G+
12. Rock 'n' Roller Coaster Starring Aerosmith ☑ G+
13. Meet Disney Stars at *Red Carpet Dreams* ☑
14. Slinky Dog Dash ☑ G+
15. Star Tours—The Adventures Continue ☑ G+
16. Star Wars Launch Bay
17. Star Wars: Rise of the Resistance ☑ ILL
18. Toy Story Mania! ☑ G+
19. The Twilight Zone Tower of Terror ☑ G+
20. *Vacation Fun* at Mickey Shorts Theater
21. *Walt Disney Presents*

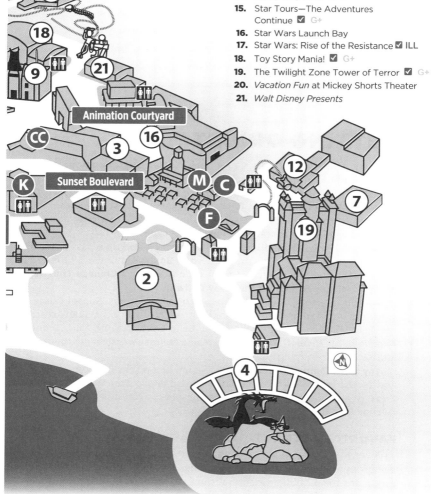

continued from page 459

HOLLYWOOD STUDIOS SERVICES

MOST PARK SERVICES are on Hollywood Boulevard, including:

ATM Just inside the park, on the right

Baby Care Center At Guest Relations; baby food and other necessities also available at Oscar's Super Service, just inside the park, on the right

Cell Phone Charging Outlets in the Hollywood Brown Derby lobby, inside Backlot Express, and near the restrooms next to Toy Story Mania!

First Aid Center At Guest Relations

Guest Relations Just inside the park, on the left

Live Entertainment and Character Information In the *Times Guide,* available at Guest Relations

Lockers Just inside the park, on the right

Lost and Found At Guest Relations

Lost Persons Report at Guest Relations/Baby Care Center

MagicBands At The Darkroom on the right side of Hollywood Boulevard as you enter the park, just past Oscar's Super Service

Wheelchair, ECV (Scooter), and Stroller Rentals At Oscar's Super Service, just inside the park, on the right

GETTING ORIENTED

ON YOUR LEFT AS YOU ENTER THE PARK, **Guest Relations** serves as the Studios' information center. Go there to pick up a park map or entertainment schedule (*Times Guide*); to report lost persons; or to access the **Baby Care Center, First Aid Center,** and **Lost and Found.** To the right of the entrance, at **Oscar's Super Service,** are **locker, stroller, ECV,** and **wheelchair rentals** and **Package Pickup.**

As in the Magic Kingdom, you enter the park and then pass down a main street. In this case, it's the **Hollywood Boulevard** of the 1930s and '40s. At the end is a replica of the iconic **Grauman's Chinese Theatre,** home of **Mickey & Minnie's Runaway Railway.**

As you face the Chinese Theatre, two themed areas, **Sunset Boulevard** and **Animation Courtyard,** branch off Hollywood Boulevard to the right. Branching off to the left is **Echo Lake.** Beyond that, **Grand Avenue** holds *Muppet*Vision 3D* and **Mama Melrose's Ristorante Italiano,** a table-service Italian restaurant.

Toy Story Land's attractions are located behind the Chinese Theatre and to the left of Animation Courtyard. Finally, **Star Wars: Galaxy's Edge** is in the upper-left corner of the park, accessible from Grand Avenue and Toy Story Land.

FAVORITE ATTRACTIONS BY AGE GROUP

THE TABLE OPPOSITE SHOWS the 10 most popular attractions by age group. Below are the average ratings for DHS attractions, by age group, for the 32,000 attraction ratings we received in the past year:

PRESCHOOL	GRADE SCHOOL	TEENS	YOUNG ADULTS	OVER 30	OVER 65
4.2 stars	4.4 stars	4.3 stars	4.4 stars	4.4 stars	4.4 stars

DISNEY'S HOLLYWOOD STUDIOS MOST POPULAR ATTRACTIONS BY AGE GROUP

PRESCHOOL	GRADE SCHOOL	TEENS	YOUNG ADULTS	OVER 30	OVER 65
Meet Olaf at Celebrity Spotlight	Droid Depot	Star Wars: Rise of the Resistance	Savi's Workshop	Star Wars: Rise of the Resistance	Star Wars: Rise of the Resistance
Disney Junior Play and Dance!	Fantasmic!	Rock 'n' Roller Coaster	Star Wars: Rise of the Resistance	The Twilight Zone Tower of Terror	Beauty and the Beast— Live on Stage
Alien Swirling Saucers	Meet Chewbacca at Star Wars Launch Bay	Savi's Workshop	The Twilight Zone Tower of Terror	Meet Chewbacca at Star Wars Launch Bay	Toy Story Mania!
Mickey & Minnie's Runaway Railway	Toy Story Mania!	Meet Chewbacca at Star Wars Launch Bay	Rock 'n' Roller Coaster	Savi's Workshop	Meet Chewbacca at Star Wars Launch Bay
For the First Time in Forever	Slinky Dog Dash	Toy Story Mania!	Meet Chewbacca at Star Wars Launch Bay	Toy Story Mania!	Fantasmic!
Alien Swirling Saucers	Meet Disney Stars at Red Carpet Dreams	Fantasmic!	Fantasmic!	Fantasmic!	Encounter Darth Vader at Star Wars Launch Bay
Toy Story Mania!	Star Wars: Rise of the Resistance	Slinky Dog Dash	Encounter Darth Vader at Star Wars Launch Bay	Slinky Dog Dash	The Twilight Zone Tower of Terror
Meet Disney Stars at Red Carpet Dreams	Savi's Workshop	Droid Depot	Toy Story Mania!	Mickey & Minnie's Runaway Railway	Mickey & Minnie's Runaway Railway
Beauty and the Beast— Live on Stage	Mickey & Minnie's Runaway Railway	Millennium Falcon: Smugglers Run	Droid Depot	Encounter Darth Vader at Star Wars Launch Bay	Walt Disney Presents
Meet Chewbacca at Star Wars Launch Bay	Encounter Darth Vader at Star Wars Launch Bay	Encounter Darth Vader at Star Wars Launch Bay	Slinky Dog Dash	Meet Disney Stars at Red Carpet Dreams	Meet Disney Stars at Red Carpet Dreams

GENIE+, INDIVIDUAL LIGHTNING LANE, AND THE TOURING PLANS

NOTE: See page 49 for detailed information and strategy suggestions for Genie+ and Individual Lightning Lane. The big questions answered in this section are:

1. Is Genie+ worth paying for in Disney's Hollywood Studios?
2. Which attractions benefit most from Genie+ or Individual Lightning Lane?
3. How can you avoid paying for Individual Lightning Lane?
4. How do Genie+ and Individual Lightning Lane work with the touring plans?

Is Genie+ Worth Paying For in Disney's Hollywood Studios?

Along with the Magic Kingdom, the Studios can potentially be one of the best uses of Genie+, especially if you meet any of these criteria:

- You'll arrive at the park after Early Theme Park Entry begins. This includes off-site guests who aren't eligible for Early Entry and on-site guests who want to sleep in.
- You won't be using a touring plan.

GENIE+ AND INDIVIDUAL LIGHTNING LANE (ILL) SELECTIONS IN DHS
ANIMATION COURTYARD • *Disney Junior Play and Dance!*
ECHO LAKE • *For the First Time in Forever—A Frozen Sing-Along Celebration* • *Indiana Jones Epic Stunt Spectacular!* • Meet Olaf at Celebrity Spotlight • Star Tours—The Adventures Continue
GALAXY'S EDGE • *Millennium Falcon:* Smugglers Run • Star Wars: Rise of the Resistance *(ILL)*
GRAND AVENUE • *Muppet*Vision 3D*
HOLLYWOOD AND SUNSET BOULEVARDS • *Beauty and the Beast—Live on Stage* • Mickey & Minnie's Runaway Railway • Rock 'n' Roller Coaster Starring Aerosmith • The Twilight Zone Tower of Terror
TOY STORY LAND • Alien Swirling Saucers • Slinky Dog Dash • Toy Story Mania!

Some character greetings were not offered with Genie+ and Lightning Lane at press time. We expect them to be added.

ESTIMATED TIME SAVINGS WITH GENIE+ BY CROWD LEVEL			
CROWD LEVEL	**TYPICAL USE**	**OPTIMISTIC USE**	**PERFECT USE**
LOW	45 minutes	65 minutes	80 minutes
MEDIUM	70 minutes	100 minutes	120 minutes
HIGH	90 minutes	120 minutes	180 minutes

DHS ATTRACTIONS THAT BENEFIT MOST FROM GENIE+ AND INDIVIDUAL LIGHTNING LANE (ILL) *(Highest Priority to Lowest)*	
ATTRACTION	**AVERAGE TIME IN LINE SAVED (IN MINUTES)**
SLINKY DOG DASH	53
STAR WARS: RISE OF THE RESISTANCE *(ILL)*	52
MILLENNIUM FALCON: SMUGGLERS RUN	39
MICKEY & MINNIE'S RUNAWAY RAILWAY	36
THE TWILIGHT ZONE TOWER OF TERROR	35
TOY STORY MANIA!	34
ROCK 'N' ROLLER COASTER STARRING AEROSMITH	32
ALIEN SWIRLING SAUCERS	16
STAR TOURS—THE ADVENTURES CONTINUE	13

We have not seen evidence that Genie+ reduces waits at shows.

Regardless of the time of year you visit, arriving before park opening should allow you to see one or two of the Studios' headliners without significant waits. Since only 13 attractions participate in Genie+ or Individual Lightning Lane, you'll be competing with lots of people for reservations, which pushes out return times and limits how many you can use in a day. Above we break down how much time we think you can save using Genie+, based on algorithms that optimize the use of Genie+ to various degrees, given what we know about sell-out times and standby waits avoided. See page 370 for more on the usage levels.

Which Attractions Benefit Most from Genie+ and Individual Lightning Lane?

For Genie+, the table above shows the attractions that might benefit most from using Genie+, based on current wait times and historical

ATTRACTION	LOW ATTENDANCE	MODERATE ATTENDANCE	HIGH ATTENDANCE
ALIEN SWIRLING SAUCERS	8 p.m.	8 p.m.	6 p.m.
BEAUTY AND THE BEAST—LIVE ON STAGE	4:30 p.m.	4:30 p.m.	4:30 p.m.
DISNEY JUNIOR PLAY AND DANCE!	5 p.m.	5 p.m.	5 p.m.
FOR THE FIRST TIME IN FOREVER	6 p.m.	6 p.m.	6 p.m.
INDIANA JONES EPIC STUNT SPECTACULAR!	4 p.m.	4 p.m.	4 p.m.
MEET OLAF AT CELEBRITY SPOTLIGHT	5 p.m.	5 p.m.	4 p.m.
MICKEY & MINNIE'S RUNAWAY RAILWAY	8 p.m.	7 p.m.	4 p.m.
MILLENNIUM FALCON: SMUGGLERS RUN	9 p.m.	8 p.m.	4 p.m.
MUPPET*VISION 3D	8 p.m.	8 p.m.	8 p.m.
STAR WARS: RISE OF THE RESISTANCE (ILL)	10 a.m.	9 a.m.	8 a.m.
ROCK 'N' ROLLER COASTER	7 p.m.	5 p.m.	2 p.m.
SLINKY DOG DASH	3 p.m.	11 a.m.	9 a.m.
STAR TOURS—THE ADVENTURES CONTINUE	8 p.m.	8 p.m.	8 p.m.
TOY STORY MANIA!	8 p.m.	8 p.m.	5 p.m.
THE TWILIGHT ZONE TOWER OF TERROR	8 p.m.	6 p.m.	3 p.m.

WHEN GENIE+ AND INDIVIDUAL LIGHTNING LANE (ILL) RESERVATIONS RUN OUT BY ATTENDANCE LEVEL*

*Information is applicable until July 24, 2024.

LOW ATTENDANCE Crowd levels 1–3 on the TouringPlans crowd calendar

MODERATE ATTENDANCE Crowd levels 4–7   **HIGH ATTENDANCE** Crowd levels 8–10

Genie+ and Individual Lightning Lane data. Attractions are listed in descending order of priority.

When Do Genie+ and Individual Lightning Lane Reservations Run Out in the Studios?

The table above shows the approximate time at which the Studios' attractions run out of Genie+ or Individual Lightning Lane capacity, by crowd level. Use this table along with the "Attractions That Benefit Most" table, opposite, to determine which reservations to get first.

How Can You Avoid Paying for Individual Lightning Lane?

The easiest way to avoid paying for Individual Lightning Lane at Rise of the Resistance is to be at the park for Early Entry, then head for Rise as soon as you enter. Note that Rise averages over an hour of downtime daily. It frequently opens significantly earlier than any other attraction in the park. But ask a cast member if it's running because it is also broken down about half the time at park opening.

How do Genie+ and Individual Lightning Lane Work with the Touring Plans?

See our advice on page 372.

DINING IN DISNEY'S HOLLYWOOD STUDIOS

ON THE NEXT PAGE IS A QUICK RECAP of the Studios' top restaurants, rated by readers from highest to lowest. See Part 6 for details.

DHS RESTAURANT REFRESHER	
COUNTER SERVICE	**FULL SERVICE**
Ronto Roasters (⊕ 94%/MAA), Galaxy's Edge	The Hollywood Brown Derby (⊕ 90%/AA), Hollywood Boulevard
The Trolley Car Cafe (Starbucks) (⊕ 92%/AA), Sunset Boulevard	Hollywood & Vine (⊕ 89%/A), Echo Lake
Woody's Lunch Box (⊕ 91%/A), Toy Story Land	50's Prime Time Café (⊕ 88%/A), Echo Lake
ABC Commissary (⊕ 90%/A), Commissary Lane	
Docking Bay 7 Food and Cargo (⊕ 90%/A), Galaxy's Edge	
Milk Stand (⊕ 87%/A), Sunset Boulevard	

Restaurants not listed are rated below average or lower.

DISNEY'S HOLLYWOOD STUDIOS ATTRACTIONS

HOLLYWOOD AND SUNSET BOULEVARDS

PALM-LINED **Hollywood Boulevard** re-creates Tinseltown's main drag during the Golden Age of Hollywood. Most of the Studios' service facilities are located here, interspersed with eateries and shops.

Evoking the glamour of the 1940s, **Sunset Boulevard**—the first right off Hollywood Boulevard—provides another venue for dining, shopping, and street entertainment.

KEY TO ABBREVIATIONS In the attraction profiles that follow, each star rating is accompanied by a category label in parentheses (see page 368 for details). E means **Exceptional**, MAA means **Much Above Average**, AA means **Above Average**, A means **Average**, BA means **Below Average**, and MBA means **Much Below Average**.

Beauty and the Beast—Live on Stage / Theater of the Stars ★★★★

PRESCHOOL ★★★★½ (AA)   GRADE SCHOOL ★★★★½ (AA)   TEENS ★★★★ (BA)
YOUNG ADULTS ★★★★ (BA)   OVER 30 ★★★★ (A)   OVER 65 ★★★★½ (E)

What it is Live musical performed in an open-air theater. **Scope and scale** Major attraction. **When to go** Check *Times Guide* for showtimes; arrive 15 minutes in advance. **Duration** 25 minutes. **ECV/wheelchair access** May remain in wheelchair. **Participates in Genie+** Yes. **Early Theme Park Entry** No. **Extended Evening Hours** No.

DESCRIPTION AND COMMENTS This long-running show combines a shortened (but complete) retelling of the story with all of the major musical numbers, tons of characters, and beautiful sets. The theater affords a clear view from almost every seat. A canopy protects the audience from the Florida sun (or rain), but it still gets mighty hot in the summer.

TOURING TIPS *Beauty and the Beast* usually runs from midmorning to around 5 p.m. The show is popular, so arrive extra early for the best seats.

Fantasmic! ★★★★½

GRADE SCHOOL ★★★★ (E)   ALL OTHER AGE GROUPS ★★★★½ (MAA)

What it is Mixed-media nighttime spectacular. **Scope and scale** Super-headliner. **When to go** Check *Times Guide* for schedule; if two shows are offered, the second show will be less crowded. **Duration** 25 minutes. **ECV/wheelchair access** May remain in wheelchair. **Participates in Genie+** No. **Early Theme Park Entry** No. **Extended Evening Hours** No.

DESCRIPTION AND COMMENTS Off Sunset Boulevard behind the Tower of Terror, this spectacular is staged on an island opposite the 6,900-seat Hollywood Hills Amphitheater. By far the largest theater facility ever created by Disney, it can accommodate an additional 3,000 standing guests for an audience of nearly 10,000.

Fantasmic! is one of the most innovative outdoor spectacles at any theme park. Starring Mickey Mouse in the role of the Sorcerer's Apprentice, the production uses lasers, fireworks, lighting effects, music, and images projected on a shroud of mist in stunning and powerful combinations. The theme is simple: good versus evil.

We don't receive many reports of young children being terrified by *Fantasmic!*, but you should still spend some time preparing your kids for what they'll see. The theme of evil means some focus on villains and their nefarious deeds.

Hang on to your kids after the show and tell them what to do should you get separated. The postshow crowd is particularly crushing.

TOURING TIPS *Fantasmic!* is to the Studios what *Happily Ever After* is to the Magic Kingdom: While it's hard to imagine a 10,000-person amphitheater running out of space, that's exactly what happens almost every time the show is staged. On evenings when there are two shows, the second will always be less crowded. If you attend the first (or only) scheduled performance, then arrive at least an hour in advance; if you opt for the second, arrive 45 minutes early.

A multigenerational family from Ontario, Canada, makes this suggestion for guests who are short on nature's upholstery:

Bring pillows or towels to sit on. We were sitting on those benches from 6 p.m. for the 7:30 show, and boy, did our rears hurt by the end!

Rain and wind sometimes cause *Fantasmic!* to be canceled; unfortunately, Disney usually doesn't make a final ruling about whether to proceed or cancel until just before showtime. On rainy or windy nights, pursue your own agenda until 10–20 minutes or so before showtime; then head to the stadium to see what happens.

***FANTASMIC!* DINING PACKAGE** If you're planning to eat at any of the park's table-service restaurants, you can obtain a voucher for the members of your dining party to enter *Fantasmic!* via a special entrance and sit in a reserved section. This saves you 30–90 minutes of waiting in the regular line to be admitted. If you know you're going to eat at one of these restaurants, the dining package is a better way to see *Fantasmic!* than lining up in advance.

Fixed-price menus are included in the package; prices listed below are the most recent available for adults and kids ages 3–9:

- **50'S PRIME TIME CAFÉ:** Lunch and dinner $54 (child $23)
- **HOLLYWOOD & VINE:** Breakfast $59 (child $39), lunch and dinner $75 (child $49)
- **THE HOLLYWOOD BROWN DERBY:** Lunch and dinner $77 (child $31)
- **MAMA MELROSE'S RISTORANTE ITALIANO:** Lunch and dinner $56 (child $23)
- **SCI-FI DINE-IN THEATER RESTAURANT:** Lunch and dinner $51 (child $23)

Nonalcoholic drinks are included; tax, tips, and park admission are not. Prices may vary seasonally, so call ☎ 407-WDW-DINE (939-3463) to confirm.

You'll receive your vouchers at the restaurant during your meal. Then, at least half an hour before the show, you'll report to the theater entrance. A cast member will collect your vouchers and point you to the reserved-seating section of the amphitheater. The reserved seats are in the center of the stadium; you won't have assigned seats—it's first come, first served—so arrive early for the best choice. If the show is canceled due to weather or other circumstances, you'll get a voucher for another performance within five days.

My family used the *Fantasmic!* dining package with a meal at 50's Prime Time Café in September 2023. The slight upcharge for the package earned us an extra 45 minutes in the parks, less time waiting in the amphitheater for the kids, and third-row seats for the show just barely 30 minutes before showtime, when the entire arena filled in with people before the spectacular started.

Lightning McQueen's Racing Academy ★★½

PRESCHOOL ★★★ (A)	GRADE SCHOOL ★★★½ (MBA)	TEENS ★★★ (MBA)
YOUNG ADULTS ★★★ (MBA)	OVER 30 ★★★ (MBA)	OVER 65 ★★★ (MBA)

What it is Wide-screen movie of Lightning McQueen's racing tips. **Scope and scale** Minor attraction. **When to go** Anytime. **Duration** Continuous 10 minutes. **ECV/wheelchair access** May remain in wheelchair. **Participates in Genie+** No. **Early Theme Park Entry** No. **Extended Evening Hours** No.

DESCRIPTION AND COMMENTS This theater show features *Cars* superstars Lightning McQueen, Cruz Ramirez, and Tow Mater. The last two are only screen appearances, but Lightning McQueen is front and center as a full-size animatronic.

The show starts slowly, but it becomes mildly impressive once the simulation starts. Using the huge screens, Lightning mimes racing as a track flies by around you. As usual, things don't quite go as planned when an old adversary shows up, but it's all settled by a race, of course.

TOURING TIPS *Lightning McQueen's Racing Academy* is located in one of the most remote corners of the park: past the end of Sunset Boulevard, then past the end of the Rock 'n' Roller Coaster plaza. Because it's hard to find, it's rarely crowded. A photo op with Cruz Ramirez is outside the show.

Mickey & Minnie's Runaway Railway ★★★★

PRESCHOOL ★★★½ (E)	GRADE SCHOOL ★★★★½ (AA)	TEENS ★★★★ (AA)
YOUNG ADULTS ★★★★½ (AA)	OVER 30 ★★★★½ (AA)	OVER 65 ★★★★½ (AA)

What it is Indoor dark ride. **Scope and scale** Headliner. **When to go** Early or late. **Duration** 5 minutes. **Loading speed** Moderate. **ECV/wheelchair access** Must transfer to the ride vehicle. **Participates in Genie+** Yes. **Early Theme Park Entry** Yes. **Extended Evening Hours** No.

DESCRIPTION AND COMMENTS Disney restarted regular production of Mickey Mouse cartoons in 2013. Mickey and Minnie sport a 1930s look, complete with "pie eyes." The Mouses, Goofy, Donald, and the rest of the gang embark on wild adventures that always seem to end up just fine.

Runaway Railway places you in the center of one of those cartoons. You careen, gently, through 10 large cartoon show scenes, from tropical islands to cities to out-of-control factories. In each scene, Mickey and Minnie attempt to save you from disaster, with mixed results.

In each scene, Disney uses a mix of traditional, three-dimensional painted sets and the latest in video projection technology to show movement and special effects. It's very well done, and there are so many things to see that it's impossible to catch everything in one or two rides.

TOURING TIPS Runaway Railway is one of the Studios' rare all-ages hits, so expect long lines for most of the day.

Rock 'n' Roller Coaster Starring Aerosmith ★★★★

PRESCHOOL NA	GRADE SCHOOL ★★★½ (A)	TEENS ★★★★★ (E)
YOUNG ADULTS ★★★★★ (E)	OVER 30 ★★★★½ (AA)	OVER 65 ★★★★ (A)

What it is Rock music–themed roller coaster. **Scope and scale** Headliner. **When to go** Early or late. **Comments** Must be 48" tall to ride; Rider Switch option provided (see page 303). **Duration** Almost 1½ minutes. **Loading speed** Moderate-fast. **ECV/wheelchair access** Must transfer from ECV to provided wheelchair, then to the ride vehicle; transfer device available. **Participates in Genie+** Yes. **Early Theme Park Entry** Yes. **Extended Evening Hours** Yes.

Motion Sickness

DESCRIPTION AND COMMENTS Rock 'n' Roller Coaster is made for fans of high-speed thrill rides. Although the synchronized music adds measurably to the experience, the ride itself is what you're here for. Its loops, corkscrews, and drops make Space Mountain seem like It's a Small World. What really makes this coaster great is that it's in the dark (like Space Mountain) and you are launched up the first hill like a jet off a carrier deck. By the time you crest the hill, you'll have gone from 0 to 57 mph in less than 3 seconds. When you enter the first loop, you'll be pulling almost 5 g's—2 more than astronauts experienced at liftoff on a space shuttle.

Reader opinions of Rock 'n' Roller Coaster are predictably mixed, and colored by how the reader feels about roller coasters in general.

From an Australian couple:

My wife and I are definitely not roller-coaster people. However, we found Rock 'n' Roller Coaster quite exhilarating—and because it's dark, we didn't always realize that we were being thrown upside down. We rode it twice!

TOURING TIPS Rock 'n' Roller Coaster is not for everyone— skip it if Space Mountain or Big Thunder Mountain Railroad pushes your limits. This is a "real" roller coaster, and you should only ride if you enjoy intense thrill rides. A single-rider queue is offered, but, oddly, it frequently has a longer wait than the standby line. Don't count on it as a time-saver. Plus, even when you exclude the lengthy planned downtime for refurbishment, this attraction *still* has the most unplanned downtime of any attraction in any park—almost 90 minutes per day. That makes figuring out a good strategy for when to ride even trickier.

The Twilight Zone Tower of Terror ★★★★★

PRESCHOOL ★★½ (MBA)	GRADE SCHOOL ★★★★ (BA)	TEENS ★★★★½ (MAA)
YOUNG ADULTS ★★★★★ (E)	OVER 30 ★★★★½ (E)	OVER 65 ★★★★½ (AA)

What it is Sci-fi–themed indoor thrill ride. **Scope and scale** Super-headliner. **When to go** Early or late. **Comments** Must be 40" tall to ride; Rider Switch option provided (see page 303). **Duration** About 4 minutes plus preshow. **Loading speed** Moderate. **ECV/wheelchair access** Must transfer from ECV to provided wheelchair, then to the ride vehicle. **Participates in Genie+** Yes. **Early Theme Park Entry** Yes. **Extended Evening Hours** No.

DESCRIPTION AND COMMENTS The Tower of Terror is peak Imagineering— the perfect combination of story and thrill. The story is that you're touring a Hollywood hotel gone to ruin. The queuing area immerses you immediately as you pass through the hotel's once opulent public rooms. From the lobby, you are escorted into the hotel's library, where *Twilight*

Zone creator Rod Serling, speaking from an old black-and-white television, greets you and introduces the plot.

The Tower of Terror is a whopping 13 stories tall. The ride vehicle, one of the hotel's service elevators, takes guests to see the haunted hostelry. At about the fifth floor, things get pretty weird, as you are subjected to a full range of eerie effects as you cross into the Twilight Zone. The sudden drops and ascents begin when your ride vehicle travels horizontally across the building into a second elevator shaft. There are several lift-and-drop sequences that are selected randomly, keeping you guessing about when, how far, and how many times the elevator will fall.

An older guest from the United Kingdom loved the Tower of Terror:

I was thankful I had read your review of the Tower of Terror, or I certainly would have avoided it. As you say, it's so full of magnificent detail that it's worth riding even if you don't fancy the drops involved.

TOURING TIPS Newer attractions draw crowds away from Tower of Terror. If you can't ride first thing in the morning, waits should be shorter in the last hour the park is open.

To save time once you're inside the queuing area, when you enter the library waiting room, stand in the far back corner across from the door where you entered and at the opposite end of the room from the TV. When the doors to the loading area open, you'll be the first admitted. Once you get into the second queueing area and the line splits, don't turn right. Continue straight for an almost-always shorter wait.

ECHO LAKE

THIS MINIATURE LAKE near the middle of the Studios, to the left of Hollywood Boulevard, pays homage to its real California counterpart, which served as the backdrop for many early motion pictures.

For the First Time in Forever: A Frozen Sing-Along Celebration ★★★½

PRESCHOOL ★★★★½ (MAA)	GRADE SCHOOL ★★★★½ (AA)	TEENS ★★★★ (A)
YOUNG ADULTS ★★★★ (BA)	OVER 30 ★★★★½ (AA)	OVER 65 ★★★★½ (AA)

What it is Sing-along stage show retelling the story of *Frozen*. **Scope and scale** Minor attraction. **When to go** Check *Times Guide;* arrive 15 minutes before showtime. **Duration** 30 minutes. **ECV/wheelchair access** May remain in wheelchair. **Participates in Genie+** Yes. **Early Theme Park Entry** No. **Extended Evening Hours** No.

DESCRIPTION AND COMMENTS This musical recap of the iconic Disney hit *Frozen* includes songs from the movie and visits from Anna, Kristoff, and Elsa. Scenes from the movie, projected on a drive-in-size screen, provide continuity and bring those who haven't seen the film up to speed. Live performers, including two "royal historians," retell the story with corny humor.

Most of the show unfolds at a leisurely pace, but the ending is presented in a nanosecond. The finale features Anna and Elsa and another rousing belting of "Let It Go." If you're a *Frozen* fan, you probably won't care about the weak points. Even if you're not a fan, you'll enjoy the show's spirit as well as that of a theater full of enraptured kids. Yes, it's contagious.

Most readers really like the sing-along, including this mom from Texas:

I'm glad we didn't skip it, because it was a total hoot—my husband and I loved it, and it turned out to be the highlight of our DHS visit! When we got home, my husband and 9-year-old son, neither of whom had seen the movie before, watched Frozen *with my daughter.*

TOURING TIPS The indoor theater is one of Disney World's largest and most comfortable, with excellent sight lines from every seat.

Indiana Jones Epic Stunt Spectacular! ★★★½

| PRESCHOOL ★★★½ (MBA) | GRADE SCHOOL ★★★★ (A) | TEENS ★★★★ (A) |
| YOUNG ADULTS ★★★★ (BA) | OVER 30 ★★★★ (BA) | OVER 65 ★★★★ (A) |

What it is Movie-stunt demonstration and action show. **Scope and scale** Major attraction. **When to go** Anytime. **Duration** 30 minutes. **Comment** Arrive 20–30 minutes before showtime. **ECV/wheelchair access** May remain in wheelchair. **Participates in Genie+** Yes. **Early Theme Park Entry** No. **Extended Evening Hours** No.

DESCRIPTION AND COMMENTS Educational and entertaining, this popular production showcases professional stuntpeople who offer behind-the-scenes demonstrations of their craft. The sets, props, and special effects are very elaborate.

TOURING TIPS The Stunt Theater holds 2,000 people; capacity audiences are possible. The first performance is always the easiest to see. If the first show is at 11 a.m. or earlier, you can usually walk in, even if you arrive 5 minutes late. If you want to beat the crowd out of the stadium, sit on the far right (as you face the staging area) and near the top.

Meet Disney Stars at *Red Carpet Dreams* ★★★★

| PRESCHOOL ★★★★½ (AA) | GRADE SCHOOL ★★★★½ (MAA) | TEENS ★★★★ (A) |
| YOUNG ADULTS ★★★★½ (A) | OVER 30 ★★★★½ (AA) | OVER 65 ★★★★½ (AA) |

What it is Character-greeting venue. **Scope and scale** Diversion. **When to go** First or last hour the park is open or during mealtimes. **Duration** About 2 minutes. **Queue speed** Slow. **ECV/wheelchair access** May remain in wheelchair. **Participates in Genie+** No. **Early Theme Park Entry** No. **Extended Evening Hours** No.

DESCRIPTION AND COMMENTS This is the venue for meeting Mickey and Minnie Mouse in Disney's Hollywood Studios. Minnie's greeting area is the set of her latest film, a musical blockbuster. Mickey is dressed as the Sorcerer's Apprentice from *Fantasia.*

TOURING TIPS The meet-and-greet entrance is found on Commissary Lane, between the entrance to the ABC Commissary and the entrance to the Sci-Fi Dine-In Theater. Long lines form once the park is full but drop considerably during lunch and dinner.

Meet Olaf at Celebrity Spotlight ★★★½

| PRESCHOOL ★★★★½ (E) | GRADE SCHOOL ★★★★½ (A) | TEENS ★★★★ (A) |
| YOUNG ADULTS ★★★½ (MBA) | OVER 30 ★★★★ (BA) | OVER 65 ★★★★ (A) |

What it is Character-greeting venue. **Scope and scale** Diversion. **When to go** First or last hour the park is open or during mealtimes. **Duration** About 2 minutes. **Queue speed** Slow. **ECV/wheelchair access** May remain in wheelchair. **Participates in Genie+** Yes. **Early Theme Park Entry** No. **Extended Evening Hours** No.

DESCRIPTION AND COMMENTS Though this is a low-frills photo shoot, Olaf puts forth a ton of effort. And I hear he loves warm hugs.

TOURING TIPS Wait times are lowest during lunch and after 4 p.m.

Star Tours—The Adventures Continue ★★★½

| PRESCHOOL ★★★½ (BA) | GRADE SCHOOL ★★★★½ (AA) | TEENS ★★★★ (A) |
| YOUNG ADULTS ★★★★ (A) | OVER 30 ★★★★ (A) | OVER 65 ★★★★ (A) |

What it is Indoor space-flight-simulation ride. **Scope and scale** Major attraction. **When to go** During lunch or after 4 p.m. **Comments** Pregnant guests and anyone prone to motion sickness should not ride; must be 40" tall to ride; Rider Switch option available (see page 303). **Duration** About 7 minutes. **Loading speed** Moderate.

ECV/wheelchair access Must transfer from ECV to provided wheelchair, then to the ride vehicle. **Participates in Genie+** Yes. **Early Theme Park Entry** Yes. **Extended Evening Hours** No.

Motion Sickness

DESCRIPTION AND COMMENTS Based on the *Star Wars* saga, this was Disney's first modern simulator ride. Guests ride in a flight simulator, experiencing dips, turns, twists, and climbs. The ride film, projected in high-definition 3D, has more than 700 combinations of possible scenes, including ones from *Andor, Ahsoka,* and *The Mandalorian*. You could ride Star Tours all day without seeing the same combination of scenes twice.

TOURING TIPS Most crowds skip over this attraction and head straight to Galaxy's Edge. Make sure you ride this one at least once if you're a *Star Wars* completionist!

Vacation Fun at Mickey Shorts Theater ★★★½

PRESCHOOL ★★★★ (A)	GRADE SCHOOL ★★★★ (BA)	TEENS ★★★★ (A)
YOUNG ADULTS ★★★½ (MBA)	OVER 30 ★★★★ (BA)	OVER 65 ★★★★ (BA)

What it is Cartoon featuring Mickey Mouse. **Scope and scale** Diversion. **When to go** Anytime. **Duration** 10 minutes. **ECV/wheelchair access** May remain in wheelchair. **Participates in Genie+** No. **Early Theme Park Entry** No. **Extended Evening Hours** No.

DESCRIPTION AND COMMENTS The Mickey Shorts Theater shows a new 10-minute Mickey Mouse cartoon called *Vacation Fun,* which combines clips from several of the newest and best Mickey Mouse cartoons. If you loved Mickey & Minnie's Runaway Railway, here's your chance to see more of the new-style cartoons.

TOURING TIPS Even if you've seen some of the clips, the theater is large, comfortable, and air-conditioned—perfect for a short break on a hot day.

GRAND AVENUE

THIS THEMED AREA has just one attraction, two restaurants, and a bar. The street sets serve as a pedestrian thoroughfare to Galaxy's Edge.

*Muppet*Vision 3D* ★★★★

PRESCHOOL ★★★★ (A)	GRADE SCHOOL ★★★★ (MBA)	TEENS ★★★½ (MBA)
YOUNG ADULTS ★★★★ (MBA)	OVER 30 ★★★★ (MBA)	OVER 65 ★★★★ (A)

What it is 4D movie starring the Muppets. **Scope and scale** Minor attraction. **When to go** Anytime. **Duration** 17 minutes. **Preshow entertainment** The Muppets on TV. **Probable waiting time** One show or less. **ECV/wheelchair access** May remain in wheelchair. **Participates in Genie+** Yes. **Early Theme Park Entry** No. **Extended Evening Hours** No.

DESCRIPTION AND COMMENTS *Muppet*Vision 3D* provides a total sensory experience, with wacky 3D action augmented by auditory, visual, and tactile special effects. If you're tired and hot, this zany show will make you feel brand-new. Although the film hasn't been updated in decades, the comedic timing and dialogue still make us laugh.

TOURING TIPS Waits generally peak around lunchtime, and it's unusual to find a wait longer than one show. If there is a long line, try again later.

TOY STORY LAND

THIS 11-ACRE LAND opened in 2018. The idea is that you've been shrunk to the size of a toy and placed in Andy's backyard, where you get to play with other toys he's set up.

Toy Story Land's attractions are designed to appeal to young children. Because there are so few other options for young kids in the park, you should expect long waits throughout the day.

Toy Story Land is one of two ways to access Galaxy's Edge, the other being **Grand Avenue.**

Alien Swirling Saucers ★★½

PRESCHOOL ★★★½ (MAA)   GRADE SCHOOL ★★★★ (BA)   TEENS ★★★ (MBA)
YOUNG ADULTS ★★★½ (MBA)   OVER 30 ★★★½ (MBA)   OVER 65 ★★★½ (MBA)

What it is Spinning car ride. **Scope and scale** Minor attraction. **When to go** After 3 p.m. **Comment** Must be 32″ tall to ride. **Duration** 3 minutes. **Loading speed** Painfully slow. **ECV/wheelchair access** Must transfer to the ride vehicle. **Participates in Genie+** Yes. **Early Theme Park Entry** Yes. **Extended Evening Hours** No.

Motion Sickness

DESCRIPTION AND COMMENTS Alien Swirling Saucers is themed around *Toy Story*'s Claw-obsessed aliens. Ride cars move, whiplike, in an elongated figure-eight around three circular tracks embedded in the ground. The ride experience is much milder than the Magic Kingdom's Mad Tea Party.

TOURING TIPS For the shortest waits, ride during the first or last hour the park is open. We recommend skipping the Saucers if the posted wait is more than 20 minutes.

Slinky Dog Dash ★★★★

PRESCHOOL ★★★★ (A)   GRADE SCHOOL ★★★★½ (MAA)   TEENS ★★★★½ (AA)
YOUNG ADULTS ★★★★½ (AA)   OVER 30 ★★★★½ (MAA)   OVER 65 ★★★★½ (AA)

What it is Mild outdoor roller coaster. **Scope and scale** Headliner. **When to go** As soon as the park opens or just before closing. **Comment** Must be 38″ tall to ride. **Duration** 2 minutes. **Loading speed** Moderate. **ECV/wheelchair access** Must transfer from ECV to provided wheelchair, then to the ride vehicle. **Participates in Genie+** Yes. **Early Theme Park Entry** Yes. **Extended Evening Hours** No.

DESCRIPTION AND COMMENTS Slinky Dog Dash is a long outdoor children's roller coaster designed to look as if Andy built it out of Tinkertoys. The trains are themed to *Toy Story*'s Slinky Dog. As for intensity, it's less intense than the Magic Kingdom's Seven Dwarfs Mine Train—lots of turns, dips, and hills but no loops or high-speed curves—and not nearly as rough as Big Thunder Mountain Railroad. For adults, it's more fun than you might expect, but not worth the very long waits it usually attracts.

TOURING TIPS Slinky Dog Dash gets crowded as soon as the park opens and stays that way all day. Visit at park opening or right before closing. It also experiences a significant amount of downtime.

Toy Story Mania! ★★★★½

PRESCHOOL ★★★★½ (AA)   ALL OTHER AGE GROUPS ★★★★½ (MAA)

What it is 3D ride through a shooting gallery. **Scope and scale** Major attraction. **When to go** Early or late. **Duration** About 6½ minutes. **Loading speed** Fast. **ECV/wheelchair access** Must transfer from ECV to provided wheelchair. **Participates in Genie+** Yes. **Early Theme Park Entry** Yes. **Extended Evening Hours** No.

DESCRIPTION AND COMMENTS Toy Story Mania! ushered in a new generation of Disney attraction: the virtual 3D dark ride. Conceptually, it's an interactive shooting gallery much like **Buzz Lightyear's Space Ranger Spin** (see page 388), but in Toy Story Mania!, your ride vehicle passes through a totally virtual midway, with booths offering games such as ring tossing and ball throwing. You use a cannon on your vehicle to play as you move from booth to booth. Each booth is manned by a *Toy Story* character in 3D glory, cheering you on.

The ride begins with a training round, then continues through a number of "real" games in which you compete against your riding mate. There are plenty of easy targets for small children to reach. If you're competitive, your elbow and shoulder will ache after one ride, but you'll want to ride again immediately anyway to improve your score.

TOURING TIPS Toy Story Mania! is one of the most reliable rides in the park and is often the first spot guests go to when Slinky Dog Dash is down. If you find yourself behind a large crowd, come back in an hour or try Genie+.

ANIMATION COURTYARD

THIS AREA IS TO THE RIGHT of Mickey & Minnie's Runaway Railway in the middle of the park. It holds a large theater used for live stage shows, a walk-through display of *Star Wars* movie props, and several character-greeting locations.

Disney Junior Play and Dance! ★★

PRESCHOOL ★★★★½ (E)	GRADE SCHOOL ★★★★ (BA)	TEENS NA
YOUNG ADULTS NA	OVER 30 ★★★ (MBA)	OVER 65 ★★★ (MBA)

What it is Live show for preschoolers. **Scope and scale** Minor attraction. **When to go** Check *Times Guide* for showtimes. **Comment** Audience sits on the floor; arrive 10–15 minutes before showtime. **Duration** 25 minutes. **ECV/wheelchair access** May remain in wheelchair. **Participates in Genie+** Yes. **Early Theme Park Entry** No. **Extended Evening Hours** No.

DESCRIPTION AND COMMENTS This high-energy music-and-video show features Disney Channel characters from *The Lion Guard, Doc McStuffins,* and *Vampirina,* along with Mickey Mouse and a DJ, who all rile up the kids. A simple narrative guides all the singing, dancing, and audience participation. The audience sits on the floor so that kids can spontaneously erupt into motion when the mood strikes (it does, and they do). Watching them live their best lives evokes those contagious feelings of Disney magic.

TOURING TIPS Staged in a huge building on the right side of the courtyard. Get here around 10 minutes before showtime, pick a spot on the floor, and relax until the action begins.

Star Wars Launch Bay ★★★

PRESCHOOL ★★★★ (AA/Chewbacca)	GRADE SCHOOL ★★★★½ (E/Chewbacca)
ALL OTHER AGE GROUPS ★★★★½ (MAA/Both)	

What it is Character greetings, along with displays of a few *Star Wars* movie models and props. **Scope and scale** Diversion. **When to go** Anytime. **Comment** There are separate lines for each character greeting. **Probable waiting time** 20–30 minutes each for the character greetings. **ECV/wheelchair access** May remain in wheelchair. **Participates in Genie+** No. **Early Theme Park Entry** No. **Extended Evening Hours** No.

DESCRIPTION AND COMMENTS Launch Bay opened when the Studios needed more things for guests to do while new rides were being built; now it's essentially a walk-through commercial for the latest *Star Wars* films. There are a few interesting models on display for the serious fan to admire, but the real draw is the character greetings.

Three characters hold court: currently Chewbacca, Darth Vader, and BB-8. Waits in line for Chewie and Vader usually run about 20–30 minutes. Chewie gives the best hugs of any character in any park. Prove me wrong.

Walt Disney Presents ★★★

| PRESCHOOL NA | GRADE SCHOOL ★★★ (MBA) | TEENS ★★★½ (MBA) |
| YOUNG ADULTS ★★★★ (BA) | OVER 30 ★★★★ (A) | OVER 65 ★★★★½ (AA) |

What it is Disney-memorabilia collection and short film about Walt Disney. **Scope and scale** Minor attraction. **When to go** Anytime. **Duration** 25 minutes. **Probable waiting time** For the film, less than one show. **ECV/wheelchair access** May remain in wheelchair. **Participates in Genie+** No. **Early Theme Park Entry** No. **Extended Evening Hours** No.

DESCRIPTION AND COMMENTS *Walt Disney Presents* consists of an exhibit area showcasing Disney memorabilia and recordings, followed by a film about Walt Disney's life and achievements, narrated by Julie Andrews. (The film is sometimes replaced with previews of upcoming Disney or Pixar films). On display are various innovations in animation developed by Walt, along with models and plans for Disney World and other Disney theme parks.

TOURING TIPS Every minute spent among these extraordinary artifacts will enhance your visit, taking you back to a time when the creativity and vision that created Disney World were personified by one struggling entrepreneur.

STAR WARS: GALAXY'S EDGE

STAR WARS HAS SO MANY DEDICATED FANS that it was only a matter of time before the movies became a real-life set.

In 2015, Disney announced its plans for Galaxy's Edge, arguably the biggest bet made on its US theme parks since EPCOT in 1982. Two nearly identical 14-acre versions were built (the other at Disneyland); together they're rumored to have cost more than $2 billion. By way of comparison, Disney bought the whole *Star Wars* franchise for $4 billion, and building the 500-acre Animal Kingdom cost $1.5 billion in today's dollars.

Disney's goal with Galaxy's Edge was to redefine the entire theme park experience. It put more money, technology, and storytelling effort into this one project than it had put into anything in a long, long time. Disney incorporated the *Star Wars* alphabet of Aurebesh to spell out signage. Disney cast members were provided background stories about their lives in Galaxy's Edge and used invented terminology and idioms in conversation with guests: "Hello!" became "Bright suns!" (or "Bright moons!" after dark). Even soda bottles got out-of-this-world redesigns and became collector items.

The expectations were impossible to live up to. The first ride to open in Galaxy's Edge was *Millennium Falcon:* Smugglers Run, to mixed reviews. The land itself, while looking reasonably like a *Star Wars* planet's outpost, doesn't include moving features like waterfalls to give visual interest, and guests didn't appreciate having to navigate the land's language idioms when all they wanted was directions to the nearest bathroom. Most cast members have abandoned their stories and verbiage. And while Rise of the Resistance is the best ride Disney has built in decades, it exhibits more operational delays and problems than almost any other Disney World ride. Its unsteady operation, coupled with its incredible popularity, means long lines throughout the day.

The biggest gamble was Disney's decision to place Galaxy's Edge at a very specific time in the *Star Wars* canon: during the third trilogy, between *The Last Jedi* and *Rise of Skywalker*. That means the land doesn't have any characters from the original trilogy (though Disney has added characters from the hit Disney+ series *The Mandalorian*). Disney thought this would make the land future-proof, able to host new stories and new characters that are written into subsequent films in the *Star Wars* franchise. And the problem, of course, is that not only do those stories or characters not yet exist, but many *Star Wars* fans love the characters from the original three films most.

unofficial **TIP**
Costumes are prohibited at Galaxy's Edge for guests age 14 and up.

THE LAND Galaxy's Edge is an outpost in the village of Black Spire Outpost, on the planet of Batuu. Formerly a busy trading port and waypoint, it's now a dusty backwater filled with bounty hunters, smugglers, and those who make a living by not being recognized. As if that weren't enough, members of the Resistance and the First Order live in and around the town in an uneasy coexistence.

Galaxy's Edge has two access points: on **Grand Avenue** and in **Toy Story Land.** Entering through Grand Avenue puts you in the middle of the Resistance's encampment, while the side closest to Toy Story Land is controlled by the First Order.

Galaxy's Edge Attractions
Millennium Falcon: Smugglers Run   ★★★★

PRESCHOOL ★★★½ (BA)	GRADE SCHOOL ★★★★½ (AA)	TEENS ★★★★½ (AA)
YOUNG ADULTS ★★★★½ (A)	OVER 30 ★★★★ (A)	OVER 65 ★★★★½ (AA)

What it is Interactive simulator ride. **Scope and scale** Super-headliner. **When to go** As soon as it opens or after 6 p.m. **Comments** Could've been great; must be 38" tall to ride; Rider Switch option available (see page 303). **Duration** 4½ minutes. **Loading speed** Moderate-fast. **ECV/wheelchair access** Must transfer to the ride vehicle. **Participates in Genie+** Yes. **Early Theme Park Entry** Yes. **Extended Evening Hours** No.

Motion Sickness

DESCRIPTION AND COMMENTS Smugglers Run lets guests fly Han Solo's *Millennium Falcon,* the "fastest hunk of junk in the galaxy." Guests approaching the attraction will see a life-size *Millennium Falcon* parked outside the spaceport, periodically venting gas as technicians tinker with the temperamental craft.

To board, you're recruited by Hondo Ohnaka, an animatronic pirate who has cut a deal with Chewbacca to use the *Falcon* for some sketchy transportation business. After Hondo explains the mission, you enter the *Falcon* through a bridge and are assigned to a flight crew of up to six people. While awaiting your turn, you can relax in the ship's instantly recognizable main hold, complete with a holographic chess board from the movies.

When the time arrives, your flight crew walks down the ship's curving corridors and appears to enter the *Falcon*'s one and only cockpit, thanks to a patented carousel system that keeps the small simulator cabins hidden from each other. Your mission has you stealing supplies from the First Order to sell on the black market. Each rider is assigned their own station: pilots up front, two gunners in the middle, and a pair of engineers in the rear to repair the ship. Scenery is projected on an ultra-HD dome outside the windshield.

What separates this ride from other simulators (such as Star Tours) are the 200 buttons, switches, and levers in the cockpit, each of which does something when activated. Indicator rings illuminate certain controls, cluing you in to the correct moment to punch them. Another difference is that the video screens displaying the action aren't attached to the ride vehicle. This not only allows for a more realistic display of the action but also reduces the potential for motion sickness.

The problem for *Millennium Falcon* is that the experience is pretty disappointing for anyone who doesn't get to be a pilot. Seats for these unfortunate souls are far enough back that it's like watching a drive-in movie through a tunnel. Worse, the controls for those four seats are on a wall next to you, at a 90-degree angle from the video screen with all the action. If you're in one of these seats, you can either look at the screen or the controls you're supposed to be working—but not both.

TOURING TIPS If you use the single-rider line, you'll usually have little to no wait. But you'll also almost always be in the back of the ride vehicle.

Star Wars: Rise of the Resistance ★★★★★

PRESCHOOL ★★★½ (MBA)   **GRADE SCHOOL ★★★★½ (MAA)**   **TEENS ★★★★★ (E)**
YOUNG ADULTS ★★★★★ (E)   **OVER 30 ★★★★★ (E)**   **OVER 65 ★★★★½ (E)**

Note: Rise of the Resistance is the highest-rated attraction in any Disney or Universal theme park in the United States.

What it is Next-generation dark ride. **Scope and scale** Super-headliner. **When to go** First thing or late at night. **Comments** Not to be missed; must be 40″ tall to ride; Rider Switch option available (see page 303). **Duration** About 25 minutes with all preshows; about 5 minutes for ride. **Loading speed** Moderate-fast. **ECV/wheelchair access** Must transfer to the ride vehicle. **Participates in Genie+** No (it offers Individual Lightning Lane). **Early Theme Park Entry** Yes. **Extended Evening Hours** No.

DESCRIPTION AND COMMENTS This is easily the most epic indoor dark ride in Walt Disney World history. It is an innovative attempt to integrate at least four different ride experiences—trackless vehicles, a motion simulator, walk-through environments, and even an elevator drop—into Disney's longest and most complex attraction ever.

The adventure begins when BB-8 rolls into the first preshow room, accompanied by a hologram of Rey. Fifty guests at a time exit the briefing room to board a standing-room-only shuttlecraft piloted by Nien Nunb from *Return of the Jedi*. As the ship breaks orbit, you can feel the rumble and see Poe Dameron accompanying you in his X-Wing, until a Star Destroyer snags you in its tractor beam.

When the doors to your shuttlecraft reopen, you've been convincingly transported into an enormous hangar, complete with 50 Stormtroopers, TIE Fighters, and a 100-foot-wide bay window looking into outer space. Cast members clad as First Order officers brusquely herd captive guests into holding rooms to await their interrogation.

Before long, you're making a break for it in an eight-passenger (two four-seat rows) troop transport with an animatronic droid as your driver. The ride blends dozens of robotic characters and enormous sets with video projections to create some of the most overwhelming environments ever seen in an indoor ride. One sequence sends you between the legs of two towering AT-ATs while dodging laser fire from legions of Stormtroopers, while another puts you face-to-face with Kylo Ren. In the epic finale, you'll survive an escape pod's dramatic crash back to Batuu, a heart-stopping multistory plunge enhanced by digital projections.

TOURING TIPS We think Rise of the Resistance is the best ride Disney has produced in decades. It's the most popular ride in the park and the most complex ride Disney has ever made. That complexity makes it prone to breakdowns—last year, it didn't open with the rest of the park on about 40% of days. It averaged just under 2 hours of outages per day, usually two 1-hour intervals.

The best way to experience Rise without a long wait is to stay at a Disney resort and use Early Entry to get in line as soon as the park opens. Alternatively, purchasing Individual Lightning Lane reservations will save you significant time on crowded days.

Galaxy's Edge Shopping, Dining, and More

SHOPPING Outside of the two headliner rides, Galaxy's Edge boasts a labyrinth of shops selling unique in-universe merchandise; some of the shops are practically attractions themselves. None of the items for sale bear the standard *Star Wars* or Disney logos, to maintain the illusion that everything on offer was actually crafted by and for the Black Spire Outpost villagers.

At **Savi's Workshop,** small groups are led by "Gatherers" through the process of building their own lightsabers, from picking a colorful kyber crystal to selecting customizable handles. The cost of this experience is around $266; reservations via Disney's website or app are strongly recommended, and you pay when you make the reservation. (A small number of same-day reservations might be available for spots starting 2 hours from reservation time.) Despite the steep price tag, it's one of the best things we experienced in Galaxy's Edge—and not for the final product; it's the experience that you're after.

If you want to build a lightsaber of your own, make reservations for Savi's up to 60 days in advance. You can proudly pair your saber with a screen-accurate Jedi tunic ensemble from **Black Spire Outfitters,** but you may wear it only outside of Galaxy's Edge.

At **Droid Depot,** you can pick robot parts from conveyor belts to build your own pint-size R-series or BB-series droid (for around $120), which will then communicate with its counterparts around the land; preassembled droids are also available. Reservations for Droid Depot can be made 60 days in advance and are strongly recommended.

DINING When you get hungry, you'll find that just as much attention has gone into the food and drink at Galaxy's Edge as everything else; even the Coca-Cola sodas come in spherical bottles emblazoned in Aurebesh, the *Star Wars* alphabet. There's no sit-down service, but Galaxy's Edge has the two highest-rated counter-service restaurants in the park: Rustle up galactic food-truck grub from **Docking Bay 7** or grab a sausage grilled under a podracer engine at **Ronto Roasters.** Wash it down with a cold glass of blue or green (nondairy) milk from the **Milk Stand. Oga's Cantina** pours exclusive adult drinks, from Spice Runner cider to Jet Juice cocktails; reservations are strongly recommended. See pages 225–238 for reviews of these four venues.

INTERACTIVITY IN GALAXY'S EDGE Perhaps the most intriguing elements of Galaxy's Edge are its experiments in live interaction, both digital and analog. Live performers, actor-controlled creature puppets, and roving droids can engage with guests. Characters include Rey, Chewbacca, Kylo Ren, and various Stormtroopers.

DISNEY'S HOLLYWOOD STUDIOS ENTERTAINMENT

IN ADDITION TO THE SHOWS and performances profiled earlier in this chapter, the Studios offers the following. Check your *Times Guide* for showtimes.

CHARACTER GREETINGS Chip 'n' Dale, Daisy, and Donald can often be found near Mickey & Minnie's Runaway Railway or Animation Courtyard, from around 10 a.m. to 5 p.m. *Toy Story* characters appear in Toy Story Land from around noon until dinnertime. Sully from *Monsters, Inc.* and many of the *Incredibles* characters (including Edna Mode, Frozone, and some of the famous family) meet in Pixar Place throughout most of the day.

WONDERFUL WORLD OF ANIMATION This 12-minute nighttime projection show displayed on the front of Grauman's Chinese Theatre (home of Mickey & Minnie's Runaway Railway) shows classic clips from Disney and the studios it has acquired. It's not the best (or the second-, third- or fourth-best) projection show Disney has done, but it's a nice way to end the evening, if you're around, and can be a low-hassle substitute for seeing *Fantasmic!*

DISNEY'S HOLLYWOOD STUDIOS TOURING PLAN

OUR HOLLYWOOD STUDIOS TOURING PLAN (see pages 561–562) has two versions: one for Disney resort guests and one for off-site guests; the plan for on-site guests uses Early Theme Park Entry (see page 30) to minimize waits in line. Because Early Entry means thousands of guests will already be in lines and on rides before off-site guests set foot in the park, the touring strategy for off-site guests must be different.

The plan does *not* assume the use of Genie+ or Individual Lightning Lane. If you opt for these, just use the free touring plan software to adjust the plan (see page 46).

PART 15

DISNEY'S
WATER PARKS

KEY QUESTIONS ANSWERED IN THIS CHAPTER

- What are Disney's water parks, and how much do they cost? *(see below)*
- How do we get there, and when should we go? *(see below and opposite)*
- Which water park is best for my family? *(see opposite)*
- How do we prepare for a day at a water park? *(page 482)*
- Are there touring plans? *(page 493)*
- What attractions are offered at the water parks? *(pages 489 and 493)*

OVERVIEW

DISNEY OPERATES TWO WATER PARKS alongside its Orlando theme parks: **Blizzard Beach** and **Typhoon Lagoon.** Both are much larger and more elaborately themed than the local or regional water parks you may have visited. Almost all the waterslides, wave pools, and lazy rivers at these parks are larger and longer than those at other water parks, too.

COST One day of admission to either park costs around $79 for adults and $72 for kids, including tax. Peak season is late May–late September. If you visit outside of that window, Disney offers a discount of around $10 per ticket.

Most visitors to Walt Disney World will spend only one day at a water park, if they choose to go to one at all. If you are planning to visit only one theme park per day during your trip, and then spending one day in a water park, buying separate water park admission is almost always cheaper than buying the **Park Hopper Plus** add-on (see page 64). And even more important, all Walt Disney World resort guests in 2025 receive **free water park admission** on their check-in day. This can be an excellent way to spend time on your arrival day, and a way to experience a water park for free!

GETTING THERE Disney provides regular daily bus service between its resorts and water parks. However, the bus service might route you through other hotels or Disney Springs, and when it does, it takes a long time to get there. If you're staying at a Disney hotel and don't have a car, a ride-sharing app or taxi is the quickest way to go. If you do have a car, parking is free.

WHEN TO GO

DISNEY GENERALLY OPENS at least one of its water parks every day of the year. Even in the winter, Orlando temperatures can vary from the high 40s to the low 80s. When it's warmer out, these off-season months can make for a great water park experience, as an Ohio reader confirms:

unofficial **TIP**
A good time to visit the water parks is midafternoon to late in the day, when the weather has cleared after a storm.

> *Going to Blizzard Beach in December was the best decision ever! They told us at the entrance that if the park didn't reach 100—yes, I said 100—people by noon, they would be closing. I guess they got to 101, because it stayed open but was virtually empty. There was no wait for anything all day! In June we waited in line for an hour for Summit Plummet, but in December it was just the amount of time it took to walk up the stairs. We had the enormous wave pool to ourselves. We did everything in the entire park and ate lunch in less than 3 hours. It was perfect. The weather was slightly chilly at 71°F and overcast with very light rain, but the water was heated, so we were fine.*

The water parks may close if the daytime high temperatures are forecast to be below 60°F or so. If you're visiting when temperatures are low, check the park's website before you visit.

AVOIDING LINES The best way to avoid standing in lines is to visit the water parks when they're least crowded. Because most visitors on any given day are tourists, not locals, the water parks tend to be less crowded on weekends, when many out-of-towners are traveling to or from Orlando. In fact, of the weekend days we evaluated, the parks never reached full capacity; during the week, Thursday had the most closures for capacity, and both parks closed at least once every other weekday. A visitor from New York shares her crowd-avoidance strategy:

> *On our second trip to Typhoon Lagoon, we dispensed with the locker rental (having planned to stay for only the morning, when it was least crowded), and at park opening we just took right off for the Storm Slides before the masses arrived—it was perfect! We must have ridden the slides at least five times before any kind of line built up, and then we were also able to ride the tube and raft rides (Keelhaul and Mayday Falls) in a similar uncrowded, quick fashion because everyone else was busy getting their lockers!*

When a water park reopens after inclement weather has passed, you'll almost have a whole place to yourself.

WHICH WATER PARK TO VISIT?

WE ASK *UNOFFICIAL GUIDE* READERS to rate water park attractions, just like they do for those in the theme parks. The one over at Universal (**Volcano Bay**) ranks first overall; you can read about it in

MOST POPULAR WATER PARKS BY AGE GROUP					
PRESCHOOL	**GRADE SCHOOL**	**TEENS**	**YOUNG ADULTS**	**OVER 30**	**SENIORS**
Blizzard Beach	Blizzard Beach	Volcano Bay	Typhoon Lagoon	Volcano Bay	Typhoon Lagoon
Typhoon Lagoon	Typhoon Lagoon	Blizzard Beach	Blizzard Beach	Blizzard Beach	Blizzard Beach
Volcano Bay	Volcano Bay	Typhoon Lagoon	Volcano Bay	Typhoon Lagoon	Volcano Bay

The Unofficial Guide to Universal Orlando. Blizzard Beach and Typhoon Lagoon tie for second.

If you're looking for the best choice for a diverse group, Blizzard Beach is probably your best bet because it's rated first or second by every age group. A couple from Illinois agrees:

> *If you have time to go to only one water park, definitely go to Blizzard Beach. It seems like they took everything from Typhoon Lagoon and made it better and faster. Summit Plummet was awesome—a total rush. The toboggan and bobsled rides were exciting—the bobsled really throws you around. The family tube ride was really good—much better and longer than the one at Typhoon Lagoon.*

A mother of four from Virginia gives her opinion on choosing between Typhoon Lagoon and Blizzard Beach:

> *At Blizzard Beach, the family raft ride is great, but the kids' area is poorly designed. As a parent, when you walk your child to the top of a slide or the tube ride, they're lost to your vision as they go down because of the fake snowdrifts. There are no direct ways down to the end of the slides, so little ones are left standing unsupervised while parents scramble down from the top. The Typhoon Lagoon kids' area is far superior in design.*

That said, since 2020, Disney typically opens only one water park per day. If you're intent on visiting a specific water park, check Disney's website for its operating status before purchasing tickets.

PLANNING YOUR DAY

DISNEY WATER PARKS are almost as large and elaborate as the major theme parks. You should be prepared for a lot of walking, exercise, sun, and jostling crowds. To have a great day and beat the crowds, consider:

1. GETTING INFORMATION Call ☎ 407-WDW-MAGIC (939-6244) or check disneyworld.disney.go.com the night before to verify when the park opens.

2. TO PICNIC OR NOT TO PICNIC Guests are permitted to take coolers into the parks, so decide whether you want to carry a picnic lunch. Alcoholic beverages, glass containers, and loose ice and dry ice are prohibited; reusable ice packs are permitted. Only one cooler per family is allowed. The in-park food is comparable to fast food, but the prices are a bit high.

3. GETTING STARTED Get up early and have breakfast. If you have a car, drive instead of taking a Disney bus. If you don't have a car, ask a cast member at your hotel if direct bus service to the water park is available. If it is, take the bus; if not, use a ride-sharing service or take a taxi instead. Either way, plan to arrive at the park 20 minutes before opening.

4. USING A GOOD TOURING PLAN The touring plans on pages 563 and 564 are designed to help you avoid crowds and bottlenecks at Disney water parks. If you're attending on a day of moderate to heavy attendance (see the Crowd Calendar at **TouringPlans.com**), consider using one of these tested plans. More touring plans are also available on the website.

5. ATTIRE Wear your swimsuit under shorts and a T-shirt so you don't need to use lockers or dressing rooms. Be advised that it's extremely common for those wearing two-piece swimsuits to accidentally lose one of the pieces on the slides. Also, the walking paths and beach sand get incredibly hot during the summer, so some form of foot protection is a must. Water shoes or sandals that strap to your feet are best. Shops in the parks sell sandals, water shoes, and other protective footwear that can be worn in and out of the water.

6. WHAT TO BRING You'll need a towel, sunscreen, and money. If you don't have towels, they can be rented for $2 each. Sunscreen is available in all park shops. Because wallets and purses get in the way, leave them at your hotel (or lock them in your car's trunk if you must). Carry your Disney resort ID (if you have one) and enough money for the day in a plastic bag or other waterproof container, or use your MagicBand to pay for things.

One reader cautions against keeping items in your pocket:

Our family absolutely loved Summit Plummet, but it claimed all four of our park passes/room-key cards as its victims. My husband had the four cards in an exterior pocket of his swimsuit, secured closed by Velcro AND a snap. But after doing Summit Plummet and Slush Gusher twice apiece and Teamboat Springs once, he looked down, noticed the pocket flapping open, and found all four cards missing! So we had to cancel all the cards (they had charging privileges) and couldn't purchase any food or drinks while we were there (we didn't bring any cash because we planned to charge with our cards)!

We've worn MagicBands at the water parks, and they're much more secure. The point is that anything in your pockets—cash, keys, and the like—may come out.

Though nowhere is completely safe, we usually feel comfortable hiding our money in our cooler. Nobody disturbs our stuff, and our cash is much easier to reach than if we'd stashed it in a locker across the park. If you're carrying a wad or you worry about your belongings being stolen, rent the locker.

A Canadian reader suggests the following option if you don't feel comfortable stashing your valuables in a locker, a cooler, or the like:

As our admission was from an all-inclusive ticket [not a MagicBand], I was concerned about our passes being stolen or lost, yet I didn't

SOGGY TIPS FROM A WATER-LOVING FAMILY

A New Hampshire family—who are evidently working on a PhD in Disney water parks—were kind enough to share their knowledge.

IF YOU'RE GOING TO THE WATER PARKS, **train on a StairMaster** prior to going, especially if you visit Blizzard Beach. For Runoff Rapids, you climb 125 stairs (yes, I counted). Imagine doing that three times in a row, trying to keep up with kids who want to go down the slide multiple times. In addition, there are at least (and here, I'm guessing) 300 stairs if you choose the Alpine Path instead of the chairlift to get to Summit Plummet. At Typhoon Lagoon, each slide, except Miss Adventure Falls, has about 60 steps, so at either park you have quite a bit of stairs to climb or go down.

We were at Blizzard Beach 15 minutes before park opening in late August, and we felt that this was plenty of time to beat the crowds. We noticed crowds building [about an hour after opening]. If you are there at park opening, **stash your things as quickly as possible while you take the chairlift to Summit Plummet.** We were first in line for the chairlift, and we were at the top with no lines. The chairlift is definitely faster if you are one of the first in line, and you won't get winded from walking the Alpine Path. However, if you arrive later in the day, the line for the chairlift builds, and you'll be left having to climb the Alpine Path—great if you're in shape, but not so much if you're not!

Check the closing time of the water parks if you plan on arriving in late afternoon. When Typhoon Lagoon closed at 8 p.m. and we arrived shortly after 2 p.m., lines tended to thin out by 4 p.m. However, when we tried that same tactic (arriving in the afternoon) when Typhoon Lagoon closed at 6 p.m., we noticed that the lines were still long, and it seemed like the crowd wasn't thinning at all. On those days, we wished that we had been there for park opening and left when crowds started to build.

We enjoyed the water parks, but **we only stayed about 3 hours max.** Though the water parks are big (as in spread out), there weren't enough attractions to keep us there the entire day. Yes,

want the hassle of a locker. I discovered that the gift shop sells water-resistant plastic boxes (with strings to go around your neck) in two sizes for around $5, with the smallest being just big enough for passes, credit cards, and a bit of money. I would've spent nearly as much on a locker rental, so I was able to enjoy the rest of the day with peace of mind.

Finally, a limited number of **wheelchairs** are available for rent for $12 per day with a $100 refundable deposit. Personal flotation devices (life jackets) can be rented for free with a refundable deposit.

7. WHAT NOT TO BRING Personal swim gear (fins, masks, rafts, and the like) isn't allowed. Everything you need is provided or available to rent or purchase.

they have slides, but not as many as I expected a Disney park to have. When lines started to build, it became less fun to wait 15-plus minutes for a slide that takes less than 2 minutes to go down. Also, the less popular attractions, such as the lazy river, got really busy, and there were hardly any tubes to be found.

Some of the slides at Blizzard Beach, such as the **Downhill Double Dipper,** take *forever* in line because you're waiting for a tube to make it from the pool up the conveyor belt to the slide stairs. Once the tube finally arrives, you still have to wait for both parties to go down together and to exit the pool. This process takes a long time. If this slide is important to you, make it one of the first things you do. The toboggan rides can also take a while because there is no clear system of who can take the mat when it finally arrives at the top (two mat rides are at the top of the mat conveyor belt: **Toboggan Racers** and **Snow Stormers**).

Some of the slides aren't very comfortable. At Typhoon Lagoon, the **Humunga Kowabunga** should be called the Wedgie Maker. Also, if your family will be going to both water parks (like we did), I sug-gest **skipping Gangplank Falls at Typhoon Lagoon and doing Teamboat Springs at Blizzard Beach instead.** Not only is Teamboat Springs *a lot* longer than Gangplank Falls, but it's also more fun.

The wave pools at both parks are very different. At Typhoon Lagoon, it's "The Wave" pool—as in, there's only one HUGE wave that you can try to bodysurf (good luck with that!). At Blizzard Beach, it's more like "The Waves" pool, where waves are put out at a continual rate, at all times, like a gentle rocking motion, and there are tubes you can use. Typhoon Lagoon has no flotation devices of any kind because, well, they'd be dangerous to everyone involved.

If you have something electronic like a smartphone or tablet that you need to stay dry at the water parks, **buy a waterproof con-tainer BEFORE you go.** The water parks sell only water-resistant containers, and even though the one we bought didn't seem to leak, it would have given us more peace of mind to have a water-proof bag/container.

8. ADMISSION Buy your admission in advance or at least 45 minutes before official opening. Guests staying five or more days should con-sider the **Park Hopper Plus** add-on (see page 64), which provides admission to either Blizzard Beach or Typhoon Lagoon.

9. LOCKERS Keyless rental lockers are $10 per day for a standard and $15 per day for a large. Standard lockers are roomy enough for one per-son or a couple, but a family will generally need a large. You can access your locker freely all day, but not all lockers are conveniently located. Getting a locker is truly competitive. When the gates open, guests race to the rental desk. The rental procedure is somewhat slow; if you aren't among the first in line, you can waste a lot of time waiting. We recom-mend skipping the locker. See No. 6 (page 483) for alternatives.

10. TUBES for bobbing on the waves, floating in the creeks, and riding the tube slides are available for free.

11. GETTING SETTLED Establish your base for the day. There are many beautiful sunning and lounging spots throughout both parks—arrive early and you can have your pick.

The breeze is best along the beaches of the surf pools at Blizzard Beach and Typhoon Lagoon. At Typhoon Lagoon, if there are children younger than age 6 in your party, choose an area to the left of Mount Mayday (ship on top) near the children's swimming area.

Also available are flat (nonadjustable) lounges and chairs (better for reading), shelters for guests who prefer shade, picnic tables, and a few hammocks. If you want more dedicated space, private cabanas are available by reservation for up to six guests. Named **Polar Patios** at Blizzard Beach and **Beachcomber Shacks** at Typhoon Lagoon, these come outfitted with lounge chairs, tables, towels, private lockers, a refillable drink mug, and an attendant who'll be at your beck and call. Cabanas run from around $250 to $500 (plus tax) depending on the season. Call ☎ 407-WDW-PLAY (939-7529) to reserve.

unofficial **TIP**
Blizzard Beach fills early during hotter months. To stake out a nice sunning spot and to enjoy the slides without long waits, arrive at least 20 minutes before the official opening time (check hours the night before).

12. SLIDES Waterslides come in many shapes and sizes. Some are steep and vertical, and some are long and winding. Some resemble corkscrews, while others imitate the pool-and-drop nature of whitewater streams. Depending on the slide, swimmers ride mats, tubes, or rafts. On body slides, they slosh to the bottom on the seat of their pants.

Though both parks are huge, with many slides, armies of guests overwhelm them during busy season. If your main reason for going to a water park is the slides and you hate long lines, be among the first guests to enter the park. Go directly to the slides, and ride as many times as you can before the park fills.

For maximum speed on a body slide, cross your legs at the ankles, and cross your arms over your chest. When you take off, arch your back so almost all your weight is on your shoulder blades and heels (the less contact with the surface, the less resistance). Steer by shifting most of your upper-body weight onto one shoulder blade. For top speed on turns, weight the shoulder blade on the outside of each curve. If you want to go slowly, distribute your weight equally, as if you were lying on your back in bed. For curving slides, maximize speed by hitting the entrance to each curve high and exiting the curve low. Physics!

Some slides and rapids have height requirements (see tables on pages 489 and 493). Riders for **Humunga Kowabunga** at Typhoon Lagoon and **Slush Gusher** and **Summit Plummet** at Blizzard Beach, for example, must be 4 feet tall. You shouldn't ride if you are pregnant or have back problems or other health difficulties.

13. LAZY RIVERS Each of the water parks offers a lazy river. These long, tranquil streams flow ever so slowly around the entire park, through caves, beneath waterfalls, past gardens, and under bridges, offering a relaxing alternative to touring on foot. Lazy rivers can be reached from several put-in and take-out points. There are never lines; just wade into the creek and plop into one of the inner tubes floating by. Ride the current all the way around or get out at any exit. It takes 30–35 minutes to float the full circuit.

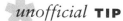

*un*official **TIP**
When lines for the slides become intolerable, head for the surf or wave pool or the lazy river.

14. BAD WEATHER Thunderstorms are common in Florida. On summer afternoons, storms can occur daily. Water parks close during a storm. Most storms, however, are short-lived, allowing the parks to resume normal operations. If a storm is severe and prolonged, it can cause a logistic mess: In addition to the park's closing, guests compete aggressively for shelter, and Disney resort guests may have to joust for seats on a bus back to the hotel.

You should monitor the local weather forecast the day before you go, checking again in the morning before leaving for the water park. Scattered thundershowers are no big deal, but moving storm fronts are to be avoided.

15. ENDURANCE The water parks are large and require almost as much walking as the theme parks. Add to this wave surfing, swimming, and all the climbing required to reach the slides, and you'll be exhausted by the end of the day. Unless you spend your hours like a lizard on a rock, don't expect to return to the hotel with much energy. Consider something low-key for the evening. You'll probably want to fall asleep early.

16. LOST CHILDREN AND LOST ADULTS It's even easier to lose a child or become separated from your party at one of the water parks than it is at the theme parks. Upon arrival, pick a very specific place to meet should you get separated. If you split up on purpose, set times for checking in. Lost-children stations are so out of the way that neither you nor your child will find them without help from a Disney cast member. Explain to your children how to recognize cast members (by their distinctive name tags) and how to ask for help.

BLIZZARD BEACH

BLIZZARD BEACH, Disney's water-adventure park, arrived with its own legend. The story goes that an entrepreneur tried to open a ski resort in Florida during a particularly savage winter. Alas, the snow melted; the palm trees grew back; and all that remained of the ski resort was its alpine lodge; the ski lifts; and, of course, the mountain. Plunging off the mountain are ski slopes and bobsled runs transformed into waterslides. Visitors to Blizzard Beach experience the big thaw—icicles drip, and patches of snow remain. The melting snow has formed a lagoon (the wave pool), which is fed by gushing mountain streams. In the ski resort's lodge area are shops; counter-service food; restrooms; and tube, towel, and locker rentals. Blizzard Beach has its own parking lot but no lodging, though **Disney's All-Star** and **Coronado Springs Resorts** are almost within walking distance.

Both Disney water parks are distinguished by their landscaping and the attention paid to executing their themes. The layout of Blizzard

Blizzard Beach

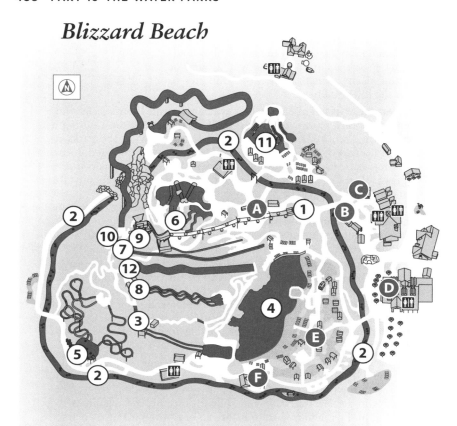

Attractions

1. Chairlift
2. Cross Country Creek
3. Downhill Double Dipper
4. Melt-Away Bay
5. Runoff Rapids
6. Ski Patrol Training Camp
7. Slush Gusher
8. Snow Stormers
9. Summit Plummet
10. Teamboat Springs
11. Tike's Peak
12. Toboggan Racers

Restaurants

A. Avalunch
B. Cooling Hut
C. Frostbite Freddy's
D. Lottawatta Lodge
E. Polar Pub
F. Warming Hut

Restrooms

Beach (and Typhoon Lagoon, described next) is a bit convoluted. Blizzard Beach has 19 waterslides. With slides on both the front and back of the mountain, it isn't always easy to find a path leading to where you want to go.

As you enter Blizzard Beach, you face the mountain. To the left is the wave pool, **Melt-Away Bay,** with gentle, bobbing waves. Coming off the highest peak and bisecting the area at the mountain's base are two long slides: Slush Gusher and Summit Plummet. On either side of the highest peak are tube, raft, and body slides. On the right, a **chairlift** carries guests to the mountaintop (you can also walk up), where

BLIZZARD BEACH ATTRACTIONS

CHAIRLIFT UP MOUNT GUSHMORE **Minimum height: 32″.** Great ride even if you go up just for the view. When the park is packed, use the singles line.

CROSS COUNTRY CREEK **No height requirement.** Lazy river circling the park; grab a tube.

DOWNHILL DOUBLE DIPPER **Minimum height: 48″.** Side-by-side tube-racing slides. At 25 mph, the tube zooms through water curtains and free falls. It's a lot of fun, but it's rough.

MELT-AWAY BAY **No height requirement.** Wave pool with gentle, bobbing waves. Great for younger swimmers.

RUNOFF RAPIDS **No height requirement.** Three corkscrew tube slides to choose from. The center slide is for solo raft rides; the other two slides offer one- or two-person tubes. The dark, enclosed tube gives you the feeling of being flushed down the john.

SKI PATROL TRAINING CAMP **Maximum height: 60″ for T-Bar (zip line).** Place for preteens to train for the big rides.

SLUSH GUSHER **Minimum height: 48″.** 90-foot double-humped slide. Cling to those swimsuit tops and hang on for your lives.

SNOW STORMERS **No height requirement.** Consists of three mat-slide flumes; you go down on your belly.

SUMMIT PLUMMET **Minimum height: 48″.** 120-foot free fall at 60 mph. Needless to say, this ride is very intense. Make sure your child knows what to expect; being over 48″ tall doesn't guarantee an enjoyable experience. If you think you'd enjoy being washed out of a 12th-floor window during a heavy rain, then this slide is for you.

TEAMBOAT SPRINGS **No height requirement.** 1,200-foot group whitewater raft flume. Wonderful ride for the whole family.

TIKE'S PEAK **Maximum height: 48″.** Kid-size version of Blizzard Beach. Recently rethemed to Disney's *Frozen* films. This is the place for little ones.

TOBOGGAN RACERS **No height requirement.** Eight-lane race course. You go down the flume on a mat. Less intense than Snow Stormers.

they can choose from Slush Gusher, Summit Plummet, or Teamboat Springs, all described below. For all other slides, the only way to reach the top is on foot. To the right of the mountain are the children's swimming areas, **Tike's Peak** and **Ski Patrol Training Camp,** and the chairlift. The children's areas are creatively designed, nicely isolated, and—like the rest of the park—visually interesting. Tike's Peak was rethemed in 2022 with characters from Disney's *Frozen*. The lazy river, **Cross Country Creek,** circles the park, passing through the mountain.

For our money, the most exciting and interesting slides are the Slush Gusher and Teamboat Springs (on the front right of the mountain) and Runoff Rapids (on the back side). **Slush Gusher** is a speed slide with hills; we consider it as exciting—but not as bone-jarring—as the more vertical **Summit Plummet,** Disney World's longest speed slide, which begins with a 120-foot free fall. On **Teamboat Springs,** a 1,200-foot-long water-bobsled run, you ride in a round raft that looks like a children's blow-up wading pool.

Runoff Rapids, accessible from a path that winds around the far-left bottom of the mountain, consists of three corkscrew tube slides, one of which is enclosed and dark. As at Teamboat Springs, you'll go much faster on a multiperson tube than on a one-person tube. If you lean so that you enter curves high and come out low, you'll really fly. Because we like to steer the tube and go fast, we much prefer the open slides (where we can see) to the dark, enclosed tube. Crashing through the pitch-dark tube isn't a pleasant feeling.

The **Snow Stormers** mat slides, on the front of the mountain, are fun but not as fast or as interesting as Runoff Rapids or Downhill Double Dipper, on the far-left front. **Toboggan Racers,** at the front and center of the mountain, consists of eight parallel slides where riders are dispatched in heats to race to the bottom. The ride itself is no big deal, and the time needed to get everybody lined up ensures that you'll wait extra long to ride. The side-by-side slides of the hilly **Downhill Double Dipper** are a faster, more exciting race venue—competitors here can reach speeds of up to 25 miles per hour.

TYPHOON LAGOON

WITH A TYPHOON-AFTERMATH THEME, Typhoon Lagoon is comparable in size to Blizzard Beach. The park has 15 waterslides, some as long as 420 feet, and two streams. Most of the slides drop from the top of a 100-foot-tall artificial mountain. Guests enter the park through a misty rainforest and emerge in a ramshackle tropical town where concessions and services are situated. Rides have a sense of adventure, as swimmers encounter bat caves, lagoons and pools, spinning rocks, and formations of dinosaur bones.

If you indulge in all features of Typhoon Lagoon, admission is a fair value. If you go primarily for the slides, you'll have just 2 early-morning hours to enjoy them before the waits become annoying.

Typhoon Lagoon provides something for all ages. Activity pools for young children and families feature geysers, tame slides, bubble jets, and fountains. For the older and more adventurous are the enclosed **Humunga Kowabunga** speed slides; the corkscrew **Storm Slides;** and three whitewater raft rides: **Gangplank Falls, Keelhaul Falls,** and **Mayday Falls. Crush 'n' Gusher,** billed as a water roller coaster, consists of a series of flumes and spillways that course through an abandoned tropical fruit–processing plant. It features tubes that hold one or two people, and you can choose from three routes—Banana Blaster, Coconut Crusher, and Pineapple Plunger—ranging from 410 to 420 feet long. Only Crush 'n' Gusher and the Humunga Kowabunga speed slides (where you can hit 30 mph) have a minimum height requirement of 48 inches.

An Ontario, Canada, mom found Typhoon Lagoon more strenuous than she'd anticipated:

I wish I'd been prepared for the fact that we'd have to haul the tubes up the stairs of Crush 'n' Gusher. My daughter was not strong enough to carry hers, so I had to lug them up by myself. I was exhausted by the end of the day, and my arms ached for a couple of days afterward. Had I known that was the case, I would have started lifting weights several months before our trip in preparation!

Those of you who share the sentiments of the mom above will appreciate **Miss Adventure Falls,** near Crush 'n' Gusher. Riders hop into a circular, four-person raft at the bottom of the slide, then ride a conveyor belt up to the top in about a minute. Though the rafts hold four, the ride works just as well for singles and couples too. The queuing area is inadequate, making for major jams on busy days. Because the attraction is suitable for all ages, expect big crowds and long waits unless you ride just after park opening.

Those looking for a more relaxing experience will also enjoy the meandering, 2,000-foot-long **Castaway Creek,** which floats tubers through hidden grottoes and rainforests.

SURF POOL

WHILE BLIZZARD BEACH has a wave pool, Typhoon Lagoon has a Surf Pool. Most people will encounter larger waves here than they have in the ocean. The surf machine puts out a wave about every 90 seconds (just about how long it takes to get back in position if you caught the previous wave). Perfectly formed and ideal for riding, each wave is about 5–6 feet from trough to crest. Before you join the fray, watch two or three waves from shore. Because each wave breaks in almost the same spot, you can get a feel for position and timing. Observing other surfers is also helpful.

The best way to ride the waves is to swim about three-fourths of the way to the wall at the wave-machine end of the pool. When the waves come—trust us, you'll feel and hear them—swim vigorously toward the beach and try to position yourself one-half to three-fourths of a body length below the breaking crest. The waves are so perfectly engineered that they'll either carry you forward or bypass you. Unlike ocean waves, though, they won't slam you down.

A teenage girl from Illinois notes that the primary hazard in the Surf Pool is colliding with other surfers and swimmers:

The Surf Pool was nice, except I kept landing on really hairy guys when the big waves came.

The best way to avoid collisions while surfing is to paddle out far enough that you'll be at the top of the wave as it breaks. This tactic eliminates the possibility of anyone landing on you from above and ensures maximum forward visibility. A corollary to this: The worst place to swim is where the wave actually breaks. You'll look up to see a 6-foot wall of water carrying eight dozen screaming surfers bearing down on you.

A Virginia mom was caught off-guard by the size and power of the waves:

I had forgotten how violent the wave pool is at Typhoon Lagoon. Thinking I'd be able to hold on to two young(ish) nephews is a mistake I made only once before getting them back to shallower water.

As noted earlier, life jackets are available at the parks' entrances for free with a refundable deposit.

A reader from New Jersey alerted us to another problem:

Typhoon Lagoon is a great family water park—our unexpected favorite. However, please tell your readers not to sit on the bottom of the wave pool—I got a horrible scratch/raspberry and saw about five others with similar injuries. The waves are stronger than they look.

Typhoon Lagoon

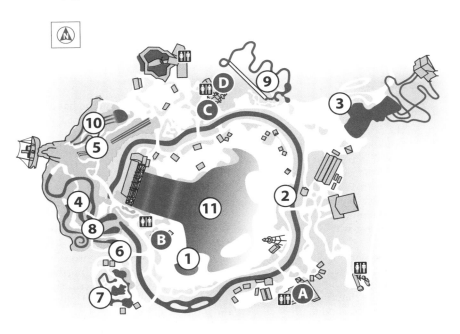

Attractions

1. Bay Slides
2. Castaway Creek
3. Crush 'n' Gusher
4. Gangplank Falls
5. Humunga Kowabunga
6. Keelhaul Falls
7. Ketchakiddee Creek
8. Mayday Falls
9. Miss Adventure Falls
10. Storm Slides
11. Surf Pool

Restaurants

A. Leaning Palms
B. Lowtide Lou's
C. Snack Shack
D. Typhoon Tilly's

👫 Restrooms

Either in the early morning before the park opens or in the evening after the park closes (hours vary), you can take **surfing lessons,** with an actual surfboard. Practice waves range from 3–6 feet tall; most students are first-timers. The cost is $229 per person for 3 hours, including tax; minimum age is 8, and classes are limited to 12 guests. Equipment is provided, but park admission is not included. For details and to see if lessons are being offered, call ☎ 407-WDW-PLAY (939-7529).

TYPHOON LAGOON ATTRACTIONS

BAY SLIDES Maximum height: 60″. Miniature two-slide version of Storm Slides designed for small children. The kids splash down into a far corner of the Surf Pool.

CASTAWAY CREEK No height requirement. Half-mile lazy river in a tropical setting with cool mists, waterfalls, and a tunnel through Mount Mayday. Wonderful!

CRUSH 'N' GUSHER Minimum height: 48″. Water roller coaster where you can choose from three slides—Banana Blaster, Coconut Crusher, and Pineapple Plunger—ranging from 410 to 420 feet long. This thriller is not for the faint of heart. If your kids are new to water park rides, this is not the place to break them in, even if they're tall enough to ride.

GANGPLANK FALLS No height requirement. Whitewater raft flume in a four-person tube.

HUMUNGA KOWABUNGA Minimum height: 48″. Speed slides that hit 30 mph. A five-story drop in the dark rattles even the most courageous rider. If you want to try this one, we recommend doing it in a one-piece swimsuit.

KEELHAUL FALLS No height requirement. Fast whitewater ride in a single-person tube.

KETCHAKIDDEE CREEK Maximum height: 48″. Toddlers and preschoolers love this area reserved only for them.

MAYDAY FALLS No height requirement. Wild single-person tube ride. Hang on!

MISS ADVENTURE FALLS No height requirement. Gentle family raft ride down a well-themed slide.

STORM SLIDES No height requirement. Three body slides plunge down and through Mount Mayday.

SURF POOL No height requirement. World's largest inland surf facility, with waves up to 6 feet high. Adult supervision required. Surfing lessons may be offered (see page 492).

AFTER HOURS EVENTS As we went to press, Disney was holding After Hours events at Typhoon Lagoon during summer months, from roughly mid-May through early September. Usually staged on Saturday from 8–11 p.m., with ticket holders admitted into the park at 6 p.m., these events include access to all of the park's major rides and slides. Tickets cost $80 for adults and $75 for children.

WATER PARK TOURING PLANS

ONE-DAY TOURING PLANS for Typhoon Lagoon and Blizzard Beach can be found on pages 563 and 564, respectively. These plans are for parents with small children. Touring plans for adults, along with our online reader survey, are available at **TouringPlans.com.**

The plans presented in this book include all the slides, flumes, and rides appropriate for kids in both parks. We've also included tips on which slides to try first if this is your child's first water park experience. For example, at Typhoon Lagoon we suggest the family whitewater raft ride Miss Adventure Falls as the first attraction. If your child enjoys that, we list Gangplank Falls and then Keelhaul Falls as the next steps up in waterslides. If that seems a bit much, however, the touring plan recommends the Ketchakiddee Creek play area as an alternative.

BEHIND-THE-SCENES *and* VIP TOURS

IF YOU'RE INTERESTED IN THE MOUSE'S INNARDS—um, make that inner workings—several tours offer a glimpse of what goes on behind the scenes. Reservations must be guaranteed with a credit card, and you must cancel at least 48 hours in advance for a full refund. Many tours require that you also buy park admission; we note where it isn't mandatory. Prices do not include tax. Some tours are available only on certain days of the week (search for them online to confirm). For reservations and details, call ☎ 407-WDW-TOUR (939-8687).

unofficial **TIP**
Many tours involve lots of walking, standing, and time spent outdoors, so check the forecast before you head out.

BEHIND *the* SCENES *at the* MAGIC KINGDOM

AS ITS NAME SUGGESTS, **Disney's Keys to the Kingdom Tour** takes you behind the scenes at the Magic Kingdom, providing a detailed look at the park's logistical, technical, and operational sides, including the parade-assembly area, the waste-treatment plant, and the utilidor network beneath the park. You'll also usually get to ride a few attractions, like the Jungle Cruise. The program ($129–$149 per person) includes lunch and runs about 5 hours; guests must be at least 16 years old. Annual Pass holders and DVC members receive a 15% discount.

A private **Fireworks Cruise** (2–2½ hours, $449, up to 10 guests) offers a guided sailing in Seven Seas Lagoon, followed by a viewing of the *Happily Ever After* fireworks from the water. On select nights, the voyage also includes a viewing of the Electrical Water Pageant. You can arrange departure from the marinas at the Contemporary, the Grand Floridian, Fort Wilderness, the Polynesian, or Wilderness

Lodge. Each cruise is conducted by a captain and includes snacks and soft drinks. Also included are decorative banners and balloons, if you are celebrating a special occasion (request these when you book). Cruises depart 1 hour and 15 minutes before the fireworks start.

BEHIND *the* SCENES *at* EPCOT

THE HOUR-LONG **Behind the Seeds** tour ($39–$45 per guest, age 3 and up) takes you through the vegetable gardens and aquaculture farms in The Land. The quality of the experience—a cross between science lecture and Willy Wonka factory tour—depends heavily on the guide's presentation. Requires reservations and park admission; make reservations online, or you can try in person on the lower level of The Land (next to the entrance to Soarin' Around the World). We used to tout this as the best-value behind-the-scenes tour, but the price has almost doubled since 2017. Still, if you like Living with the Land, this is the tour for you.

If you have divers in your group, **DiveQuest** at The Seas with Nemo & Friends Pavilion ($229–$249 per guest, age 10 and up with proof of scuba certification) is the most unique way to experience the 5.7-million-gallon aquarium and its 2,000-plus sea creatures. The tour of the tanks at The Seas lasts 2 hours, including about 40 minutes of diving. You'll also get a backstage tour of the inner workings of this massive aquarium. Any members of your party who don't want to participate or aren't scuba-certified can watch from the 56 windows in The Seas and see you swimming with the fishes. All diving equipment is provided—you can't bring your own, other than your own dive mask. Swimsuits are required, and shorty wet suits are provided.

If you're not scuba-certified and still want to interact with the citizens of The Seas, **Dolphins in Depth** ($209 per guest, must be at least 4 feet tall) is the choice for you. This 2-hour experience allows you to talk to the experts who work with and care for the dolphins in The Seas every day. The tour includes about 30 minutes with the dolphins in the water (waist-deep on a platform). You'll also get to view backstage areas where dolphin care happens and learn more about dolphin training and research. Bring a swimsuit for when you get in the water! Shorty wet suits are also provided in adult sizes.

BEHIND *the* SCENES *at* DISNEY'S ANIMAL KINGDOM

MY PICK FOR BEST TOUR at Walt Disney World, the **Wild Africa Trek** (3 hours, $219–$229) takes groups of up to 12 on forest hiking trails, suspension bridges high above hippo and crocodile pools, and a private safari complete with a gourmet meal in the middle of the savanna. Open to guests age 8 and up. Extensive walking is required; guests must weigh 45–300 pounds and be at least 4 feet tall for the safety gear. You'll need to wear closed-toe shoes and clothing you'd be comfortable wearing on a ropes course (no skirts or dresses, please). Photos are included in this excursion, and you'll want proof that you walked on a rope bridge over bloats of hippos and floats of crocodiles. If you'd rather just have the safari and food/drinks without the hiking and rope bridges, opt for **Savor the Savanna** ($189–$199 per person).

The **Starlight Safari,** previously offered only to guests of Animal Kingdom Lodge & Villas, is now open to all Disney resort guests. For $75–$89 per guest, you can board a safari truck and explore the savannas of Animal Kingdom Lodge. Look for the residents by using the provided night-vision devices. Tours are limited to guests age 8 and older and typically last about an hour.

Caring for the Giants is a 1-hour tour led by an animal-care specialist, focusing on the care of the park's elephants. The minimum age is 4 years, so this tour is great for your younger animal lovers. In fact, my family did it with our 4-year-old during a recent trip. The tour guide will always keep guests engaged, whether they are 4, 44, or 84. The cost is $39 per person. You'll get to walk backstage to a van that will drive you around the back of the savanna to a viewing platform where the elephants will usually be 80–100 feet away as you observe them and learn all about their care and behavior.

Up Close with Rhinos, focusing on the care of the park's rhinos, is also a 1-hour tour led by an animal-care specialist. This is another great option for families with younger kids; guests age 4 and up are welcome. The cost for this one is slightly higher, at $49 per person. But that's because instead of viewing the animals from a platform 100 feet away, you'll go backstage to get up close and personal with the white rhinos.

VIP TOURS

I CAN TELL by the book you're reading that you're smart, and probably hilarious, kind, and patient to boot. If you're also flush with disposable income and looking to avoid every possible line at Disney World while having most of your whims catered to, then a **private VIP tour** is what you want.

For $450–$900 per hour (depending on the season; 7 hours minimum), a Disney VIP host will pick you up at your resort (or meet you at the park of your choosing), precheck your admission tickets, and whisk you and up to nine of your friends through a private entrance to a Disney theme park. Once in the park, your VIP guide will ensure that you wait as little as possible for whatever attractions you want to see (usually by taking you through the Lightning Lane, even if you don't have reservations) and make sure you get prime spots for viewing parades and fireworks. If you want to visit multiple parks, the VIP guide will drive you in a private car.

Unofficial Guide readers rave about the guides, who do everything from entertain the kids to regale the adults with obscure theme park trivia. They also provide lots of snacks and can arrange meals.

VIP tours can be booked 3–90 days in advance by calling ☎ 407-560-4033. You must cancel at least 48 hours in advance to avoid a charge of 2 hours at the booked rate.

DISNEY SPRINGS, SHOPPING, *and* NIGHTLIFE

A DISNEY WORLD VACATION isn't just theme parks and attractions. If you want to shop, see live entertainment, or just have something to do after the parks close, this chapter is for you.

Walt Disney World has a huge outdoor mall complex with restaurants, shopping, and theaters, so guests of its hotels and theme parks never need to go somewhere else to spend their money. This chapter covers that complex, called **Disney Springs.** In addition, it explores the best **shopping** in the theme parks and nearby in Orlando. Finally, it lists the great **nightlife** options at the Disney resorts and elsewhere in the World.

DISNEY SPRINGS

ARRIVING AT DISNEY SPRINGS

BY CAR Guests driving to Disney Springs will take Buena Vista Drive from Disney property, and Hotel Plaza Boulevard from the Disney Springs resorts and FL 535. I-4 westbound offers direct access to the complex via Exit 67.

There are three parking garages and four surface lots. The **Lime** garage serves The Landing, Town Center, and Marketplace areas of Disney Springs. The **Orange** garage is closest to the West Side, the AMC 24 movie theater, and Planet Hollywood. The third garage,

Disney Springs

Disney's Saratoga Springs Resort & Spa

Strawberry Parking Lot

Lake Buena Vista

water taxi

water taxi

water taxi

West Side Dock

The Landing Dock

West Side

Parking

Orange Garage

WEST SIDE Shopping

1. Disney's Candy Cauldron
2. DisneyStyle
3. M&Ms Store
4. Pelé Soccer
5. Star Wars Galactic Outpost
6. Sunglass Hut
7. Super Hero Headquarters

WEST SIDE Dining

8. City Works Eatery & Pour House
9. Food Trucks at Exposition Park
10. House of Blues Restaurant & Bar
11. The Smokehouse
12. Jaleo/Pepe by José Andrés
13. Splitsville
14. Starbucks
15. Summer House on the Lake

THE LANDING Shopping

16. Chapel Hats
17. **Group 1:** Erwin Pearl, Oakley, Sanuk, Savannah Bee Company
18. Havaianas

THE LANDING Dining

19. The Boathouse
20. Chef Art Smith's Homecomin'
21. The Edison
22. Enzo's Hideaway
23. Erin McKenna's Bakery NYC
24. The Ganachery
25. Gideon's Bakehouse
26. Jock Lindsey's Hangar Bar
27. Joffrey's Coffee & Tea
28. Maria & Enzo's
29. Morimoto Asia/ Morimoto Street Food
30. Paddlefish
31. Paradiso 37
32. Pizza Ponte
33. Raglan Road/ Cookes of Dublin
34. STK Orlando
35. Terralina Crafted Italian
36. Vivoli il Gelato
37. Wine Bar George

TOWN CENTER Shopping

38. Coca-Cola Store
39. **Group 1:** American Threads, Johnston & Murphy, Tommy Bahama, Fit2Run
40. **Group 2:** Columbia, Everything but Water, Free People, Johnny Was, Kate Spade New York, Lilly Pulitzer, Rothy's, Sperry, Sugarboo, Vera Bradley
41. **Group 3:** Coach, MAC, Jo Malone
42. **Group 4:** Lacoste, Luxury of Time
43. **Group 5:** Lovepop, Ron Jon Surf Shop, Sephora, Shore, Stance, Superdry
44. **Group 6:** Levi's, Orlando Harley-Davidson, TUMI, Volcom
45. **Group 7:** Alex and Ani, Anthropologie, Ever After Jewelry Co., Fabletics, Francesca's, Kendra Scott, lululemon, Melissa Clube, L'Occitane en Provence, Rustic Cuff, Under Armour, UNOde50

Grapefruit, sits opposite the Lime garage on the other side of Buena Vista Drive. It is connected to Disney Springs via a raised walkway. There is no charge to park in the garages.

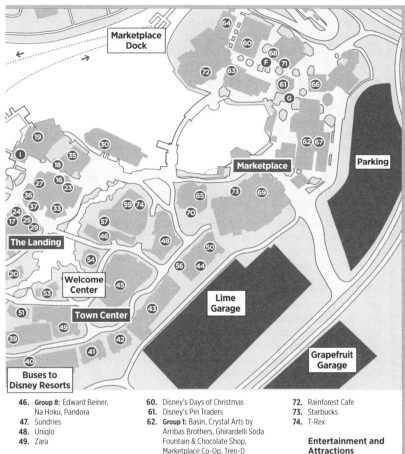

46. **Group 8:** Edward Beiner, Na Hoku, Pandora
47. Sundries
48. Uniqlo
49. Zara

TOWN CENTER Dining
50. Amorette's Patisserie
51. Blaze Fast-Fire'd Pizza
52. Chicken Guy
53. D-Luxe Burger
54. Frontera Cocina
55. Planet Hollywood
56. The Polite Pig
57. Sprinkles
58. Wolfgang Puck Bar & Grill

MARKETPLACE Shopping
59. Build-a-Dino/Dino Store

60. Disney's Days of Christmas
61. Disney's Pin Traders
62. **Group 1:** Basin, Crystal Arts by Arribas Brothers, Ghirardelli Soda Fountain & Chocolate Shop, Marketplace Co-Op, Tren-D
63. **Group 2:** Goofy's Candy Co., Star Wars Trading Post, Swings N' Things
64. **Group 3:** The Art of Disney, Disney's Wonderful World of Memories
65. The Lego Store
66. Once Upon a Toy
67. PhotoPass Studio
68. The Spice & Tea Exchange
69. World of Disney

MARKETPLACE Dining
70. The Daily Poutine
71. Earl of Sandwich

72. Rainforest Cafe
73. Starbucks
74. T-Rex

Entertainment and Attractions
A. Aerophile
B. AMC Disney Springs 24/ MacGuffins
C. AMC Disney Springs 24 Dine-In Theatres
D. Cirque du Soleil
E. House of Blues
F. Marketplace Carousel
G. Marketplace Train Express
H. Splitsville Luxury Lanes
I. Vintage Amphicar & Italian Water Taxi Tours

An LED display on each level of the garages indicates how many open spaces there are on each level. Typically, the lower levels fill up first, with more open spaces available on each successive level up.

You'll ultimately want to navigate down to Level 2, where all guests are funneled through security. If there are no spots on that level, park as close as possible to the center of the level where you find a spot and walk down to the security checkpoint. There's also "preferred" parking available in the Lemon and Mango surface lots for $20. We're not sure why you'd pay this much to park, but it's there if you can't find a spot and you're desperate.

BY DISNEY TRANSPORTATION All Disney resorts and theme parks offer **bus transportation** to Disney Springs; some bus routes are shared with **Typhoon Lagoon,** one of Disney's two water parks. The Disney bus area is centrally located between the Orange and Lime parking garages. **Saratoga Springs Resort, Old Key West Resort**, and the **Port Orleans Resorts** offer boat transportation to the Disney Springs dock at The Landing.

BY TAXI/RIDESHARE Drop-off and pickup are at the **Cirque du Soleil** theater on the far west side of Disney Springs and at the far east side of the Marketplace.

ON FOOT Saratoga Springs Resort has walking paths to Disney Springs, and guests staying at hotels in the **Disney Springs Resort Area** (see page 166) can walk to Disney Springs on walkways and pedestrian bridges to avoid traffic.

GETTING ORIENTED

DISNEY SPRINGS IS DIVIDED INTO FOUR AREAS, each with its own theme. **Marketplace,** on the east side of Disney Springs, is the most kid-friendly, with the **World of Disney** store and many activities for children. It has a small carousel and minitrain rides for a fee. A free splash area is great for cooling down, and free concerts take place in the amphitheater across from World of Disney.

The Landing is the waterfront section of Disney Springs. Open, winding paths offer sweeping views of the water and Saratoga Springs as you walk between the Marketplace and the West Side.

The third area is the Old Florida–style **Town Center,** which has most of the well-known retail stores in Disney Springs (**Uniqlo** and **Zara** are the largest). If you've ever found yourself at Pirates of the Caribbean and thought, "What this place needs is upscale shopping," you'll love this section. Town Center sits between The Landing and the parking lot.

On the **West Side,** a Disney-themed **Cirque du Soleil** production called *Drawn to Life* opened in 2021. **Jaleo by José Andrés** (see page 260), an **AMC** multiplex theater, the **Splitsville** bowling lanes, and **Starbucks** are the biggest draws here.

DISNEY SPRINGS SHOPPING AT A GLANCE
Marketplace

DISNEY'S DAYS OF CHRISTMAS This shop is sheer holiday magic, with hundreds of holiday decorations for sale. We especially like the ornament personalization—for a small fee, an artist will handwrite your name and a phrase or date. What better way to remember your Disney vacation than an ornament you put on your tree every year?

THE ART OF DISNEY Browse fine art, watch artists draw characters, or pick up some postcards as fun and cheap souvenirs.

BASIN If you want fancy soaps and other scented products, this is the place to go.

CRYSTAL ARTS BY ARRIBAS BROTHERS Sparkly collectibles and works of art abound in this shop full of Arribas Brothers products. Avoid it if you have clumsy family members!

GOOFY'S CANDY CO. Interactive show kitchen with lots of sweets. Enjoy create-your-own pretzel rods, marshmallows, and candy apples.

THE LEGO STORE This hands-on outdoor play area has bins of Legos that kids can get creative with. Inside you'll find an impressive selection of all the latest Lego sets. Photo ops with life-size Disney characters surround the shop.

unofficial **TIP**
At **Ghirardelli Soda Fountain & Chocolate Shop,** near Basin and Crystal Arts, you can smell the chocolate when you walk in. Chocolate souvenirs abound, but go ahead and treat yourself to a "world famous" sundae topped with hot fudge made daily. The line for ice cream often winds out the door—it's that good.

MARKETPLACE CO-OP The Co-op has six pop-up-style retail experiences within one shop. Shops rotate depending on what is popular at the time.

ONCE UPON A TOY This is the place to find toy sets and a huge selection of plushies. We also appreciate that Once Upon a Toy is far less crowded than World of Disney. You're less likely to lose your kids (or partner) here.

STAR WARS TRADING POST Although *Star Wars* merchandise can be found in other stores, this is the largest consolidated collection anywhere on-property outside of Galaxy's Edge in Hollywood Studios. Shop here for collectibles and Galaxy's Edge merch specifically.

THE SPICE AND TEA EXCHANGE Carries flavored salts and sugars, teas, and spice mixes. You can also purchase wines and cookbooks.

TREN-D Women's apparel and accessories, plus exclusive items from cutting-edge designers.

WORLD OF DISNEY With the largest selection of Disney merchandise in the world, World of Disney can get oppressively crowded. It has a little bit of everything. If you can't find something to love here, you won't find it anywhere on-property.

Town Center

AMORETTE'S PATISSERIE Beautiful cakes and pastries, including Disney character–themed cakes, large and small, that you won't see anywhere else, plus sandwiches.

COCA-COLA STORE A fun visit, especially for fans of soda. The roof deck has a bar with Coke flights and views of Disney Springs.

JO MALONE Perfumes, candles, and other scented lifestyle items.

KATE SPADE NEW YORK What sets this location apart from the one at your local mall is that it often has Disney-themed bags and accessories only available here or online.

LILLY PULITZER Bright, fun prints synonymous with summertime.

PANDORA The jewelry retailer has an agreement with Walt Disney World that includes another shop on Main Street, U.S.A. Many Disney-exclusive charms sell out quickly.

SUPERDRY Fun casual wear for teens and young adults.

TOMMY BAHAMA One of the few shops at Disney Springs with a decent selection of casual menswear. It also has a nice selection of swimwear for both men and women.

UNIQLO Fast fashion and exclusive Disney apparel. Uniqlo is handy if you need to buy basics such as sweatshirts and T-shirts.

VERA BRADLEY The ubiquitous quilted bags with a fanatical following. You'll find both Disney-exclusive and mainline prints here.

Other shops in Town Center include **American Threads, Anthropologie, Coach, Columbia Sportswear, Fabletics, Francesca's, Free People, Johnny Was, Lacoste, Levi's, L'Occitane, Lovepop, Lululemon, Mac Cosmetics, Na Hoku, Harley-Davidson, Ron Jon Surf Shop, Rothy's, Sephora, Sperry, Sugarboo & Co., Under Armour, Volcom,** and **Zara.**

The Landing

THE GANACHERY Exquisite handmade chocolates in gourmet flavor combinations. This Disney-run shop may be more pricey than you're expecting, but—coming from a chocolate connoisseur—it's worth it. Don't skip the old-fashioned flavored chocolate, if it's available. They card you for it for a reason.

GIDEON'S BAKEHOUSE This bakery/coffee shop serves cookies that weigh almost half a pound, admirably attempting to redefine the phrase *single serving*. Expect a line of at least 30 minutes most of the day.

JOFFREY'S COFFEE & TEA COMPANY You can purchase leaves to take home or enjoy a hot or cold tea at the counter. Very pleasant and less hectic than Starbucks for your caffeine needs.

You'll also find kiosks selling everything from wind chimes to yo-yos as you walk through The Landing.

West Side

DISNEY'S CANDY CAULDRON Watch as gooey treats are made in the open kitchen. Dipped candy apples (befitting the Snow White theme) are the house specialty. There's also a decent selection of bulk candies.

DISNEYSTYLE Packed full of the trendiest Disney apparel and accessories you'll find on the West Side.

M&M'S A large store selling everyone's favorite melt-in-your-mouth chocolates in every flavor and color imaginable, along with clothing, mugs, and other merchandise.

PELÉ SOCCER A store for the biggest soccer fans in your life.

STAR WARS GALACTIC OUTPOST A large selection of *Star Wars* souvenirs, from T-shirts to Stormtrooper helmets. Focuses more on clothing and "fun" than the Marketplace's Star Wars Trading Post.

SUNGLASS HUT Got to sunny Florida and forgot your shades? This is the place to pick up a pair to save your retinas.

SUPER HERO HEADQUARTERS Guardians of the Galaxy: Cosmic Rewind is the only Marvel-themed ride at Walt Disney World and, oddly, it chose not to deposit you directly into the Marvel-themed gift shop. So if you're missing Marvel merch, head here instead.

BARS AND NIGHTLIFE AT DISNEY SPRINGS

DISNEY SPRINGS IS A POPULAR DESTINATION after dark for folks who aren't ready to sleep but don't want to burn park admission for just a few hours in the evening. You'll find street entertainment, including singers, musicians, and performance artists, spread throughout Disney Springs. There's even more entertainment at many of the restaurants, including bands and singers at **House of Blues** (pages 260 and 509) and **Splitsville Dining Room** (page 275) and music and Irish dancers at **Raglan Road Irish Pub & Restaurant** (page 269).

Some of our favorite places to grab a drink are at Disney Springs. Raglan Road has multiple bars and a fantastic menu of appetizers. **Jaleo by José Andrés** (page 260) and **Wine Bar George** (page 284) have excellent drinks and tasty small-plate menus. **The Boathouse** (page 248) and **Morimoto Asia** (page 265) both have bars worth a visit. Reader ratings for **The Edison, Enzo's Hideaway,** and **STK Orlando** are so low that we don't recommend them.

TAKE IT ON THE RUN, BABY

FOR AN EVENING OF DRINKING and strolling, Disney Springs has you covered. Starting with the **AmphiBar** outside the entrance to The Boathouse, the restaurants quickly figured out that there was a market for cocktails to go. Find Guinness outside **Raglan Road** and margaritas at **Frontera Cocina** and **Dockside Margaritas.**

SHOPPING *in* WALT DISNEY WORLD *and* ORLANDO

SHOPPING AT DISNEY WORLD

EACH THEME PARK has at least one major retail space, several minor ones, and gift shops attached to most attractions. While we occasionally groan about how the merchandise selection at each store and park gets more and more similar every year, this does mean that if something catches your eye, you'll most likely see it again. Ditto for prices; pricing is consistent throughout the resorts—an item on sale in one location will be the same price at all locations.

See the following pages for a quick-reference guide to which theme park shops carry what you're looking for.

Magic Kingdom Shopping

BIBBIDI BOBBIDI BOUTIQUE Located in Cinderella Castle, this salon for kids ages 3–12 will give princess hopefuls a royal makeover. Packages range from $107 to above $500, plus tip. Photo packages, a Knight Package (for those who don't want to be princesses), and other add-ons are available for an extra charge.

MAGIC KINGDOM SHOPPING SAMPLER	
I WANT . . .	**FIND IT AT . . .**
• One-stop shopping	• **The Emporium,** Main Street
• Candy, pastries, and fudge	• **Main Street Confectionery,** Main Street • **Big Top Souvenirs,** Fantasyland
• Disney art and collectibles	• **Main Street Cinema,** Main Street
• Holiday décor	• **Olde Christmas Shoppe,** Liberty Square
• Memory cards and batteries	• **Box Office Gifts,** Main Street
• Personalized mouse ears	• **Box Office Gifts,** Main Street • **Fantasy Faire,** Fantasyland
• Princess wear	• **The Emporium,** Main Street
• Tech gifts	• **Space Mountain Gift Shop,** Tomorrowland
• Women's jewelry, handbags, and accessories	• **Main Street Jewelers** (has a **Pandora** shop)

Reservations can be made up to 60 days in advance (70 days for Disney resort guests); call ☎ 407-939-7895 for information or reservations. Allow 30 minutes–1 hour for the whole makeover.

EPCOT Shopping

Retail is a big part of the **World Showcase** experience in EPCOT, much more so than in the other theme parks. This is one of the rare times that most merchandise you see will be unique. With a selection that ranges from affordable trinkets to $99,000 pieces of art, the shops in World Showcase have something for everyone. Walking clockwise, you'll find the following:

★ **MEXICO** Probably the most immersive shopping experience in all of World Showcase, **Plaza de los Amigos** is a re-creation of a Mexican shopping village at dusk. You'll find all manner of sombreros, Día de los Muertos (Day of the Dead) items, Oaxacan carved wooden animals, and blankets. Along the side of the shopping area is **La Princesa de Cristal,** with crystal jewelry and trinkets, and another shop with leather items, women's dresses and blouses, and other accessories.

★ **NORWAY The Fjording** is a series of small shopping galleries with popular imports such as trolls (from $15) and wooden Christmas ornaments (from $5). Other hard-to-find imports include Scandinavian foods and candies, Laila perfume and body lotion, and Helly Hansen and Dale of Norway clothing, including thick woolen sweaters. You'll also find all things *Frozen* here.

★ **CHINA** This pavilion features one of our favorite shops, piled with imports such as real silk kimonos, cloisonné, and thick silk rugs. **House of Good Fortune** is more like a rambling department store than a shop. You'll find everything here, from silk fans to $4,000 jade sculptures to antique furniture. The silk dresses and robes are competitively priced. Darling handbags are $10 and up, and silk ties are around $20. We always admire the handwoven pure-silk carpets, starting at about $300 for a small rug and topping out around $2,500 for a 4-by-8-foot rug. The prices are comparable to what you'd pay outside the World.

EPCOT SHOPPING SAMPLER	
I WANT . . .	**FIND IT AT . . .**
• One-stop shopping	• **Creations Shop,** World Celebration
• Disney art and collectibles	• **The Art of Disney,** The American Adventure Pavilion
• Disney comics and books	• **ImageWorks,** Imagination! Pavilion
• Eco-friendly gifts	• **Outpost,** World Showcase
• Kitchen supplies and décor	• **Port of Entry,** World Showcase
• Memory cards and batteries	• **Camera Center,** World Celebration
• Personalized mouse ears	• **Creations Shop,** World Celebration
• Princess wear	• **The Wandering Reindeer,** Norway Pavilion
• Tech gifts	• **Creations Shop and Camera Center,** World Celebration

Village Traders, a shop between China and Germany, sells beautiful, handmade African woodcarvings. Another specialty here is bead jewelry, crafted in Uganda from repurposed Disney paper products such as old handout guides.

★ **GERMANY** Shops interconnect on both sides of the cobblestoned central plaza. From left to right, you'll first find **Karamell-Küche** which has take-home candies in addition to its wide array of snacks. If you can tear yourself away from that amazing smell, next you'll get to **Die Weihnachts Ecke,** where Christmas ornaments (pick up a pickle!) and handmade nutcrackers are on display year-round. Next is the **Weinkeller,** with nearly 300 varieties of German wine and liqueur to sample or bring home. Farther on is another shop that people of the clumsy persuasion (like me) should avoid: **Kunstarbeit in Kristall** carries a fabulous collection of Swarovski crystal, including pins, glassware, and Arribas Brothers collectibles (check out the limited-edition $37,500 replica of Cinderella Castle or the $99,000 Spaceship Earth Beacon of Magic). Across the plaza, **Stein Haus** is stocked with limited-edition steins and glassware, as well as Biergarten gear. Prost! Tiny **Das Kaufhaus** stocks a nice selection of Adidas sportswear. Next door is **Volkskunst,** where the walls are covered with Schneider cuckoo clocks and the shelves are lined with German candies and souvenirs. On your way to the next pavilion, you'll find yet another shop, **Glaskunst,** featuring glass boots and steins, with options for personalization. Who knew Germans liked shopping so much?

★ **ITALY** At **Il Bel Cristallo,** find sportswear, Bulgari and Emilio Pucci fragrances, Murano figurines, elaborate Venetian masks, wine by the bottle, and a small selection of Christmas decorations in the back room.

★ **JAPAN** An outpost of the country's 350-year-old **Mitsukoshi Department Store** stretches along one entire side of the Japan Pavilion. Kid-friendly merchandise (Hello Kitty, Naruto, and Yu-Gi-Oh! are often seen) fills the front, with kimonos, slippers, handbags, and lots more at the back. Mitsukoshi's expanded culinary display includes a sake-tasting bar, along with chopsticks, pretty rice bowls, a large variety of teas and teapots, and imported snacks. The selection of products

DISNEY'S ANIMAL KINGDOM SHOPPING SAMPLER	
I WANT . . .	**FIND IT AT . . .**
• One-stop shopping	• **Discovery Trading Company,** Discovery Island
• African souvenirs	• **Mombasa Marketplace,** Harambe, Africa
• African wines, cookbooks, and Flame Tree Barbecue Sauce	• **Zuri's Sweets Shop,** Africa
• Dinosaur kitsch and toys	• **Chester and Hester's Dinosaur Treasures,** DinoLand U.S.A.
• Memory cards and batteries	• **Island Mercantile,** Discovery Island
• My own shoulder-top banshee or glowing Pandora merch	• **Windtraders,** Pandora—The World of Avatar
• Personalized mouse ears	• **Island Mercantile,** Discovery Island

related to anime is great as well. Tourists line up for an oyster that is guaranteed to have a pearl in its shell (pearls are polished for you by the salesperson). And there is an entire room dedicated to Japanese snacks, which can be a fun culinary adventure.

★ **MOROCCO** Several shops populate this pavilion, although many remain closed, including **Tangier Traders, The Brass Bazaar,** and **Casablanca Carpets.** Instead, head to **Souk-al-Magreb** (beside Spice Road Table), where you can find authentic Moroccan clothing, Morocco Pavilion souvenirs, and colorful lanterns.

★ **FRANCE** The courtyard at the France Pavilion has some *merveilleux* shopping opportunities. A dedicated Guerlain shop, **La Signature,** offers cosmetics and fragrances from the French house, along with makeup consultations. **Plume et Palette** has fragrances, cosmetics, and women's accessories from Christian Dior, Givenchy, Kenzo, Le Tanneur, and Thierry Mugler, to name a few.

Find wines and kitchen goods, including a Champagne-tasting counter, at **Les Vins de Chefs de France** and **L'Esprit de la Provence,** which are connecting shops. And finally, at the back of the pavilion, **Souvenirs de France** sells a smattering of everything French, from berets and Eiffel Tower models to T-shirts and language books.

★ **UNITED KINGDOM** **The Toy Soldier** sells costumes, books, and plush toys featuring English characters from favorite films and television shows, as well as British rock and roll–themed items. You'll find plenty of Alice in Wonderland, Peter Pan, and Winnie the Pooh merchandise too. Stop at **The Crown & Crest** to look up your family name in the coat-of-arms book, and the shop will create your family's insignia in a beautiful frame of your choice. At the adjacent **Sportsman's Shoppe,** you'll find plenty of football (soccer) apparel, balls, and books.

Across the street, you'll find **The Queen's Table,** a gift shop with UK-themed clothing (and commemorative tartan), glassware, and more. The quaint **Lords and Ladies** offers lotions, soaps, scarves, jewelry, and perfume from the United Kingdom. **The Tea Caddy** stocks Twinings tea, biscuits (cookies), and candy.

★ **CANADA** There's not much shopping here, but **Northwest Mercantile** has a wide selection of merchandise, including NHL jerseys, T-shirts, sweatshirts, aprons, and pajamas, especially flannel.

DISNEY'S HOLLYWOOD STUDIOS SHOPPING SAMPLER	
I WANT . . .	FIND IT AT . . .
• One-stop shopping	• **Mickey's of Hollywood,** Hollywood Boulevard
• Clothes and accessories tied to Disney's current marketing promotion	• **Keystone Clothiers,** Hollywood Boulevard
• Holiday décor	• **It's a Wonderful Shop,** Streets of America
• MagicBands and other Disney gifts	• **The Darkroom,** Hollywood Boulevard
• Personalized mouse ears	• **Legends of Hollywood,** Sunset Boulevard
• Princess wear	• **Legends of Hollywood,** Sunset Boulevard
• *Star Wars* souvenirs	• **Black Spire Outfitters,** Galaxy's Edge
• Women's jewelry, handbags, and accessories	• **Keystone Clothiers,** Hollywood Boulevard

Our Favorite Free Souvenirs from Walt Disney World

BIRTHDAY TREATS Be sure to mention any special occasions you're celebrating when you check in for your meal at a table-service restaurant. You may get a surprise dessert.

CELEBRATION BUTTONS Just married? Just graduated? Just happy to be nominated? There's a button for that. Get one when you check in to your hotel or from Guest Services.

KIDCOT FUN STOPS Kids love collecting and coloring the postcards from each pavilion.

STICKERS Cast members give out so many of these, we're afraid there might be an adhesive shortage.

TRANSPORTATION TRADING CARDS Did you know that monorail and bus drivers have trading cards to give out?

If you realize on your flight home that you forgot to buy mouse ears for your niece, don't worry. **ShopDisney** online (shopdisney.com) has a dedicated section of parks merchandise.

SHOPPING OUTSIDE DISNEY WORLD

Upscale Shopping

The Mall at Millenia (mallatmillenia.com) is anchored by **Bloomingdale's, Macy's,** and **Neiman Marcus.** You'll find designer boutiques, such as **Burberry, Chanel, Gucci, Hermès,** and **Louis Vuitton,** and the closest **Apple Store** to Walt Disney World. Millenia also has fast-fashion staples such as **H&M** and **Forever 21,** as well as the usual suspects, including **Gap, Victoria's Secret,** and **J.Crew.**

Midscale Shopping

The Florida Mall is home to **Dillard's, JCPenney, Macy's,** and **Sears.** Apart from the anchors and high-end designer shops, it has many of the same stores as The Mall at Millenia. Visit simon.com/mall/the-florida-mall.

Outlet Shopping

If you think the crowds at the parks are overwhelming, then you'll want to avoid the two **Orlando Premium Outlets** at International Drive and

TIPS FOR AVOIDING BUYER'S REMORSE
1. Know ahead of time how much things cost. You can browse many theme park items at disneystore.com.
2. Be specific. Disney collecting can spiral out of control if you don't narrow your focus. Pick a character or movie you love, and stick to that.
3. Don't buy merchandise with a date on it. That Walt Disney World 2025 T-shirt you buy to commemorate your vacation isn't going to look as fresh on January 1, 2026. There's a reason you see so much of this stuff at Disney outlets.
4. Buy lower-priced Disney souvenirs at local big-box stores.
5. Don't fall for limited editions. If they make 2,000 of something, is it really limited?
6. Wait. Don't make your purchases until you've been to more than one shop.
7. Some of the best things in life are free. Consider our favorite freebies at Walt Disney World (see page 507) and skip the cash register.

Vineland Avenue (premiumoutlets.com/outlet/orlando-vineland). Tourists arrive here by the busload, and the experience will leave you questioning everything from consumer culture to your own judgment. For the theme park visitor, the only redeeming aspect of these two malls is the **Disney Character Warehouse** (there are locations at both outlets).

Disney Shopping Outside of Walt Disney World

The Disney outlet at Vineland is about twice the size of the location on I-Drive. To get an idea of what you'll find there, check out Derek Burgan's past **"The Magic, The Memories, and Merch!"** entries on the **TouringPlans.com** blog.

Fans seeking one-of-a-kind souvenirs, including costumes, props, and local art, should check out **TD Collectibles** (☎ 407-347-0670; tdcollectibles.net).

Orlando International Airport has three Disney shops, one at each terminal, for making purchases on the way home. The shops are fairly large and well themed for what they are; plus, they're run by Disney.

NIGHTLIFE *at* WALT DISNEY WORLD RESORTS

DISNEY'S BOARDWALK OFFERS two adult-oriented venues, Jellyrolls and Atlantic Dance Hall. **Jellyrolls** is a dueling-piano bar that's open nightly, 7 p.m.–2 a.m. (cover charge applies). It's one of the few age-21-and-up places you'll find at Walt Disney World. The entertainment is usually outstanding. Across from Jellyrolls is **Atlantic Dance Hall**. It's often booked for private events, but on weekends it's generally open in the evenings (and has free admission). The house DJ spins everything from '70s disco to top 40 and EDM. Like Jellyrolls, Atlantic Dance Hall is age 21 and up.

At **Coronado Springs Resort,** you'll find **Rix Sports Bar & Grill.** It usually isn't busy unless there's a convention at the resort. Other Disney resort bars with live entertainment are **Scat Cat's Club** at **Port Orleans French Quarter** and **River Roost** at **Port Orleans Riverside.**

Trader Sam's Grog Grotto (inspired by the bar at the Disneyland Hotel in California) at the **Polynesian Village Resort** is a delight. If you've ever found yourself at *Walt Disney's Enchanted Tiki Room* and thought, "You know, booze would really make this better," then this is your place.

Our favorite nightspot at Walt Disney World, **Top of the World** at the Contemporary Resort's **Bay Lake Tower,** is for Disney Vacation Club members and their guests. If you're a member or you can talk one into letting you in, try to stay after the Magic Kingdom fireworks—the view and setting are outstanding.

unofficial **TIP**
Nightlife doesn't just mean stuff for the adults to do. There are plenty of kid-friendly activities after dark for the young ones. Check your resort's recreation schedule for campfires, movies on the beach or at the pool, and more.

Free Concerts at Walt Disney World

EAT TO THE BEAT For this concert series, classic and once-in-the-news acts accompany your trip around EPCOT's World Showcase during the fall **International Food & Wine Festival.** Featured artists tend to be from the 1980s and later.

EPCOT INTERNATIONAL FESTIVAL OF THE ARTS This festival takes place in January and February and includes concerts at the America Gardens Theatre. The Disney on Broadway series is often featured.

GARDEN ROCKS Held during the International Flower & Garden Festival in the spring, this series features acts from the 1960s onward.

House of Blues

Type of show Live concerts with an emphasis on rock and blues. **Tickets and information** ☎ 407-934-BLUE (2583); houseofblues.com/orlando. You can also purchase tickets in person at the box office Tuesday–Thursday, noon–7 p.m., and after noon on show days. **Nights of lowest attendance** Monday and Tuesday. **Usual showtimes** Between 7 and 9:30 p.m., depending on who's performing.

DESCRIPTION AND COMMENTS Developed by Blues Brother Dan Aykroyd, House of Blues consists of a restaurant and blues bar, as well as a concert hall. The restaurant is one of the few late-night dining options in Walt Disney World. Live music cranks up every night at 10:30 p.m. in the restaurant and blues bar, but even before then, the joint is way beyond 110 decibels. The music hall next door features concerts by an eclectic array of musicians and groups. Genres have included gospel, blues, funk, ska, dance, salsa, rap, zydeco, hard rock, groove rock, and reggae.

TOURING TIPS Ticket prices vary from night to night according to the fame and drawing power of the featured band. They ranged from $29 to $135 in early 2024, with the higher-cost tickets for better-known performers.

The music hall is set up like a nightclub, with tables and barstools for only about 150 people and standing room for a whopping 1,850. The tables and stools are first come, first served, with doors opening an hour before showtime on weekdays and 90 minutes before showtime on weekends. Shows are all ages unless otherwise indicated.

PART 18

RECREATION *and* SPAS

KEY QUESTIONS ANSWERED IN THIS CHAPTER

- What is RunDisney and how do I participate? *(see below)*
- What are the best places to relax on property? *(page 512)*
- Where can I play minigolf with my family? *(page 514)*
- How can I get out onto the water while at Walt Disney World?? *(page 514)*
- Can I learn any new skills while on vacation? *(page 515)*

MOST WALT DISNEY WORLD GUESTS never make it beyond the theme parks, water parks, or Disney Springs. Those who do, however, will be rewarded with an extraordinary selection of recreational opportunities. From guided fishing adventures and archery lessons to horseback (or Segway) riding, fitness center workouts, world-class massages, and golf (miniature or original), there is something for everyone.

▌▌ RUN, DISNEY, RUN

RUNDISNEY is a completely different way to experience the Walt Disney World theme parks (and the roadways that connect them). Themed race events held at Walt Disney World throughout the year allow participants to run or walk around the property. Frequently, runners will dress up inspired by Disney characters and will get to meet Disney characters, enjoy live entertainment, and participate in photo opportunities and other fun activities along the course. If you complete any RunDisney race, you'll be rewarded with a Disney-themed medal. Depending on the event, you may be able to complete a 5K, 10K, 10-miler, half-marathon, or full marathon.

WALT DISNEY WORLD RUNDISNEY EVENTS

TYPICALLY, FOUR RUNDISNEY EVENTS are hosted at Walt Disney World every year:

WALT DISNEY WORLD MARATHON WEEKEND is already scheduled for January 8–12, 2025. This event offers a 5K, 10K, half marathon, and full marathon. Participants can also complete the Goofy's Race and a Half challenge by finishing the half marathon and full marathon, or the Dopey challenge by finishing all four races during the weekend.

DISNEY PRINCESS HALF MARATHON WEEKEND is scheduled for February 20–24, 2025. This event offers a 5K, 10K, and half marathon. Participants can also complete the Disney Fairytale challenge by finishing the 10K and half marathon.

SPRINGTIME SURPRISE WEEKEND is scheduled for April 3–6, 2025. This newer event offers a 5K, 10K, and 10-miler. Participants can also complete the Springtime Surprise challenge by finishing all three races.

DISNEY WINE & DINE HALF MARATHON is typically held in early November. This event offers a 5K, 10K, and half marathon. Participants can also complete the Two Course challenge by finishing the 10K and half marathon.

REGISTRATION

REGISTERING FOR A RUNDISNEY EVENT is typically its own competition. It's not uncommon for a race to sell out the same day it opens for registration—sometimes within an hour if it's a popular event or a new theme. So make sure you know the basics if you want to try out one of these popular events!

To register efficiently, you'll need to create an account on the RunDisney website before registration day. Set up your profile and store your payment information so that you can get through the registration process quickly. Once registration opens, "Register Now" buttons will appear below each race for the event. Once you click to register, you'll be placed into a virtual queue. The wait times in this "waiting room" can last more than an hour. Be patient and remain on that page until you reach the end of the countdown, when you will be moved into the actual website to start your registration. At this point, you should be able to register for any of the (non-sold-out) races or challenges for the weekend, regardless of which "Register Now" button you clicked. Be prepared with your name, email address, phone number, physical address, and emergency contact information.

COST

RUNDISNEY RACES ARE NOT a cheap way to experience the Walt Disney World theme parks. Still, the unique entertainment offered along each course, the exclusive medals, and the opportunity to run with thousands of other Disney fans mean that events are still in high demand despite the cost. Prices for the 2024 season were as follows:

- **5K:** $108–$112
- **10K:** $151–$155
- **10-miler:** $212
- **Half marathon:** $219–$240
- **Marathon:** $221
- **Challenge:** $389 (Disney Fairytale) to $672 (Dopey)

The costs at the higher end of the range are all for the Wine & Dine weekend because they include access to the post-race party on Sunday night in EPCOT. Your registration fee includes your race bib(s), your finisher medal(s), and a race shirt. After the race you'll also receive a snack box and hydration. It doesn't include theme park admission, a resort stay, your race photos, or any merchandise.

RUNDISNEY EXPO

YOUR RUNDISNEY RACE WEEKEND will start at the RunDisney Expo at the ESPN Wide World of Sports Complex. That's because this is where you'll pick up your race bib. If you're staying at a Walt Disney World resort, there will be buses to take you to the expo. Otherwise, arrange your own transportation by driving (parking is free) or using a ride-sharing service or Minnie Van. Once you have your bib, then you can pick up your race shirt. At the expo, you'll also have access to all kinds of running gear and other merchandise.

TREAT YOURSELF *in* WALT DISNEY WORLD

YOU'VE JUST COMPLETED another mini marathon day in the theme parks, and after you get the kids into bed you realize you barely have enough energy to crawl into bed yourself. Fortunately, there are plenty of ways to pamper yourself and your ailing body in the World.

SENSES SPA

LOCATED AT THE GRAND FLORIDIAN, Senses is easily the best spa in the Disney area. It has all the bells and whistles (actually, that doesn't sound very relaxing—make that tranquil music and soft lighting) you could hope for. The décor is tasteful, and everything from the entry process to the lounge area to your actual treatment exudes elegance, pampering, and relaxation.

You can book spa treatments online, but they don't integrate well with My Disney Experience, so make sure you remember or create a reminder for your appointment time. Keep in mind, you're welcome (and encouraged) to check in 30–60 minutes before your treatment to enjoy the lounge. And you absolutely should spend time enjoying the lounge. It's one of the best parts of the whole experience!

Senses offers massages (solo or couples), facials, nail services, haircuts and styling, and makeup consultations. There is also a dedicated menu of experiences for kids and teens. Prices range from $55 for an express manicure to $295 for an 80-minute Grand Signature Massage.

Once you check in for your appointment, you'll be asked to pick a stone from a table in the entryway that will set the tone for your experience. Mostly, it will help determine the lighting in your treatment room or the scents of the products used. Then, you'll be escorted to the appropriate lounge based on your gender. If you're a new visitor, you'll be given a small tour and be informed of the lounge rules.

In the lounge, you'll find a locker room, well-appointed bathrooms, lounge chairs (with blankets and curtains if you choose to use them), and a wet room. If you'd like to use the wet lounge, you'll need to bring a swimsuit. You'll find a sauna, hot bath area and heated tile loungers in the wet room—this is my favorite part of the entire spa!

At your appointment time, an attendant will escort you to your treatment room and then back to the lounge after your treatment is complete. Then you'll pay for your services before leaving.

The spa at the Grand Floridian is certainly a big treat, with a price tag to match. A massage will truly melt away all the stress and physical exertion of all those park days.

IN-ROOM OPTIONS

IF YOU'RE LOOKING FOR SOMETHING more private, or perhaps even more reasonably priced, an increasing number of options have proliferated after the pandemic. The **Ear for Each Other** Facebook group (facebook.com/groups/earforeachother) was created to support laid-off or furloughed cast members. Some of these cast members started up services that helped replace offerings that were suspended at Disney at the time (like Bibbidi Bobbidi Boutique or the spa). Even now that Disney services are available again, many guests found they liked the flexibility and customer support these small businesses provide.

MASSAGES One such option that's directly comparable to Senses Spa is an in-room massage at your Walt Disney World resort. Denise from **Sol, A Wellness Company** (solwellnessllc.com) offers a variety of massage options, all in the comfort of your room. Times are flexible, and prices are reasonable. In 2024, I paid $180 (plus tax and tip) for a 50-minute massage at Senses Spa, and $130 (again, before tip) for a 60-minute massage with Denise in my room at the Riviera Resort. What are the trade-offs? There's no lounge area, and you'll have to keep your room tidy enough for a heated massage table to be set up. But as someone who likes to both treat myself and get a good deal, the savings of more than 25% helped me feel even more relaxed. And not having to figure out transportation to the Grand Floridian, plus getting to be in the comfort of my own room without worrying about the other guests around me at the spa, was a big incentive.

MAKEOVERS This is another option for the adults or kids in your party. These services exploded during the pandemic when the popular Bibbidi Bobbidi Boutique and Harmony Barber Shop were both closed. A search on Ear for Each Other for these services returns countless options. You can get haircuts (even first haircuts), extensions, hairstyling, makeup, and more. We got our younger daughter's first haircut from **Selina Ashley,** one of the vendors on Ear for Each Other, in our room at Caribbean Beach in 2022. Both of our girls also got their hair curled (and glittered, of course) and a little princess makeup applied for our day at the Magic Kingdom. It was an unforgettable experience. One vendor (**@two4art** on Instagram) will even apply custom henna in your room—much of it Disney-themed and all of it beautiful.

SPECIAL DELIVERIES If you've never treated yourself with chocolate or other goodies at Walt Disney World, there are many vendors ready to deliver them directly to your resort. One of my family's favorites is **A New Hope Confections,** which makes some of the most delicious and beautiful chocolate we've ever had—and we're a family of chocolate-consuming experts. Jenna and Dean, who design, make, and deliver it themselves, are both former Disney cast members. I'm not exaggerating when I say that once when I picked up my chocolates from bell services, Goofy and Donald were in the lobby greeting guests and they came over to try to "steal" my chocolates—they're that good.

The WILDERNESS MUST *be* EXPLORED

THERE ARE MORE RECREATIONAL OPPORTUNITIES at **Fort Wilderness** than at any other Walt Disney World resort. And you don't have to be staying at the cabins or campsites to participate in these activities. Some need to be scheduled in advance, and others can be arranged upon your arrival.

Tri-Circle-D Ranch (located just behind Pioneer Hall, which hosts the *Hoop-Dee-Doo Musical Revue*) is easily accessible by boat from the Magic Kingdom or Wilderness Lodge. This is where many of the horses and ponies that serve Walt Disney World spend their time when they're not working. You can visit the animals or even take a carriage ride or pony ride.

If you'd like to tour more of the resort, you can take a **Segway tour** for $90–$99 per person or rent bikes, canoes, or kayaks to explore by land or water. Fort Wilderness even offers **archery lessons** for $49 per person, if you really want to feel like you're at summer camp.

BIG COMPETITION *at* MINIATURE GOLF

DECADES AGO, the Walt Disney World powers that be noticed that families were escaping the WDW bubble in search of a little friendly competition on the minigolf course. The natural response was to start offering courses on-property. The result was **Fantasia Gardens and Fairways Miniature Golf,** an 11-acre complex that offers two 18-hole courses. The Fantasia Gardens course is an "adventure" course themed after Disney's animated film *Fantasia*. The Fantasia Fairways course is geared more toward older children and adults, and it's a very convincing miniature golf course in the truest sense of those words. Complete with sand traps and water hazards, it could be a real golf course shrunk down by Ant Man. Both courses are beautifully landscaped and creatively executed. They feature fountains, statues, topiaries, flower beds, and many more touches that make it a magical and top-notch minigolf option.

Fantasia Gardens is located on Epcot Resorts Boulevard, across the street from the Swan resort. To reach the course, you can either arrange your own transportation or take a bus or boat to the Swan and walk over. The Fantasia Gardens course is open daily, 10 a.m.–10 p.m., while the Fantasia Fairways course closes an hour earlier. The cost to putt is $19 for adults and $12 for kids ages 3-9 (plus tax). It's expensive minigolf, but you can't put a price on defeating your loved ones at Disney.

Winter Summerland Miniature Golf is the other minigolf facility on Disney property. Located next to the Blizzard Beach water park, this location also offers two 18-hole courses. The Winter Course has a "blizzard in Florida" theme, and the Summer Course boasts a tropical-holiday theme. Both courses are much easier than the Fantasia Gardens and Fairways courses, which makes them a good choice for families with young children. Daily operating hours for both courses are 10 a.m.–10 p.m., and the cost is the same as Fantasia Gardens.

◧▮ SKILL UP!

LOOKING TO PICK UP A NEW TRICK or two while on vacation in Orlando? There are many ways to learn something new while at Walt Disney World, and picking up a new skill while on vacation will help you remember your time at Disney anytime you apply that new skill once you get home.

Coronado Springs is a surprising hot spot for learning something new, with two offerings you won't find at other resorts. First, you can enroll at **Sangria University** at Three Bridges Bar and Grill. It's a 90-minute afternoon class offered on Saturdays and Sundays that discusses the history of sangria and reveals the recipes for all the house-made varieties of sangria served at this location. Of course, you'll also get to taste all four varieties, along with a light appetizer to keep you somewhat level-headed. Once you're all trained up, you'll be given the opportunity to make your own glass of sangria from a selection of fruits and spirits. Obviously, you have to be age 21 or older to participate. The price is $69–$79 per person (plus tax and tip).

Every Friday afternoon at Coronado Springs, you can tap into your inner artist by attending the 2-hour **Colors of Coronado Painting Experience,** facilitated by a local artist. For $40 (plus tax), you can follow along as you paint an 11-by-14-inch canvas with a Disney-themed design—the painting changes monthly—while enjoying great views from Toledo, where the class is held.

Over at **Disney Springs,** you can practice a different type of artistry at **Amorette's Patisserie Cake Decorating Experience.** Typically offered once per day, in the morning, this 90-minute class allows you to create a culinary show-stopper. A reservation costs $199 (plus tax) and gets you a table for up to two people (but you'll pay the same price if you're solo). The class sizes are small, so you'll get plenty of hands-on instruction, insider stories, and tips and tricks and you create a Mickey Mouse or Minnie Mouse dome cake. (Mickey is offered Sunday, Tuesday, Thursday, and Saturday. Minnie is offered Monday, Wednesday, and Friday). Each has different flavors, so make sure you book the one that sounds better to you. Your reservation also includes some beverages while you decorate.

The **Ear for Each Other** Facebook group (see page 513) also has a bevy of options for upskilling while in your own hotel room or elsewhere at your Disney resort. I'll highlight a couple of these options, but you should explore them all for yourself.

Before the pandemic, one of the most popular experiences at Hollywood Studios was **Jedi Training.** Families would rope-drop sign-ups for this free show, where their children would learn the ways of the force before battling a *Star Wars* baddie. Unfortunately, this show never returned after the pandemic. Thankfully, **Justin Aldridge,** one of the Jedi masters who participated in the show, is still around the World and willing to train new apprentices in private sessions at your resort. My daughters learned the ways of the Force from Justin during our 2023 vacation. We met up at a gazebo at Animal Kingdom Lodge, and the kids brought the lightsabers they'd built at Tatooine Traders the previous day (Justin can also provide lightsabers to use during training).

I could not have been more impressed with the experience. Justin emphasized the importance of remaining focused and in control rather than . . . running at your sibling and flinging your weapon around. He explains what the colors of the lightsabers mean; he talks about how Jedi keep the peace and fight only as a last resort; and he regularly refers to the need to practice any skill you want to hone—so many good lessons that are transferrable beyond lightsaber wielding.

At the time of our lesson, Justin charged $75 for one participant and $25 for each additional participant. The base lesson is 30 minutes, but Justin happily sticks around for more-advanced training or answering questions about the parks. Our session ended up being about 45 minutes.

If you're more inclined toward artistic activities, you may want to check out the services offered by **Jason Zucker.** Jason is a Disney animator who has created designs for pins, watches and collectibles and now offers in-person and virtual **animation classes.** If you love the Animation Academy offered at Animal Kingdom or on Disney Cruise Line, this is the option for you. It's more personalized, and you'll definitely learn some real drawing skills, rather than simply following along. He'll come to your resort for a one-on-one or small group session, or you can bring a little of the Disney magic home and do a virtual lesson after your vacation!

ACCOMMODATIONS INDEX

Note: Page numbers in **bold** indicate a resort's main entry.

See also the Restaurant Index on pages 522–524 and the Subject Index on pages 525–545.

See also the Restaurant Index on pages 522–524 and the Subject Index on pages 525–545.

See also the Restaurant Index on pages 522–524 and the Subject Index on pages 525–545.

See also the Restaurant Index on pages 522–524 and the Subject Index on pages 525–545.

See also the Restaurant Index on pages 522–524 and the Subject Index on pages 525–545.

RESTAURANT INDEX

Note: Page numbers in **bold** indicate a restaurant's main entry.

See also the Accommodations Index on pages 517–521 and the Subject Index on pages 525–545.

See also the Accommodations Index on pages 517–521 and the Subject Index on pages 525–545.

See also the Accommodations Index on pages 517–521 and the Subject Index on pages 525–545.

SUBJECT INDEX

See also the Accommodations Index on pages 517–521 and the Restaurant Index on pages 522–524.

See also the Accommodations Index on pages 517–521 and the Restaurant Index on pages 522–524.

See also the Accommodations Index on pages 517–521 and the Restaurant Index on pages 522–524.

See also the Accommodations Index on pages 517–521 and the Restaurant Index on pages 522–524.

See also the Accommodations Index on pages 517–521 and the Restaurant Index on pages 522–524.

See also the Accommodations Index on pages 517–521 and the Restaurant Index on pages 522–524.

See also the Accommodations Index on pages 517–521 and the Restaurant Index on pages 522–521.

See also the Accommodations Index on pages 517–521 and the Restaurant Index on pages 522–524.

See also the Accommodations Index on pages 517–521 and the Restaurant Index on pages 522–524.

See also the Accommodations Index on pages 517-521 and the Restaurant Index on pages 522-524.

See also the Accommodations Index on pages 517–521 and the Restaurant Index on pages 522–524.

See also the Accommodations Index on pages 517–521 and the Restaurant Index on pages 522–524.

See also the Accommodations Index on pages 517–521 and the Restaurant Index on pages 522–524.

See also the Accommodations Index on pages 517-521 and the Restaurant Index on pages 522-524.

See also the Accommodations Index on pages 517–521 and the Restaurant Index on pages 522–524.

See also the Accommodations Index on pages 517–521 and the Restaurant Index on pages 522–524.

TOURING PLANS

"Not a Touring Plan"
TOURING PLANS

MAGIC KINGDOM

FOR ALL GUESTS If Tron Lightcycle/Run or Tiana's Bayou Adventure is using a virtual queue, obtain a boarding group as soon as they're available (7 a.m. for all guests, 1 p.m. if you've already tapped into the park). If you're willing to purchase Individual Lightning Lanes, you should do so as early as possible to get the best selection of return times. If using Genie+, get the first available reservation for Tiana's, Big Thunder Mountain Railroad, Jungle Cruise, Peter Pan's Flight, Seven Dwarfs Mine Train, or Space Mountain. Fit that return-time window into the plan. Throughout the day, continue obtaining the earliest available Genie+ reservation for any of the next few attractions you're visiting.

FOR ALL GUESTS USING EARLY ENTRY Arrive at the Magic Kingdom entrance 40 minutes–1 hour before official opening. If you are driving and parking, add 20 minutes to get from the Transportation and Ticket Center to the entrance.

FOR ALL OFF-SITE GUESTS ARRIVING AT OFFICIAL OPENING Arrive at the park entrance 30–60 minutes before official opening.

FOR PARENTS WITH ONE DAY TO TOUR AND USING EARLY ENTRY See Fantasyland first, starting with Peter Pan's Flight. See Frontierland, then Adventureland. Consider a midday break at the hotel if the park is open past 8 p.m. Then tour Tomorrowland and Liberty Square (if your kids are interested in Haunted Mansion).

FOR PARENTS WITH ONE DAY TO TOUR AND ARRIVING AT OFFICIAL OPENING Begin a clockwise tour of the park in Fantasyland, skipping Seven Dwarfs Mine Train and Peter Pan's Flight. After Fantasyland, tour Tomorrowland, then Adventureland. Experience Seven Dwarfs Mine Train and Peter Pan's Flight in the late afternoon or evening, or use Genie+.

FOR ADULTS WITH ONE DAY TO TOUR AND USING EARLY ENTRY Start in Tomorrowland, including an early boarding group or Individual

Lightning Lane for Tron. Tour the headliner attractions in Frontierland and Adventureland next, saving shows for the middle of the day. Tour Liberty Square around dinner. End the day with Fantasyland, saving Seven Dwarfs Mine Train for as late as possible, or use Genie+.

FOR ADULTS WITH ONE DAY TO TOUR AND ARRIVING AT OFFICIAL OPENING Start touring in Frontierland, then tour Adventureland and Liberty Square. Visit Fantasyland in the late afternoon and Tomorrowland after dinner.

FOR PARENTS AND ADULTS WITH TWO DAYS TO TOUR AND USING EARLY ENTRY On Day One, tour Fantasyland's headliner rides first, starting with Seven Dwarfs Mine Train. Tour Frontierland next, then Liberty Square. Finish up with Fantasyland's secondary rides. Start Day Two in Tomorrowland, then tour Adventureland and any favorites you'd like to repeat.

FOR PARENTS AND ADULTS WITH TWO DAYS TO TOUR AND ARRIVING AT OFFICIAL OPENING On Day One, tour Frontierland first, then Liberty Square, followed by Fantasyland. Finish with Peter Pan's Flight and Seven Dwarfs Mine Train in Fantasyland. Start Day Two in Adventureland, and then see Tomorrowland.

FOR PARENTS AND ADULTS WITH AN AFTERNOON AND A FULL DAY For the afternoon, tour Frontierland and Tomorrowland. On your full day of touring, see Fantasyland, Liberty Square, and Adventureland.

EPCOT

FOR ALL GUESTS If Disney is using a virtual queue at Guardians of the Galaxy, obtain one as soon as they're available on the day of your visit (7 a.m. for all guests, and 1 p.m. if you've already tapped in). If you're willing to purchase Individual Lightning Lane for Guardians, do so as soon as possible on the day of your visit to get the best selection of return times. Likewise, if you're using Genie+, obtain the earliest possible reservation for Remy or Test Track. Throughout the day, continue obtaining the earliest available Genie+ reservation for any of the next few attractions you're visiting.

FOR ALL GUESTS USING EARLY ENTRY Enter EPCOT at the International Gateway if possible, and ride Remy, followed by Frozen Ever After and Test Track. Tour World Discovery, then World Nature, then World Celebration. Begin a clockwise tour of World Showcase starting with Mexico. For dinner, snack at the food booths or quick-service spots in World Showcase. Finish the day by viewing *Luminous* and/or the light shows on Spaceship Earth. If you're entering from the main entrance, start at Frozen and Test Track, saving Remy for late in the evening.

FOR ALL GUESTS ARRIVING AT OFFICIAL PARK OPENING Enter EPCOT at the main entrance and ride Test Track as soon as you're admitted to the park. Tour to World Nature, then visit World Discovery and World Celebration. Begin a clockwise tour of World Showcase at Mexico. For dinner, snack at the food booths or quick-service spots in World Showcase. Finish the day by viewing *Luminous* and/or the light shows on Spaceship Earth.

DISNEY'S ANIMAL KINGDOM

FOR ALL GUESTS If you're willing to purchase Individual Lightning Lane for Avatar Flight of Passage, do so as soon as possible on the day of your visit. Likewise, if you're using Genie+, obtain the earliest possible reservation for either Na'vi River Journey or Kilimanjaro Safaris. Throughout the day, continue obtaining the earliest available Genie+ reservation for any of the next few attractions you're visiting. Don't use Genie+ for shows unless it's a very crowded day and you'd like to see *Festival of the Lion King*.

FOR PARENTS AND ADULTS USING EARLY ENTRY Begin a land-by-land, clockwise tour of the park, starting in Pandora. Work in shows like *Feathered Friends in Flight* as you near them. If the park is open past dark, eat dinner, then end the night with *Awakenings* at the Tree of Life and a tour of the Valley of Mo'ara in Pandora.

FOR PARENTS AND ADULTS ARRIVING AT OFFICIAL PARK OPENING Begin a land-by-land, clockwise tour of the park starting at Kilimanjaro Safaris in Africa. Work in shows like *Feathered Friends in Flight* as you near them. Save the attractions in Pandora for last. If the park is open past dark, eat dinner, then end the night with *Awakenings* at the Tree of Life and a tour of the Valley of Mo'ara in Pandora.

FOR PARENTS AND ADULTS ARRIVING IN LATE MORNING Begin a clockwise tour of the park, starting in Africa and saving Pandora for last. If the park is open past dark, eat dinner, then end the night with *Awakenings* at the Tree of Life and a tour of the Valley of Mo'ara in Pandora.

DISNEY'S HOLLYWOOD STUDIOS

FOR ALL GUESTS If you're willing to purchase Individual Lightning Lane for Star Wars: Rise of the Resistance, do so as soon as possible on the day of your visit. Likewise, if you're using Genie+, obtain the earliest possible reservation for Slinky Dog Dash. If it's not available, try *Millennium Falcon:* Smugglers Run, Rock 'n' Roller Coaster, Mickey & Minnie's Runaway Railway, or Toy Story Mania! Throughout the day, continue to obtain the earliest available Genie+ reservation for that same list of time-saving attractions.

FOR GROUPS WITH OLDER CHILDREN, TEENS, AND ADULTS USING EARLY ENTRY Ride Rise of the Resistance as soon as you're admitted into the park. It is usually the only attraction to open before Early Entry officially begins. Next, begin a clockwise tour of the Studios in Toy Story Land with Slinky and Toy Story Mania, followed by Runaway Railway, and then the attractions on Sunset Boulevard just before or after lunch. Spend the afternoon watching shows, and revisit Galaxy's Edge in the evening, when crowds start to thin. Finish the night at *Fantasmic!*

FOR ADULTS ARRIVING AROUND LUNCHTIME Begin a tour of the park in Galaxy's Edge, then visit the attractions on Sunset Boulevard. Ride Mickey & Minnie's Runaway Railway in midafternoon, and save Toy Story Land for last, when crowds have started to thin. Get in line for Rise of the Resistance during the last 2 hours the park is open. Use Individual Lightning Lane and/or Genie+ as described above.

The Magic Kingdom

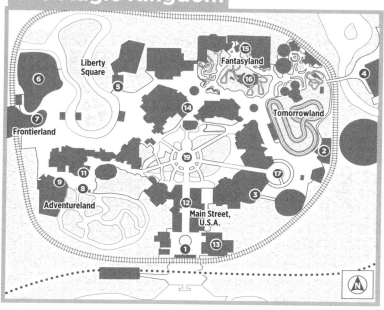

EARLY-ENTRY ONE-DAY TOURING PLAN FOR ADULTS

If Tron Lightcycle/Run or Tiana's Bayou Adventure is using a virtual queue, obtain a boarding group as early as possible on the day of your visit.

1. Arrive at the Magic Kingdom entrance 45 minutes before official opening on days of normal attendance, and 1 hour before official opening during holidays and busy times. Take pictures on Main Street, U.S.A., before the park opens.
2. As soon as the park opens, ride Space Mountain in Tomorrowland.
3. Try Buzz Lightyear's Space Ranger Spin.
4. Redeem boarding group or Individual Lightning Lane for Tron Lightcycle/Run.
5. Tour The Haunted Mansion in Liberty Square.
6. Ride Big Thunder Mountain Railroad in Frontierland.
7. Ride or redeem boarding group for Tiana's Bayou Adventure.
8. Take a Jungle Cruise if the posted wait is under 40 minutes. Otherwise skip for now
9. Experience Pirates of the Caribbean in Adventureland. Order lunch using mobile

ordering while in line. The highest-rated spot is Columbia Harbour House, which is nearby.
10. Eat lunch.
11. Experience *Walt Disney's Enchanted Tiki Room.*
12. Explore Main Street USA, including shopping and catching performances by the Dapper Dans or the Casey's Corner Pianist
13. If time permits, meet Mickey Mouse in Town Square Theater
14. See *Mickey's PhilharMagic* in Fantasyland.
15. See *Enchanted Tales with Belle* or ride Under the Sea: Journey of the Little Mermaid, both in Fantasyland.
16. Ride Seven Dwarfs Mine Train.
17. Ride the Tomorrowland Transit Authority PeopleMover.
18. If time permits, revisit favorite attractions, try new ones, or tour the park.
19. See the *Happily Ever After* fireworks show.

To use Genie+ with this plan: The most useful Genie+ reservations for this plan are for Tiana's Bayou Adventure, Space Mountain, Big Thunder Mountain Railroad, Haunted Mansion, and Jungle Cruise. Get the first available reservation for any of those, and fit that return-time window into the plan. Once you're able to get your next Genie+ reservation, look for the earliest return time for any of the next few attractions in the plan. **If using ILL,** try to get a reservation for Tron Lightcycle/Run with a return time as close to park opening as possible and a Seven Dwarfs Mine Train reservation for midmorning.

See **theugseries.com/free-touring-plans** to customize this plan at no charge, including the attractions and your walking speed, plus real-time updates while you're in the park.

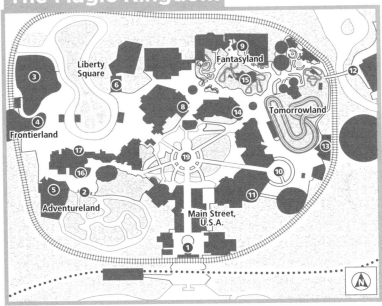

The Magic Kingdom

NON-EARLY-ENTRY ONE-DAY TOURING PLAN FOR ADULTS

If Tron Lightcycle/Run or Tiana's Bayou Adventure is using a virtual queue, obtain a boarding group as early as possible on the day of your visit.

1. Arrive at the entrance 30 minutes before official opening on days of normal attendance and 1 hour before official opening during holidays and busy times.
2. As soon as you're admitted to the park, take the Jungle Cruise in Adventureland.
3. Ride Big Thunder Mountain Railroad in Frontierland.
4. Ride or redeem boarding group for Tiana's Bayou Adventure
5. Experience Pirates of the Caribbean in Adventureland.
6. Tour The Haunted Mansion in Liberty Square. While in line, use mobile ordering for lunch. The best spot nearby is Columbia Harbour House in Liberty Square.
7. Eat lunch.
8. See *Mickey's PhilharMagic*.
9. Ride Under the Sea: Journey of the Little Mermaid.
10. Ride the Tomorrowland Transit Authority PeopleMover.
11. Ride Buzz Lightyear's Space Ranger Spin.
12. Redeem boarding group or Individual Lightning Lane for Tron Lightcycle/Run.
13. Ride Space Mountain.
14. Ride The Many Adventures of Winnie the Pooh in Fantasyland.
15. Experience Seven Dwarfs Mine Train.
16. See *Walt Disney's Enchanted Tiki Room* in Adventureland.
17. See the *Country Bear Jamboree*.
18. If time permits, revisit favorite attractions, try new ones, or tour the park.
19. See the *Happily Ever After* fireworks show.

To use Genie+ with this plan: The most useful Genie+ reservations for this plan are for Tiana's Bayou Adventure, Big Thunder Mountain Railroad, Space Mountain, Haunted Mansion, and Buzz Lightyear. Get the first available reservation for any of those, and fit that return-time window into the plan. Once you're able to get your next Genie+ reservation, look for the earliest return time for any of the next few attractions in the plan. **If using ILL,** try to get a reservation for Tron Lightcycle/Run with a return time in the middle of the afternoon and a Seven Dwarfs Mine Train reservation for midmorning

See **theugseries.com/free-touring-plans** to customize this plan at no charge, including the attractions and your walking speed, plus real-time updates while you're in the park.

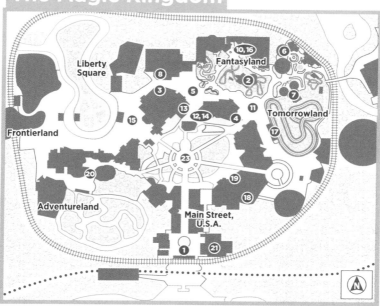

EARLY-ENTRY ONE-DAY TOURING PLAN
FOR PARENTS WITH SMALL CHILDREN

Review the Small-Child Fright-Potential Table on page 304. Attractions shown should be suitable for most children ages 5 and up. Interrupt the plan for meals, rest, and bathroom breaks.

1. Arrive at the entrance 45 minutes before official opening on days of normal attendance, and 1 hour before official opening during holidays and busy times.
2. As soon as the park opens, head toward the right-hand side of Cinderella Castle and ride Seven Dwarfs Mine Train in Fantasyland.
3. Take Peter Pan's Flight.
4. Ride The Many Adventures of Winnie the Pooh.
5. Ride Prince Charming Regal Carrousel.
6. Meet the characters at Pete's Silly Sideshow.
7. Take a spin on Dumbo the Flying Elephant.
8. Try the It's a Small World boat ride. Use mobile ordering to order lunch while in line. The best nearby spot is Columbia Harbour House in Liberty Square.
9. Eat lunch.
10. Ride Under the Sea: Journey of the Little Mermaid.
11. Give the Mad Tea Party a whirl.

12. Meet one pair of princesses at Princess Fairytale Hall.
13. See *Mickey's PhilharMagic*.
14. Meet one pair of princesses at Princess Fairytale Hall.
15. Catch the afternoon parade from Liberty Square.
16. See *Enchanted Tales with Belle*.
17. Take a spin on the Tomorrowland Speedway in Tomorrowland.
18. Ride Buzz Lightyear's Space Ranger Spin.
19. See *Monsters, Inc. Laugh Floor*.
20. If time permits, ride The Magic Carpets of Aladdin in Adventureland.
21. Meet Mickey Mouse at Town Square Theater on Main Street, U.S.A.
22. If time permits, revisit favorite attractions, try new ones, or tour the park.
23. See the *Happily Ever After* fireworks show.

To use Genie+ with this plan: The most useful Genie+ reservation for this plan is for Peter Pan's Flight (by a wide margin), then the Mickey Mouse meet and greet, Buzz Lightyear, and The Many Adventures of Winnie the Pooh. Get the first available reservation for any of those, and fit that return-time window into the plan. Once you're able to get your next Genie+ reservation, look for the earliest return time for any of the next few attractions in the plan. **If using ILL,** try to get a reservation for Seven Dwarfs Mine Train in the morning..

See **theugseries.com/free-touring-plans** to customize this plan at no charge, including the attractions and your walking speed, plus real-time updates while you're in the park.

The Magic Kingdom

NON-EARLY-ENTRY ONE-DAY TOURING PLAN FOR PARENTS WITH SMALL CHILDREN

Review the Small-Child Fright Potential Table on page 304.
Interrupt the plan for meals, rest, and bathroom breaks.

1. Arrive at the Magic Kingdom entrance 30 minutes before official opening on days of normal attendance, and 1 hour before official opening during holidays and busy times.
2. As soon as the park opens, head to Fantasyland and ride The Many Adventures of Winnie the Pooh.
3. Give the Mad Tea Party a whirl.
4. Try The Barnstormer.
5. Ride Dumbo the Flying Elephant.
6. Meet some characters at Pete's Silly Sideshow.
7. Ride Under the Sea: Journey of the Little Mermaid.
8. Try the It's a Small World boat ride. Use mobile ordering to order lunch while in line. The best nearby dining location is Columbia Harbour House in Liberty Square.
9. Eat lunch.
10. See *Mickey's PhilharMagic*.
11. Meet princesses at Princess Fairytale Hall.
12. Ride The Magic Carpets of Aladdin in Adventureland.
13. Catch the afternoon parade from Frontierland.
14. Take the raft over to Tom Sawyer Island in Frontierland.
15. See *Monsters, Inc. Laugh Floor* in Tomorrowland.
16. Take a spin on the Tomorrowland Speedway.
17. Ride Buzz Lightyear's Space Ranger Spin.
18. Ride Seven Dwarfs Mine Train in Fantasyland.
19. Take Peter Pan's Flight.
20. If time permits, meet Mickey Mouse at Town Square Theater.
21. If time permits, revisit favorite attractions, try new ones, or tour the park.
22. See the *Happily Ever After* fireworks show.

To use Genie+ with this plan: The most useful Genie+ reservation for this plan is for Peter Pan's Flight (by a wide margin) and then the Mickey Mouse meet and greet, Buzz Lightyear, and The Many Adventures of Winnie the Pooh. Get the first available reservation for any of those, and fit that return-time window into the plan. Once you're able to get your next Genie+ reservation, look for the earliest return time for any of the next few attractions in the plan. **If using ILL,** try to get a reservation for Seven Dwarfs Mine Train in the early evening.

See **theugseries.com/free-touring-plans** to customize this plan at no charge, including the attractions and your walking speed, plus real-time updates while you're in the park.

The Magic Kingdom

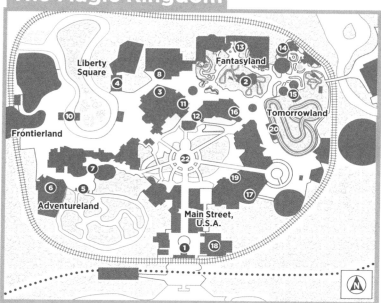

EARLY-ENTRY DUMBO-OR-DIE-IN-A-DAY
TOURING PLAN FOR PARENTS WITH SMALL CHILDREN

Review the Small-Child Fright Potential Table on page 304. Interrupt the plan for meals and rest.

1. Arrive at the entrance 45 minutes before official opening on days of normal attendance, and 1 hour before official opening during holidays and busy times.
2. As soon as the park opens, ride Seven Dwarfs Mine Train in Fantasyland.
3. Take Peter Pan's Flight.
4. Tour The Haunted Mansion in Liberty Square.
5. Take the Jungle Cruise in Adventureland.
6. Experience Pirates of the Caribbean.
7. Ride The Magic Carpets of Aladdin.
8. Take the It's a Small World boat ride. While in line, use mobile ordering to order lunch. The closest good spot is Columbia Harbour House in Liberty Square.
9. Eat lunch.
10. Take the raft over to Tom Sawyer Island in Frontierland.

11. See *Mickey's PhilharMagic* in Fantasyland.
12. Meet princesses at Princess Fairytale Hall.
13. Ride Under the Sea: Journey of the Little Mermaid.
14. Meet the characters at Pete's Silly Sideshow.
15. Ride Dumbo the Flying Elephant.
16. Ride The Many Adventures of Winnie the Pooh.
17. Try Buzz Lightyear's Space Ranger Spin in Tomorrowland.
18. Meet Mickey Mouse at Town Square Theater.
19. If time permits, see *Monsters, Inc. Laugh Floor* in Tomorrowland.
20. Take a spin on the Tomorrowland Speedway.
21. Circle back to any skipped attractions, or revisit favorites.
22. See the *Happily Ever After* fireworks show.

To use Genie+ with this plan: The most useful Genie+ reservations for this plan are for Haunted Mansion, Jungle Cruise, the Mickey Mouse meet and greet, The Many Adventures of Winnie the Pooh, and then Buzz Lightyear. Get the first available reservation for any of those, and fit that return-time window into the plan. Once you're able to get your next Genie+ reservation, look for the earliest return time for any of the next few attractions in the plan. **ILL reservations** shouldn't be needed for this plan.

See **theugseries.com/free-touring-plans** to customize this plan at no charge, including the attractions and your walking speed, plus real-time updates while you're in the park.

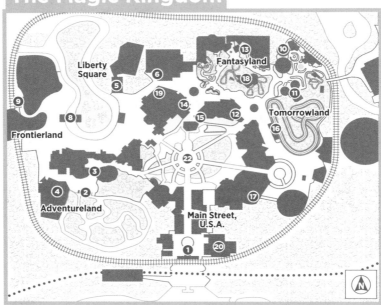

The Magic Kingdom

NON-EARLY-ENTRY DUMBO-OR-DIE-IN-A-DAY TOURING PLAN FOR PARENTS WITH SMALL CHILDREN

Review the Small-Child Fright Potential Table on page 304. Interrupt the plan for meals and rest.

1. Arrive at the entrance 30 minutes before official opening on days of normal attendance, and 1 hour before official opening during holidays and busy times.
2. As soon as you're admitted to the park, take the Jungle Cruise in Adventureland.
3. Ride The Magic Carpets of Aladdin.
4. Experience Pirates of the Caribbean.
5. Tour The Haunted Mansion in Liberty Square.
6. Take the It's a Small World boat ride. While in line, use mobile ordering to order lunch. The best spot nearby is Columbia Harbour House in Liberty Square.
7. Eat lunch.
8. Take the raft over to Tom Sawyer Island in Frontierland.
9. Take the Walt Disney World Railroad from Frontierland to Fantasyland.
10. Meet the characters at Pete's Silly Sideshow.

11. Ride Dumbo the Flying Elephant.
12. Ride The Many Adventures of Winnie the Pooh.
13. Ride Under the Sea: Journey of the Little Mermaid.
14. Watch *Mickey's Philharmagic*.
15. Meet princesses at Princess Fairytale Hall.
16. Take a spin on the Tomorrowland Speedway.
17. Try Buzz Lightyear's Space Ranger Spin in Tomorrowland.
18. Ride Seven Dwarfs Mine Train in Fantasyland.
19. Take Peter Pan's Flight.
20. If time permits, meet Mickey Mouse at Town Square Theater.
21. Circle back to any skipped attractions, or revisit favorites.
22. See the *Happily Ever After* fireworks show.

To use Genie+ with this plan: The most useful Genie+ reservation for this plan is for Peter Pan's Flight (by a wide margin), the Mickey Mouse meet and greet, and then Buzz Lightyear and The Haunted Mansion. Get the first available reservation for any of those, and fit that return-time window into the plan. Once you're able to get your next Genie+ reservation, look for the earliest return time for any of the next few attractions in the plan. **If using ILL,** try to get a reservation for Seven Dwarfs Mine Train in the early evening..

See **theugseries.com/free-touring-plans** to customize this plan at no charge, including the attractions and your walking speed, plus real-time updates while you're in the park.

The Magic Kingdom

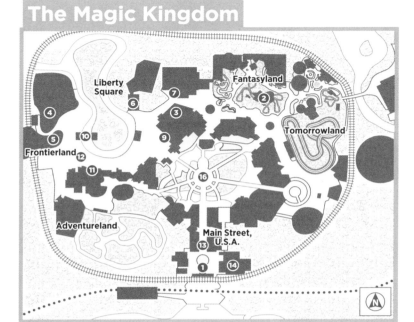

EARLY-ENTRY TWO-DAY TOURING PLAN FOR ADULTS: DAY ONE

If Tiana's Bayou Adventure is using boarding groups, join as early as possible on the day of your visit.

1. Arrive at the entrance 45 minutes before official opening on days of normal attendance, and 1 hour before official opening during holidays and busy times.
2. As soon as the park opens, ride Seven Dwarfs Mine Train in Fantasyland.
3. Ride Peter Pan's Flight.
4. In Frontierland, ride Big Thunder Mountain Railroad.
5. Ride or redeem boarding group for Tiana's Bayou Adventure.
6. In Liberty Square, ride The Haunted Mansion.
7. Ride It's a Small World in Fantasyland. Order lunch using mobile ordering. The best nearby spot is Columbia Harbour House, next door.

8. Eat lunch.
9. Watch *The Hall of Presidents* in Liberty Square.
10. Explore Tom Sawyer Island in Frontierland.
11. Work in a viewing of *Country Bear Jamboree* in Frontierland.
12. Watch the afternoon parade from Frontierland.
13. Explore Main Street, U.S.A., including shopping and catching performances by the Dapper Dans or the Casey's Corner pianist.
14. Meet Mickey Mouse in Town Square Theater
15. Revisit any favorite or skipped attractions.
16. See the *Happily Ever After* fireworks show.

To use Genie+ with this plan: The most useful Genie+ reservations for this plan are for Tiana's Bayou Adventure, Peter Pan's Flight, Big Thunder Mountain, Pirates of the Caribbean, Haunted Mansion, and meeting Mickey Mouse. Get the first available reservation for any of those, and fit that return-time window into the plan. Once you're able to get your next Genie+ reservation, look for the earliest return time for any of the next few attractions in the plan. **ILL reservations** shouldn't be needed for this plan.

See **theugseries.com/free-touring-plans** to customize this plan at no charge, including the attractions and your walking speed, plus real-time updates while you're in the park.

(see next page for Day Two)

The Magic Kingdom

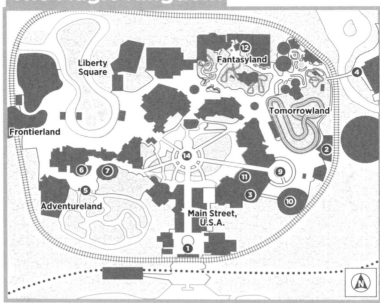

EARLY-ENTRY TWO-DAY TOURING PLAN FOR ADULTS: DAY TWO

If Tiana's Bayou Adventure is using boarding groups, join as early as possible on the day of your visit. Interrupt the plan for meals and rest.

1. Arrive at the entrance 45 minutes before official opening on days of normal attendance, and 1 hour before official opening during holidays and busy times.
2. As soon as the park opens, ride Space Mountain.
3. Ride Buzz Lightyear's Space Ranger Spin.
4. Redeem boarding group or Individual Lightning Lane for Tron Lightcycle/Run.
5. In Adventureland, take the Jungle Cruise.
6. See *Walt Disney's Enchanted Tiki Room.* Use mobile ordering to order lunch.
7. Tour the Swiss Family Treehouse.
8. Eat lunch.
9. Ride the Tomorrowland Transit Authority PeopleMover in Tomorrowland.
10. See *Walt Disney's Carousel of Progress.*
11. See *Monsters, Inc. Laugh Floor.*
12. Ride Under the Sea: Journey of the Little Mermaid
13. Revisit any favorite attractions or tour the rest of the park.
14. If you've not already done so, see the *Happily Ever After* fireworks show.

To use Genie+ with this plan: The most useful Genie+ reservations for this plan are for Space Mountain, Jungle Cruise, and Buzz Lightyear. Get the first available reservation for any of those, and fit that return-time window into the plan. Once you're able to get your next Genie+ reservation, look for the earliest return time for any of the next few attractions in the plan. **If using ILL,** make reservations for Tron for in the morning.

See **theugseries.com/free-touring-plans** to customize this plan at no charge, including the attractions and your walking speed, plus real-time updates while you're in the park.

EARLY-ENTRY ONE-DAY TOURING PLAN

If Guardians of the Galaxy: Cosmic Rewind is using boarding groups (see page 49), obtain a reservation at 7 a.m. or 1 p.m. on the day of your visit, and interrupt the plan when it's time to ride.

1. Arrive at the International Gateway or main entrance 50 minutes before official opening (70 minutes on busy days and holidays).

2. If entering from International Gateway, you will likely be able to get into the queue for **(2a)** Remy's Ratatouille Adventure before Early Entry begins. Ride it first. If entering from the main entrance, head straight to **(2b)** Frozen Ever After.

3. Ask a cast member if Test Track in World Discovery is operating. If it is, ride. You can use the single-rider line if it's open.

4. If your group includes teens, ride Mission: Space in World Discovery and skip Living with the Land in step 7.

5. Ride Spaceship Earth in World Celebration. Skip this step if the posted wait time at Soarin' is already over 30 minutes.

6. Ride Soarin' Around the World in The Land Pavilion in World Nature.

7. Ride Living with the Land. Skip it if you have teens, to save time.

8. Eat a light lunch. Sunshine Seasons is the closest option, but Connections Eatery is good and offers mobile ordering.

9. Tour The Seas main tank and exhibits. Watch *Turtle Talk with Crush* if you have time.

10. Walk through Journey of Water, Inspired by Moana.

11. Begin a clockwise tour of World Showcase at Mexico, including Gran Fiesta Tour.

12. Tour the Norway Pavilion and ride Frozen Ever After.

13. See the China Pavilion. Skip the film—it's not rated highly by any age group.

14. Check out the Germany Pavilion.

15. Tour the Italy Pavilion.

16. Watch Voices of Liberty in The American Adventure Pavilion.

17. Tour the Japan Pavilion and exhibits.

18. Tour the Morocco Pavilion and exhibits.

19. Tour the France Pavilion. The sing-along here is skippable.

20. Tour the United Kingdom Pavilion

21. Tour the Canada Pavilion and see the film.

22. See the fireworks show. Good viewing locations should be available around the Mexico Pavilion; in front of World Showcase where it meets Future World; and between Canada and France.

To use Genie+ with this plan: The most useful Genie+ reservations for this plan are for Remy's Ratatouille Adventure, Frozen Ever After, Test Track, and Soarin' Around the World (in that order). Get the first available reservation for one of those, and fit that return-time window into the plan. Once you're able to get your next Genie+ reservation, book one of the remaining four attractions in the plan. **If using ILL,** try to get a Guardians reservation for as close to park opening as possible, when the wait will be shortest.

See **theugseries.com/free-touring-plans** to customize this plan at no charge, including the attractions and your walking speed, plus real-time updates while you're in the park.

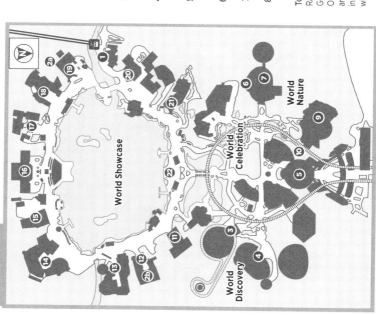

EPCOT

NON-EARLY-ENTRY ONE-DAY TOURING PLAN

If Guardians of the Galaxy: Cosmic Rewind is using boarding groups (see page 49), obtain a reservation at 7 a.m. on the day of your visit and interrupt the plan when it's time to ride.

1. Arrive at EPCOT's main entrance 30 minutes before official opening (50 minutes on busy days and holidays).

2. As soon as the park opens, ask a cast member if Test Track in World Discovery is operating. If yes, ride Test Track. You can use the single-rider line if it's open.

3. If your group includes teens, ride Mission: Space in World Discovery and skip Living with the Land in step 6.

4. Ride Spaceship Earth in World Celebration. Skip this step if the posted wait at Soarin' is already over 30 minutes.

5. Ride Soarin' Around the World in The Land Pavilion in World Nature.

6. Ride Living with the Land. If you have teens, skip it to save time.

7. Eat a light lunch. Sunshine Seasons in The Land is the closest option, but Connections Eatery is good and offers mobile ordering.

8. Tour The Seas main bar and exhibits.

9. Walk through Journey of Water, Inspired by Moana.

10. Begin a tour of World Showcase at Mexico. Skip the Gran Fiesta Tour to save time.

11. Tour Norway and ride Frozen Ever After.

12. See the China Pavilion. Skip the film—it's not rated highly by any age group.

13. Check out the Germany Pavilion.

14. Tour the Italy Pavilion.

15. See Voices of Liberty in The American Adventure Pavilion.

16. Tour the Japan Pavilion and exhibits.

17. Tour the Morocco Pavilion and exhibits.

18. In France, ride Remy's Ratatouille Adventure. To save time, skip the film shown elsewhere in the pavilion.

19. If you have more than 2 hours before the park closes, tour the Canada Pavilion and see *Canada Far and Wide*.

20. Return to World Discovery. Ride Guardians of the Galaxy if you haven't already.

21. See the evening fireworks. Good viewing locations should be available around the Mexico Pavilion; in front of World Showcase where it meets Future World; and between Canada and France.

To use Genie+ with this plan: The most useful Genie+ reservations for this plan are for Remy, Frozen Ever After, Test Track, and Soarin' (in that order). Get the first available reservation for one of those, and fit that return-time window into the plan. Once you're able to get your next Genie+ reservation, book one of the remaining four. Once those are used or booked up for the day, look for the earliest return time for any of the next few attractions in the plan. **If using ILL,** try to get a Guardians reservation for before noon to avoid a walk back from the World Showcase.

See **theugseries.com/free-touring-plans** to customize this plan at no charge, including the attractions and your walking speed, plus real-time updates while you're in the park.

Disney's Animal Kingdom

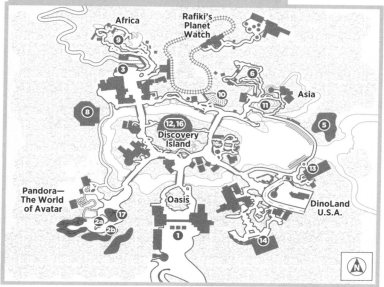

EARLY-ENTRY ONE-DAY TOURING PLAN

1. Arrive at the main entrance 50 minutes before official opening on days of normal attendance (70 minutes during holidays and busy times). Follow cast member instructions to line up for Avatar Flight of Passage.

2. Ride Avatar Flight of Passage (**2a**), then Na'vi River Journey (**2b**) in Pandora.

3. Ride Kilimanjaro Safaris in Africa

4. Sign up for Wilderness Explorers at any booth or dedicated space you pass that has booklets.

5. Ride Expedition Everest in Asia.

6. Walk the Maharajah Jungle Trek. Use mobile ordering to order lunch. Satu'li Canteen in Pandora and Flame Tree Barbecue on Discovery Island are both good options.

7. Eat lunch.

8. Work in the next showing of *Festival of the Lion King* in Africa around the next two steps.

9. Walk the Gorilla Falls Exploration Trail.

10. See *Feathered Friends in Flight!* in Asia.

11. Get wet on Kali River Rapids in Asia, if temperatures permit.

12. Tour the Discovery Island Trails and any other animal exhibits that interest you.

13. See *Finding Nemo: The Big Blue . . . and Beyond!* in DinoLand U.S.A.

14. Ride Dinosaur.

If the park is open past dark:

15. Eat dinner in the park— try Nomad Lounge or book a meal at a table-service restaurant like Tusker House or Yak & Yeti.

16. See *Awakenings* at the Tree of Life. Check *Times Guide* for start time.

17. Tour the Valley of Mo'ara in Pandora.

To use Genie+ with this plan: The most useful Genie+ reservations for this plan are for Na'vi River Journey and Kilimanjaro Safaris, then Expedition Everest and (during summer) Kali River Rapids. Get the first available reservation for one of those, and fit that return-time window into the plan. Once you're able to get your next Genie+ reservation, look for the earliest return time for any of the next few attractions in the plan. **ILL reservations** shouldn't be needed for Flight of Passage as long as you head there first thing during Early Entry.

See **theugseries.com/free-touring-plans** to customize this plan at no charge, including the attractions and your walking speed, plus real-time updates while you're in the park.

Disney's Animal Kingdom

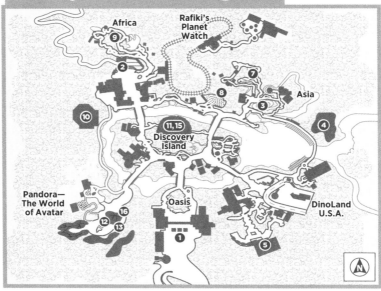

NON-EARLY-ENTRY ONE-DAY TOURING PLAN

1. Arrive at the main entrance 30 minutes before official opening on days of normal attendance (50 minutes during holidays and busy times).
2. As soon as you're admitted into the park, take the Kilimanjaro Safaris tour in Africa.
3. Get wet on Kali River Rapids in Asia, if temperatures permit.
4. Ride Expedition Everest.
5. Ride Dinosaur in DinoLand U.S.A. Use mobile ordering to order lunch in advance. The best restaurants in the park are Satu'li Canteen in Pandora and Flame Tree Barbecue on Discovery Island.
6. Eat lunch. On your way to lunch, sign up for Wilderness Explorers at any booth or dedicated space that has booklets. Play a few games as you tour the rest of the park.
7. Walk the Maharajah Jungle Trek.
8. See *Feathered Friends in Flight* in Asia.
9. Walk the Gorilla Falls Exploration Trail.
10. See *Festival of the Lion King.*
11. Tour the Discovery Island Trails and any other animal exhibits that interest you.
12. Ride Avatar Flight of Passage in Pandora.
13. Take the Na'vi River Journey boat ride.

If the park is open past dark:

14. Eat dinner in the park.
15. See *Awakenings* at the Tree of Life. Check *Times Guide* for start time.
16. Tour the Valley of Mo'ara in Pandora.

To use Genie+ with this plan: The most useful Genie+ reservations for this plan are for Na'vi River Journey and Kilimanjaro Safaris, then Expedition Everest and (during summer) Kali River Rapids. Get the first available reservation for one of those and fit that return-time window into the plan. Once you're able to get your next Genie+ reservation, look for the earliest return time for any of the next few attractions in the plan. **If using ILL,** obtain a reservation for Flight of Passage for around 4 p.m.

See **theugseries.com/free-touring-plans** to customize this plan at no charge, including the attractions and your walking speed, plus real-time updates while you're in the park.

Disney's Hollywood Studios

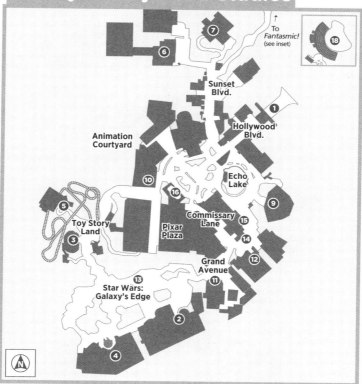

To
Fantasmic!
(see inset)

Sunset Blvd.

Hollywood Blvd.

Animation Courtyard

Echo Lake

Toy Story Land

Pixar Plaza

Commissary Lane

Grand Avenue

Star Wars: Galaxy's Edge

EARLY-ENTRY ONE-DAY TOURING PLAN

1. Plan to arrive 60 minutes before official park opening on non-peak days (90 minutes during holidays and other busy times).
2. If the park opens 15-20 minutes before Early Entry, immediately ride Star Wars: Rise of the Resistance (**2**) in Galaxy's Edge. Otherwise, go straight to Slinky Dog Dash (**3**).
3. If you rode Rise and the park still isn't officially open, ride Slinky Dog Dash.
4. Ride *Millennium Falcon: Smugglers Run.*
5. Ride Toy Story Mania!
6. Ride Rock 'n' Roller Coaster on Sunset Boulevard.
7. Ride The Twilight Zone Tower of Terror. Use mobile ordering to order lunch. The highest-rated spots are Docking Bay 7 and Woody's Lunch Box.
8. Eat lunch.

9. Watch *For the First Time In Forever, Indiana Jones Epic Stunt Spectacular!,* and *Beauty and the Beast—Live on Stage* sometime in the early afternoon.
10. See *Walt Disney Presents* in Animation Courtyard. If you have small children, try *Disney Junior Play and Dance!,* instead.
11. Watch *Muppet*Vision 3D.*
12. Ride Star Tours—The Adventures Continue.
13. Explore the rest of Galaxy's Edge.
14. Meet Mickey and Minnie at *Red Carpet Dreams.*
15. Meet Olaf at Celebrity Spotlight.
16. Ride Mickey & Minnie's Runaway Railway.
17. Experience Rise of the Resistance (**2**) or Slinky Dog Dash (**3**) if you haven't already.
18. End the night with *Fantasmic!*

To use Genie+ with this plan: The most useful Genie+ reservations for this plan are for Slinky Dog Dash, Tower of Terror, *Millennium Falcon:* Smugglers Run, Toy Story Mania!, and Rock 'n' Roller Coaster. (During summers and holidays, almost any Genie+ reservation except Star Tours will save time.) Get the first available reservation for one of those, and fit that return-time window into the plan. Once you're able to get your next Genie+ reservation, look for the earliest return time for any of the next few attractions in the plan. **If using ILL,** book one for Rise only if it's broken down at the start of the day

See **theugseries.com/free-touring-plans** to customize this plan at no charge, including the attractions and your walking speed, plus real-time updates while you're in the park.

Disney's Hollywood Studios

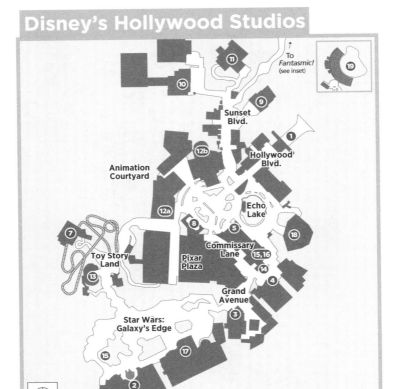

NON-EARLY-ENTRY ONE-DAY TOURING PLAN

1. Check official park hours the night before your visit, and plan to arrive 50 minutes before official park opening (70 minutes during holidays and other busy times.)

2. As soon as you're admitted into the park, ride *Millennium Falcon:* Smugglers Run in Galaxy's Edge.

3. See *Muppet*Vision 3D* in Grand Avenue.

4. Experience Star Tours—The Adventures Continue in Echo Lake.

5. Work in a showing of *For the First Time in Forever* around the next few steps. Use mobile ordering to order lunch. The best spot nearby is Docking Bay 7 in Galaxy's Edge.

6. Eat lunch.

7. Ride Toy Story Mania! in Toy Story Land.

8. Try Mickey & Minnie's Runaway Railway on Hollywood Boulevard.

9. Work in *Beauty and the Beast—Live on Stage* around the next two steps.

10. Ride Rock 'n' Roller Coaster.

11. Ride The Twilight Zone Tower of Terror.

12. See *Walt Disney Presents* (**12a**) in Animation Courtyard. If you have small children, try *Disney Junior Play and Dance* (**12b**), also in Animation Courtyard, instead.

13. Ride Slinky Dog Dash in Toy Story Land.

14. Meet Mickey and Minnie at *Red Carpet Dreams.*

15. Meet Olaf at Celebrity Spotlight.

16. See *Vacation Fun* in Echo Lake.

17. Ride Star Wars: Rise of the Resistance and explore the remainder of Galaxy's Edge.

18. See the *Indiana Jones Epic Stunt Spectacular!*

19. See the evening fireworks and/or *Fantasmic!*

To use Genie+ with this plan: The most useful Genie+ reservations for this plan are for Slinky Dog Dash, Tower of Terror, *Millennium Falcon:* Smugglers Run, and Rock 'n' Roller Coaster. (During summers and holidays, almost any Genie+ reservation except Star Tours will save time.) Get the first available reservation for one of those, and fit that return-time window into the plan. Once you're able to get your next Genie+ reservation, look for the earliest return time for any of the next few attractions in the plan. **If using ILL,** try to obtain one for Rise of the Resistance for around 5 p.m.

See **theugseries.com/free-touring-plans** to customize this plan at no charge, including the attractions and your walking speed, plus real-time updates while you're in the park.

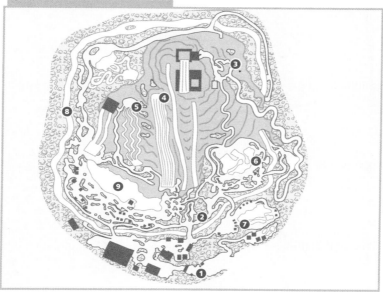

BLIZZARD BEACH ONE-DAY TOURING PLAN
FOR PARENTS WITH SMALL CHILDREN

1. Arrive at the park entrance 30 minutes before opening. Take care of locker and towel rentals at Lottawatta Lodge, to your left as you enter the park. Find a spot to stow the remainder of your gear, noting any nearby landmarks to help you find your way back.

2. Take the chairlift up Mount Gushmore to the Green Slope. *Note:* It might be faster—though more tiring—to walk to the top.

3. Raft down Teamboat Springs. Repeat as much as you like while the park is still uncrowded.

4. If your kids are up for it, try the Toboggan Racers.

5. If the kids enjoyed the Toboggan Racers, try the Snow Stormers next.

6. Visit the Ski Patrol Training Camp.

7. Visit Tike's Peak.

8. Grab some tubes and go floating in Cross Country Creek.

9. Swim in Melt-Away Bay's Wave Pool for as long as you like.

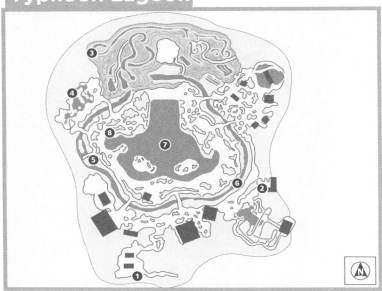

TYPHOON LAGOON ONE-DAY TOURING PLAN
FOR PARENTS WITH SMALL CHILDREN

1. Arrive at the park entrance 30 minutes before opening. Take care of locker and towel rentals at Singapore Sal's, to your right after you've walked along the winding entrance path and emerged into the park. Find a spot to stow the remainder of your gear, noting any nearby landmarks to help you find your way back.

2. Ride Miss Adventure Falls as many times as you like.

3. Ride Gangplank Falls as many times as you like.

4. If your kids enjoyed Gangplank Falls, try Keelhaul Falls if it seems appropriate.

5. Enjoy the Ketchakiddee Creek kids' play area.

6. Grab some tubes and ride Castaway Creek. A complete circuit takes 20–25 minutes.

7. Swim in the Surf Pool as long as you like.

8. Ride the Bay Slides in the Surf Pool.

9. Repeat your favorite attractions as desired.

MAGIC KINGDOM TOURING PLAN COMPANION
ATTRACTION INFORMATION

Attraction | Location | When to Go | Authors' Rating | Comments

Ariel's Grotto (*Genie+*) | Fantasyland | Early or late | ★★★

Astro Orbiter | Tomorrowland | Before 11 a.m. or before park closing | ★★ | Fright potential*

The Barnstormer (*Genie+*) | Fantasyland | Early or late | ★½ | 35" minimum height; fright potential*

Big Thunder Mountain Railroad (*Genie+*) | Frontierland | Early or late | ★★★★ | 40" minimum height; pregnant guests should not ride; fright potential*

Buzz Lightyear's Space Ranger Spin (*Genie+*) | Tomorrowland | First or last hour the park is open | ★★★★ | Fright potential*

Casey Jr. Splash 'N' Soak Station | Fantasyland | When it's hot | ★★½

Country Bear Jamboree | Frontierland | Anytime | ★★★

Dumbo the Flying Elephant (*Genie+*) | Fantasyland | Early or late | ★★½ | Fright potential*

Enchanted Tales with Belle | Fantasyland | Early or late | ★★★★

The Hall of Presidents | Liberty Square | Anytime | ★★★

The Haunted Mansion (*Genie+*) | Liberty Square | Early or late | ★★★★½ | Fright potential*

It's a Small World (*Genie+*) | Fantasyland | Early or late | ★★★½

Jungle Cruise (*Genie+*) | Adventureland | Early or late | ★★★½ | Fright potential*

Liberty Belle Riverboat | Liberty Square | Anytime | ★★½

Mad Tea Party (*Genie+*) | Fantasyland | Anytime | ★★ | Motion sickness potential; pregnant guests should not ride

The Magic Carpets of Aladdin (*Genie+*) | Adventureland | Before noon or after dark | ★★ | Fright potential*

The Many Adventures of Winnie the Pooh (*Genie+*) | Fantasyland | Early or late | ★★★½ | Fright potential*

Meet Mirabel at Fairytale Garden | Fantasyland | Early or late | ★★★½

Mickey's PhilharMagic (*Genie+*) | Fantasyland | Anytime | ★★★½

Monsters, Inc. Laugh Floor (*Genie+*) | Tomorrowland | Anytime | ★★★

Peter Pan's Flight (*Genie+*) | Fantasyland | First or last 30 minutes the park is open | ★★★★

Pete's Silly Sideshow | Fantasyland | Early or late | ★★½

A Pirate's Adventure: Treasure of the Seven Seas | Adventureland | Afternoon | ★★½

Pirates of the Caribbean (*Genie+*) | Adventureland | Anytime | ★★★★ | Fright potential*

Prince Charming Regal Carrousel | Fantasyland | Anytime | ★★★

Princess Fairytale Hall (*Genie+*) | Fantasyland | Early or late | ★★★

Seven Dwarfs Mine Train (*ILL*) | Fantasyland | As soon as the park opens | ★★★★ | Fright potential*

Space Mountain (*Genie+*) | Tomorrowland | At park opening or during the last hour before closing | ★★★★ | 44" minimum height; pregnant guests should not ride; motion sickness and fright potential*

Swiss Family Treehouse | Adventureland | Anytime | ★★★ | Fright potential*

Tiana's Bayou Adventure (*formerly Splash Mountain*) | Frontierland | At park opening or use Genie+ | *Too new to rate* | 40" minimum height; pregnant guests should not ride; you'll get wet; fright potential*

Tom Sawyer Island and Fort Langhorn | Frontierland | Afternoon | ★★★ | Fright potential*

Tomorrowland Speedway (*Genie+*) | Tomorrowland | Not in the hot sun | ★★ | 54" minimum height for kids to drive unassisted; motion sickness potential

Tomorrowland Transit Authority PeopleMover | Tomorrowland | Anytime | ★★★½

Town Square Theater Meet and Greets (*Genie+*) | Main Street, U.S.A. | Early or late | ★★★★

Tron Lightcycle/Run (*ILL*) | Tomorrowland | When your boarding group is called | ★★★★ | Fright potential*

Under the Sea: Journey of the Little Mermaid (*Genie+*) | Fantasyland | Early or late | ★★★ | Fright potential*

Walt Disney's Carousel of Progress | Tomorrowland | Anytime | ★★★

Walt Disney's Enchanted Tiki Room | Adventureland | Anytime | ★★★ | Fright potential*

Walt Disney World Railroad | Multiple stations | Anytime | ★★★

* See Small-Child Fright-Potential Table on page 304.

DINING INFORMATION Counter Service

Restaurant | Location | Quality | Value | Selections

Aloha Isle | Adventureland | Excellent | B | Soft-serve, ice-cream floats, pineapple juice

Casey's Corner | Main Street, U.S.A. | Good | C | Hot dogs, plant-based "sausage" dogs, corn dog nuggets, fries, Baseball Brownie

Columbia Harbour House | Liberty Square | Good | B | Grilled salmon, fried fish and shrimp, lobster roll, fried chicken, plant-based "crab" cake sandwich, grilled shrimp, salads, hush puppies

Cosmic Ray's Starlight Café | Tomorrowland | Fair–Poor | C | Burgers (including plant-based), hot dogs, Greek salad, chicken sandwich, chicken strips, hot dogs, seasonal dessert; some kosher

DINING INFORMATION Counter Service *(continued)*

Restaurant | Location | Quality | Value | Selections

The Friar's Nook | Fantasyland | Good | B | Hot dogs; bacon mac and cheese; bacon, egg, and cheese breakfast croissant with tots

Gaston's Tavern | Fantasyland | Good | B | Ham-and-Swiss sandwich, cinnamon rolls, Grey Stuff, LeFou's Brew

Golden Oak Outpost *(seasonal)* | Frontierland | Fair | C | Fried-fish sandwich, chicken strips, chili-cheese fries, chocolate chip cookies

Liberty Square Market | Liberty Square | Good | C | Hot dogs, fresh fruit, pretzels, packaged drinks and snacks

The Lunching Pad | Tomorrowland | Fair | C | Hot dogs, pretzels, specialty frozen drinks

Main Street Bakery (Starbucks) | Main Street, U.S.A. | Good | B | Coffees, pastries, breakfast sandwiches

Pecos Bill Tall Tale Inn and Cafe | Frontierland | Fair | C | Pork carnitas and chicken fajita platter, nachos, rice bowl with veggies, salad, burgers, strawberry-limeade slush, shortcake, doughnut holes, yogurt

Pinocchio Village Haus | Fantasyland | Fair-Poor | D | Flatbread pizzas, chicken strips, fries, Caesar salad

Tomorrowland Terrace Restaurant *(seasonal)* | Tomorrowland | Fair | C– | Varies

Tortuga Tavern *(seasonal)* | Adventureland | Fair | B | Chicken strips, sandwiches, hot dogs

DINING INFORMATION Table Service

Restaurant | Meals Served | Location | Price | Quality | Value | Selections

Be Our Guest Restaurant | L-D | Fantasyland | Expensive | ★★ | ★★ | *Lunch and dinner:* French onion soup, pork tenderloin, Grey Stuff, filet mignon with Robuchon potatoes, pan-seared scallops with risotto; kids' menu

Cinderella's Royal Table | B-L-D | Fantasyland | Expensive | ★★★ | ★★ | *Breakfast:* Eggs, bacon, sausage, pastries, shrimp and grits, quiche, French toast, beef tenderloin frittata. *Lunch and dinner:* Lamb, filet, fish, chicken, vegetarian pasta; kids' menu

The Crystal Palace | B-L-D | Main Street, U.S.A. | Expensive | ★★½ | ★★★ | Buffet with fried chicken, prime rib, Southern Fried Cauliflower, seasonal salads; character meals

Jungle Navigation Co. Ltd. Skipper Canteen | L-D | Adventureland | Expensive | ★★★½ | ★★★ | Char siu pork, Korean barbecue–inspired crispy fried chicken, grilled steak with adobo, corn pancakes with pork and avocado cream; chocolate cake with caramelized bananas; plant-based options; kids' menu

Liberty Tree Tavern | L-D | Liberty Square | Expensive | ★★★ | ★★★ | All-you-can-eat platter with roasted turkey, pork roast, mashed potatoes, stuffing, vegetables, and mac and cheese; Impossible Meatloaf; toffee cake

The Plaza Restaurant | L-D | Main Street, U.S.A. | Moderate | ★★ | ★★ | Old-fashioned diner and ice-cream shop fare: bacon cheeseburger, chicken sandwich, sundae; kids' menu

Tony's Town Square Restaurant | L-D | Main Street, U.S.A. | Moderate-Expensive | ★★★ | ★★ | Spaghetti with meatballs, shrimp fettuccine Alfredo, chicken parmigiana, butcher's steak; kids' menu

Advance Reservations are recommended for most Magic Kingdom full-service restaurants; call ☎ 407-WDW-DINE (939-3463) *or visit disneyworld.disney.go.com/reservations/dining.*

GOOD REST AREAS

Back of Storybook Circus, between Big Top Treats and the train station | Fantasyland | Covered plush seating with electrical outlets and USB phone-charging stations

Covered porch with rocking chairs on Tom Sawyer Island | Frontierland | Across the water from the *Liberty Belle* Riverboat dock; bring refreshments from Frontierland; closes at sunset

Cul-de-sac | Main Street, U.S.A. | Between the china shop and Main Street's Starbucks on the right side of the street as you face the castle; refreshments nearby

Picnic tables | Fantasyland | Near the *Tangled*-themed restrooms, between Peter Pan's Flight and The Haunted Mansion; outdoors but has phone-charging stations

Quiet seating area | Tomorrowland | Near restrooms on the right as you approach Space Mountain. Near building to the right of Space Mountain's entrance, near the trees, there's a covered seating area farther back in that corridor; refreshments nearby

Second floor of train station | Main Street, U.S.A. | Refreshments nearby; crowded during fireworks and parades

Upstairs at Columbia Harbour House | Liberty Square | Grab a beverage and relax upstairs; restrooms available

EPCOT TOURING PLAN COMPANION

ATTRACTION INFORMATION

Attraction | Location | When to Go | Authors' Rating | Comments

The American Adventure | United States, World Showcase | Anytime | ★★★½

Awesome Planet | The Land, World Nature | Anytime | ★★½

Beauty and the Beast Sing-Along | France, World Showcase | 11 a.m.–6 p.m. | ★★

Canada Far and Wide | Canada, World Showcase | Anytime | ★★★

Disney & Pixar Short Film Festival (*Genie+*) | Imagination! Pavilion, World Nature | Anytime | ★★½

DuckTales World Showcase Adventure | World Showcase | Anytime | ★★★

Frozen Ever After (*Genie+*) | Norway, World Showcase | Before noon or after 7 p.m. | ★★★★ | Fright potential*

Gran Fiesta Tour| Mexico, World Showcase | Anytime | ★★½

Guardians of the Galaxy (*ILL*) | World Discovery | As soon as the park opens, using Early Entry, if possible. | ★★★★ | 42" minimum height; fright and motion sickness potential*

Impressions de France | France, World Showcase | 7–8:45 p.m. | ★★★

Journey into Imagination with Figment (*Genie+*) | Imagination! Pavilion, World Nature | Anytime | ★★½ | Fright potential*

Journey of Water, Inspired by Moana | World Nature | Anytime | ★★★★

Living with the Land (*Genie+*) | The Land, World Nature | Anytime | ★★★★

Meet Anna and Elsa at Royal Sommerhus | Norway, World Showcase | At park opening, at lunch or dinner, or during the last hour the park is open | ★★★★

Mission: Space (*Genie+*) | World Discovery | Anytime | ★★★ | Orange version not recommended for pregnant guests or anyone prone to motion sickness or claustrophobia; 40" minimum height for Green version and 44" for Orange version; c

Reflections of China | China, World Showcase | Anytime | ★★½

Remy's Ratatouille Adventure (*Genie+*) | France, World Showcase | At park opening | ★★★★ | Fright potential*

The Seas Main Tank and Exhibits | The Seas, World Nature | When you need a break from the heat, sun, or rain | ★★★½

The Seas with Nemo & Friends (*Genie+*) | The Seas, World Nature | Anytime | ★★★ | Fright potential*

Soarin' Around the World (*Genie+*) | The Land, World Nature | First 2 hours the park is open or after 4 p.m. | ★★★★½ | 40" minimum height; fright potential*

Spaceship Earth (*Genie+*) | World Celebration | Midday | ★★★★

Test Track (*Genie+*) | World Discovery | First 30 minutes the park is open or just before closing, or use the single-rider line | ★★★★ | 40" minimum height; pregnant guests should not ride; fright potential*

Turtle Talk with Crush (*Genie+*) | The Seas, World Nature | Anytime | ★★★★

* See Small-Child Fright-Potential Table on page 304.

DINING INFORMATION Counter Service

Restaurant | Location | Quality | Value | Selections

L'Artisan des Glaces | France, World Showcase | Excellent | C | Gourmet ice cream and dairy-free sorbet

La Cantina de San Angel | Mexico, World Showcase | Good | B | Tacos; fried cheese empanada; grilled chicken with cascabel pepper sauce; guacamole; churros; margaritas

Connections Café and Eatery | World Celebration | Good | C | Burgers, pizza, salads, plant-based options

Fife & Drum Tavern | United States, World Showcase | Fair | C | Turkey legs, hot dogs, popcorn, soft-serve ice cream, slushies, beer, alcoholic lemonade, root beer floats

Les Halles Boulangerie–Pâtisserie | France, World Showcase | Excellent | B | Sandwiches (ham and cheese; Brie, cranberry, and apple), quiches, soups, bread, pastries

Katsura Grill | Japan, World Showcase | Good | B | Sushi; udon noodle bowls; chicken, beef, or shrimp teriyaki; ramen; edamame; miso soup; yuzu tea cheesecake; Kirin beer, sake, plum wine

Kringla Bakeri og Kafe | Norway, World Showcase | Good–Excellent | B | Norwegian pastries and desserts, iced coffee, imported beers and wines

Lotus Blossom Café | China, World Showcase | Fair | C | Egg rolls, pot stickers, orange chicken, chicken fried rice, Mongolian beef with rice, caramel-ginger or lychee ice cream; plum wine, Tsingtao beer

Refreshment Outpost | Between Germany and China, World Showcase | Good | C | All-beef hot dogs; slushies, soft-serve, soda, draft beer

Refreshment Port | Near Canada, World Showcase | Good | C | Soft-serve, specialty alcoholic drinks, beer

Regal Eagle Smokehouse | United States, World Showcase | Good | B | Regional barbecue specialties, burgers, salads, vegetarian options; beer, hard cider, wine, and specialty cocktails

Rose & Crown Pub | UK, World Showcase | Good | B | Fish-and-chips, Scotch egg; beer and spirits

Sommerfest | Germany, World Showcase | Fair | C | Bratwurst, pretzel bread pudding, jumbo pretzel; beer

DINING INFORMATION Counter Service *(continued)*

Restaurant | Location | Quality | Value | Selections

Sunshine Seasons | The Land, World Nature | Good | B | Rotisserie and wood-fired meats and fish; soups, salads, sandwiches, flatbreads

Tangierine Café | Morocco, World Showcase | Good | B | Kebabs; hummus; Moroccan wine and beer

Yorkshire County Fish Shop | United Kingdom, World Showcase | Good | A | Fish-and-chips, draft ale

DINING INFORMATION Table Service

Restaurant | Meals Served | Location | Price | Quality | Value | Selections

Akershus Royal Banquet Hall | B-L-D | Norway, World Showcase | Expensive | ★★ | ★★★ | Family-style dining with Norwegian meatballs, grilled salmon, chicken and dumplings, lefse, mashed potatoes, green beans, mac and cheese, corn dogs; full bar, including aquavit cocktails; character meals

Biergarten Restaurant | L-D | Germany, World Showcase | Expensive | ★★★ | ★★★★ | Traditional German sausages, homemade spaetzle, rotisserie chicken, braised red cabbage; full bar; kids' menu

Le Cellier Steakhouse | L-D | Canada, World Showcase | Expensive | ★★★★ | ★★★ | Canadian Cheddar soup, filet mignon, mac and cheese, loaded mashed potatoes, poutine, chocolate tart; full bar and Canadian wines; kids' menu

Chefs de France | L-D | France, World Showcase | Expensive | ★★½ | ★★★ | Boeuf Bourguignon, French onion soup topped with Gruyère; vegetarian options; beer, wine, cocktails; kids' menu

Coral Reef Restaurant | L-D | The Seas, Future World | Expensive | ★★★ | ★★ | Steak and seafood; chocolate cake; full bar; kids' menu

La Crêperie de Paris | B-L-D | France, World Showcase | Moderate | ★★★½ | ★★★ | Chèvre, spinach, and walnut savory crepe, banana-filled dessert crepe; full bar; kids' menu

Garden Grill Restaurant | B-L-D | The Land, World Nature | Expensive | ★★★ | ★★★ | Grilled beef with chimichurri, turkey with stuffing and gravy, BBQ ribs, mashed potatoes, veggies, salads; berry shortcake; plant-based options; full bar; character meals; kids' menu

La Hacienda de San Angel | D | Mexico, World Showcase | Expensive | ★★★½ | ★★★ | Flautas, guacamole, queso fundido, carne asada-style New York strip, fried-shrimp tacos, tenderloin fajitas; full bar with margaritas and specialty tequilas; kids' menu

Monsieur Paul | D | France, World Showcase | Expensive | ★★★ | ★★ | Black-truffle soup, black sea bass in potato "scales," roasted duck; full bar; no kids' menu

Nine Dragons Restaurant | L-D | China, World Showcase | Moderate | ★★★ | ★★½ | Crispy duck bao buns, honey-sesame chicken, salt-and-pepper shrimp; full bar; kids' menu

Rose & Crown Dining Room | L-D | United Kingdom, World Showcase | Moderate | ★★★½ | ★★★ | Fish-and-chips, bangers and mash, shepherd's pie (with vegetarian option), Scotch egg; sticky toffee pudding; full bar; kids' menu

San Angel Inn Restaurante | L-D | Mexico, World Showcase | Expensive | ★★★ | ★★ | Queso fundido, rib eye tacos, vegetarian huarache; sweet corn ice cream; full bar; kids' menu

Shiki-Sai | L-D | Japan, World Showcase | Moderate | *Too new to rate* | Sushi and sashimi; full bar

Space 220 | L-D | World Discovery | Expensive | ★★½ | ★½ | Seared tuna, burger, vegetarian stuffed shells, chicken with potato gratin, spaghetti with shrimp, miso-glazed salmon, salads; full bar; kids' menu

Spice Road Table | L-D | Morocco, World Showcase | Expensive | ★★★★ | ★★★ | Mediterranean-style small plates including fried calamari and hummus fries, lamb kefta, spiced shrimp and chicken; full bar

Takumi-Tei | D | Japan, World Showcase | Expensive | ★★★★★ | ★★★½ | Traditional Japanese kaiseki cuisine; Wagyu beef, sushi; full bar; multicourse kids' menu

Teppan Edo | L-D | Japan, World Showcase | Expensive | ★★★★ | ★★★ | Chicken, shrimp, beef, scallops, and veggies stir-fried on teppanyaki grill; full bar; kids' menu

Tutto Italia Ristorante | L-D | Italy, World Showcase | Expensive | ★★★★ | ★★ | Pasta, steak, salmon, chicken, fried calamari; wine flights; kids' menu

Via Napoli Ristorante e Pizzeria | L-D | Italy, World Showcase | Expensive | ★★★½ | ★★★ | Wood-fired pizzas, pastas, filet, Mediterranean sea bass, chicken Parmesan; tiramisu, panna cotta, Torta Della Nonna, cheesecake; beer and wine; kids' menu

Advance Reservations recommended for most EPCOT full-service restaurants; call ☎ 407-WDW-DINE (939-3463) or visit disneyworld.disney.go.com/reservations/dining.

GOOD REST AREAS

Benches | Mexico, World Showcase | Inside the pavilion against the inside of the wall that forms the walking ramps to the retail space; air-conditioned

Benches | The Seas, World Nature | Air-conditioned

Japan gardens | Japan, World Showcase | To the left of Katsura Grill, a set of tables overlooking a lovely garden and koi pond; outdoors but shaded, with refreshments nearby

Rotunda and lobby | The American Adventure, World Showcase | Air-conditioned; refreshments nearby; usually quiet

UK Rose Garden benches | United Kingdom, World Showcase | Behind the pavilion

DISNEY'S ANIMAL KINGDOM TOURING PLAN COMPANION

ATTRACTION INFORMATION

Attraction | Location | When to Go | Authors' Rating | Comments

The Animation Experience at Conservation Station (*Genie+*) | Rafiki's Planet Watch | Check *Times Guide* | ★★★

Avatar Flight of Passage (*ILL*) | Pandora | At park opening or after 3 p.m. | ★★★★½ | 44" minimum height; pregnant guests should not ride; fright potential*

The Boneyard | DinoLand U.S.A. | Anytime | ★★★½

Conservation Station and Affection Section | Rafiki's Planet Watch | Anytime | ★★★

Dinosaur (*Genie+*) | DinoLand U.S.A. | Early or late | ★★★½ | Fright potential; 40" minimum height; pregnant guests should not ride; fright potential*

Discovery Island Trails | Discovery Island | Anytime | ★★★

Expedition Everest (*Genie+*) | Asia | Early or late | ★★★★½ | 44" minimum height; motion sickness potential; pregnant guests should not ride; single-rider line available; fright potential*

Finding Nemo: The Big Blue . . . and Beyond! (*Genie+*) | DinoLand U.S.A. | Check *Times Guide* | ★★★★

Feathered Friends in Flight! (*Genie+*) | Asia | Anytime | ★★★★ | Fright potential*

Festival of the Lion King (*Genie+*) | Africa | Earlier or later showtimes | ★★★★

Gorilla Falls Exploration Trail | Africa | Before or after Kilimanjaro Safaris | ★★★★

It's Tough to Be a Bug! ★★½ (*Genie+*) | Discovery Island | Anytime | Fright potential*

Kali River Rapids (*Genie+*) | Asia | Before 11 a.m. or last hour the park is open | ★★★½ | 38" minimum height; pregnant guests should note that the ride is bouncy; you'll get wet; fright potential*

Kilimanjaro Safaris (*Genie+*) | Africa | At park opening or after 3 p.m. | ★★★★★

Maharajah Jungle Trek | Asia | Anytime | ★★★★ | Fright potential*

Meet Favorite Disney Pals at Adventurers Outpost (*Genie+*) | Discovery Island | First thing in the morning or after 5 p.m. | ★★★½

Na'vi River Journey (*Genie+*) | Pandora | Before 9:30 a.m. or during last 2 hours before closing | ★★★½ | Fright potential*

Awakenings | Discovery Island | Anytime | ★★★½

TriceraTop Spin | DinoLand U.S.A. | Anytime | ★★ | Fright potential*

Wilderness Explorers | Parkwide | Sign up in the morning and complete activities throughout the day. | ★★★★

Wildlife Express Train | Africa | Anytime | ★★

* See Small-Child Fright-Potential Table on page 304.

DINING INFORMATION Counter Service

Restaurant | Location | Quality | Value | Selections

Creature Comforts (Starbucks) | Discovery Island near Africa | Good | C | Coffee and espresso drinks, teas, sandwiches, pastries

Flame Tree Barbecue | Discovery Island | Good | B | Pulled-pork sandwich, ribs, smoked half-chicken, mac and cheese with pulled pork, plant-based "sausage" sandwich; beer, frozen rum drink

Harambe Market | Africa | Good | B | Grilled chicken or ribs served over rice and salad greens; salads; plant-based "sausage"

Kusafiri Coffee Shop and Bakery | Africa | Good | B | Impossible empanadas; flatbreads; pastries; cookies; sausage, egg, and cheese biscuit; coffee and beer; some kosher

Pizzafari | Discovery Island | Poor | C | Chicken Parmesan sandwich; personal pizzas; Caesar salad; cannoli cake

Restaurantosaurus | DinoLand U.S.A. | Fair | C | Burgers, chili-cheese dog, chicken sandwich, chicken nuggets, Cobb salad, breaded shrimp, plant-based Southwestern burger

Royal Anandapur Tea Company | Asia | Good | B | Hot and iced teas, hot chocolate, coffee and espresso drinks, frozen chai, pastries

Satu'li Canteen | Pandora | Good | A | Customizable bowls with chicken, beef, shrimp, or fried tofu; steamed "pods" (stuffed bao buns)

Yak & Yeti Local Food Cafes | Asia | Fair | C | Honey chicken with steamed rice, cheeseburger, teriyaki chicken salad, vegetable tikka masala, Korean fried-chicken sandwich, tempura shrimp, egg rolls, fried rice; American-style breakfast fare

DINING INFORMATION Table Service

Restaurant | Meals Served | Location | Price | Quality | Value | Selections

Rainforest Cafe | B-L-D | Park entrance | Moderate | ★½ | ★★ | Spinach-and-artichoke dip, coconut shrimp, burgers, ribs; brownie cake with ice cream; full bar; kids' menu

DINING INFORMATION Table Service (*continued*)

Restaurant | Meals Served | Location | Price | Quality | Value | Selections

Tiffins Restaurant | L-D | Discovery Island | Expensive | ★★★½ | ★★½ | Charred octopus and honey-glazed pork belly appetizers, tamarind-braised short rib, butter chicken; full bar; kids' menu

Tusker House Restaurant | B-L-D | Africa | Expensive | ★★★ | ★★★ | Buffet with roast pork, beef, and chicken; character meals; full bar next door; kids' selections

Yak & Yeti Restaurant | L-D | Asia | Expensive | ★★★ | ★★ | Lo mein noodle bowls, coconut shrimp, chicken tikka masala, Korean fried-chicken tenders, firecracker shrimp; full bar; kids' menu

Advance Reservations recommended for most Animal Kingdom full-service restaurants; call ☎ 407-W D W-D I N E (939-3463) *or visit* disneyworld.disney.go.com/reservations/dining.

GOOD REST AREAS

Gazebo behind Flame Tree Barbecue | Discovery Island | Follow the path toward the water, along the left side of Flame Tree Barbecue; gazebo has ceiling fans

Outdoor covered benches near exit from Dinosaur | DinoLand U.S.A. | Gazebo-like structure with nearby water fountain

Seating area adjacent to Dawa Bar | Africa | Refreshments nearby; outdoors and can be noisy from street performers

Walkway between Africa and Asia | Plenty of shaded rest spots, some overlooking streams; refreshments nearby; a favorite of *Unofficial Guide* researchers

DISNEY'S HOLLYWOOD STUDIOS TOURING PLAN COMPANION

ATTRACTION INFORMATION

Attraction | Location | When to Go | Authors' Rating | Comments

Alien Swirling Saucers (*Genie+*) | Toy Story Land | After 3 p.m. | ★★½ | 32" minimum height; motion sickness potential

Beauty and the Beast—Live on Stage/Theater of the Stars (*Genie+*) | Sunset Boulevard | Check *Times Guide* | ★★★★

Disney Junior Play and Dance! (*Genie+*) | Animation Courtyard | Check *Times Guide* | ★★

Fantasmic! | Check *Times Guide*; if two shows are offered, the second will be less crowded | ★★★★½ Fright potential*

For the First Time in Forever (*Genie+*) | Echo Lake | Check *Times Guide* | ★★★½

Indiana Jones Epic Stunt Spectacular! (*Genie+*) | Echo Lake | Anytime | ★★★½

Lightning McQueen's Racing Academy | Sunset Boulevard | Anytime | ★★½

Meet Disney Stars at *Red Carpet Dreams* | Echo Lake | First or last hour the park is open or during mealtimes | ★★★★

Meet Olaf at Celebrity Spotlight (*Genie+*) | Echo Lake | First or last hour the park is open or during mealtimes | ★★★½

Mickey & Minnie's Runaway Railway (*Genie+*) | Hollywood Boulevard | Early or late | ★★★★ | Fright potential*

Millennium Falcon: Smugglers Run (*Genie+*) | Galaxy's Edge | At opening or after 6 p.m. | ★★★★ | 38" minimum height; pregnant guests shouldn't ride; motion sickness and fright potential*; single-rider line available

Muppet*Vision 3D (*Genie+*) | Grand Avenue | Anytime | ★★★★

Rock 'n' Roller Coaster (*Genie+*) | Sunset Boulevard | Early or late | ★★★★ | 48" minimum height; pregnant guests shouldn't ride; motion sickness and fright potential*; single-rider line available

Slinky Dog Dash (*Genie+*) | Toy Story Land | At opening or just before closing | ★★★★ | 38" minimum height; fright potential*

Star Tours—The Adventures Continue (*Genie+*) | Echo Lake | During lunch or after 4 p.m. | ★★★½ | 40" minimum height; pregnant guests shouldn't ride; motion sickness and fright potential*

Star Wars Launch Bay | Animation Courtyard | Anytime | ★★★

Star Wars: Rise of the Resistance (*ILL*) | Galaxy's Edge | First thing or late at night | ★★★★★★ | 40" minimum height; pregnant guests shouldn't ride; motion sickness and fright potential*

Toy Story Mania! (*Genie+*) | Toy Story Land | Early or late | ★★★★½

The Twilight Zone Tower of Terror (*Genie+*) | Sunset Boulevard | Early or late | ★★★★★ | 40" minimum height; pregnant guests shouldn't ride; fright potential*

Vacation Fun at Mickey Shorts Theater | Echo Lake | Anytime | ★★★½

Walt Disney Presents | Animation Courtyard | Anytime | ★★★

* *See Small-Child Fright-Potential Table on page 304.*

DINING INFORMATION Counter Service

Restaurant | Location | Quality | Value | Selections

ABC Commissary | Commissary Lane | Fair | C | Pork carnitas or shrimp tacos, Buffalo chicken grilled cheese, Mediterranean salad (vegetarian option available), chicken club sandwich, plant-based burger; some kosher; beer

Backlot Express | Echo Lake | Fair | C | Angus bacon cheeseburger, chicken strips, Cuban sandwich, Southwest salad, teriyaki chicken or tofu bowl

Catalina Eddie's | Sunset Boulevard | Fair | D | Cheese and pepperoni pizzas, Caesar salad

Docking Bay 7 Food and Cargo | Galaxy's Edge | Excellent | A | Smoked ribs served with blueberry corn muffins, roasted chicken served on salad greens or with mac and cheese and roasted veggies, tuna poke

Dockside Diner | Echo Lake | Fair | D | Hot dogs with over-the-top toppings

Fairfax Fare | Sunset Boulevard | Fair | B | Waffle bowls with chicken, pork, brisket, or plant-based option

Milk Stand | Galaxy's Edge | Fair | F | Frozen nondairy drinks, with or without alcohol

Oga's Cantina | Galaxy's Edge | Fair | D | Batuu Bits snack mix; sampler platter with cured and roasted meats, cheese, and pork cracklings; alcoholic and nonalcoholic cocktails; wine and beer | Online reservations available

PizzeRizzo | Grand Avenue | Poor | C | Personal pizzas, meatball subs, salads

Ronto Roasters | Galaxy's Edge | Good | B | Pita wrap filled with roast pork, grilled pork sausage, and slaw; pork rinds; nonalcoholic fruit punch; breakfast wraps

Rosie's All-American Cafe | Sunset Boulevard | Fair | C | Burgers, hot dogs, chicken nuggets, fries, plant-based "lobster" roll; child's chicken nuggets with a yogurt smoothie and fruit

DINING INFORMATION Counter Service *(continued)*

The Trolley Car Cafe (Starbucks) | Hollywood Boulevard | Good | C | Coffee and espresso drinks, tea, breakfast sandwiches, pastries
Woody's Lunch Box | Toy Story Land | Excellent | A– | *Breakfast:* Lunch Box Tarts; breakfast bowl with scrambled eggs, potato barrels, and country gravy *Lunch and dinner:* Sandwiches (BBQ brisket, smoked turkey, grilled three cheese); tomato-basil soup; "totchos" with chili, queso, and corn chips

DINING INFORMATION Table Service

Restaurant | Meals Served | Location | Price | Quality | Value | Selections

50's Prime Time Café | L-D | Echo Lake | Moderate | ★★★ | ★★★ | Pot roast, meat loaf, fried chicken, PB&J milkshake, warm apple crisp, chocolate–peanut butter layer cake; full bar; kids' menu
Hollywood & Vine | B-L-D | Echo Lake | Expensive | ★★ | ★★★ | *Breakfast:* Bananas Foster French toast, eggs Benedict, chicken with Mickey waffles *Dinner:* Beef tenderloin, roast chicken, mac and cheese with shrimp, roast pork, plant-based option; character breakfast; full bar
The Hollywood Brown Derby | L-D | Hollywood Boulevard | Expensive | ★★★★ | ★★½ | Cobb Salad (named after the owner of the original restaurant), pork, lamb, chicken breast; grapefruit cake; kids' menu. Patio lounge serves cocktails and small plates.
Mama Melrose's Ristorante Italiano | L-D | Grand Avenue | Expensive | ★★★ | ★★ | Seasonal pastas, fresh mozzarella, campanelle with shrimp, flatbread "pizzas," charred strip steak; tiramisu, chocolate-and-cherry torte, cannoli; full bar; kids' menu
Roundup Rodeo BBQ | L-D | Toy Story Land | Expensive | ★★★ | ★★★ | Family-style barbecue, cheddar biscuits with sweet pepper jelly, salmon, mac and cheese, corn on the cob, potato barrels
Sci-Fi Dine-In Theater Restaurant | L-D | Commissary Lane | Moderate | ★★ | ★★ | Sandwiches, burgers (plant-based option available), pasta; shakes and sundaes; full bar; kids' menu

Advance Reservations recommended for DHS full-service restaurants; call ☎ 407-WDW-DINE (939-3463) or visit **disneyworld.disney.go.com/reservations/dining.**

GOOD REST AREAS

Animation Building | Animation Courtyard | Benches in and around Star Wars Launch Bay; refreshments nearby
Benches along Echo Lake | Some shaded; refreshments nearby
Covered seating behind Sunshine Day Bar | Sunset Boulevard | Refreshments nearby; ample seating